Jason and the Argonauts
through the Ages

ALSO BY JASON COLAVITO

*Knowing Fear: Science, Knowledge and the
Development of the Horror Genre* (2008)

EDITED BY JASON COLAVITO

*"A Hideous Bit of Morbidity": An Anthology
of Horror Criticism from the
Enlightenment to World War I* (2012 [2008])

Jason and the Argonauts through the Ages

JASON COLAVITO

McFarland & Company, Inc., Publishers
Jefferson, North Carolina

LIBRARY OF CONGRESS CATALOGUING-IN-PUBLICATION DATA

Colavito, Jason.
Jason and the Argonauts through
the ages / Jason Colavito.
p.   cm.
Includes bibliographical references and index.

ISBN 978-0-7864-7972-6 (softcover : acid free paper) ∞
ISBN 978-1-4766-1566-0 (ebook)

1. Jason (Greek mythology)   2. Argonauts (Greek mythology)   I. Title.
BL820.A8C63 2014   398.20938'02—dc23   2014007615

BRITISH LIBRARY CATALOGUING DATA ARE AVAILABLE

On the cover: Statue of Jason, Schönbrunn Palace, Vienna
(Dreamstime); inset graphic © 2014 iStockphoto

Manufactured in the United States of America

*McFarland & Company, Inc., Publishers
Box 611, Jefferson, North Carolina 28640
www.mcfarlandpub.com*

Table of Contents

Preface

When I was young, I found an old copy of Edith Hamilton's *Mythology*, and I was immediately taken by the story of Jason and the quest for the Golden Fleece. Later, I read the account of the same journey in Bulfinch's *Mythology*, and I wondered why the details did not entirely match. Additional investigation in other collections of the Greek myths yielded similar results. Sometimes Jason seemed the hero of the story, sometimes almost the sidekick to Medea. Sometimes Jason's father Aeson is overthrown by Pelias, but sometimes he surrenders power voluntarily, or was never king at all. Sometimes Pelias forces Jason to undertake the quest for the Fleece, but sometimes the idea comes from Jason, or Hera. Even the details of the voyage of the *Argo* did not agree. Did Jason and his companions travel to Aea or to Colchis? The general outline of the story remained, but the details almost always differed.

There was no such ambiguity about the other great epics of the Greco-Roman world. Homer's *Iliad* and *Odyssey* were always the same in every summary, as was Virgil's *Aeneid*. These poems were complete works, and their adventures and characters were fixed by the poets' creation, enshrined in texts passed on unchanged for centuries. No compilation of mythology failed to list the stops on Odysseus' voyage, or the successions of conflicts the preceded the fall of Troy. And yet Jason was somehow different, and I wanted to know why.

In my search for answers, I discovered that there was no one book that examined the history of the Jason myth comprehensively, or placed it in its archaeological and cultural context. No fewer than a dozen poets told Jason's story in some way, but where was a discussion of the development of the myth across time? Where the story was discussed, it was usually briefly, as in the mythological compendia, or in passing in works on other myths. Those few books that did discuss Jason at length were usually very old; or inaccessible to me for being written in German, a language I do not speak or read; or in almost all cases of a heavily academic nature, treating specific aspects of the myth, or offering literary criticism of specific authors' poems about Jason. The exceptions were the travelogues that retraced the Argonauts' presumed paths, which were of little interest to me. What light did it shed to know that three millennia after the Argonauts' passage one could buy discount carpets where once sandaled feet had trod? For the general reader interested in the context, history and development of the myth, there was a void.

A great deal of exceptionally interesting work exploring the Jason myth has appeared in academic journals and scholarly books over the past two decades, but for general readers, these are often difficult to find and frequently are highly technical, presupposing a great deal of knowledge of the classical world and ancient literature that the academic audiences for which they were written know but which nonspecialists may not have. Academic articles and chapters, by their nature, treat only slices of the story, single aspects and angles that, to my knowledge, have yet to be assembled into a broader exploration of the changing nature of the Jason story. Even the most thorough academic article cannot cover in its twenty or thirty pages the scope of material a book can explore.

The present work is not a specialist's book. It is, instead, the book I wished I could have read when I first became interested in the Jason story. It aims to synthesize the scholarly work being done in the classical, artistic and archaeological fields, and to carry the story forward past the classical world and follow the development of the myth down to the present day. I hope that this book will answer the question posed in this preface—why Jason?—and in so doing show that the history of the Jason myth is every bit as epic as the Greek legend itself.

Introduction

Beginning with thee, O Phoebus, I will recount the famous deeds of men of old, who, at the behest of King Pelias, down through the mouth of the Pontus and between the Cyanean rocks, sped well-benched *Argo* in quest of the golden fleece.

—Apollonius of Rhodes, *Argonautica* 1.1–4.
Trans. Robert Cooper Seaton

The legendary hero Jason and I share a name, and this is no coincidence. I was named for him, and he is one of the few Greek heroes whose name is still commonly given to children. Turn back the clock a century or two, and you will find any number of classical heroic namesakes: Achilles, Alexander, Cyrus, Hector, Hercules, Julius, Marcus, Nestor, Ulysses, and more. One American president (Grant) shared his name with the adventurer of the *Odyssey*, and all across early America new cities were founded in honor of the Classical world: Aurelius, Cicero, Homer, Scipio, and more in upstate New York alone. Of those names that belong only to legend and not to history, Jason remains the most common classical name given to children, the fourth most popular boy's name in the year I was born, though now eclipsed by biblical names such as Jacob and Daniel.

Part of this popularity may be due to the name's joint Greek and Hebrew heritage. While the Greek version of the name Jason is ancient, going back into the darkest recesses of myth and legend, a phonetically similar name is also a variant of Joshua, or Yehoshua, also transliterated as Jesus, and meaning "Yahweh is salvation." A certain Jason of that Hebrew name, later St. Jason of Tarsus, appears in the Book of Acts and in Romans as an apostle and relative of St. Paul. But of him, we are not concerned. Our Jason, the Jason of Greek myth, takes his name, as we shall see, from the ancient word for "healer," and this Jason stands as one of the first heroes of the ancient people who would one day become the Greeks of the Classical Age.

To some extent, we are all familiar with at least part of the story of Jason and his Argonauts, if only from the 1963 movie version. They are the mighty band of adventurers who set sail from the sun-dripped coasts of Greece and crossed the storm-tossed sea to reach the outer limits of civilization, the very edge of the world itself, in order to retrieve the Golden Fleece and return with it to Greece to win back a kingdom wrongly usurped. This story has been told a thousand times, from the ancient, unnamed, and forgotten bards who sang unrecorded songs of the *Argo*'s thrilling trip across what Homer, in both the *Iliad* and the *Odyssey*, would describe as the "wine-dark sea," to the great poets Pindar and Apollonius, who gave us the versions of the story we know today, to the filmmakers in Hollywood who placed Jason and his Golden Fleece upon a silver screen and introduced him anew to generations unborn and un-conceived when the first tales of his epic voyage formed on the lips of Mycenaean tellers of tales in a time so long ago that even the Greeks themselves thought of it as belonging more to myth than to history.

But while most of us know at least the outlines of Jason's adventure, few of us know the epic of the Jason legend itself, the story behind the story. As we shall see, the Jason story is one of the oldest in all Greek mythology, predating even what we think of as Ancient Greek civilization itself. Its origins reach back, past the Classical Greece of Plato and Socrates, past the Archaic civilization of Homer and Hesiod, past the Greek Dark Ages, that vast period of barbarism and creativity, back all the way to the Mycenaean civilization, which occupied Greece before there was a culture we would today call classically Greek. Recent research has traced the Jason story back to these people, a warrior race who ruled Greece between 1600 BCE and 1100 BCE largely coterminous with the Bronze Age in the region. They spoke an early form of Greek, recorded in a mysterious script known as Linear B, and their civilization—along with many in the Bronze Age world—began to collapse around 1200 BCE leaving spectacular ruins and a raft of legends which the peoples who succeeded them would transform into the familiar mythology of Hellas.

Before there was Greece, there was Jason.

So old is the Jason story, "ever one of the most popular of the Greek myths,"[1] that even Homer at the dawn of recorded Greek literature need only allude to it elliptically in the *Iliad* and the *Odyssey*, assuming his audience in the eighth century BCE already knew the details, as well or better than the stories of the Trojan War and its aftermath he came to sing. In the *Odyssey*, Homer refers only to Jason reaching the Clashing Rocks, an allusion standing for the adventure as a whole. He has the enchantress Circe tell Odysseus:

> The only coursing ship that ever passed this way was *Argo*, famed of all, when voyaging from Aeëtes: and her the waves would soon have dashed on the great rocks, but Here [Hera] brought her through from love of Jason.[2]

Homer (or the poet or poets known now by that name), it is frequently argued, incorporated information, ideas, and legends from the Mycenaean period when he composed his masterworks in the eighth century or so, across a distance of three or four hundred years from the events he described.[3] If Homer knew much of what we consider the story of Jason and the Argonauts, it must have been a myth already hoary with age, a tale that had been told and retold for centuries. This in itself is somewhat astounding, since in Homer even the very gods themselves lack some of the attributes we see in them in the high civilization of Classical Greece and its Hellenistic and Roman successors. Apollo, for example, is in Homer only the warrior god of prophesy, not yet the lord of the Muses, the patron of music, or the god of healing (that god was then the Mycenaean Paean or Paiawon, with whom he later merged). Jason, then, in his essential functions predates even some of the gods themselves as we have come to know them. One of his few rivals in that regard is Heracles (Latin: Hercules), another legendary character of ancient provenance, whom we shall encounter again in tracing the arc of the Jason story.[4]

But if age were the defining aspect of a myth, then Jason would have no claim on our imaginations, outpaced as he is by the truly primordial myths of the ancient world, the earliest Egyptian myths and the Sumerian *Epic of Gilgamesh*. Indeed, the best-known and fullest version of the Jason story is not very ancient at all, composed only at the tail end of the Greek epic tradition. The Hellenistic poet Apollonius of Rhodes composed his *Argonautica* only in the third century BCE, a thousand years after the origins of the myth, and with many updates, additions, and changes. No, it is not the age of the myth that draws us in.

Instead, the Jason story compels us for another reason. It is an epic adventure, a compelling quest, a story of courage, of love, and of betrayal. It is also the tale of a man who, in Apollonius' version, is all-too-human and striving to complete feats typically reserved for demigods while shouldering the responsibilities and weight of his own humanity. The story of the voyage of the Argonauts is laden with iconic imagery, of the Golden Fleece and the Clashing Rocks, of the Harpies and Sirens, and the great ship *Argo*. And, in the final analysis, the epic of Jason is also a great deal of fun. While the scholar G. S. Kirk once complained that the Jason story was "enthralling but bland, even superficial,"[5] I hope this book will show that the myth is anything but, that the story of its evolution is itself an epic, one that reaches back to a lost period of history and embodies mysteries and rites practiced for gods no longer remembered.

The myth of Jason underwent enormous changes in its evolution, even in some of the aspects that seem most important to the story. For example, though the myth of Jason is very old, it is only in the seventh century BCE that we know for sure that Jason was seeking the Golden Fleece. What, if anything, was he after before this? And how did we end up with the myth we know today? As we shall see, there is good reason to suspect that the Jason story originated in an ancient tale of a fertility god who died, traveled to the Underworld, and was resurrected to marry a goddess.

* * *

This book will attempt to trace the history of the myth of Jason and the Argonauts. To do so, I will draw on a range of evidence, including the many versions of the myth recorded by ancient poets, the writings of ancient historians who attempted to place the legend in the real world, and the ancient art that depicted scenes from the voyage of the Argonauts, including variants of the story that remain unrepresented in the extant literature. This book will also examine later variants and interpretations, including medieval, Renaissance, Victorian, and modern retellings.

But these primary sources are only a part of the story. In addition, this book will draw on the work of scholars who have studied the many aspects of the Jason legend and will attempt to correlate their findings with the literary and archaeological records. Together, these sources provide a cross-disciplinary approach to the myth from multiple perspectives, including the literary, historical, and archaeological, because only by viewing the story of Jason through a variety of lenses and contexts can we begin to see the legend in its full richness, not just as an ancient adventure, but as an attempt to tell a universal story through the detritus of a vanished Bronze Age world. Of course, the primary sources disagree, as we shall see, and scholars have myriad interpretations and understandings of the myth, not all of which agree. For some, Jason is a mythic tale of initiation, for others a literal record of an expedition to a far-off gold mine. I began with the position that most theories have something to recommend them, and this book will attempt to review these disparate opinions and ideas, emphasizing some above others in an attempt to create a coherent account of the myth's development. Of course, there will be some loose ends and a few parts that do not entirely fit.

To tell the story of the myth of Jason and the Argonauts, in Part One, this book will first set the stage by relating the origins of the mythic imagination in the Paleolithic and Neolithic worlds before focusing on the first recorded mythological systems, including that of the Near East, which is a likely influence on Greek myths. The origins of Greek mythology and the beginnings of the Greek epic tradition will be discussed. Following this, an archaeological survey of the late Bronze Age in Greece will be presented, including a discussion of the Mycenaean city where the Jason story is set. Mycenaean trade missions will be explored, including the tradition of sailing, along with evidence for possible voyages to the Black Sea region, as depicted in later versions of the Argonaut legend.

Part Two will explore the development of the Jason story from Mycenaean Greece down to the Hellenistic and Roman periods. Drawing on recent scholarly research, I will attempt to reconstruct the earliest versions of the Jason stories and analyze the important differences between what we know of them and the later versions of the tale as it has come down to us. Following this, the story as known to Hesiod and Homer will be discussed, and then in turn, the definitive versions presented by Pindar and Apollonius, as well as additional depictions in other ancient authors. This section will emphasize the changing nature of Jason's character across the centuries, as the figure of Jason transforms from a possible Mycenaean god into a demigod, a hero, and finally an all-too-human character undertaking an expedition worthy of the gods.

Part Three will explore the many facets of the Jason myth in three contexts: within the myth itself, within Greek mythology as a whole, and within the broader context of Near Eastern and Indo-European mythologies. Literary analysis, mythological investigation, history, and archaeology will illuminate the origins and impacts of the most iconic aspects of the legend, including the Golden Fleece, the Dragon's Teeth, and the sorceress Medea. This investigation will show that Jason was once imagined to have undertaken a descent into the Underworld, known as a *katabasis*, with clear parallels in Greek and Near Eastern mythology. I will also offer a new theory explaining the Golden Fleece in mythic and archaeological context. Taken together, this evidence indicates that Jason's original Underworld voyage involved his death and resurrection, culminating in his ritual marriage to a pre–Greek earth goddess.

Part Four will trace the afterlife of the Jason myth from the Middle Ages to today. This section will look at medieval attempts to link Jason to Christ and the plethora of modern retellings in prose, in poetry, and in such modern media as television, video games, and graphic novels. This section will also evaluate scholarly and not-so-scholarly attempts to investigate the Jason myth, ranging from efforts to pinpoint the exact route taken by the *Argo* to fanciful attempts to read into the Jason story an ancient record of extraterrestrial visitation.

Finally, I will offer some concluding thoughts on the changing nature of Jason, the way he and his story reflect the needs and values of the people telling his story, and the reasons the Jason myth remains relevant in the twenty-first century world.

The Story of Jason

In order to explore the epic history of the Jason legend, we must first review the story of Jason and the Argonauts as it has come down to us, following in general the most familiar version of the story, the one told by Apollonius of Rhodes in his *Argonautica*, supplemented as needed by additional details drawn from other authors to cover the sections of the myth excluded from the *Argonautica*. This is the version of the story told in truncated form in Thomas Bulfinch's *The Age of Fable, or Stories of Gods and Heroes* (1855) and at greater length in the later mythological compilations by such luminaries as H. J. Rose, Edith Hamilton, and others. Let us call this the Standard Version, to borrow a phrase from another branch of criticism, though I remind readers that even this is merely my own retelling of the story and cannot be considered in any way the "official" or "definitive" version, there being no such thing.[6]

It is from this baseline that we can begin to analyze the origins of the myth and the permutations it has undergone as it travelled from Mycenae to Alexandria to Rome and to us in the modern world. Let us also pause here to offer a brief definition of what I mean by *myth*. Among anthropologists, classicists and others, terms such as *myth, epic, legend, folktale,* and *saga* all have multiple if somewhat overlapping meanings,[7] with *myth* tending to refer to traditional stories of the doings of gods and heroes in a timeless past. Legends, sagas, and epics, on the other hand, tend toward adventure and are frequently assumed by their composers to have a basis in historical truth. Later, in modern usage, *myth* came to represent stories that were unverifiable and likely untrue, as opposed to *history*, which claimed to speak for truth. For our purposes, *myths* will refer to the body of stories told about the gods and heroes of ancient times. The adventure of Jason, as a type of myth, is also an epic for its length and scope. I will also refer to it on occasion as a legend, both because its tellers assumed it had a basis in fact, and because there are too few synonyms for myth and epic to repeat only those two too frequently.

Since no one ancient source presents the entirety of the Jason cycle from beginning to end, let us summarize the Standard Version of the myth.

PROLOGUE

Before the story of Jason properly begins, Phrixus and Helle set events into motion when their mother Nephele sought to secure their safety, fearful that the new wife of her one-time husband Athamas, King of Thessaly, would do the children harm. The god Hermes came to her aid, providing a flying ram bearing a magnificent golden fleece to spirit the boy and the girl to safety. The two rode upon the creature's back as it flew from Thessaly deep into the east. However, Helle lost her grip on the ram's fleece and fell to her death in the waters separating Europe from Asia, thereafter called the Hellespont in her honor, known today as the Dardanelles.

Phrixus landed safely on the eastern shore of the Black Sea, where the ram deposited him in the kingdom of Colchis, whose king, Aeëtes, offered him welcome and shelter. In thanks for his salvation, Phrixus sacrificed the golden ram to Zeus, and he presented its fleece to Aeëtes, who hung it in a sacred grove, under the protection of a dragon who never slept. Aeëtes would thereafter attribute the prosperity of his kingdom to the presence of this divine ram's skin.

THE CALL TO ADVENTURE

Jason was born the son of Aeson, king of Iolcus, and was only a small child when his uncle Pelias took the throne in Aeson's place. Some versions of the story claim that Aeson had tired of the burdens of government and surrendered his crown willingly, making his half-brother regent only until Jason would come of age; other versions claim that Pelias seized power by force, driving out Aeson and seeking to murder his offspring to secure his dominion. In the time of Pelias's ascension, Jason's mother successfully hid him from Pelias's wrath by claiming the baby was stillborn and then spiriting Jason away to the centaur Chiron to be educated and trained in safety. Still wary, Pelias consulted an oracle, which told him to beware the appearance at court of a man wearing but one sandal.

Long years passed, and Jason grew into young manhood and set out to claim his birthright and restore the throne of Iolcus to its rightful dynasty. On his journey to Iolcus, Jason came to the River Anaurus, where an old woman sought his help in crossing. In aiding her, Jason lost one of his sandals, but he gained her blessing, worth all the more for she was none other than the great goddess Hera, wife of Zeus, in disguise. Jason continued on to Iolcus, where a frightened Pelias received him during games and a sacrifice honoring Pelias's father, the god Poseidon.

Both Pelias and Jason understood that Jason was the rightful king, but Pelias had no intention of giving up his throne. Instead, he told Jason that he would only surrender the crown if Jason could prove himself the rightful heir by performing a great feat, journeying to Colchis (called Aea in the earliest tales) to retrieve the Golden Fleece, which Pelias claimed was by right the property of their family, since Athamas, father of Phrixus, was their shared relative. Pelias believed this an impossible task. He hoped, and Jason feared, that he was sending the young man to certain death.

Nevertheless, Jason accepted the challenge.

THE JOURNEY TO COLCHIS

In those days, there was no easy way to travel to the distant kingdom of Colchis, for the only boats yet known were small, hollowed tree trunks fit only for short travel along the coasts. Jason employed the craftsman Argus to create a vessel capable of carrying fifty men across the limitless seas, all the way to Colchis at the edge of the world. This he did, a feat of engineering celebrated for its audacity, and the boat took the name *Argo*, after its maker (literally, "made by Argus," in the Greek dative). Some said the goddess Athena helped design the vessel, and others that a plank incorporated into the ship came from the oracular grove of Zeus at Dodona, which had the power to speak and give prophesy. Hera watched over and protected the boat and its occupants.

Knowing the odds against him, Jason sought to bolster his chance of success by calling for companions to sail with him, a band of fifty heroes known as the Argonauts after the ship they sailed. By tradition, it is said that the greatest heroes and demigods of Greece sailed in the *Argo*, including Heracles, Peleus, Nestor, Orpheus, the twins Castor and Pollux, and a woman, the huntress Atalanta.

The Argonauts' first adventure found them stopping on the Isle of Lemnos, where the island's women had murdered all the men and lived by themselves under their queen, Hypsipyle. Hypsipyle gave Jason a wonderful robe as a prize for winning games on Lemnos. The Argonauts and the women of Lemnos found each other enjoyable company, and soon the women gave birth to a race of Argonaut children, known as the Myniae, with Jason fathering twins by the queen herself. Heracles protested at the immorality of this carnal recreation, and the troop moved on.

The Argonauts lost their bearings and landed at the port of a friendly king, who mistook them for enemies, and the ensuing battle left many of the Doliones dead when the dawn came and the Argonauts realized the terrible error that had occurred. Later, they found themselves on the island of Mysia, where water nymphs kidnapped Heracles' favorite, the boy Hylas, prompting Heracles to abandon the Argonauts forever in a fruitless search for his friend.

In Thrace, the Argonauts sought counsel from the blind prophet Phineus, who had the gift of prophecy but lost his sight for revealing too much of the gods' plans. Phineus was tormented by the Harpies, ugly winged women who stole his food, rendering him but skin and bones. After Jason killed the Harpies (or, in other versions, after the flying Argonaut twins Calais and Zethes chased them away), Phineus returned the kindness by pointing the way to Colchis and explaining how the Argonauts could cross the dangerous Symplegades, the Clashing Rocks that guarded the passage to the east, crushing between them anything that attempted to pass through.

The secret, Phineus said, was to release a dove between the rocks. If it made it to the other side, so too would the *Argo*. Jason did as Phineus instructed, and the dove passed unharmed, except for a few tail feathers clipped as the cliffs smashed into one another. When next they opened, the Argonauts rowed furiously and passed through the clashing rocks, suffering only minor damage to the ship's stern.

Now the path to Colchis lay clear.

THE ACHIEVEMENT OF THE FLEECE

The Argonauts sailed across the Black Sea until they came to its eastern extreme where lay the kingdom of Colchis and its king, Aeëtes. Jason sent word to the king that he had come to take back the Fleece, and the wily king promised that he would willingly surrender his treasure, if only Jason would prove his worth by completing three impossible tasks. Perhaps having grown weary of undertaking so many unattainable adventures, Jason became overwhelmed with sadness but steeled himself to attempt the impossible. In this he found aid at the hands of King Aeëtes' daughter, Medea, a sorceress of some renown who fell madly in love with Jason by the hand of Eros (Cupid), son of Aphrodite, at the specific request of Hera. Jason promised Medea marriage if she would help him attain the Fleece.

Jason's first task was to yoke two fire-breathing bulls with bronze hooves, and then use them to plow the Field of Ares. His second task was to plant the field with the teeth of the dragon slain by the legendary hero Cadmus, teeth that would sprout into fully armed men who would attack whosoever had raised them up. Only after defeating these warriors would Aeëtes consider Jason worthy of receiving the Fleece. The third task would be to retrieve the Fleece from the sleepless dragon that guarded it.

Medea gave Jason the keys to performing each of these feats. First, she gave him a magical ointment which protected him from the bulls' flames. With this, he calmly approached the bulls and slipped the yoke over their heads, amazing the Colchians and sending up cheers from the assembled Argonauts. Jason then plowed the field and planted the dragon's teeth. Under Medea's instructions, when the warriors rose from the ground, Jason threw a large stone into their midst, confusing the armed men and causing them to turn on each other, fighting until all were slain. Again the Colchians gasped in amazement, and again the Greeks cheered.

Now Jason proceeded to the sacred grove wherein the Fleece stood, protected by the dragon that never sleeps. Once more, Medea's aid proved essential. She had given Jason a sleeping potion whose scent quickly put the dragon to sleep, and Jason seized the moment to attain the Fleece. Aeëtes, of course, had no intention of letting his divine charm escape, and he moved to stop Jason, who fled from Colchis with the Argonauts, Medea, and her brother in tow. Aeëtes gave chase in ships of his own. Medea stopped Aeëtes' pursuit by killing her brother Apsyrtus and chopping the corpse into pieces, scattering them into the sea, knowing that by unbreakable law Aeëtes could allow no corpse to rest in the sea. Other versions of the legend have Jason murder Apsyrtus, but the result is the same.

THE RETURN VOYAGE

In punishment for the murder of Apsyrtus, Zeus caused great storms to blow the *Argo* off course until the oracular plank built into the boat spoke and told the Argonauts that they needed to seek absolution from the witch Circe on her magical island of Aeaea. Only after they had done this would they be allowed to journey home.

This cleansing they duly received, and they proceeded homeward toward Iolcus. However, en route they needed to first pass the Sirens, those magical women who lived on three small islands and sang songs so beautiful that sailors plunged to their deaths trying to reach the source of the music. Following remembered advice from the centaur Chiron, Jason instructed Orpheus to play his lyre, and the great musician played music more beautiful than even the Sirens' song, letting the Argonauts pass safely by.

The final test before returning to Colchis lay on the island of Crete. There, the bronze giant Talos blocked the path back to Iolcus, hurling rocks that threatened to destroy the *Argo*. In order to pass safely by, Talos had to be destroyed. Medea lulled the metal man to sleep with a spell and then removed the bronze bolt that held fast his one artery. He bled to death, and the *Argo* sailed for home.

Now arrived at Iolcus, Jason produced the Fleece and demanded that Pelias surrender his throne, but the tyrant refused. Nevertheless, Jason celebrated the triumph of the Fleece, setting up the *Argo* on land as a monument to Poseidon. Jason was sad that his aged father could not participate in the rejoicing. He then asked Medea to take years from his own life to give to his father. Medea instead restored Aeson's youth at no cost to Jason, cutting the old man's throat and rejuvenating him in an herb-filled cauldron. Pelias' daughters looked in awe at the restoration of the old man and begged Medea to restore their own father. This Medea pretended to consent to do, but instead she killed Pelias without resurrecting him, and Pelias's son exiled both Medea and her husband to Corinth.

DOWNFALL AND DEATH

In Corinth, Jason fathered two boys with Medea but grew tired of her. He abandoned the sorceress and became engaged to Creusa (or Glauce—the ancients disagreed), the daughter of the city's king. Medea did not take this betrayal well. She sent the bride for a wedding gift a poisoned robe which burst into flames upon the wearing, and she murdered her children by Jason to spare them from the ignominy of her actions. Then she set the palace of Corinth aflame and flew off into the night in a serpent-drawn chariot sent by the sun god Helios, her grandfather, eventually to land in Athens where she married the king, the father of the Athenian hero Theseus.

Jason eventually achieved his first objective, though he no longer felt joy in the attainment. With the help of Peleus, the father of Achilles, Jason defeated Pelias' son to become the king of Iolcus, which was his birthright. There he reigned in relative peace for many years, but he had lost the love of Hera because of his betrayal of Medea. As a result, Jason ended his days alone and sad. Finally, the gods meted out his final punishment for his betrayal of Medea. When he was an old man, he slept one day under the decaying hulk of the *Argo*, dreaming of his youth, when the ship fell down on him, killing him. Thus ended the life of the hero Jason.

The gods, however, honored the achievement of Jason, if not the man, and called the *Argo* up into the sky where it became the constellation of that name, one of the largest in the empyrean. Of the Fleece, however, no more is recorded, though it was believed that the Fleece, in the form of the sacrificed ram, joined the *Argo* in the sky as the constellation Aries.

Such is the story of Jason, at least as the storybooks would have it. Of course the Standard Version is neither the first version nor the definitive one. Unlike the poems of Homer, which forever embody the stories of Achilles and Odysseus, there is no one authoritative text for the Jason story, not even Apollonius' late *Argonautica*, which self-consciously reworked and, indeed, altered older versions to tell its story in a new way. As C. J. Mackie explained, "Jason is clearly one individual whose heroic character is transformed very significantly through time within the literary tradition."[8] He is by turns a hero, a villain, a man, a superman—in short, a very human character. This, in turn, makes his journey from prehistoric legend to Hellenistic epic that much more interesting, and that much more compelling, in its way, than the relatively static and unchanging figure of Odysseus, forever captured in the *Odyssey*.

As we shall see, there is evidence that the oldest Jason stories derive from the mysterious rituals performed for the lost gods of Mycenaean Greece, and Jason may well have once been a god, one who lost his divine stature as Mycenaean practice gave way to Greek. And as we shall see, his first quest may not have been for the Golden Fleece but instead to win the hand of a goddess. But in order to fully appreciate Jason's gradual metamorphosis from godlike hero to fallible human, it is first necessary to understand where Jason came from, in both the metaphorical and literal senses. A myth can only be understood in context—in the context of the story it tells, in the context of the culture in which it was told, and in the broader context of the many competing and complementary cultures and belief systems through which its ideas developed and changed. Only by viewing the myth through the multiple prisms of these overlapping contexts can the myth's many meanings begin to be understood. To that end, we must journey back to where it all began. First, we will need to understand the origins of the mythological imagination and trace the beginnings of Greek mythology and the Greek epic tradition. Then, we must examine the Bronze Age world the Jason story purports to depict and seek in its archaeological remains an understanding of the raw material that gradually fashioned itself into the story of Jason and the Argonauts.

As with any hero, the first chapter must be the origin story. For the subject of our study, the myth of Jason and the Argonauts, that origin story begins in a dark cave a long, long time ago with the very first tellers of tales and the stories they told.

PART ONE

ORIGINS

1

The World of Myth

In the beginning, there were no myths because there were no words. The first anatomically modern humans emerged more than one hundred thousand years ago. The species we call *Homo sapiens* shared their world with other human species, including the Neanderthals, the miniature humans of what is now Indonesia, and a genetically distinct species in Siberia.[1] At first, our species was silent, but eventually, after long spans of time, language developed through methods we can only guess and do not yet fully understand. It has been argued that Neanderthals also had a form of language, possibly a practical form of speech unable to convey symbolic meanings, but this claim is controversial, and so far as we can prove, fully modern symbolic language emerged only with us.[2]

But with the emergence of language, storytelling soon followed; presumably truth came first and made up stories came later, though obviously there is no way to know for sure. It is, of course, impossible to know the exact beliefs, stories, and myths of the people who lived in the Upper Paleolithic (35,000 BCE–12,000 BCE), the long period that begins with the first humans and ends with the Ice Age. This was a world of hunter-gatherers who archaeology says lived in small, nomadic groups wandering through a landscape pregnant with powerful forces they neither understood nor could control—predatory animals, violent weather, and the recurring cycles of nature—all forces humans would wish to master, or at least temper through appeal to the supernatural forces they would come to believe lay behind them.

These Paleolithic people left no written language, but they did leave behind art, and this art provides an entry point into the development of the modern imagination and the types of stories humans around the world had begun to tell. It is during this period that archaeological evidence emerges for the first known religious activity, with the implication that such rituals required stories to convey the rituals' symbolic meanings.

This cultural complex is most spectacularly displayed in the cave paintings of Western Europe, including the famous images of Lascaux, where long caves were elaborately decorated with depictions of wildlife, including horses and bulls along with some human and abstract images, 17,000 years ago. Other evidence comes from carved statuettes, the so-called Venus figures, which were carved as far back as 35,000 years ago and depict heavily stylized women, often overweight (or perhaps pregnant), with large breasts and buttocks buttressed by tiny heads and legs. These have been variously interpreted as fertility idols or even ancient pornography, but so little evidence exists that no definitive interpretation has emerged.

In *The Mind in the Cave*, David Lewis-Williams argued that the structure of the human brain was responsible for the florescence of Paleolithic art and for the origins of belief in the supernatural—in gods and monsters.[3] Lewis-Williams presented evidence that certain activities, including meditation, fasting, and the consumption of hallucinogenic plants, can induce altered states of consciousness and hallucinations that manifest as a set of symbols that are consistent across time and space, the result of the wiring of the human mind. Such hallucinations can be deep and intense, so much so that they can appear to be more real than the material world, and the gateway to the supernatural. Common themes seen in these altered states of consciousness include vast caverns filled with geometric abstractions, the appearance of animals or animal-human hybrids, and meetings with terrifying monsters, though the exact content of a hallucination is governed by one's cultural expectations acting on the raw material in the mind. For example, one culture might interpret a zigzag shape as a geometric abstraction and another as a snake; one culture's animal-headed god might be another culture's chimerical animal-human abomination. These creatures would lay behind the monsters of myth.

Upon entering this altered state of consciousness, the brain produces a number of fixed sensations, which our consciousness interprets based upon cultural expectations. Some of these sensations include the feeling of entering a vortex, the feeling of suffocation or difficulty breathing, and strange sounds ringing in the ears. Ancient cultures, and modern hunter-gatherer groups, interpreted these as trips underground, underwater, or to the underworld. Other sensations include feelings of weightlessness and dissociation from the body, which translate into experiences of flight or trips to the sky or the spirit realm. In this sense, the biology of the brain provides the template for the division of the universe into the earthly plane, with an underworld below and a celestial realm above.[4] That such patterns manifest in world mythologies is surely no coincidence, and as will be seen, the early Jason stories reflect this primordial cosmology, as well as the shaman's journey from the waking world into the spirit realm accessible only through altered consciousness.

Across cultures, access to this spirit realm has frequently been restricted to a special class of seers, known anthropologically as shamans.[5] They usually have a monopoly on communing with the spirits and bringing back boons or effecting medical cures via their altered states of consciousness, interpreted as their travels across time and space. The shaman must be equipped with specialized ritual knowledge imparted by tradition hoary with age, knowledge that gives the shaman the power to intercede in the realm of the supernatural, and knowledge that protects him or her from the threats of the spirit realm. The shaman is a healer, a sorcerer, an intermediary between the gods and men, and a journeyer who brings prosperity to his or her people by traveling across time and space and returning with a divinely sanctioned boon. And of course the shaman must also be able to battle evil spirits, monsters, and the forces of dark magic that threaten his community. The shaman may also suffer ritual death and dismemberment, often in a cauldron, and he or she has access to the powers of divination and prophecy.[6] Many of these elements are recognizable, if in altered form, in the Standard Version of the Jason story, and as we shall explore more fully later on, this is not a coincidence.

Whether one chooses to accept that the origins of the supernatural realm and thus the mythological stories told about the supernatural are biologically induced, the evidence for organized ritual activity becomes increasingly overwhelming as the Paleolithic gives way to the Neolithic (c. 9500 BCE to the beginning of the Bronze Age), the period defined by the rise of farming and the beginnings of permanent settlements. At the astonishingly early date of eleven thousand years ago, the people of central Turkey began the ritual construction of stone pillars at Göbekli Tepe, many of which were elaborately carved with depictions of animals—foxes, scorpions, lions. The largest stones weigh more than seven tons and stand sixteen feet high, and most are shaped like the letter T, with a tall pillar spreading its arms wide to the heavens. Göbekli Tepe predates the well-known site of Stonehenge by six thousand years, and to archaeologists working there, the site suggests that ritual and myth were not aspects of civilization that emerged as it developed but instead the root cause of civilization itself. First came the rituals and the myths, then came the will to build shrines and temples, and finally came the infrastructure to house, feed, and support the workers who labored to cast myth into stone.[7] This contrasts with the classical view of civilization, which posited that population or environmental pressures created a need for a stable food supply, and farming in turn helped create cities and the complex cultures they bring. No matter which view is ultimately the better explanation, the development of mythology was intertwined with the flowering of civilization.

This eighteenth-century copper carving depicts a Sámi shaman from the Scandinavian Arctic. He holds a ritual drum on which are runes through which he could divine the future. Shamans the world over were believed to have special access to the supernatural when in altered states of consciousness.

Within a few centuries of Göbekli Tepe's construction, farming had appeared in the area around the site, and with it the hunter-gatherer societies of the Near East began to settle down and adopt the elements we recognize as a civilization—cities, temples, social hierarchy, writing, and religion. By the time of the early Turkish city of Çatal Höyük around 6000 BCE archaeological evidence indicates that the community was already worshipping a supreme goddess connected to the cycles of nature and a subsidiary male god who took the form of a bull, a theme that will reappear later in our story. David Lewis-Williams and David Pearce suggest that Göbekli Tepe and related early sites were likely tied to myth cycles whose heroes' "cosmological exploits were probably linked symbolically to the animals carved on the Göbekli stone pillars. Myth and cosmology were thus consonant with architecture."[8] For these researchers, the mythological heroes must have been characters who represented the transition from hunting (animals, nature, chaos) to farming (plants, civilization, order). They may also have been mediators between the shamanic world of the hunter-gatherer and the more formal and organized world of the temple priests.

Exactly how much continuity existed between the presumed myth cycle of the early Neolithic world of Göbekli Tepe and Çatal Höyük and the first recorded Near Eastern mythology thousands of years later is uncertain, and necessarily speculative. As archaeologist Gary Rollefson told *Smithsonian* magazine, "There's more time between Göbekli Tepe and the Sumerian clay tables [etched in 3300 BC] than from Sumer to today.... Trying to pick out symbolism from prehistoric context is an exercise in futility" (brackets in original).[9] We can presume the existence of myth before Sumer, but of its content we can only guess. The builders of the stone pillars are mute; their carvings are all that speak for them. Writing would not be developed until ancient Sumer six millennia afterward when the first words were etched in cuneiform on clay tablets.

The Proto-Indo Europeans

Chronologically between Çatal Höyük and Sumeria but geographically removed from both were the Proto-Indo-Europeans, a group named from a scholarly reconstruction of their language. Many European, Anatolian, and Indo-Iranian languages, including Latin (and its descendants), Greek, Sanskrit, and others derive from a common source, and due to their geographic distribution from India to Iberia are termed Indo-European languages. Their hypothetical common ancestor is therefore known as Proto-Indo-European (PIE), which may have been spoken by a group living somewhere in central Asia, perhaps in the Black Sea-Caspian Sea steppe, sometime before 3400 BCE though the exact dates are speculative and vary among scholars.[10] Scholars have reconstructed a vocabulary for this language by comparing commonalities among its descendants, and from this vocabulary they are able to deduce certain facts about the social structure of PIE society and its functions. PIE society was hierarchical in nature, with a high-ranking warrior caste whose exploits were recorded in heroic poetry as a way of guaranteeing immortality through continued fame.[11] This reconstruction is based on three pillars: first, shared linguistic terminology (such as the words for warriors, gods, etc.); second, shared mythic motifs (including heroic exploits and dragon-slaying); and third, shared function or formula in myth (such as the pattern of interaction between characters, regardless of their specific form). Only when all three appear together can we be reasonably certain that a common PIE ancestor exists.[12]

The Proto-Indo-European people worshipped a pantheon of gods, of whom several appear to be the most important: a sky god, *Dyēus, viewed as the cosmic father; the sun god, who rides in a chariot and lives on an island across the ocean in the realm of the dead; a storm god, who wields thunder and lightning; a goddess of the Dawn; and possibly an earth goddess.[13] According to Calvert Watkins, the PIE people had a foundational heroic myth which is summarized succinctly in the formula "HERO SLAY SERPENT," which reappears in Indo-European myths from India to Ireland.[14] This phrase refers to a poetic formula (a standard line in a poem) rather than to the action itself; in other words, while heroes slay serpents the world over, in PIE-derived poems, the use of this specific poetic formula marks its ancient pedigree. The hero can be either explicitly a god (like Zeus or Apollo), or a man (such as Perseus or Cadmus), but his original was probably a god. The myth, in its manifold forms, appears to relate to a common Indo-European theme, in which a god encounters the power of chaos, frequently equated with death and symbolized by the serpent, and in killing the monster restores order and secures new life, immortality, or rebirth. This dragon, scholars claim, probably guarded treasure, symbolizing the prevention of gift exchange and the free-flow of wealth necessary for elite PIE society to function.[15]

However, critics have noted that reconstructions of this PIE myth are quite speculative,[16] and if the proto–Greeks moving into the Balkan Peninsula brought with them a PIE dragon-slaying myth, they would have entered an Aegean and Near Eastern world that already had several non–Indo-European monster-slaying stories of its own.

The Near East

In his recent book *Travelling Heroes*, Robin Lane Fox argues that much of the body of what became Greek mythology could be traced to travelers from the Greek island of Euboea, whose adventures across the Mediterranean world served to connect ancient stories from Assyria (the successor to Sumer) and Phoenicia to the developing tradition of Greek culture and adding Near Eastern stories to the lexicon of Greek myth. Scholars place this great cross-pollination in the eight century BCE, the Orientalizing Period in Greek art, when Near Eastern influences were well-documented and manifest in Greek interpretations of Near Eastern artistic motifs and images; but Lane Fox recognizes that the core of the Jason story predates this influx of Near Eastern influence.[17] Others have argued that the communication between Greece and the civilizations of the Near East, including Egypt, Sumer, Assyria, Babylon, the Hittite Empire, and Phoenicia, was much closer than typically believed, and much of what we think of as Greek mythology has been adapted and from antecedents found in the Levant and the Mediterranean coasts of Asia and Africa, perhaps beginning as early as the Mycenaean period, though not taking full form until the age of Homer.[18] This does nothing to diminish the Greeks' originality or inventiveness, any more than it harms Shakespeare to note that his *Hamlet* derived from a medieval legend. The source is not the invention; it is what the artist does with it that marks a work of genius.

It would hardly be surprising that at least some elements of the Near Eastern tradition would have found their way to Greece during the Mycenaean period. By the time the Myce-naean people were constructing their stone palaces and plotting the destruction of Troy (see chapter 2), the mythology of Sumer and its successors was already four millennia old, and that is a very long time for stories to sit in one place without escaping their borders. If only by diffusion, it seems likely that the Mycenaean people must have known something of the Near East. As M. L. West discussed in his study of Near Eastern influence on Greek myth, by the seventeenth century BCE, the grave goods of Mycenaean lords included exotic items from all across the Near Eastern world, including Mesopotamia and Syria, which speaks to trade with those regions; and after the fifteenth century Mycenaean pottery is found far abroad from its Greek homeland, attesting to trade relationships with Egypt, Syria, and else-where.[19] There were, therefore, two primary period of heavy Near East influence, in the Mycenaean Age and the eighth century BCE, and both left their mark on Jason.

None of this is to suggest, however, that the Jason myth originated in the Near East, though as we shall see it is likely that many of the incidents in the epic were influenced by stories told in Mesopotamia and elsewhere. The first extant references to the developed Argonaut story come from the Orientalizing Period, when Near East influence was at its height, so the influence of the Near East is pertinent to our discussion for both its direct and indirect antecedents to the Jason tale. Indeed, West has suggested that the bards who first sang of Jason may have drawn on ideas from the *Epic of Gilgamesh* in developing his adventures,[20] and as we shall see, the Medea tale has clear antecedents in popular Hittite myths. The connections, of course, are necessarily speculative and though suggestive cannot be said to be conclusive.

MESOPOTAMIA

The oldest recorded myths belong to Sumer, an ancient civilization of Mesopotamia in what is now Iraq. The Sumerians are traditionally reckoned the "Cradle of Civilization," and the first identifiably Sumerian settlement, Eridu, dates back to the sixth millennium BCE. By around 5300 BCE Sumer had cities, and these large centers subsisted on agriculture, and also practiced warfare. The march of civilization made their society more complex, and by 3500 BCE records were being kept in a form of writing, cuneiform, made from pressing a stylus into clay. Soon, writing leapt from mercantile pragmatism to artistic and ritual purposes, and the first written literature in the world took shape.[21] Of the myths of Sumer, we know of their pantheon of gods, led by An, the god of heaven, and including Enki, the god of water; Enlil, the god of magic; and Inanna (the Ishtar of the Babylonians), the Queen of Heaven, a goddess of love and war. The stories of Sumer's gods and heroes were recorded in short, probably unrelated poems, and were depicted in their art, including statues and seals, which were cylindrical in form.

Gradually, the Semitic-speakers of Akkad superseded the Sumerians, and in so doing, they took over much of Sumer and assumed much of Sumerian mythology, though the Akkadian versions sometimes differ, in small or significant ways, from their precursors, as might be expected after thousands of years of change. The Akkadians were succeeded by the Babylonians, who adopted the Akkadian myths more or less intact. It was the Akkadians who began the process of merging short poems about heroic deeds into the first true epic.

The best known Mesopotamian myth is the *Epic of Gilgamesh*, which was first recorded in Sumerian, though the extant Gilgamesh tales were written as separate stories and may never have been put together as a single epic. Unfortunately, many Sumerian tales exist only as fragments, and it is the later Akkadian and Babylonian versions of the epic that give us the most complete versions, though sometimes with differing details from the source material as the later authors reworked and altered ancient sources[22]—not unlike the changes the Jason story would experience. In one of the oldest texts, a poem known as "Gilgamesh, Enkidu, and the Netherworld," the hero kills a serpent at the base of a sacred tree in the presence of the goddess Inanna before his friend Enkidu descends into the Netherworld. The sun god Utu (= Shamash) opens a hole in the Netherworld to let him out. This tale, partially included in the later Giglamesh epic, bears a clear echo of the tasks Jason performs in Colchis. In another Sumerian poem, "The Death of Ur-Nammu," Gilgamesh is himself explicitly the king of the Netherworld.

The most complete text is known as the Standard Version. Most translators, however, reconstruct the story by correlating passages from several of the extant texts, Sumerian, Akkadian, and Babylonian, to piece together what is otherwise an epic of lacunae since no one set of the twelve clay tablets telling the story survives intact. What is perhaps interesting to note is that Gilgamesh is not a wholly fictive figure, and inscriptions confirm that he was a historical king of Uruk around 2750 BCE[23] who became mythologized over time, perhaps absorbing earlier stories told of other heroes of ancient times. But in so doing, Gilgamesh serves as a precursor to the later claims that Greek myths, including Jason, preserve a kernel of truth beneath their magic.

As the first recorded epic adventure, composed around 2000 BCE *Gilgamesh* is an important precursor to the voyage of the Argonauts, and Greek epics as a whole. Some have argued, often persuasively, that *Gilgamesh* influenced Homer's *Odyssey*,[24] which in turn has also been argued to have drawn from an early, unrecorded version of the Jason story.[25] Homer, of course, had indicated as much in his references to Jason passing through the same mythological landscape that Odysseus was travelling. The *Odyssey*, too, of course, influenced Apollonius in composing his own *Argonautica*. We shall have occasion to tangle with this web of mutual influence again when we explore the Jason story proper, but for now, let use examine the Standard Version of the *Gilgamesh* tale.

Gilgamesh, king of Uruk, is born two-thirds god and one-third man, rendering him abnormally powerful but still mortal. This great power Gilgamesh uses to tyrannize his people, who cower in fear and ask the gods for help. The gods seek to balance Gilgamesh by giving him a counterpart, Enkidu, a man born in nature and reared in the wild. When the two meet upon Enkidu's arrival in Uruk, they come to blows, but soon become the best of friends when Enkidu accepts Gilgamesh's superior strength and skill. Together, they leave Uruk in search of fame and fortune in the Forest of Cedars, where, against the wishes of the council of elders and the entreaties of Enkidu, Gilgamesh plans to slay the giant Humbaba. In the first Sumerian versions of this tale, Gilgamesh sets out on this adventure with fifty companions, though in the Standard Version he and Enkidu are alone.

Gilgamesh's goddess mother secures for him the protection of the sun god, and when Gilgamesh and Enkidu make camp in the Cedar Forest, Gilgamesh dreams of monsters, including wild bulls and a thunderbird with flaming breath. Enkidu interprets these as good omens, despite Gilgamesh's fears, and together they slay Humbaba with the help of the sun god, who binds the giant while they slay him. They then return to Uruk on a raft.

In Uruk, the goddess Ishtar (Inanna) attempts to seduce Gilgamesh, who rejects her advances. In her wrath, she has her father Anu send the Bull of Heaven to punish Gilgamesh, and the Bull causes the waters to dry and the plants to die. Gilgamesh slays the Bull without divine help, but amidst Uruk's rejoicing, Enkidu dreams that the gods will punish him with death in vengeance for the death of the Bull of Heaven. Enkidu curses the gods and wishes he never left the wild. The sun god reaches out to tell Enkidu that his death will devastate Gilgamesh and that it is unfair to blame the gods for his fate. Enkidu recants, but dies and descends to the netherworld.

Gilgamesh, overcome with grief, sets out for the netherworld, across the Sea of Death, where lives Utnapishtim and his wife, the two humans who survived the Great Flood that destroyed the old world, in their ark which came to rest atop a mountain. They are immortal, and Gilgamesh hopes to gain from them the secret of immortality to avoid Enkidu's fate. Gilgamesh takes a ferry piloted by Urshanabi, whose crew of stone men, invulnerable to death, he kills. He must therefore cut down trees to make punting poles to cross the water, and Ursinabi's boat travels at superhuman speed, covering six weeks' journey across the sea in three days' time. Utnapishtim refuses Giglamesh's request, and instead shares the story of the Flood, but eventually takes pity and tells Gilgamesh of a plant that will restore his youth. Gilgamesh seeks out the plant at the bottom of the ocean, but a serpent steals it from him, and with it his chance at immortality. He returns to Uruk heartbroken but upon seeing the city's massive walls rejoices at the form of immortality his and his countrymen's works provide.

A twelfth tablet, unrelated to the rest of the Assyrian epic but copied largely from the Sumerian "Gilgamesh, Enkidu, and the Netherworld" poem not otherwise included in the *Epic*, concludes the story with Enkidu rising from the dead to rejoin Gilgamesh after the sun god intervenes. Interestingly, long after this text was complete, the Babylonians invoked Gilgamesh as the judge of the dead, king of the Underworld gods, and as a god whose chthonic power could be used in rituals of exorcism and supernatural healing of afflictions caused by spirits. In several Assyrian incantations, Gilgamesh piloted a ship that ferried the dead to and from the Netherworld, complete with a crew of sailors.[26]

Immediately, several parallels to the Jason story attract out attention:

- Both (the Sumerian version of) Gilgamesh and Jason have fifty companions and are associated with healing.
- Both receive divine protection (from the sun god and from Hera).
- Both are involved in the slaying of a giant (Humbaba and Talos), with help from others (from Enkidu and Medea).
- Both journey to a realm beyond the known world by water (to the Netherworld and Colchis/Aea).
- Both are at first refused the prize they seek (the plant of immortality and the Fleece).
- Both must battle a bull (the Bull of Heaven and the fire-breathing bulls).
- Both defeat a series of men with earth-like qualities (the stone men and the dragon's tooth warriors who spring from the ground).
- Both face the wrath of a powerful female figure (the goddess Ishtar/Inanna and the sorceress Medea).

These parallels are suggestive, but they are hardly conclusive. There remains a chasm of centuries separating the composition of Gilgamesh (c. 2000 BCE) and the first recorded allusions to the Jason myth (c. 800 BCE), centuries during which the Sumerian tales of Gilgamesh and his fifty companions transformed into the tale of the deep friendship of Gilgamesh and Enkidu. M. L. West has argued that the early Jason tales were "influenced by a version—surely a Greek version—of the Gilgamesh epic"; however, he draws no specific parallels between the elements I have identified and the Jason story.[27] Indeed, it would seem highly unlikely that the fifty companions made it from Sumer to Greece, though as always we have no knowledge of what oral traditions existed outside the formal written texts.

Instead, West sees four parallels between *Gilgamesh* and the presumed original Jason myth, which, as we shall see in chapter 4, he has reconstructed from parallel events in Homer's *Odyssey*. These four parallels are not the only ones connecting Jason to Gilgamesh, but are instead those that are identifiable through material presented in the *Odyssey*:

- The land of Aea (the first name of Colchis, and the Argonauts' original destination) resembles that of Aya, the Babylonian goddess of the dawn. Aea was a land in the farthest east, the land where the sun rose. (West would later claim also it shares a close connection with the most ancient Indo-European words for dawn.[28])
- Gilgamesh is sad and dejected after Enkidu's death, which "might well have been" paralleled in the version of the *Argonautica* Homer used in composing a similar scene in the *Odyssey*.
- Gilgamesh must cross the Waters of Death to reach Utnapishtim, which may have parallels in an older Jason story of the Argonauts passing the gates to Hades, inspiring Homer's hero to actually travel to the underworld.
- Gilgamesh must fell trees to make stilts on which he will cross the deadly waters. Odysseus, too, must fell trees to leave Calypso's island by raft. West speculates that Jason may once have needed to haul his boat across land on wooden rollers.[29]

These parallels are of course highly speculative, relying as they do on reconstructed events, and there is no incontrovertible evidence that the Jason story known to Homer contained any of these elements. However, when we explore the earliest Greek tales of Jason in chapters three and four, the relationship between our hero and Gilgamesh will become clearer, and possibly more striking. For example, the earliest form of Medea was a goddess, tying her much closer to Near Eastern tradition. This association is strengthened some when we note that the traditional iconography of Heracles, including the clubbed figure in lion's skin, the hero who battles a seven-headed serpent, the hero who frees an imprisoned god from a mountain, and the hero who is the son of the god of thunder, all can be found in (presumably unrelated) Sumerian cylinder seals from the third millennium BCE.[30] However, as Walter Burkert noted in reference to Heracles, but which could equally apply to Jason, "It is possible indeed that individual motifs were taken over [...] Iconography may easily cross the borders of language [...] Yet there must be some organizing force to integrate the details."[31] It is important to emphasize that the existence of parallels, or even outright borrowing, does not constitute proof that the Greeks simply adopted Gilgamesh, changed his name, and set him afloat in the sea. Jason is a much different character than Gilgamesh, and if they shared some adventures in common, this speaks more to the mythic imagination than to slavish copying.

Another Near East poem, an unnamed Sumerian description of the Underworld known from a single damaged tablet, depicts a land quite similar to Jason's Aea. Here the sun lives in the hours of night, just as on Aea the sun stores his rays; and here a pit to the deepest part of the Underworld is symbolized by the gaping jaws of a large monster, much like the dragon Jason would fight, and indeed, in some versions, descend into. The sun in this realm is considered both a god of the heavens and a god of the Underworld. A related myth cycle dating back perhaps as far as the fourth millennium BCE[32] tells of the courtship of Inanna and the (probably mortal) shepherd king Dumuzid (better known by his Akkadian name, Dumuzi). Inanna later visits the underworld and is trapped there. None of the gods would sacrifice himself to rescue her until Ea the wise finally resurrects her. However, a replacement in the Underworld must be found, and Inanna sends her husband, Dumuzi, to the underworld to take her place, and he is dismembered by the devils which come to claim him. After a confusing series of events, Inanna agrees to resurrect Dumuzi for half the year, alternating with his sister, who agrees to relieve him in six month spells. Intriguingly, thereafter Dumuzi makes his journey to and from the underworld by boat, apparently in the care of the sun god, after which Dumuzi weds the goddess anew.[33]

Dumuzi is thereafter worshipped as a dying and rising god, associated by 1000 BCE with the death of crops in Mesopotamia's hot and dry summer and their rebirth when the cooler, wetter period arrives at the end of August. Dumuzi's name means "producer of healthy young ones" or "the one who makes the young one all right" (remarkably similar to the Greek meaning of "Jason"—"healer") and referred to his role supervising the production of crops and young farm animals.[34] Sumerian kings would identify as Dumuzi through a mystical marriage to Inanna which was a feature of their cultic worship,[35] just as Jason would wed the mystical sorceress Medea before he became king in Iolcus. Like the later Medea, Inanna appears in this myth cycle as deeply in love with her husband, but also capricious, intermittently cruel and violent to him, and possessed of magical power. Inanna also shares characteristics with Hera (as Queen of Heaven), Aphrodite (as goddess of love, with whom the Greeks equated her), and Athena (a warrior goddess, who may have derived from Inanna[36])— all three goddesses who aid Jason in variations of his myth. Related to the myth of Dumuzi and Inanna is the character of Ningishzida, the Sumerian god of medicine who was also an underworld deity closely associated with a monstrous dragon. He and Dumuzi guard the palace of heaven in one myth.

The myth of Dumuzi and Inanna originated in Sumeria, and it was told later in Akkadia. Under the names Tammuz and Ishtar, the story was retold in Babylon and remained current in the Near East down until the Christian era. The Bible makes reference to the women who wept for Tammuz during the annual festival celebrating his death and rebirth.[37] It is from the Babylonian version preserved by the Semitic people of Syria that the myth enters Greek mythology as the tale of Adonis and Aphrodite and clearly influenced other divine-mortal couplings,[38] but given the myth's widespread currency from the third millennium BCE, it is possible that the older version of it underlay the stories told of other dying and rising gods (or they may descend from a prehistoric common source), including those worshipped on Crete and in the Mycenaean lands, and may well underlay the story of Jason himself, as we will explore in chapters two and three. The likelihood that these gods descend from a Neolithic version whose locus was in Anatolia is strengthened by the proximity of the Adonis myth, known as Attis in Anatolia, to the ancient civilizations of Göbekli Tepe and Çatal Höyük, but there is not enough evidence for firm conclusions.[39] Another interpretation suggests that the god Dumuzi is a deification of the Sumerian king "Dumuzid the Shepherd" (c. 2900 BCE) who may have conducted a sacred marriage to the goddess Inanna in order to heal the land and guarantee the growth of crops, a ritual that was translated into a mythological event, as also happened with Gilgamesh. (Of course, the king might just as well have been named for the god, and primacy cannot be established.) Could King Dumuzid have been the original Jason?

For now, the best we can say is that there are some suggestive parallels between the Near East and Jason stories, and given the Greek adoption of many Near Eastern myths and motifs at many times in their history, it is probable that at least some of the Gilgamesh epic and Inanna story influenced the development of the Jason myth. This conclusion is, of course, both speculative and tentative, like so much about the ancient past, and can only be couched in the conditional tense. As we progress in our study, we will try to fill in some of these conditionals with additional evidence.

THE HITTITES

Mesopotamian, especially Akkadian, mythology heavily influenced the Hittite people who occupied Anatolia, modern Turkey, during the Bronze Age. Additional sources of influence came from the Hurrian people, whose pantheon of gods, including the mighty weather god Teshub (derived from the earlier Hattian god Taru), combined Mesopotamian and Indo-European deities and formed the core of the Hittite religion and mythology. The Hittites absorbed myths and gods from across the Near East, and boasted of living in the "land of a thousand gods."[40] Among the most important were the Storm God and the Sun God, who together gave the Hittite kings their power, and both of whom had both heavenly and chthonic aspects.[41] The Hittites flourished from 1750 BCE to 1180 BCE before their state collapsed into smaller city-states that continued Hittite culture and traditions into the eighth century BCE. The Hittites wrote in cuneiform, and many of their mythological beings have clear antecedents in Mesopotamia. They translated the *Epic of Gilgamesh* into their language (with some adaptations, including a new visit to a personified Sea[42]), and the Hittites, whom the Mycenaeans knew, worshipped Inanna (as Ishtar) probably before the fourteenth century BCE,[43] and must therefore have known some version of the Dumuzi myth. The supreme god was the storm god Teshub, under the name Tarhun, later identified with Zeus. (I will refer to him as Teshub for clarity.)

The Hittites had another story that has historically been compared to the Dumuzi legend. In the Hittite tale, Teshub's son, Telipinu, becomes enraged and leaves the heavens. As a result, crops wither and animals die. No one can find Telipinu until at last a small bee locates him sleeping in a meadow. The bee stings him to wake him, but this only makes Telipinu angrier. He unleashes violence upon the land and upon mankind. Teshub sends the goddess of magic, Kamrusepas (the "Healer"), to soothe his son's anger, and she cleanses him of his rage. After doing so, the pair return home, and the crops and animals once more thrive.[44] Beside Telipinu is raised a pole or tree "and from this pole the hunting bag made from a sheep's skin is suspended. Within lies the fat of the sheep, within lies corn, asses, and wine."[45] However, this myth is not seasonal or annual in nature, and it does not involve the death of a god or hero figure, or a divine consort. Some see the hunting bag, or *kurša*, on a pole as the prototype of the Golden Fleece.

Because the Hittite Empire reached into Asia Minor, its myths and legends were but a stone's throw from the Mycenaean lands and those of the Dark Age Greeks, with whom they had contact through trade. A Hittite god of lightning may have been the inspiration for Pegasus, the flying horse of the Greeks. It has also been fairly well established that Hittite myths decisively influenced Hesiod's depiction of Cronus, the first king of the gods, and Typhon, the monster who sought to overthrow Zeus in the *Theogony*. These stories may be related to the Babylonian creation myth, in which the creator god Marduk slays the chaos goddess Tiamat, who is sometimes identified with the serpents or dragons to which she gave birth. There is, though, no ancient confirmation of her dragon appearance. Hittite depictions of dragons have also been connected to the Greek myth of Python, the serpent slain by Apollo.[46] The Hittite story of the defeat of the dragon is known in two variants. Both variations have been closely associated with the story of Zeus and Typhon. The first relates how the sky god and his son defeated the dragon, but the second variation is interesting in that it shows a theme that resonates with the Jason story.

The storm god Teshub had been defeated by his enemy, the dragon Illuyanka, and he sought out his daughter, the goddess Inara, for aid. Inara recruited the hero Hupasiyas to help defeat the dragon, which he consented to do only in exchange for becoming the goddess's lover. The pair then set the trap. Inara invited the dragon to a banquet, and she fed the dragon large quantities of food and drink until the mighty monster passed out from too much gorging and intoxication. Once subdued, Hupasiyas bound the dragon, and the storm god came and slew the dragon.[47] But Hupasiyas and Inara did not live happily ever after. Inara locked Hupasiyas in a stone house and forbade him from gazing out the window, lest he see his wife and child. One day, he looked out the window and thereafter begged to return home. Inara became enraged, but the results of her rage are unrecorded.[48] The extant written account breaks off here, but it has been suggested that she killed Hupasiyas in her wrath.

The parallels to elements of the Jason-Medea story are interesting, especially when we consider, as we will in chapter 3, that the Medea figure was originally depicted as a goddess:

- The male character (Hupasiyas and Jason) is involved in an intimate relationship. with a woman of great power (Inara and Medea).
- The man cannot defeat the dragon without the woman's help.
- The woman devises a plan to subdue the dragon, to which the hero agrees.
- The woman uses intoxication (strong drink or a magic potion) to render the dragon unconscious.
- The woman becomes enraged when the male character wishes to exit the relationship.

Indeed, Jan N. Bremmer, following Volkert Haas, specifically cited this myth as the possible foundation of the Jason-Medea story, and Bremmer further notes the presence among the Hittites of ritual artifacts called *kurša*, which were sheepskins sewn into a bag and ritually filled with fertility amulets to guarantee prosperity, much as Aeëtes would claim the Golden Fleece provided to Colchis.[49] In this theory, the Hittite festival of Purulli, in which the kurša was rededicated and during which the story of the killing of Illuyanka was told or reenacted, formed the template for Jason's achievement of the Fleece. And as with Inanna and Dumuzi, the springtime Purulli festival culminated with the Hittite king and queen reenacting the sacred marriage of Teshub and his divine consort to guarantee the fertility of the fields.

We will examine this and other explanations for the origins of the Fleece later, in chapter 11, but for now it is important to note that during the age immediately before the Jason story emerged, during the Mycenaean period in Greece, stories were circulating not far away about a hero who became consort to a powerful female and through her aid defeated a dragon. However, as with the story of Gilgamesh, influence is not the same as wholesale adoption, and nowhere in the Hittite story is there a quest aspect to the hero's need to defeat the dragon, or a sea voyage to distant shores. Indeed, Hupasiyas is not the focus of the Hittite tale but acts as a pawn manipulated by Inara to serve the storm god's ends, something very different than Medea's lovelorn efforts to aid Jason in his attempt to seize the Fleece.

UGARIT

Flourishing from the fifteenth to the thirteenth centuries BCE, Ugarit was a Mediterranean city in what is now Syria, and it had documented trade relationships with Cyprus and the Mycenaeans, as evidenced by pottery found in the city. From this source, it is possible that Near Eastern myths entered into Mycenaean consciousness. The most important Ugarit myth is that of Baal, the warrior god of rain and fertility, who, like Jason, must defeat a monster, and, like Dumuzi, dies and ventures to the Underworld before a resurrection. Baal was originally a title used for the god Hadad, who is cognate with the Akkadian storm god Adad whom we shall meet again. His myth exists in two parts, his defeat of the dragon and his triumph over death, which scholars believe are variants of the same story, with later writers replacing the dragon with a personification of death.[50]

In the first version, which is known only from incomplete and fragmentary tablets, the chief god, El, commissions the craftsmen of the gods to build a palace for Yam, the personification of the sea, who is closely related to serpents and is the father of a seven-headed dragon. A palace is the physical symbol of power and kingship. El has given Yam divine authority and the power to oust Baal from heaven. Baal is taken to the underworld, but (in a missing portion of the text) escapes, and uses two magic weapons created by Kothar wa–Hasis, the god of craftsmen, to defeat Yam.[51]

In the second version, which is more complete, Baal receives permission from El to build a palace, symbolizing his kingship, and Baal proclaims his power across the world and even in the Underworld, inviting the god of death, Mot, to celebrate. Mot, instead, orders Baal to the Underworld, and the gods find his dead body and mourn for him. Baal's sister and wife, the war goddess Anat, is bereaved and in her rage at Baal's death seizes Mot, dismembers him, grinds him like wheat, and sows the pieces into the ground.[52] The text breaks here, and it is unclear how Baal returns to life, but, resurrected, he returns to heaven. Baal, who is frequently depicted as a bull-horned god, mates with a cow (possibly a bovine Anat) eighty-eight times,[53] symbolizing the return of fertility. Mot, too, regenerates and the two have a confrontation seven years later, followed by a battle neither wins. The sun goddess intervenes, and rebukes Mot, and Baal reigns triumphant.

As in the Sumerian underworld, the sun deity is conceived as ruler of the dead, just as Jason's object is Aea, the kingdom of the resting sun. Additionally, Baal defeats the monster with magic weapons, just as Jason defeats the dragon through magic. And Anat's dismemberment and planting of Mot recalls both Medea's dismemberment of Pelias and Jason's challenge in planting the teeth of the dragon. While Mot is only described as a monster of ravenous jaws, other Near Eastern people associated the jaws of the underworld with a dragon. However, because the text is missing, we cannot say how Mot's dismemberment and burial played out or how closely it may have paralleled the sowing of the dragon's teeth.

PHOENICIA

Another Near Eastern people whose mythology plays some role in the Jason story are the Phoenicians, a maritime people who lived in independent city states on the coast of the Mediterranean, in what is now Lebanon and Syria. They shared much of their mythology, including the Baal stories, with the Ugarits and other Canaanite peoples, and they worshipped a version of Dumuzi named Eshmun, who was beloved by the amorous goddess Astarte or Ishtar (= Inanna), and who castrated himself to avoid her advances, thus dying. Astarte revived him and caused him to become a god of healing.[54] The Phoenicians invented an alphabet which came to Greece probably around 800 BCE possibly via trade on the island of Euboea,[55] and was adapted into the Greek alphabet we now know, sparking a wave of literacy that saw the first recorded literature—including the poems of Homer and Hesiod's early references to the Jason story. They flourished between 1500 BCE and 300 BCE which places the Phoenicians' most active phase, 1200–800 BCE right around the time that the Jason myth was taking shape. The Phoenicians navigated epic journeys across the known world, reaching distant shores that may well have contributed to the Argonaut legend as travelers' tales became known through commerce and trade.

The spring of Paraporti in Thebes (center) is the traditional site of the sowing of the dragon's teeth. The Greeks believed that the dragon Cadmus slew lived in the cave seen at left as it appeared in 1903. According to myth, half this dragon's teeth ended up in Colchis, where Jason would later sow them (Library of Congress).

Phoenician mythology shows a blend of influences, including Akkadian and Egyptian motifs and ideas, as well as some that are parallel to Hebrew myths found in the Old Testament. Their pantheon featured many deities whose names are familiar to us, including the sky god El, the storm god Baal, and the fertility goddess Astarte, the equivalent of Ishtar or Inanna, whom we recall from the *Gilgamesh* epic.[56] Important for our purposes is one myth that has a claimed relationship to Phoenicia, the myth of Cadmus, which like most myths, has many variants. Scholars have disagreed on whether the Cadmus story derives from Phoenicia, but there is evidence that the core of the story originates in Near Eastern tales of a hero's battle with a dragon, as discussed above in our section on Hittite myths.[57] If this suggestion is correct, it would imply that both the Cadmus story and the episode in which Jason defeats the dragon to gain the Fleece are derived from the same mythic tradition, making, I suppose, Jason and Cadmus unintentional players in alternate tellings of the same drama. (Jason was reckoned to be a descendent of Cadmus' daughter's brother-in-law, for what it's worth.)

Cadmus (or Kadmos) was a prince in Phoenicia who wandered around the Mediterranean world in search of his sister, Europa, whom Zeus had taken. The Oracle at Delphi told Cadmus to stop his search and instead found a city whose everlasting fame would be his reward. The site would be chosen by a cow, which Cadmus followed across the countryside until it came to rest at what would become Thebes. There Cadmus paused to collect water from a spring, only to find it guarded by a dragon, a son of the war god Ares (Jason's dragon lives in the "Grove of Ares"). Cadmus slew the dragon, and Ares cunningly sought revenge by encouraging Cadmus to plant the dragon's teeth to make Thebes great in war. When he did so, the teeth sprouted into warriors, the Spartoi (Sown Ones), who rose up fully armed and ready to attack. Athena, the goddess of wisdom, saved Cadmus by giving him a stone, which he hurled into the midst of the warriors who, confused, attacked one another until only five were left. These five then helped Cadmus raise up the new city. Ares, appalled at his creations' defeat, gave his daughter to Cadmus as a wife, and together the couple ruled over Thebes.[58] Cadmus was credited with bringing his alphabet with him from Phoenicia and teaching it to the Greeks. Elements of the Cadmus story reflect those of Baal's, including the presence of a monster, a cow, the sowing of a dismembered enemy, and a final battle against that which grew from the planted remains. Indeed, the Greeks held that Cadmus was the nephew of Belus of Egypt, who may have been a Hellenized form of Baal.[59]

The relevance of this tale to the Jason story is obvious, and the Greeks themselves explained it thusly: Cadmus had planted but half the dragon's teeth; the other half traveled to the court of Aeëtes, where Jason would later sew them. It is commonly thought that the Cadmus story was told first, with Jason's reenactment of the battle with the Spartoi added to his myth at a later date, though with all things mythological, this is not certain, and Jason's battle with the Earthborn Men is attested from at least the sixth century BCE. Cadmus the Phoenician was likely not so much a literal retelling of a genuine Phoenician myth (though likely inspired by one) as he was the Greeks' interpretation of Phoenician civilization and the benefits conveyed by it onto them, namely the alphabet. Remarkably enough, the transmission of the Phoenician alphabet to Greece is thought to be the work of a single literate Phoenician individual (possibly a scribe or merchant), probably not named Cadmus, teaching his script to a single Greek recipient, who adapted it to his (or, less likely, her) language.[60] Within a few years, the innovation had spread into a florescence of Greek writing, the first since the disappearance of the Mycenaean Linear B four centuries before.

Egypt

Lastly, no exploration of Near Eastern myth, no matter how cursory, can fail to mention the civilization of Egypt, which in the Classical and Hellenistic periods would loom so large in the Greek imagination as an improbably old and rich culture. The Greeks themselves attempted to find parallels between their mythology and that of the Egyptians, and when Alexander conquered Egypt, he was proclaimed the son of Ammon (or Amun), who as king of the Egyptian gods, was identified with Zeus, king of the Greek gods, and received homage under the Ptolemaic rulers as Zeus-Ammon, and under the Romans as Jupiter-Ammon (Jupiter, of course, being the Roman equivalent of Zeus, from an older king of the Latin gods).

However, the mythology of Egypt does not appear to play much of a direct role in the Jason story, aside from the common themes of Near Eastern mythology already discussed. One exception of some interest is the story of Osiris and Isis, an Egyptian god and goddess who were both husband and wife and brother and sister. Osiris was a giver of civilization and served as pharaoh of Egypt until his brother Set, whom the first century BCE Sicilian historian Diodorus Siculus equated with Typhon[61] (who in turn was the dragon of the Hittites and possibly of Jason's story, too), grew jealous and murdered Osiris and set his body adrift in the Nile. Isis found her husband-brother's body in Phoenicia and brought it back to Egypt. Set, angered, cut Osiris' body into six (or fourteen) pieces and scattered them across Egypt, but Isis pieced Osiris back together and used magic to resurrect Osiris, who impregnated her before dying again. This story has echoes of Medea chopping Aeson and Pelias into pieces and cooking them in her cauldron. For Aeson, the mystical dismemberment restored him to life, as it did Osiris.

It used to be argued in the Victorian period that the soul of Osiris was associated with the ram and was frequently depicted as a ram-headed man. Osiris' priests were said to have kept sacred rams at a shrine in Mendes, and mummified them after their deaths to be buried at the holy necropolis of the rams. However, such claims apparently referred to Osiris in a limited capacity as a composite with the ram-headed god Re, Re being closely associated with Ammon in *his* composite form, Ammon-Re, and modern studies of Osiris no longer refer to a close association with rams.[62] The exception is at Mendes, where the sacred ram embodied the soul of *both* Osiris and the sun god Re, as the Golden Ram would be said to embody the soul of Phrixus in some versions of the Jason myth. The ram had four heads and may have represented the four Egyptian gods who ruled as earthly pharaohs. The ram also had oracular powers and, like the *kashut* of the Hittites, was associated with fertility and sexuality.[63]

These parallels, however, are not so much direct influences on the Jason story as they are a part of the same body of symbols, beliefs, and traditions that informed the mythology and ritual of the Near East and therefore the developing mythology of the Greeks.

Greece

We have no written records of the myths and legends told in the lands of Greece before the time of Homer and Hesiod in the eighth century BCE, but we know that stories had been told. Images, medallions, and figurines preserve some indication of these stories. Some of these stories had come down from Mycenae, and through them from the Minoans, as we shall see in chapter 2. Though the Mycenaean people had writing, Linear B, they did not use it to record poems, songs, or myths. Instead, they used their writing for record keeping and inventories—the workaday business of trade. After them, the peoples living in Greece ceased recording even those details for four centuries, until a Phoenician brought letters back to Greece and writing began anew. Soon, in the eighth century BCE, the poems of Homer—the *Iliad*, the tale of the Trojan War, and the *Odyssey*, about Odysseus' struggle to return home to Ithaca—were written down, and Hesiod composed the first major works of Greek theology, mythology, and cosmology, the *Theogony* and *Works and Days*. If these works seem to emerge fully formed *ex nihilo*, it is because they are written forms of stories that must have existed in oral form before they were set down in the newfangled writing from over the sea.

It has been argued at length in the scholarly literature, for example, that Homer's *Odyssey* incorporates ancient folktales and legends that must have been current in oral form at the time that Homer created his epic, and one of those sources was likely an oral form of the voyage of the *Argo*. It is also a near certainty that the Homeric epics were originally oral in form and developed gradually during the Dark Ages from folk tales, legends, and, yes, Near Eastern stories. These were only written down once writing had reemerged, the *Iliad* around 750 BCE and the *Odyssey* by 720 BCE. The same process applied to other Greek myths and legends, as (presumably) bits of Minoan and Mycenaean mythology, historical memory, folk tales and legends, and Near Eastern influences mixed and merged and transformed into the stories that came to be recorded in the Archaic and Classical periods.

Scholarly work on the Homeric epics might be taken as a guide to the function of the oral tradition in the Greek world before writing.[64] Research suggests, and the stories of Homer themselves imply, that the earliest pieces of the Greek epics came from Mycenaean sources. For example, the cities Homer describes as power centers in the *Iliad*, including both Mycenae and Troy (Ilium), were major centers during the Mycenaean era, but much less powerful, if not abandoned, during the Archaic period when Homer composed. Troy itself was unoccupied from its fall at the end of the Mycenaean period down until 700 BCE well past Homer's age. The poems also describe warfare by chariot and the use of bronze weapons, tools of older generations not found in eighth century Greece. For the stories to include such material in an age without written historical records, they must have called back to genuine memories of a time when the Mycenaean world was in full flower. We will explore what we know of the Mycenaeans' specific beliefs and their origins, including from the Minoans, in the chapter 2.

For this to have occurred, bits of Mycenaean history and legend must therefore have been preserved in folk tales and poems circulating in the Dark Age world that followed the Mycenaean collapse. Eventually, it would be shown that Homer's poems were written down from originals composed in this oral age. In the 1920s, the American Homeric scholar and linguist Milman Parry noticed that Balkan folk singers composed long epics in an essentially formulaic manner, in which stock phrases of set metrical length were used to build the meter of poems that were more or less improvised as the storyteller recited them. Thus, repeated phrasing like "earth-shaking Poseidon" indicated that the originals of the Homeric works derived from this oral tradition. Therefore, as the Homeric works developed, bits of Mycenaean lore, Near Eastern myths, and, probably, some original material came together gradually, as themes, ideas, and incidents were mixed and remixed into new confections. The incidents on which Homer drew were probably already a part of folklore, or, as we have briefly mentioned, part of an earlier *Argonautica*, and the characters in his poems along with their stories were almost certainly already formed before he sang of Odysseus and Achilles and Troy. Instead, Homer's contribution was to give these many stories a single form, which he (or she or they—Homer's identity—or reality—has been debated and is not conclusive[65]) cast as two epic poems and fixed into the versions of the stories we know today.

These new poems were not accurate reflections of their original Mycenaean source poems or culture, however, and their component folk stories, incidents, and characters had changed greatly over the centuries between Mycenae and Homer. Archaeologists examining Homer's descriptions of warfare, for example, note that Homer's descriptions reflect contemporary practices more than they do genuine Mycenaean ways of war, implying that for all their references to the deep past, the Greek stories of the eighth century are only distorted mirrors of the most distant time, memories to be sure, but faded, twisted, and partial memories. As an example Homer's mixing of old traditions and new practices, he describes cremations when Mycenaeans buried their dead (though they may not have done so when far from home), but he accurately describes boar's tusk helmets used only in the Bronze Age (before 1200 BCE).[66] This is not unlike what we find in Shakespeare's *Julius Caesar*, which while hewing closer to the facts of Roman history, includes details like "chimney-tops" that were part of the author's London but not Caesar's Rome. It goes without saying that the Mycenaean and Dark Age stories the poet or poets we call Homer inherited must have changed and mutated as they were told and retold down until the time when Homer merged them into single works that eventually came to be recreated as written works at the dawn of ancient Greek writing. In this way, bits of genuine Bronze Age material became embedded in an essentially Archaic work of synthesis. We shall return to Homer later on when we attempt to reconstruct the version of the Jason story known to him.

The Jason stories must have followed a similar trajectory to the composition of the *Iliad* and *Odyssey*, finding their origins in tales, incidents, and bits of remembered fact and fancy from the Mycenaean world. The stories would have grown and developed like the Homeric stories, experiencing changes as they were told and retold, and absorbing new influences and adventures as smaller stories became attached to one another, and to the longer narrative. Eventually an epic was born, but unlike Homer's tale, the Jason story found no eighth century writer who would cast it in ink on parchment in immortal prose. As a result, the story never became fixed in a final form, remaining mostly an oral tradition throughout the Archaic period.

Conclusions

In the world where the Jason story was first told, Near Eastern mythology provided mythic precedents for many aspects of the Jason story. These included:

- A hero who had fifty companions.
- A hero who received the protection of the gods.

- A hero who went on an epic quest to retrieve an important treasure.
- A hero who traveled across water to reach a mysterious land.
- A hero who reached the land where the sun rested and a dragon lurks.
- A hero who fought and defeated (a) bull(s).
- A hero who sewed dragon's teeth and fought warriors who sprang from them.
- A hero who fought and slew a dragon.
- A hero who received the help of a powerful woman to subdue the dragon.
- A hero who became the consort of the powerful woman.
- A hero who faced the wrath of the powerful woman after abandoning her.

Here in précis we have the outline of the story of Jason, the Argonauts, and Medea. However, these elements were scattered across many myths from many cultures, and they had never before been united into the tale we know as the *Argonautica*. While some of these elements may have come directly from their Near East counterparts, it is also possible that others were developed independently in Greece. At this distance in time, there is no way to know for sure which might belong to which set. However, in order to trace what we do know of the history of the Jason myth and how these pieces came together around an original, autochthonous Mycenaean core, we must begin where it started, in Mycenaean Greece, and survey the history of that society, and its successors in the Greek Dark Ages before we can begin to put together the pieces of the story of Jason and the Argonauts.

2

Mycenaean Greece

For most of the period between the age of Homer and the late nineteenth century, mythology was the only window into the world that had come before classical Antiquity. The ancients considered stories like the voyage of the Argonauts, the siege of Troy, and the wanderings of Odysseus to be mostly factual accounts of events that had occurred in the deep past (though recognizing the differing renditions of these stories were sometimes at odds), and upon these writings the ancients composed their histories and sought the origins of their families and their communities. Through the myths, the writers of Antiquity proposed a succession of pre–Homeric peoples, including the Pelasgians, the first peoples of Greece, and the Achaeans, the people of whom Homer sang. (Today the former are sometimes identified with the Neolithic or early Bronze Age occupation, and the latter are usually identified with the Mycenaeans, though both names are later inventions.[1] No one knows what the Mycenaeans called themselves, though their ruling class may have called themselves Ionians.) The stories and myths were simultaneously a repository of historical knowledge and a genealogy through which the families of the ancient world could trace their ancestry back to heroes like Jason and Theseus, and through them to the gods.

The evidence confirming the truth of the myths was everywhere. Cities featured in the myths still existed, and monuments to the great heroes and events of the mythic past littered the landscape. Who could doubt the reality of the Greek heroes, known to be giants, when their very bones (actually mammoth or other large mammal bones) were on display at temples across the Mediterranean world?[2] And did not the myths explain the origins of far-distant peoples through the adventures of the Greeks? The Roman-era Greek geographer Strabo, for example, sought to affirm the connection between the voyage of the Argonauts and the peoples of Georgia and Armenia, which "all admit" to be plausibly true history. It was a story with special meaning for the geographer, whose great-uncle was governor of Colchis,[3] and therefore one he returned to time and again to link Colchis back to the Greek world through a long and honored history:

> For, as all admit, the original voyage to Phasis [western Georgia] ordered by Pelias, the return voyage, and the occupation, however considerable, of islands on the coasting-voyage thither, contain an element of plausibility, as do also, I am sure, the wanderings which carried Jason still further—just as there is an element of plausibility in the wanderings of both Odysseus and Menelaus—as evidenced by things still to this day pointed out and believed in, and by the words of Homer as well. For example, the city of Aea is still shown on the Phasis, and Aeëtes is believed to have ruled over Colchis, and the name Aeëtes is still locally current among the people of that region. Again, Medea the sorceress is a historical person; and the wealth of the regions about

Colchis, which is derived from the mines of gold, silver, iron, and copper, suggests a reasonable motive for the expedition, a motive which induced Phrixus also to undertake this voyage at an earlier date. Moreover, memorials of both expeditions still exist: the sanctuary of Phrixus, situated on the confines of Colchis and Iberia, and the sanctuaries of Jason, which are pointed out in many places in Armenia and Media and in the countries adjacent thereto. More than that, it is said that there are many evidences of the expeditions of Jason and of Phrixus in the neighborhood of Sinope and the adjacent sea-board and also about the Propontis and the Hellespont as far as the regions about Lemnos.[4]

These "sanctuaries of Jason" were called *Jasonia*, and were claimed to be memorials to sites where the Argonauts had once crossed on their voyage, even as far as modern Tajikistan. The discovery of these monuments in a wild and distant land confirmed for the court of Alexander the Great that his mission to the east was not without precedent, for had not Jason been here before? Did not the land of Armenia recall the Argonaut Armenos, whose existence could not be doubted? In truth, these monuments were simply "places of worship" (temples, altars, and other sacred spots) known by the Median word **yazona*, equivalent to the Persian word *ayazana* or *ayadana*, which had nothing to do with Jason but which the Greeks imagined sounded like the word Jasonia[5]; however, the presumed fact of the Argonautic voyage gave credence to this interpretation. It was, for the Greeks, the only deep history they had.

The situation did not improve appreciably until the end of the nineteenth century. The distant past was still deeply mysterious, and the Greek myths reigned as the only guide to this wild period of European history. In 1830, for example, the Rev. Royal Robbins produced a universal geography and history of the world, and the earliest sections present the biblical narrative as the true history of Israel, and noted that the Greek myths are "all we know" of the prehistory of Europe:

> These fables, however, are supposed to be founded on facts [...] The first great enterprise of the Greeks was the Argonautic expedition, 1263 years BC. Its destination was to Colchis, the modern Mingrelia, in Asia Minor. It was led by Jason, and is supposed to have been both a military and mercantile adventure. According to some, the object of was to open the commerce of the Euxine [Black] Sea, and to secure some establishment on its coast. According to others, Jason wished to avenge the death of his kinsman Phryxus, and to recover his treasures, which had been seized by the king of Colchis. Hence, in the language of fiction or figure, it was the "Golden Fleece" that was the object to be recovered.[6]

Here, on the very cusp of the Victorian age, historians claimed a historical reality for the Greek myths beneath the veneer of fable, and the Argonauts' voyage was treated as a historical happening, essentially as Apollonius of Rhodes had written it. Similarly, the works of Homer were taken to have a historical reality and, until around 1870, a presumed privilege in depicting the customs and practices of the otherwise unknown world of Greek prehistory. However, a countercurrent had formed in the Victorian era which dismissed the Greek myths as flights of fancy, corrupt borrowings from Scripture, or otherwise folk legends that could not be profitably disentangled from the accretions of fiction that grew like barnacles on scattered kernels of historical truth. As history increasingly came to rely on the methods of science, Greek myths no longer offered the sort of provably documentary truth scientific historians sought. In the latter nineteenth century, scholars influenced by rationalism and evolutionary theory reversed the prevailing view of Greek prehistory and instead claimed that phases of Greek history before Homer were instead the result of heavy "Phoenician" influence, including the Greek myths.[7] Greek prehistory, therefore, was the history of Phoenicia. Nothing before the institution of the Olympic Games in 776 BCE could be assumed to be scientifically provable history.[8]

Due to the Ottoman occupation of the Greek mainland (until independence in 1832), the Aegean islands, and the Turkish coast, there was little field research done on the ground in the early nineteenth century (and what artifacts did arise were claimed to be "Phoenician"), so little was known about the earliest history of the region. Eventually scholars began to doubt that even Ancient Greece's most famous event, the Trojan War, had any reality outside of Homer.[9] Then, in 1870, the German archaeologist Heinrich Schliemann made a find that changed everything with astonishing speed. As one twentieth century historian wrote, "it was almost universally admitted, from the first moment of the discovery that the whole question of early Greek traditions had entered upon a new phase."[10] By claiming to follow the geographical clues in Homer's *Iliad* and the works of later Classical writers (though actually retrofitting a discovery made by Frank Calvert to the geographical speculations of Charles Maclaren), Schliemann had uncovered the site of Troy and proved that the ancient legend had a basis in fact.[11] If Troy were real, what other myths might be as well?

Moving his operation to Greece in 1876, Schliemann astounded the world again. He discovered at the previously known citadel of stone at Mycenae a culture that he attributed to Agamemnon, Homer's king of Mycenae, and which was unlike anything then known. And he found treasure, a lot of treasure. Sumptuous and golden, the artifacts he uncovered amidst the colossal ruins of the city were the work of a high civilization, but one very different from the styles known from the Classical world. A particular gold mask depicting a man with facial hair Schliemann announced was the very burial mask of Agamemnon himself. The *Iliad*, in short, was no longer myth but fact.

Though the mask would turn out to be far too old to belong to Agamemnon, the civilization at Mycenae that Schliemann uncovered would revolutionize the discipline of ancient history and extend our knowledge of Greek prehistory deep into the past. Today we call this civilization Mycenaean, after the site where it was first discovered, though what these people called themselves we cannot say, though the Hittites may have called them the Ahhiyawa, suggesting Homer's Achaeans had the right name. When Mycenaean civilization was revealed, scholars did not know exactly what to make of it or exactly where in the history of Greece to assign it, and into the early twentieth century, the civilization was variously attributed to a number of (real and imagined) early Greek tribes and foreign nations, including "to the Dorians, to the Achaeans, to the Pelasgians, to the Carians, to the Phoenicians, and even to the Hittites," with the consensus favoring "a composite culture ... produced either by many peoples, or under the influence of many."[12] Today, we have a very different view of Mycenaean civilization, one that focuses on its original achievements. This civilization, which flourished between 1600 and 1200 BCE the Greeks later commemorated as the Age of Heroes. It was also the civilization that gave birth to Jason.

The Mycenaean Era

In the Greek myths, the monumental stone city of Mycenae was said to have been founded by Perseus, a son of Zeus by a mortal woman. Perseus was considered the first of the heroes, that race that would include such luminaries as Theseus, Heracles, and Jason, and his city was therefore held to be among the oldest founded in Greece. Though Perseus was mythological, Mycenae, which is located on the Peloponnesian peninsula in the region known as Argolis, was quite real, and its old position as a major center of the late Bronze Age and a dominant force in the prehistory of Greece was preserved long after its fall in the myths of subsequent millennia. It is from Mycenae, for example, that Agamemnon gathers the peoples of Greece to attack Troy.

The historical Mycenae began as a community of farmers and herders around 2000 BCE though their ultimate origin is unknown, perhaps coming from an area north of the

The ruins of Mycenae were known before Heinrich Schliemann excavated them, but his work helped to place the cyclopean stone structures like those pictured above into a mysterious period before Homer, a time we now call the Mycenaean Age. This was the period the Greeks called the Age of the Heroes (Library of Congress).

The massive Mycenaean tombs, like this one, testify to the wealth and power of the Bronze Age monarchs. Centuries later, grave goods stolen from these tombs served the later Greeks as Heroic artifacts from a forgotten age of power and glory (Library of Congress).

Black Sea in what is now the Ukraine. As these speakers of a proto–Greek dialect settled in what is now Greece around 1600 BCE a time called the Late Helladic Period, they absorbed cultural influences from the Egyptians, the Hittites, and the Minoans—the seafaring merchants who had a prosperous and lavish rival civilization on the island of Crete—and developed their own unique civilization, first at Tiryns and Lerna, and later elsewhere across the Peloponnese and neighboring areas. These centers would be remembered long into historical times, preserved in the *Iliad*'s Catalogue of Ships long after many had fallen into ruin. In the 1930s, Martin P. Nilsson noticed the coincidence and deduced from it the Mycenaean origin of the myth:

> [A] close inspection shows that the mythical importance of a site closely corresponds to its importance in Mycenaean civilization. The mythical importance of a city is, to use a mathematical term, a function of its importance in Mycenaean civilization. This close and constant correspondence precludes any thought of casual coincidence.[13]

The most important settlements lay around the Plain of Argos, but others lay beyond. Among the ancient sites whose Mycenaean historicity archaeologists have proved is Iolcus, city of Aeson and Jason, in Thessaly, which was a powerful and active Mycenaean center, as we shall see.

The first identifiably Mycenaean traits are evidenced in the archaeological record in the form of burial customs. Between 1650 and 1600 BCE burials shifted from single interments in rectangular stone-faced graves known as "cist graves" to new methods, including shaft graves and large tombs holding multiple burials. The most famous of the Mycenaean burial styles is the *tholos* tombs, beehive-shaped false domes made from inset rings of stone above a stone-built circular burial chamber. These were usually set into hillsides and typically featured a broad paved avenue leading to a stone entranceway that would have been flanked with Minoan-style pillars. Inside, bodies would be laid to rest on the tomb floor or in shafts. The whole was then covered with an earthen mound. These tombs are no longer seen after the period of Mycenaean collapse in the thirteenth century.[14] Additionally, between 1650 and 1600 BCE and only during this period, high ranking bodies wore gold burial masks, likely an imported custom, though of uncertain (perhaps northern) origin. Such evidence indicates the arrival of a new people and a new culture in the lands of Greece.

MINOAN INFLUENCE

The Mycenaeans came into contact with the old and rich society of the Minoans on Crete, and from them they borrowed much of their iconography and art, and also their writing. The Minoans flourished from roughly 2700 BCE to 1450 BCE and the Mycenaeans would have become aware of them not long after their civilization had begun to grow. The Minoan civilization was based in a series of large, complex "palaces" of many rooms in which the population lived and worshipped. These were later remembered as the Labyrinth of Minos in which the Minotaur roamed. The name Labyrinth in fact descends from a pre–Greek word for "double-axe," referring to the Minoan religious symbols that decorated the palace.[15] The seafaring Minoans had a far reaching trade network stretching from Egypt to Anatolia, a system of writing, and a rich artistic culture which included frequent depictions of religious rites revolving around bulls. From the Minoans, the Mycenaean people and then the later Greeks would inherit cult practices and possibly some myths and legends.

Based upon interpretations of Minoan art, it is frequently claimed that the Minoans had a matrilineal society and a powerful and socially prominent female priesthood who performed rites in honor of one multiform goddess or a series of goddesses, much as the later Medea was a powerful priestess or goddess in Colchis.[16] The pantheon of the Minoans may have been led by a goddess, to which some scholars believe an inferior male god, known later as Velchanos, paid homage through his death and annual rebirth, representing the cycle of nature and possibly male initiation rites.[17] In some theories, he annually enacted a sacred marriage to the goddess. This god (or another like him) is represented in the exquisite Palaikastro Kouros, a gold and ivory statue of a young god, possibly representing a Cretan form of the dying and rising Egyptian god Osiris or even a Cretan version of the serpent-slaying storm god.[18] Within the shrine dedicated to this statue, a small repository may even have served as the hiding place of the image when the god was deemed to be "dead" and in the Underworld, though this is speculation.[19] Minoan religious rites appear closely connected to rituals of regeneration, rebirth, and resurrection, presided over by an earth goddess.[20] There is perhaps

This rhyton in the form of a bull's head is one of many pieces of Minoan art depicting bulls. Scholars are divided whether the Minoans considered the bull sacred to a deity or perhaps a form of a deity itself. The later Greeks would remember the Minoan bulls in the form of the Minotaur and Talos, the bull-formed sun god of Crete (Walters Art Museum).

a relationship, or at least a parallel, to the marriage of Inanna and cyclically-dying Dumuzi in the Sumerian pantheon. The Cretan god would eventually be identified with Zeus, who was traditionally born on Crete, and he would come to supersede his matron. The Minoan goddess may have been a single Great Mother with many aspects, or she may have been multiple goddesses; the exact relationship between and among the female deities is unclear. She is perhaps a triple goddess of the heavens and/or the sun (with her doves), the earth (as mistress of animals with her lions), and the underworld (as the goddess of snakes). But in some form she and her cohorts traveled to Greece.[21] Rodney Castleden believed that the Minoans also paid respect to a male deity, an earth god, who had the shape of a bull and was worshipped in three forms, as a god of the underworld (bringer of earthquakes), a god on earth (in the form of a bull), and as a heavenly god (the god of the sun),[22] though his interpretation is extremely speculative, especially since Nanno Miranatos identifies the Minoan sun goddess as female—and as an underworld goddess as well.[23] Some scholars believe that there was no bull god[24] and that the bull instead represented either a symbol of the earth goddess or even Velchanos himself.[25] The Minoan deities, whoever they were, apparently each had overlapping responsibilities in the heavens, on earth, and beneath it, something carried over into Mycenaean and early Greek cults.

Additionally, the Minoans sometimes carried shrines to their gods on board their ships, as depicted in the gold ring of Mochlos. This image has been interpreted as the Goddess of Navigation, and the practice recalls the legend of the oracular plank included in Jason's *Argo*. The best evidence indicates most Minoan vessels were generally quite small, though some may have been nearly as large as the *Argo*. No Minoan vessel's remains have yet been found, but a Minoan seal depicts a ship with thirty oars, the possible forerunner of the later eighth century BCE *pentekonter*, or fifty-oared ship.[26] Another goddess, the snake-goddess, is depicted in Minoan statuary as a woman entwined with snakes, though there is some doubt about whether some of these images are of priestesses or snake-charmers rather than goddesses.[27] Snakes in the Minoan and later Mycenaean context were considered guardians of houses,[28] just as the serpent-dragon guards the Fleece. Such evidence recalls, to an extent, the important role played by female figures such as Medea and Hera in the seagoing voyage of the *Argo*, especially when we recall Medea's association with serpents in her flight from Corinth to Athens, and her knowledge of how to charm the dragon, which is usually depicted as a large snake. A direct connection is speculative but not impossible. The parallels demonstrate that the Mycenaeans would have come into contact with elements familiar to the Jason story by 1500 BCE at the latest.

Finally, the later Minoans apparently believed that the Land of the Dead existed across a large sea or river, and that a boat was necessary to cross this sea. The Ayia Triada sarcophagus of c. 1370 BCE depicts the deceased receiving a model boat as an offering, which many archaeologists have interpreted as representing the ship the dead use to travel to the afterlife. This belief may have derived from the ancient Egyptians, who imagined their dead rulers sailing on a bark into the netherworld, though it may also derive from a more common cross-cultural set of beliefs (typically but not exclusively associated with Indo-Europeans) found from Ireland to India in which a ferryman and a boat are necessary to cross water to the land of the dead.[29] However, the evidence used to support the Minoan concept of an afterlife reached by water derives from a later period, when the Mycenaeans had taken over Crete, and it is unclear whether the belief originated with the Minoans, was an import from the Mycenaeans, or something else entirely.[30] The other images on the sarcophagus are sometimes interpreted as either a cult of the dead or as representing a dying and reborn vegetation god on the order

In this drawing of a detail from the Aiya Traida sarcophagus three men carry young calves and a model boat (right) as offerings for the deceased. The presence of the boat implies a belief that the soul of the deceased crossed water to reach the land of the dead (author's drawing).

of Velchanos or Dumuzi.[31] A scene of a boat travelling to the Underworld appears again on later Mycenaean funerary art near Thebes (see chapter 7).

The Mycenaeans observed with great interest the culture and economy of Crete, and when Minoan civilization went into decline, the Mycenaeans stepped in (see below). From the Minoans they borrowed the construction and style of their ships. The very first artistic depiction of a Mycenaean vessel comes from Iolcus, where Jason caused the *Argo* to be built. There, a fragment of a vase depicts this vessel, with its extended keel and raised stern, and its many pairs of oars, historical counterpart to the *Argo*.[32] A later vase, from Tragana, comes to us from the twelfth century BCE, right after the collapse of Mycenaean power, but depicts the type of boats that would have been in use in the Mycenaean era. The ship is long, with a central mast from which billows a single sail. The stern post seems to take the form of "fish tail or possibly an animal head."[33] There are cabins at the stern and the prow, a large forecastle, and what is perhaps a banner displayed atop it. Such ships would have held about thirty oarsmen, and a gangplank rises above them to allow passage from end to end without interference in their rowing.[34] Such ships must have been the model for the legendary *Argo*.

THE PALACES

The most distinctive features of Mycenaean civilization are the large palace citadels that formed the major centers. These palaces were derived from two sources, the large, multi-room palace complexes of the Minoans to the south and the heavily fortified citadels of the Hittites to the east.[35] Drawing on features of the both, the Mycenaean peoples created stone fortresses on high, defendable sites within which sat the residences of the elite, including the city's leadership. A typical palace was surrounded by stone fortifications, often with guard towers. Beneath the walls, the shops and residences of the common folk spread. Beyond these would have been the fields and farms that supported the city.

The palaces incorporated within themselves a key aspect of their Minoan progenitors, a court that served as a temple and gathering hall. In Mycenaean centers, such a court is known as a *megaron*, and its form is instantly familiar to anyone who has studied the layout of Athens' famous Parthenon. A porch, typically fronted by two columns, opens onto a large, rectangular hall, whose roof was usually supported with more columns. At the center of this hall was a large hearth (or possibly a round offering table or altar), above which opened a skylight, called an oculus, in the roof above. In Mycenaean times, these structures had both sacred and secular functions, serving as both places of worship and as throne rooms for the kings of the cities and council chambers for the elite. Bernard Clive Dietrich argued that the Mycenaean rulers, following the models of the Near East, were priest-kings, and each city would have had its own protective deity to whom the king was closely allied. Such relationships, he said, underlay the close relationships between gods and heroes in myth, including Athena's aid in helping Jason to design and construct the *Argo*.[36] Others, however, noted that this speculation is based on a "web of associations and assumptions" and that the presence of free-standing megara outside the palaces argues for their function as temples rather than as royal homes.[37]

Regardless of their secular functions, as the power of the kings declined at the end of the Mycenaean age, the sacred functions continued after the secular authority had vanished. The Mycenaean megara gave way to Greek temples, and over the centuries the sites retained the air of sanctity. New temples sprang up where palaces and their megara had been; a temple to Hera sat atop the palace of Tiryns, and one to Athena, the Parthenon and its predecessors, stood on the Acropolis at Athens.[38] The freestanding megara, too, eventually found new temples sitting atop them, including the famous temple of Demeter at Eleusis.

MYCENAEAN RELIGION

Archaeological evidence alone cannot prove whether the Greek myths had already emerged in some form during the Mycenaean period. Martin P. Nilsson made a persuasive case on literary grounds in *The Mycenaean Origins of Greek Mythology* (1932) that the genesis of many Greek myths can be traced back to the Mycenaeans; however, critics argued that the Mycenaean myths cannot be securely adjudged because no texts from the period contain the myths as they were then told and almost no surviving Mycenaean art depicts mythological scenes.[39] Against this view, two arguments have been forwarded: First, the Geometric Period also featured remarkably few depictions of myth in art, but myth is well attested from that era, which terminated at the time of Homer. Second, a few Mycenaean works of art do show mythological scenes, including images that closely parallel the myth of Zeus carrying off Europa while disguised as a bull, as well as images of such mythological creatures as the chimera and, important for our purposes, centaurs, like Chiron, who raised and taught the young Jason.[40] With the full decipherment of Linear B, scholars were able to find scattered references to the Mycenaean gods on written tablets and could draw some general conclusions.

The exact nature of Mycenaean religious belief cannot now be reconstructed, but some educated guesses can be made based on documentary evidence and archaeological remains. We know from Linear B inscriptions found on tablets at Pylos (and to a lesser extent elsewhere) that by the time the Mycenaean centers had fallen, the major gods of classical Greece had acquired their names: Zeus, Hera (as *Era*), Athena, Artemis, Hermes, and Poseidon, though there were many additional gods whose worship did not survive.[41] A form of Ares was present, too, under a different name. Another god, Paiawon, a healer (perhaps only of war wounds), later lent his name to Apollo as Paean when Apollo arrived in Greece and the earlier god ceased to be worshipped.[42] The goddesses Athena, Artemis, and (later) Demeter derived some of their aspects from the Minoan Great Goddess(es) of household, animals, and vegetation, but it is not known how closely these or other godly names were tied to forms of they took in the Classical Age; for example, we cannot know whether the Mycenaean Athena was yet the goddess of wisdom or possessed of aegis and owl. She is instead mostly likely connected to the Shield Goddess, a war goddess who holds a large shield which symbolizes her potency.[43] At this early date, however, Hera is already closely tied to Zeus, though in what capacity is unknown. To Hera, the oldest Greek temples were dedicated, and she was frequently equated with the ancient Mother Goddess of Crete and the earth/fertility goddess or Heavenly Queen of the Near East, for whom a young male god died and was resurrected each year.[44] Hera's original association with an earth goddess figure survived deep into antiquity through her Homeric description as "cow-eyed" and her association with cows, the female bovine counterpart to the bull-formed earth god. Hera grew increasingly important over the course Mycenaean culture,[45] and it is worth noting the role she takes as the most active divine agent in the Jason story. The other important goddess to Jason was

Athena, and she and Hera may—but it is by no means certain—have been the Two Queens[46] who were the wives of the chief god of the Mycenaeans—a god who was *not* Zeus.

Based on the extent of offerings to the gods that have survived from the Mycenaean era, the scholarly conclusion is that Poseidon, not Zeus, was the chief (or at least most important) god of the Mycenaeans, known in the Greek of Linear B as *Po-se-da-wo-ne*, possibly meaning "Lord (or Husband) of Earth" (the etymology is disputed[47]). The best evidence of Poseidon worship comes from tablets found at Pylos, and in the Jason myth this close connection is shown in the king of Pylos, Neleus, who is the brother of Pelias, both sons of Poseidon.[48] The future god of the sea seemed to hold his kingship in his aspect as the god of earthquakes, "earth-shaking Poseidon," equivalent to Near Eastern gods of earth who held vaunted positions in the Sumerian and Hittite pantheons.[49] He is not associated with the sea on any surviving Mycenaean tablet; perhaps this became an aspect of his power when the Greeks' sea power grew and required a divine patron. He is also the god of oracles, and the first oracle at Delphi, before Apollo.[50] There may be an echo of his supremacy in the scene when Jason first appears at the court of Pelias when the king is making a sacrifice to Poseidon, his father and patron. Given that Phrixus had sacrificed the golden ram to Zeus, and Jason went to fetch its Fleece from Colchis in order to supplant Pelias (and therefore Poseidon), it becomes tempting to conclude that at one level the myth of Jason captures within it the transition from the supremacy of Poseidon to that of the new king of the gods, Zeus.[51] This conclusion is all the more intriguing when we remember that the goddesses who might have been Mycenaean Poseidon's wives, Hera and Athena, became the consort and daughter of Zeus after his chairmanship of the gods became established. It was almost as if the goddesses were party to a conspiracy to overthrow Poseidon.

This admittedly speculative idea finds confirmation in another aspect of Mycenaean cult practice. From the Minoans, the Mycenaeans had borrowed a series of religious symbols. Important among these was sanctity of the bull, the sacred animal of the Minoans. Among the Mycenaeans, Poseidon the Earth Shaker (rather than the later sea god version) was especially the god of the bulls, whom Rodney Castleden equated, speculatively, with a Cretan god. He suggested that just as the Greek myth of the Cretan Labyrinth of Minos is a reflection of the Minoan palace, so too is the Minotaur a memory of the potent bull-god Poseidon.[52] In the Greek myth, Poseidon demands the sacrifice of a bull, setting off the chain of events that would culminate in the birth of the Minotaur. In Minoan palaces, a bull-leaping ceremony was performed whereby youths would tease a bull and perform acrobatic feats over him before (possibly) sacrificing the animal to Poseidon. It might therefore be important to note that the Greeks later identified the river Oceanus, source of all waters on and beneath the earth, as bull-headed,[53] as they would many river gods, a possible memory of this early form of Poseidon. Indeed, across the Near East at the time, a number of gods with bull's heads are known, including the Canaanite chief deity El, creator of earth and master of its waters, and the Vedic figure Yama, ruler of the underworld, of primordial Indo-European descent. The Greeks recalled an ancient, mostly-forgotten god called Zagreus who was the bull-headed consort of the earth goddess and was the greatest of the gods, according to the lost epic poem *Alcmeonis*.[54] Zagreus later became identified with Dionysus, and some scholars think he began as a Semitic god, another Near Eastern connection.[55]

Among the Mycenaeans, the bull appeared both in art (such as in the depiction of Europa on the bull's back) and architecturally in the form of "sacral horns," through which sculptural bulls' horns on buildings and altars symbolized the animal, and thus the divine. The Mycenaeans imported the image of bull-leaping from Crete, if not necessarily the practice, and they sacrificed bulls to the gods, especially Poseidon, as well as possibly human sacrifices.[56] The image of the powerful, divine bull is, of course, reminiscent of the two fire-breathing, brazen-hoofed bulls Jason must yoke in Colchis. Perhaps we have here another distorted account of the transition from Poseidon's supremacy to that of Zeus, when en route to the Zeus-inspired Fleece, Jason tames Poseidon's sacred beasts. Could this be another recollection of the old form of Mycenaean worship which was no longer practiced after the fall of Mycenae, a reconfiguration of an old myth of the earth god in a new Zeus-dominated era?

Unfortunately, at such a distance, it would be impossible to say for certain, though the symbolism is appropriate. Further confirmation for this idea comes from the suggestion (admittedly quite speculative) that the Mycenaeans once worshipped Poseidon in three forms corresponding to the underworld, earth, and heavens: as the god of earthquakes, the god of bulls, and the god of the sun. In Mycenaean Greece and on Crete, some believe the sun god role and the bull god role were once combined, as in the later Greek description of the ancient Cretan sun god Talos as bull-formed.[57] When we recall that Aea/Colchis was deemed the land where the sun stored his rays, and King Aeëtes the son of the sun, the symbolism becomes even starker. The fire-breathing, brazen hoofed bulls could be solar symbols, as the bull's fiery breath recalls the solar rays emerging from artistic depictions of bulls' heads. The men born of dragon's teeth (if they were original to the myth) are earth symbols, and the dragon the underworld symbol. We shall return to this hypothesis in chapter 3.

IOLCUS: THE CITY OF JASON

In the Jason legend, our hero is the heir to the throne of Iolcus (also transliterated from the Greek as Iolkos), a city in Thessaly in east-central Greece, somewhat beyond the main power center of the Mycenaeans in Argolis. In the *Odyssey* Homer describes the city of Iolcus as "spacious" and is obviously aware of its Mycenaean-era greatness. Just as all of the other places Homer attributed to the Achaeans in the *Iliad* were major centers of Mycenaean power, so too was Iolcus a powerful center of Mycenaean culture in Thessaly. An important sea-faring center, the somewhat inland Iolcus reached the sea by a long inlet, known in Greek as an *ialka* (perhaps giving the town its name), that led to the port of Pagasae, which served as a major Thessalian shipyard and port from the Mycenaean age until another port, Demetrias, was constructed to the north in 293 BCE. Archaeological research indicates that when Iolcus was founded, it was close to the sea, but over time the coastline retreated as the local river washed down soil from the highlands.[58] A brief tour of the Mycenaean city of Iolcus will help us to set the beginning of the Jason story in its archaeological and cultural context.

The Mycenaean area formerly known as Iolcus is located just beyond the modern city of Volos, at the foot of the Pelion, the mountain where the centaur Chiron was said to live. In later times, and perhaps as early as the Mycenaean era, rams would be sacrificed to Zeus and townsfolk would climb Pelion wearing their fleeces in a ritual of symbolic rebirth, echoes of Phrixus' sacrifice of the golden ram, about which more in chapter 3.[59] On the plain below, the dry bed of the river Xerias was once the flowing Anaurus, where Jason lost his sandal. Nearby stand the ruins of the Neolithic settlement of Dimini, with its acropolis, walls, and

Ships docked at Volo beneath Mt. Pelion, as seen in 1903. The scene would have been much the same in the Bronze Age, when Mycenaean ships gathered at Pagasae, the port near Jason's Iolcus, contributing to the legend of the Argonauts. The city of Iolcus was eventually abandoned, and the nearby city of Volos replaced it, assuming even its name. Modern Volos grew on the Anaurus River atop the ancient ports of Pagasae and Demetrias in the nineteenth century (Library of Congress).

tombs, the oldest of which date back to the middle Bronze Age, around 4000 BCE. The Neolitihic Dimini comprised a village at whose center stood a well-built megaron, which archaeologists believe to have been the home of a high-status individual or family, perhaps a village chief or headman, due to the absence of cult objects and the presence of domestic tools and remains. Other houses in this ancient Stone Age village were smaller but also laid out in the style of a megaron.[60] Based on pottery similarities, this settlement may have had contact with Anatolia during the Late Neolithic or Early Bronze Age.[61] The beliefs and legends of the village's people are, unfortunately, unknown, but may have included an earth goddess and a bull-formed earth god, a belief system common across the Aegean region at least since the Neolithic and Çatal Höyük.

Atop this village rose a Bronze Age settlement that the director of excavations at Dimini, Vassiliki Adrimi-Sismani, identified as Jason's Iolcus, with its Mycenaean cultural features, an assessment that is generally accepted by archaeologists today. In the past, it had been assumed that Dimini was abandoned long before the Mycenaean occupation, but newer evidence suggests that the site was continuously occupied and gradually grew from a Neolithic settlement into a Bronze Age city.[62] Mycenaean Iolcus was best represented until quite recently by the area's well-known tholos tombs, among the few located outside southern Greece. Archaeologists excavating at Dimini unearthed eleven city blocks between 1977 and 1997, and they discovered the remains of the palace or temple of Mycenaean Iolcus in 1997. Today, the city represents the most complete Late Bronze Age settlement known in Greece, and it is from these excavations that we have received a glimpse into the city of Jason at the time of the Argonauts' expedition.

The Mycenaean settlement began in the fifteenth century BCE and reached its greatest extent in the fourteenth and thirteenth centuries BCE. In its earlier Mycenaean phase (fourteenth century BCE), a large paved road, approximately 15 feet (4.5 meters) wide and 300 feet (95 meters) long ran through the center of the city, with rectangular houses lining both sides. These houses were built on stone foundations with superstructures of mud brick. Most of the homes were designed with a central courtyard containing a hearth and a well, with additional rooms behind. In one of the homes, a household altar was found, with a bull figurine, perhaps representing Poseidon in his bull-god form.[63] A megaron served as an administrative center for the city, and was later replaced with much larger structures.

During the thirteenth century BCE, the population of the city grew, as evidenced from the increased number of houses, additions to existing houses, and the expansion of the city to around 24 acres (10 hectares). However, experts are unable to estimate exactly how many people might have lived in Mycenaean Iolcus.[64] What they do know, however, is that the city was well-organized and evinced evidence of centralized planning, indicating a strong central authority, such as a king, and also shows evidence of craft specialization, which indicates that the city was wealthy and had an ample supply of food from the surrounding plains.

Unlike most Mycenaean centers, whose "palaces" sat atop high hills, the early megaron of Iolcus and the two larger, connected megara that later replaced it are located at the foot of a hill (the hill being too small to support a major construction), and there appears never to have been a temple atop the hill. The two megara are known archaeologically as Megaron A and Megaron B, and they probably were two stories tall. They stand astride a central court and are flanked by rooms believed to be workshops and residential quarters. The site, as a whole, is thought to be an "administrative center," and it is the largest and most complex Mycenaean "palace" known in all Thessaly.[65] Within the megara, evidence has been found for artisanal work, including metal work, and ritual activity in the form of cult objects, including terracotta figurines of women, cows and/or bulls, and a throne with a seated figure. Megaron A appeared to have more secular functions, and religious activity is in greater evidence in Megaron B. The implication is that the rulers of Iolcus employed royal craftsman in the service of the king and his cult. As Adrimi-Sismani notes, "Possibly when their access to raw materials was limited they did not hesitate to organize great overseas expeditions in order to acquire them."[66] This, she implied, might have been the historical background for the Jason story.

The city's two megara were destroyed sometime between 1292 and 1132 BCE according to radiocarbon tests done on datable material (pottery shards) found in the layer of debris that marked the end of the two buildings. Megaron B burned, but the causes of the fire and of the destruction of Megaron A are unknown, though work on the site continues. No evidence of natural disaster, such as earthquake, has yet been discovered. It is known that across the ancient world formerly sacred sites were ritually destroyed when they were rebuilt or abandoned. The Etruscans and Romans practiced destructive rituals to deconsecrate temples and "unfound" cities. Such practices were necessary to remove an old god from his or her temple when rededicating a site to a new deity.[67] The Archaic Etruscan meeting hall, functionally similar to a megaron, at Poggio Civitate was ritually torn down in the sixth century BCE, its walls knocked over, its statuary carefully buried. Other Etruscan temples show evidence of ritual destruction.[68] Similar practices occurred in Hellenistic Greece. In 312 BCE Ptolemy I conquered the city of Marion on Cyprus and ritually deconsecrated the temples of Zeus and Aphrodite by burning them, relocating their cults to the new city of Arsinoe.[69] Could the destruction of Iolcus' megara reflect a deconsecrating, or even a transition to a new form of worship? This is one possible explanation, though certainly not the only one. There is simply not enough evidence to know for sure; however, the supposition takes on added weight in light of the fact that the nearby settlement of Volos-Palia expanded rapidly at the time of Iolcus' abandonment, and later assumed the name of Iolcus. Across the region of Thessaly, populations shifted from old Mycenaean centers to new nearby settlements that would come to prominence in the Dark Age and beyond.[70] Perhaps after the fall of Mycenaean power, a new center and new rituals were needed.

What is known is that after the destruction, the residents of Iolcus reoccupied Megaron A—but not Megaron B, the one associated with cult activity—for a short period after its destruction. Changes in the type of pottery found above and below the layer of destruction imply a cultural change at the time of destruction. The residents of Iolcus finally abandoned the megaron altogether right around the time that Mycenaean power across the Greek world faded away. In this, Iolcus followed the pattern of most other Mycenaean centers.

The excavations at Iolcus tell us much about the culture and practices of the people who lived there in the age of Jason, much of which agrees with the myth:

- The city was likely ruled by a king.
- The city was connected to the port of Pegasae, and through it to sea travel.
- Ritual bull figurines imply the worship of the Mycenaean Poseidon.
- The nearby Mt. Pelion was associated with the sacrifice of rams.

There remains, however, a crucial missing element. The Jason story is primarily one of the quest, the epic voyage from Thessaly to Aea/Colchis at the far edges of the world. Is there an archaeological basis for suspecting the Mycenaeans of such sea voyages?

THE MYCENAEAN SEA EMPIRE

We know from exotic materials found in Mycenaean sites that Bronze Age Greece had a wide trade network that stretched across central and southern Europe, perhaps as far to the north as Britain. Mycenaeans would not have gone that far themselves; instead, goods would be traded from one community to another across the continent until they reached Greece, traveling along well-developed trade routes. Inevitably, stories about these far-flung places must have travelled back to Greece with goods like gold, amber, and tin. The Mycenaeans did, however, sail to the east, travelling from island to island across the Aegean Sea, establishing networks of commerce. At first they did so in competition with the Minoans, but eventually they achieved dominance over the Aegean Sea routes. In the fourteenth century BCE, the Mycenaeans established ties with Egypt and the eastern coast of the Mediterranean; a century later, they dominated eastern Mediterranean trade and could bring increasing amounts of Near Eastern goods to Mycenaean centers. They also sailed westward to Italy, a land well-known by the Archaic Period.[71] Mycenaean pottery has been found from southern Italy to Egypt to the Levant.

Because mainland Greece has relatively few resources, the Mycenaeans needed foreign trade to supply their elite with luxury goods, and to grow their economy beyond the subsistence agriculture that had characterized Greek life before 1600 BCE. This impetus pushed the Mycenaeans to sea, and these trade missions are often claimed to lay behind the legend of Jason and the Argonauts. After all, if precious metals, exotic stones, ivory, and glass beads all had to be imported, trade was necessary, and missions would have to be sent out to find resources and arrange for their purchase and transport. And something would need to be traded in return. Exactly what the Mycenaeans sold is unknown. It may have been wool, as the Minoans did, or perhaps slaves. However they did it, the Mycenaean elite grew enormously wealthy.

The most important event in the development of Mycenaean sea trade was the collapse of Minoan power following the powerful volcanic eruption on Thera, an event dated somewhere within fifty years of 1570 BCE. The geological and climate changes unleashed by this massively destructive event created powerful tsunamis of around 60 feet (20 meters), lowered temperatures by several degree Celsius, and devastated Crete's population when the volcanic ash killed at least two years' crops. The weakened Minoan civilization became prey to outside forces. Its vitality sapped, it gradually but inexorably declined. Power passed to the Mycenaeans. Around 1380 BCE the Mycenaeans gained effective control of Crete, though they likely left the local elite in charge of domestic affairs, based on the relative lack of evidence for destructive conquest. However, megara began to replace Minoan construction; pottery switched to Mycenaean forms, and Linear B became the language of trade. Within fifty years, the Mycenaeans had absorbed the Minoan trade empire, and Mycenaean sites could be found all across the eastern Mediterranean. The Egyptians recognized the change and repainted scenes of Minoan traders to reflect the costumes of their new Mycenaean trading partners.[72]

But did the Mycenaeans travel to the Black Sea? For a long time the answer to that question was a decisive "no," and no Mycenaean relics were found in the Black Sea region. However, in 1991, Stefan Hiller surveyed the evidence and concluded that the few bits of Mycenaean pottery and Mycenaean-style stone anchors found on the southwest portion of the Black Sea coast argued for a Greek presence there in the Bronze Age. Further, he described bronze axes found in the southern Ukraine that resembled those made at Troy, and objects used in hitching horses to chariots that were possibly from Mycenae, though no absolute connection can be proved. Decorative items originating in Mycenaean patterns were found in an arc stretching from Mycenae to Transylvania to the Ukraine, arguing for "influence" if not direct contact between these regions. Further, swords found in the northeastern coast of the Black Sea are similar in design to Mycenaean originals. Taken together, Hiller argued, these lines of evidence demonstrate that Mycenaeans sailed the Black Sea. Consequently, Hiller wrote, the Argonauts' voyage could well have been founded on Mycenaean-era voyages, a proposition made stronger by the clear reality of Iolcus as a Mycenaean center.[73] However, the evidence does not necessarily prove Mycenaean voyages, or sustained contact. For example, goods can be traded from hand to hand over long distances. In North America, a medieval Norse coin may have traveled thousands of miles from Greenland to Maine via the Inuit of the Arctic without a concomitant movement of Vikings.[74] Closer to our purpose, the Mycenaeans received trade goods from as far afield as Britain and the Baltic, but they almost certainly never travelled there, instead receiving goods through a trade network.[75] Nevertheless, if only by hearsay, there would have been some understanding of these faraway lands in the heartlands of the Mycenaeans.

Therefore, by the time the Mycenaean centers fell, it was not uncommon for a person living at, say, Iolcus to be familiar with lands ranging from Italy in the West to Anatolia and Syria in the East, Egypt in the south, and, further afield, rumored lands of half-mythical peoples spoken of in merchants' and travelers' tales. In this age, the Black Sea was considered an entry point to the great Oceanus, the river that surrounded all the land in the world, and it was not yet known to be an enclosed sea. Any lands that lay across far Ocean, like Aea, were a sort of never-never land cloaked in fantasy and myth. When the earliest Jason set sail for Aea, he was heading not on a typical Mycenaean trade mission, but instead going far beyond the well-plotted and familiar journeys of Mycenaean trade to the very ends of the earth.

THE FALL OF THE MYCENAEANS

Near the end of the Mycenaean period, around 1250 BCE Hittite archives report the activity of a group of foreigners known as the Ahhiyawa who were a great sea power and who conducted war in Anatolia, against a city once ruled by a king or prince named Alaksandus. Scholars identify these people as the Achaeans (the Mycenaeans), who fought a war in Troy against Priam and his son, Prince Alexander, better known as Paris. The story of the Trojan War seemingly had a basis in truth, in frequent raids by Mycenaeans along the Anatolian coast.[76] However, only fifty years after the Trojan War, Mycenaean civilization vanished, quickly.

The fall of the Mycenaeans has been attributed to a variety of causes, including civil war, invasion, climate change, and natural disaster. The great megaron temple-palaces were destroyed, and many were either torn down or burned. Many were empty inside when destroyed, which can point either to looting or to deliberate evacuation before an enemy or ritual deconsecration. No definitive explanation for the fall of the Mycenaeans exists, and what evidence exists can support a number of hypotheses. A fire could well be arson, ritual, or the result of natural disaster. The Greeks themselves attributed the end of the Heroic Age to the invasion of the Dorians, a northern people for whom no archaeological evidence exists. Homer suggests that feuds and open warfare between the Achaean centers led to their weakening and downfall. It is also possible that the common people rose up town by town against weakened elites paralyzed by bureaucracy and ritual, and destroyed the symbols of elite power, the megara and the massive walls of the citadels. These would be replaced later by new temples and smaller rebuilding efforts, in keeping with the idea of a new, popular-based culture succeeding a former elite who were dead or in disrepute. At any rate, by 1120 BCE the trappings of elite culture, including Linear B writing and tholos tombs, had vanished, and with it the Mycenaean Age. The Dark Ages had begun.[77]

In the end, the less civilized Greeks who came after the Mycenaean Age stood in awe of the giant ruins scattered across the landscape, which they imagined to have been constructions so much beyond them that they must have been the work of a race of heroes or giants. Mycenae and its sister cities became associated with the Cyclopes, titanic sons of the primordial gods Uranus (Sky) and Gaia (Earth), divine blacksmiths and architects. The colossal citadels passed from history into legend, and the "cyclopean" walls became places where mythology was made real.[78]

The Dark Ages

What came next was a period of darkness and decline. The Dark Age Greeks are in many ways parallel to people everywhere who carried on after the end of a powerful elite culture, like the western Europeans after the fall of Rome, or the Maya after the end of their pyramid cities. Writing was no more, gone until the legendary Cadmus brought it from Phoenicia in the eighth century. Nearly half the known Mycenaean gods ceased to be worshipped. Old religious practices were revitalized with new deities and new rituals from the Near East, perhaps via the cult centers of Cyprus,[79] that combined with the surviving Mycenaean cults and formed the new Greek religion that would continue on into Late Antiquity. Old centers lost population, and new centers formed. Mycenae, for example, faded while nearby Argos grew so powerful that the playwright Aeschylus would later place his *Agamemnon* there instead of the king's Homeric capital of Mycenae. The styles of art changed dramatically, and by the end of the period Near Eastern influences became paramount. Populations declined; subsistence farming became a way of life again, and foreign trade all but vanished.[80] The great sea voyages became memories, Jason perhaps standing for them all.

In the Dark Ages, the worship of Zeus definitively superseded that of Poseidon and Hera, and Zeus became the chief god of the Greek pantheon, perhaps when the old Indo-European-inspired sky god (*Dyēus/Zeus) took over the attributes of a Near Eastern storm god, those beings originally being separate.[81] Exactly when this occurred is unknown, and it is unlikely to have happened all at once all across Greece. (Some suggest the process began in Mycenaean times, but this cannot be proved.) However, by the time of the shepherd-poet Hesiod at the end of the Dark Ages, Zeus is clearly the king of the gods. Hesiod (or the poets represented by that name) was something of an evangelist for Zeus and told the story of Zeus' accession to the divine throne in the form of a myth which adapted motifs from Near Eastern mythology, common during the Orientalizing Period and its influx of new beliefs. The story begins with Cronus usurping control of the heavens by castrating Uranus, the sky god:

> Then the son [Cronus] from his ambush stretched forth his left hand and in his right took the great long sickle with jagged teeth, and swiftly lopped off his own father's members and cast

them away to fall behind him. And not vainly did they fall from his hand; for all the bloody drops that gushed forth Earth received, and as the seasons moved round she bare the strong Erinyes and the great Giants with gleaming armour [...][82]

Cronus' wife Rhea spirited away their son Zeus to Crete, where he grew to manhood and then overthrew his father, assuming the kingship of the gods and receiving the lightning bolt as his weapon from the Giants Cronus had bound.

In this story, the common Near Eastern myth of a primordial deity who is torn asunder in order to cleave sky and ground is plainly visible. Additionally, the story shows clear echoes of the Hittite and Hurrian myth of the three gods who succeed each other as ruler of heaven. Anu (Uranus) is deposed by Kurambi (Cronus) who gives birth to a storm god son, Teshub (Zeus), who overthrows him in turn. However, the identity of the Greek Cronus (also transliterated as Kronos) is not clear-cut, and according to Robin Hard, Cronus and the Titans may have been imported wholesale from the Near East.[83] For the Archaic and Classical Greeks, Cronus was not a god so much to be worshipped (unlike his Roman counterpart, Saturn) as to serve as a placeholder, a mythological figure who filled the genealogical gap between Uranus and Zeus as the Near Eastern story was refashioned for the Greek tradition. Indeed, there is no pre–Archaic mention of Cronus as the King of the Gods. He had no identifiable cult, and apparently only a single temple near that of Zeus at Athens, and a small altar at Olympia, both with his wife Rhea in their function as Zeus' parents. On symbolic grounds Bernard C. Dietrich equated Cronus with a god of grain, but expressed some consternation that his Hittite and Hurrian counterpart, Kumarbi, was identified with the Sumerian god Enlil, the god of the Earth, instead.[84] This, however, may be a key to disentangling the story.

If it is true that the Mycenaeans worshipped Poseidon as the earth god, then it is possible that at first it was Poseidon who filled the role taken by Cronus in Hesiod's day. One tantalizing thread that connects these two deities is the possible—but highly speculative—nineteenth century identification of Cronus' name with the Semitic term *k-r-n* or *q-r-n*, meaning "horned."[85] Could this reflect the horned bull-god of the earth, Poseidon the Earth-Shaker? A. P. Bos notes the parallels between the Cronus story and another Near East bull god, the creator god Ilu, whom the weather god replaces, though Bos equates Cronus with the weather god and not the creator god.[86] Additionally, Cronus stands in relation to his sons Zeus (of the storms), Poseidon (of the sea), and Hades (of death) just as the bull-formed head of the Mesopotamian pantheon, El (who is cognate with Ilu), stands in relation to his sons Adad (or Baal, of the storms), Yam (of the sea), and Mot (of death). Perhaps Cronus was a Near Eastern epithet of an old chief god that eventually took on a life of its own when Zeus replaced Poseidon as king of the gods. Obviously, in such a situation, Poseidon simply could not be both the deposed king and also Zeus' brother, the sea god. This is of course only speculation, but it may be possible that the Dark Age Greeks separated the sea god from the older Mycenaean earth god and, calling the latter by another name, left him to his fate, deposed by Zeus in imported myth as the Zeus cult took over the head of the Greek pantheon in practice following the Mycenaean collapse.

One possible confirmation of this comes from a myth associated with Cronus. It is said as early as the Archaic period that he took the form of a horse and impregnated the nymph Philyra on the coast of the Black Sea. She fled in shame to Thessaly where she gave birth to a human-horse hybrid, the centaur Chiron, who would become Jason's tutor.[87] This of course is in contradiction to the later myth of Poseidon, who is said to have been the god who created horses by spilling his semen on the ground (or mating with a monster who became the mother of horses), or to have taken the form of a horse to pursue Demeter.[88] Cronus could not logically have had the form of a horse or created horse hybrids before the animal existed, unless, of course, at one time Cronus and Poseidon were one and the same. As we shall see in chapter 3, evidence indicates the centaurs, and by extension Chiron's father, once had the form of a bull.

This is only speculation, no matter how suggestive; however, it does offer an intriguing interpretation of Jason's quest. Jason travels *east*, to the region whence came the storm god attributes of the composite Zeus, to retrieve his symbol, the Fleece, and return it to Mycenaean Greece. His aim is to replace Pelias, son of Poseidon, with himself, under the aegis of the Fleece and its patron, the new king of the gods, Zeus. Given that the Jason story developed in oral tradition during the Greek Dark Ages when the forms of Greek religion we recognize today were taking shape, it seems possible that the Jason story reflects in a very indirect way the transformation of the Greek pantheon in the years between the fall of Mycenaean rule and the establishment of the new Archaic order, a subject to which we will return in our next chapter.

What is certain, however, is that the Dark Age Greeks told stories, stories about the vanished Mycenaean world, and stories derived from the myths and legends of the peoples the Mycenaeans had traded with and interacted with. In the minds of the Greeks who gaped in awe at the ruins around them as they squatted in their small, flimsy houses and huts, the former world of cyclopean stone had been one of giants, of heroes, of demigods. These people must have done great things and experienced great adventures. Gradually, the stories of the Mycenaean people coalesced into the mythology we know today. The new mythology of the gods took shape in the forms recorded in Hesiod's *Theogony*. The stories of the Trojan War solidified into a series of long oral poems known as the Epic Cycle: *Kypria, Iliad, Aithiopis, Little Iliad, Ilioupersis, Nostoi, Odyssey,* and *Telegoneia,* of which only two survive complete.

Another series of stories, that of an epic journey to the ends of the earth to retrieve the Golden Fleece, also came together in oral tradition. It is to this story that we now turn.

PART TWO

DEVELOPMENT OF THE MYTH

3

The God

The First Jason Stories

G. S. Kirk, the great British scholar of the classics, believed that the story of Jason and the Argonauts originated centuries before the corpus of mythology that developed around the Trojan War. He argued that while the heroes of the *Iliad* and the *Odyssey*—Agamemnon, Menelaus, Achilles, Odysseus, etc.—participated in events that were complex and semi-realistic, if not based on fact, another group of heroes, including Perseus, Cadmus, Heracles, and Jason, were the subject of imaginative fantasies, "simple episodes that nevertheless seize the imagination." The two types of stories, the complex and the simple, the realistic and the fantastic, appear to be younger and older myths. Jason and his fellow heroes, importantly, were placed into a mythical context decades or centuries before the Trojan War, in "an earlier heroic generation." If the Greeks recognized these heroes as being more ancient than the warriors at Troy, who it is now understood were based upon Mycenaeans at the end of their cultural age, then it stands to reason that Jason and the other heroes must have stretched back still farther. Jason must have been a hero whose story was first told in some form by the Mycenaeans themselves in the time before the Dark Age.[1] Kirk, in *The Nature of Greek Myths*, suggested that the Jason story indeed began in Bronze Age Greece and only later, after 1000 BCE gained its specific geographic footing in the Black Sea.[2] As we have seen, the Near Eastern stories of the hero who slays the dragon and the hero who undertakes a great quest were extant before this time, and thus the Jason story may well have begun in this age.

However, these original stories of Jason are long lost. The classics professor and cryptanalyst Henry D. Ephron thought he had found a piece of one in 1961 when he attempted to translate a tablet from Enkomi, Cyprus, written in a mysterious and un-deciphered language from the island known as Cypro-Minoan. The tablet dated to sometime around 1200 BCE and in Ephron's translation formed part of a poem dealing with Jason, "lord of the wandering Argo," and Medea, and seemed to relate an incident in which the hero sacrificed a goat so that a seer would perform a secret rite.[3] This would be the oldest reference to Jason's adventures yet found; however, Ephron's work was based on an assumption that Cypro-Minoan was a form of simplified Mycenaean Greek, which later scholarly work has not borne out. Ephron's largely fanciful translation has found little support, and Cypro-Minoan remains undeciphered.

Our first securely attested written references to Jason's legend occur only with Homer in 750 BCE and Hesiod not long after, and after them only in fragments of poetry. The full story of Jason and his quest survives in its oldest form only in the Fourth Pythian Ode of

Pindar, composed in 462 BCE a thousand years after Mycenaean culture ruled the Aegean, though earlier written versions existed but were lost. By this time, the story had grown and changed and had taken on the form, more or less, in which we know it today. The fifty Argonauts, once anonymous, may not have had their roster filled with all the heroes who would later row the *Argo,* but the outlines were there. Three hundred years had passed between Pindar and Homer, and five centuries between Homer and the fall of Mycenaean culture. If it is true that Jason originated among the Mycenaeans, the story that bore his name in the time of Homer and Pindar may have been very different from the story as it was told in the megara of Iolcus in the Bronze Age, just as the Jason of the many forms of his later legend differed in his personality and in his details. Kirk describes the Jason tale of ten centuries of myth as "an amalgam of diverse elements,"[4] and indeed, it is the changeable and mutable nature of the Jason story that sets it apart from the fixed forms of the Homeric heroes, or even the relatively stable characterizations of Heracles and Perseus. Each generation and successive age found in the Jason tale what they wished to see. As a consequence, the Jason of Pindar and the Jason of Apollonius are very different men; was the Jason of the Mycenaeans different still?

This chapter intends to explore this question by attempting to pull together what scholars have reconstructed about the earliest Jason stories and evaluate the figure of Jason in light of shamanism and cult initiation in the period between the fall of the Mycenaeans and the Archaic Age. However, reconstructions are necessarily tentative and each, to a greater or lesser extent, is speculative. Hence, any attempt to imagine the early adventures of Jason is an exercise in creativity as much as it is a deduction from fact. These reconstructions cannot be perfect mirrors of the past, and some of the elements of the recreated stories may be extremely close to the lost original while other aspects may be very much wrong. Before we begin to sift the evidence for the first Jason stories, let us conduct a thought experiment of our own to illustrate the problems of reconstructing myths from what is known through their later forms.

A Thought Experiment

Let us imagine ourselves as archaeologists a few thousand years from now, an age when the written word has been replaced by technologies that stream thoughts directly into our heads and reading has been all but forgotten. From an examination of movies that survive from the dark ages of the twentieth and twenty-first century, English has been deciphered, but while we can understand its spoken form, all we know from these films is that written words existed primarily to record the titles and functions of the ritual experts who created movies, and to provide signage and record economic transactions. Nevertheless, an interesting discovery indicates that at one point movies had been preceded by written texts, something called "books."

A cache of ancient video recordings has been uncovered, and it is up to us to reconstruct the original lost texts upon which they must have been based. These movies include four versions of *Hamlet* and four versions of *Dracula*:

- *Hamlet* (1948, with Laurence Olivier).
- *Hamlet* (1964, with Richard Burton).

- *Hamlet* (1990, with Mel Gibson).
- *Hamlet* (1996, with Kenneth Branaugh).
- *Dracula* (1931, with Bela Lugosi).
- *Son of Dracula* (1943, with Lon Chaney, Jr.).
- *Dracula* (1992, with Gary Oldman).
- *Dracula*: *Dead and Loving It* (1995, with Leslie Neilson).

From these films, how accurate might our hypothetical reconstructions of Shakespeare's play *Hamlet* and Bram Stoker's novel *Dracula* be? To take *Hamlet* first, we would immediately be struck by the fact that all four versions are nearly word-for-word the same, and we would rightly conclude that the lost text contained those words. In reconstructing the text, we would, of course, note that some of the films contain scenes not included in others. We might feel that the longest of the films, the 1996 version, is the most complete and therefore closest to the original; or, we might equally conclude that only the scenes each film has in common are derived from Shakespeare, and any others are interpolations or corruptions. We would also note that three of the four films use medieval or Renaissance costumes and sets (Branaugh instead moved the period to the Victorian era), and would have a good idea of the time period of the original, if not an exact idea. We would end up with a reconstruction that was, perhaps, only a few lines or scenes off from the original play, a fairly good estimate given the time that had passed.

    Dracula on the other hand is more problematic. The four versions we have to work with are very different in their details and share only the broadest plot outline in common— that a vampire arrives from Eastern Europe, attacks a young woman, and is destroyed by a team composed of a romantic interest for the woman and a scientist. It will be obvious that the 1995 film is a burlesque, a Mel Brooks parody of the other *Dracula* titles. How would we go about correlating the various films and their conflicting accounts of the vampire to determine what might or might not have been a part of the written text that inspired them all?

    First, we would draw on similarities. The 1931 and 1992 *Dracula* movies tell substantively the same story, and they share a number of scenes in common, including a male character's first meeting with Dracula at his castle, the vampire's voyage by sea to England, and his attacks on young women in London. These, then must be a part of the original. The differences, though, would be confounding. We would be hard pressed to assign the characters to their correct places, since the two films have different figures with different relationships to each other perform key actions. For example, in 1931 (and in the 1995 comedy) Renfield voyages to Transylvania, but in 1992 it is Jonathan Harker. In 1931 and 1995, Dracula is dispatched in London, while in 1992 he is chased back to Transylvania and killed at his castle. Was this an original action, or would our archaeologist find it a "separate tradition" that has unknowingly duplicated the hypothetical novel's first scene again at the end of story? The fact that *Son of Dracula* essentially retells the same plotline in a new location, New Orleans, might lead us to conclude that it was either meant as an extension of the novel or perhaps as a localized tradition intended to connect the vampire to Louisiana. We would finally note that all of the movie versions emphasize the vampire's romantic attachments to the young women he pursues, and conclude that the theme must have been essential to the novel.

    Our hypothetical reconstruction of *Dracula*, therefore, would contain some elements that are correct (the outline of the plot, a few of the key characters, many of the locations) and many that seemed probable but are in fact incorrect (the identities and relationships of some characters, the final scenes of the novel, the explicit love theme). It would likely have missed out on the epistolary structure of the novel, and would be able to verify only a few lines of dialogue that must have been in the original book given their later repetition ("I bid you ... welcome." "I never drink ... wine."). The accuracy of the reconstructed story would be significantly less than with *Hamlet*, and necessarily incomplete.

Reconstructing the story of Jason from its later surviving versions is far closer to trying to rebuild Stoker's *Dracula* than it is to transcribing *Hamlet*, known as it is from differing poetic treatments, later attempts to connect the legend to the city of Corinth, sequels (such as the *Medea* plays), and even from comedic versions recorded on pottery. This thought experiment begins to hint at the challenges of attempting a reconstruction of an ancient tale from its later versions. With those caveats firmly noted, we can begin to weigh the evidence and assess what *might* have been in the earliest Jason stories.

Jason and Chiron

The character we know in English as Jason is more properly Iason in Greek, the letter "J" being a medieval invention applied to words beginning with "I" to soften their hard sound. His name derives from the Greek *iasthai* ("to heal") and means "healer." It may be first attested in a name found on a Linear B tablet at Pylos, *i-wa-so* (the Mycenaean *w*, or digamma, drops out in later Greek), but this is uncertain, for that word has also been plausibly explained as a place name along the border of Achaea and Arcadia (Homeric Iasos), an ethnic name for a group or individual from that region, or a military term for lookouts (who may have been from Iasos).[5] In most versions of the myth this is Jason's only name; however, this was sometimes held to be a name bestowed upon him by his teacher after his escape from Iolcus, based on Pindar's statement that the centaur Chiron chose to address the hero as "Jason." A later Alexandrine commentator, or *scholiast*, on Pindar wrote in a marginal note known as a *scholium* that Jason was given his name by Chiron, and the Renaissance mythographer Natalis Comes misread the Greek text of another scholium to make this name Dolomedes (no Classical authority gives any earlier name), and still later writers confused Dolomedes for Diomedes and repeat this claim down to the present day, usually citing the Pindar scholia as the putatitve source.[6] Since this claim dates only to the Renaissance, it does not reflect a genuine Archaic or Dark Age tradition about Jason's name. Etymologically, Jason's name is probably related to that of Iasion, a consort of the earth goddess Demeter, though the two characters' only mythological connection is a shared family relationship to Cadmus.

In the Standard Version, the etymology of Jason's name makes little sense, since in none but the most metaphorical of ways is he a healer.[7] He does not heal wounds, nor does he use medicinal herbs or drugs. These aspects are associated instead with the sorceress Medea, who knows well the magic of potions. However, in the Standard Version, the young Jason is sent to a cave on Mount Pelion to be tutored by the centaur Chiron, an ancient creature who provided many of the epic heroes of Greek myth with knowledge of the healing arts, especially the use of potions and drugs. That this is a very ancient tale is confirmed by its repetition in Hesiod, one of the oldest surviving Greek authors, as early as the eighth century BCE.[8] According to the classical scholar C. J. Mackie, this may hold the key to unraveling the earliest version of Jason.

As noted previously, the centaur Chiron was the son of the soon-to-be-deposed king of the gods, Cronus, conceived on the shores of the Black Sea during his reign and born to the nymph Philyra in Thessaly, near where Jason would be born. He was half man and half equine, sharing the upper body of a man and the hindquarters and four legs of a horse. As a result of his divine parentage, Chiron was blessed with great wisdom and nobility, and later tradition makes him the teacher of "Peleus, Achilles, Telamon, Theseus, Machaon, Podaleirios, Cephalus, and even Apollo," in addition to his most famous pupil, the healer Asclepius, and Jason and Jason's son by Medea, Medeus.[9]

We know that the Mycenaeans depicted centaurs in their art, possibly in imitation of Minoan practice where bulls were sometimes depicted with human heads.[10] Chiron was also said to have suffered an irreparable knee wound as the result of Heracles' actions, a clay figurine found at Lefkandi and dated at 900 BCE clearly shows a beautifully decorated centaur with that self-same knee wound.[11] However, horses were introduced to Greece only in the second millennium BCE, so whether there had been an earlier Chiron who had once borne the body of a different animal (say, a bull), he would only have been a horse since the terminal Mycenaean period, right around the time the Jason myth would have begun. Our word "centaur" derives from the Greek *kentauros*, which, while its etymology is obscure, is frequently argued to contain the root *tauros*, indicating a bull, perhaps referring to the Near East bull gods.[12] This agrees well with the bull of Mycenaean Poseidon, who it is possible once served in place of Cronus as the previously reigning king of the gods (and therefore as Chiron's father). Does this indicate that Jason was reared in the worship of the earth god, or had once served him?

Given the age of the Chiron story, it would seem most likely that he was Jason's teacher in myth before he was made the teacher of the other heroes. Perhaps Achilles was made his pupil in imitation of Jason, whose tutelage to Chiron was therefore the model for other heroes' mythic education. Alternately, it is also possible that the Jason myth came first, and Chiron became associated with Jason later on. In the classical age Chiron was the model teacher, but references to him in the Homeric poems make clear that his myth stretched back as far as Greek memory allowed. It is not, however, entirely clear whether Chiron was always considered a centaur, and in the *Iliad*, there are no references to his equine qualities. Could his conflation with an animal-human hybrid perhaps represent a literalized understanding of the shaman's ability to commune with the spirit world and transform into animals? If so, this would imply that Chiron was passing on his shamanic (or priestly) knowledge to Jason, something that agrees with Mackie's interpretation of the myth, which we will now explore.

Jason the Healer

In other myths, Chiron teaches Achilles and the healer Asclepius the secrets of medicinal plants and drugs. Asclepius, Chiron's best student, so masters the arts of healing that he can even revive the dead, which earns him the punishment of Zeus. Since the healing arts were a major portion of Chiron's curriculum, and since Jason's own name implies a healing function, Mackie concludes that the weight of evidence suggests Jason originally had a mastery of pharmacy.[13] Evidence for this can be found on a Greek krater vase from Corinth from c. 575 BCE which depicts a scene from the voyage of the Argonauts when Jason approaches the blind seer Phineus to learn the will of the gods. In the Standard Version, Jason and the Argonauts aid Phineus by freeing him from the harpies, but in the krater a different story emerges. Here, Jason is depicted standing behind a seated Phineus, both of whom are explicitly named on the vase. Jason's hands are placed over the eyes of the seer, and Mackie, following the German scholar M. Vojatzi, identifies this as Jason healing Phineus of his blindness.[14] This evidence fits well

Detail from a Corinthian column-krater vase from c. 575 BCE depicting Jason (standing at left) healing the blind Phineus (seated at right) by placing his hands across the king's eyes. On the fragment from which this drawing was made (in a private collection), the artist inscribes both Phineus' and Jason's names beside the figures (author's drawing).

with literary accounts of Chiron's ability to heal blindness, as well as his student Asclepius' similar power. Jason might well, therefore, have once possessed great healing powers. However, no later literary sources explicitly discuss Jason as a master of medicine.

There is another adventure associated with Jason that is known only from visual imagery. A series of Greek and Etruscan images ranging in age from the late sixth to the early fifth centuries BCE depict Jason descending into the mouth of the dragon and emerging from the monster's mouth before claiming the Golden Fleece. The oldest of these images, vases from Corinth, are in fact the first known images of Jason,[15] and must have represented a variant story that later authors did not record. An Etruscan hand mirror shows Jason, explicitly named, emerging from the mouth of the dragon while clutching the Golden Fleece, while an Etruscan scarab medallion shows the hero emerging from the dragon but no Fleece. These pieces are usually assigned to the fifth century. Another Etruscan image, without Jason, shows Athena and Artemis standing beside the dragon and the Golden Fleece, usually interpreted as depicting the moment when Jason is within the dragon. Around 480 BCE an Athenian red figure cup by the painter Douris gives the most elaborate depiction of this story. In the image, a bearded serpent or dragon is seen on the left of the image, his mouth open, sharp teeth visible. Behind him, the Golden Fleece hangs limply from a tree bearing apples. Within the dragon's mouth, a limp bearded man, Jason, is seen emerging, his long hair falling over his head. Beside him stands the helmeted goddess Athena, recognizable by her aegis and owl. It has been suggested that this image represents Jason cutting the tongue from the serpent to win the Fleece, but Jason holds no tongue in any of these images, so this seems a less likely explanation.

These images are noteworthy for several reasons. First, they represent a version of the story not found in any written account of the myth. Second, they depict Jason defeating the dragon either unaided or with the help of the goddess Athena—not the Medea of later telling. Finally, they are noteworthy for what is absent. Medea is depicted not at all. Jason's descent into the dragon's belly is not attested in the surviving literature, Apollonius may have had this alternative version of the snake story in mind when in his *Argonautica* Jason and Medea confront the serpent in the Grove of Ares and the snake was "eager to enclose them both in his murderous jaws,"[16] and Pindar when he implies that the Golden Fleece rested in the serpent's jaws.

Mackie suggests that the literary Jason is almost purposely reconfigured to eliminate references to his "otherworldly" adventures, such as healing the blind or descending into the serpent's belly, rendered less magical and more realistic.[17] The original mythical figure, as displayed in the oral tales recorded on pottery and medallions, instead was closer kin to Orpheus and Heracles (both of whom descended into Hades), taking part in adventures with a decidedly magical or otherworldly component. In fact, Mackie suggests that the journey Jason makes to the land of Aea to retrieve the Fleece and the journey into the dragon's belly are intentionally meant to evoke a journey to the Underworld. Evidence can be found in Pindar's description of Jason calming the anger of the dead Phrixus by retrieving the Fleece, which symbolizes his soul.[18] "Jason's task is to restore harmony to the upper and lower worlds. His quest therefore ... restores the peaceful coexistence of the living with the dead."[19] Jason, in short, heals the rift between the earthly plain and that of Hades.

But we can go beyond this and suggest that at first the trip to Aea was a *literal*, not symbolic, trip to Hades, or *katabasis* ("descent") in Greek.[20] The imagery of Jason within the dragon is striking for its similarity to Near Eastern conceptions of the Underworld, especially the common motif that the large jaws of a monster form the entrance to Hades—a close duplicate of the descent into the dragon's belly in the Jason story. And the dragon lived in the "Grove of Ares," the war god who in his first conception was originally an Underworld or chthonic god[21] equated with the Mesopotamian underworld god Nergal, who was also seen as the same as or the brother of the chthonic Gil-

The Etruscans frequently depicted a variant version of the Jason story where the hero is swallowed by the dragon and emerges from its belly. This drawing depicts the underside of a Etruscan sard scarab of c. 500 BCE on which is carved a scene of Jason (with petasos, sword, and shield) emerging from or being swallowed by the dragon. The scarab is currently in the Boston Museum of Fine Arts (author's drawing).

gamesh in his role as underworld god and ferryman. Joseph Fonten-rose also notes that the *Argo*'s steers-men were forms of Charon, guide of the dead, which we will look at in greater detail in chapter 6. Given also the fact that Near East mythol-ogy assigned the Underworld the role of nighttime resting place of the sun's rays, an image that reappears nearly word-for-word in many ancient descriptions of Aea, this identity seems plausible. In this case, Jason as "Healer" and master of plants would equate quite well with Dumuzi, the god of vegetation who "healed" the dry earth each year when he returned from the Under-world to restore plant life. It corre-lates also with the ancient claim that Jason had a passion for agriculture, a claim dating back to Pherecydes.[22] Dumuzi's name, it will be recalled, means the "producer of healthy young ones" (crops and sheep)[23] remarkably close in meaning to Jason as "healer" in the sense of "guarantor of health." Dumuzi was

This image from a red figure cup painted by Douris c. 480 BCE and now in the Vatican's Museo Gregoriano Etrusco is among the most important for understanding how the story of Jason was told outside elite epic poetry. Here, in a version of the story not found in written accounts, the hero emerges from the mouth of the bearded dragon as the warrior goddess Athena, holding her owl, stands guard. The Golden Fleece hangs on the tree behind the dragon.

also sometimes prayed to for healing,[24] and his Phoenician adaptation, Eshmun, was explicitly the god of healing at Sidon.[25] In this sense, Jason can also be compared to the related Mesopotamian god Ningishzida who was a god of healing (or sometimes the son of one). This figure was closely associated with the underworld in at least one poem and was closely tied with his guardian monster, a horned serpent-dragon.[26] In some texts and myths, Dumuzi and Ningishzida have become partially conflated, with the former borrowing aspects of the latter.[27] He was variously considered an aspect of Dumuzi/Tammuz, a companion of Tam-muz, or Tammuz's father.[28] It is likely that both figures were once gods of similar function in different cities and were later worked into a unified though obviously not completely con-sistent mythology. Serpents and healers are of course close cousins because the snake sheds his skin and thus seems to "heal" himself and be "reborn" time and again.

Angelo Brelich, the historian of religion and anthropology, also saw in Jason a cult figure who was once associated with healing; and the German scholar Otto Pressen stated simply that Jason was once a god of wellbeing.[29] Indeed, John Pinsent argued that the images of Jason's descent and return from the snake represented a death and rebirth of the hero, whose quest was, therefore, "as befits a man whose name is 'Healer,' for immortality, and that he ... died and was rejuvenated."[30] Such a tradition, if it in fact existed, would be entirely consistent with the hypothesis that a Mycenaean god underlay the hero Jason, a possibility that G. S. Kirk pointed out likely underlay many of the Greek heroes, whose dramatic achievements likely once belonged to Mycenaean gods before being assigned to Greek heroes.[31] The Mycenaeans had a god of healing, Paiawon (Paean), who at the end of their reign ceased to be worshipped. His divinity and name transferred to Apollo, a newer god from the east. We know nothing of Paiawon's mythology other than Homer's association of him with healing and a mastery of plants and herbs. It may be possible that a story told of Paiawon served as the model for Jason. Or, if Ian Rutherford is right that Paiawon was originally a military god whose healing functions were limited at first to the battlefield,[32] "Jason" may instead have been an epithet of another god with more general healing functions, one who faded into a hero after the fall of the Mycenaeans. Duplication would not be unprecedented; Athena and Ares both presided over aspects of war (strategy and violence, respectively), for example, and Apollo and Asclepius shared the role of healing god in later Greek and Roman times. The Hittites knew of a powerful Mycenaean healing god, whom they did not name, but whom they called overseas (possibly by borrowing a cult statue) from Ahhiyawâ (believed to be the Homeric Achaeans, either in Greece or a Mycenaean colony) to aid their ailing king, Mursili II (c. 1320 BCE), who like Aeëtes was identified with the Sun.[33] Physicians travelled from court to court in the Late Bronze Age, bringing their skills with herbal remedies and surgery to foreign kings.[34] Such travels of men and gods parallel Jason's voyage to the land of the sun. As we will see in chapter 8, there is also reason to suspect that the Mycenaeans linked healing powers metaphorically to slaying a serpent.

After Mycenae, Jason became a human hero, albeit one with some divine powers. Mackie believes the Greeks of the Archaic Age took a dim view of trespassing on the territory of the gods, especially in the realm of supernatural healing. Asclepius transgressed, and his supernatural abilities found themselves suppressed in Homer, where he becomes instead a mortal doctor. Chiron, too, eventually becomes a teacher rather than a medicinal wonder-worker.

> Likewise the apparent healing of blindness, when such a condition has been ordained by the heavens, is a fundamental challenge to the order of the world. In all likelihood therefore Jason at some early stage stirs the same moral dilemmas in the poets as Asclepius and Chiron do. Magical healers are perceived as dangerous, and their activities are deemed essentially inappropriate for Greek heroes like Jason.[35]

As a result, Jason's healing functions are transferred to the figure of Medea who is a foreigner and a sorceress and not subject to the same laws as the Greeks. Scholars have long asserted that Medea must once have been a goddess who was later reduced to a sorceress, and indeed Hesiod includes Medea among the list of immortal and divine figures.[36] This agrees well with the suggestion that her intervention in the Jason tale derives from the goddess figure in the Hittite story of the storm god and the dragon, or from the Inanna or Hera figure in the Dumuzi or Velchanos stories, or both.

Jason the Shaman

But we can go beyond Mackie's analysis and find additional evidence that Jason performed magical feats that speak to an original role as a shamanic figure. The Archaic writers Pherecydes and Simonides state that Jason underwent a rejuvenation, having been dismembered and resurrected, his flesh boiled in Medea's cauldron.[37] This story is hinted at in the Hellenistic writings of Lycophron as well. Since Jason was about twenty when he undertook his adventure, he clearly was not in need of rejuvenation; however, the dismemberment and recreation of the human body is an essential element of the shaman's initiation, undertaken (mentally) in the trance state when the shaman has entered the nether-world. "In order to become a shaman, a person might have to undergo a symbolic dissolution, dismemberment and reconstruction by the spirits" including by cooking in a cauldron.[38] Thus, as Yulia Ustinova recently suggested, Jason's dismemberment and reconstitution represent a shamanic initiation.[39] If so, his original quest, travelling to Aea to kill the dragon and win the hand of a goddess, can be interpreted in shamanic terms. Dismemberment is also a part of the death and resurrection of Dumuzi in Sumerian myth, another possible origin for this strange rite of "rejuvenation," and the roles of shaman and god are not as distinct as they might appear. Gods such as Dionysus display shamanic traits, and shamans (and priests) could at any time become possessed by the gods that they served. Certainly individuals and characters have crossed between roles. Heracles is just one example of an originally shamanic figure who eventually becomes mythologized as a god. The shaman was believed to be able to walk with the gods, and even gods might be imagined to perform the same roles as their representatives on earth, though on a grander scale. Both god and shaman are healers.

As discussed in chapter 1, the shaman was the earliest form of human religious expression, and the shaman was considered a type of culture hero who was able to mediate between the spirit world and the mortal plain—much as Pindar has Jason "calm" the angry spirit of Phrixus to restore harmony between the living and dead. How closely does Jason conform to the anthropological definition of shamanism? In *The Quest for the Shaman*, Miranda and Stephen Aldhouse-Green set out a series of traits that the shaman expresses across cultures. In addition to the power to heal, which we have already discussed, these include: entering a trance state to travel to the supernatural realm and commune with the spirits, the ability to cross boundaries or become 'two-spirited,' the ability to change shapes or become an animal, the use of special structures and equipment to attain the transformative state, a belief in a tiered cosmos, access to the otherworld, symbolic dismemberment, and the power of divination.[40] Let us evaluate the Jason story in light of these traits.

TRAVEL TO A SUPERNATURAL REALM

The shaman will induce a trance state through meditation, sensory deprivation, or hallucinogenic drugs in order to enter the realm of the supernatural. The shaman will undertake this psychic journey and go to the land of the spirits, where he will interact with divine forces. The equivalent action in the Jason story is the journey from the "normal" world of Iolcus to the supernatural realm of Aea, in a land that was originally considered a "fabulous" kingdom beyond the known world, far out into the River Ocean, where the sun stored his beams,[41] a version of the Underworld. Only in the sixth century would this supernatural realm be converted into the very real land of Colchis on the Black Sea's southeastern shore, after the Greeks had colonized the land. During the Dark Age, the Black Sea's shores were unknown, and possibly limitless, and Jason's adventure there surely was meant to represent a trip beyond the known world. The similarity here between Jason's voyage across the waters to Aea, Dimuzi's journey to the Underworld by boat, and Gilgamesh's voyage across the waters of death to visit Utnapishtim reinforces the identification of a sea voyage with a journey through the trance state to the realm of the spirits, a journey shamans frequently describe as travelling through water.[42]

The Ability to Communicate with the Supernatural

The shaman undertakes the voyage to the supernatural realm in order to commune with the spirits. This can take the form of a conversation with a god or a monster, as well as a battle with the same. Jason, of course, has interactions with many supernatural entities, including the goddess Hera and battles with the monsters in Aea, not least the dragon.

The Ability to Cross Boundaries or Become Two-Spirited

The shaman is typically described as having "two-spirits," and they can cross boundaries, both real and symbolic. These boundaries may include those dividing the genders, human and animal, and the human and spirit worlds. Chiron obviously fits this category, as a creature between the animal and human state, a shaman with healing power. Jason frequently crosses between the human and supernatural worlds. He leaves Iolcus to enter the shamanic realm of Chiron. He then crosses back in Iolcus and leaves again to cross into the supernatural realm of Aea. Jason's "two-spirited" nature is depicted in Pindar's Fourth Pythian Ode where Jason is first seen carrying two spears and wearing two cloaks,[43] the first the civilized cloak of the Greeks, the second the pelt of a leopard. He thus embodies both civilization and the wild, his two natures united in his single figure.[44]

Shape-Shifting

The shaman frequently has an animal helper or is able to transform into an animal. This may take a literal form, believing he has become the animal, or it may be symbolic in the shaman's application of animal elements such as horns, skins, or pelts to take on an animal form. The shaman believes that he and the animal share one nature and have a complete identity. Jason is not specifically identified with an animal in the surviving myths, but his quest is to retrieve the pelt of a ram, which is described by Pindar as the "soul" of the shamanic character Phrixus, who also underwent a journey to a supernatural realm and an (attempted) sacrifice. Additionally, as noted, in Pindar he wears the pelt of a leopard, which may have originally been his spirit animal.

Special Structures and Equipment

The shaman may make use of special symbols or equipment to essentially separate himself from society attain the supernatural realm. These may include caves or mountains, sacred pools or rivers, drums and costumes, and more. Chiron's cave on Mount Pelion is one such place, a shaman's sacred space where the supernatural impinges on reality. The Grove of Ares, where the dragon lives in Aea/Colchis may be considered another such sacred space.

A TIERED COSMOS

Shamanic societies believe in a tiered cosmos, with an upper world where the spirits or gods reside, a middle plain on which mortals live, and an underworld that is home to the dead and from which evil and disease may rise. This obviously corresponds to the Greek cosmos, as well as to the specific mythic geography of the Jason story, in which the supernatural realm of Aea is conceived as being beyond the waters (and therefore symbolically below) the mortal realm of Iolcus, literally so if Aea truly were originally the Underworld itself.

ACCESS TO THE OTHERWORLD

The shaman will have access to the spirits through special places, such as natural formations potent with supernatural energy, usually located at the edge of the inhabited world. Again, Chiron's cave located on Mount Pelion, just beyond Iolcus, serves as one such place. Jason's access to the Grove of Ares, and thus to the dragon, repeats this idea of the shaman being able to enter the otherworld through places just beyond the realm of civilization.

SYMBOLIC DISMEMBERMENT

We have already seen that an ancient tradition had Jason dismembered and "rejuvenated," which was known to Greek writers, including Pherecydes. As Mackie has noted, the circumstance whereby Jason found himself in the belly of the dragon are unknown. It is not impossible that the hero found himself dismembered and consumed by the dragon only to emerge restored to his original form, perhaps through the aid of a divine figure, such as Athena (as in the Douris painter's krater) or Hera. This would be thematically quite similar to Dumuzi, his possible progenitor, who is dismembered by devils with axes and knives before being sent to the Underworld, from which he requires the goddess Inanna's permission and aid to return.[45] Athena, it will be remembered, shares traits with the earlier goddess Inanna, who may have inspired the Greek figure.[46] This may well have been the origination of this event in Jason's story, but nonetheless an echo of the shamanic. In a later telling this event could have been transposed to the cauldron of Medea, and then, in the written tradition, moved entirely from its initial place at the climax of the hero's quest to its appendix, when Medea uses the cauldron on Pelias and Aeson. There is precedent for this type of relocation, as we shall see, in the movement of the Argonauts' encounter with the Clashing Rocks from its initial position in the myth.

THE POWER OF DIVINATION

Jason himself does not appear to have the power of prophesy, but he does exist in a matrix of divination. An oracle warns Pelias of his coming; Phineus the seer provides him with guidance, and the Oracle of Zeus at Dodona provides a magical plank for the *Argo* which also utters prophesies. There is not enough evidence to say that the first Jason would have possessed divinatory powers himself, but the myth as it has come down to us shows him to be the recipient of prophesies from the gods, as are shamans.

Miranda and Steven Aldhouse-Green provide copious evidence for the survival of shamanism in Europe into the Roman period, not least in the oracles at Dodona and Delphi and the mysteries of Demeter at Eleusis, who engaged in trance states to channel the gods. There is little doubt that shamans existed in Europe during the Neolithic. The Aldhous-Greens also explain that shamanic elements survived in classical Greek and Roman religious rituals, including soothsaying, divination, and other ritual acts.[47] Consequently, Greco-Roman religion can be said in a sense to have grown out of an earlier religious tradition that originated in shamanic practices in Bronze Age Greece (or earlier).

We could, therefore, conclude simply that the earliest Jason represents a shaman on his journey to the spirit realm. However, the Mycenaeans are not known to have used shamans during the period when the Jason story emerged. There is another possibility that better fits the remaining evidence for the origin of the Jason story. The shamans had their successors in the priests of Mycenaean and then Greek religious cults, who appropriated the practices and beliefs of the shamans. These figures would have gradually grown into their formal religious roles as society grew more complex and their jobs became more formalized. While Jason's story includes shamanic elements, it is also possible that his story is a survival of a shamanic-influenced religious cult, and that Jason reflects either a young man's initiation ritual into the priesthood, or as Fritz Graf argued, into the caste of aristocratic warrior kings, or as Angelo Brelich preferred, representing an adolescent's initiation into manhood.[48]

The Zeus Cult

In chapter 2 we examined the evidence for the primacy of Poseidon in the Mycenaean pantheon and his later displacement by Zeus. Whether this event was remembered by the Dark Age and Archaic Greeks who developed the Jason story is an open question, but what is certain is that the Jason myth as it has come down to us contains a close relationship between the heroic actions of Jason and the worship of the greatest of the gods, Zeus. As we saw in chapter 1, the story of Jason, Medea, and the dragon parallels the Hurrian and Hittite story of the hero Hupasiyas whom the goddess Inara employed to help the weather-god Teshub slay the dragon who threatened him.

Teshub wielded a thunderbolt and was identified with a sacred bull. In this, he appears to combine aspects of the Indo-European weather god and the bull-formed Near Eastern earth god, and indeed is sometimes described as the lord of heaven and earth. He was, however, primarily the storm god, for whom the bull represented the bellowing thunder. Teshub is the equivalent of Zeus (who also absorbed the sacred bull aspect, as evidenced in his rape of Europa in the form of a bull), who was himself the god of sky and had been since the earliest Indo-European times, when he was known as Dyēus, the god of the daytime sky, possibly three millennia before the gods of Greece sat upon their Olympian thrones. Versions of sky gods with names that are variants of Zeus, Deus, or Divus occur from India to Anatolia and beyond, but this god, while conceived as the father of the gods, was a relatively minor figure who was distinct from the storm god and almost certainly not the gods' king.[49] In Greece, he was always addressed as Zeus the Father, or in the vocative, *Zeu pater* (hence his Latin form Jupiter, or Iuppiter—Jove the Father). It is believed Zeus is the only Proto-Indo-European god to have survived into historic times.[50]

However, the Zeus cult was not always a cult of the Greeks. The weather god's worship is well attested across the Near East going back into the Bronze Age; however, the first written evidence we have for Zeus worship in the Greek mainland comes from the Mycenaean city of Pylos, around 1200 BCE. On a tablet written in Linear B we find reference to sacrificial victims brought to Zeus and to Hera—human or animal is unclear, though the accompanying image shows a man and woman.[51] Was Zeus originally a god who demanded human sacrifice? We will return to this point in a moment. The Mycenaean Zeus also had a month named for him and a festival likely celebrated in that period. Consequently, given the complex development of his cult at the end of the Mycenaean period, he must have joined their pantheon before 1200 BCE but exactly how far back, it is impossible to know. Nor can it be assumed that the Storm God of the Near East simply crossed the Aegean and took up residence in Greece. The Mycenaeans, like the later Greeks, would have adopted and adapted any new deity so that the new god would have a composite character, part Near Eastern storm god, part whatever indigenous deity with whom he might have been identified, and part ancient Sky Father. It is quite possible that the Mycenaean Zeus was closer to the Proto-Indo-European Sky God, and only in the Dark Ages absorbed the additional functions or the PIE or Near East storm gods, under Near East influence (as evidenced by his iconic depiction with a Near East divine thunderbolt instead of a PIE-style thunder hammer or mace), which helped his promotion to the head of the pantheon. It is interesting to note that the thunderbolt of Zeus, the Keraunos, is very similar to the names of other Indo-European storm gods, suggesting that Zeus took over the functions of a storm god of that name.[52] Did the Near East Storm God bring with him the story of the defeat of the dragon, if not in Hurrian form, then in whatever form was ancestral to it? Or did the story only arrive in Greece later, when the Dark Age Greeks absorbed much more of Near Eastern mythology?

The evidence for human sacrifice in the Mycenaean era is inconclusive, but mythology suggests that such practices could have occurred, if rarely. Agamemnon sacrifices his daughter to guarantee success in war, and the Jason story begins with the failed sacrifice of Phrixus whom a false oracle of Zeus demands be sacrificed to appease the god. Clearly, if human sacrifice to Zeus were unprecedented, the false oracle could never have pulled off such a ruse. On the other hand, scholars like Dennis D. Hughes and Walter Burkert propose that myths of human sacrifice arose to explain animal sacrifice, as a substitution, and therefore of quelling unease about the killing of animals to please the gods.[53] The Greeks themselves believed that human sacrifice had been practiced in the distant past but, a few aberrant (and likely fictitious) examples aside, no longer was by the Archaic era. The myth of the failed sacrifice of Phrixus and successful sacrifice of the Golden Ram depicts just such a human sacrifice replaced by an animal sacrifice. This is reflected in a ritual carried out at Mt. Laphystios, near Corinth, as reported by Herodotus, who tells of its occurrence when the Persian king Xerxes fought his way across Greece in 480 BCE:

> When Xerxes was come to Alus [Alos, or Halos] in Achaea, his guides, desiring to inform him of all they knew, told him the story that is related in that country concerning the worship of Laphystian Zeus: how [Phrixus' father] Athamas son of Aeolus plotted Phrixus' death with Ino, and further, how the Achaeans by an oracle's bidding compel Phrixus' posterity to certain tasks: namely, they bid the eldest of that family forbear to enter their town hall (which the Achaeans call the People's House), and themselves keep watch there; if he enter, he may not come out, save only to be sacrificed; and further also, how many of those that were to be sacrificed had fled away in fear to another country, but if they returned back at a later day and were taken, they had

been brought into the town hall; and the guides showed Xerxes how the man is sacrificed, with fillets covering him all over and a procession to lead him forth. It is the descendants of Phrixus' son Cytissorus who are thus dealt with, because when the Achaeans by an oracle's bidding made Athamas son of Aeolus a scapegoat for their country and were about to sacrifice him, this Cytissorus came from Aea in Colchis and delivered him, but thereby brought the god's wrath on his own posterity. Hearing all this, Xerxes when he came to the temple grove forbore to enter it himself and bade all his army do likewise, holding the house and the precinct of Athamas' descendants alike in reverence.[54]

Hughes argues that this story represents a series of events in a prescribed ritual of initiation, distorted through Herodotus' secondhand account. Though Herodotus' text is unclear and apparently corrupt in parts, it appears that in the ritual, the head of the Athamid family, descended from Phrixus' father Athamas, is forbidden from entering the hall. The younger Athamids enter, and are spotted. The guardians of the hall tell them they are to be sacrificed, and they flee. They return, and the eldest Athamid is "sacrificed" in their place, likely represented in the ritual by a ram, as evidenced by the fact that the oldest Athamid performs this ritual drama dressed in "fillets," strips of wool likely representing sheep's or ram's fleece.[55] Hughes therefore sees in the Phrixus myth and the attendant ritual undergone by his father's descendants an echo of ancient rites of initiation, noting that the false sacrifice, the escape, and the period of exile are

> common elements of "rites of passage" and together may suggest that the ritual functioned to initiate a young member of the family into the priesthood of Zeus. Or possibly, the fifth-century ritual represented a survival of old initiation rites undergone by all young males in the area, but now conserved only in the family which claimed direct descent from Athamas.[56]

Here we have Phrixus, the Golden Fleece, and the priesthood of Zeus united in a ritual that must have had antecedents that stretched back into the past. A similar ritual, also related to rams and the cult of Zeus, occurred nearby at Jason's hometown of Iolcus, on Mt. Pelion, well into the Hellenistic era, as reported by Heraclides in the third century BCE:

> On the heights of Mt. Pelion, there is a cave, the so-called Cave of Cheiron, and a shrine of Zeus Aktaios. At Sirius' rising, which is the time of the greatest heat, the most prominent citizens, those in the prime of their lives, climb up to the cave. They are chosen by the priest and girded with fresh, thrice-shorn sheepskins. This shows how cold it must be on the mountain![57]

By analogy, it seems clear that this ritual again has a relationship to initiation into the cult of Zeus, a caste under his protection (perhaps originally aristocratic or kingly), or perhaps his ancient priesthood. Once again, the younger members of the community ("in the prime of their lives") enact an initiation rite, and ritually "become" the ram who would originally have been sacrificed to Zeus. Over the generations the original meaning was lost, and the pantomime of dressing in the skin of the rams for Zeus' sake was continued. Note especially the presence of a priest of Zeus overseeing the ceremony.

Given the elements of the Jason story that closely resemble shamanic activity and the close ties between Phrixus, rams, and Zeus, it seems impossible not to equate Jason's quest to achieve the Fleece with the rituals of initiation involving the meaning behind the ram sacrifice to Zeus. Indeed, this was the opinion of the nineteenth century German classist Karl Otfried Müller (1797–1840), the first to scientifically study Greek mythology, though he went too far in arguing that the Fleece was conceived as the symbol and seal of Zeus' covenant with the Greeks. However, the conclusion, which seems to follow from the myth and the ritual, is that Jason became closely related to the Zeus cult, and his story may represent the quest of the shamanic priest of Zeus or an initiate into a cult or group under his protection enacting a sacred rite or mystery in honor of Zeus. This Zeus symbolism appears to have been laid atop the older myth of Jason the Healer who quested for the earth god to win the hand of a goddess, thus changing the story. Indeed, the Fleece's earliest mention in the Jason story is in the seventh century (though it must have begun somewhat earlier), when Zeus had already triumphed over the earth god. Perhaps only with this change is the Golden Fleece attached to the story of Jason and his descent into or defeat of the underworld dragon.

And what is a (golden) ram if not a male sheep? Hesiod and Homer both describe Jason as a "shepherd of the people," an epitaph repeated by other authors and a common phrase referring to Greek military leaders in Homeric-era epic poetry (Agamemnon and Hector share the title in the *Iliad*),[58] referring not the owner of a flock but him who cares for them on behalf of another.[59] It is interesting to note that the phrase originates with titles of authority in the Near East where gods like Shamash and, interestingly, Dumuzi were described as "shepherd" and kings such as Hammurabi claimed the title "shepherd of the people" before 1750 BCE.[60] From the Near East also may have come the story of Jason and the dragon, and the classic form of Zeus himself. If it could be proved that the title "shepherd of the people" was used for the earliest Jason, long before the age of Homer, it could be argued that the epitaph is a remembrance of a Near East royal title borne by a kingly hero, or even by the dying and rising god with whom he may have been once equated. But this cannot be proved, and so this is, like so much in the reconstruction of lost myths, only speculation.

The Hera Cult

In Mycenaean times Zeus had a consort (or perhaps sister) named Diwija (the female form of Zeus' name) before he was married to Hera. Nothing is known of this goddess, and she disappears from history with the Mycenaeans, part of the shakeup in religious beliefs that reconfigured the Greek pantheon. By analogy with Zeus and Diwija, it has been suggested that the Mycenaean Hera, whose name appears in the ancient tablets at Pylos alongside Zeus's but not with him elsewhere, would have had a male consort, whose name is suggested as Heros, the male form of Hera. This name does not appear in any of the tablets of Pylos, or anywhere in Linear B, and is speculative at best. However, Walter Pötscher suggests that Hera had the function of the Minoan earth goddess,[61] whose consort Velchanos died each year with the vegetation he symbolized and was reborn and contracted a sacred marriage to the goddess. That such a story could also reflect an Indo-European inheritance can be found in the widespread Northern European stories of spring maidens like the May Queen, a goddess figure who contracts a sacred May-time marriage with a green-clad youth before a decorated tree like the Maypole—or the Fleece-bedecked oak. In Latvian myth, the Sun Maiden stands before just such a tree, the *Austras koks*, waiting to take a divine suitor in marriage to mark the start of summer.

Hera herself probably originated as a Proto-Indo-European goddess, at least in name, though one who absorbed many Minoan goddess functions in the Mycenaean era.[62] This likely included the Minoan tree goddess, the goddess of nature symbolized in a tree, which would account for the sacred oak included in the design of the *Argo* (only later the oak of Zeus) and perhaps even the oak at Colchis on which the Fleece rests.[63] She would also have had the function of goddess of war (later assigned to Athena), and goddess of the citadel, and in some places she was also the goddess of sexuality before the advent of Aphrodite in the Greek pantheon.[64] It is likely no coincidence that three separate forms of this goddess enter Jason's myth, with the classical Athena, Aphrodite, and Hera substituting for the original multiform, multifunction universal goddess. (As we shall see, this also closely parallels the triple-form of Inanna, the Sumerian goddess.) If Hera was in fact originally an earth goddess associated with trees and annual vegetative rites, it lends credence to the idea that the heroes closely associated with her, such as Jason, were originally dying-and-rising seasonal gods that belonged the vegetation cycle and the annual death and rebirth of nature.

After the fall of Mycenaean Greece, when the pantheon underwent dramatic changes, Diwija disappeared and Hera abandoned "Heros" (or perhaps Poseidon) for Zeus, her earth goddess aspects giving way to the heavenly Queen of the Gods. (Around this time the people of Crete also began identifying Velchanos with Zeus.) In so doing, the Heros figure became downgraded from god to demigod, since the new and revised Hera could now have no consort but Zeus, lending his name to the race the Dark Age Greeks imagined the Mycenaeans to be—*heroes*.[65] Hera, in this theory, became the patron of the heroes under the all-seeing beneficence of Zeus.[66] Additional confirmation can be found in the attested superimposition of the rites of Zeus on those formerly associated with Hera at Argos during the Geometric Period, and the gradual fusing of Hera and Zeus rituals and cults elsewhere, culminating in the downgrading of the goddess in *The Iliad*.[67] The Hera myths about her heroes would be no different.

If this theory is true—and it is a big if—it provides another clue to the antiquity of the Jason story, for Jason's divine patron in his quest is none other than Hera, and as we have seen Jason's quest may originally have involved a symbolic death and resurrection through dismemberment, much as the presumed story of Heros (and the Sumerian Dumuzi myth) would have had it. In this reading, the original Jason story may well have been a Mycenaean religious mystery or initiation rite on the Sumerian or Minoan order bastardized into an adventure tale when the original cult of Heros and Hera dissolved in the transformation to the Olympian religion of Zeus and his consort Hera. Thus, Heros becomes the hero Jason, and his religious function is transferred to the new supreme deity, Zeus. Or, the myth may have been an early Mycenaean or Dark Age Greek adaptation of the Inanna and Dumuzi story (as the developing myth of Heracles absorbed and included elements from Gilgamesh and other Near East myths in the same period), with the roles recast with more familiar characters, giving Hera the role of Inanna, both of whom share aspects of the early earth goddess as well as the title Queen of Heaven. Dumuzi would therefore become Jason in a partial translation of his ancient name.

Partial confirmation of this idea can be found in the myth of Iasion and Demeter. Iasion (also spelled Jason or Iasos) was the Crete-born son of Zeus and Electra who mated with Demeter in a thrice-plowed field, leading to the birth of Plutus, or wealth. For his hubris in mating with a goddess, Zeus killed Iasion with a lightning bolt.[68] Demeter is another goddess who, like Hera, traces her ancestry back to the Minoan earth goddess, and Iasion is her mortal consort who causes the spring child Plutus to be conceived, just as Heros (or Velchanos on Crete) was consort to Hera. Fontenrose, agreeing with K. O. Müller, claimed that out "of Iasion, I think, came the hero Jason,"[69] etymologically if no other way, and if so, we have a clear myth of a Jason figure coupled to an earth goddess. It is also worth mentioning here that many scholars hold that some (though by no means all) of the oldest hero figures, those belonging to the time before the historicizing myths of the Trojan War, were formerly deities, "faded gods," who even in the Archaic age maintained a clear association with exercising power under the earth (i.e. in the Underworld) and received sacrifices and worship,[70] especially at former Mycenaean tombs and ruins, which became the sites of cultic hero worship.[71] As Walter Burkert noted, this conception emerged when the old earth gods of the Mycenaeans gave way to the sky-focused, ethereal religion dominated by the newly-promoted Zeus. The older, Mycenaean cult sites, places where the earth gods had been worshipped, now became the site of localized hero worship, with the heroes stepping in to fill the chthonic void when the Olympians sailed upward to become celestial gods under Zeus.[72]

This theory would thus explain another aspect of the Standard Version of the Jason story, Hera's overwhelming love of Jason, an aspect he shares with later heroes such as Achilles, but to a greater extent. In the past, this was attributed to the influence of Corinth (whose patron was Hera) in the later development of the myth, but this cannot be because Homer already knows of Hera's involvement long before the Corinthians adapted a version of the Jason story for their purposes. Hera is typically seen as a jealous and wrathful goddess and is usually depicted as punishing mortals. If the theory is true, then her rather anomalous love of Jason (and the other heroes) would be a remembrance of Hera's original consort Heros, later rationalized as her supporting Jason because Pelias failed to honor her, inspiring her wrath.

An immediate objection that could be raised is that if Jason were merely a downgraded Heros, it would seem to contradict the suggestion that he was involved in the cult of Zeus, since the Hera and Zeus cults were separate in Mycenaean times. This objection, of course, assumes that the myth as we know it is a lineal successor of a single Mycenaean story. It is also possible—in fact likely—that the Jason story represents a merging of many tales and traditions, perhaps including the rites of Dumuzi/Velchanos/Heros and the story of Zeus and the slaying of the dragon. For example, one could speculate that as the Jason story took shape, the epic was formed from the merging of many stories, just as the *Odyssey* was formed from a core myth of Odysseus and the addition of many folktales and pieces of other stories, including the *Argonautica*. Perhaps the prominence of Hera in the early phases of the Jason story reflects a portion of a Heros myth that survived into a later, more Zeus-centered narrative tradition.

A Tentative Evolution

As the reader has likely noted, the origin of the Jason story is not simple, and the pieces that can be inferred from the evidence at hand do not fit neatly into a single picture. In part, this is due to the tentative nature of reconstructions. But it is also due to the complexity of teasing out a single meaning from a story that may have many component parts and may also have encoded a number of meanings across both time and space. From the evidence we have examined so far, we can begin to construct a tentative developmental evolution of the early Jason stories.

FIRST STAGE: THE EARLIEST PERIOD

From Near East models, we can imagine an inferior young male god or semi-divine hero (on the order of Velchanos or the conjectured as Heros among the Mycenaeans) who serves the powerful earth goddess or goddess of renewal (possibly the Mycenaean Hera, almost certainly part of the tree cult). His rites apparently involved yearly death and rebirth, and he would become identified with Zeus. There may have also been a male god or gods who operate in the underworld (god of earthquakes), on earth (as a bull), and in the heavens (god of the sun). It is unknown whether there was a connection between Velchanos and these gods, though it is not impossible that the Velchanos/Heros figure descends into the underworld and receives the permission of the underworld/sun god to be reborn, culminating in a sacred marriage to the goddess, as in the Dumuzi-Inanna myth, or, perhaps as in the sacred marriage of Teshub and his consort in the Hittite Purulli fertility festival, though this god was certainly not the inferior partner. Dietrich, incidentally, suggests that the bull itself represented the dying and reborn god to the Minoans,[73] thus possibly connecting these figures in an older layer of myth when once they were one.

SECOND STAGE: THE MYCENAEAN PERIOD

The story would not have been the same in Mycenaean Greece, if only because the supreme deity there was the god Poseidon rather than the goddess, so Poseidon's aspects would likely have become more important than the goddess's. The underworld adventure would become the focus of the telling of the Heros/Jason story, quite possibly influenced by contact with the Near Eastern myth of Inanna and Dumuzi. Given that Aeëtes was the father of Medea, and Cronus (previously linked to an earth god) was the father of Hera, perhaps this form of Poseidon was the father or guardian of the earth goddess whose challenges must be surmounted to win the goddess' hand. In the similar story of the Greek Persephone, the goddess requires the permission of Zeus to escape from Hades to return to her mother Demeter, who also shares aspects of the Mycenaean earth goddess. In the myth of Inanna and Dumuzi, the shepherd god must receive the permission of Inanna before he can rise again.

As we have seen, a healer, god, or demigod of great power, Jason, ventures across the waters (likely, given the Mycenaean-Minoan Ayia Triada sarcophagus, via a boat voyage to the Underworld) to reach the land where the Underworld god dwells, likely seen as similar to the Sumerian Underworld. Here he confronts challenges representing a god or the gods (or, perhaps, goddess—the snake was a symbol of the Minoan earth goddess[74]) in their roles as sun god, god of the earth, and god of the Underworld, possibly, like Dumuzi (and, as we shall see, also the Greek Theseus), to bring the earth goddess back from the Underworld. These challenges take the form of the yoking of the solar bulls, battling the earth men (though this may not have been original to the myth), and the descent into the dragon's belly, which are attested from the earliest recorded Jason stories and must therefore be quite ancient. It is possible that the descent into the dragon resulted from a literal-minded Mycenaean adaptation of the Near Eastern monster whose jaws formed the entrance to the underworld.

Through these challenges, which closely resemble elements of the Sumerian underworld where the sun rests, Jason is dismembered and resurrected, and emerges from the mouth of the underworld monster who swallowed him. He may then have won the hand of the goddess, or perhaps immortality, or both.

How closely this reconstructed story is related to an early Minoan-Mycenaean original is debatable, and it cannot be clearly determined whether the two were once separate or if the presumed Mycenaean story was an interpretation of the Minoan myth mixed with Near East influence, with the Velchanos or Dumuzi figure downgraded into a supernatural healer. Alternately, it is possible that Jason was at this period a Dumuzi-type god and only lost his divine stature in the Dark Ages when the old rites of the earth god and goddess were again reinterpreted in light of Near Eastern myths and the supremacy of Zeus. The sacred marriage to Hera would survive as Jason's marriage to the downgraded sorceress Medea, who stands in for the missing goddess.

THIRD STAGE: THE DARK AGE

As Dietrich discussed in *The Origins of Greek Religion*, by the Dark Age the Mycenaean religion had fused with new Near Eastern influences, and the Hittite version of Zeus, Teshub, merged with what he presumed to be the Mycenaean tradition of the young man who died for the goddess each year.[75] How and why this happened is unknown, but on Crete the successors to the Minoans identified Velchanos with the young Zeus, and he retained that identification into historic times. However, it is not necessarily the case that the identification occurred outside of Crete in the same way. Indeed, figures such as Hyacinthus, Erechtheus, and Iasion/Plutus also are descended from Mycenaean divinities (or the same one, transforming at different places) and are divine youths associated with the earth goddess and the rebirth of nature in the spring,[76] yet were not identified as Zeus. The Mycenaeans already had a god named Zeus, and he was *not* their Velchanos figure, Heros. It would therefore be unsurprising if a young god figure once associated with Hera degraded, like Hyacinthus, into the hero Jason.

No matter how it happened, no later than the ninth century BCE (and probably long before), the myth of the Teshub, his daughter, the hero, and the dragon crossed the Aegean and became a part of the Jason story. Teshub was identified as Zeus, and the Near Eastern myths associated with the god were integrated into Greek practice, as evidenced by Hesiod's clearly Near Eastern-inspired *Theogony*. This is the period in which Zeus, with his Near Eastern pedigree, ascended to the peak of the reforming Greek pantheon, and the earth god lost his primacy. The old Mycenaean earth god stopped being worshipped; Poseidon became a sea god, having abdicated his earthly and heavenly powers. Myths involving him needed to be rewritten, or else would stop being sacred mysteries and initiation rites and instead descend into folk tales. Perhaps both happened to Jason, and the mystery story became an adventure tale when the cult behind him lost its followers in the changing religious environment of the post–Mycenaean era. Thus, the solar aspect of the story focused Aeëtes, son of the sun (Helios) and his fire-breathing bulls; the underworld aspect is no longer a sacred serpent or the monster whose jaws lead to Hades but instead a simple dragon guarding the Golden Fleece in the Grove of Ares.

At this point, for whatever reason, an identity must have been made between the heroic healer who descends into the dragon's belly and the Near Eastern hero who helps slay the dragon. Whether this was the result of purposeful synchretization or natural evolution as two similar stories were told side by side is impossible to know, but in reconciling the two stories, the core of the later Jason myth developed. The eastern goddess Inara, the daughter of Teshub, becomes the female figure who now aids Jason in his battle with the dragon. Perhaps this identification led Douris to paint Athena as Jason's helper, on analogy with Inara as the daughter of Teshub/Zeus. (It may also be that Athena was equated with Inanna, or that all were seen as versions of one another.) Velchanos' sacred marriage to Hera becomes Inara's and then Medea's marriage to Jason. Increasingly active in the story, the female figure is assigned the powers of drugs and healing that Jason once held, for it would be manifestly redundant to have two actors reduplicating their efforts. The goddess needs something to do since the quest is no longer to win her hand, and in the Hittite myth she serves the brew that sedates the dragon, so her takeover of Jason's pharmacological skills is logical. In the Hittite myth Teshub completes the slaying of the dragon initiated by the Jason figure. In the Mycenaean story, Jason triumphs over the dragon himself. Zeus therefore becomes a symbolic presence, evidenced in the Fleece that was consecrated to him and which the dragon guards (which entered the myth perhaps as recently as the seventh century and likely in connection with Hittite influence). Therefore, while Jason retains the ability to defeat the dragon, Zeus is not wholly absent, and his battle with the dragon, like that of the Hittite hero, is conducted under the inspiration of Zeus.

In this syncretic story, Jason travels to a distant land, as before, but now his quest has a different purpose. The deposed earth god is no longer the object of the voyage to the Underworld, but the obstacle on a trip to the ends of the earth. His symbols are now downgraded to challenges preventing Jason from reaching his true object, the Fleece. The story of initiation into the mysteries of the earth god and goddess and the sacred marriage to Hera are now simply an adventure. The hero's original vegetative function was remembered as Jason's otherwise anomalous love of agriculture. Whether this suggestion is correct (and it is only informed speculation—many other explanations are possible), what is certain is that sometime around 900 BCE the fundamentals of the Jason story were in place.

However, this development was not complete, and may have occurred differently in the various places where the story was told. Given the pottery evidence, it is clear that the old form of Jason descending into the serpent's belly remained current through the fifth century. Evidence from the fragments of the ancient *Naupaktia* and the poet Eumelus confirms that multiple versions were known—they describe the yoking of the bulls in the sixth century but do not describe Medea as Jason's helper in his adventure with the dragon. Obviously, the process of transformation was gradual and incomplete. What remained in the development of our myth was to turn the story of a healer who battled a dragon into an epic involving a great sea journey of many episodes. As the Jason story grew, new adventures were attached to the skeletal framework, and the hero's voyage over the waters became a magnet attracting a range of folk stories, eventually crystallizing into the Standard Version. This process we will explore in our next chapter.

4

The Hero

The Making of an Epic

We have so far seen the gradual development of several key aspects of the Jason myth, including the figure of Jason himself, his education on Mount Pelion, and his adventures in the land of Aea/Colchis. However, these elements, while essential, are not the aspect of the story that best defines the Jason myth. That element is, of course, the great sea voyage aboard the *Argo* and the many adventures its fifty occupants had along its passage. G. S. Kirk believed that the details of this great voyage became fixed only around 1000 BCE when the Greeks began to colonize the lands that would become the Argonauts' route, "but the voyage itself is older."[1]

Because every version of the Jason story, whenever it was told, discusses Jason's voyage in some form, if only tangentially, as in Hesiod's reference to Jason's "swift ship," the trip by water must have been an important element of Jason's story from the first. There was, of course, the logical issue of translating Jason from his home to the distant land (or, originally, the Underworld) where he must accomplish his labors. Gilgamesh crossed the waters of death on stilts to reach Utnapishtim, and Dumuzi went to and from the Underworld by boat. In the Minoan and Myceanaean belief systems, a boat carried travelers to the Under-world. Jason's voyage, too, was conceived as a journey across the waters. It is entirely possible that early story-tellers recognized that the events in Teshub's battle with the dragon occurred in the east, and perhaps for that reason Jason was made to travel there, or it is also possibly that the Dumuzi's water journey or Minoan-Mycenaean funerary beliefs influenced the ear-liest versions of Jason's journey on the strength of the parallels between Dumuzi and Inanna and Heros and Hera. This is especially likely given Fontenrose's suggestion that the men who steered the *Argo* were closely modeled on Underworld deities and ferrymen, who brought the dead to the Underworld by ship, as we will explore further in chapter 6. Unlike many Near Eastern heroes who could travel by land, the route from Greece to the east had no choice but to cross water, given the geographical knowledge of the early Greeks. In going east, Jason had to cross into the Black Sea, the boundaries of which were then unknown. This landscape, still wild and mostly mythic, became the backdrop for the story.

It is possible that the voyage was first placed in more familiar waters, perhaps repre-senting a trip to Anatolia, before being relocated to the Black Sea; but this intermediary step, proposed by literal-minded scholars who assume the story originated in real life voyages,[2] is unnecessary if one instead believes that Jason precedes his epic voyage. It is, however, interesting to note the parallels between Jason's journey across the waters and the mythic significance of the very real journeys of the Mycenaeans' trading partners far to the North. The Bronze Age peoples of Britain, Ireland, and Northern Europe, the builders of the stone monuments of those regions, are believed to have made long-distance trade journeys in sewn-plank boats that held twenty or more sailors, from after 2000 BCE down until around the time of the Mycenaean collapse. Among the British, these long-distance journeys were seen as partly ritual acts, associated with achieving honor for or the blessing of the ancestors (much as Jason quests to retrieve the Fleece of his ancestor Phrixus) and to retrieve "exotic goods and esoteric knowledge."[3] Those who undertook these journeys were said to undergo a process of "transformation and regeneration," again paralleling Jason's journey.[4] Further, like Jason's Argonauts, these British seafarers would have included members of the elite, those aspiring, like Jason, to leadership roles, who would benefit through the acquisition of "magical" knowledge and linkage to the realm of the ancestors via navigational knowledge of the stars. Those who undertook these journeys were buried in rich graves indicating either honor as heroes or deification as living gods.[5] This is not to say that the Mycenaeans were directly aware of the beliefs of these British seafarers far to the north, though it is possible that myths or stories associated with these journeys came to Greece with the amber and metals traded from distant parts of Europe. Such ideology may instead suggest that similar processes were at work in Greece, and that this type of "mythologizing" of early seafarers may lay behind the earliest depictions of Jason's voyage and the inclusion of such a ritual journey over the waves in a myth that is otherwise concerned with dragon slaying and goddess marriage. That the Jason story was a myth later applied to real geography was the opinion of Demetrius of Scepsis as early as the second century BCE, much to the ire of Strabo, who assumed the Argonaut story was history, not myth.[6]

For whatever reason, once it was established that Jason's journey would parallel Dumuzi's in travelling across the sea to reach the enchanted land where the sun stored his rays, the temptation to fill in the details of this voyage must have been irresistible. He obviously needed a ship, like Dumuzi had, which grew in stature into the greatest (or first) built, and certainly he must have had adventures between leaving Iolcus and arriving at Aea. Every storyteller must have had a story to add, and eventually they would make an epic.

What is certain is that by the time of Homer, the journey of Jason and his ship *Argo* were already legendary. This chapter will attempt to examine the process whereby the early story of the healer who defeated the dragon became the story of the hero who voyaged to the ends of the earth to achieve the Golden Fleece. To do so, we will attempt to reconstruct the version of the *Argonautica* known to Homer and then trace the subsequent development of the voyage of the *Argo* in the Archaic Age, down to just before the time of Pindar, whose Fourth Pythian Ode presents our fullest accounting of the myth until Apollonius centuries later.

Black Sea Voyagers

In the Greek cosmology recorded by Hesiod, the sun was imagined to rise and set in a single location, neither east nor west, but a singular edge of the earth that could be reached by travelling either east or west until one hit the bronze gate that marked the rising and

The Black Sea acquired the euphemistic name Euxine (Hospitable) Sea to replace its older moniker, the Axeine (Inhospitable) Sea. This stretch of coast at Gagra, near ancient Colchis, was the most distant eastward point the Greeks would colonize on the Black Sea coast. While some believe the Mycenaeans reached this point, no archaeological evidence can confirm such claims (Library of Congress).

setting place of the sun, and the entrance to Tartarus, the deepest Underworld (see chapter 7).[7] In Homer, there was a bifurcation of this portal into gates for the eastern and western transit of the sun, resulting in a duplication of peoples and myths on both sides of the divide, exemplified by the Ethiopians, believed to live at both the farthest east and west, closest to the sun.[8] Since it was early established that Jason must travel to the land where the sun stores his rays, on the banks of Ocean, there was really little choice but to approach via the Black Sea.[9] Further to the south, Anatolia loomed, and more southerly still, the coasts of Syria, Phoenicia, and Egypt formed an arc of land sealing off the eastern seas. Only the Black Sea, whose boundaries were still unknown and possibly limitless, offered the possibility of a sea voyage eastward toward the great river Ocean and the endless waters that were believed to circumscribe all land. For this reason, if for no other, Jason's travels had to go outward into the Black Sea, known in classical times by the purposely misleading name the Hospitable Sea (*Euxeinos Pontos*), itself a replacement for its first title, the Inhospitable Sea (*Axeinos*

Pontos), strange, foreign, and difficult to navigate. To cross it was an adventure worthy of a great hero.

In myth, this was the land of the Cimmerians, a tribe living at the gates of Hades, often identified with the fearsome Scythians. At first the Greeks associated the Black Sea with the Ocean surrounding all land. As Homer put it, this was "earth's limits, the deep stream of Okeanos, where the Kimmerian people's land and city lie, wrapt in a fog and cloud."[10] Though Homer did not specifically name this place as the Black Sea, Herodotus did, equating the Cimmerians with the Scythians who ruled the Black Sea's north coast.[11] Later, after the Greeks had explored the Black Sea's coast in the seventh century and recognized it as an enclosed sea, they imagined that the Caspian Sea was in fact the true arm of Ocean (even though it was salt water and Ocean was imagined to be fresh) and that only a narrow isthmus separated the Black Sea from the end of the earth, with the River Phasis (the modern Rioni) connecting the Black and Caspian Seas. Hecataeus, of Miletus, a Greek city on the coast of Asia Minor, depicts the world just this way in his map of 500 BCE as scholars have reconstructed it.[12] Hecataeus also proposed that the Argonauts sailed up the Phasis to reach the Ocean via the Caspian and then travelled Ocean's lengths to where it met the Nile, returning to Greece along that route. It is frequently suggested that it was in Miletus that storytellers first connected Jason to the Black Sea since sailors from this Greek colony were among the first Greeks to explore the Black Sea and both Miletus and Iolcus claimed their people to be Minyae, descendants of King Minyas of Thessaly, like most of the Argonauts.

There is some slight evidence that Mycenaeans may have visited the Black Sea from time to time,[13] but even if this is the case, this does not prove what Stefan Hiller argued, that the Argonauts' voyage was a literal memory of these Black Sea trips. He believed that because Iolcus was a real Mycenaean center, and because the Mycenaeans had sailed the Black Sea, we could conclude that Aea had an independent Black Sea reality as well. But even if the Mycenaeans traveled the Black Sea, and even if those voyages informed the first Jason stories, it does not prove, as Hiller thought, that Aea was always conceived as a Black Sea settlement rather than a fantastic, mythic space outside the normal world—in fact, the Gate of the Sun and the Underworld. The reality of Iolcus does not imply the reality of Aea any more than the reality of Heracles' home of Thebes proves the reality of the Garden of the Hesperides, or the Underworld. Most fantasies have the real world as an entry point, all the better to move the audience from their everyday world to the mythic space.

At any rate, these voyages, if they ever existed, ended with the Mycenaean collapse, and they left little trace among the Greeks, except, perhaps, as a distorted, impressionistic memory in the Jason myth. This memory, though, probably more specifically recalled a time when Mycenaeans sailed the Aegean, a type of large-scale sailing and trade that declined precipitously after the Mycenaean collapse. The first secure evidence for Greeks in the Black Sea comes in the form of pottery from the seventh century BCE. Sporadic interaction may have taken place before this in the Dark Ages, and some controversial evidence suggests contact, trade, and possible settlement in the eighth century BCE[14] which finds some support in eighth century literature[15]; however, Greek presence cannot be securely proved prior to the seventh century. Since Homer and Hesiod were already familiar with the fully developed Jason story in the early to mid-eighth century, the myth must have predated the Greek exploration of the Black Sea in those decades, rather than emerging as a result of those explorations. Symbiotically, however, these voyages would have informed later versions of the Jason story as new details filled in old outlines.

Greek pottery shows up at Colchis in modern Georgia by the late seventh century, likely via trade from Greek colonies on the Black Sea's southern coast, and Greek colonies emerged in Colchis not long after, in the sixth century BCE. Colchis was first mentioned by name by Eumelus, who lived in the eighth century BCE, but it is unclear that he meant the name to refer to the Black Sea coast. Additionally, there is controversy about whether the texts attributed to him can be dated to the eighth century. They may reflect seventh or sixth century revisions or the work of another author.[16] By the end of the seventh century, colonies were also established on the north coast, in the area of the Crimea and the straights that lead to the Sea of Azov. Unfortunately, there is not enough evidence to say conclusively whether contact before the colonial period was the result of Greeks traveling on trade missions, Black Sea residents returning home with Greek objects, or objects traveling along trade routes without the movement of peoples.[17] However, the most compelling conclusion is that before the seventh century BCE, Greek "penetration" of the Black Sea occurred primarily through cultural transmission between peoples and not necessarily actual voyages into the Black Sea.[18]

According to David Braund, as the Greeks expanded their explorations and trade missions into the Black Sea, and eventually came to colonize its coasts, they employed the preexisting myth of Jason and the Argonauts as a sort of mythic origin story for their own adventures.[19] (It couldn't have happened the other way around, since the Greeks placed Jason before the Trojan War and clearly understood that their own expeditions to the Black Sea were more recent than the Trojan War.) In so doing, they came to incorporate increasing geographic knowledge and details about the Black Sea into the developing story, until eventually Jason's quest to the (mythical) river Phasis in Aea, somewhere on the shores of Ocean beyond the edge of the known world, settled on the real world coast of Georgia, in the land of Colchis, whose main river, the modern Rioni, absorbed the name Phasis and into which Aea disappeared. One impetus for the identification of Aea with Colchis may have been the name of the Armenian people living beyond Colchis, the Hay or Hayk, possible descendants of the inland Anatolian Bronze Age kingdom of Hayasa, whose name recalls Aea, but which is now believed to have been situated near Lake Van in the east rather than the Black Sea in the north as once thought. Another may well have been the mythology the Greeks encountered when they first landed on Georgian shores. If the reports of early Christian missionaries can be taken to represent more ancient beliefs, the native people worshipped gods influenced by other Near East deities, including those of Mesopotamia and Anatolia. Their chief gods were probably the Moon God and the Sun God, just as Aea was the dawn-land of the Sun. They worshipped a version of the Hittite god Teshub, and the material remains from the Caucasus show the ancient Proto-Indo-European motif of a hero's battle with a dragon depicted frequently on Bronze Age religious art.[20] In much later myth, it was said that a Georgian hero named Amirani fought a giant from whose body emerged three dragons. Amirani killed the first two dragons, but the third swallowed him whole, just like Jason in the Douris cup; and Amirani's brothers needed to free the hero by cutting the dragon open with an axe (or he cuts himself out in another variant). Amirani eloped with a princess clothed in golden garments more beautiful than the sun (shades of the Golden Fleece), and who was able to save his life through her knowledge of a magic herb (shades of Medea, but without the necromancy—a mouse told her the secret).[21] How much of this story was known in the eighth century BCE is unclear; the oldest recorded versions are medieval in date but are evidently based on a mythic hero who predated the arrival of the Greeks in the Caucasus region,[22] and almost certainly some Proto-Indo-European-derived dragon myth would have been known, too. But, equally possible, Jason may have influenced Amirani instead.

When the Greeks arrived and found a land ruled by the Sun in which a hero battled a dragon and won a princess's hand, it would only have been natural to associate it with their own Jason story. To the Greek mind, standing before a sun temple by the Black Sea surrounded by images of a hero battling a great serpent they must have thought they had come to Aea itself and had found the very spot where Jason had killed the guardian of the Golden Fleece. In fact, they had merely stumbled on another mythology that grew from the same mixture of Mesopotamian and Indo-European motifs as had the Greeks' own.[23]

The Fantastic Voyage

In 1869 the German classical scholar Johann Wilhelm Adolf Kirchoff, a professor of classical philology at the University of Berlin, proposed that Homer's *Odyssey* was a composite work, and that a significant number of passages derived from an early version of the Jason and the Argonauts story. In Kirchoff's view, the original *Odyssey* had at its nucleus the myth of the "return of Odysseus" from Troy, and comprised the stories of his encounters with the Cyclops, Calypso, and Phaeacians. To this, the epilogue in Ithaca, where Odysseus confronts Penelope's suitors, and the adventures of Telemachus, his son, were later added. Following these changes, an additional set of adventures, including Circe, the Sirens, the cattle of the sun, and Scylla were imported into the *Odyssey* from their original context, the Argonaut myth.[24] German scholars expanded and refined this thesis in the nineteenth and twentieth centuries, though most of this literature was (and remains) un-translated into English. In 1879 British the classical scholar Frederick A. Paley presented this idea for English-speaking audiences in a lengthy if somewhat faulty *Dublin Review* article.[25]

Kirchoff's thesis has found wide scholarly acceptance, even if specific details are sometimes questioned, or alternative arguments for which sections are original and which are later interpolations are sometimes proposed. From the conclusion that whatever version of the Jason story was current at the time that the *Odyssey* took its final form served as an inspiration for Homer, it was therefore possible to use these aspects of Homer's poem to work backward to draw conclusions about the content of this older *Argonautica*. Karl Meuli, a professor in Basel, Switzerland, approached the Argonauts' story in just this way in his book, *Odyssee and Argonautika* (1921), which attempted to demonstrate Homer's reliance on an early form of the Jason story, and offered a tentative reconstruction of the events that must have been part of that first *Argonautica*. More recently, M. L. West reevaluated the evidence for the early *Argonautica* found in the *Odyssey*, and in so doing allows us a glimpse at the original oral tradition.

According to West, the following elements from the *Odyssey* are likely to have been present in the version of the *Argonautica* known in the ninth and eighth centuries:

- The Clashing Rocks.
- Circe the Sorceress.

- The Sirens.
- The Laestrygonians.
- The Cimmerians and the approach to Hades.
- The Cattle of the Sun.[26]

To this list of original Argonaut adventures, we can add the Lemnian women, attested in Homer's *Iliad*. Together, they demonstrate that Homer was acquainted with a version of the legend that had already begun to be located in the still mostly-uncharted Black Sea, and one that was already replete with adventurous episodes.

THE LEMNIAN WOMEN

In Book VII of the *Iliad*, Homer alludes to Jason's liaison with Hypsipyle, the queen of the women of the northeastern Aegean island of Lemnos, and the son, Euneus, she bore to him during the Argonauts' stay on her island.[27] Euneus is mentioned elsewhere in the *Iliad* as the king of Lemnos who orders the provisioning of the Greek fleet on their long voyage. A son of Jason, unnamed but probably Euneus, also buys Priam's son Lykaon as a slave, and Euneus possesses a silver mixing bowl that he gives to Patroclus. It is perhaps interesting that Homer devotes more references to Euneus that he does to his more famous father, Jason, which as Mackie suggests may have to do with Jason's ambiguous status as a healer whose power defied Homeric conceptions of mortals' proper sphere.[28]

According to ancient tradition, the women of Lemnos insulted Aphrodite and as a result the goddess cursed them with a bad smell that drove their husbands to take mistresses on the mainland. Enraged, the women murdered their husbands and lived on the island by themselves until Jason and his men came and impregnated the sexually frustrated women. Burkert has connected the episode on Lemnos to a Near East-inspired New Year's festival conducted on the island each year since pre–Greek times, which involved the women and men separating, the men symbolically dead. The women then lived alone for a period, and sacrificed a ram whose blood was used to call "secret gods from under the earth" and whose fleece was used for ritual purification. The rites apparently end with the men, symbolizing the gods, returning by ship, bringing new life (as dead Dumuzi returned to the murderous Inanna by ship) and involved sexual license in which women were the aggressors.[29]

The similarities between these rites and the Dark Age Jason story must have proven irresistible. Burkert suggests that the Argonauts were substituted into the festival's mythology in place of the original earth gods, the Cabeiri (Kabeiroi), chthonic deities who were the patrons of sailors and who were worshipped on Lemnos. They were grandsons of the islands' patron, Hephaestus, the blacksmith of the gods, who was equated on Lemnos with the dying and rising god Baal. Connected to an ancient earth goddess, the Cabeiri were worshipped in mystery rites known only to initiates. It is interesting to note that at Thebes, the Cabeiri are associated with bull sacrifices, and small bronze bulls were given as offerings.[30] They would have been the original mythic group to sail to Lemnos (from the Underworld, perhaps) to repopulate the island[31]; however, it may well be that the association emerged because of Jason's own earlier identification with a similar dying and rising earth god. Early Greek visitors could have made the equation with their own myth of Jason, just as they identified foreign gods and heroes with their own, and then incorporated the Lemnian version of the myth into the growing cycle of Jason poems as an episode of Jason's adventures.

At any rate, the identification of the Argonauts with the Lemnian episode must have occurred in the Dark Ages since it is well-known to the *Iliad* poet and is thus the oldest adventure associated with Jason's journey, one that predates the Greek conquest of non–Indo-European Lemnos in the sixth century BCE. As one of the oldest urban centers in the Aegean, settled from the fourth millennium BCE, the fortified Lemnian town of Poliochni was a wonder of the world, but it was abandoned sometime before 2000 BCE. There was no large-scale settlement again until the end of the Mycenaean Age. For the Mycenaeans, Lemnos was a source of slave women, and the Mycenaeans had settlements on the island,[32] which apparently imported pottery from Iolcus.[33] Around 2000 BCE Lemnian pottery is found in the region of Jason's hometown of Iolcus, indicating early contact.[34] Lemnos also had direct and indirect trade relationships with Troy, Anatolia, and the Black Sea beyond, from which it imported metals for metalworking. For these reasons Lemnos may have entered into the Jason myth as an obvious stop on an eastward mission from Mycenaean Iolcus. It is interesting, though, that this early adventure is at its core a minor-key recapitulation of the climax of the Jason story, with a ritual male death, holy ram's fleece, and marriage to a high-powered woman. It is almost as if a competing Jason-like story and ritual from Lemnos became incorporated into the Greek Jason myth.

THE CLASHING ROCKS

As we have seen, Homer references the Jason story at times in both the *Iliad* and the *Odyssey*. In the latter poem, one of his longest references has Circe tell of the voyage of the *Argo* past the Planctae, an etymologically difficult term which apparently meant "wandering," "jostling," or "clashing" rocks.[35] They were identified with the Clashing Rocks, also known as Symplegades, as early as Pindar, only to be separated later on.[36] In the *Odyssey*, Circe states:

> The only coursing ship that ever passed this way was *Argo*, famed of all, when voyaging from Aeëtes: and her the waves would soon have dashed on the great rocks, but Here [Hera] brought her through from love of Jason.[37]

From this brief reference to the Argonaut story, we can deduce many points about the Archaic oral tradition that informed it:

- Jason's ship was already named *Argo*.
- The king of Aea (later Colchis) was already named Aeëtes ("the man of Aea").
- Jason passed through the clashing rocks.
- Hera loved and protected Jason.
- The Argonauts passed the clashing rocks while *leaving* Aea, not going to it.

Because the Argonaut story is consistent in its description of the voyage moving eastward from Iolcus to the Black Sea on its outward journey, this means that the clashing rocks were not synonymous with the narrow strait of the Bosporus, as they would become in later times. They are, apparently, positioned instead somewhere along the return path, which could not have been identical to the outward trek. Since the Greeks before the Archaic period did not yet understand the Black Sea to be enclosed, they first conceived of the return

The Bosporus became identified with the Clashing Rocks of the Argonaut myth because the narrow strait was the smallest opening along the water route from Iolcus to Colchis; however, the position and identity of the Symplegades has varied widely through time, sometimes identified with the Homeric Planctae and othertimes thought to be separate mythic rocks (Library of Congress).

journey as moving from the Black Sea into the waters which led outward to the great river that surrounds all land. Consequently, West argues, the *Argo*'s return journey was meant to follow the River Ocean from Aea back to Greece.[38] As for the Clashing Rocks, expanding geographical knowledge in the sixth century would force them from the end of the journey to the beginning, to agree with the new discovery that the Black Sea was enclosed, and "the myth was modified" to claim that the rocks stopped clashing after Jason's passage.[39] We know this must have occurred around the sixth century because in Homer's *Odyssey* the rocks still clash, despite Jason's passage, and Odysseus chooses the "easier" way of travelling between Scylla and Charybdis.

West goes further, and argues that the Clashing Rocks were a mythological portal, which like other such gates in folk legends and fairy tales worldwide, closes shut behind a hero escaping with the elixir of life. He reads the Golden Fleece to be a stand-in for the life-giving ambrosia of the gods, on analogy with the golden apples of the Nordic myths and the Soma of Indian myth, and which also in Homer passes through the clashing rocks on the wings of doves.[40] Jason is thus a hero seeking the secret of renewed life, just as Gilgamesh was. In myth, ambrosia was grown on the banks of Oceanus, just the spot where Jason sails. If true, this origin for the Golden Fleece would agree well with the idea that Jason was originally the Velchanos figure who needed to descend into the underworld to receive the gift of rebirth.

CIRCE

In the *Odyssey,* the sorceress Circe is Aeëtes' sister and also has a home in the farthest east, where the sun's rays are stored for the dawn. The east is the direction of Jason, but fits ill with Odysseus' westward voyage, implying that this episode (despite later attempts to retroactively remove Circe to the vicinity of Italy) belonged first to Jason. Confirmation can be found in Pherecydes, who recorded in the fifth century BCE that the Golden Fleece resided on the "Aeaean isle," a reference to Circe's home.[41] West believes that as she does with Odysseus, Circe must have served to give Jason and Medea advice about their escape from Aea,[42] but having two sorceress women with overlapping powers seems unnecessarily redundant. An answer might lie in Hittite myth. Judith Yarnall connects Circe to, among others, Kubaba, consort of Teshub (Zeus), and suggests that Circe originates in an ancient Anatolian earth goddess who degraded into various sorceresses and lesser deities as the male-centered worship of Zeus triumphed over goddess worship.[43] This is only a stone's throw from Inara, Teshub's daughter, who was possibly the first Medea figure. This may explain Circe's presence in the Argonaut story, as the mother whose daughter the hero has won by triumphing over the dragon, or even as a replacement for Hera, the earth goddess, at this stage of the journey. Alternately, other scholars have followed the suggestion of Strabo that Homer (or some tradition before him) created Circe's island of Aeaea from Aea and Circe from Medea herself.[44] This explanation would also remove the redundancy of populating Aea with a multiplicity of semi-divine sorceresses who mate with mortals and master the use of herbs.

THE SIRENS

The Sirens are the bird-bodied, woman-headed creatures who living on an island and draw sailors to their ends by singing irresistible songs. Odysseus passes the Sirens by stuffing wax in his crew's ears to block out the enchanting melody that drives men to their deaths. After he passes, the Sirens commit suicide for their failure to charm a victim from his ship. West argues, persuasively, that in myth such acts of self-slaughter are the result of losing a contest, as when the Sphinx dies when Oedipus solves its riddle. The conclusion is that this action originally belonged to the Argonaut story, and the Sirens died after recognizing the superior beauty of Orpheus' music. West notes that Orpheus is not attested as an Argonaut before the sixth century, but believes he must always have been one.[45] This not necessarily the case. The earliest sculpture of this scene, from the Treasury of Sicyon at Delphi (560 BCE), shows *two* lyre players on the prow of the *Argo.* The implication, as Graf suggests, is that there was once another singer and Orpheus was added later and gradually replaced him.[46] This solution allows us to keep the Sirens without postulating a "celebrity" Argonaut whose fame would have eclipsed the hero Jason had he been included before the time of Homer.

THE LAESTRYGONIANS

In the *Odyssey,* the Laestrygonians are violent, human-consuming giants who destroy eleven of Odysseus' twelve ships by throwing rocks at them in a sheltered cove. Since the nineteenth century, this episode was compared to the incident in Apollonius' *Argonautica* where six-armed giants hurl rocks at the moored *Argo* in a sheltered cove at Cyzicus, the land of preternaturally long days and long nights. German scholars believed the Argonautic version must have preceded the Homeric, and West has argued persuasively that the origin of the Laestrygonian story comes from travelers' tales of the Balaclava region of the Crimea, whose geography the *Odyssey* apparently describes quite closely, and whose vicious barbarian inhabitants, the Tauroi (who Herodotus reported made human sacrifices of passing sailors) compare equally well to the Laestrygonians. Another detail, the claim that the land of Czyicus had exceptionally long days and nights, is possibly a traveler's tale of far northern Europe, brought along the amber routes, which became conflated with the story of Laestrygonians. West notes that such correlations imply a journey north from the Black Sea, something closely related to the Argonauts but less likely to have been an original part of Odysseus' wanderings in the western Mediterranean.[47] However, Dimitri Nakassis makes the intriguing suggestion that the Laestrygonians of perpetual day and the Cimmerians of perpetual night (see below) were originally a single people who lived at the entrance to Tartarus (the Underworld gate where the sun rose and set) but were bifurcated into opposites to conform to a new mythic geography that separated the sun's transit into eastern and western poles. Thus, in the *Argonautica*, both would have been a single hostile people surrounding Aea, associated at some point with the Crimean Tauroi, before being divided in half and flung across the world.[48]

A Passage to Hades

Among the landscapes of the Black Sea is the rather dramatic vista from the Sea of Azov, which contains a confluence of rivers, mud volcanoes, and poplar forests, scenes which parallel Odysseus' trip to the gates of Hades. The Cimmerians, who occupy a benighted land of mists and clouds, are said in Homer to live beside Hades at the edge of the Ocean, and Herodotus and Strabo both located the Cimmerians' home on the north shore of the Black Sea, which in Homer's day was considered an arm of Ocean. Herodotus discussed a real tribe of that name, and Strabo equated them to their Homeric namesakes, as surely other ancient sources did. Again, West held that such parallels hold for an *eastern* voyage rather than the westward track of Odysseus, reinforcing the connection to the Argonauts and their Black Sea passage. West suggested that the Argonauts sailed past these places but did not stop at Hades to communicate with the dead. Instead this hypothetical episode inspired Homer to have Odysseus do so.[49] These suppositions are a bit complex, and somewhat tautological.

A more parsimonious reading, in keeping with the idea that Jason's voyage was a shamanic trip to the underworld or netherworld is that Aea was originally conceived as the underworld, and this description would have carried over into Dark Age and Archaic versions of the story as geographic rumors of the Black Sea transformed the mystical underworld into a forbidding land on a more realistic sea coast. Homer wrote that "Never on them [the Cimmerians] does the shining sun look down with his beams, as he goes up the starry sky or as again toward earth he turns back from the sky, but deadly night is spread abroad over these hapless men."[50] The Cimmerians live in darkness because they were once thought to exist beyond or beside the land of Aea, the place of the dawn. This entrance to the Underworld, associated with the Cimmerians in Homer, is dark because the sun rises from the gate and travels over Ocean and onward toward land, thus bypassing these people and denying them light. In short, the landscape details from the real Black Sea were grafted on to a pre-existing conception of a voyage to the underworld. In the final phase, the underworld would vanish altogether (it appears in no extant version of the Jason story) because it has no independent purpose. Aea or Colchis stands for it by itself. (See chapter 7.)

THE CATTLE OF THE SUN

The principle antagonist for Odysseus is Poseidon, which has given many commentators to wonder why it is Helios whose wrath destroys all of Odysseus' companions when they kill one of his sacred cattle. These cattle, three hundred fifty in number, represent the days of the lunar year, as Aristotle noted.[51] Beginning with Meuli, scholars have proposed that the cattle incident belongs properly to the Argonauts, who triggered the wrath of the sun by humiliating his son Aeëtes and taking his daughter Medea. West suggests that the Argonauts merely viewed the cattle but did not touch them. This solution is strangely passive. What purpose would it serve to view but not touch the sacred cattle? A more integrated thesis would suggest that the bulls Jason must yoke, whom we have considered solar symbols of the earth god's solar form, are two of the solar cattle, accounting for their flaming power. This solution neatly integrates two sets of bulls/cows with solar imagery and places them in the context of the parts of the Jason story we know to have been extant in the Dark Age, without the need to hypothesize a second foray of Argonaut tourists in the sun's pastures, or an actual Greek presence in the Black Sea prior to the earliest archaeological evidence. Thus, both the entrance to Hades and the cattle of the sun would have originated in the older *Argonautica*'s description of Aea as the Gate.

Interestingly, as we have noted, the equation of Aea with an older version of the underworld quite closely matches the description of the underworld in an ancient Sumerian poem. There a god of the underworld, unnamed, describes his realm. It is located beside a river and includes "the mountains of the sunrise" and the "house of the setting sun." The sun is conceived as both the god of heaven and the judge of the dead. The sun's house has at its door a "monster with jaws that gape" and a furious guard lion. The goddess Inanna has a garden there, too.[52] Here, as we do with Aea, we have an association with the resting sun and a monster or dragon whose jaws give entrance to the pit. The garden of Inanna recalls the enchanted isle of Circe, an earth goddess figure, whose home of Aeaea was likely originally conceived as a part of Aea. Given this information, the idea of Aea as an equivalent of Hades is increasingly plausible. We will explore this connection in greater detail in chapter 7.

Of course, it can be objected that the Greeks and other Near Eastern people conceived of the entrance to the Underworld as being the west, not the east, the place where the sun sets.[53] The German scholar Carl Robert in fact proposed in 1920 that the Argonauts originally travelled west, not east, and that only after the opening of the Black Sea was the story relocated. Though his argument is not entirely convincing, it might account for the discrepancy between the apparently western location of the underworld and Jason's eastward progress. However, all of this presumes that Jason's voyage was always conceived as a literal trip on real waters. The original was likely not geographically centered (stories such as Prometheus' mountain enchainment were not given fixed locations in those days either), and only later became associated with a specific direction of travel, as the Black Sea became the locus of action. Besides, Strabo had no trouble identifying Homer's Cimmerians who encamp beside

Hades' entrance with the people of the Black Sea region, indicating that Hades was not always exclusively conceived as being to the west of Greece. The Mesopotamians, in fact, considered an important entrance to Underworld to lie at the gate through which the sun emerged at dawn to start each new day.

If this reading is correct, it means that Jason's three tasks at Aea become still more potent: He tames the fiery bulls who represent the days of the year (and thus time itself), fights the earthborn men to master this plane, and descends into the underworld to triumph over death. He is thus thrice a hero, above, below, and upon the earth, master of them all.

The Transformation: Hesiod and the Homeric Fragments

Having now rung as much blood from the Homeric stone as we are likely to get, we might profitably move on to Homer's rough contemporary, Hesiod. Hesiod was a Boetian shepherd who, according to legend, met the Muses on Mount Helikon and under their tutelage composed two great poems, the *Theogony*, an account of the origin and genealogy of the gods, and *Works and Days*, which gave agricultural instructions. Hesiod was regarded as an historic figure in ancient times and usually considered a contemporary of Homer. Alcidamas in the fourth century BCE paired the two poets in a fictitious "contest," which Hesiod won. However, modern scholars increasingly favor identifying Hesiod as a composite figure to whom a number of Archaic poems were attributed. Dates for the works attributed to Hesiod range from 720 BCE to 650 BCE for their oral forms, and it is believed they were first written down by no later than 600 BCE.[54] These poems reveal a poet who is an acolyte of Zeus, one who holds an "exalted view of Zeus," glorifying in the "exaltation of Zeus' power."[55] Indeed, Hesiod is essential in transmitting the new version of the triumphant, universal Zeus who by the eighth century had become the supreme Greek deity, definitively suppressing the old Poseidon earth god and co-opting the Mycenaean earth goddess Hera as the more ethereal Queen of Heaven.

Among many other poems that were attributed to Hesiod off and on in historical times is the *Catalogue of Women*. It was a sort of sequel to the *Theogony*, relating the genealogy of the demigods and heroes. This poem does not survive in its entirety and is known only from fragments, which are now frequently considered a later revision or summary of an original Hesiodic poem (or competing poems) and have been variously dated between 776 BCE and 476 BCE with many scholars favoring the sixth century. It incorporated oral traditions stretching back much farther as well parts of a genuine Hesiodic original from the eighth century.[56]

In the *Theogony*, Hesiod references the Jason story and provides our earliest mentions of Aeson, Aeëtes, and Pelias, as well as Medea. In one passage, the genealogies of Aeëtes and Medea are given, including Aeëtes' and Circe's divine parents: Helios and the daughter of Ocean, Pereseïs. Another Oceanic daughter, Idyia, becomes Aeëtes' wife, and the mother of Medea, who, it is implied, is an immortal (by dint of being included in the section of the *Theogony* on unions between gods and mortals), like her divine ancestors. A longer passage gives the most direct reference to the Argonaut story:

> And the son of Aeson by the will of the gods led away from Aeëtes the daughter of Aeëtes the heaven-nurtured king,[57] when he had finished the many grievous labours which the great king, overbearing Pelias, that outrageous and presumptuous doer of violence, put upon him. But when

the son of Aeson had finished them, he came to Iolcus after long toil bringing the coy-eyed girl with him on his swift ship, and made her his buxom wife. And she was subject[58] to Iason, shepherd of the people, and bare a son Medeus whom Cheiron the son of Philyra brought up in the mountains. And the will of great Zeus was fulfilled.[59]

What is interesting in this brief précis of the Jason myth is that Aeëtes is not assigned a role in imposing labors on Jason. Here, it is Pelias who is the sole villain, and it is intriguing that he is assigned "many grievous labors" to impose on Jason, not just the one he is credited with in later versions. The implication is that Pelias assigned Jason to voyage to Aea and to perform the three tasks that later writers have Aeëtes ask him to do. This is confirmed by the poet's note that Aeëtes is "Zeus-cherished" or the "foster son of Zeus" (a more literal translation of διοτρεφέος, given above as "heaven-nurtured") and that winning the hand of Medea was the will of Zeus, as (presumably) was securing Zeus' Golden Fleece (though Hesiod's only mention of the Fleece, in the *Catalogue of Women*, is in conjunction with Phrixus and not related to Jason[60]). It is almost as if Hesiod, who could not completely change the received tradition of the sun god's role at Aea, purposely recast Aeëtes in a more Zeus-friendly light. If he could not be Zeus' literal son, he could be Zeus' favorite or a foster son. It would be logically strained therefore to have Zeus' king, Aeëtes, standing as an obstacle to Jason's quest to fulfill Zeus' will. Thus, Poseidon's son Pelias is the sole villain of the story, and this transformation resolves another problem inherent in the later Argonaut stories.

Critics have noted for centuries that Aeëtes essentially functions as a second Pelias in later Argonaut tales, a parallel made explicit in Valerius Flaccus' Roman *Argonautica*. Both kings initially promise to submit to Jason, and then both kings impose "grievous labors" upon him. Finally, both kings fail to yield to him upon completion of these labors. This close similarity implies that at one point either Aeëtes and Pelias were the same character (perhaps the earth god), or that Pelias' demands were once more extensive and later poets divided them among the two kings for dramatic effect. Hesiod appears to identify the Aeëtes-Medea relationship as essentially the same as the relationship between Zeus/Teshub and Inara in the Hittite myth of the dragon, with which the poet must have been familiar given the close parallels between the *Theogony* and Hittite and Near East cosmology. In that story, the goddess's father was no villain, either. It is interesting to note that Aeëtes is named in Hesiod as an adopted son of Zeus rather than emphasizing him as a son of Helios, the sun. Thus, only Pelias is a Poseidon/earth god figure, and the villain. Every other character has been made into an instrument of triumphant Zeus. Given Aeëtes,' and Aea's, relationship to the three forms of the earth god and his underworld, this must be no coincidence.

Hesiod seems to have purposely recast the Jason myth in a way favorable to the Zeus cult, minimizing any remnants of the old earth god, and in fact any deity other than Zeus. Not even Hera, whom we would expect from Homer to have warranted a mention, is present, perhaps because in Homer she still maintains traces of her former, pre–Zeus status as his superior and must therefore have held that status in the pre–Homeric *Argonautica*. There is now only Zeus.

Lastly, Medea appears here only as an adjunct to Jason, and apparently a figurative descendant of Zeus, the prize from his voyage, rather than an essential helpmeet. She is not associated with any earth deities, as she would be again in her frequent associations with Hecate. This brief passage seems, therefore, like most of the *Theogony*, propaganda for Zeus against the older earth god and goddess religion. It is not, in all likelihood, a simple, unfiltered transmission of the Jason myth but a purposely revised version, just as Hesiod recast other myths, such as Prometheus' deception of Zeus, into terms more favorable to the deity.

THE CATALOGUE OF WOMEN

Hesiod's only other recorded mention of Jason's name comes in a fragment of the *Catalogue of Women*, preserved in a note from a scholiast writing on Homer's *Odyssey*:

> Tyro the daughter of Salmoneus, having two sons by Poseidon, Neleus and Pelias, married Cretheus, and had by him three sons, Aeson, Pheres and Amythaon. And of Aeson and Polymede, according to Hesiod, Iason was born. "Aeson, who begot a son Iason, shepherd of the people, whom Chiron brought up in woody Pelion."[61]

This fragment tells us little, except that Hesiod's *Catalogue of Women* must have listed the genealogy of Jason, and explicitly linked Pelias to Poseidon; whereas Jason's lineage is carefully separated from that of the evil, Poseidon-born Pelias. Finally, the scholiast records either a mistaken or variant version from that given in the *Theogony* in which it is Jason rather than his son who is given over to Chiron. It is probably also worth noting that Jason's mother, here given as Polymede in our earliest surviving text to name her, was of such little importance that at least ten names for her exist in ancient literature: Alcimede, Amphinome, Arne, Eteoclymene, Polymede, Polymela, Polypheme, Rhoeo, Scarphe, and Theognete.[62]

A few other fragments[63] bear relevance on the Argonauts' journey. In a fragment from the scholiast to Apollonius of Rhodes, we learn that Hesiod did not include Iphiclus among the Argonauts.[64] This implies that Hesiod had a list of Argonauts who were already among Jason's companions at this early date. A fragment attributed to the Alexandrian librarian Eratosthenes informs us that Hesiod and Pherecydes both confirm that Helle and Phrixus received transport on a golden ram.[65] Curiously it is said to be "immortal," which raises the question of how it could be sacrificed.

Another fragment from the Apollonius scholiast records two variants of the myth of the seer Phineus, first that he was blinded "because he revealed to Phrixus the road," presumably to Aea, and that he was blinded because he "preferred long life to sight."[66] The Harpies are separately described as taking Phineus on a journey around the world, "to the land of milk-feeders who have waggons for houses,"[67] whom the scholiast appears to equate with the Scythians of the Black Sea. Following this, two fragments from the same source, tell of the defeat of the Harpies at the hands of the sons of Boreas, who, crucially, "prayed to Zeus" to defeat the Harpies, and Zeus apparently answered their prayer, though the Harpies "were not killed."[68] It is unclear whether Hesiod meant this as an episode in the journey of the Argonauts (many scholars feel it was not originally so meant), but it appears as such in later versions. However, given that the artistic evidence from pottery possibly records a much different tradition—that Jason cured Phineus' blindness—we may have another case where Hesiod is purposely revising a myth to remove traces of Jason's godly powers and transferring his heroic deeds to the intervention of all-powerful Zeus. Alternately, there may have been two separate myths—first that the Boreal twins drove out the Harpies, and second that Jason later restored Phineus' sight—that became conflated later on when the twins were drafted aboard the *Argo*.

In three fragments preserved in Philodemus and Strabo, and the Apollonius scholiast, it is very briefly noted that Hesiod mentions the Argonauts' adventures with pygmies, half-dog people, and great-headed people. He then notes that they left Aea via the river Phasis, entered the Ocean, and sailed around it to Libya (the ancient name for Africa), carrying the *Argo* overland to the Mediterranean.[69] This might represent the first attempt to integrate the mythic edge of the world with early reports of geographic discoveries in the farthest east, though M. L. West believes Hesiod meant it as purely mythic, derived from the Indo-European word for "radiant," *Bhā-tis*, a reference to its role as the place where the sun rose, in Aea, the land of the Dawn.[70] In two fragments from the Apollonius scholiast, Hesiod is said to have related Circe's involvement in the Argonaut story as well as the sailors' involvement with the Sirens.[71] The scholiast states that Apollonius followed Hesiod in bringing Circe to Italy, but this must be a Hellenistic interpretation since Italy had only just begun being colonized in Hesiod's day.

Several other fragments provide additional genealogical discussions related to the families of Jason, Phrixus, and the Argonaut Eumeleus. However, these discussions are related to the broader development of Greek mythological storytelling and do not directly impact our study of the Argonaut story proper. A final fragment of interest from the Apollonius scholiast states that Hesiod had already attached Heracles to the Argonauts' journey, and that the hero did not complete it, having been abandoned while searching for water in Magnesia.[72] This fragment comes from the *Wedding of Ceyx*, which was thought in ancient times to be Hesiod's but seems instead to be a later expansion of an episode from the *Catalogue of Women*. As such, it probably belongs to the sixth century, when Heracles had been interpolated into the Argonauts' journey.

THE HOMERIC FRAGMENTS

Homer's and Hesiod's poems were only a few of many epics that existed in the Archaic world. The Dark Ages had bequeathed a number of oral traditions—the *Argonautica* among them—and over time, a number of these poems began to overshadow the others. By the Hellenistic Period six poems originating in the Archaic period—*Kypria, Iliad, Aithiopis, Little Iliad, Ilioupersis, Nostoi, Odyssey,* and *Telegoneia*—became known as the Epic Cycle because these works treated episodes related to the lead up to, conduct of, and aftermath of the Trojan War. Aside from the two works of Homer included in the list, the authors of the other six poems are unknown. The ancients had their theories, but they were little more than conjecture.[73] These poems, which exist only in a few scattered fragments and summaries, are also of uncertain age, usually dated somewhere between the eighth and sixth centuries, though likely drawing on oral traditions from the age of Homer.[74]

Of these poems, there is only one fragment that deals with an Argonautic theme. It is uncertain why the poem *Nostoi* ("The Returns"), which is concerned with the returning heroes of the Trojan War, should hark back to the Argonauts. Perhaps the author had meant to draw comparison between the two expeditions to the east, or it might have been related to Achilles' imagined marriage to Medea in the afterlife. The fragment is preserved in the argument to Eurpides' *Medea*:

Forthwith Medea made Aeson a sweet young boy and stripped his old age from him by her cunning skill, when she had made a brew of many herbs in her golden cauldrons.[75]

This fragment presents a different story than Pherecydes and Simonides (see below), who claimed Medea had restored Jason. As we have seen, this type of shamanic restoration may have been involved with the resurrection rites of the early Jason story. Here we seem to have evidence that at least one strand of tradition had already removed this event from the climax of Jason's heroic venture to its aftermath, translating the resurrection into a rejuvenation of Jason's father.

A final Homeric fragment, from the *Oechaliae Halosis* ("The Taking of Oechalia"), preserved in the scholia to Euripides' *Medea*, describes an early version of Medea's life after Jason:

[W]hile Medea was living in Corinth, she poisoned Creon, who was ruler of the city at that time, and because she feared his friends and kinsfolk, fled to Athens. However, since her sons were too young to go along with her, she left them at the altar of Hera Acraea, thinking that their father would see to their safety. But the relatives of Creon killed them and spread the story that Medea had killed her own children as well as Creon.[76]

However, the mention of Corinth, which came to prominence in the Archaic period rather than the Mycenaean period, argues that this is a later layer of myth and, combined with the previous fragment, "doubtless represent the kind of accretions which the central narratives regularly received in early epic poetry until at last a cycle was formed."[77] Indeed, the *Oechaliae*, which is of uncertain provenance, is usually dated to the seventh century, right around the time that Corinth began associating the Jason story with its own history of glorious seafaring.

Therefore, at the end of the seventh century, we have clear evidence that the core of the Jason story had begun developing accretions. The original journey to Aea had been expanded into a series of adventures, including the interlude on Lemnos, and Jason's crew must have been at least partially named. Based on linguistic evidence, some have proposed that those Argonauts whose names end in the Mycenaean-era suffix "*-eus*" are most likely to have been original Argonauts: Caeneus, Cepheus, Lynceus, Oileus, Orpheus, and Peleus, later the father of Achilles.[78] However, this is uncertain, and no list of Argonauts exists from the oldest sources. Instead, it would seem most likely that Jason's companions, like those of Gilgamesh, were formerly anonymous, and the names of Mycenaean-era and Dark Age folk heroes became attached to the voyage in the telling, probably in different combinations at different times and under different poets. Eventually, even the greatest heroes of the Greece, including Heracles, Castor and Pollux, and the sons of the Boreal wind, found themselves drawn into Jason's journey. Their adventures, however, were likely at first separate from the Argonautic voyage and only later adopted into the legend.

It is to this process of accretion that we now turn.

Enter the Fleece

Surprisingly, the story of the Golden Fleece, so important in the later versions of the Jason legend, is not directly attested in any of the ancient sources before the seventh century. The Fleece of Phrixus is alluded to in Hesiod's *Catalogue*, and in a fragmentary epic poem preserved in the scholia to Apollonius called the *Aegimus* (traditionally dated to the seventh century BCE), Phrixus purified the Fleece and "Holding the Fleece he walked into the halls of Aeëtes."[79] But in neither author is Jason directly linked to the Fleece in the extant fragments, and indeed many scholars believe the story of Phrixus and the Fleece was originally unconnected with Jason's voyage.[80] They were apparently two separate and smaller myths later joined. It seems that the earliest Jason stories had him conducting his quest for other reasons, perhaps to win the hand of a goddess, as our proposed reconstruction notes. Perhaps the Fleece joined the story when Jason's voyage was placed in the Black Sea, to a distant land similar to which Phrixus and Helle had fled. The ancients apparently first held that the Golden Ram *swam* away with Phrixus and Helle, as attested by a majority of the ancient authors, only later to be held to fly in a popular tradition perhaps derived from depictions of the ram on the Attic stage[81]; and so the ram's swim might first have been seen as parallel to Jason's voyage and thus united the two legends through their common passage by sea. If Phrixus' ram swam out into the sea and onward to Ocean, and if Jason passed the same way, he would necessarily run into the Fleece.

The seventh-century poet Mimnermus (flourished c. 630–600 BCE) is the first to affirm the object of Jason's quest in a fragment preserved in Strabo, who also quotes the poet's fixing of Aea's location beyond the edge of the world:

> Never would Jason himself have brought back the great fleece from Aea, accomplishing his mind-racking journey and fulfilling the difficult task for insolent Pelias, nor would they have come even to the fair stream of Oceanus.... To the city of Aeëtes, where the rays of the swift Sun lie in a chamber of gold beside the lips of Oceanus, whither glorious Jason went.[82]

Another fragment describing the sun's glorious nighttime bed may have come from the same elegiac love poem describing Medea's and Jason's love, but this is uncertain. What is certain is that Aea was still a fantastic, mythical land in the seventh century, not yet part of the real world of the Black Sea the Greeks were starting to colonize. And now, finally, the most recognizable aspect of Jason's quest, the Golden Fleece, that very symbol of his story, is at last an attested part of the Argonaut myth. When and how it became a part of Jason's story is unknown, but as we have seen it appears to be related to a reconstruction of an older Mycenaean era story in light of more recent developments in the Greek pantheon: the ascension of Zeus.

Surely Mimnermus did not invent the Fleece, or the Phrixus story it first belonged to. Homer and the earliest Hesiodic poems do not mention the Fleece, so it would seem that the oral tradition must have interwoven questing Jason and the ram sometime in the century between Homer and Mimnermus. One key may be the negative view Homer has of Jason (perhaps due to his supernatural power) and the "glorious" depiction by Mimnermus. Did adding the Golden Fleece give Jason a more appropriate object for his voyage and thus make an older, less favorable legend more appealing to the poets of the seventh century onward?

The Naupaktia

During the seventh and sixth centuries, the much-embroidered Jason story was obviously popular and circulated in many variants. There were at least two competing versions of the story's climax, involving either Jason's descent into the dragon or putting the dragon to sleep, and any number of adventures heading to and from Aea, which increasingly came to be identified with the land of Colchis, on the far shores of the Black Sea, an ancient kingdom of advanced metalworkers that had collapsed in face of invasion in the eighth century. In the sixth century, colonists from the Greek city of Miletus in Asia Minor set up a colony, Phasis, in Colchis, and thereafter the region became increasingly prominent in the Argonaut myth. It is one of these Milesians who is traditionally said to have been the anonymous author of the *Naupaktia* (also called the *Naupaktika* or *Carmen Naupactium*), an epic giving a number of famous genealogies in the style of Hesiod's *Catalogue*. The true authorship of the poem has been contested since antiquity, and it may be linked to Naupaktos, the city of the title.

Of the poem itself, only ten lines survive (mostly in the scholia to Apollonius of Rhodes' *Argonautica* and a few descriptions from later writers); however, a 1977 reconstruction from these fragments by Victor J. Matthews offers a glimpse at the earliest Argonaut epic. The theme of the poem was predominantly genealogical, and it appeared to trace the ancestors and descendants of those identified as Argonauts when the poem was written, perhaps centered around the family of Minyas, whose many sons were numbered among the Argonauts, and bequeathed the race of the Minyae in later legend. Obviously this implies that a full list of Argonauts was then in circulation, and it is likely that at this stage Heracles was not among their number.[83] The poem likely started with the story of Phrixus and the challenge Pelias gave to Jason. It describes the outward voyage from Iolcus, and it also rehearses the driving of the Harpies, relating how the Boreads drove the winged monsters to Crete. It is likely that the poem describes the killing the Harpies, possibly by Zeus.[84]

The poem then goes on to describe the moment when Aeëtes challenged Jason to yoke the bulls to secure the Fleece, apparently because an oracle warned the king to use the test to guard against the sons of Phrixus who were to murder him, a story found in Herodorus.[85] Here, "all the heroes of Argos"[86] offered to complete the challenge at first, until the Argive Argonaut Idmon, the seer, told Jason he needed to perform the task himself. (Interestingly, the *Naupaktica* lists Idmon as the ship's psychic, but Pindar assigns this role to Mopsus, and Apollonius, combining sources, simply lists both.) The story of the earthborn men does not appear in the poem, and possibly originated in the work of Pherecydes, though this is uncertain.[87] Jason then apparently kills the dragon or serpent and brings the Fleece to Aeëtes' palace. All of this is accomplished without Medea's help, magical or otherwise.

In a scene apparently intended at least partially as comedic,[88] Aeëtes rewards Jason by giving a feast for the Argonauts, and plans to burn their boat and kill them while they eat. But Aphrodite intervenes, filling Aeëtes with intense sexual desire for his wife, Eurylyte, and he excuses himself to have sex with her. The Argonauts take the opportunity to escape, and Medea follows with the Fleece. Matthews suggests that in this version of the story, Jason's protecting goddess was Aphrodite, not Hera.[89] This gives us a third goddess figure (after Hera and, in the artistic tradition represented by Douris, Athena) playing this role, suggesting perhaps that the original goddess was non–Greek or pre–Greek (on the order or Inanna or the tri-form Minoan goddess) and could be identified with many figures in the Greek pantheon as the story was transferred from its Near East, Aegean, and Mycenaean roots to a fully Greek epic. It may perhaps be helpful to think of a continuum of goddess figures across the Aegean and Near East who have dying-and-rising consorts and control fertility, the heavens, war, and sexuality. Only later did this figure become divided, which would imply Jason's story was first told before the Great Mother figure broke apart into Hera, Athena, Aphrodite, Demeter, and Persephone. It may also be significant that Aphrodite has the same function as patron of sexuality as Aya, the Babylonian dawn goddess whose name has been linked to the land of Aea.[90]

Idmon is in this poem the most important of Jason's companions (the steersman Tiphys is apparently the second), and for this reason, argues against the early inclusion of Orpheus or Heracles among the Argonauts, since their fame would easily have outstripped that of Idmon. In the *Naupaktica*, Idmon dies among the Mariandyni on the return from Aea, a story repeated in Pherecydes and Herodorus, the latter claiming that the return journey was along the same path as the outward one. Tiphys, too, dies on the return. Jason and Medea are said in the *Naupaktia* to have had only two sons, Mermeros and Pheres, so this poem predates (or is an alternate to) the versions in which the couple's many children die at Corinth. Mermeros appears in the *Odyssey*, and Matthews suggests this is based on Homer's knowledge of the coupling of Jason and Medea, though it is also possible that they were retroactively made parents to a preexisting figure.

Living for a time at Iolcus, Jason leaves after Pelias' death, apparently having no legitimate claim to Pelias' throne. The poem appears to have then discussed Jason's residence on Corcyra, an island colonized by Corinthians, and the fragments imply that Jason continued to live peacefully there together with his wife Medea. The poem is the first to indicate that Jason removed his seat from Iolcus to Corcyra, and it likely did so as part of the great Archaic hero relocation that eventually brought Jason to Corinth as king.

The Corinthian Jason

In the Archaic Period, the Greeks developed a cult of heroes, and these legendary men were seen as important patrons and protectors of cities and families. In time, this would involve the outright adoption and transfer of heroes from one location to another. At the end of the sixth century, Solon "summoned" the ancient heroes of Salamis—Periphemos and Kykhreus—and sacrificed to them to attach their loyalty to Athens in its war against Salamis.[91] Within a century, such practices had evolved into the construction of temples to foreign heroes within cities like Athens and the acquisition of heroes' relics, including their statues and bones, for the cities that came to claim them as their own. The relics of the hero Hector, for example, were transferred from Troy to Thebes and he became a protector of the city. Associating a city with a hero was a way of absorbing the hero's power.[92] The city of Corinth, which invented the trireme warship and had grown wealthy and powerful on the strength of its sea trade after 925 BCE, participated in this process by associating itself with Jason to give itself the epic history denied it in Homeric poetry.

By the end of the eighth century, Corinth, located on the isthmus connecting the Peloponnese to the rest of Greece, had developed its own cycle of Jason myths. Obviously, Jason himself had been associated with Iolcus, from which his voyage departed. Though Iolcus was now eclipsed by Pagasae, the close association of hero and city could not be entirely broken, for tradition had linked the two. Instead, the Corinthians proposed a sequel. Jason and the Argonauts docked the *Argo* at Corinth and conducted victory games there. It was then said that after Jason had returned to Iolcus with Medea, the pair removed their seat to Corinth at the invitation of the Corinthians, where, by Medea's grace, Jason reigned as king. The story is told in the epic poem, *Corinthiaca*, traditionally ascribed to the eighth-century

The city of Corinth, seen here in ruins, was not originally associated with Jason, but after it grew rich and powerful from sea-going voyages, the city adopted the Argonaut as its own, and tradition held that the Corinthian poet Eumelus created an epic poem to justify the removal of the hero from Iolcus to his new home. The Corinthians would also identify Medea with their goddess of children (Library of Congress).

BCE poet Eumelus, but now thought to have been written in the seventh, or even the sixth century.[93] This poem detailed the mythological history of Corinth's rulers, including a myth making Aeëtes its former king (and therefore originally a Greek and a Corinthian), but it survives only in fragments. The second-century CE writer Pausansias preserved a summary of the section concerned with Jason:

> Eumelus said that Helius (*Sun*) gave the Asopian land to Aloeus and Ephyraea [i.e. Corinth] to Aeëtes. When Aeëtes was departing for Colchis he entrusted his land to Bunus, the son of Hermes and Alcidamea, and when Bunus died Epopeus the son of Aloeus extended his kingdom to include the Ephyraeans. Afterwards, when Corinthus, the son of Marathon, died childless, the Corinthians sent for Medea from Iolcus and bestowed upon her the kingdom. Through her Jason was king in Corinth, and Medea, as her children were born, carried each to the sanctuary of Hera and concealed them, doing so in the belief that so they would be immortal. At last she learned that her hopes were vain, and at the same time she was detected by Jason. When she begged for pardon he refused it, and sailed away to Iolchus. For these reasons Medea too departed, and handed over the kingdom to Sisyphus.[94]

If Pausanias correctly reported Eumelus' words, this would be our first mention of Aeëtes' kingdom being called Colchis, which argues for a composition date in the seventh century, when such territory was familiar to Black Sea explorers. Slightly later, Epimenides of Knossos wrote a "poem of six thousand five hundred verses on the building of the *Argo* and the expedition of Jason to Colchis,"[95] according to Diogenes Laertius, but nothing of this poem remains. It did, however, apparently follow the Corinthian version of Jason's return, according to later writers.

As we can see, the Corinthians sought to adopt Aeëtes and Medea as two of their own, by associating Corinth with Aeëtes as its former king and native son, and therefore heralding Medea as a combination of heroine, queen, and goddess. In contrast to the version reported in the *Oechaliae*, Eumelus has Medea killing her children by accident while attempting to secure immortality for them, an unforgivable sin that caused Medea and Jason to separate. Unlike the *Oechaliae*, this version is apparently more sympathetic to Medea, befitting a city that would worship Medea as a local goddess, and offer sacrifices to her two slain children in a temple dedicated to Hera. The connection between Medea and the temple of Hera reinforces the Victorian-era suggestion that Medea was once viewed as a form of that goddess, and thus was especially important at Corinth, whose patron goddess was Hera.

Sarah Iles Johnston goes so far as to suggest that the Corinthians identified a preexisting protector (earth) goddess of children with Hera in the Archaic Period, with Hera displacing the older goddess, who then became a sort of "demon of childbirth" attached to Hera's cult, a dark figure who represented the negative aspects of the goddess, including the disasters that can befall children. Fourteen youths were committed to her (and/or Hera's) service each year, shorn of hair and dressed in black, symbolically dead and sacrificed to the goddess. For this reason, the Corinthians erected a statue known as "The Terror" in the temple of Hera, and this terrifying woman apparently represented Medea, the demon goddess.[96] The Corinthians equated this proto–Medea figure with her counterpart in the Jason legend—who must in those days have still been identified with the earth goddess of the original story—as part of the great Archaic trend of connecting cities to the great epics like the *Argonautica*.[97] Perhaps the wrath of the child killer seemed similar to the jealous rage of the Innana or Inara figure of the Jason story. It is unknown, however, whether the Aean or Corinthian goddess was the original bearer of the name Medea, but if Hesiod knew her by name, it would seem logical to assume her name belonged first to Aea and the Corinthian goddess possessed a different name. By this process, the Corinthians brought the Argonautic adventure to Corinth and created the lengthy sequel involving Jason, Medea, and the murdered children out of the rites of symbolic child sacrifice practiced there to ensure the safety of the city's youths. One other connection is worth noting. Medea in later tradition is closely associated with the goddess of black magic, Hecate. This goddess was not always infernal in association, and in Hesiod she begins as an honored "nurse of the young."[98] There is therefore a very close parallel between the child protecting goddess of Corinth and Hecate in both their original function and their later devolution into goddesses of terror and fear, a change in function associated with a souring of Greek attitudes toward the use of magic and therefore of magic's patrons (see chapter 8).

The upshot was that an alternate Medea entered the Jason cycle, and the subsequent adventures of this Corinthian Medea became a mythic cycle of their own. In creating this connection between Medea and Corinth, Corinth received Jason for a mythic king, and an epic voyager to serve as a powerful hero for Corinth's lucrative trade ventures overseas.

Stesichorus, Simonides and Ibycus

Stesichorus (c. 640–555 BCE) wrote a poem on the funeral games for Pelias, of which only fragments survive. These fragments discuss a chariot race, leaping, boxing, and a javelin event, with the participation of Meleager and Castor and Pollux.[99]

Ibycus, a lyric poet of the sixth century BCE, was considered a canonical poet in Hellenistic Alexandria, but little of his work survives. He must have written lyric poetry about episodes from the Argonauts' voyage. In the scholia to Apollonius' *Argonautica*, we learn that Ibycus was the first to write that Hera promised Thetis that Achilles would marry Medea when both had passed into the Underworld after their deaths.[100] He also recorded an otherwise unseen sister for Jason, Hippolyta, who seems to have been removed from the later poetic tradition to make Jason's situation that much more heroic as an only child.[101]

Simonides of Ceos (c. 556–468 BCE) composed poetry in Athens and was credited as the inventor of the Memory Palace, a system for remembering complex information by assigning it to "rooms" in an imagined building for later retrieval. He composed at least one, but possibly several, lyric poems on Argonaut themes, especially dealing with Medea. What is known of Simonides' Argonaut writings comes from the scholia to Apollonius, for whom he was a source, as well as the scholia to Euripides' *Medea*. In the latter work, the scholiast records that Simonides, "in his hymn to Poseidon, says [the Fleece] was dyed with purple from the sea,"[102] a departure from the tradition of a Golden Fleece, but in keeping with Simonides' love of dramatic color imagery.[103] Simonides also discussed such episodes of the Argonauts' voyage as the Clashing Rocks. He is the earliest to have recorded the Argonauts' competition on the island of Lemnos to win a cloak, and he also may have been the first to link the Argonauts to a battle against the bronze giant Talos, whom he described, according to the Plato scholia, as burning to death anyone who approached Crete.[104] Talos, as we shall see in Part Three, was originally conceived as a bull representing the Cretan sun god, who was also a form of the earth god. Whether Simonides mentioned him in an Argonautic context is, however, uncertain. Simonides, as we have seen, also asserts that Medea rejuvenated Jason by dismembering and boiling him.

Simonides repeats the story of Ibycus that Hera told Thetis that Achilles was fated to wed Medea, which Simonides apparently used as a tragic juxtaposition for the love of Jason and Medea at Colchis, which he told in apparently sensual and erotic detail.[105] He then follows the now-standard Corinthian conclusion to the Jason story.

Between Homer and the sixth century poets, we have witnessed a florescence of the Jason myth, growing from a relatively simple story to a complex epic of many episodes and adventures and an expanding roster of characters. The expansions and accretions are inconsistent, contradictory, and sometimes redundant. They bear the traces of many hands working toward many purposes. We have seen Jason's voyage move from the mythical land of Aea to a newly explored land on the coast of the Black Sea. We have seen the divine figure of Jason's helping goddess melt into a (mostly) human sorceress, and then a murderess. We have seen Jason's quest accrue a sequel in Corinth, and we have seen the early legend of the hero who sought to win the hand of the goddess acquire a new objective, the Golden Fleece. In short, by the end of the sixth century BCE, we have seen the ancient tale transformed, in its essentials, into the story as it would be known for the next two and half millennia.

But something is still missing. For all that we know of the plot of the story, the characters are still something of a mystery. Who was Jason? Who was Medea? Why did they do what they did? These are the questions taken up in our next chapter, as we explore the full flowering of the myth in the Classical, Hellenistic, and Roman eras.

5

The Man

From Hero to Human

With the major events of the Argonauts' voyage rather well-established by the start of the fifth century, the evolution of the Jason tale turned toward the characterization of the hero and his retinue. What kind of man was Jason to be? Would he be a hero like Achilles, confident and proud? Would he be more like Odysseus, wise and wily? Or like Heracles, prone to fits of rage? The Jason of oral tradition is unknown; we can deduce his deeds, but of his character there is little to say. He did not become a well-defined figure like Homer's heroes, and over time several interpretations of Jason would compete to define that man at the center of the myth. Similarly, the character of Medea was open to interpretation. Was she a dewy-eyed ingénue or a wily temptress? Was Medea a bystander to Jason's heroics, someone who aided the hero, or the prime mover in the adventure at Colchis? There were as many Medeas as there were Jasons.

This chapter will survey the most important works in the evolution of the Argonauts' adventure, those written during the period between 500 BCE and 90 CE. If the first five hundred years of Jason described the transformation of a god into a demigod, and the second five hundred years the transformation of a demigod into a hero, these five hundred (or so) years chronicled a hero's transformation into a man. This may be contrasted with the evolution of Heracles, who shared with Jason shamanic traits, an influx of Near East imagery, and a penchant for acquiring mythological adventures, but who followed the opposite trajectory, rising from an originally human figure to a hero eventually worshipped as a god.[1] And like Jason, no epic poet sang of a complete Heracles cycle until quite late in his evolution, when around 600 BCE an epic fixed his cycle in twelve canonical labors. Heracles, who was once human, and in the *Iliad* still mortal, eventually rose to the heights of Olympus, and his cult spread from one end of the Mediterranean to the other (except, oddly, for Crete). He was even identified with the Phoenician god Melqart.[2]

For Jason, the opposite occurred. A character who may have originated in the divine consort to the earth goddess lost his divinity and became a hero, performing great deeds with preternatural power and skill. Over the course of the period under discussion, this hero inexorably became a man, one who was all-too-human and subject to the failures and foibles inherent in the human condition. What he lost in superhuman powers from the Age of Heroes he gained in becoming a human who could do the work of the gods. If Heracles was a man made a god, Jason was a god made into a man.

Perhaps it was fated that the two heroes should cross paths. As Jason and Heracles competed to acquire new adventures to their myths, Heracles came aboard the *Argo*, and in time, some would even begin to say that he, not Jason, was the true leader of the Argonauts.

Jason in Prose

The Greek historian and philosopher Pherecydes (c. 600–550 BCE), however, was adamant that Heracles was *not* among Jason's Argonauts, despite the apparently popular tradition by the end of the sixth century that had begun to connect the two heroes. The *Argo*, Pherecydes said, could not support his weight, and he must have remained in Thessaly, at Aphetae. We have on occasion made reference to this scholar, who sometime in the sixth century wrote a prose version of Jason's voyage as part of his ten-volume *Theologia*,[3] which provided the genealogies and adventures of the gods and heroes, much as Hesiod had done. This work is known primarily in fragments preserved in the writings and scholia of others. We have already discussed his allusions to the story of the Harpies and Phineus and his claim that Medea dismembered and boiled Jason into renewed life. Pherecydes also preserved the tradition that Jason had a deep love of agriculture, possible a memory of his origins as a god of vegetation.

Pherecydes said the *Argo* was named for Phrixus' son Argus. He described the Golden Fleece as hanging on an island, Aeaea, in the middle of the river Phasis, and in the fifth book of the *Theologia*, he describes how Ares and Athena split the teeth of the dragon Cadmus killed between that hero and the Aean king, Aeëtes. In the sixth book, he tells how Aeëtes was master of the brazen-hoofed, fire-breathing bulls, which he used to plow fifty acres. Pelias, he said, asked the newly-arrived, one-sandaled Jason how he would respond to an oracle prophesying his death at the hands of a citizen. "Jason responded that he would send him to Aea to retrieve the Golden Fleece from Aeëtes. Hera suggested the idea to him so that Medea might come as an evil for Pelias." A fragment from the seventh book tells that "Jason killed the dragon," and later the scholar introduces the killing of Medea's brother. In his version, Medea, on Jason's word, seizes Apsyrtus, who in this telling is an infant. She takes him to Jason, and when Aeëtes gives the Argonauts chase, she kills and dismembers the baby, throwing the remains into the Phasis. Pherecydes then relates Medea's dismemberment and rejuvenation of Jason, and concludes by telling how Jason and the Argonaut Peleus conquered Iolcus together after the death of Pelias and the ascension of Pelias' son Acastus.[4] As Braswell notes, taken together, this collection of fragments indicates that in Pherecydes' day the three challenges Jason faces in Aea were all assembled: the yoking of the bulls, the battle with the Spartoi, and the slaying of the dragon.[5]

At the end of the fifth century, the mythographer Herodorus (not to be confused with Herodotus), wrote a treatise on Heracles and another on the Argonauts. He agreed with Pherecydes that Heracles was too heavy for the *Argo*. According to Plutarch, Herodorus also denied that Theseus was an Argonaut,[6] which implies that in at least some traditions the Athenian hero was already aboard Jason's ship. Herodorus' purpose was not to record the myth as it was then told but instead to explore his ideas about science and philosophy, and he purposely altered the content of the myths he recorded—including Jason's—to glorify his hometown of Heraclea, a Greek city on the south coast of the Black Sea.[7] Local tradition had made the city into the site of the deaths of Jason's companions, the seer Idmon and the steersman Tiphys, and Herodorus "confirmed" the story in his telling. The city fathers claimed the site for Heraclea was chosen specifically to mark Idmon's grave, which was said to rest in the center of the town's agora. In Herodorus' Argonautic account, rationalism predominated, and the mythic and magical elements of the story were given speculative and sometimes specious "explanations," most of which are now lost, but would have paralleled his other rationalizations. For instance, he explained Prometheus bound to a rock in the Caucasus Mountains while an eagle ate his liver as "really" the story of an Asian king who was imprisoned by his countrymen when the river "Eagle" flooded, a sign of divine disfavor.[8] As we have seen, he also insisted that the *Argo* followed the same path to and from Colchis, logical of course, but also all the more glorious for Heraclea, which would have received *two* visits from the illustrious crew. Herodorus reworked the Argonaut story to make both Idmon and Tiphys die at the future site of Heraclea on the Argonauts' *second* docking at the site, on their way home.

Herodorus' surviving fragments make no mention of Medea's magic, and she may not have helped Jason in any significant way—reflecting perhaps the older tradition of Jason descending alone into the dragon's belly rather than the newer story of him working with Medea to charm him. He does, however, preserve a possibly older legend which claimed that Aeëtes had received a prophesy of his own death at a descendant's hand, inspiring the trial of the yoking of the bulls to spot any wayward family who might show up, since the sun's own bloodline alone could control the solar bulls. It is perhaps noteworthy that Aeëtes is here acting again in parallel to Pelias, with both issuing challenges in response to similar prophesies.

Hellanicus of Lesbos (fifth century BCE) followed Herodorus in creating a genealogy and history of the heroes, and he wrote that the Medes of northwestern Iran derived their name from Jason's wife Medea, who fled there after her adventures in Corinth and Athens. This same story appears in Herodotus' *Histories*,[9] which volume begins by relating that the Greeks refused Aeëtes' demand for compensation for Medea's abduction.[10] Herodotus also included an explanation for the Greek settlement of Libya (North Africa) in the history of the Argonauts. According to Herodotus, after the completion of the *Argo*, Jason sailed to Delphi with one hundred cattle and a bronze tripod to make a sacrifice, but a wind blew the Argonauts off course, landing them at Lake Tritonis, a body of water the Greeks believed to have existed in southern Tunisia, and one associated with Poseidon's son Triton. There, Triton agreed to show the Argonauts the way to navigate the lake's marshes to return to the Mediterranean in exchange for the tripod. Triton then prophesied that a descendent of the Argonauts would carry off the tripod someday, and a hundred Greek cities would bloom on Lake Triton.[11] Herodotus agreed with the other prose writers that Heracles did not complete the Argonauts' voyage, but he reported that Heracles was abandoned in Magnesia, a part of Thessaly, when looking for water.[12]

Overall, the impression the prose writers leave is that they are attempting to rein in a narrative tradition that had grown wild with agglomerations and additions, and to which all the heroes of Greece had been drafted for service. While these writers are unable to completely eliminate the fantastic "improvements" the oral epics had devised, or all the extraneous heroes sailing aboard the *Argo*, their efforts to rationalize Jason's adventures, deny or minimize the presence of certain heroes, and historicize the legend into a plausible (for their era) narrative speak to a story that had acquired great currency, great power, and a bewildering variety of permutations, many of which were contradictory in their elements. Did Jason descend into the dragon, or charm him? Was Medea a prize to be won, or an essential helpmeet? Did the Argonauts sail out to Aea on the Ocean or Colchis on the Black Sea? Which among Greece's legendary heroes accompanied him? With no fixed form to follow, the germ of the Jason story had blossomed into a thousand forms.

The Fourth Pythian Ode of Pindar

Given the multiplicity of Jason stories, eventually some traditions gained greater weight and respectability through inclusion in the works of the great poets. As one of the nine canonical poets of the Greek world, Pindar (522 or 518–443 BCE) gave grandeur and heft to the Jason story when he cast it into the form of a victory ode, known as the Fourth Pythian Ode after the traditional numbering of the poems written to commemorate the victors of the quadrennial Pythian Games at Delphi. Pindar's life is known only in outlines; the oldest extant biographies of the poet are medieval in date and somewhat suspect for their far remove from events. Scholars instead have constructed their view of Pindar's life from clues left in his body of poetry. Born in the years when Persia invaded Greece, Pindar would grow into young manhood in Thessaly in a Greek world menaced from many sides, from Persians in the east, but also from Carthaginians in the west. He trained in Athens and called Thebes home, though Thebes would fine Pindar for praising Athens in his poetry. The two cities were enemies, and Pindar stood between them. Thebes accused Athens of creating an empire (she was), and Athens claimed to be guarding Greece against the Persian menace (she was). When Pindar wrote his poems, he did so to place the dramatic events of his century in a mythological context.[13] For him myth and history were inseparable, but myth needed to serve as precedent for modern events.

In 498 BCE Thorax of Larissa in Thessaly commissioned the young Pindar to compose the first of his victory odes to survive, *Pythian 10*, to celebrate the victory of Hippokleas of Pelinna in a double race for boys. He would compose poetry for more than fifty years, and the last poem scholars can date, *Pythian 8*, was written when the poet was about seventy-two years old, in 446 BCE. Throughout his life, he received the patronage of powerful men, including the tyrants Hieron and Theron of Syracuse, and in his odes Pindar expresses confidence in the immortality of his own words. His surviving poems sing the praises of the victors of the games which drew athletes from across the Greek world to compete in athletic and literary challenges, the forerunner of the modern Olympic Games. The games were held on staggered schedule: quadrennial Olympic and Pythian Games and biennial Nemean and Isthmian Games at their host cities across Greece. During the three months of each set of games, war was forbidden and competitors were guaranteed safe passage across Greece. Jason and the Argonauts were credited in one epigram with competing in and winning the first Isthmian Games.[14]

It is important to understand that the odes Pindar composed to memorialize the victors of these games existed in a specific context. These odes were written to be performed. In the Archaic Period, it was considered unseemly to directly praise a human being, an affront to the gods. Therefore, the achievements of a man were related to the mythological accomplishments of a hero or a god, usually one considered an ancestor of his family. Similarly, contemporary events were reflected and refracted through the lens of long ago actions of heroes and gods. Thus, when Pindar composed his Fourth Pythian Ode, he did not set out to tell the story of Jason and the Argonauts from start to finish as an attempt to preserve and propagate a myth; instead, Jason's story was used for Pindar's own purposes, and in so doing, adaptations occurred.

Pindar's Fourth Pythian Ode is his longest extant poem, more than twice the length of any other, and the longest surviving piece of poetry between the Homeric age and the dramas of Aeschylus.[15] It is the oldest telling of Jason's story to survive in full. Pindar composed the poem in 462 BCE to honor Arkesilas IV, King of Cyrene (in North Africa) upon the occasion of his victory in the chariot race at the Pythian Games at Delphi. However, it is Pindar's Fifth Pythian Ode that contains the actual celebration of Arkesilas' victory. Instead, the Fourth had a different purpose. Pindar intended his poem as a plea to Arkesilas to return a man of his acquaintance named Damophilos from exile in Thebes, and to that end, the myth of Jason was consciously adapted. It is unknown whether Damophilos paid for the poetic plea, or whether Pindar added it to a poem the Cyrene royal house paid for on his own initiative.[16] Arkesilas claimed descent from Battos I of Thera, founder of Cyrene, and through him to the otherwise unimportant Argonaut Euphamos, from whose loins came the Greeks of North Africa. On this basis, Pindar connected Arkesilas to the Jason myth, and constructed his story to present Arkesilas with two opposing paths: He could be a tyrant like Pelias, or he could be glorious like Jason and recall Damophilos to Cyrene. The city of Cyrene, famous for its doctors, had special resonance with Jason's name (= healer), and Pindar appears to have purposefully used this symbolism to urge Arkesilas to heal the rift with Damophilus.[17] No record of the king's reaction survives.

JASON IN THE ODE

The Ode opens with the Argonauts returning from Colchis with Medea. She hails the mighty seamen and issues a prophecy that one of them, Euphamos, shall eventually found a race that will come to colonize Libya (and thus found Cyrene). Pindar then relates this prophecy to another, one the Delphic Oracle gave to Battos urging him to found Cyrene. The poem then shifts quickly to telling the story of Jason's voyage, thematically linking it through another prophecy, one delivered to Pelias, warning him of the danger of a man who would come to him from the mountains with a single sandal. He came, and Pindar provides the first and most impressive description of Jason in literature:

> So in the fulness of time he came, wielding two spears, a wondrous man; and the vesture that was upon him was twofold, the garb of the Magnetes' [= Magnesian] country close fitting to his splendid limbs, but above he wore a leopard-skin to turn the hissing showers; nor were the bright locks of his hair shorn from him but over all his back ran rippling down. Swiftly he went straight on, and took his stand, making trial of his dauntless soul, in the marketplace when the multitude was full.
>
> Him they knew not; howbeit some one looking reverently on him would speak on this wise: "Not Apollo surely is this, nor yet Aphrodite's lord [Ares] of the brazen car; yea and in glistening Naxos died ere now, they say, the children of Iphimedeia, Otos and thou, bold king Ephialtes: moreover Tityos was the quarry of Artemis' swift arrow sped from her invincible quiver, warning men to touch only the loves within their power."[18]

In Pindar's description, Jason was a man in full, glorious enough to be mistaken for a god as beautiful as Apollo or as puissant as Ares. He wears the hunting costume of Magnesia, the region surrounding Iolcus, whose traditional garb included a single sandal so that one would have a free foot to better grab slippery terrain.[19] Like Heracles and his lion skin, Jason comes wrapped in leopard skin, his long hair indicative of an adolescent on the verge of manhood, aged twenty years. Clearly, Jason is intended to be every bit the hero.

THE ARGONAUTS' ADVENTURE

Pelias arrives, and he demands the stranger explain himself, which Jason does in gentle words, relating first the circumstances of his long ago escape from Pelias, which builds to a dramatic statement of identity: "it shall hardly be said that a son of Aison, born in the land, is come hither to a strange and alien soil. And Jason was the name whereby the divine Beast [Chiron] spake to me."[20] Jason, maintaining the most civilized of dialogues, argues that by divine right the throne does not belong to Pelias, but that he might keep all the lands and wealth he usurped so long as justice is done and the scepter returns to its rightful king, Jason.

Pelias, who is here claimed to be a second cousin of Jason rather than his uncle, then challenges Jason to retrieve the soul or spirit of Phrixus in the form of the Golden Fleece, a task the Oracle at Delphi apparently commanded. Successful completion, Pelias says, will earn Jason the throne. From this point, Pindar's narrative follows the familiar outlines of the story. Jason assembles the Argonauts, and Pindar lists some (but not all) of them: three sons of Zeus (including Heracles), two sons of Poseidon (including Euphamos), Orpheus, two sons of Hermes, the Boreas twins, and Mopsus (not Idmon) the seer, who cast auguries at the launch of the *Argo*. Hera makes her appearance to fill the heroes with courage, and they sail for Colchis under good omens sent from Zeus. Pindar records no incidents along their outward voyage except a sacrifice to Poseidon performed at the Bosporus and an allusion to the passage through the Clashing Rocks (here relocated to the start of the journey), and he skips instead to the story's climax at Colchis, where Aphrodite uses a woodpecker (the wry-neck) as a love charm so Jason might detach Medea from her parents and fill her with love for him. Medea then anoints Jason with an olive oil solution to protect him from his upcoming ordeal.

Aeëtes challenges Jason to yoke the fire-breathing, brazen-hoofed bulls, and he demonstrates his mastery of them by performing the task first himself. Protected by Medea's oil, Jason does not hesitate, and manfully plows a field with the flaming bulls. "And a cry without speech came from Aietes in his agony, at the marvel of the power he beheld."[21] The Argonauts cheer on their hero, and Aeëtes grimly reveals the Golden Fleece's resting place, protected by a dragon larger than the fifty-oared *Argo*. Unfortunately, this most dramatic of encounters Pindar chooses not to relate, saying only that his ode is running long and he knows a "shortcut" to the end of the story. He briefly indicates that Medea's "wiles" helped Jason defeat the dragon, and that she helped the hero carry her off from Colchis.

Pindar says the Argonauts sailed Ocean to the Red Sea and then north (over land through Libya) to the Aegean where they reached Lemnos and fathered the Lemnian women's children. Apparently Jason must be extremely charming to seduce Hypsipyle while engaged to Medea and not earn the sorceress's immediate wrath. The Lemnian episode, traditionally placed at the start of the journey, is here moved to the end to provide Euphamos with the

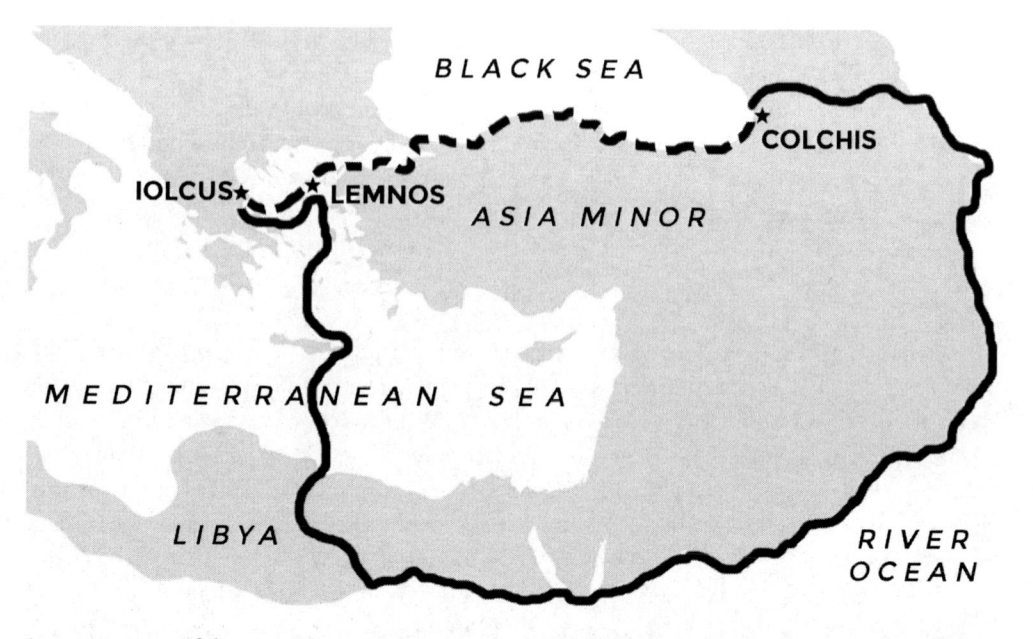

In every version of the story, the Argonauts travel out along a similar route (broken line). In the Fourth Pythian Ode, Pindar has the Argonauts return (solid line) from Colchis by sailing along the Ocean to the Red Sea, and then across Libya to the Aegean. In Pindar's time, the true extent of Arabia and Africa were unknown, with much of their area thought to be Ocean, and the Caspian Sea was thought to be an arm of the Ocean. This southerly route was also used by Hecataeus of Miletus, though with one difference. He made the Argonauts travel up the Nile instead of across Libya because he believed the Nile's source was the River Ocean (author's drawing).

opportunity to father the race that would include Arkesilas chronologically close to the Argonauts' stop on Thera from the opening of the ode, when Medea can prophesy the glorious future of his progeny. Thus, the ode returns to its opening and closes the circle. The poem then concludes by telling Arkesilas that he, like Jason, is a healer and should consider healing the rift in Cyrene by recalling Damophilos, whose praises Pindar sings at great length.

PINDAR'S ADAPTATION OF MYTH

As has been noted by many scholars, Pindar did not intend to tell a complete version of the Argonauts' adventures. Only a few of their many episodes appear in the Ode, and these are condensed or merely alluded to, like the Clashing Rocks. They are also arranged for Pindar's purposes, such as his relocation of the stop at Lemnos. The poem is impressionistic, emphasizing above all else the diplomatic but dramatic confrontation between Jason and Pelias, the key moment in the myth for the audience Pindar wished to reach: Arkesilas. The Ode recalls the great Homeric epics but is compressed into but three hundred lines. As Bruce Karl Braswell put it, "In short, while Pindar is indeed concerned to produce the effect of heroic narrative, he has written not a real epic but a grand choral lyric on an epic scale."[22] It is, quite possibly, the best of the ancient Jason stories.

Pindar's Jason is not merely noble, but the very embodiment of the virtues of the legitimate king, the same virtues Hesiod outlined in the *Theogony* centuries earlier: mastery of oratory, judiciousness, and a godlike presence.[23] Indeed, in his combination of aristocratic heroism, romance, and virtue, "for the first and last time in classical literature, there appears in full expression the idea of Chivalry."[24] Based on this image, medieval writers would come to see in Jason an important forerunner of the ideal Christian knight (see Part Four). These virtues are further magnified by Pindar's artistic choice to minimize the role of the other Argonauts, including Heracles, and also to minimize the role of Medea. This heroic Jason, however, cannot be entirely the work of Pindar; tradition must have afforded Jason a similar heroic stature, or else the poem would not be as effective, depending as it does on familiarity with the motifs of the myth to achieve its effects.

This would be the high point for Jason as glorious hero.

Jason in Images

Around the same time Pindar was composing his Fourth Pythian Ode for a North African king, Jason's image and story began showing up in the art of the Etruscans, the native inhabitants of northern and central Italy. The Greeks colonized Sicily and southern Italy in the eighth century BCE, and they came into contact with the Etruscans, to whom Greek stories and the Greek alphabet soon spread. These stories were adopted and adapted into the Etruscans' own rich preexisting mythology, and Greek heroes became favorites of the Etruscans. In Etruscan art, Jason was a Pindaric hero of full stature, but back in Greece he would be less fortunate.

JASON IN ETRURIA

The Etruscans did not depict Jason frequently in their art, but when they did, they tended to depict scenes that do not survive in the versions of Pindar or Apollonius. Beginning in the fifth century BCE and continuing into the fourth, the Etruscans created images of Jason emerging from the dragon's jaws, usually with a sword, sometimes clutching the Golden Fleece. These appeared on mirrors as well as on carved gemstones in the shape of Egyptian scarabs, such as the one held in Boston's Museum of Fine Arts. The inscribed reverse of a bronze mirror in the Villa Giulia depicts the confrontation between Jason and the dragon, and a mirror in Tübingen depicts Athena and Artemis looking at the dragon, which has been interpreted as showing the time in which Jason is inside the dragon. According to Jennifer Neils, the Etruscans viewed Jason's battle with the dragon as a death and resurrection,[25] a subject of fascination for a people who believed in life after death and that the souls of the dead could, in some cases, become gods—and who also believed golden sheep were a sign of coming prosperity.[26] We know this version of the story was not an Etruscan invention because these motifs appear on Greek vases dating back to the late seventh century BCE, two centuries before the first Etruscan examples.[27] This Jason is puissant, heroic, and dynamic.

An Etruscan bronze mirror of the third century BCE shows "HEASUN" (Jason) on a stool, taking a potion from a woman labeled "METVIA" (Medea) in the presence of "MENRVA" (Athena/Minerva), traditionally interpreted as representing the "rejuvenation" of Jason, but more likely representing his restoration after his death and resurrection within the dragon.[28] Another shows Jason (or possibly Aeson) emerging from a cauldron while an old man, possibly Pelias, looks on. A similar Greek vase found in Etruria depicts Jason standing beside a cauldron in which Medea has rejuvenated a ram. The constant presence of Athena is especially interesting, reflecting as it does the Douris cup, but wholly separate from the literary tradition, which gives Athena a role in building the *Argo* but not at Colchis. Neils argued that Athena is present because she is the goddess of warriors and would be expected to be present in such situations.[29] Is this simply because she is the goddess of heroes, or is it because aspects of Near Eastern goddesses such as Inanna or Inara who first held this position in the myths that preceded Jason could be and sometimes were equated with Hera, Aphrodite, or Athena? However, it is not unprecedented to show Athena beside a warrior where she is not present in the literary myth. A kylix by the Athenian painter Aison from the late fifth century BCE depicts Theseus and the Minotaur with Athena rather than Ariadne standing beside him.

A final mirror, from Bolsena in Italy, shows a scene depicting Eiasun (apparently Jason) groveling and beseeching Fufluns (often identified with Dionysus), who stands with Areatha (Ariadne) while the Argonaut Castor looks on. No parallel is known in Greek or Roman myth, though it was suggested in the Victorian era that the Etruscan artist conflated elements of the Theseus story with that of Jason on account of Ariadne's presence[30]; however, Ariadne was the mythological bride of Dionysus so this is not likely. It is possible that the image depicts an unrecorded story from the Argonaut cycle,[31] or an Etruscan adaptation perhaps reflecting Orphic traditions (see below), with Jason, in his role as healer, asking for Fulfuns' assistance in obtaining or using a magical plant, since Fulfuns was, besides a patron of gaiety and happiness, a god of vegetation and healing, a role with which Jason had been associated in the ancient oral traditions. It is also possible that the vase represents an Etruscan version (taken literally or otherwise) of a satire of the Jason story featuring Dionysus (see below). However, the Greeks of southern Italy identified Dionysus with death and the underworld (and sometimes with Hades himself) since the god had been dismembered and resurrected (like Jason in Medea's cauldron or in the dragon), implying that this scene may also represent an unrecorded version of Jason in the deepest Underworld.[32]

Besides Jason, the Etruscans made a number of mirrors depicting Castor and Pollux battling Talos, the bronze giant. Some of these mirrors from the fifth century BCE seem to show Talos defeating his adversaries, an apparently purposeful reinterpretation of the Greek myth, perhaps related to the Etruscans' desire to identify with a powerful figure who protected his homeland just as the Etruscans stood ready to protect Etruria from the rising Roman Republic.[33]

JASON IN GREEK ART

The first images of Jason in Greece date back to the seventh century BCE, in Corinth, where vase fragments show a man emerging from a dragon's mouth. Though Jason is not named, the scenes are quite similar to the famous Douris drinking cup (kylix) depicting Jason emerging from the dragon's mouth in the presence of Athena, which was discussed in chapter 3. These are among the earliest images of Jason to survive, and they depict him performing heroic actions, if not always, as in the case of the Douris kylix, in the most heroic of poses. There is a clear contrast between the limp, exhausted Jason of Douris and the glorious, invincible Jason of the near-contemporary Pindar. Jason also appeared on the fabulous Chest of Cypselus—Cypselus was the seventh century BCE tyrant of Corinth—an apparently magnificent work that Pausanias described at length in the second century CE.[34] Jason and Aphrodite flank Medea in his wedding scene.

Medea is rarely depicted before the fourth century BCE, and then typically as a sorceress. For example, the fifth century "Talos Painter" showed Medea preparing to slay Talos while Castor and Pollux hold him fast. Medea holds a basket of herbs signifying her magical powers. After this century, Medea is seen much more frequently and in many new actions, primarily those from the incidents at Corinth rather than the adventures in Colchis. However, a late fourth century BCE red figure vase now in Naples shows Jason removing the Fleece while Medea feeds a sleeping potion to a large snake wrapped around a tree, ratifying Medea's increasingly prominent role at the center of the Argonaut myth.

Jason himself does not fare so well. After Douris, his image becomes less heroic, overshadowed by those around him. On an Athenian column krater of 470–460 BCE exactly contemporary with Pindar, the Orchard Painter depicts a crouching Jason about to snatch the Golden Fleece while Athena and an unidentified man with his hand on the *Argo* stand by. The unidentified man has been suggested to be Zeus,[35] but this is uncertain. In the words of Gisela M. A. Richter, "The rather emaciated, bearded, and hairy Jason does not exactly tally with Pindar's description of young

Although Jason is not named in this image from a seventh-century BCE Corinthian vase, the similarity to the Douris cup and Etruscan images in which Jason is named make it virtually certain that this is the oldest surviving image of Jason. The original is very badly preserved, with the greatest damage to the head of the serpent and to Jason; therefore, the jaw line seen in this drawing is the author's own hypothetical reconstruction (author's drawing).

Jason. Instead he is that rather rare product in Greek art—an individualized human being."[36] It is true that to modern eyes the crouching Jason looks puny in comparison with the glorious goddess standing at full height beside him. However, using a high quality reproduction of the vase image, measuring the bent Jason's body from ankle to knee, knee to hip, torso, and head, and adding these measurements reveals that were he to stand at his full height Jason's size would be identical to Athena's height from heel to helmet. Further, the width of his arms almost exactly matches that of Athena's, implying he is not noticeably slimmer. He is shown in profile, making his lithe and muscled body appear thinner than the goddess, who is seen straight on. The arrangement of elements is unfortunate to modern eyes accustomed to attempts to render objects in three-dimensional perspective, something that did not exist until the Renaissance. In terms of ancient art, in which characters are flat and occupy a single two-dimensional plane, Jason and Athena are the same size, and would have appeared that way to Greek eyes. A parody version of this same scene also exists, on a matching column

This krater from c. 470–460 BCE attributed to the Orchard Painter, gave rise to the modern claim that the ancients had a tradition of a "puny" Jason. Here, Jason (left) seizes the Golden Fleece from the snake, while Athena presides and a man variously identified as Aeëtes, Zeus, or an Argonaut stands beside the oracular plank of the *Argo*, symbolized by a talking head. Jason's crouched posture led many modern scholars to claim Jason is "puny" compared to Athena, but were he standing at his full height, he would be the same size as the goddess (author's drawing).

krater by the Orchard Painter now in Bologna, with a satyr performing Jason's role and Dionysus standing in for Athena. On the Jason krater the front of the Fleece is seen; on the satyr krater the rear.

As a result of his interpretation of the Jason krater and the later literary depictions of Jason as something less than a demigod, Moses Hadas concluded in 1936 that there must have been a tradition of a "feeble Jason," if only in Greek comedy, a man helpless, overshadowed, and dominated by the women around him—the ultimate sin in the Greek idea of manhood. Hadas wondered whether Pindar's Jason was "an orthodox poet's resentment of such a tradition" and an attempt to counter it,[37] but this could not be the case since it would have been highly inappropriate to compare a reigning king (Arkesilas) to a character deemed to be effeminate if this were the dominant view of Jason in the fifth century. Obviously, the Argonaut legend would not have persisted if this were the original Jason; however, as Medea grew in stature and importance in the telling of the Argonaut myth, Jason suffered a concurrent loss of stature.

If there were a tradition of a "feeble Jason" (most likely in comedy) it would seem to be a reflection of the changes in his story as the epilogue at Corinth came to overshadow and reconfigure the adventures that came before. During this period, in the fifth century, the rivalry between Athens and Corinth grew heated, both in the realm of trade and in politics, especially over the colony of Corcyra—the same city where the Corinthians claimed Jason made his home. This led in part to the outbreak of the Peloponnesian War between Athens and the Peloponnesian League, led by Corinth's ally Sparta, in 431 BCE. It was, therefore, no surprise that the Athenians frequently depicted their rival's adopted hero, Jason, as effeminate or weak, and their goddess-heroine Medea as psychotic and a witch. And because it is the Athenian versions that survive, this is how the story was remembered in later centuries.

Nowhere was this clearer than on the Greek stage.

Jason on the Stage

Aristotle wrote that the Greek stage featured tragedies and comedies because those forms of art descended from choral hymns sung to Dionysus during the festival of the Dionysia performed in Athens each year. These expanded into full-length plays performed from the mid-sixth century BCE down to about 220 BCE. Originally, only tragedies were produced, but after 486 BCE comedies were added, along with short satyr plays, which were burlesques of Greek myths, often with graphic sexual content. One of these burlesques is perhaps depicted on the Bologna krater's image of a satyr and Dionysus reenacting the seizing of the Fleece.

The earliest Athenian playwright, Aeschylus (c. 525/4-c. 456/5 BCE), composed around ninety plays, of which only seven survive intact. None of the extant plays deal with the Argonauts; however, Aeschylus appears to have written a series of tragedies based on Jason with the titles *Argo (The Rowers)*, *Lemnioi*, *Hypsipyle*, and *Kabeiroi*. These plays were likely unrelated. In *Argo*, the ship's prophetic beam speaks and refuses to allow slaves to row the ship. Nothing is known of the *Lemnioi*, which might have dealt with a different episode at Troy rather than the Argonautic cycle. *Hypsipyle* focused on the women's refusal to let the Argonauts disembark until they agreed to couple with the women. Finally, *Kabeiroi* depicts Jason and the Argonauts as drunken louts interacting with the Cabeiri on Lemnos.[38] It is not known which (if any) of these may have been intended as a satyr play or whether all were tragedies, though it is usually thought that the *Kabeiroi* was meant as a satyr play from the comedic implications of the surviving fragments, with the Cabeiri of the chorus taking the role of satyrs while the Argonauts roll about drunkenly on stage.

Sophocles (c. 497/6 BCE-c. 407/6 BCE) also composed a series of plays related to the Argonauts' story. He wrote two plays about Athamas, the father of Phrixus, of which only one survives, as well as tragedies with the titles *Phrixus* and *Ino* which treated the events of Ino's attempt to have Phrixus sacrificed and the events after Phrixus arrived in Colchis. Only two lines of *Phrixus* survive: "Hound-like they howled, as it were whimpering..." and "Goal of our journey, precincts of this land," presumably Colchis.[39] Another series of plays, of which only a few fragments remain, covered episodes from the Argonauts' voyages. *The Lemnian Women* described the Argonauts' meeting with the women of Lemnos. Two plays about Phineus, *Phineus* and (possibly) *Tympanistae* dealt with the seer's deliverance from the Harpies and possibly the fates of his blinded children. The *Women of Colchis* related the love of Jason and Medea. A few surviving fragments give a flavor of the work. Medea asks Jason, "Do you promise with an oath to return the kindness?" This must come when Medea offers her help in exchange for marriage, right before the scene where the bulls appear and "with limbs of brass they breathe out from their lungs—and their nostrils blaze."[40] After the yoking of the bulls, Aeëtes describes the Spartoi:

> Did not the offspring of the earth forth-spring?
> Ay truly, bristling fierce, with a plumed crest,
> In arms of brass, forth from their mother's womb
> Dauntless they sprang![41]

Though Pindar had left the Spartoi out of his Pythian Ode, the near-contemporary work of Sophocles shows this was considered a standard part of the myth in the fifth century. A further play, *Scythians*, treated Medea's murder of Apsyrtus, and *The Root-Cutters* dealt apparently with Medea's aborted rejuvenation of the aged king Pelias. Fragments of this play depict Medea as a dark sorceress, consorting with serpents and Hecate, goddess of witches, collecting roots for her potions "that she reaped with bronze blades while naked, crying out, and shouting."[42] This depiction, which varies greatly from the goddess-like version of the Corinthian Medea, is in keeping with the attitudes at Athens in the run-up to the Peloponnesian War.

The story of Medea provided material for Euripides' (c. 485 or 480–406 BCE) greatest play, *Medea*, composed in 431 BCE—the year of the Peloponnesian War—and the winner of third prize in that year's Dionysia competition. Euripides had told some of Medea's story in the lost play *Aegus*, about an attack she made on Theseus, and in composing the *Medea* he may have drawn on a tragedy of the poet Neophron, whose *Medea* followed the same outline as his own, with a few minor differences. Neophron's play survives only in fragments, but these show that the poet had used Medea's emotional turmoil, a hallmark of Euripides' play, as an essential element of the tragedy. He differed from Euripides in making Medea prophesy that Jason would die by hanging himself rather than die beneath *Argo*. However, Neophron's chronology is disputed, and it is uncertain whether he or Euripides wrote his *Medea* first.[43]

Euripides' play begins with Medea's servant announcing her wish that Jason had never come to Colchis and bemoaning the loutish Argonaut's abandonment of his wife and children for the hand of the Corinthian king Creon's daughter, Glauce, and the royal power that would bring. Creon has decided to drive Medea and her sons from Corinth forever, and Medea becomes suicidal over Jason's betrayal, wishing for his utter destruction. When Jason comes to visit her on the eve of her exile Medea reminds Jason how much he owes to her:

> I will begin at the very beginning. I saved thy life, as every Hellene knows who sailed with thee aboard the good ship *Argo*, when thou wert sent to tame and yoke fire-breathing bulls, and to sow the deadly tilth. Yea, and I slew the dragon which guarded the golden fleece, keeping sleepless watch o'er it with many a wreathed coil, and I raised for thee a beacon of deliverance.[44]

Note that at this stage, Medea is no longer mere bystander or even helper, but now claims full credit for Jason's heroism, reinforcing the "unmanliness" of the "villain." Here Jason is in eclipse, Medea in command. Having abandoned Colchis for Jason, she cannot return to her father; having killed Pelias for Jason, she cannot return to Iolcus. Jason has left her no option but death. Jason retorts by "turn[ing] orator" (an echo of Pindar's depiction), arguing that Medea is exaggerating her claims and has no real cause for anger. Did she not benefit from living in glorious Greece rather than benighted Colchis? Did he not make her famous? He proposes to keep her and their sons in comfort and someday welcome her back into his new family, as his mistress. Enraged, Medea belittles Jason's "specious words" and the falseness of his oratory. Jason, she said, should have asked Medea's permission if marrying Glauce was such a good idea. They argue and part on bad terms.

Medea then secures protection from the King of Athens, to whom she will flee after conducting her revenge. To Glauce she sends a wedding gift, a golden robe and crown, poisoned. It will soon kill her and Creon, who touches the garments in an attempt to save her. Meanwhile, Medea calls for Jason to falsely apologize, and Jason, boorishly, accepts: "Lady, I praise this conduct, not that I blame what is past; for it is but natural to the female sex to vent their spleen against a husband when he trafficks in other marriages besides his own."[45]

Medea sends her children off to the palace with the poisoned gifts, and decides, despite her motherly instincts, that to ruin Jason the children too must be sent to their deaths. She is momentarily overcome with emotion:

> O my babes, my babes, let your mother kiss your hands. Ah! hands I love so well, O lips most dear to me! O noble form and features of my children, I wish ye joy, but in that other land, for here your father robs you of your home. O the sweet embrace, the soft young cheek, the fragrant breath! my children! Go, leave me; I cannot bear to longer look upon ye; my sorrow wins the day. At last I understand the awful deed I am to do; but passion, that cause of direst woes to mortal man, hath triumphed o'er my sober thoughts.[46]

But it is for naught. Her vengeance wins.

Jason arrives to forestall Medea's hand, but too late. The children are dead. Medea appears in a chariot drawn by dragons, sent by the Sun to rescue her and take her to Athens. Jason curses Medea, curses her barbarism and her un–Greekness, and her unbridled, hormonal passions that led her to marriage and to murder. Medea curses him back for his infidelity and betrayal and prophesies his death beneath *Argo*'s rotting hulk. They argue; Medea departs. Both are grieving. Jason is ruined. The play ends with the chorus solemnly claiming it was Zeus' will.

Critics have debated whether the play is proto-feminist or misogynistic, whether Medea is heroine or villain.[47] In truth she is both, and neither. Euripides apparently purposefully reinterpreted the deaths of Medea's children (or drew on a variant tradition), making them the object of Medea's rage when the traditional myth had them killed by the Corinthians themselves. She would forever after be a child murderer. Her actions, though formally a triumph and victory, elicit revulsion and horror. In the context of fifth century Athens, she is a foreigner and a barbarian, a woman ruled by passion and standing outside the rules of civilized society. Under Athenian law of Euripides' era, as a foreigner she is also illegitimately married, her children bastards. Jason is a civilized orator; in places Medea's emotions prevent her from completing sentences.

Jason in this play has been depicted as a callous egoist, boorish, and despicable. Though "a selfish ass" in modern eyes, Jason is a man that the men of fifth century Athens could understand. He is a failed hero, his glory behind him. His only chance at being remembered after his death is through his family, and for this he needs legitimate heirs, which his children with Medea cannot be under the law. This is why he wants a new marriage, and from this rational (though obviously insensitive) position, his actions and behavior become understandable. Medea's actions are therefore that much more dramatic: She kills not only Jason's family, but his only chance at remaining a part of the Greek community. Nor can he find yet another new bride, for Medea still lives, and would continue her vengeance. She has robbed him of his immortality.[48] But even in the most sympathetic of readings, Euripides' Jason is not the youthful hero of legend. He is no longer the man of destiny but instead one on whom destiny acts, passive recipient of fate's fickle fortunes, his grand quest now a curse, his life turned to dust. He is now just a man.

A further diminution occurred in other authors' later plays. A tragedy of the fourth century BCE by an unknown author, preserved only in an outline in the late Latin poet Dracontius (fifth century CE), depicts Medea as a performer of human sacrifices, a practice she surrenders only when Aphrodite appears to forestall her sacrifice of Jason.[49] Jason, so subsumed beneath Medea (the subject of Dracontius' story), owes not just his heroics but his very life to Medea, and nearly died at the hands of a foreigner and woman, humiliating for any ancient Greek man, and far from Pindar's glorious hero. The Jason story would also continue to figure in poetry. Antimachus of Colophon told of Jason's and Medea's doomed love around 400 BCE as part of his massive *Lyde*, a compilation of heroes' tragic loves, of which eighteen lines survive. He may have invented the tradition Apollonius would follow in which Medea charms the snake to sleep instead of having Jason kill it outright, and it is possible that his account included a more elaborate taking of the Fleece which involved several Argonauts and a battle with royal guards, similar to the account of Dionysus Schytobrachion (see below).[50]

Jason's fate on the Greek stage was not just his own. The Athenian Euripides himself gave a revisionist take on the god Apollo as immoral and a tyrant in *Electra* (420 BCE after the deity's oracle at Delphi sided with enemy Sparta in the Peloponnesian War. The hero Odysseus also fared poorly on stage, and writers like Sophocles increasingly depicted him as mendacious, deceitful, and wily instead of simply cunning. This was part of a widespread fifth century desire to rework Greek myths to expose new themes, comment on contemporary events, and to recreate heroes as more human figures, figures with the flaws and foibles of humans.[51] To an extent, part of the entertainment of a Greek drama was to see a "new" take on an old myth.

If the Jason of the stage was now a man, how would that man have handled the adventures the hero Jason once performed? There were two answers to that question. The first was to deny any hint of the divine, and the second was to re-imagine the epic in new, more modern terms. Both forms found their voice in Greece.

Denying Jason

In the first century BCE, the historian Diodorus Siculus included a rationalizing account of Jason in his *Library of History*,[52] one that drew on the work of Dionysus Schytobrachion (c. third century BCE), who created an *Argonautica* of six books, which is unfortunately lost. Dionysus attempted to reinterpret the story of Jason in terms of logic and reason, avoiding godly intervention and the supernatural, in keeping with his belief that the gods were ancient kings and generals who were later worshipped as divinities. In this he followed a trail blazed by Herodorus, and in both cases "rationalizing" was taken rather liberally and had only a superficial relationship to seeking out truth. Instead, Dionysus wanted to provide explanations, no matter how strained, that sought to remove the supernatural from myth. Diodorus summarized Dionysus' rationalist account, and he added variants he encountered in other versions of the myth. Dionysus apparently thought little of Jason and instead assigned Heracles primacy in the venture.

According to Dionysus, Jason was an arrogant and presumptuous youth who got it in his head to seek out the Golden Fleece to gain glory for himself. Pelias, now viewed as, if not good, neutral, gave permission in the hope that he would die and thus prevent him from succeeding Pelias on the throne. Jason built a boat that was larger than any other, named not for Argus the builder but for the Greek word for speed (*argon*), and he sailed to the wild lands of Colchis where cannibals lived. The Argonauts chose Heracles as leader, and he commanded the expedition all the way to Colchis. At Troy Heracles defeated a sea monster and received honors from the Trojans. During a storm, Orpheus gave a sacrifice to the gods to secure calm seas, and Dionysus reinterprets the episode with Phineus as Heracles' defeat of a hostile king.

Dionysus reports that the Argonauts saw the land of Taurica (the Crimea), where it was the custom (as we saw in chapter 4) for inhabitants to sacrifice visitors to Artemis. He rationalizes Hecate as a queen of Taurica and the wife of Aeëtes, thus the mother of Medea who is made a sister of Circe, all three of whom were mistresses of pharmacology (especially poisons), but not magical. Medea and Jason become betrothed out of his gratefulness for her warning about the custom of sacrifice in those lands. The Golden Fleece is stored in this version in a temple of Ares surrounded by cruel Taurican soldiers whose name, being like the word for bull (*tauros*) gave rise to the myth of the fire-breathing bulls. The golden ram of Phrixus, too, was little more than the figurehead on his boat. The Fleece, instead, was the skin of Phrixus' tutor Krios ("ram" in Greek), who was sacrificed to the gods and his pelt dipped in gold. As the king's daughter, Medea could command the temple gates open, and the Fleece was secured. This is similar to the rationalizing account given by the possibly fourth-century BCE author Palaephatus, who claimed that a man named Ram took a gold statue of a woman named Fleece to Colchis with him, "and this is the true story."[53]

On the way back, the Trojans mistreated the Argonauts when Heracles demanded the Trojans give him his reward for saving them from the sea monster. A battle ensued, which Heracles won, installing Priam on the throne and precipitating the later Trojan War. Back home, Pelias thought the Argonauts dead and forced Aeson to commit suicide. However, Medea plotted a stratagem to win back the kingdom. She used makeup to make Pelias' daughter look young again, and, thinking her rejuvenated, Pelias asked for the same treatment. Instead, he was killed. Jason (for no clear reason) then places Pelias' son on the throne, and Heracles suggests that the Argonauts form a mutual defense league, to be honored with sporting games, which he would found—the Olympic Games. The tragedy at Corinth then occurs to Jason as Euripides would have it, and, "not being therefore able to bear the insupportable weight of his calamities, he killed himself."[54]

Of this account, two primary themes emerge: First, the true hero of the story was Heracles, who commanded the expedition and performed its most important mission: setting the stage for the even more important Trojan War. (This was originally a separate myth of Heracles and Hesione, folded now in the Argonauts' journey.) In this Dionysus denies Jason, rendering him not just human but utterly unimportant, a colorful character who stumbled into historical events that had resonance far beyond him and without his direct understanding or intervention. Such views would come to a head with the unreliable author Ptolemaeus Chennus, who wrote in his *New History* of the second century CE that the *Argo* had been built by Heracles himself and that he had fallen in love with Jason's son Argos and named the boat after him![55]

Second, Jason never performed any truly heroic deeds. Instead, he was a presumptuous youth whose entirely human acts were later mythologized into heroics by later writers. This was entirely in keeping with the philosophy of euhemerism, founded by Euhemerus (fourth century BCE), which held that mythology could be explained as natural processes transformed into the supernatural by poets. The truth of this speculation was self-evident in the recent career of Alexander the Great, who was obviously a man, but who had already become the subject of myths and had been deified in Egypt. Surely, though, there would be someone to stand up for Jason, to see in him something of the old hero of Pindar? The Hellenistic librarian Eratosthenes (or rather someone writing under his name) did his part, claiming in the *Catasterismi* that the *Argo* was the first ship ever to sail,[56] a departure from all previous versions that merely made it the biggest and the best. This may have been done to justify *Argo's* position among the stars in an age that was no longer impressed with mere primacy in Black Sea voyaging.[57] (This tradition was followed by Roman-era authors, including Catullus, Valerius Flaccus, and the poet of the *Orphic Argonautica*.[58]) Jason's great champion, though, would be Apollonius of Rhodes, but his would be a Jason reflective not of the old style of Homeric heroics but of the new Greece created after the political and philosophical upheavals of Alexander the Great.

The Alexandrian Epic

The Peloponnesian War left Greece divided and devastated. Athens had fallen, its government replaced with repressive oligarchs. Militaristic Sparta gained hegemony in Greece, and soon Sparta found itself at war with the Persian Empire. Thereafter Thebes gained primacy in Greece, but the internecine conflicts among the city states left Greece vulnerable to foreign intervention. Phillip II of Macedon forced himself on Greece, and in 338 BCE Greece became a province of his kingdom. His successor, Alexander the Great (356–323 BCE king from 336), conquered most of the known world and spread Greek culture from Egypt to India. His seemingly superhuman feats earned him comparisons with Heracles, deification in Egypt, and his own cycle of Greek myth. In Armenia, Alexander famously found the Jasonia, the monuments to Jason, which were nothing of the sort. He also founded in Egypt the new city of Alexandria, named for himself. When his empire broke apart at his death, Alexandria became the capital of a Greek-dominated Egyptian kingdom whose rulers, the Ptolemies, made it the predominant center of culture, learning and trade. It was here, in the shadow of the great Library of Alexandria, that Apollonius was born in the third century BCE, at a date uncertain, in a time when the old heroes and myths were increasingly seen not as the primary province of certain cities, such as Jason with Corinth, but instead as pan–Hellenic, the patrimony of a civilization that began to recognize itself as not Athenian or Spartan but Greek. In this way Jason would come to Egypt.

What we know of Apollonius comes from two biographies in the scholia to his work, both derived from a lost original. They report that Apollonius composed the first version of his *Argonautica* as a young man, but it garnered a poor reception (condemned, in fact), and he departed for Rhodes. There he revised the poem into the version known today. This poem received acclaim in Rhodes, and as a result Apollonius declared himself a man of Rhodes. At some point he also became the librarian of Alexandria in honor of his fame and learning. He is sometimes said, on disputed evidence, to have had a feud with Callimachus, another poet and scholar at the Library and his former teacher. Callimachus urged poets to try new forms and to stop creating epics in the outdated mold of Homer. He told part of Jason's flight from Colchis in his compilation of elegiac poems, the *Aitia*, which exists only in fragments. Apollonius died in 246 BCE but the two biographies differ whether he died in Rhodes or Alexandria.

As a scholar, Apollonius was familiar with the many extant and contradictory elements of the Jason story as they had come down to him. Working from these sources, he attempted to pull together as many details as possible and work them into a coherent whole, one inspired by and conforming to an extent to the models provided by Homer, especially the *Odyssey*.[59] In this, a layer of intertextuality emerges in which Apollonius self-consciously and purposefully draws on and adapts Homer to model episodes in his poem, while Homer had drawn on and adapted an even older *Argonautica* in crafting the *Odyssey*. Apollonius' epic would differ from Homer's work in one respect: his would run fewer than six thousand lines, just over a third the length of the *Iliad*. It also would differ in its style, representing the culture and ethos of Hellenistic Greece, with a hero more human than the demigods of Homer.

Apollonius' *Argonautica* is a powerful and rich work, one that no thumbnail sketch can capture with true justice. Indeed, entire books have been written explicating the *Argonautica* in all its poetic, scholarly, and cultural wealth, as well as the debt it owes to the *Odyssey* which it liberally reworks and adapts in both language and incident.[60] Unfortunately, such artistic considerations lie beyond our scope, which instead will focus on mythic developments in the poem. The plot of the epic parallels that of the Standard Version for the most part, which is not saying much since generations of mythologists have derived the Standard Version primarily from the *Argonautica*. Therefore, the plot can be sketched quickly, noting primarily aspects unique to Apollonius' telling.

THE STORY AS GIVEN BY APOLLONIUS

Book One covers the setting off of the *Argo* and the adventures on the journey to Colchis. Surprisingly, the events leading to Jason's quest are treated quickly, with only brief allusions to Jason fulfilling a prophecy given to Pelias (more of the story is given in dialogue later). He arrives in Iolcus having lost a sandal in the mud when crossing the river Anaurus during a festival when Pelias honors Poseidon but neglects to honor Hera, but this take only a few lines. The building of the *Argo* by Argus with Athena's aid is alluded to briefly, and then the genealogies of the fifty Argonauts are expounded. The most important event in Book One occurs when the Argonauts have gathered, and Jason asks them to elect a leader for the expedition. Here Apollonius nods to the changing mythic tradition that had steadily eroded Jason's stature. The assembled heroes elect Heracles to lead the mission, after Jason diplomatically enjoins them to select the bravest; but Heracles declines and defers to Jason. The Argonauts then meet Hypsipyle on Lemnos and, after she lies to them about the murder of the men, they couple with the women of the island. Jason takes Hypsipyle as consort. Following this, the Argonauts reach the Doliones and mistakenly kill King Cyzicus and his men due to misunderstanding. This causes much grief. At their next stop, Cius, water nymphs abduct Heracles' companion Hylas, and Heracles stays behind on the island to search for him, crazed in his despair.

Book Two chronicles the Argonauts' adventures among the colorful peoples met en route to Colchis, described in anthropological detail, too numerous to detail here. At the Bosporus the Boreal twins, Zetes and Calais, free Phineus from the Harpies, and Phineus explains how to navigate the Clashing Rocks and reach Colchis. The rocks are to be passed watching for a dove to fly through, and Apollonius adds to this story the aid of Athena who holds the rocks apart and pushes the *Argo* quickly through. After encounters with the Amazons and the mountain of Prometheus, among other adventures, the Argonauts arrive in Colchis. The seer Idmon and Tiphys die along the way.

Book Three describes the Argonauts in Colchis, beginning with the forbidding Plain of Circe where corpses wrapped in ox hides hang from willow trees and then the great palace of Aeëtes, constructed by the god Hephaestus himself in thanks to the sun god and a wonder of stone and engineering. Resolving the disparate traditions of which goddess aided Jason, Apollonius simply includes them all: Hera and Athena work together to help Jason, asking Aphrodite to have her son Eros pierce Medea with a love arrow. Aeëtes issues his challenges to Jason to yoke the bulls (now all of brass, a gift of Hephaestus) and battle the Spartoi, and Medea, overcome with love, prays to Hecate, the dark goddess of witches, to deliver him.

And before her eyes the vision still appeared—himself [Jason] what like he was, with what vesture he was clad, what things he spake, how he sat on his seat, how he moved forth to the door—

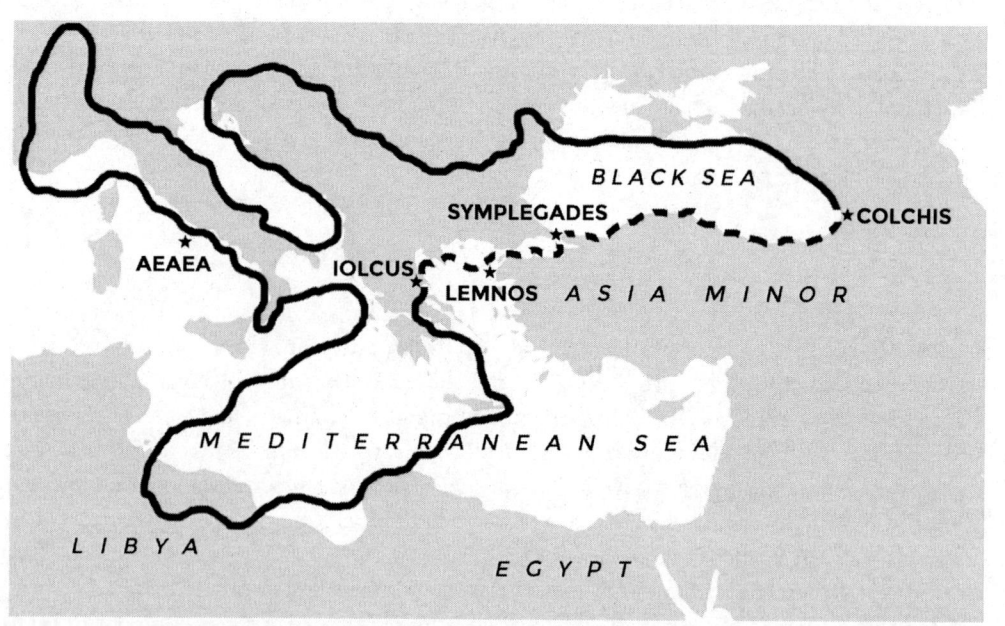

The geography of Apollonius' *Argonautica* differs markedly from that of Pindar, though they share a similar outward route (broken line). Apollonius has his heroes travel back (solid line) across Europe and Italy in an attempt to reconcile the Argonaut myth with what the ancients had come to believe were the physical locations of places mentioned in the *Odyssey*. This route is often taken as canonical by rationalizing modern scholars who attempt to retrace Jason's "real" route to and from Colchis (author's drawing).

and as she pondered she deemed there never was such a man; and ever in her ears rung his voice and the honey-sweet words which he uttered.[61]

The development of the pair's love is among the most beautiful passages in the epic, and the most admired. Hera drapes Jason in glory that he might be even more attractive to Medea in both appearance and in words, "like Sirius coming from Ocean."[62] In the temple of Hecate, Jason comes to Medea for aid, unaware of the love spell, and pleads with her in gentle oratory. Medea provides him with drugs in exchange for a harrowing sacrifice to Hecate and a marriage vow.

> And she would even have drawn out all her soul from her breast and given it to him, exulting in his desire; so wonderfully did love flash forth a sweet flame from the golden head of Aeson's son; and he captivated her gleaming eyes; and her heart within grew warm, melting away as the dew melts away round roses when warmed by the morning's light. And now both were fixing their eyes on the ground abashed, and again were throwing glances at each other, smiling with the light of love beneath their radiant brows.[63]

With Medea's secret aid, Jason accomplishes the tasks asked of him, but Aeëtes refuses to give Jason the Fleece.

In Book Four, Medea gives Jason her aid in putting the dragon to sleep and stealing the Fleece. She departs with the Argonauts, pursued by Medea's brother Apsyrtus, in this version older than she. Jason proposes to abandon Medea, leading to an outburst of rage that prefigures her later career in Corinth; but Jason explains this is a trap for Apsyrtus, which leads to Jason (rather than Medea) murdering Apsyrtus in the Adriatic after travelling the Ister (Danube). They seek out Circe in Italy, where Homer had placed her, for absolution, which she grants. To agree with Homer's mythic geography from the *Odyssey*, Apollonius has the Argonauts pass through a second set of rocks, the Planctae, on their route home (for Homer had placed the clashing rocks in the west). The Colchians again intercept the *Argo* and demand Medea, but surrender her when she and Jason consummate their union. The Argonauts have a few more adventures en route home, including an interlude at Lake Tritonis, which they reach by carrying the *Argo* on their shoulders which follows the same plan as the version in Pindar. To agree with Pindar, Apollonius includes a second seer, Mopsus, who dies on this leg of the voyage. At Crete, Medea uses her spells to slay Talos, and the Argonauts finally arrive home in Thessaly:

> Be gracious, race of blessed chieftains! And may these songs year after year be sweeter to sing among men. For now have I come to the glorious end of your toils; for no adventure befell you as ye came home from Aegina, and no tempest of winds opposed you; but quietly did ye skirt the Cecropian land and Aulis inside of Euboea and the Opuntian cities of the Locrians, and gladly did ye step forth upon the beach of Pagasae.[64]

Thus ended Apollonius' *Argonautica*.

APOLLONIUS' JASON

Any summary of the *Argonautica* makes it sound more active and direct than it is by virtue of relating events, which in the poem are widely scattered among a great number of anthropological and geographical digressions, typical of Hellenistic interests. However, even by these standards ancient critics still found the poem somewhat unsatisfying. The author known as Longinus (first century CE) considered Apollonius technically perfect but soulless[65] while the Roman Quintilian thought it an example of "evenly sustained mediocrity" but not without its merits.[66] Modern critics have been divided as well, primarily over Apollonius' depiction of Jason in the epic. Until the late twentieth century, critics faulted Apollonius for failing to make his Jason a full hero in the style of Homer. His Jason has been seen as weak, ineffective, subordinate to his comrades and to Medea, colorless, uninteresting, repellent, and, fatally, a hero only in matters sexual and romantic.[67] Worse, though Medea loves him, he does not return her love, and appears to use her as a means to an end, just as Theseus used Ariadne.[68]

Heracles appears to best him among the Argonauts; Medea controls his fate at Colchis. Jason's frequent bouts of uncertainty, anguish, and self-doubt—despite their precedents in the despair of Agamemnon and Achilles—are read as weakness, and his reliance on a team of heroes is seen as undercutting his individual glory. But Jason is not simply a puppet in Apollonius; his anguish comes out of the responsibility he deeply feels for the safety of his crew, which he knows will not all survive.[69] Leadership lies heavy on his head, not because he is weak but because he is human. He feels emotions because he is a man, and his crew—for whom he is responsible—depend on him, and he is uncertain whether he can succeed. For R. L. Hunter, Jason's gradual acquisition of the trappings of a Greek warrior—heroic rhetoric, the arms of a *hoplite* or infantryman, puissance—mark him as an initiate into manhood, into the caste of warriors, and finally, a very human hero.[70] For Stephen Jackson, Jason is a brave man, a thinking man, a true Hellenistic hero, but a human one—willing to do anything to survive. "He has proved himself to be a man, with all man's faults—a human being in an epic scenario."[71]

Apollonius' Jason is not a demigod, nor is he a Homeric epic hero. He is, for perhaps the first time in the Western cannon, a hero entirely human acting in world forever just beyond his power. He has no supernatural powers like the Boreads or Heracles, no preternatural skill like Idmon and Mopsus, but in the end it is Jason, a man, who, through means lofty and base, honest and deceptive, achieves what the heroes on the *Argo* cannot. He wins the Fleece, and this human hero of Apollonius is the version of Jason against which all others would be measured.

Jason in Rome

Though ancient critics were ambivalent about the *Argonautica*, it found a welcome reception in Rome among the elite, especially after its translation into Latin by Varro Atacinus in the mid first century BCE. In 146 BCE the Romans, who had absorbed Greek myths and gods from the Etruscans, absorbed Greece itself into their expanding empire, creating the province of Achaea in the Peloponnese and Thessaly. Alexandria fell in 30 BCE becoming the capital of Roman Egypt. In Rome, Greek tutors became sought-after teachers for the children of the elite, and the Romans themselves recognized the debt their culture owed to the Greeks in architecture, art, religion, and literature. As the first century CE poet Horace put it, *Graecia capta ferum victorem cepit* ("When Greece was captured, she herself made a slave of her savage subduer"[72]). Every educated Roman was expected to know the myths of the Greeks, which were also the Romans' own. The simplistic and derivative mythological compilation prepared by Gaius Julius Hyginus, a freedman of Augustus and librarian of the Palatine Library, preserves the myth of Jason as known to the Romans around 1 CE and as it would be taught by Greek *rhetors* to Roman youths. Primarily the *Fabulae* summarizes the *Argonautica*, with the episodes at Iolcus and Corinth drawn from other Greek sources. It is interesting for including two versions of Jason's missing sandal: telling both of its accidental loss due to haste and its loss when carrying a disguised Juno (Hera) across a river,[73] without attempting to explain the contradiction, and apparently without care that the summary includes the Juno story twice.[74] The Jason story remained popular under Rome, and when the Emperor Titus captured Jerusalem and made off with the Temple treasure, the Romans likened it to Jason's seizure of the Golden Fleece.[75] Hadrian named the colonnade surrounding the Temple of Neptune in Rome the Portico of the Argonauts, and statues and paintings of Medea were common throughout the empire, including a painting in the Forum of Caesar, and a famous statue in the baths of Antioch in Syria.

MEDEA UNDER THE EMPIRE

The writers of Rome's golden age of poetry made ample use of Greek themes, and they produced a number of Latin versions of Greek literature, both in direct translation as well as in adaptation, with Euripides' *Medea* among the most translated and adapted. Among the most admired original adaptations was Ovid's version of *Medea*, of which only a few lines survive. The story was also told in dramatic versions by Ennius, Accius, Curiatus Maternus, and Lucan, none of which survive, and the Stoic philosopher Seneca (c. 4 BCE-65 CE), the tutor of Nero, whose *Medea* we possess.

Seneca's *Medea* was not meant to be presented on stage, though it takes the form of a play. It follows the outline of Euripides' tragedy, but like any remake, it is both more violent and more direct than its predecessor, making explicit events and actions implicit in the older play. In this version, Medea is more closely aligned with the infernal powers, praying to Hecate, Pluto (Hades), Proserpina (Persephone), and the Furies, and mixing witchy potions with bloody rites and prayers. This Medea is more vengeful, more violent, more conscious of her wickedness, but not without remnants of her humanity. She still loves Jason, after a fashion: "If possible may he live, my Jason, as once we was; if not, still may he live and, mindful of me, keep unharmed the gift I gave" [i.e. his life].[76] Though she avenges herself mightily on Corinth and her children, she spares Jason, for somehow she still feels for him. Jason, by contrast, is less contemptible than his Euripidean counterpart. Seneca's Jason is genuinely concerned for Medea, but ultimately helpless before powers greater than himself—a continuation of the theme of the ineffective or weak Jason carried over from Greek literature. He offers his death to quench her rage but to no avail. Seneca implies that Medea murders her children (seen on stage, unlike in Euripides) because the angry spirit of her brother Apsyrtus, who appears on stage, demands blood vengeance. Jason is heartbroken, and shouts to the fleeing Medea in her serpent-drawn chariot: "Go on through the lofty spaces of high heaven and bear witness, where thou ridest, that there are no gods."[77]

In Seneca's hands, Medea completes her centuries-long transition from divine goddess to hellish witch. Seneca's Medea is the prototype for Shakespeare's Lady Macbeth, and this play a likely source for the Bard's own.[78]

Though Ovid's (43 BCE-17 or 18 CE) *Medea* does not survive, he discusses the sorceress at length in the *Metamorphoses* as well as *Heroides* and *Tristia*. In *Metamorphoses* he beautifully retells the Argonauts' adventure from Medea's lovelorn perspective, and he foreshadows the disaster at Corinth by having his heroine reflect on what she would do if the object of her love ever chose another woman over her. Ovid has Jason charm the dragon himself (but has Medea do it in *Heroides*), though otherwise he follows the *Argonautica* before relating Medea's rejuvenation of Aeson, aborted rejuvenation of Pelias, and alluding to the Corinthian tragedy and her career at Athens. The earlier *Heroides*, by contrast, tells the same material in the form of a poison pen letter from Medea to Jason, filled with her bile, reflecting on events just before the action of what would have been Ovid's play, *Medea*. A section of *Tristia* ("Sorrows") tells of Medea's murder and dismemberment of Apsyrtus, a pointed contrast to Apollonius' less violent variant. Again, Ovid uses the incident to foreshadow Corinth, implying that the maid Medea was already corrupted, turning into the vengeful witch of legend even on the *Argo*.

JASON AND THE CAESARS

The Romans clearly found Medea a fascinating figure, but Jason, too, had his moment in the empire of the Caesars, not least for his spiritual connection. His adventures in Colchis, including both the bulls and the dragon, were frequent motifs on Roman sarcophagi, and several beautiful examples survive, most depicting the hero nude except for a warrior's helmet. Once such sandstone sarcophagus from Viminacium, now in Serbia, depicts among its mythological scenes Jason holding the Golden Fleece, while the serpent (dragon) entwines a tree. Other images include Perseus and Dionysus. Such motifs suggest, according to Sanja Pilopović, that the Romans considered the quest for the Fleece symbolic of the triumph over death and the attainment of immortality and rebirth,[79] consonant with the earliest versions of the story, as reconstructed in chapter 3. This suggests that these associations—kept alive in Etruria even after the myth was changing shape in Greece—persisted among the Romans. The combination of Jason and Dionysus on the same sarcophagus recalls the Etruscan image of Jason and the Etruscan Fufluns (Dionysus) from several centuries before. The implication of the frequent images of Jason (sometimes with Medea) is that Roman oral tradition preserved an alternate reading of Jason, associated with rebirth and resurrection, that the literary tradition, which followed Greek models, did not. That literary tradition, however, would contribute to two Latin epics that would prove highly influential in world literature, one directly and the other less so.

When speaking of ancient epics, Virgil's *Aeneid*—the story of the Trojan hero Aeneas' departure from Troy and his foundation of the race that would someday found Rome—is spoken of in the same breath with the *Iliad* and the *Odyssey*—a cornerstone of Western literature. In constructing his epic, Virgil (70 BCE-19 CE) obviously studied the models of Homer, but as has been shown in many scholarly studies, Virgil also drew heavily on the *Argonautica* to model Aeneas' adventures in the Mediterranean and especially the love Dido of Carthage feels for Aeneas, a tragic romantic interlude drawn from Apollonius' romantic treatment of Medea's love for Jason in Book IV of the *Argonuatica*.[80] Virgil also understood Jason's voyage to be a symbolic trip to the Underworld, with Colchis standing in for Hades and the Golden Fleece corresponding the golden bough Aeneas seeks during his descent in Book VI.[81] It is an exaggeration, but not much of one, to suggest that without Jason and Apollonius we would not have the *Aeneid* we know today.

As an interesting footnote to Virgil and Jason, around 203 CE the African play-wright Hosidius Geta created a version of the tragedy *Medea* composed entirely of fragments extracted from the collected works of Virgil, a Roman literary exercise known as a "cento," and the only known cento to take the form of a tragedy. In doing so, he purposely echoed the language of Ovid's and Seneca's *Medea*, and he drew extensive fragments of Virgil from Book IV of the *Aeneid* to provide Medea her dialogue, especially from the sections with Dido that Virgil had himself modeled on the Medea in Apollonius' *Argonautica*.[82] The poem itself is (understandably) somewhat bloodless and artificial, but interesting nonetheless.

The other Roman epic derived from Jason's story is a much more direct interpretation.

THE ROMAN ARGONAUTICA

Gaius Valerius Flaccus (died c. 90 BCE), about whom relatively little is known, was a poet under the Flavian emperors. Based on allusions in his work, it is usually assumed that Valerius read the Latin translation of the *Argonautica* of Apollonius in a scholarly edition with commentary and discussions of the Greek sources Apollonius used,[83] and he may have employed the services of a Greek scholar in discussing mythological themes and learning about Greek sources.[84] Around 70 CE Valerius began composition of his own *Argonautica*, modeled on Apollonius as well as on Virgil's *Aeneid*, but the composition took a long time. The poem references the eruption of Mount Vesuvius in 79 CE suggesting that Valerius worked on the epic for at least those nine years. He was probably still working on it in 90 CE when he died, leaving his *Argonautica* unfinished (though some believe it was finished, but part lost). The story ends abruptly right after Medea's marriage to Jason, in mid-speech. Quintilian reported that Valerius' death was a great loss to Roman poetry.[85]

The outline of Valerius' *Argonautica* follows closely the version of Apollonius in most episodes and adventures (down to the doubling of seers in Mopsus and Idmon), but some of the details differ, reflecting alternative traditions about Jason's voyage. In Valerius' version, Pelias is well aware of Jason long before the latter arrives in Colchis, and has spent years plotting the death of a man who already has a formidable heroic reputation. According to Valerius, an oracle specifically warned Pelias about Jason, rather than the more ambiguous "man of one sandal." Aeson here commits suicide early on to keep Pelias from using him as a weapon against Jason. There will be no rejuvenation for him, but in the carefully described Underworld he shown his reward and the punishment that awaits the wicked Pelias.

Valerius also makes Chiron come to the Argonauts so Peleus might give his son Achilles into the great teacher's charge, part of a continuing theme in the poem that the Argonauts' journey prefigures the Trojan War. Valerius follows the adventure of Hercules and the sea monster at Troy told in the version of Dionysus Schytobrachion, foreshadowing the Trojan War to come—a decisive reading that influenced medieval and modern interpretations of the myth. However, because Hercules leaves the Argonauts in Valerius, the raid on Troy would come at the hands of ex–Argonauts after the voyage ends. In the Roman era, Apollo became identified with the sun, replacing Sol (Helios), and he is here seen as the lord of Colchis. Valerius adds to the adventures in this land a war between the Scythians and Colchians, modeled on historical events involving the warlike Scythians in that region, all the better to set up rival martial suitors for Medea, making her escape from Colchis doubly dramatic and giving a rational reason for her to aid Jason beyond simply her emotional attachment.

Under the threat of foreign war, Aeëtes promises the Fleece in return for the Argonauts' martial aid. Valerius, interestingly, notices that Pelias and Aeëtes act with extremely similarity, and he makes Jason point to this coincidence of motive and manner when Aeëtes announces the new tests Jason must perform even after delivering Colchis from the Scythians:

> Where have his promises gone? What deceits is he plotting to order? Another Pelias I see here, another ocean. Why not come and thrust your imperious hatred down upon this head? Never shall my right hand nor my hope be found wanting.[86]

Valerius reinstates some of Jason's heroic stature and shows that despite Medea's help it is Jason whose active role ensures his triumph over the bulls and the Spartoi. These he defeats by throwing not a rock but a helmet filled with Medea's poisons into the throng of men, who, intoxicated, kill one another. Interestingly, in this instance, Medea is explicitly compared to the Anatolian version of Inanna, Cybele, mourning for Attis (= Dumuzi) as a poetic invocation of the power she holds over the Spartoi, who cut and tear themselves just as Cybele's anger causes her worshippers to rend themselves for Attis each spring. Later, Valerius compares her marriage to Jason to Cybele's rejoicing at Attis' rebirth.

The most important difference between Valerius' and Apollonius' poems, and one in keeping with evolving religious traditions in the Greco-Roman world, was the increasing role of omniscient Jupiter (Zeus) in the undertaking, subordinating all the other divine helpers to adjuncts of a fate planned in advance by Jove and directed entirely for his ends. This idea Valerius borrowed from Virgil.[87] Early on Idmon the seer has extremely specific visions of all the Argonauts' fates, and the point is stressed repeatedly that their destinies are as fixed as the rotation of the stars in the heavens. The past serves to control the present, and the present shapes an unavoidable future. In Valerius, Jason is a man in the hands of fate, his destiny foreordained on Olympus long before he attempts action.

The *Argonautica* of Valerius Flaccus differs from its Greek prototype in the vividness and directness of its imagery and language. Where the earlier poem was more discursive, allusive, and languid, the Roman version mirrors the virtues of Latin poetry. Images are starker; the language more energetic. The poem is, to modern readers, more entertaining than Apollonius,' even if it suffers somewhat in being almost completely unoriginal. One wishes Valerius had lived to finish it. The poem was not widely circulated, but as we shall see, it came to be highly influential in defining the medieval Jason.

Orpheus, Jason, and Cultic Worship

An anonymous writer history assigned the name Apollodorus, writing in Greek, created a grand summary of Greco-Roman mythology at an uncertain date, perhaps the first century CE, maybe later. Apollodorus retold the Standard Version of the Jason story, drawing explicitly on older authors such as Pherecydes, Herodorus, and primarily Apollonius. He preserved a few choice variants, including the suggestion, apparently from Pherecydes, that Jason lived in the country because of his love of husbandry and agriculture, and that Pelias summoned him to Iolcus to attend his sacrifice to Poseidon, therefore becoming the author of his own downfall when Jason lost his sandal en route, fulfilling a prophecy. Strabo (63 BCE–24 CE) tried to find a historical basis for the Argonauts' voyage in the gold mining operations of Colchis (see Book Four). But aside from scattered allusions to Jason and Medea in later Greco-Roman writing, Valerius' account might have been Antiquity's last word on Jason.

However, an anonymous author of the fourth century CE, writing at the very end of pagan Antiquity, composed a final ancient Jason epic, the so-called *Orphic Argonautica*. Running about 1,400 lines in classical hexameter (about a fifth the length of Apollonius), the Orphic poem retold the Jason story from the first-person perspective of Orpheus, an Argonaut who had otherwise become a cult figure. By the sixth century BCE, Orpheus was hailed as the hero who gave the art of medicine to humanity; the hero who founded cults of Apollo, Demeter, Dionysus, and Hecate (originally an Anatolian earth goddess before becoming the goddess of ghosts and black magic[88]); and the hero who provided his followers with mystical rites and rituals of purification and initiation. In myth he descended into and returned from the Underworld in search of his dead love, Eurydice, whom he rescues in early versions and loses in later ones. He was dismembered by the worshippers of Dionysus when he declared Apollo, the Sun, the only true god. His cult, the Orphics, believed that earthly life was a punishment and in the immortality of the soul, a transfiguration that helped men become gods after they shed their bodies and took up eternal life in the Elysian Fields of the Underworld. They worshipped Orpheus, Persephone, and Dionysus, all figures who had descended to Hades and returned.[89]

The *Orphic Argonautica* was written to sound older than it was, recalling the language of Homer, but infused with errors of more recent vintage.[90] The Orphic poem takes its plot and events (and much of its language) from Apollonius and Valerius Flaccus, but Orpheus is given a role more fitting to his exalted standing within his cult. Orpheus, not Heracles, returns the Argonauts from their revels on Lemnos. It is he, and not Medea, who charms the dragon to sleep in order to secure the Golden Fleece. The dragon—here a large snake curled around an oak tree like a caduceus—lives within a fifty-four foot tall enclosure of seven walls and three gates guarded by a statue of a

> far-seeing queen, scattering with her motion the radiance of fire, whom the Colchians propitiate as Artemis of the gate, resounding with the chase, terrible for men to see, and terrible to hear, unless one approaches by the sacred rites and purification, the rites kept hidden by the priestess who was initiated, Medea, unfortunate in marriage, along with the girls of Cyta. No mortal, whether native or stranger, entered that way, crossing over the threshold, for the terrible Goddess kept them away by all means, breathing madness into her fire-eyed dogs.[91]

Beyond this lay a field filled with powerful magic roots and herbs. At the center stood an oak on which the Golden Fleece was draped. To open the gates, Orpheus conducts hideous rites of dog sacrifice with magic herbs that call up the Furies, Pandora (as an earth goddess), and Hecate, with three heads: a horse, a dog, and a boar. The writer seems to identify Hecate with Artemis (as she frequently was in late Antiquity), and the scene is terrible to behold. After the magical rites, she lets Jason, Medea, Mopsus, and Orpheus in. Orpheus sings the hissing snake to sleep, and Medea tells Jason to take the Fleece from the oak beside the "tomb" of Zeus Chamaizelos, a chthonic form of Zeus often identified with Hades, "the Other Zeus." (Indeed some suggest Hades originated as an aspect of Zeus, who had absorbed the earth god's dominion over the dead.) They then race back to the *Argo* where the Argonauts rejoice in their triumph.

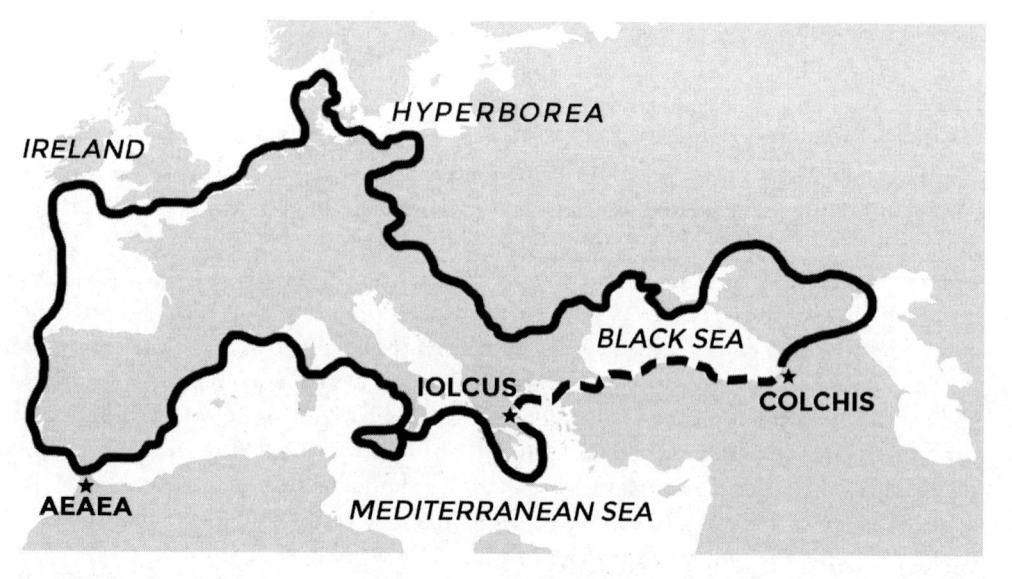

While sharing the same outward journey (broken line) as Apollonius, the *Orphic Argonautica* sent the Argonauts on a northward return voyage (solid line) that some have interpreted as reaching the Arctic, while others, like Judith Bacon, whose reconstructed Orphic route is seen here, took them across in Northern Europe. Because the Orphic poem was for many years considered the oldest version of the *Argonautica*, it gave rise to many speculative theories about ancient Greek voyages to Scandinavia, Ireland, and farther afield (author's drawing).

The return journey Orpheus describes is different from that of Apollonius in its route (but not outcome), perhaps travelling as far as Britain and Ireland, beyond which they encounter the pine-covered Island of Demeter, where two primeval temples mark the spot where Hades seized Persephone. An analysis by J. R. Bacon suggested that the poem was drawing on an Orphic tradition about the Argonauts' voyage dating back to the early fifth century BCE.[92] Since the Orphics were intimately connected with the Mysteries of Dionysus, it is interesting to compare this suggested tradition with the Etruscan Jason mirror featuring Fufluns/Dionysus at around that same time. Orphism was especially prevalent in Greek Italy and Sicily, and was perhaps even the faith's birthplace, as early as the sixth century BCE but certainly by the fifth century BCE,[93] and the Etruscans were known to have absorbed Orphic ideas, especially those about the afterlife.[94] Could this mirror represent an early episode from a lost Orphic Argonautic tradition?

While the *Orphic Argonautica* is no masterpiece of literature (though much better than its reputation suggests[95]), it does, in its rough way, return the story of Jason to where it began in the Mycenaean era. Orpheus assumes the magical and pharmacological role Medea once held, which in turn originally belonged to Jason. In the cult version of Orpheus we again have a hero who descends into the Underworld and returns from it, a hero dismembered, and a hero who spoke to the possibility of renewed life after a properly sanctified death. The only complication was that this hero was no longer Jason but instead Orpheus, a mythological figure whose complex mythology is much more recent than the older Jason he was attempting to replace (he does not appear in Homer or Hesiod).[96] Jason, however, would still have his due, after a fashion. In the city of Abdera on the Thracian coast, Strabo reported a Temple of Jason, built by Alexander's general Parmenion. Monuments to Jason, Strabo said, marked the path of the *Argo* in Armenia and were "evidence of the expedition of Jason."[97] In Iran, then called Media, the highest mountain was known as Mt. Jasonium, now known as Mt. Damavand. Jason, Strabo added, was also honored as the founder of the Doric temple of Hera at Foce del Sele in Lucania, fifty stadia (5 mi/8 km) from the Greek city of Paestum (Poseidonia) in Italy.[98] Though this might seem like just another myth (Greek settlement began only around 600 BCE and the temple dates from after 575 BCE), archaeological investigation uncovered a Bronze Age settlement at Paestum with Mycenaean pottery.[99] It is just possible that Hera and Jason in different, older forms came this way before. But if in places like Abdera Jason was worshipped once more as a god, it was a very different form of devotion than the earliest Jason had received. The Temple of Jason was likely an import from campaigns soldiers from Thessaly fought in Armenia under Parmenion,[100] derived from the *ayazana* they encountered there and which the Greeks mistook for monuments to Jason (see chapter 2). This newly divine Jason was the result of fortuitous coincidence that accidentally restored an old god to his throne.

Perhaps in keeping with the new, imperial ideology of the years of Alexander and of Rome, a new epilogue for the Jason story emerged, replicating and repurposing parts of the original story. According to Gnaeus Pompeius Trogus and Strabo, both writing in the first century BCE, after his time in Colchis, Jason conquered all of Armenia, a forerunner of Alexander the Great, who was jealous of his temples, the Jasonia.[101] Trogus, as preserved by Justin, reports a *second* voyage to Colchis, apparently unique to him, though believed to derive from Hellenistic Greek sources, possibly Timagenes of Alexandria. (A century later, Tacitus, probably drawing on Trogus or a shared source, agrees that Jason returned to Colchis at a later date.[102]) Justin says that Jason, expelled by Pelias' sons, "set out on a second voyage for Colchis, accompanied by a numerous train of followers (who, at the fame of his valour, came daily from all parts to join him), by his wife Medea, whom, having previously divorced her, he had now received again from compassion for her exile."[103] Yes, they improbably reconciled in this version, despite her murderous temperament. Then, to make restitution to Medea's father for taking the Golden Fleece and despoiling his daughter, he "carried on great wars with the neighbouring nations; and of the cities which he took, he added part to the kingdom of his father-in-law, to make amends for the injury that he had done him in his former expedition."[104] Justin said that this was the true origin of the Jasonia, and that Alexander's jealous general Parmenion (*contra* Strabo) smashed the temples of Jason wherever they were found so Jason could not rival the divine Alexander. He did not get them all.

On the most significant headland on the northern shore of Anatolia, two thirds of the way between Byzantium and Colchis, a temple to Jason stood on a windswept promontory known in Latin as the Jasonium or in Greek as the Jasonion (Cape Jason, modern Yasun Burnu in Turkey). Passing sailors made sacrifices there to calm the inhospitable waters of the Black Sea, and a passage often considered an interpolation has Xenophon pass through here in the *Anabasis*.[105] But like so much of Jason's antique legend, this cape too was an interpolation. The Jason temple of Anatolia was merely another *ayazana*, a Persian or Persian-influenced cult site that the Classical Greeks misinterpreted as one devoted to Jason.[106] It was at the very edge of the old Median territory, which once reached to Cappadocia in Asia Minor. After the Greek gods and heroes lost their last worshippers, the pagan temple to Jason was replaced by a Christian church, a restored version of which stands today, and in much the same way the living pagan Jason would be replaced a new Jason, a literary rather than mythic figure, a now medieval man destined to embody the new virtues of the Christian faith.

At the end of Antiquity, there were many competing versions of Jason: the demigod and the weakling, the hero and the human. With changing of the age, Jason no longer commanded a presumed reality, but as a new era dawned, the ancients left us his myth in all its diversity and color, preserved in their texts as though in amber, to be told and retold for millennia to come. Before we continue with that part of the story, we should first pause to analyze Jason and his myth as they stood at the end of Antiquity in light of all we have learned. This mythic context will be the subject of Part Three.

PART THREE

THE MYTH IN CONTEXT

6

The Archetype

Heroes and Villains

There is no single date that marks the end of Antiquity, but a series of events slowly dissolved the ancient pillars of civilization that had propped up the Classical world from the Archaic period straight through until what Gibbon called the "glorious afternoon" of the Antonine emperors of Rome. In 330 CE the Roman emperor Constantine moved the capital of the Roman Empire to Byzantium, renamed Constantinople, on the Bosporus, near where Helle had fallen from the golden ram. However, this would be no pagan city. The "New Rome" would be very different from the Greek and Roman cities that preceded it. It would grow into a Christian city in a Christian empire. In 337 CE Constantine converted to Christianity. In 363, the last pagan to rule the Roman Empire, Julian the Apostate, died. In 380 the emperor Theodosius I declared Christianity the empire's only official state religion, and over the next few years he harshly persecuted pagans. In 388, he ordered the pagan temples closed or destroyed, and in 391 the ancient rite of animal sacrifice was forbidden. In 393 the last of the Olympic Games founded by Heracles were held. In 529, Justinian I closed the Platonic Academy in Athens.

Belief in the Greek myths did not end all at once, but rather faded away gradually as Christianity washed over the Roman Empire. In time, however, the citizens of Christian Constantinople—Greek speakers who considered themselves citizens of the Eastern Roman Empire—forgot their old gods and their old heroes. Their statues still stood across the empire, and in Constantinople itself statues of the gods, heroes, and statesmen lined the streets as masterworks of ancient art. But, eventually, it came to pass that even the educated no longer knew who many of the figures were. In the eighth century CE, a group of philosophers in the capital tried to identify the subjects of the old statues, but there were many they could not understand or misunderstood, and they made up stories to explain statues that confused them, attributing to most malevolent power.[1]

The story of Jason and the Argonauts lived on, however, in works preserved from Antiquity, foremost among them the *Argonautica* of Apollonius and the *Library* of Apollodorus. The latter work was perhaps the most complete expression of a trend in mythography originating centuries earlier, the desire of the Greeks to weave together into a coherent whole the disparate myths and legends that had come down to them from the remote past. Though even Apollodorus' workmanlike effort was unable to completely unify Mycenaean myths, Dark Age legends, and Archaic reinventions, the body of mythology that the Hellenistic

Greeks and the Romans would have known was heavily integrated, with every character and occurrence worked into a web of allusions that served to imagine the ancient past as a long, epic saga of gods, heroes, and humans whose every action was a part of the great panorama of history, from the creation of the world down to the age of Alexander, the man who became a god. This tendency toward seeking unity in Greek myths continued deep into the Middle Ages, when the three so-called Vatican Mythographers, from the eighth to the twelfth centuries, created their compendia of Greek myths intended to provide a handbook for Christians to use and exploit the myths for godly purposes, including the teaching of virtue.[2]

Of course not all the Greek myths were originally connected; many began life as independent stories of local gods and heroes spread throughout the Aegean, originating in different dates and times, from the Mycenaeans down to the allegorical myths created as late as the Roman era. Therefore, before we examine the medieval, Renaissance, and modern afterlife of the Jason myth, we should pause to examine Jason in his mythological context, including his relationships with and comparisons to other mythic figures. A myth and the symbols included within it cannot be treated in isolation; they exist in multiple, overlapping contexts. These include the context of the story itself, the context of its place within and relationships to Greek mythology as a whole, and the broader context of the regional cultures and mythologies within which Greek myths developed and were situated. Only by examining and interrogating the myth within these contexts can its multiple, overlapping, and sometimes contradictory symbolic meanings be most fully understood. This Book will explore first Jason's relationships to other human characters, followed by chapters examining the lands to which he travelled and the mythological creatures and objects he encountered.

Jason and the Heroes

Jason, of course, was hardly the only hero in ancient Greek myth; unlike most world mythologies, which concentrate primarily on the actions of the gods, the Greek myths are somewhat overstuffed with heroes. Many of these heroes may have begun their careers as local gods who were integrated into the Greek pantheon as something less than divine, much the way the medieval cult of saints superseded the manifold pagan divinities and heroes, proposing Christian alternatives who either absorbed the old gods and heroes or replaced them in function, deed, and honor.[3] Whether Jason himself began as a Mycenaean god or as a hero invented to replace one, he shares traits with many of his mythological cousins, especially three of the most important heroes: Perseus, Theseus, and Heracles. Two of these would be numbered among the Argonauts by the end of Antiquity; Perseus, the mythological founder of Mycenae, was reckoned too far in the past to have been an Argonaut. He was the great-grandfather of Heracles.

PERSEUS

The story of Perseus is among Greek mythology's most familiar. Zeus came to his mother Danaë as a golden shower and impregnated her in Argos. Danaë's father, the king of Argos, cast her and her son into the sea in a casket, for an oracle had foretold that his daughter's son would kill him one day. They washed ashore on Seriphos, where years later the king, Polydectes, determined to remove Perseus and marry Danaë. To do this, he demanded a gift of horses from every man invited to the royal banquet. Unable to provide a horse, Perseus, now a youth on the verge of manhood, promised the king whatever else he asked, and the king demanded the head of the Gorgon Medusa, whose hair was made of snakes and whose gaze turned men to stone.

Unable to refuse, Perseus went in search of the Gorgon. Athena came to his aid, telling him to seek out the Graeae, three old sisters of Medusa who shared one eye and one tooth. These Perseus stole and ransomed for guidance to the grove of the Hesperides, who gave him magical weapons to defeat the Gorgon, including winged sandals, a satchel to carry her head, and Hades' helmet of invisibility to make his escape. To avoid Medusa's gaze, Perseus viewed her only in reflection in his polished mirror, and he beheaded her. Her two sister Gorgons chased him, and he escaped by crossing the great Ocean. On his return to Seriphos, Perseus rescued the maid Andromeda, whose father had chained her to a rock as sacrifice to a sea serpent, under orders from the Oracle of Ammon. Perseus killed the serpent and took Andromeda as a wife. According to Apollonius in the *Argonautica*, as Perseus flew home, Medusa's head dripped blood into the sands of Libya, and where it hit serpents grew. One of these serpents would eventually kill the Argonaut Mopsus.

The Perseus story appears to contain two separate myths, the Gorgon and the serpent, which gradually merged into a single myth cycle.[4] Perseus is alluded to in Homer, though not as a Gorgon slayer, and the core of his myth is given in Hesiod. Therefore, it seems that as a myth Perseus is somewhat younger than Jason, who was already well-known to Homer. The individual episodes of Perseus' story may date back to the Mycenaean era,[5] but the complete Perseus myth only took its modern shape in the writings of Pherecydes (who also wrote of the Argonauts) in lost portions of his work summarized in the scholia to Apollonius and in Apollodorus.[6]

Even a cursory reading of the myth produces obvious parallels to Jason's story:

- A far-flung adventure undertaken by an adolescent hero.
- The presence of two wicked kings who wish to be rid of the hero.
- A king deceptively sending a hero to his death through an impossible mission.
- The aid of a goddess in the hero's quest.
- The slaying of a serpent and marriage to a king's daughter.
- The use of magic to defeat the monsters.[7]

However, at a deeper level, the Perseus myth displays striking parallels not just with the Argonaut story as given in the Hellenistic era but also with the reconstruction of the Jason story proposed in chapter 3. For this analysis, we will concentrate on the core of the Perseus story, the defeat of the Gorgons, which was likely the oldest and original section of the myth. The Andromeda section was likely tacked on later, reproducing ideas and motifs from the Medusa episode mediated through Near Eastern iconography (e.g., cylinder seals depicting a god slaying a serpent in the presence of a female figure[8]). Interestingly in one version of the serpent slaying the monster swallows Perseus and he kills it from within, much as the iconographic tradition shows Jason being swallowed.[9]

The Gorgons—the three snake-haired sisters—lived in what was Daniel Ogden described as a "never-never land" that in the oldest myths was simply located far away, at the farthest points of the compass,[10] typically in the west, just like Jason's Aea in the east. Only later did they acquire a fixed geographic location, in the deserts of Libya, just as Aea became identified with Colchis. The Gorgons in the earliest tales are clearly associated with death and its companions, terror and fear. Homer in the *Odyssey* described the "Gorgon head of some fell monster high Persephone might send out of the house of Hades."[11] Like Jason's adventures, Perseus' death-dealing Gorgons have a Near East counterpart. Their image has been linked to depiction of the giant Gilgamesh slays, Humbaba, whose severed head is depicted as covered in wavy lines (representing intestines) with a grimacing mouth and protruding teeth, very similar to the earliest images of the Gorgon. Humbaba's breath was said to cause death, and he guarded evil spirits in the realm of the dead on behalf of Tammuz (Dumuzi) and the sanctuary of Ishtar (Inanna) for that goddess.[12] Gilgamesh travels to the far distant realm of the Cedar Forest, where dwelled the gods, to kill the demon, just as Perseus travels to the unknown lands to slay the Gorgon. Additionally, Medusa herself has been seen, like Medea, as a mother goddess figure who over the centuries faded into a wicked demon, equivalent to Hera or Inanna.[13] Thus, to gaze upon Medusa is to die, just as it is impossible to gaze upon the countenance of a god(dess) and live.[14] It is not impossible that the Gorgon resulted from the conflation of a Humbaba demon type and a decaying goddess. After all Humbaba was originally Ishtar/Inanna's guardian, and the two figures may have merged in the telling.

In truth, the Greek myth, like that of Jason, probably is not a literal translation of a Near East story but instead a mixture of Near East iconography, Mycenaean heroes or deities, ancient folk tales and myths, and a large dash of Archaic invention. However, within this heady brew we can identify an important and highly relevant theme. King Polydectes' name means "much receiving" and is also one of Hades' titles as he who receives the many dead.[15] This is not unlike the relationship Pelias and Aeëtes share with the old Mycenaean earth god. Additionally, the Gorgons, whatever their origin, cause death and are related to the Graeae, symbols of old age. G. S. Kirk speculated therefore that the earliest Perseus story involved the hero, whose name means "destroyer" (the opposite of Jason the "healer"), attacking the kingdom of the dead, or even death itself[16] and then returning to the mortal world. This is thematically akin to the ancient Near East tales of the god who dies and rises again, as well as the suggested early versions of Jason's own story. Perseus the Destroyer and Jason the Healer are thus mirror images of one another. The early Jason travels to a distant land beyond the eastern horizon to defeat a monster and return with a goddess in marriage. The early Perseus travels to a distant land beyond the western horizon to destroy a goddess and returns with a monstrous weapon, the Gorgon's head. It would be wondrously appropriate to find that both shared some ancient Mycenaean relationship, but, alas, there is no evidence suggesting it. Fontenrose, however, argued that Perseus' story originated as one told of Baal, with Polydectes as death symbol playing the role of the death-god Mot.[17] As we have seen, this Near East story is thematically similar to the Inanna-Dumuzi story to which Jason appears to have become attached, and the two stories represent the two variant models of the hero's triumph over the underworld, through love and through war.

Just as Jason's story grew less heroic over time, so too was Perseus' softened. In the early Archaic period Perseus beheaded an angry Medusa, and her two sisters gave chase; but after the fifth century BCE this changed and instead Perseus was said to have sneaked up to the sleeping Gorgons and removed Medusa's head without her sisters' notice. Similarly, while Jason's Medea grew more wicked over time, by the Hellenistic period depictions of Medusa transformed her from hideous into a great beauty. Thus in both the stories of Jason and Perseus, the processes of Greek mythological transmission gradually altered stories that shared a similar theme and origin.

THESEUS

An even closer similarity exists between Jason and his companion aboard the *Argo*, Theseus, added to the roster of Argonauts in traditions followed by Apollodorus and Hyginus, though not by Apollonius or Valerius Flaccus. His story begins with King Minos of Crete, a son of Zeus who married Pasiphae, a daughter of Helios (and thus a half-sister of Aeëtes and aunt of Medea), who also possessed magical powers, cursing Minos to ejaculate serpents and insects when he attempted to seduce a mistress. In most of Greece, Minos was known as a just and righteous king who presided over a great empire, but in Athens he was reconfigured as a tyrant. One year he failed to sacrifice a promised bull to Poseidon, who became so angry that he caused Pasiphaë to lust for the bull and mate with it while disguised as a cow. Thus she conceived the Minotaur, a man with a bull's head and tail (though early images depict him as a bull with a man's head). Minos demanded Athens send a ship filled with seven male and seven female youths to Knossos each year to feed the Minotaur, who lived in an elaborate maze beneath the palace, the Labyrinth, to keep him confused and unable to escape.

Meanwhile, Theseus was born in Troizen, across from Athens, to a woman the Athenian king impregnated and abandoned without meeting the child. He engaged in a series of adventures similar to those of Heracles on route to Athens. Jason's ex-wife, Medea, fled to Athens after killing Jason's sons, and there she married Theseus' father, Aigeus, now the Athenian king. Theseus arrived in Athens, and Medea figured out the stranger's identity before Aigeus, and conspired to persuade Aigeus to rid Athens of her son Medus' rival for the throne. She tried several tricks to kill Theseus, including poison and sending him on a fruitless quest to kill a magic bull. But Aigeus eventually recognized a sword and sandals he had left behind in Troizen and knew Theseus as his son. Medea and Medus were banished, travelling to Persia where Medus founded the Median race. Theseus volunteered to travel to Crete as one of that year's sacrificial victims. The ship hoisted black sails to signify death, with the promise of white sails should Theseus return to Athens alive. In a variant version, Theseus is said to be Poseidon's son, and Minos makes him prove his divinity by fetching a ring from beneath the sea.

The core story of Theseus, what happens next, is very ancient indeed. Theseus arrived on Crete, and Minos' daughter Ariadne fell deeply in love with him. She gave Theseus a ball of string to unwind as he wandered the Labyrinth that he might retrace his path to escape, and he promised to take Ariadne back to Athens as his wife. In the oldest versions of the story, she handed him a glowing wreath or crown instead. Theseus killed the Minotaur with a sword at the center of the maze, and he followed the thread back out. He and Ariadne escaped with the other youths, and they prevented Minos from giving chase by punching holes in the Cretans' ships to sink them. On the way back to Athens, Theseus abandoned Ariadne on the island of Naxos, originally because he loved another, but in later versions because the god Dionysus wanted her for a wife. Theseus returned to Athens, but he forgot to change the ship's sails. Seeing the black banners, Aigeus killed himself, thinking Theseus dead. Theseus became king.

Scholars have shown that the Theseus figure began his existence as a local hero in the area of Athens and was consciously remodeled by the Athenians into a great hero, meant to be the Attic equivalent of the Peloponnesian Heracles. Originally Theseus' adventure with the Minotaur took place in an ancient mythological past, seven generations before the Trojan War; but later this was revised to merely two generations prior.[18] This process contributed to the reorientation of the Argonaut myth, whereby Heracles and Theseus stopped over at Troy and precipitated the events that would cause the Trojan War. Thus, through them was Jason dragged out of the past and into the historicized world immediately before the war.

As R. L. Hunter has shown, the stories of Theseus and Jason are strikingly similar, a fact that was not lost on Apollonius in writing the *Argonautica*, which has Jason and Medea themselves note the parallels. (Obviously, the chronology of Theseus and Jason varied by author—only some make him an Argonaut, and Apollonius thought him older than Jason.) Both Jason and Theseus return to the cities of their fathers as strangers and as heirs to the throne. Theseus' sandals recall Jason's one-sandaled arrival. Both travel over the sea to distant and menacing kingdoms in ships bearing the fruit of the land's youth. Both face tests at the hands of a son of a god who intends to kill them. Both receive aid from a king's daughter, who has fallen in love with him.[19] Obviously, both must battle supernatural bulls who represent the earth god. Both also promise engagement to their respective helpers, and Ariadne, like Medea, was originally a goddess on Crete, one of vegetation and fertility, and a major one at that.[20] (The glowing crown was the vegetation goddess's leafy wreath.) Both abandon their foreign wives to take up with more suitable Greek brides. Both also lose their fathers (at least in some versions) as a result of their adventures. Both eventually become kings in tragic circumstances.

Some have argued that both myths are based upon rituals intended to usher young men into manhood.[21] This is an outgrowth of a school of thought that assumed that myths are *post hoc* rationalizations explaining the origin and functions of preexisting ritual acts. While there is undoubtedly an element of the young man's journey to manhood in these stories, it is difficult to imagine what other age the heroes could have in undertaking their adventures. Logically, there is a brief window between the end of childhood and the assumption of marriage and community responsibilities when young men could serve as symbolic or actual warriors and go out on an epic quest. Middle aged men or prepubescent boys would not fare as well.

Instead, there is another connection between Jason and Theseus that is much more intriguing. Nilsson argued that since Ariadne was a Minoan vegetation goddess, Theseus (whose name means, apparently, "the acknowledged one") was originally a Minoan male divinity or hero who descended into the Labyrinth, which represents the Underworld, to defeat the earth god (symbolized in the Minotaur), seize the goddess, and carry her off in marriage. This same story was retold more literally in a variant version in which Theseus attempts but fails to abduct Persephone, also originally a vegetation goddess, directly from the Underworld itself. Both variants became a part of the Theseus cycle, though not entirely harmoniously. The older version represented the pre–Greek idea of the triumph over death, and the latter the Archaic conception of the irresistible triumph of death.[22]

We thus have reproduced again the core actions of the Jason story, and again the reproduction of the old Mycenaean-Minoan relationship between the dying and rising god, his earth goddess consort, and the bull-form earth god who opposes him. The relationship between Theseus and Jason is perhaps therefore not one of shared ritual rites but instead of shared origin, variant local versions of the ancient god who may have been their shared progenitor.

HERACLES

The life of Theseus was modeled on that of Heracles, and like Theseus, Heracles was something of a latecomer to the roster of Argonauts, and not one who fit in particularly well with the existing myth. At times, it is denied that he ever sailed with Jason. At other times it is said that he began the voyage and left partway through. Still other, later writers make Heracles the commander of the mission and see him through to the end. This changing role for Greece's greatest hero reflects Heracles' increasing stature in mythic history over the course of centuries.

Heracles' mythic exploits are so numerous that an entire book would be required to do them justice; for our purposes only the merest sketch will have to suffice. Heracles was born in Thebes to a foreigner of Argive stock, a descendent of Perseus. He was a son of Zeus, but Hera was enraged by Zeus' infidelity and became Heracles' lifelong enemy. Hera tricked Zeus into promising his mistress's firstborn son would be king of Mycenae and then undercut Zeus by making his mistress first give birth to Heracles' twin by another father, Eurystheus. Heracles thus became subject to Eurystheus and was forced to perform twelve arduous labors for that king in penance for a murder he committed in a fit of madness. These labors are well known, including bouts of monster slaying or capture, voyages to distant realms, and a trip to the Underworld. He also undertook many other random adventures before, between, and after the labors. Originally, this entire body of myth had no fixed form (indeed they were likely once separate myths entirely), and only after the sixth century did the myriad tales of Heracles take shape as Twelve Labors and Incidental Adventures.[23] Finally, at the end of his life, Heracles fell victim to an angry wife, upset that he was taking up with another bride. She poisoned his tunic with the blood of a centaur, causing the hero's flesh to burn away. He built a funeral pyre and immolated himself. In the age of Homer and Hesiod, Heracles then dies and descends into the Underworld, where Odysseus encounters him. However, in the seventh a century BCE a new story took hold. Heracles instead became a god, rising up to join his father on Mt. Olympus and marry the goddess of youth. Copyists added this new information to passages in Hesiod and *The Odyssey* (where the Underworld Heracles is now merely an image of the hero) to reflect Heracles' now-divine status, in lines widely considered interpolations.[24]

There are two essential parallels to the Jason myth that are important for our purposes. First is the piecemeal way in which the Heracles cycle formed, and second is the similarity of some episodes of Heracles' labors to the mission Jason undertook. Let us begin with a brief discussion of Heracles' evolving myth.

Burkert, writing in the 1970s, suggested as others have, that the core Heracles myth dates back to the Neolithic—or even Paleolithic—in the form of a shaman who uses hunting magic to quest for powerful animals.[25] Given what we know about the standard set of images that emerge from altered states of consciousness, it is evident that no single heroic figure had a story told continuously from the Ice Age to the Roman Era; instead, the character of Heracles drew upon iconography and adventures of ancient vintage that emerged in many places from shamanic and priestly spirit voyages in which the hierophant became a powerful intercessor with animals and monsters. However, another school of thought sees in Heracles a Near Eastern god or analog of Gilgamesh who was transformed into a Greek hero in the adaptation.[26] These ideas are not mutually exclusive, though the degree to which one aspect of another predominates is debatable.

The iconography of Heracles draws on Near Eastern prototypes, including both Gilgamesh and the Sumerian-Akkadian god Ninurta ("Lord of Earth"). The latter personage was a renowned monster-slayer who killed twelve fabulous beasts, including a seven-headed serpent exactly parallel to the multi-headed Hydra Heracles felled. He further conducted battles in the Underworld. Ninurta is also the son of the storm god, just as Heracles was the son of Zeus the Thunderer.[27] However, as Jan N. Bremmer noted, the correspondences are not exact, and Heracles is not simply a literal translation of Ninurta to Greece. The idea of a series of labors may have carried through, with the Greeks adapting, subtracting from, and adding to the corpus at will. In different towns and at different times, different stories were told all across the Greek world. Only many centuries later did the labors take their standard form, and even then, new adventures continued to accrue to Heracles' expanding myth, including his voyage on the *Argo*, whose captain saw his own share of mythic accretions.

Among Heracles' canonical labors are three that are of especial interest to our inquiry, as well as Homer's report that Heracles' wounded Hades with an arrow. To take these in the order of most to least clear, we will begin with Heracles' descent into Hades to retrieve the hell-hound Cerberus, guardian of the Underworld, and bring him to King Eurystheus. This myth, which is the oldest of the above for which literary evidence remains, is literally a descent into the Underworld and clearly of a piece with the motif in the Jason, Perseus, and Theseus myths of the triumph over death. In the Underworld, Heracles threatened Hades with an arrow; freed Theseus, who became trapped fetching Persephone; and slaughtered some of Hades' cattle, about which more anon. Cerberus had three dogs' heads and a snake's tail, and he is the equivalent of the two monstrous lions that guard the Sumerian underworld and the composite monster (crocodile, lion, and hippopotamus) that lurked in the Egyptian underworld to eat the souls of the unworthy. Heracles' victory over Cerberus is therefore conceivably a Greek version of an ancient story of the admission of the soul to eternal life.[28]

In the *Iliad* Homer describes Heracles wounding Hera with a trident and then smiting Hades with an arrow, wounding the god so badly before the very gates of the Underworld that he fled to Olympus to seek Paean to heal him; yet as Nilsson noted, the name of the Underworld gates (*púlai*) was conflated with that of the city of Pylos (*Púlos*), and the myth later remodeled to represent Heracles' war on Pylos.[29] But before the Greeks transferred the story from the Underworld to the mortal plain, the story must once have been almost a repetition of the Cerberus episode, featuring the hero descending to the Underworld to attack Death himself, and thus overcome it. Later Greeks, as we have now repeatedly seen with Theseus and others, believed death unconquerable, and the older myths about gods or heroes who descended to the Underworld and returned were remodeled, removing the Underworld context or remaking it in the image of the new Greek Underworld of the Archaic age. It may also be significant that Homer ties this myth to the wounding of Hera, who in the age before Homer would have been an earth goddess also associated with the Underworld and the cycle of life and death. Like Perseus, Heracles attacks the goddess rather than marries her, and returns from the Underworld encounter much improved.

In a third instance of the repetition of this theme, Heracles travels west across the Ocean to the island of Erytheia where the monster Geryon, who combined three men into one, tended his cattle alongside those of Hades himself. En route, the heat of the sun so annoyed Heracles that he threatened Helios with an arrow, and the sun god gave him use of his golden cup to ride back to Greece across the Ocean after completing his labor. This cup was the bark whereby the sun rode from sunset to the land of sunrise each night, traveling across Ocean. Like Aea before it, Erytheia was once a fabulous land before being localized in the Atlantic Ocean. Heracles rustled the cattle by killing their guardians, Eurytion and his two (or more) headed dog Orthos. (Though, as Bruce Lincoln points out, the grammar in Hesiod's version of the story makes it possible that Geryon killed Eurytion and the dog in the oldest versions and was therefore a cattle rustler himself.[30]) Geryon then attacked, and Heracles killed him with an arrow and took the cattle. G. S. Kirk suggested that Geryon's cattle were originally the same as Hades,' possibly representing the souls of the dead, and Orthos originally Cerberus.[31] All of these cattle, Dimitri Nakassis argued, were identical with the cattle of the sun. The solar cattle and the underworld cattle are bifurcated version of a single herd which once grazed at the sun's gate to the Underworld before the unipolar vision of cosmic geography gave way to a bipolar east-west axis, separating the sun from the Underworld and the living from the dead.[32]

Thus Erytheia is yet another version of the Underworld, and the story another version of the myth of the hero descending into Hades and triumphing over death. This suggestion is paralleled in Watkins' linguistic evidence, which suggests the episode began as a Proto-Indo-European dragon-slaying myth,[33] which he elsewhere linked to the PIE hero's triumph over death, reinforcing the underworld imagery in the story by another means. Especially noteworthy is the depiction of this Underworld stand-in as a fantastic island, much like Aea, along the path of the Sun, again like Aea, and from which one returns by sailing on Ocean along the return route of the Sun. Not only is this identical in concept to Jason's journey, but as M. L. West noted in discussing Heracles, this conception of an Underworld where the sun traveled at night by ship is the same as the Egyptian Underworld,[34] and to which we can add the Sumerian. On that equation, incidentally, with the Near East sun god as the judge and ruler of the dead, Hades' and Helios' cattle are indistinguishable, reinforcing what we learned in chapter 3 about the cattle Jason encountered in an early *Argonautica* and Homer's appropriation of the incident for Odysseus in the *Odyssey*.

If this were not enough, Heracles made a thematically indistinguishable trip yet another time, in search of the Golden Apples of the Hesperides. These apples grew on a tree guarded by a dragon in a sacred grove on an island out on the far side of Ocean, originally in the west but later relocated in the north, at the end of a route complex enough to rival Jason's as the myth grew through accretion. The parallels to the Golden Fleece in its sacred grove are obvious, made more so by the observation of R. Roux that the Greek words for "apple" and "sheep" were the same, represented by *mêlon*, and suggesting a common origin for the symbols.[35] The islands of the Hesperides appear to be connected, Kirk says, to "the idea of an afterlife" or even the "Elysian Fields" of the blessed dead, according to Nilsson.[36] Indeed, the Greeks of the sixth century BCE saw the episode as a precursor to Heracles' apotheosis. The apples themselves may have originated as the food of the gods, a fruit of immortality or perhaps youth, which recalls the ambrosia the doves brought through the Clashing Rocks, which as we have seen may have in fact been related to the Golden Fleece in the earliest Argonaut epics. In the oldest version of the story, Heracles kills the dragon and takes the apples, while in later ones he tricks Atlas into performing the task. Either way the combination of golden treasure, tree, dragon, and island on the shore of Ocean irresistibly recalls the object of Jason's quest. Apollonius mentions the incident in the *Argonautica*, and there the serpent is named Ladon, which was seen as related to the name of one of the Underworld's rivers, Lethe,[37] thus again reinforcing the connection between the island of the Golden Apples, the island of the Golden Fleece, and the Underworld. It is unclear whether the Hesperides' adventure is an old myth or is a recent addition, so whether Jason's or Heracles' episode came first cannot be determined.

Heracles' name, "The Glory of Hera," has variously been reckoned as ironic, confusing, derived from a non–Greek word, or an attempt to appease the angered goddess. However, given the close similarities of Heracles' early exploits with those associated with the ancient earth deities, a more intriguing possibility is to suggest that the oldest Heracles was a hero or subsidiary divinity in service to an older form of Hera (the earth goddess) who was reconfigured as a son of Zeus after the old Mycenaean (or pre–Mycenaean) religion gave way to the supremacy of Zeus and a very popular hero needed a new divine patron.[38] West implies as much, in fact, suggesting that in the distant past Heracles may have originated as one of Hera's "year spirits,"[39] the dying and rising figure; but this was long forgotten by the Archaic, surviving only in scattered moments of myth. Burr C. Brundage argued that Heracles' mother Alcmene was in fact originally Hera herself, though his reason for doing so was a passage in Diodorus describing Hera's symbolic birthing of Heracles after his apotheosis.[40] It might be better instead to suggest that among those episodes folded into the legend of the strong man who came to be known as Heracles were several versions of the ancient Mycenaean tale of the hero who entered the Underworld for Hera. That in later myth Hera's opposition caused Heracles to suffer and die mirrors the story of the earth goddess and Velchanos or Inanna and Dumuzi; and it is not hard to see how in patriarchal, Zeus-centric stories the older Mycenaean mystery of the god who must die for his goddess could be re-imagined as the goddess's hatred for the dying hero.

Thus, in Perseus, Theseus, and Heracles we see the same basic story that forms the core of Jason's own tale—that of the hero who descends to the Underworld and returns. Two of these heroes, Perseus and Heracles, do so to kill and thus by violence triumph over death on the model of Baal. Two, Jason and Theseus, descend, defeat a monster, and in the process win the hand of a goddess, which is the reward for triumphing over death, on the model of Dumuzi. Whether one chooses to believe, as Kirk apparently felt, that this coincidence of motifs is the result of a common fairy-tale form, or whether the repetition points to an old Mycenaean (or earlier) story repeated and reinterpreted across many myths, the fact remains that Jason shares this motif with three Greek heroes of undoubted ancient origin. I would suggest that the inclusion of four versions of the story in Heracles' tale and two in Theseus' implies that the original story of the harrowing of hell was very old and told of many heroes in many cities. Perhaps each Mycenaean center had its own, or developed one from a common source: Perseus in Argolis, Theseus in Attica, Jason in Thessaly, and Heracles, well, most places and repeatedly. (His battle with a monstrous lion is repeated twice, too, indicating his myth was localized in many places simultaneously.) Versions of these stories mutated and some lost their Underworld connotation, and these stories recombined in the adventure cycles associated with the heroes who now bear multiple iterations of the same story.

Jason and the Gods

G. S. Kirk maintained that Jason, Perseus, and Heracles were "surely not" minor gods of any kind, faded or otherwise.[41] Yet he also maintained that these heroes' adventures might well trace their origins back before the Mycenaeans, long before Zeus reigned on Olympus and when the gods lived in the sea and under the earth. Elsewhere, he offered several other disconnected premises that together contradict his beliefs about the heroes' divine status:

- The women in many of these heroes' stories were once earth goddesses.
- The villains in many of these heroes' stories were once solar, earth, or underworld gods.
- The heroes interact with gods on more or less equal terms in the oldest versions of their stories.
- The lands to which these heroes traveled were originally either Underworld or divine territories.
- Heroic stories of monster slaying and city founding originally belonged to gods.
- Prior to Archaic Greece, Near East and Aegean mythological stories were told primarily if not exclusively about the gods.

Granted these premises, it seems logically impossible to make such a clean distinction between heroes and divinities. At some point, finding divine origins for every other aspect of a hero's tale must imply that the hero himself belonged once among the gods as well.

In the end, however, it matters little whether stories about gods devolved onto humans raised to heroic stature or whether former gods were reconceived as heroes.[42] Most mythological characters contain elements of both. It would be as useful to argue whether the chess board is white with black squares or black with white squares when it is in truth a patchwork composite. However, in the final analysis the oldest sections of the heroic myths must originally have been told of gods of some sort, and arguing whether Jason or Perseus acquired a god's tale or whether the god became the hero is a semantic difference that tells us nothing in particular about either hero or legend since the heroic name merely signifies a collection of human and superhuman attributes that blended into one whether there ever was a man or god by that name.

However, the gods themselves in their Olympian splendor are close compatriots of heroes, and in the case of Jason, three goddesses and Zeus dominate his divine retinue. In the oldest known version of Jason's story, the one recorded in Homer, it is Hera who is Jason's divine helper, the goddess who loved the hero greatly. On the oldest known images of Jason, it is Athena who stands beside him. Among the Archaic poets, Aphrodite takes the lead in aiding Jason in achieving his triumph. Much later, Apollonius would weave these disparate stories together and imagine Hera working with Athena to employ Aphrodite's aid. But this is simply an attempt to reconcile divergent and contradictory traditions, much as Apollonius would include both Mopsus and Idmon aboard the *Argo* when the ship's seer's name differed in variant tales.

Given that there was no fixed form for the Argonauts' voyage or a fixed catalog of ship mates and each poet reinterpreted them anew, the implication, therefore, is that many variants of Jason's story existed prior to Homer. Some of these must have featured Hera as the hero's helper, in keeping with her most ancient role from Mycenaean days as the patron and guardian of heroes. Other versions must have made the divine helper Athena, who succeeded to Hera's old role as the patroness of heroes. Finally, versions with Aphrodite must also have existed, perhaps abstracting from the marriage and love of Jason and Medea.

And yet this solution, while logical, seems somewhat incomplete. Is it entirely coincidence that the three Greek goddesses who feature as Jason's helpers in versions of his story are also the three goddesses most closely tied to aspects of the Near East goddess Inanna/Ishtar? That goddess, who was coeval with the Mycenaeans and predated them by a millennium was one of the most widespread and most worshipped in the Near East under her plethora of names: Innana, Ishtar, Astarte, etc. In her sphere of influence she possessed powers that are later associated with many of the Greek goddesses:

- She is a goddess of fertility and agriculture.
- She is a goddess associated with sexuality.
- She is a goddess who presides over marriage, especially sacred royal marriages.
- She is a goddess who oversees the course of earthly life.
- She is a goddess who is the Queen of Heaven.
- She is a goddess who presides over war, known as the "dance of Inanna."
- She is a goddess who serves as the personal protector of the deserving.[43]

It is commonly thought that Aphrodite is a Greek importation of Inanna, not least because Aphrodite is associated in myth with the dying and rising Adonis, who is closely modeled on Tammuz/Dumuzi. However, it can equally well be argued that in receiving myths from the Near East, a goddess like Inanna could be interpreted in her many aspects as not just Aphrodite (goddess of sexuality) but also Athena (warrior, protector) and Hera (Queen of Heaven, goddess of marriage, and, in her oldest form, earth goddess of fertility). I would suggest that the oldest Jason myths in the Mycenaean (or even pre–Mycenaean era) would have featured a goddess who shares these multiple and overlapping traits. This goddess was probably known as Hera among the Mycenaeans (though they also had their Shield Goddess, who was probably Athena). As the Greek pantheon was remodeled in the wake of Zeus' ascendency, the powers of the former chief goddess were apportioned among the other goddesses. Demeter inherited fertility (and Iasion); Aphrodite love. Athena took over war (likely during the Mycenaean period itself), and Hera retained little but marriage and preeminence in heaven. Thus, in the hero tales, including Jason's, the interventions of the goddess became divided among several as the old tale was reworked, thus producing the confusing cacophony of goddesses who aid Jason and the sometimes strained logic used to introduce all of them into his myth. And of course, the original goddess figure herself was remade as Medea (see below).

By the same token, the ascendency of the worship of Zeus over his rival Poseidon led to another interesting facet of the myth, the increasingly prominent role of Zeus in the proceedings. The earliest Jason stories say little of Zeus for the most part. In fact, even Zeus' most prominent aspect in the myth, the Golden Fleece dedicated to him, is not universally recognized as his. Some authors report instead that Phrixus dedicated the Golden Fleece to Ares, and it is always said to hang in a grove or temple to Ares—not Zeus. It would make logical sense to have the Fleece belong to the god in whose enclosure it hangs, and this may well have been the original version of the story. This is reinforced when we recognize that Ares—the god of violence whose companions are *Phobos* and *Deimos*, Fear and Terror— may originally have been situated in the Underworld,[44] and may have been a god of Death before the characters of Hades and Ares were entirely separate. And of course, as at Thebes, Ares is associated with a large snake, another Underworld symbol.[45] Once again, the land of Aea is closely tied to the Underworld, even in its most sacred grove, which retains memories of the old chthonic gods.

But later Zeus became more important, reflecting his growing role in the Greek pantheon after the Mycenaean age and his eventual identification as the central, ethereal, and somewhat remote figure in Greek religious life. The Golden Fleece became attached to Zeus; Zeus the all-seeing was said to have ordained Jason's quest in order to make up for the lie that Phrixus had to die in Zeus' name. It is by Zeus' grace that the *Argo* is granted immunity from destruction or shipwreck. As though to solidify the connection, myth began to speak of a plank of oak from Zeus' sacred grove in Dodona being placed in the *Argo* itself. It is Zeus who must consent to allowing the Argonauts to drive away the Harpies he had sent to Phineus. Zeus too takes anger at the murder of Apsyrtus and orders Jason's and Medea's purification by Circe. True, Apollonius' Zeus is a remote figure and in Apollonius, the poet explains that Hera and the other goddesses are acting largely and initially without the knowledge of Zeus. This may be a memory of an older story that lacked the king of the gods; however, Apollonius specifically compares Jason to Zeus in describing his armor as glimmering like lightning during a storm.[46] Both god and hero are reared in a remote cave (Chiron's and the cave on Crete), both struggle against tyrannical kings (Pelias and Cronus), and both, of course, are married to a goddess following an epic struggle. Where Pindar had seen Jason as the image of Apollo or Ares, now he is Zeus. (Apollonius also repeats the earlier authors' comparisons to Apollo and Ares in the preceding lines.[47]) In Valerius Flaccus, Jupiter (Zeus) is not only supreme but ubiquitous. He is omniscient, and his will puts all actions into motion and determines their outcome.

Jason and the Villains: Pelias and Aeëtes

But if Jason's divine helpers gained Olympian stature until even Zeus himself entered into his myth, those who opposed Jason shared a less august fate. We have already seen that the king who sent Perseus on his quest, Polydectes, seems to have originally been an Underworld god, identified with Hades. We have also seen that the king who challenged Theseus, Minos, though named a son of Zeus, is through the Minotaur if in no other way closely related to the Cretan religion and its bull symbols. And we have seen that Heracles encountered stand-ins for the Underworld god. Another of his labors, the cleaning of King Augeas' stable, is closely related to the sun god. The cattle of Augeas are those of the sun, and Augeas' name ("the shining one") belongs etymologically to words associated with the sun. However, since in ancient Near East mythologies the sun god and the underworld/earth god were the same or close partners, it is no wonder that the ancient sources are divided whether Augeas was the son of Helios or Poseidon. At any rate, since Perseus, Theseus, and Heracles all encountered villains who were degraded versions of or replacements for the former Mycenaean (or pre–Mycenaean) earth gods, it is unsurprising that the two kings who challenge Jason to his tasks display these same affinities.

Pelias was reckoned the son of Poseidon, and he made sacrifices to that god while denying honors to Hera (or, in the more lurid version, committed murder in her sanctuary).

Pelias had his own mythology independent of Jason. Born to Poseidon by a mortal, he was suckled by a mare and his twin, Neleus of Pylos, by a dog. Later, Pelias promised his daughter's hand to the one who could yoke a boar and a lion to a single chariot, an adventure won when Apollo deceived him by giving King Admetos of Pherai a chariot with the beasts already bound to it. This little story has clear echoes of Jason, Medea, Aeëtes, and the bulls. According to myth, Pelias found his mother being abused at the court of Cretheus of Iolcus by Sidero, the king's wife. Pelias killed her in Hera's sanctuary, and Cretheus married Pelias' mother, thus allowing Pelias to assume the throne even though his mother had borne a son, Aeson, to Cretheus. Pelias is an ancient mythological figure, mentioned in both the *Iliad* and the *Odyssey*, though strangely not as Jason's villain. Homer merely states that "Poseidon, shaker of the land" fathered him, that he lived at Iolcus, and that his mother gave birth to Aeson. Given that the former Mycenaean earth god Poseidon is his father, it is perhaps significant that Pelias shares his name with Mt. Pelion, and both derive from the pre–Indo-European word *pala*, for rock[48] (though the ancients fancifully argued that his name derives from the bruise, or *pelion*, left on his face when a horse stepped on him[49]). In some form, there must have been once a connection between Pelias, a chthonic power such as an earth god, and Mt. Pelion, the spot of rock where Jason grew up. It is possible that "the rocky one" was an epithet for the old earth god, much the way Polydectes seems to reflect an old name for Hades, and that the god was replaced with a king in the myth.

As Jason himself notes in Valerius Flaccus' *Argonautica*, Pelias finds his functional twin in Aeëtes of Colchis, who shares with Pelias a desire to rid himself of a troublesome stranger by demanding Jason perform tasks and then refusing the hero a promised boon. Aeëtes' name tells us rather little, since it means simply "the man of Aea."[50] However, as we have seen, the land of Aea may take its name from the Akkadian and Babylonian goddess of the dawn, Aya, wife of the sun, or from an Indo-European word for the sun's radiance,[51] so in this sense Aeëtes may be some garbled transmission of an old name or epithet for a sun god. This suspicion finds confirmation in the universal description of Aeëtes as the son of Helios, the Greek sun god. Since we have so far seen that in the oldest myths kings seem to take the place of gods and share their names with aspects of the deities, it is not very far-fetched to presume that the oldest layers of the Jason myth must have featured the Sun God himself rather than a mortal king. Indeed, for other reasons, several scholars have suggested this same point.[52] If it was recognized that the Near Eastern sun god operated under the earth as well as in the sky, then it must have been easy to connect the underground sun erupting with each dawn to the god whose most terrible power was the shaking of the earth. Therefore, it seems unlikely to be coincidence that Pelias, son of chthonic Poseidon and the substitute earth god, functions identically with Aeëtes, son of the Sun and the substitute sun god. When operating under the ground they became functionally the same.

Jason and Medea

Further, as we know, in Near Eastern belief, the sun god was not merely the light of the earth but also an underworld deity who descended into the underworld each night and judged the dead as he travelled back to the gate of dawn. Thus it surprises us very little that the Gate of Aya, through which the sun rose each morning, was in Mesopotamian belief also an entrance to the Underworld itself.[53] Once again the Underworld motif makes itself plain. The voyage to Aya is a trip to the gate of the Underworld, which came to be taken as a name for the whole.[54] It is also interesting to note that the Gate of Aya was also the Gate of Inanna (because her evening star, Venus, rose there).[55] If a hero were to seek a goddess in the Underworld, the gate of Inanna and Aya is the place to find her. It is surely no coincidence that the goddesses Jason finds there, including Hera, Aphrodite (Venus), and Medea all share aspects of Inanna.

Medea is a special case, but not entirely unique. We have seen that in the time before Hesiod she was counted among the immortals. She is, depending on the tradition, either the sister or niece of the great sorceress Circe; and many scholars beginning as far back as Strabo have plausibly argued that both Medea and Circe were originally a single divine figure. The name of Circe at first seems unrelated to our discussion, since it derives from the Greek word for hawk or falcon (*kirkos*). However, in the Semitic languages the word for falcon was "*ayyah*" (Hebrew), which M. L. West suggests gave us the name Circe when the old goddess of the dawn and sexuality, Aya, was brought into Greek from a Semitic source which had jumbled the Akkadian name with a Semitic sound-alike. Circe, in the oldest references, in the *Odyssey*, lives in a land where the sun rises and the goddess of Dawn lives. This island was named Aeaea, obviously derived from Aea, and was originally positioned in the river Phasis and held the Golden Fleece.[56] Circe would therefore have originally been Aya, the wife of the Sun,[57] but a version who absorbed other Near East goddess attributes, including those of various earth and underworld deities.[58] It has been suggested, plausibly though not definitively, that Circe was originally Jason's helper,[59] and only later did the character fully differentiate from the incipient Medea, with whom she shares so much common heritage, when Homer appropriated Circe from Jason for Odysseus. If so, there would then exist a much closer etymology related to the sun, as opposed to Medea, whose etymology is uncertain but may relate to the Greek word for "to plan" or "to contemplate"[60] and apparently referred to the idea of cunning or intelligence. If so, it is interesting that this name draws on an attribute, though not necessarily a Mycenaean one, of Athena, the hero's guide and Jason's companion on the Douris cup—the goddess of wisdom. In the nineteenth century it was suggested that Medea's name derives from a word meaning "to care for,"[61] also appropriate for a hero's helper, and especially for a goddess who loves a hero, such as Aphrodite or Inanna. The name may otherwise be of non–Greek origin.

Medea herself is a complex figure. She is Jason's helper, the murderess of Pelias, the restorer of Aeson, the slayer of Jason's children, the attempted killer of Theseus, the ancestor of the Medes of Iran, and the wife of Achilles in the afterlife. However, as Fritz Graf discussed, the earliest Medea is simply the divine daughter who helps the hero (if she did even that much at first); "all the other episodes appear to be chance additions, accrued during centuries of storytelling."[62] Therefore, in seeking out her origins, we can discard the episode at Corinth and its aftermath, stories that belong properly to a study of Medea rather than one concerned primarily with Jason, the hero who through the unfortunate waxing of Medea's fame and influence found himself brought low when myth demanded a victim for Medea's wrath. Instead, we can turn toward those scholars who sought the origins of Medea in goddess figures who would have decayed or been transfigured into a princess, much the way Ariadne had once been a Minoan goddess. In this, the most common suggestion is that Medea was once an "earth mother" or even "a goddess comparable to Hera."[63] The idea being that originally divine female figures were all aspects of a single earth goddess whose powers became divided among more specialized deities and whose divided characters gave rise to the princesses and sorceresses of myth. Of course, just as the heroes combined aspects of gods and men, Medea was not "merely" Hera or Inanna reduced, but a composite figure drawing on goddesses and the needs of narrative.

Thus, approaching the story from this angle we once again confirm that like Ariadne and Medusa before them, Medea and Circe hold within themselves elements of the earth goddess, elements we already inferred from studying Jason's role in the descent narrative and its clear parallels with the spectrum of goddesses with annually dying consorts, such as Hera-Velchanos and Inanna-Dumuzi. This offers additional support for the hypothesis that Jason's voyage was first imagined as a trip across the waters of death to the Underworld, and Medea's love for the hero originally a sacred marriage of the dying-and-rising vegetation god with the earth goddess.

Jason, the Argonauts and the Ship of the Dead

A final word needs to be said about Jason's steersmen, whom Fontenrose has linked to Charon, the ferryman who carries souls across the waters of death to their final reckoning in the depths of the Underworld.[64] In the earliest Greek myths, it is unclear how the dead were envisioned as traveling to Hades, and the first known guide of the dead was Hermes, attested in the Archaic period. There is no mention of Charon in Homer or Hesiod, and it is assumed that he became attached to the Underworld sometime during the Archaic period, though his exact origin is unknown. He is first mentioned only in the sixth century BCE,[65] in a poem called *Minyas*, of which a fragment survives in Pausanias: "Then the boat on which embark the dead, that the old ferryman, Charon, used to steer, they found not within its moorings."[66] Given that the Jason story predates that of Charon, Fontenrose's claim cannot be exactly accurate, but his general point is likely quite correct: The passengers on the *Argo* have a clear relationship with death and the dead, and the voyage of the *Argo* is very much a voyage into the realm of death.

The first to pilot the *Argo* was Tiphys, whose name recalls that of Typhon, the monster who attacked Zeus and was sometimes identified with Charon. Another who helmed the boat after Tiphys' death was Erginos (according to Herodorus and Valerius Flaccus). This figure was variously called the son of Poseidon, Klymenos or Periklymenos. The latter names are epithets associated with Hades. Hades, Charon, and Erginos all share a pair of traits: Stark white hair and unnatural strength. Fontenrose further discusses the coincidence of Tiphys' and Idmon's deaths among the Mariandyonoi, a tribe who worshipped a dying and rising vegetation god, who along the Black Sea routes had various names, including those of the Argonauts Tiphys, Idmon, and Hylas. This vegetation god had a dual nature, as god of vegetation and also as demon of death.[67] The implication, of course, is that the Greeks who told the story of the one-time vegetation god Jason identified these characters as analogs to Jason's own story and brought them aboard his ferry to the Underworld as fellow-travelers.

The steersman after Tiphys was Ankaios according to Apollonius, who was again a son of Poseidon, but whose brothers were named Eurypylos and Periklymenos, again both names given to Hades.[68] Another Periklymenos was commonly reckoned an Argonaut himself, and this Periklymenos was the warrior who opposed Heracles at Pylos. As we have seen, the Pylos incident was an attempt to transfer the Homeric tale of Heracles' wounding of Hades at the gates (*púlai*) of the Underworld to the city of Pylos. Thus, Periklymenos, too, originated in the god Hades. Fontenrose argued that Ankaios was also a vegetation god in origin,[69] and this Argonaut's death at the hands of boar recalls the myth of Attis, the dying and rising vegetation god who originated in Tammuz and died the same way.

Another who volunteered to steer the *Argo*, Nauplios, was again a son of Poseidon, and also associated with death. In myth, one of his name killed unruly children sent to him and sailed the waters bringing death to unfortunate mariners who crossed his path. Finally, Euphemus, yet another son of Poseidon, is sometimes said to have steered the *Argo*. His name, "the original euphemism," was apparently meant to conceal his true name, again identified by Fontenrose as Hades.[70] In short, in the Argonaut myth, the sea appears to originally have been synonymous with the Underworld, and Poseidon's sons with Hades and his ferryman, Charon. Given that the oldest form of Poseidon likely rested on his subterranean earth-shaking functions (where the sun went at night), this identification is unsurprising, and takes us back to Mycenaean myths.

The very builder of the *Argo* shares some of these selfsame traits. In later Antiquity Argus the shipbuilder was considered distinct from the other two Argus characters of mythology, the hundred-eyed monster devoted to Hera and the hero Argus who killed the monster Echidna and a terrible bull. The hero and the monster originated in the same figure, and both wore a bull's hide as their chosen costume, a costume Apollonius assigned to the *Argo's* builder, implying a familial relationship if not identification. Fonterose believed that the shipbuilder derived from the ancient "hero-monster," and noted that all three of these characters were closely associated with underworld or chthonic power, as well as the goddess Hera.[71] This same Hera was once the Minoan-Mycenaean earth goddess, so the relationship of the earth goddess to chthonic powers is obvious.

The name of the *Argo* itself, alternately said by the ancients to descend from the name Argus or from the word *argos* meaning "swift," brings to mind Bürger's line from "Leonore," that "the dead travel quick,"[72] which has an echo in the twelfth century Byzantine *Digenes Akrites* cycle where in one episode the dead carry off the living on a swift horse (as in later Greek folklore, when Charon carries off the dead thusly), and in the Book of Job where the days of life are said to pass away like swift ships.[73] In Virgil, Charon's boat travels lightly on the Styx because souls have no weight, but when Aeneas boards the boat, it lowers down into the waters of the river, the sutures cracking, and water seeping in. More directly, *Argo* echoes the *Epic of Gilgamesh*, when Gilgamesh rides Urshanabi's swift boat across the Waters of Death to the land of Utnapishtim and covers a journey that should take six weeks in only three days. Recall, too, the Babylonian belief that Gilgamesh was in death himself the ferryman of the dead.

Of course, we have no way of knowing how fast the Greek dead were thought to fly, but Mycenaean and Homeric imagery gives the soul wings, implying a belief in quick travel, just as the original Greek guide of the dead, Hermes, was the supernaturally swift messenger of the gods, who, interestingly, was also the killer of the hundred-eyed monster Argus, the "Argeiphontes." The latter's name, like that of *Argo*, comes from *argos*, which has an additional meaning, "white," "shining," or "bright," as in his all-seeing eyes. (For this reason, Arthur B. Cook identified the *Argo* and Argus with Argive Zeus, making the ship Zeus' own.[74]) It may derive ultimately from the Proto-Indo-European root *Ar* in the sense of "to get" or "to earn," a reference to *Argo*'s mission to retrieve the soul of Phrixus from Aea, or the Underworld. However, just to make things interesting, S. Davis held in the 1950s on the grounds of comparative mythology that Argus was originally a dragon or serpent slain by a pre–Greek god replaced later by Hermes Argeiphontes, whose unusual epithet was etymologized backward into the word *argos*, swift or bright. This reading was confirmed via linguistic analysis in Calvert Watkins' more recent massive study of ancient Proto-Indo-European serpent myths, *How to Kill a Dragon* (1996).[75] Thus the whole complex of Argus and *Argo* images was in truth yet another iteration of the hero vs. serpent myth (with the *Argo* as the ship of the underworld dragon?) since, as Davis wrote, "Apollo, Kadmus, Perseus, Jason, Heracles, and perhaps Hermes, and their subsequent successors in European literature, are all varied aspects of one and the same hero who is reputed to slay a dragon."[76] And the serpent, of course, is associated with the underworld and chthonic power.

As Fontenrose summarizes:

> Hence every steersman, lookout, builder, seer, and guide of the *Argo* proves to have manifold connections with demonic powers of sea, land, and the underworld. It is likely that every one is a form of the boatman of the dead, Charon, who, as I have pointed out, has also a more general character of a spirit of death. [...] If the *Argo*'s pilot is drawn ultimately from the Stygian boatman, then we are justified in agreeing with those scholars who have held that the Argonautic voyage has its roots in tales of voyages to the other world.[77]

However, since Jason and the *Argo* seem older than Charon and his ferry, it would be closer to the facts to say that the pilots of *Argo* and their passengers are quite closely tied to the realm of the dead. Perhaps in the evolving myth, characters who in their home cities were once thought to have descended to the Underworld and returned became passengers on Jason's ship, companions in a voyage of the damned. They may have been brought aboard by a process of synchretism whereby lesser characters were magnetically attracted to the greater hero whose tale mirrored their own. Thus, the dying vegetation deities encountered en route to Colchis were subsumed by Jason just as the vegetation god Hyacinthus was subsumed by Apollo and any number of local strongmen disappeared into Heracles.

If the steersmen of the *Argo* were truly ferrymen of the dead, they would have to have come into the myth not from Charon but from the ferrymen or dread pilots who ferried souls across the waters of death in other mythologies, both Indo-European and non–Indo-European. The pilot of the boat that crosses the waters of death in the *Epic of Gilgamesh* is one such figure; the ferryman of the dead who personifies old age is a common feature of Indo-European mythologies and is apparently quite ancient, perhaps a common Proto-Indo-European inheritance.[78] We have seen in the Greek lands that the Minoan-Mycenaean Ayia Triada sarcophagus and later Mycenaean funerary art suggests that a journey the underworld was conceived as a voyage by boat over the sea as early as the fourteenth century BCE. If a specific ferryman did not exist in Mycenaean mythology per se, he must have existed in the stories the Greeks took over in assimilating and creating the Jason epic from their Minoan, Mycenaean, and Near East sources.

However, the exact configuration of the Minoan and Mycenaean underworlds is unknown, so the degree to which Jason's Aea/Colchis matches these realms of the dead cannot be determined with specificity, only perhaps in the most general terms. In our next chapter we will compare Aea to the Greek and Near East lands of the dead to show just how closely Aea conforms to ancient conceptions of the underworld.

7

The Traveler
The Descent into the Underworld

When Apollonius of Rhodes set about creating his epic *Argonautica*, he drew inspiration from Homer's *Odyssey*, a complex and colorful poem which in turn had drawn on a still earlier version of Jason's voyage in order to flesh out the itinerary of Odysseus. Apollonius included encounters with or equivalents to nearly all of the adventures that Odysseus had experienced in the long slog from Troy to Ithaca, all that is except for one notable exception:

> And now she [Odysseus' ship] reached earth's limits, the deep stream of the Ocean, where the Cimmerian people's land and city lie, wrapt in a fog and cloud. Never on them does the shining sun look down with his beams, as he goes up the starry sky or as again toward earth he turns back from the sky, but deadly night is spread abroad over these hapless men. On coming here, we beached our ship and set the sheep ashore, then walked along the Ocean-stream until we reached the spot foretold by Circe. [...] So when with prayers and vows I had implored the peoples of the dead, I took the sheep and cut their throats over the pit, and forth the dark blood flowed. Then gathered there spirits from out of Erebus[1] ["darkness," i.e. the Underworld] of those now dead and gone,— brides, and unwedded youths, and worn old men, delicate maids with hearts but new to sorrow, and many pierced with brazen spears, men slain in fight, wearing their blood-stained armor. In crowds around the pit they flocked from every side, with awful wail. Pale terror seized me.[2]

In Book XI of the *Odyssey*, Odysseus travels to an entrance to the Underworld, located like Jason's Aea, at the farthest reaches of earth along Ocean, and he converses with the shades of the dead, an action not repeated in Apollonius' *Argonautica*. Odysseus sacrifices some sheep, and their blood draws the hungry dead to the surface, where they speak with the terrified hero after consuming the sacrificial blood. In what appears to be an interpolation, Odysseus also seems to be *in* the underworld, viewing characters such as Sisyphus and Tantalus within Hades while also described as standing *outside* the underworld. Apparently, someone added material from a poem about a downward descent to Odysseus' necromancy at the Underworld's edge.[3]

A dramatic encounter with the Underworld is one of the epic hero's most important tasks, yet Apollonius neglected to assign one to Jason. There are two schools of thought as to why. One set of scholars argues that Apollonius purposely omitted an Underworld itinerary to reinforce his status as a poet independent of slavish devotion to Homeric models.[4] This may have been true for Apollonius, but it does not explain the absence of an Underworld

This eighteenth-century illustration from a German edition of the *Odyssey* depicts Odysseus calling forth the shades of the dead by digging a pit and conducting a sacrifice. The poet of the *Orphic Argonautica* used this scene as a model for the dark rites Orpheus uses to call up Hecate and Pandora from the Underworld in order to secure the Golden Fleece (Beinecke Rare Book and Manuscript Library, Yale University).

voyage in the writings of every other ancient writer whose work survives. Clearly, the mythic tradition does not include an explicit trip to the House of Hades. The other school believes that Apollonius viewed the entire Argonautic journey as a *katabasis*, thus rendering redundant another explicit voyage to Hades.[5] This idea comes closer to the weight of the evidence, which, as this book has made clear, finds the impetus for Jason's journey to Colchis in an ancient deity's descent into the Underworld. Expanding this idea beyond the special case of Apollonius is not without its critics, of course. Classical philologist Paul Dräger emphasized that "People's opinion that the *Argonautica* formed originally a catabasis is as old [...] as it is wrong. Only Apollonius made the voyage of the Argonauts to Colchis into a catachthonic [Underworld] journey."[6] It is difficult to disentangle exactly how much of the Argonaut myth was Apollonius' own creation and how much drew upon older sources; however, as we have seen, Underworld themes are prevalent not just in Apollonius' *Argonautica* but throughout the Jason myth in all its forms, including those that predate Apollonius. Apollonius did not invent (or make use of) the tradition of Jason's descent into the dragon's belly, an Underworld motif; nor did he invent the traditions which tied Jason's quest to the magic of healing, renewed youth, and immortality. He did not invent the imagery of the shaman's otherworldly journeys inherent in Jason's quest, nor the suggestion that the retrieval of the Golden Fleece was a mission to retrieve the "spirit" of dead Phrixus from a land of monsters, much as Orpheus tried to retrieve Eurydice from Hades. And he did not invent the connections that many of the Argonauts share with the Underworld.

However, given the lack of a direct link between the Golden Fleece and Jason before the seventh century, an objection could be raised that Aea was not associated with Jason at first either. This might seem to be confirmed by the clear link between Phrixus and Aeëtes in the seventh-century *Aegimius*, probably written sometime before Mimnermus linked Jason and the Fleece. However, Jason is clearly linked to Medea and Aeëtes in Hesiod, and to Aeëtes in Homer, so primacy must be assigned to Jason's claim on Aea, even absent the Fleece, with Phrixus becoming attached to the land later when his myth was joined to Jason's.

This chapter will examine Colchis/Aea for evidence, through comparison with other Greek myths and practices and related Near East mythology and iconography, that this fantastic land was once the Underworld in an ancient version of the Jason myth. To do so, we must first look at the real archaeology of the region of Colchis in Georgia before examining Greek and Near Eastern conceptions of the realm of the dead.

The Real Colchis

The land of Colchis occupies the western shore of the Black Sea in what is today the country of Georgia and parts of northeastern Turkey. Unfortunately, due to a combination of political isolation and instability and historic scholarly uninterest in the region, it is not as well explored as many ancient sites.[7] There is some ambiguous evidence that the name is preserved in Linear B, in the form of *ko-ki-da* (which may only be a personal, not place, name),[8] but there is no context for claiming a relationship to the story of Jason, especially since possible analogs for the more ancient and relevant names of Aeaea (Circe's island) and Aeëtes, a_3-*wa-ja* and a_3-*wa-ta* respectively, also exist.[9] *Ko-ki-da*, if it does refer to Colchis, does not appear on the same tablet—or even in the same country—as the tablet claimed to have Jason's name. The word read as "Jason" is listed on a tablet at Pylos, and *ko-ki-da* at Knossos, on Crete (but then the Aean words are also distributed among the same two cities). Based on these uncertain inscriptions, Georgian researchers have promoted the idea that the Mycenaeans had contact with, or at least knowledge of, Colchis and that an otherwise unattested Kingdom of Colchis must have existed c. 1500 BCE but this is highly speculative given the extant evidence. A stronger case could be made for Mycenaeans in the Crimea, or the Bulgarian coast. As we have seen, there is some circumstantial evidence for contact between the Black Sea and Mycenaean Greece, but this evidence is not conclusive. The oft-repeated claim that "the anchors of Mycenaean ships" have been found "all along the Black Sea coasts,"[10] thus proving Mycenaean sea voyages to Colchis, is a myth. What have been found are stone anchors *in the Aegean style* (whose manufacture cannot be determined), and even these have been found only in Bulgaria, on the Black Sea's *west* coast, far from Colchis.

Herodotus believed that the Colchians were the descendants of Egyptians, based on their shared practice of circumcision and their shared manufacture of linen.[11] The people of Colchis are described as having dark skin, not because they are Egyptian, as Herodotus thought, but because they were associated with the land of the sunrise, where early Greeks thought the rising sun burned them each dawn. Though this ancient speculation of Egyptian origin has given rise to flights of Afrocentric fantasy (whereby Jason's voyage was "really" a pilgrimage to learn from an African culture[12]), the archaeological evidence shows no sign of Egyptian presence in Colchis. Instead, the region, like most others on the Black Sea coast, had an indigenous population that gradually experienced Greek settlement in the seventh and sixth centuries BCE, becoming partially Hellenized during the period of colonization.

The ancient writers said that the Henioks (or Heniochi) were the oldest populations of Colchis, but modern researchers mostly believe that this was a composite term for a plethora of indigenous groups that later gave rise to the Abkhazians and other peoples of the Caucasian coast.[13] There has also been some unconfirmed speculation that these groups, or at least the nearby Achaioi (cf. Achaeans) were Greek migrants escaping the Mycenaean collapse,[14] but archaeology does not recognize this. The earliest cultures of the region are poorly studied, but it appears that around the third millennium BCE there were relatively few public buildings but a well-developed metalworking industry in gold, silver, and bronze. Intriguingly, the central hearths of houses were frequently decorated with images of rams.[15] A "proto-Colchian" culture developed between the middle second millennium and early first millennium BCE, the Early and Middle Bronze Age in the region, with characteristically elaborate bronze artifacts, including decorated axes and images of animals.[16] The late Bronze Age civilization of the southwestern coast of the Black Sea is referred to archaeologically as the "Colchian culture," and it is best known for its high quality metalwork, in gold, iron, and other metals, as early as the late second millennium BCE, roughly contemporaneous with early Dark Age Greece. It is frequently claimed that this culture was known as the Qulha or Qolha among the Uratians, a northern Anatolian people of the ninth to seventh centuries BCE, who in turn gave the term "Colchis" to the Greeks. This leads to a logical impasse, of course; for if Colchian culture can be traced only to the period after the Mycenaean collapse, then logically, it cannot have been the inspiration for Aeëtes' kingdom, which on other grounds we have seen was originally considered a fantastic land of no fixed geography with clear ties (via Mycenaean Iolcus) to the Bronze Age. It was only in the seventh century that the Argonauts' voyage was reinterpreted as one to Colchis.

The land of the Georgian coast does not quite conform to the impression the literary evidence leaves of Jason's Colchis, which interestingly is never clearly described, as though it were always something of a hazy fantasy that sat uneasily beside the real land identified later with it. The real-life region is swampy, frequently flooded, and (in the Bronze Age) heavily forested with deciduous trees and bushes that grew large enough to give the appearance of trees. The land is also very wet, receiving an average of roughly five to seven feet (1500–2200 mm) of rain each year.[17] While this description conforms somewhat to the heavy mist Apollonius says Hera sent to give the Argonauts cover in Colchis, this wet, swampy region is in general quite a poor analog to the glorious kingdom of the sun at the edge of the known world. The mist, incidentally, is not original to the Jason story but is Apollonius' version of the "dark clouds" with which Athena covered Odysseus on his arrival in the lands of Alcinous, which story Apollonius used as a model for the Argonauts' arrival in Colchis. The real Colchis does, however, have native oak trees, which agrees with the oak on which the Golden Fleece hung.

Settlers from Miletus founded Greek colonies in Colchis at Phasis, Dioscuria, and Gyenos by no later than the sixth century BCE. In doing so, they applied the myth of Jason and the Argonauts to the lands they colonized, drawing on ideas and themes that had been incorporated in epic poetry, such as Eumelus' *Corinthiaca* the century before. Thus, the colony at Phasis takes its name from the river in Jason's Colchis. The approach to the city of Phasis earned the name "the Plain of Circe" after the sorceress whose island stood beside Aea. The surrounding region absorbed Greek political and culture influence and in so doing became politically organized under indigenous leadership, forming the Kingdom of Colchis, which lasted from the sixth to first centuries BCE.[18] Just before the Greek conquest, the interior city of Vani in Colchis produced a great deal of gold luxury objects, and the city continued to be a metalworking center until the end of the Kingdom of Colchis. It is sometimes said that the Greeks modeled Aeëtes' city on the wealth of Vani, whose stone walls and guardian goddess recall the *Orphic Argonautica*'s description of the enclosure of the Fleece,[19] but if this happened it was only centuries after Aea had already entered myth, since the city of Vani did not exist when Jason's story was first told. Given that this kingdom came into existence far later than Jason's story, its history and achievements, while impressive, are beyond our scope.

It is therefore logically impossible that the Black Sea coast of Georgia and eastern Turkey was the original destination of Jason and his heroic crew. One more fact mitigates against Colchis as the original destination of the *Argo*'s journey. By simple syllogism, some have argued that Jason's Colchis must have been a real place for the Mycenaeans because Iolcus was real, and a myth with one real location must necessarily discuss other real places.[20] Unless one is willing to argue that every Greek mythological location, including the Islands of the Blessed, Hyperborea, and the Underworld are also real (and not just "inspired" by "rumors" of real places), this is a logically problematic argument. However, beyond that point, the real places mentioned in the Greek myths tend to have elaborate myth cycles. The old Mycenaean cities certainly figure in a range of myths as do such Argonautic places as Crete, Lemnos, and Libya, all of which are entwined with other myths and figure into them in many ways. Even the Amazons—who also live along the Black Sea coast—make more than one appearance, in the myths of Heracles, Theseus, and Bellerophon. And yet, Colchis does not have this mythological connection to other stories in the oldest layers of myth.

Unlike Mycenae, Iolcus, or Athens, Colchis has no lengthy list of kings, no connection to other heroes except for Jason. Thebes can boast Cadmus, Oedipus, Creon, Heracles, and others. Even Iolcus had a myth cycle devoted to Pelias alongside that of Jason, and a later history of warfare. But Colchis made a remarkably shallow impact in myth for a country of such import that for almost a thousand years after the Mycenaean collapse it was still supposedly commemorated—by name no less—by people who did not visit its shores again until the eighth or seventh centuries BCE. Surely, if Colchis were well-known to the Mycenaeans other heroes should have ventured to its distant shores and other figures from Colchis besides Medea should have contributed to the genealogies of the Mycenaeans' leading families. And yet they did not. Unlike the fecund Greek mythological men and women, the anonymous Colchians are remarkably infertile in cross-pollinating myths or spawning heroic sons and daughters. (Pasiphaë, mother of the Minotaur, shared parents with Aeëtes and is therefore sometimes counted a Colchian by modern writers, though her story plainly originated in Crete.) The implication, of course, is that Colchis only became attached to the Jason myth long after the most important periods of mythmaking, in the Mycenaean era and Dark Ages, had come and gone.

Since Hesiod considered Medea a goddess, it stands to reason that the land in which she dwelled and which her divine father ruled was not like the other lands of Greece or the Near East. In fact, it was no real land at all.

The Underworlds of the Near East

As we have seen, Colchis appears to have come rather late to the Jason myth, first mentioned only in Eumelus in the sixth century BCE. Prior to him, Jason's journey was instead said to be to the fabulous land of Aea. Later writers tried to harmonize the divergent traditions by making Aea the capital of Colchis, but this is a rather late development. We have also seen that Aea, the land of the dawn, shares a close affinity with Aya, the name for a Near Eastern goddess of the dawn, prompting scholars like M. L. West to suggest that the Greek land took its name from the Near Eastern goddess, who was also the wife of the sun and goddess of sexuality. Since Aya is closely linked to the Mesopotamian gate to the Underworld, the Gate of Ishtar and Aya,[21] from which the evening star (Ishtar) and the dawn (Aya) arose, we are therefore within reason in suspecting that Aea had as its original form elements drawn from the Mesopotamian Underworld. This idea is reconfirmed when we recall that scholars believe the fantasy lands visited by Perseus and Heracles were former representations of the Underworld and that in his *Theogony* Hesiod, so deeply influenced by the Near East, depicted the singular rising and setting place of the sun as a bronze gate of the Underworld, leading to deepest Tartarus:

> There stands the awful home of murky Night wrapped in dark clouds. In front of it the son of Iapetus [Atlas] stands immovably upholding the wide heaven upon his head and unwearying hands, where Night and Day draw near and greet one another as they pass the great threshold of bronze: and while the one is about to go down into the house, the other comes out at the door.[22]

Thus, farthest east and west must have been one. As Dimitri Nakassis notes, this gate becomes the center of the cosmic world, the axis mundi:

> the collocation of the gate of the sun and the gate of the dead is a recurring pattern in cosmologies of the eastern Mediterranean, and there may be Indo-European analogues as well. The

Egyptian and Near Eastern parallels reflect a compression of the functions of the axis mundi analogous to the Hesiodic description, spatially associating the life cycle with the solar cycle.[23]

In order to understand the Mesopotamian underworld's relationship to Aea, we must first briefly survey the later Greek underworld and point out some important differences which help establish the connection between Aea and the Near East rather than the Greek land of the dead.

The Greek Underworld

The Greek Underworld was ruled by Hades who became the god of the dead when he and his two brothers, Zeus and Poseidon, drew lots to rule the sky, the sea, and the underworld. He is frequently called "the Other Zeus" as a nearly equal ruler of a realm separate from the gods, and when depicted in art he shares the same appearance as his brother. Hades' name was thought in ancient times to derive from *aides*, meaning "unseen," but it may also derive from *Aia*, meaning earth, or a conjectured Proto-Indo-European term meaning "the one who presides over meeting up" (i.e., reunion in death), according to modern scholars.[24] The ultimate etymology is uncertain, however. The German philologist Ulrich von Wilamowitz-Moellendorff argued a century ago that Hades' and Aeëtes' names both derived from the same root, earth, thus indicating that Jason's voyage was to the Land of Death,[25] but his etymology of Aeëtes has been frequently disputed. *Aia* is phonetically very close to both the land of *Aea* (also transliterated as *Aia*) and the goddess *Aya*. While this would be entirely keeping with the ideas presented so far in our exploration of Jason, we unfortunately cannot attribute this to anything more than a harmonious coincidence until more evidence arises. It may also be worth mentioning another coincidence, that Aeëtes is frequently associated with wealth, while Hades' much later title of Plouton (Pluto) means "wealthy," and refers to the underground metals he controls. In Rome, he was *dives*, or wealthy, from which, Cicero argued, comes the Roman name for him, Dis Pater.

While the contours of the classical Greek Underworld are well known, the Mycenaean conception of the Underworld is almost entirely unknown. It is generally thought that the Mycenaeans believed that the soul lived on in some fashion after death, and it is usually thought based on funerary art that the soul reached the Underworld by boat, possibly one large and with many oars, crossing the waters of death. A small coffin, or *larnax*, from a Mycenaean tomb at the fourteenth and thirteenth century BCE Tanagra cemetery near Thebes has a partially preserved image showing a boat with many oars arriving at a land where human figures that resemble plants or trees wave about wildly in expressive postures of mourning. This image has been interpreted as a scene of a soul's arrival in the Underworld.[26] Other coffins from this same site show humans with bat-like or birdlike wings, and these images are believed to represent the souls of the dead flying off to the Underworld.[27] It may be significant that the souls of the Mesopotamian dead were also believed to take the form of birds (see below), though some believe that the Mycenaean images may not represent the dead and that many scholars have misinterpreted them by positing a connection to Mesopotamia that cannot be proved.[28]

In the Homeric poems, life after death seems to be cloaked in shadows, where spectral souls reenact their earthly lives in a land largely bereft of light. The souls of the dead escape from the body and flit to the Underworld where they live a hungry, shadowy half-life, unable to speak or communicate with the world above except when some mortal provides them with blood. In this land, most humans eke out an unsatisfactory simulacrum of earthly life, but there was also the Elysian Fields (in Homer), or the Isles of the Blessed (in Hesiod), where a few select heroes had a more pleasant afterlife under the benevolent rule of Cronus. This was a land, however, originally separate from the Underworld, and is in other poems identified with a White Island or White Rock. Beneath the Underworld stood the pit of Tartarus in which the Titans, the former rulers of the heavens, wait imprisoned behind bronze doors.

This Homeric Underworld was considered to lie beyond Ocean, at the confluence of great and thundering rivers. Unlike later Greek tradition and, apparently, Mycenaean belief, the souls of the dead in Homer do not need to travel by ship to the Underworld but instead simply disappear into the ground. However, it is made clear in the *Odyssey* that the dead cross a river into the Underworld, and that once they cross this river they cannot return to the land of the living. In Homer's *Iliad*, the impassable river was the Styx, but in later tradition it is the Acheron. Humans who wish to visit the Underworld must venture to places that give entrance to the Underworld, such as the opening Odysseus seeks out by traveling to the banks of Ocean.

In the twenty-fourth book of the *Odyssey*, a later interpolation into the Homeric poem describes Hermes taking souls down to Hades:

> As in a corner of a monstrous cave the bats fly gibbering, when one tumbles from the rock out of the cluster as they cling together; so gibbering, these moved together. Protecting Hermes was their guide down the dank pathway. Past the Ocean stream they went, past the White Rock, past the portals of the Sun and land of dreams, and soon they reached the field of asphodel, where spirits dwell, spectres of worn-out men.[29]

Asphodels are a family of flowering plants with gray leaves and pale yellow flowers that grow primarily on barren ground, appropriate for an underworld plant. It is the flower Persephone picked when Hades came to abduct her, and it is also the flower of the dead. Interestingly, some asphodel seeds are fatal to birds,[30] and the plant, for all its gloomy appearance, grows best in areas of bright sunshine.

Note that in this Underworld, the entrance to the realm of Hades stands beside the "Portals of the Sun" (more literally "the Gates of Helios"), just like the Gate of Ishtar and Aya in Mesopotamian mythology. In this version, the Gates of Helios stand in the farthest west, a vision carried over into later Greek belief. However, the sun had gates in both the west (sunset) and the east (sunrise), and conceivably either could be used to access the land of the dead. If we follow Hesiod, both may in fact have been a single gate conceived as existing at the singular edge of the world, at Tartarus. When Odysseus travels "west" to the land of the Cimmerians, he arrives in a place that we have seen might originally have been considered the "east," in the northern regions of the Black Sea, where the Cimmerians were later thought to live. The Underworld in Greek myth has its own separate gates. In Hesiod, Hades lives amidst vast halls, and his realm is guarded by the terrible dog Cerberus who prevents souls from escaping through Hades' and Persephone's gates. Hades is sometimes referred to as the guardian of the gates.

As the geography of Hades' shadowy kingdom developed more fully, the Underworld gained a number of rivers, symbolic of the stages of mourning: Styx ("Abhorent"), representing the horror of death; Acheron ("Woeful"), representing distress due to loss; Cocytus

("Lamentation"), representing the rites of mourning; Pyriphlegethon ("Fire"), representing the funeral pyre; and Lethe ("Forgetfulness"), representing the ultimate fate of all who walk the earth. However, these were later additions; Hesiod and Homer sang only of Styx.

Within the realm of the dead, it was first believed that Hades himself passed judgment on the dead, assigning them to happier or grimmer regions of the Underworld. In such a capacity he is referenced in the works of Aeschylus, and he is probably the mysterious "somebody" who judges the dead in Pindar. Later, Hades is replaced in this role by King Minos of Crete, who becomes the judge of the dead, possibly because Homer had suggested that in the Underworld Minos continued the royal function of judging disputes (just as all shades continued their earthly pastimes), which became generalized to judging the moral worth of the dead. This belief coincided with changing Greek beliefs about the afterlife, including the belief in the Classical and Hellenistic periods that initiation into the Eleusinian mysteries could guarantee a soul a better lot in the hereafter. Eventually, the Underworld gained more, and more specialized, judges, as well as all manner of monsters to torment the sinful dead, most clearly expressed in Virgil's *Aeneid*, but certainly prevalent in some form in the Archaic period, more so in popular Greek belief than in extant literary sources.

THE MESOPOTAMIAN UNDERWORLD(S)

It would be an oversimplification to suggest that Mesopotamia had a single conception of the Underworld that lasted for three thousand years without change. There were some differences among the Sumerians, Akkadians, and Babylonians, and from city to city within those culture areas, not to mention the other societies that adopted and adapted Mesopotamian beliefs, such as the Hittites and the Semitic peoples of the Mediterranean coast. However, we can outline some of the general concepts of the Mesopotamian Underworld as well as some of the more specific details that appear on in certain times and places. The most dramatic description of the Mesopotamian Underworld, known as *Arallu*, comes from the *Epic of Gilgamesh*, in which the dying Enkidu dreams of the kingdom from which none return:

> There is the house where people sit in darkness; dust is their food and clay their meat. They are clothed like birds with wings for covering, they see no light, they sit in darkness. I entered the house of dust and I saw the kings of the earth, their crowns put away forever; [...] I saw also Samuqan, the god of cattle, and there was Ereshkigal the Queen of the Underworld...[31]

It is altogether a gloomy and uninviting place, not very dissimilar in effect to the Greek House of Hades. Note that the god of cattle resides in the Underworld in Near Eastern belief, and compare this to the instances of cattle we have examined so far: the bull-formed god who dwells within and below the earth, the cattle of the sun, the cattle of Hades, and the bulls Jason yokes. Compare also the *Gilgamesh* description of the dead covered with feathers and possessed of wings to the images found on the Mycenaean coffins depicting souls as winged and possessed of the ability to fly. In *Gilgamesh*, Enkidu dreams that his arms have become wings, and a great bird monster forces him to fly to the Underworld.

Ereshkigal is the queen and ruler of the underworld, and she is known as the "great earth." She is the sister of the goddess Inanna, and is considered to be the underworld aspect of the Queen of the Heavens. Her husband is the god Nergal, Lord of the Underworld, who in turn was the personification of summer's high heat and the disease and pestilence it brought. As a result, he is identified with the midday sun and is sometimes considered an aspect of Shamash, the sun god. However, Nergal was originally an earth god. In myth, he descends into the Underworld, seizes the throne from Ereshkigal and reigns as king thereafter. Some believe that the Sumerians had two different underworld traditions, and the marriage of Ereshkigal and Nergal symbolized a synchretizing of the two variant beliefs about the Underworld. Nergal entered Phoenician mythology as Melqart, who absorbed Dumuzi's dying-and-rising function, and was later identified with Heracles.³² The ancients believed his name was a contraction of his formal title, *enurugal*, Lord of the Great City.³³ The Great City was another name for the underworld because so many dead souls were housed there. Nergal was also known as the "Enlil of the Underworld," after the high god of the Sumerians, just as Hades was "the Other Zeus."³⁴ Nergal becomes associated with dragons in later myth when the gods ask him to subdue a terrible serpent with forelimbs. Nergal was assimilated in the Hittite pantheon as the Sword-God who reigned in the Hittite Underworld and would therefore have been known to the Mycenaeans.³⁵

One of the most foreign aspects of the Mesopotamian underworld is its close relationship to the sun, a facet that is present in Greek belief in only the most vestigial forms, such as Hesiod's bronze gate. In Mesopotamia it is however apparent in both the sun's role as a judge of the dead and Nergal's association as both a sun god and an underworld deity. This relationship between the sun and death, so alien to modern Western thought, has made it difficult for many scholars to recognize the essential underworld motifs in the Jason story, blinded (so to speak) by the prevalent solar iconography:

> To the modern student this assimilation of the infernal and solar cult must at first seem strange. Its explanation may arise from the astronomical movement of the sun, which passes daily from the upper to the nether world. [...] [I]n the religious system of [Babylon] the sun was considered to perform the functions of a psychopomp, conducting the spirits of the dead down to the underworld.³⁶

This is one reason that Arallu is, like the Greek Underworld, considered to exist both under the ground and at the westernmost reaches of the world, where the sun descends at sunset. Among the Hittites, a similar (and Mesopotamian-derived) tradition made the sun goddess also a goddess of the underworld. The Mesopotamian underworld is surrounded by a river, traditionally known as Hubur, which is the waters of death, the primal abyss that was Tiamat. Because the Mesopotamians also believed that a great sea called the Apsû existed under the earth (manifesting as springs on the surface), the underworld therefore seemed to be an island amidst waters that could only be reached by boat. This belief appears to have arisen from a very early conflation of Apsû and the Underworld.³⁷ To cross either these waters or the waters of the river Huber, Humut-tabal, a bird-faced ferryman with four hands, took souls in his boat, just as Urshanabi did for Gilgamesh across the waters of death. Model boats were placed in the graves of Near Eastern kings to ease their passage into death.³⁸ Still another tradition identified the Underworld with a mountain because the western mountains were where the sun was believed to have the gates by which he descended into the underworld.

Once one had crossed the waters of death, one reached a forbidding land but one whose topography is not entirely clear in the extant Mesopotamian sources. It is frequently likened to a desert or a dead and barren land. In the short Sumerian poem known as "The Sumerian Underworld," an unnamed god boasts of his realm. As he describes it, the underworld exists beneath a divine mountain and is a place where a cosmic judge apportions punishments and pleasures to the dead. This underworld, unlike later tradition, is located at the "mountains of the sunrise" but it is also the "house of the setting sun." In other words, it is the place *between* the sunset and the next sunrise, the land beneath the world, with gates on both ends of the sun's nocturnal journey (or, alternately, a single gate representing both). As we have seen, the Gate of Ishtar and Aya was believed to mark an entrance to the underworld in the east. The sun is said to live in this underworld house, whose sill is the jaws of a monster and equivalent to the Canaanite Mot's jaws of death into which Baal descends and is resurrected. The river of the dead runs through the land, and a monstrous lion guards the angry dead. However "rainbow gardens" belonging to Inanna also stand here, like the Elysian Fields, to give hope of happiness.[39]

In the more famous version of the Underworld known from the Sumerian (and later Babylonian) poem cycle describing Inanna's journey to the land of the dead, the Underworld is envisioned as a palace of lapis lazuli, the rare and intensely blue stone. These halls of the dead are surrounded by seven rings of walls, and within each wall is a gate. At the center of these rings, Ereshkigal sits enthroned, attended by the seven (or fifty, or six hundred) nameless Anunnaki, who flutter like bats and dispense doom. Elsewhere, Ereshkigal's son, Ningishzida (also reckoned the son of other gods), is the patron of medicine, a deity of the underworld, and possessed of a guardian monster, a fearsome dragon or horned snake, the *basmu* serpent.[40] He is charged with calling plants back to life after the killing heat of summer, thus serving as the herald of Dumuzi's return, and he is the "Lord of the Good Tree," who is himself sometimes depicted as a serpent, perhaps from the twisting roots of the tree, which become symbolically a serpent coiled around it.[41] In this figure, we see key elements of the Jason myth: the healing power, the serpent and tree, and the underworld. Later, the Babylonians would reassign the basmu snake to Marduk, the supreme god after 1500 BCE Ningishzida was conflated with Dumuzi/Tammuz at several points. The former was sometimes the father of, companion to, or avatar of the latter. It is not impossible that at times they were considered the same deity.

THE TWO UNDERWORLDS

Many scholars believe that Near East conceptions about the Underworld influenced the Greek version at some point in the past,[42] either through direct diffusion or perhaps an intermediary such as the Hittites or another Anatolian group. If the evidence from the Mycenaean coffins has been interpreted correctly, we might posit two stages of Mesopotamian influence. First, in the period of Mycenaean expansion, Near Eastern or pan–Aegean views of the Underworld influenced Mycenaean beliefs, including the confluence of the solar and underworld gates, the crossing of water by boat to enter the underworld, the idea of the land of the dead existing at the edge of the world beyond Ocean, and the idea of the underworld as a bleak and desolate existence. Since the later Greeks of Hesiod's day recognized the sun as operating beneath the earth at night, it is not impossible that the Mycenaean sun had a role underground.

However, after the Mycenaean collapse, ideas about the afterlife evidently changed, and the Homeric underworld likely lost many of its more elaborate Mycenaean-Mesopotamian trappings, including apparently the many-oared ship that crossed the waters to the land of the dead. The new Greek underworld, too, appears to have become more generalized and considered more subterranean than a formless netherworld at the edge of the world. Finally, during the Orientalizing Period, the ferryman of the dead reappears and the underworld becomes more elaborately described, perhaps reflecting renewed Near East influence five hundred years after the first wave ended. It is in this period that the Near Eastern myth of Inanna and Dumuzi influences Greece under the guise of the myth of Demeter and Persephone, and again as Adonis (Attis) and Aphrodite. But surely we should have reason to suspect that this Archaic or late Dark Age addition to the corpus of Greek myth is not the first time Inanna and Dumuzi appeared in ancient Greece.

This scenario, though obviously speculative, could account for some of the contradictory aspects of the Greek conception of Hades' realm, including the divergent traditions of an underworld both directly beneath the earth of Greece and also on the far shore of Ocean. Homer reconciles the two visions by making a spot on the banks of Ocean *an* entrance to the Underworld where mortals may seek the dead, but this does not disguise the originally separate and somewhat oppositional accounts. Based on the stories of Heracles' trip to the edge of the world to steal the cattle of Geryon and Perseus' trip across the waters in search of Medusa, it appears that the underworld at Ocean's edge is the older version, and Near Eastern in origin. Myths such as these, and Jason's own, must have lost their Underworld associations when the Mycenaean underworld with its Near East influence gave way in the Dark Ages to a simpler and more indigenous conception of a realm of the dead directly beneath the feet of living people. As the Greek vision of the underworld changed, so too must the myths associated with an older belief system that exhibited important discontinuities between the Mycenaean era worship of immanent underworld, earth, and sky gods and the Archaic religion of more ethereal Olympian celestial beings.

This period also coincides with two other factors that support this supposition: First, the removal of the old earth gods such as Poseidon and Hera from the earth to Olympus when the sky god Zeus became the supreme deity left the earth devoid of chthonic powers that had heretofore been envisioned as living within and beneath the ground. Second, cults of local heroes were established at the Mycenaean era tombs to exercise power beneath the earth in place of the former gods. Since the heroes (or degraded earth gods, or what-have-you) were not coequal to the Olympians, they could not be exactly divine. If they were not of the same substance as the gods, then they had to be mortal. And if they were mortal and dead and under the earth, then the Underworld could no longer be beyond the edge of the world but instead beneath the soil of Greece. This version came to dominate Greek myth in time, but it left behind residue of the older conception, including the lands where the glorious ancient dead live blissfully in the farthest west, at the gates of the Sun.

Aea and the Underworld

After examining the Near Eastern and Greek conceptions of the underworld, certain parallels to the mysterious land of Aea become nearly unavoidable. It would, of course, be wrong to suggest that the Greeks simply appropriated the Sumerian underworld and translated it wholesale into their myths. Similarly, it is quite obvious that Jason is no direct copy of either Dumuzi or Ningishzida. Instead, the fabulous land of Aea and the hero who travels to it represent a conflation, adaptation, and reinterpretation of many elements, among which must have been Near Eastern conceptions of the underworld and its denizens, perhaps even the heritage of a continuum of religions stretching from the Aegean to the Persian Gulf. A look at the parallels between the two will show how ancient Near Eastern concepts survived in the Greek myth. However, a word of caution is necessary. Because so many of the oldest Jason stories are fragmentary, the following discussion necessarily draws on the entire corpus of Jason texts, including those written in the Hellenistic and Roman periods. Apollonius' story may have self-consciously invoked a katabasis, which would prejudice our discussion by confusing genuinely Archaic ideas with Hellenistic adaptations and interpolations. For example, the presence of the infernal goddess Hecate is most likely a more recent addition to the Jason myth (though not of Apollonius; she appears in Sophocles' *Root-Cutters*), and though she has clear underworld associations, we may pass over her for now except to note that she echoes the underworld aspects of the ancient earth goddess she once was and whose role in the story she partially usurps. With that caveat, some of the more important parallels between Aea and the underworld can be explored.

THE WATERY APPROACH

As we have seen, the Near Eastern underworld existed in its many forms across some sort of body of water, whether it be the great world Ocean, the underground Apsû sea, or the fatal river Hubur. Similarly, to reach Aea, Jason must cross a great uncharted sea, and to leave he follows the path of the world-encompassing Ocean. This may not seem like a dramatic parallel until we recall that both Perseus and Heracles must also cross great bodies of water to reach lands that scholars have identified as former representations of the Underworld. Taken together, it appears that in myth, the crossing of great waters is symbolic of a descent into the regions of death, another parallel that agrees well with neurological findings about the symbolism of shamanic trance states where water is associated with descent. This view carried over into the Greek conception of the sea as the "ultimate place of no return," the same term used to describe the House of Hades, where objects (or people) cast into the sea were believed to be forever lost, swallowed in an embrace that could never be broken.[43]

It may also be worthwhile to note that the river Hubur, which lay either at the farthest west or the farthest east, before the gate of the underworld, was believed to devour any who touched it, necessitating the use of a boat for souls to cross to the land of the dead. In the myth of Jason, no one enters the waters around Aea/Colchis except for one character, and he is dead. In the oldest extant versions of the myth, Apsyrtus, Medea's infant brother, is killed and his corpse dismembered and thrown into the sea. It may be permissible to speculate that this is a distortion of the idea of that the infernal waters are fatal. Perhaps originally, Apsyrtus was thrown alive into the river, which chews up and kills him in its fatal waters.

THE PLAIN OF CIRCE

The Plain of Circe is described only in Apollonius' *Argonautica*, and it has sometimes been argued that this ominous land leading up to Aeëtes' city was entirely Apollonius' invention. However, the Greek colony at Phasis, on the site of what was believed from the late Archaic to be the site of Jason's Colchis, there was a Plain of Circe, according to the fourth century BCE historian Timaeus, who wrote before Apollonius. M. L. West believed that the colonists at Phasis named the site after Circe because she was at that point (the seventh century BCE) already associated with the myth of the Argonauts[44] (see chapter 3).

Circe's Plain lay between the place where the Phasis joined the Black Sea and the uplands where Aeëtes dwelled. This plain is an eerie, death-infused place where "in line grow many willows and osiers, on whose topmost branches hang corpses bound with cords."[45] These are the bodies of men, wrapped in ox hides and suspended from trees; the women are buried. The willow tree, because it was associated with lowlands and water, places deemed close to the House of Hades, was intimately associated with death and the Underworld, as well as infertility. It was one of the trees, along with the poplar, that grew in the sacred grove of Persephone in the *Odyssey*. It was also, paradoxically, a tree of life sacred to the goddess Hera and to other earth goddesses beyond Greece.[46] Osiers are a type of willow that grow in flooded, marshy environments. Though most likely unrelated, the Colchians' manner of disposing of the dead recalls Inanna's descent to the Underworld. When the Anunnaki pass sentence on the goddess, she sickens, she dies, and her corpse is hung from a spike.

Apollonius was writing in the third century BCE, five hundred years after Aea had merged with the Black Sea land of Colchis. Clearly, such a wetland is closer to the geographic reality of Greek Phasis than to our proposed underworld, but it is telling that in adapting this physical detail from the real-life Colchis he has taken pains to associate it closely with death, both in the corpses hanging from the trees as well as the choice of foliage. In so doing, Apollonius provided an appropriate transitional land between the Apsû waters and the dusty, barren underworld otherwise missing in Near Eastern myth.

THE PALACE OF AEËTES

In the fragments of Mimnermus in the seventh century BCE, we first hear of Aeëtes' city at Aea on the banks of the River Ocean, the place where the sun god stores his rays in a chamber made of gold. As we have seen, in Near Eastern belief, derived from a geocentric model of the cosmos, the sun passed the nighttime hours beneath the earth, in the underworld, where he was also the judge of the dead. The gate by which the sun emerged from the underworld, the Gate of Aya and Inanna, was the place of the dawn, and thus geographically synonymous with Aea. The city's location along Ocean recalls simultaneously the land where Hades' cattle were pastured in the myth of Heracles, the entrance to the Underworld visited by Odysseus, the great waters associated with the Sumerian underworld, and the waters of death that led to the blessed land where Gilgamesh finds the immortal survivors of the great flood.

It is interesting to note that in Mimnertus, the "city" of Aeëtes is mentioned, while later tradition focuses instead the palace of the Colchian king, within this city. There of course is danger in making too much of a coincidence of language (the king, after all, must live *somewhere*), but it is worth noting that the Mesopotamians thought of the Underworld as both the "Great City" and also as containing the lapis lazuli palace of Ereshkigal that sat in the center of the barren wastes, surrounded by the seven gates. Of Aeëtes' palace, our primary source is Apollonius, but its presence is implied in earlier versions. The surviving fragments of the *Naupaktia*, for example, depict the king feasting the Argonauts, and this action presumably took place in his palace's great hall. Apollonius' describes Aeëtes' palace as a wonder of stone and bronze, furnished with four fountains from which flowed milk, wine, oil, and hot and cold water. Within the palace stood a courtyard off which many doors opened onto unnumbered chambers. Beyond these, well-crafted buildings housed the royal family and its attendants. In both Apollonius and Valerius Flaccus, a temple or shrine to the Underworld goddess Hecate stands adjacent to or nearby the palace complex. In Valerius, there also stands a temple to the Sun (here Apollo, identified in late Antiquity with Helios), on whose doors bronze reliefs show the voyage of the *Argo* and the future that awaits Jason. In both Apollonius and Valerius, the miracles of the Colchian building program are the work of Hephaestus (Vulcan), craftsman of the gods.

Apollonius' description of the palace is clearly influenced by the architectural wonders of Ptolemaic Alexandria, and scholars have also argued that Hephaestus' contributions to Colchian architecture derive from Apollonius' echoing of the *Odyssey*'s palace of Alcinous,[47] guarded by gold and silver dogs crafted by Hephaestus. The interlude with Alcinous from books VI to XIII contains within it the sections of the *Odyssey* most commonly identified with borrowings from an ancient *Argonautica,* in books X to XII,[48] so the possibility that this description draws on a still older palace of Aeëtes cannot be entirely excluded. Victorian scholars speculated, though on very insecure grounds, that Alcinous was originally an Argonautic figure before being taken over by Homer,[49] and M. L. West notes that the glorious description of the palace is shared with palace descriptions in other Indo-European tongues, attributing it to an ancient Proto-Indo-European poetic inheritance that figuratively linked impressive palaces to the attendant beauty of the sun and moon.[50] Erwin Cook has demonstrated that the description of the Palace of Alcinous derives from Assyrian palace architecture, though of the eighth century BCE or later, linking the palace back to the Near East.[51] (The possibility that later poets "updated" an older image of a Near Eastern palace to conform to more modern reports from Assyria cannot be excluded.) In describing the recurrence of this same palace imagery in Ovid's description of the Sun's palace in the *Metamorphoses,* Peter E. Knox notes that many of the aspects ascribed to the Sun's (and therefore Aeëtes') palace are common Hellenistic palace descriptions, including the attribution of divine craftsmanship.[52] Therefore it is probably only coincidence that in Canaanite myth, the palace of the death god Mot is also built by the craftsman of the gods.

However, Hephaestus' presence here has other echoes with underworld motifs. First, Hephaestus was the god of Lemnos, a figure the Lemnians worshipped as a form of Baal, the dying-and-rising god who fought Mot when he employed the gods' craftsman to build his palace. Additionally, Hephaestus crafted the *Iliad*'s remarkable shield of Achilles, which featured as one of its scenes a pair of lions fighting a bull near a herd of cattle. This image, of lion attacking bull, was coincidentally the same image found throughout the Near East as the symbol of the dual relationship of Nergal and Shamash, the gods of the dead and the sun.[53] Hephaestus also crafted the derivative Shield of Heracles in Hesiod's poem of that name, which is festooned with death-infused imagery of dragons. Most importantly, Hephaestus was believed to work his art deep under the earth, the smoke of his forge emerging as volcanoes such as Mt. Etna. Further, as father to the Cabeiri, the Underworld gods, he was again associated with the realm beneath the earth. Some scholars have even posited a connection between Hephaestus and the monster Typhon, noting that both are associated with volcanoes, both are cast down from Olympus, and (in some mythic variants) both are sons of Hera.[54]

This Mesopotamian cylinder seal from the third millennium BCE shows the sun god Shamash, with solar rays emanating from his shoulders, cutting his way through the earth with his divine blade to bring the dawn. To his left and right, two attendants crowned with horns (more typically represented as actual anthropomorphic bulls) pull open the Gate of Dawn. The imagery closely parallels Pherecydes' and Apollonius' claim that the solar Aeëtes plowed the dawn land with an adamantine blade and fire-breathing bulls (author's drawing).

THE FIELD AND FIRE-BREATHING BULLS

The challenge Aeëtes lays down for Jason is first to yoke the fire-breathing, brazen-hoofed bulls on the Field of Ares and with them plow a large field. This challenge is present in the oldest levels of the Jason myth and must have had great symbolic importance in the earliest Argonaut epics. In Apollonius, Aeëtes uses a plow of adamantine with the fire-breathing bulls, and this plow was another of Hephaestus' divinely-crafted gifts. Adamantine is a mythical substance that is supposed to be extraordinarily hard. It is the same substance that made up the sickle Cronus used to castrate Uranus, and it is the same substance that composed the sickle or sword Perseus used to behead Medusa. The name derives from the word *adamas*, meaning "untameable," especially appropriate given the character of the bulls. The idea of a solar figure cutting the ground with a sharp blade also closely parallels the Near Eastern sun god Shamash, who uses a serrated knife to cut through the mountains of the east in order to rise at dawn, an image reinforced by the curvature of Shamash's blade, which resembles the curvature of wooden Bronze Age plows yoked to oxen or bulls. The image of cutting through earth with a blade surely suggests the actions of a plow. Further, iconographic evidence from Babylonia shows that the sun god, who is seen aflame with rays emerging from his body, wields this earth-cutting knife when leaving the gates of the dawn, which are opened by a pair of bull-men who are his attendants.[55] Since we have seen the close connection between Aea and the Babylonian dawn goddess Aya, it seems possible that Shamash, his knife, and the bull men contributed in jumbled form to Aeëtes, his adamantine plow, and his flaming bulls.

In the first stories, Aeëtes, as the son of the Sun, demonstrates his mastery of these monstrous cattle by first performing the feat himself, yoking the bulls and plowing the field with ease. In this, he betrays his character's former designation as the sun god himself. The episode recalls the myth of Phaëton, another son of the sun. Phaëton asked his father to drive the chariot of the sun, pulled by four fiery divine horses, and Helios refused. However, Phaëton tricked his father into swearing and unbreakable oath by the river Styx to grant his wish. Unable to refuse, Helios gave Phaëton the reins, and he promptly crashed and burned to death because only a god can master the sun's chariot. In other Near Eastern contexts, the sun's chariot is variously pulled by fiery mules, oxen, griffins, or, in the later case of Medea, dragons. We have already seen that the Mycenaeans equated the bull god with the sun by placing his solar disc upon images of the bull, and the bull's flaming breath clearly recalls both this symbolism and the flaming mules Shamash yoked to his chariot. Among the Hittites and Hurrians, the storm-god Teshub (who slew the dragon) was associated with two bulls, representing Day and Night, Serri and Hurri, who pulled his chariot or wagon.[56] Though these were not, strictly speaking, solar bulls, their association with the skies is clear. This identification is made closer when we recall that the Hittites divorced Teshub from his first wife and made him the husband of their sun goddess when they took him over from the Hurrians (who inherited him from Hatti) under the name Tarhun. Here we have a clear case of a pair of yoked bulls, though obviously not used for plowing. However, since Teshub was associated with fertility in his role of bringing life-giving rain to the fields, his bulls can be said to have an agricultural function by association. Jason's bulls may take something from the Hittite god's yoked steeds and Shamash's pair of bull men, transformed somewhat as versions of the story traveled and changed from Anatolia to Greece. The Greeks, of course, would not have simply adopted the Hittite or Babylonian myth wholesale but rather incorporated it into existing beliefs. At the same time, we must also note the old Indo-European tradition using cows or bulls, especially reddish or tawny cows (such as fire-breathing brazen bulls?) to symbolize the dawn.[57] In this reading, Jason is showing his ability to do the job of the sun by mastering the bulls who control sunrise and sunset from below the earth, a feat greater than Phaëton's failed ride.

Additionally, as we have seen, M. L. West concluded that Jason and the Argonauts either saw or interacted with the cattle of Sun en route to Colchis. We have also had occasion to mention Hades' cattle in connection with Heracles' trip to a land much like Aea. The presence of these herds of cattle in connection with the Underworld has multiple echoes in Near Eastern mythology. First, the sun god was frequently associated with bulls in Mesopotamia, in Egypt, in Mycenaean lands, on Crete, and elsewhere. The sun god in Near Eastern belief was also an Underworld deity and judge of the dead. The bull was also one of the oldest symbols of the earth god, including the Mycenaean Poseidon, and indeed had been a key symbol of the earth god since at least the Neolithic period. The Babylonian god Samuqan was associated with these same functions, as a fertility god, earth god, and a god of cattle. In the *Epic of Gilgamesh*, his seat is in the Underworld. As in the myth of Heracles and Geryon, many have seen in the cattle of the Underworld mythological symbols for the souls of the dead.[58] Both the sun's and Geryon's cattle may be bifurcations of the original herd that grazed at Hesiod's singular Underworld solar gate when this original conception became translated into the dual east-west gates of later belief.[59]

Here is may be worth noting that Bruce Lincoln has reconstructed a Proto-Indo-European myth that presumably had once been told among the ancestors of the people who would populate Europe, the Near East, and India between the fifth and second millennia

BCE. This myth of the "cattle raid" in which a three-headed serpent or dragon from a foreign land steals a hero's cattle. The hero meets the serpent again, defeats the serpent, and regains his cattle. This myth, Lincoln believes, lies for example behind Heracles' raid on Geryon's cattle. However, as intriguing as this would be for Jason's confrontation with the serpent in Colchis to retrieve the "soul" of Phrixus, I cannot agree with Lincoln's reduction of the myth to a literal memory of Indo-European invaders raiding the cattle of indigenous populations who, paradoxically, are symbolically cloaked under the mythic image of serpents.[60] It seems rather contradictory to suspect the myths of symbolism only in part. Why should the cattle be literal while the serpent is metaphorical? (Lincoln's answer is that cattle were essential to the prehistoric economy, while serpents were not.) I would suggest that myths are more complex than that.

More to our purpose is H. J. Rose's suggestion that in the oldest layers of myth, a distinction was made between the chthonic gods who lived just beneath the surface and provided fertility to the soil and mineral wealth, and those gods who dwelled in the deepest Underworld, the land of the dead.[61] In this reading, the cattle of Hades are in fact from this former layer, life-giving creatures (thus equivalent to the sun cattle from which they were divided) whom the adventurer to the Underworld would pass by en route to a confrontation in the lowest depths, where the serpent dwells. This suggestion would help to explain the conception of such parallel Underworld or Netherworld realms as the Elysian Fields (living) and the House of Hades (dead) and the land of Utnapishtim (living) and that of Ereshkigal and Nergal (dead). Rose further echoes what we have seen earlier: That this realm beneath the ground was once the home of the gods, including the earth goddess Hera, until the cult of mountain-dwelling Zeus called the gods upward into the sky.[62] However, Rose's suggestion that invading "Achaeans" (Mycenaeans) imposed their cattle practices on an agricultural indigenous society cannot be true, since cattle husbandry has been attested in Greece since the Neolithic.[63] However, when the cattle-raising Indo-European people came into Greece sometime after 2500 BCE (possibly the immediate ancestors of the Mycenaeans), they brought with them the worship of the sky god Zeus, and they started the long process of creating the Greek pantheon and sending the earth gods skyward.

But as Rose admits, this Underworld where the old gods dwelled was easily and early conflated with the Underworld of the dead, which leaves us again where we began: with the Underworld, and its cattle, and the hero who descends into the land beneath the earth. Further, the fallow field that Jason must plow has clear echoes both of the "thrice-plowed field" where his namesake Iasion impregnates the earth goddess Demeter and the barren fallows that the Mesopotamians considered the Underworld to comprise. Its association with the god Ares makes perfect sense in light of Near Eastern belief (see below). The imagery used in describing Inanna's descent to the Underworld includes clouds of dust and fields of rubble ground by a "stone-breaker."[64] There are also "fields of the dead" which grow a fatal grain.

THE SOWN MEN

It is an open question whether the grim grain of Aea's fatal field, the earth-born men or Spartoi, were original to the Jason myth, an importation from the myth of Cadmus, or whether both derived from an earlier and independent source. Kirk felt that the Cadmus story was older[65]; Sir Hugh Lloyd Jones felt the influence ran the other way.[66] Since the Spartoi are said to have grown from the teeth of a dragon sacred to Ares, and the dragon Jason fights lives in the Grove of Ares, there must be some additional connection beyond a coincidence of terminology to account for the appearance of the same story in two myths. It is quite possible that two originally dissimilar stories grew closer together over time and were at some point synchretized. Certainly, Pherecydes was aware of the sowing of the dragon's teeth in conjunction with the Jason myth in the sixth century BCE, but the earlier *Naupaktia* may not have included the task. The following discussion, admittedly speculative, proceeds from the assumption—no means a certain one—that some type of event roughly analogous to the Spartoi followed the yoking of the fire-breathing bulls.

In the myth of Cadmus, the teeth are sown to grow citizens for Thebes, but Jason sows the teeth as a challenge, with the intention of killing those who rise from the ground. In this case, the chthonic action of performing a ritual of plowing a dusty field before calling up bodies "planted" beneath the ground recalls less Cadmus' actions than necromantic actions associated with the rites of the dead. For example, in the *Odyssey*, Odysseus digs a pit into which he pours offerings of blood and wine in order to call up the dead. These dead, like the Spartoi, emerged in great masses and must be controlled through the use of weaponry to prevent them from overwhelming the summoner. Significantly, the necromantic rites involve the flaying of sheep. In some ancient rites, the necromancer sleeps on this fleece atop a tomb (the rite of *incubation*) in order to experience the rising of the dead.[67] But the necromancer must be careful to control physical contact with the dead, lest they drag him to the House of Hades. In the *Orphic Argonautica,* Orpheus performs a similar rite to raise infernal Hecate in order to open the gates to the Field of Ares, here clearly a stand in for the Gates of Hades. In most versions of the story, Jason, too, digs a furrow into which he places an offering, the dragon's teeth, which result in the rising of bodies from beneath the earth. Like Odysseus' spirits, they are an insistent crowd.

The scene with the Spartoi has additional resonances with Near Eastern necromantic and Underworld traditions, and this is to be expected since the Greeks are believed to have borrowed their ideas about necromancy from the Mesopotamians.[68] In Mesopotamia, a figurine or something belonging to an intended victim could be buried in the ground, in a fresh grave, whose occupant would then rise to take the victim down into the Underworld.[69] Despite the "official" belief that the dead could not escape from the Underworld, in popular tradition revenants and spirits could and did come up from below at the performance of the proper rituals. The god Nergal performed a similar feat, digging a hole in the *Epic of Gilgamesh* and calling up the spirit of Enkidu. In the Sumerian version, it is Utu (= Shamash) the sun god who performs the feat. Similarly, Hittite priests called up the deities of the Underworld through an offering of blood and wine in pits dug with knives[70]—and plows are nothing if not oversized knives, a connection made more explicit by the linkage of Aeëtes' adamantine plow with the adamantine sickle Cronus uses to cut Uranus. If Aeëtes' palace is taken to be similar to the palace of the sun at the gates of the Underworld, then that which Jason calls up from below the ground by plowing furrows and filling the furrows with an offering must originally have been the restless dead or their chthonic gods, those who lie beneath the ground. Apollonius' description of the dead Spartoi bleeding so much that "the furrows [Jason plowed] were filled with blood"[71] surely recalls Odysseus filling the pit with sheep's blood to call forth the dead.

But contact with the dead is dangerous, and the necromancer must be properly prepared and then afterward purified. Scholars note that the ointment Jason wears on the Field of Ares in Apollonius has "strongly necromantic overtones"[72] drawn closely from Odysseus' rites on Ocean's shore (see chapter 8). Could Medea's drugs have been intended as a ritual purification meant to keep Jason safe from contact with the dead?

We know that the more recent among the ancient writers objected to the lack of explicitly necromantic invocations in the Homeric epics, and they speculated openly that the Greeks of the Late Archaic period excised direct references to necromantic activity when compiling the standard versions of Homer in the sixth century BCE.[73] We also know that many of the Greek myths were remodeled during the Archaic period to tone down the violence, render the monsters less monstrous, assuage the crudest aspects, and rationalize some of the most magical actions to conform to the changing customs and mores of a new society that prized rational thinking.[74] The same impulse that reconfigured the Land of the Dead as the islands of Geryon and Medusa could very well have substituted the planting of dragon's teeth for a thematically similar necromantic event in the most ancient Jason stories. It is not difficult to imagine Jason using the solar bulls to dig a trench from which the dead or chthonic deities might rise—or even to give entrance to the Underworld itself. In Lucian's *Menippus* of the second century CE, a necromancer in Babylon accomplished just this task. He digs a pit and performs the same sacrifices as Odysseus. "At once the whole area shook and the ground was broken open by the spell. One could hear the barking of Cerberus in the distance, and everything looked dismal and gloomy."[75] Might this then have been Jason's path downward to the pit symbolized in the dragon's jaws?

THE GROVE OF ARES

The final task Jason accomplishes is in some ways the most muddled in the sources. Leaving aside the question of whether Jason descends into the serpent, slays it, or puts it to sleep, with or without Medea's help, the location of this action is disputed. In the *Naupaktia* fragments, the Golden Fleece is seen only in Aeëtes' palace, which has led some to conclude that in this early version the Fleece was simply kept in the king's home. Pindar places the snake in a thicket of trees, but nothing more specific. In Pherecydes, the grove and snake reside on Circe's island of Aeaea in the river Phasis. In Diodorus, following Dionysus Schytobrachion, the fleece is kept in the Temple of Ares, around which a great wall stood. In the late *Orphic Argonautica* this becomes seven parapets surrounding a grove filled with the plants of the dead, including asphodel. In Apollonius, the sacred grove is dedicated to Ares but is simply a cluster of trees, without walls. Apollodorus does not give the snake a fixed home, and Hyginus merely states that he guards a "shrine," perhaps intended to reflect the Temple of Ares. From this thicket of contradictions, a few conclusions can be drawn.

First, the tradition of the Fleece residing in a sacred grove appears to predate its placement in a temple, and the variant temple tradition appears to be the result of later efforts to rationalize the Jason myth and prune away the magical or wild aspects of it. Such sacred groves are well-attested in Greek religion (they are among the earliest Greek sanctuaries[76] and probably had Mycenaean antecedents[77]). They were liminal sites where rituals of initiation and the practice of mystery religions occurred, including rites dedicated to the death and rebirth of a miraculous child or adolescent figure.[78] Examples of these cults connected to the nature cycle include those dedicated to Opheletes (a child killed by a snake and later worshipped as a hero) at the grove of Zeus at Nemea, Pelops (dismembered and cooked as a child but restored by the gods) at the grove of Zeus at Olympia, and Melicertes (a child thrown from a cliff but changed into a sea god) at the grove of Poseidon at Isthmia, not to mention Persephone and Plutus in the Eleusinian Mysteries. If we recall that Jason was an adolescent of twenty and associated with agriculture, his journey to a grove to be swallowed by a snake seems part of a larger and very ancient pattern. Such groves were also considered places of oracles and healing,[79] like the groves of Apollo and Asclepius, which again relates them to Jason the healer as well as to the oracular plank from the grove at Dodona built into the *Argo*. Many groves were closely associated with chasms and other forms of entrance to the Underworld; in myth, Theseus, for example, descends to Hades through a sacred grove at Taenarus, and Oedipus at one at Colonus.[80] In the *Odyssey*, Circe directs Odysseus to a sacred grove to perform his necromantic rites:

> When you have crossed by ship the Ocean-stream to where the shore is rough and the grove of Persephone stands,—tall poplars and seed-shedding willows,—there beach your ship by the deep eddies of the Ocean-stream, but go yourself to the mouldering house of Hades.[81]

Note that this grove appears in the exact section of the *Odyssey* M. L. West identified as working under the influence of the ancient *Argonatuica*. Outside of myth, Pausanias wrote that Ares had a sacred grove in a town called Geronthrae in the southeastern Peloponnese, and it apparently dated back to the Dark Ages or earlier.[82] Geronthrae itself was once a Neolithic settlement and had significant occupations in the Mycenaean and later periods.

Since nearly all of the gods had sacred groves, and any dozen of them could easily have filled the role of patron of Aea's grove, we must ask what role Ares specifically played in the land of Aea. On the surface it seems hardly appropriate for the land of the sun god Helios to have its most sacred grove as well as the field surrounding it dedicated to the war god Ares, a god so unloved that his worship was among the rarest in the Greek world. There is, however, a Near East parallel that explains this strange juxtaposition of Ares in the land of the sun. In Babylon, the underworld god Nergal was identified with the sun god Shamash as being one and the same, reinforcing the old idea of the sun as the judge of the dead by making him an actual god of the Underworld as well.[83] This god of death reveled in violence and slaughter, which made him a fit counterpart for the Greek god Ares. Both were also gods of pestilence. From around 3000 BCE the Mesopotamians identified Nergal with the planet Mars,[84] a planet that was believed to rise in the mountain of the rising sun, which is to say, at the very gate of the Underworld where Jason comes to seek his fortune. The planet set again in the west, at the gate of sunset. Mars is not visible in the east at sunrise or in the west at sunset, so this must have been symbolic, due to Nergal's close relationship with Shamash as an aspect of the sun. As Mars, Nergal is the "star of the judgment of the fate of the dead,"[85] an aspect also assigned elsewhere to the sun god himself. When the Greeks adopted the Near Eastern astronomical system, they reassigned Mars to Ares. The identification is evident in a fifth century BCE coin from Cilicia which shows Nergal on one side and Ares on the other.[86] Therefore, the Grove of Ares and Field of Ares at Colchis appear to encode a memory of the old death god, Nergal, and through him to a system of belief that equated the Underworld with the land of the sun.

In the center of this grove stands the oak on which the Golden Fleece hangs. The oak obviously recalls the sacred oaks of Dodona, from which the *Argo* gained its magic plank. However, the tree also parallels the *gis-kin* tree of Sumer (the *kisgun* tree of later Mesopotamia), which "is growing in the pure underworld."[87] This tree had healing powers due to its purity, a trait it shares with the ritual use of ram's fleece in the Greek world (see chapter 8). It also served as a conduit between the earth and the Underworld. A description of a portion of this tree as it protruded in the confines of a temple in the early Sumerian city of Eridu recalls Jason's Aea:

> In Eridu groweth the dark *kiškanû*,
> That springeth forth in a place undefiled,
> Whereof the brilliance is shining lapis-lazuli
> Which reacheth unto Ocean [*Apsû*];
> From Ea-Enki the way in Eridu
> Is bountiful in luxuriance,
> Where the underworld is, there is his dwelling,
> And the resting-place is the chamber of Nammu.
> In an undefiled dwelling like a forest grove
> Its shade spreadeth abroad, and none may enter in.
> In its depths (are) Shamash and Tammuz.
> At the confluence of two streams
> The gods Ka-Hegal, Shi-Dugal, (and) ... of Eridu
> [Have gathered] this *kiškanû*, [and over the man]
> Have performed the Incantation of the Deep,
> (And) at the head of the wanderer have set (it).
> That a kindly Guardian, a kindly Spirit
> May stand at the side of the man, the son of his god.[88]

In the underworld, Dumuzi and the sun god Shamash are the guardians of the sacred tree.[89] Though this tree is rooted in the underworld, it grows upward and appears on earth at the confluence of the Tigris and Euphrates rivers (the "two mouths"), though it was also placed in a mythical eastern land where the sun rises, which was the original location of the earthly paradise where Utnaphishtim lives in immortality along, in theory, with the revivified noble dead. At this important place, Gilgamesh is forbidden in an ancient Sumerian adventure from chopping down a sacred cedar tree from the divine grove of the sun god and achieving immortality,[90] a motif transformed when folded into the much later epic version of *Gilgamesh* into the twin stories of fashioning a raft from the gods' cedars and the loss of the plant of immorality to the serpent. Serpent and cedar together well represent the Grove of Ares, along with the intimation of immortality. Some version of the *Gilgamesh* epic was probably known to the Mycenaeans. This may be coincidental, of course, since there are only so many places to store a fleece in a grove, but the recurring confluence of images and symbols seems to argue against chance combination.

Finally, we cannot take leave of the Grove of Ares without noting one of its most peculiar features. In the late *Orphic Argonautica*, it is described as lying behind seven ring-walls or parapets in a circle punctured by three bronze gates. Atop one of these gates, a statue of Artemis, whom the poet identifies with the infernal goddess Hecate, presides; and only with permission of the actual Hecate can the gates be unbarred. This setup uncannily echoes the vision of the Underworld presented in the myth of Inanna's descent, where the goddess must pass through seven gates in seven great walls to reach the throne of Ereshkigal, who must give her permission, as Hecate does in the *Orphic Argonautica*, for the locks to be undone and the gates opened; otherwise no one can pass through alive. Though the *Orphic Argonautica* is a very late poem (fourth century CE at the earliest), we have seen that some scholars believe it may draw on more ancient Orphic traditions dating back to the Archaic. While it seems unlikely that this passage is a direct descendant of Inanna's journey, it certainly draws on the same bank of imagery.

In the center of this enclosure the *Orphic Argonautica* describes a field filled with plants used for the dark arts within which stood a great oak where the snake guarded both the Fleece and the "tomb of Zeus Chamaizelos"—identified sometimes in Greek religion as the Underworld god Hades, and sometimes as a subterranean snake form of Zeus himself, who symbolizes "reconciliation with the dead."[91] He is a chthonic, distorted survival of the old earth god who was worshipped before the Zeus cult gained the upper hand, before all the gods were thought to live in the sky, the god from whom the aquatic form of Poseidon probably separated, the same earth god who, in the guise of Pelias, sent Jason on his quest. We shall encounter a form of him again in chapter 8.

We shall save the dragon-serpent for the next chapter, but at the conclusion of our survey of the geography of Aea, the close relationship of its landmarks, animals, and foliage to the terrain of the Underworld has become apparent. Based on our discussion, we can deduce a story whereby the hero arrives at the gates of the Underworld (the Clashing Rocks perhaps?), which are the same as those of the rising sun. There, he uses the sun's own solar bulls to cut a furrow into which he makes ritual offerings, having purified himself with magical rites. This accomplished, the path to the Underworld opens before him and he descends. Here, the image of the dragon's jaws as a gateway to the Underworld returns to mind, and his downward journey is complete.

While individually each element in Jason's Aea may have a multiplicity of meanings and explanations, when taken in aggregate it seems impossible that pure coincidence would string together so many symbols with clear significance to the Underworld. Certainly, even if the earliest Jason story was not intended to be an Underworld narrative, later tradition has made it so. Placing Aea in the broader context of both Greek mythology and Near Eastern mythology emphasizes with uncanny results the close relationship of Aea with the land of the dead, and given the multiplicity of authors working across centuries with the mythic tradition, the most parsimonious conclusion would be that the core Jason story was a katabasis, upon which all later versions were based and to which Apollonius and the *Orphic Argonautica* consciously or not sought to return.

8

The Occultist

Magic, Monsters and the Golden Fleece

The Greeks imagined their world as suffused with magical power, and they expended immense energy pursuing advantage through magical incantations, potions, curses, and spells. Some of these magical interventions were little more than appeals to the gods through the proper and appropriate magic words needed for occult intercessory prayer. Other interventions, like the protective ointment Medea gives to Jason in Apollonius' *Argonautica*, involve the preparation of elixirs and medicines from special herbs and exotic ingredients. Magical practitioners of many stripes prowled the Greek world, including medicine men, psychics, ritual purifiers, wonder-workers, and necromancers. And of course the gods held their fair share of magic, as did the heroes who were worshipped in their chthonic homes under the earth.

In the deep past, in the time before Homer, perhaps into the Mycenaean Age, the magic of heaven, earth, and the underworld were considered all of a piece, with humans able to wield the same types of powers as the gods themselves, though to a lesser extent.[1] This is the reason, Derek Collins argued, that the *Odyssey* makes no comment on the necromantic activity of Odysseus in the grove of Persephone; necromancy had not yet been delineated as a distinct and dishonorable activity, and the close interaction of men with the magic of heaven and the Underworld was taken for granted. Only later would calling up the dead come to be seen as a thing apart from the normal rites and sacrifices of religious life, and a dark part at that. But this was long after Homer had become too canonical to remove the episode. Similarly, the use of medicinal preparations (drugs, or *pharmaka*) was afforded to the gods, humans, and chthonic powers alike. While the divine Hermes or semi-divine Circe might have special knowledge of rare medicinal plants, human doctors also had recourse to the same healing powers through their own, albeit more limited, knowledge of medical magic.[2]

However, in time the Greeks began to categorize some forms of magic as dangerous, un–Greek, and reserved only for the gods. This appears to occur at the same time that the Greeks begin to conceive of the gods as celestial and transcendent rather than chthonic and imminent, which is to say when Zeus takes his Olympian throne. These new conceptions manifest in the criticisms leveled against magic practitioners during the fifth and fourth centuries BCE when the Hippocratic physicians and Plato argued that "exploiting nature's properties in magic in some sense implies a mastery of the divine," which no pious Greek could countenance.[3] It was at this same time, according to Mackie, that the "censorious" poets removed Jason's own magical powers of healing from the literary treatments of his myth (though they were preserved in fifth century pottery images), and they transferred his magic to Medea to make him a pious and proper Greek, and to reserve for the gods such powers as the healing of blindness.[4] By the Classical period, laws begin to emerge prohibiting some types of magical actions. A "witch" named Theoris of Lemnos was tried and executed in fourth century BCE Athens for marketing harmful incantations and potions, and across Greece practitioners of dangerous magic were prosecuted or executed, though perhaps on charges of impiety for daring to suggest the ability to manipulate the gods rather than for magic per se.[5] Clearly, something changed in these centuries, with a new understanding of the relationship between men and the gods, and who has the right to manipulate supernatural power.

Therefore, it is little wonder that so many of the otherworldly and magical aspects of Jason's story have been toned down, eliminated, or otherwise imposed upon other, foreign characters as the Jason myth traveled down the centuries. This chapter will look at magic and monsters in the Argonaut saga and attempt to place them in the larger context of Greek (and non–Greek) magical thought.

Medea, Hecate and Earth Magic

If we accept that in the earliest stories the healer Jason was himself in command of his magic, the presence of the infernal goddess Hecate in the Argonaut myth starts to become more understandable. The most ancient versions of the story in the surviving fragments do not reference Hecate, and for the most part her presence is extraneous. Hera, Athena, and Aphrodite are generally assigned, in some combination, command of the situation; and it is their magic that causes Medea to fall in love and Jason to succeed. Medea, by contrast, possesses a superior but human level of medicinal skill. As late as Pindar, Medea is depicted as simply possessing the knowledge to combine herbs and olive oil, without the infernal connotations.

However, during the period when magic started to achieve a bad reputation, the time of the Hippocratic and Platonic attacks on magic, something changes in Medea and thus in the Jason story. First, Jason's magic had been transferred to Medea, a foreigner, a non–Greek, onto whom such powers could be safely disposed without compromising the hero's piety. But Medea's magic could not be the same pure, beneficent magic that the gods had shared with men in the old days. This non–Greek, foreign magic took on associations with the powers of darkness for the very logical reason that if goodness was synonymous with living a pious Greek life and leaving control of certain types of magic to the gods, then anyone who wielded such powers must be either evil, a witch, or in league with the dark powers. It is no coincidence, then, that Medea's later history becomes a tale of increasing wickedness as authors wrote of the foreign witch-queen against a backdrop where philosophers had come to interpret the practice of magic as a form of dangerous impiety. Consequently, when Sophocles causes Medea to consort with Hecate in *The Root-Cutters* and Euripides in *Medea*, the association had become entirely natural.

Hecate was a foreign goddess, and therefore one appropriate to foreigners like Medea. She was rationalized as the cousin of the huntress Artemis, but she had originated as a mother goddess or earth goddess in Asia Minor, only coming into the Greek sphere during the Dark

Ages or early Archaic, somewhat too late to have been original to the Jason story. Hesiod praises her as a great and beneficent universal goddess "whom Zeus the son of Cronus honored above all" and made a nurse of the young.[6] She is not yet identified with the Underworld, another strike against her originality in Jason's story. By the seventh century she became associated with ghosts, crossroads, and black magic, appearing at this time with dark connotations in the *Hymn to Demeter*, where she is an attendant of Persephone, queen of the Underworld. Hecate's associates are the ghosts of the restless dead, and magicians of the Classical period routinely sought her aid in performing magical rites. This change from benevolent to infernal goddess is perhaps mirrored in the transformation of Medea at Corinth from a protective goddess of childbirth into the monstrous child-killing creature commemorated in the statue known as "the Terror."

Since Medea and Hecate are closely aligned, we are not surprised to see that Medea calls upon the rites of Hecate in protecting Jason in Apollonius' *Argonautica*. As mentioned in chapter 7, the protection Medea offers Jason in this poem is necromantic in tone, and it also draws explicitly on the rites Odysseus offered to call up the dead in the *Odyssey*. The same pit is dug, and the same dark sacrifices are offered, only now they call forth Hecate rather than the spirits of the friendlier human dead:

> When at thy coming my father has given thee the deadly teeth from the dragon's jaws for sowing, then watch for the time when the night is parted in twain, then bathe in the stream of the tireless river, and alone, apart from others, clad in dusky raiment, dig a rounded pit; and therein slay a ewe, and sacrifice it whole, heaping high the pyre on the very edge of the pit. And propitiate only-begotten Hecate, daughter of Perses, pouring from a goblet the hive-stored labour of bees. And then, when thou hast heedfully sought the grace of the goddess, retreat from the pyre; and let neither the sound of feet drive thee to turn back, nor the baying of hounds, lest haply thou shouldst maim all the rites and thyself fail to return duly to thy comrades. And at dawn steep this charm in water, strip, and anoint thy body therewith water, strip, and anoint thy body therewith as with oil; and in it there will be boundless prowess and mighty strength, and thou wilt deem thyself a match not for men but for the immortal gods.[7]

As mentioned earlier, Orpheus performs a similar rite to open the great gate in the *Orphic Argonautica*, though with more explicitly necromantic activity, and in both instances the result is the same: The goddess appears in her hideousness, clothed in Apollonius with a crown of snakes and oak twigs, just as the Grove of Ares would hold a snake entwined on an oak tree. In the Orphic version, Pandora and the Furies come, too. Thus have the propitiatory rites of Odysseus been transformed into fully necromantic rites, in keeping with Classical and Hellenistic ideas about the foreign, un–Greek, and essentially impious nature of presumptuous rites intended to make demands of the gods. By contrast, Apollonius allows Jason one bit of magic, or more correctly, magical ritual. Jason imbibes and spits out the blood of Apsyrtus while ritually mutilating the dead lad's body, a magical rite associated with appeasing the ghosts of the murdered. However, it is made clear from the context that this is a reprehensible act that requires purification, which takes Jason and Medea to the island of Circe to undo the contamination they have acquired.

Similar concerns must have factored into the gradual transformation of Jason's resurrection. At first, it seems that Jason descended into the dragon and returned. Later, his resurrection takes on a more necromantic cast in Medea's cauldron, perhaps incorporating a darker take on the bath of purification[8] which was an essential aspect of initiation into sacred mysteries, marriage rites, and, therefore, of the hero's descent into the Underworld and return, which historically shared many traits in Greek conception with initiation rites. In the Homeric epics, women bathe heroes who return from conflict with cauldrons of water and anoint them with oil (which Homer metaphorically likens to making them like gods[9]), and as Jason's intended bride, Medea would have performed a ritual bath for him, and Jason would have taken one both as the returning hero and as bridegroom. That the Jason legend contains purification imagery is confirmed by the presence of a ram's fleece in the story, which since Mycenaean times was an essential element of ritual purification (see below). Thus, as the story changed through time, the bath of purification became the locus of the resurrection itself, its cleansing waters curdled into a sorceress' stew. (A modern rationalizing view instead suggests that Medea's cauldron is a memory in myth of Greeks finding early Iron Age burials in which ashes and bits of cremated bone were stored in bronze cauldrons, but it seems unlikely to me.[10]) T. T. Duke recognized Medea's cauldron as a close relative of the bathtub where in Aeschylus' *Oresteia* Clytemnestra kills her husband Agamemnon upon his return from Troy, and he concluded that it represented for Aeschylus the blood-catching bowl of a religious sacrifice, used for chthonic blood rites associated with the dying and rising vegetation god of Crete.[11] It is quite possible that the bowl of sacrifice and the cauldron of purification became conflated in the Jason myth, giving rise to the necromantic overtones of Medea's actions, and eventually to the relocation of Jason's resurrection to her bowl.

We know that Pherecydes and Simonides claimed that Medea dismembered Jason and restored him in her magic cauldron, an event that must have referred originally to ritual rebirth (like that of shamans) since Jason would, at twenty, have been too young to need "rejuvenation." We also know that this event was first displaced onto Jason's father, Aeson, and then onto Pelias, probably when the original idea of rebirth (an area best left to the gods) degraded into simple rejuvenation (which was less impious). In this final transformation, the resurrection is aborted, and the dark magic associated with this violation of the prerogatives of the gods is not actually used. A parallel can be found in the Near East, where the sixth century BCE Jewish mystic Ezekiel describes an animal sacrifice being boiled in a cauldron until all the meat is gone, thus purifying sin.[12] In Mesopotamian myth, Enki (or, later, Marduk) slaughters a god and the other gods immerse themselves in his blood, called explicitly a "purification bath," and afterward, human life is born when the slaughtered god's dismembered and rendered flesh and blood is mixed with clay in the bath.[13] Such ritual rites conducted by baths occur elsewhere in Greek myth; in the *Odyssey* and in Aeschylus, as we have seen, and Achilles is dipped into the Styx to grant him invulnerability. In another version recorded in the *Aegimius*, his mother Thetis threw her children except Achilles into a cauldron of water to test their mortality and they all died. At some point the mythic rebirth of the ritual bath took on presumptuous overtones of trespassing on the divine. In Archaic myth first recorded in Pindar, Zeus kills Asclepius for resurrecting the dead, and the poets of the Archaic emphasized the punishment imposed on Greeks who impugn on the territory of the gods. Since Homer is silent on Asclepius' fate, it is possible that like Jason his deeds were once celebrated but later remodeled to reflect a new understanding of the relationship between god, man, and magic.

Medea used a different form of magic to destroy the bronze giant Talos, bewitching him with the evil eye, which caused him to swoon, fall, and scratch the vein that ran through his ankle, making the ichor of life leak out until he died. Talos is the last survivor of the Age of Bronze, the period before modern men, and in later myth he was deemed bronze himself, through a confusion of the Bronze Age with the idea that men were then made of bronze. Following the precedents of Greek magic, Medea invokes the gods of the Underworld to achieve her aim, using the evil eye, an ancient superstition dating back to pre–Greek times. However, this episode of magical invention is a late addition to the Jason myth. According to Apollodorus, Talos existed in two mythical forms: first, as the last living man from the Age of Bronze, and second as a bull given to Minos by Hephaestus.[14] Since the Cretan word *talos* is the same as *helios* on the mainland, it has been argued since ancient times that Talos was originally a Cretan sun god, represented as a bull, a man, or a bull-headed man.[15] A remnant of his godhood remains in the ichor said to flow through his veins, ichor being the divine equivalent of blood. Apollodorus records three variants in the death of this demigod: Medea removing the nail sealing his vein, Medea driving him mad with drugs, and the great archer of the Argonauts, Poeas, shooting him in the ankle. If the pattern of Medea taking over actions formerly ascribed to other actors holds true, the story that Poeas attacked Talos would have been the oldest form, and relocated to Medea as the locus for impious acts, such as causing the death of a divine being. Of Poeas, little is written. His name apparently refers to vegetation,[16] and Quintus Smyrnaeas described him as "godlike" in his third century CE *Trojan Epic*, itself influenced by Apollonius' *Argonautica*. In Apollodorus he sets light to Heracles' funeral pyre, but in most versions another performs this task. With so little to go on, we cannot conclude that Poeas was another in the line of vegetation figures who raid the land of the sun-underworld god, but the symbolism seems right, and compares to Heracles' wounding of Hades and Hera in the *Iliad*, and the way those stories were also toned down or suppressed in subsequent versions. At any rate, the Talos incident is certainly not original to the Jason story and came in when the epic poets raided the storehouse of myth to provide new incidents for the Argonauts following Homer's own raid on the Argonauts' original stash of stories. In the visual tradition, fifth century vase images show Castor and Pollux attacking Talos, and some believe the figure removing the nail from Talos' ankle on one of the extant vases is Jason himself, a very different tradition from the Medea-centric version.[17] Obviously, an attack on a god (former or otherwise) was a tremendous act of presumption.

Such presumptive abilities were inappropriate for the (human) Jason in the highest realms of poetry but acceptable at first for his divine consort, Medea, in her early role as goddess. As she grew increasingly less divine in literature, her magical abilities became increasingly threatening and therefore impious. While the poets could displace the magic from Jason to the foreigner Medea, there was nowhere else for these powers to go, and as a result the ex-goddess became increasingly witchy and eventually an embodiment of infernal power. A similar transformation affected the other half of Jason's brush with rebirth, the serpent, as we shall see. But before we consider the snake, we should first conclude our survey of magical people in the Argonauts' adventure.

Seers and Oracles

Another form of Greek magic practice was foretelling the future, through the practice of divination from signs in the natural world, through seers who were personally connected to the divine, and through oracles where the god spoke directly to humans through a human vessel. In Pindar's Fourth Pythian Ode, Medea herself takes on the role of seer and forecasts the eventual establishment of Greek colonies in North Africa. Seers and oracles derive ultimately from the shaman who has special access to the gods. However, archaeologically, oracles are associated first with the great temples of the gods in Egypt, Asia Minor, and Mesopotamia, where the gods would deign to speak with humans. Prophets and prophesy are documented on tablets in Mesopotamia back to the twenty-first century BCE, where seers known as *maḥḥû* or *muḫḫû*, deriving from a word meaning "frenzied," offered prophesies in altered states and were associated with temple sites.[18] The chief gods associated with divination were Shamash, the sun, and his brother Adad, the storm god, whose sacred animal was the bull and who used lightning as his weapon, just like Zeus. In one prophecy given through a human mediator at the Oracle of Adad around 2000 BCE Adad demands land, an estate, as payment for giving a king the throne:

> Am I not Adad, lord of Kallassu, who raised [the king] in my lap and restored him to his ancestral home? [...] Now since I restored him to his ancestral throne, I may take the estate away from his patrimony. [If the king] fulfils my desire, I shall give him throne upon throne, house upon house, territory upon territory, city upon city. I shall give him the land from the rising of the sun to its setting.[19]

Another fragmentary prophecy appeared to warn a king to avoid travel and to neither buy nor store goods so long as his enemies circled the borders of his kingdom.[20] These prophesies, conveyed to kings, obviously parallel the warnings that the Greek oracles gave to Pelias and Aeëtes to caution them on the insecurity of their thrones. However, there is no evidence of oracles in the Mycenaean age, though the Hittites apparently had oracles in the second millennium BCE,[21] yet it is likely that the Mycenaeans practiced a form of prophecy through divination based on the flight of birds. Oracular rites in Greece, however, appear around the ninth century, possibly transmitted from the Near East via the Hittites during the Dark Age.[22] They must therefore have been added to the Jason story after then.

In the Argonaut tales, the primary role of seer is associated with Idmon and Mopsus on the *Argo*, and Phineus, whom the Argonauts visit. There were two mythic figures named Mopsus, who may have originated in one Near Eastern figure who differentiated into two, a Thessalian and an Asian one, at a later date.[23] The Asian Mopsus was apparently a historical figure, or believed to be so, long before Homer. An inscription from Asia Minor records mention of the house of Muksas in Hittite, or Mps (Mopsu) in Phoenician,[24] while another evidently refers to Moksus as far back as the fifteenth century BCE,[25] though Robin Lane Fox argued that the oldest name cannot be related to the later, eighth century versions, concluding that Mopsus was a Dark Age figure that the Greek identified with a preexisting Greek Mopsus in the eighth century BCE.[26] He had his own body of mythology as a wandering seer who founded cities in the wake of the Mycenaean collapse, and competed in tests of his psychic power according to Hesiod. Michael Attyah Flower suggests that Mopsus may represent a mythic memory of the way divination by entrails was imported to Greece from the Near East during the Greek Dark Ages, supplementing the old forms of divination by bird flight.[27] The second Mopsus was a seer from Dodona who specialized in augury by bird flight, and this Mopsus was the seer of the *Argo*. This Mopsus may appear in Linear B tablets as *Mo-qo-so* (though Lane Fox doubts this connection), and quite possibly the name was originally not a person but an ancient, Near Eastern title meaning "prophet" rather than referring to a specific individual.[28] This idea would harmonize the two characters named Mopsus as vari-

Delphi claimed to be built atop a serpent slain by Apollo, whose chthonic power inspired the Pythia to deliver prophecies. The Oracle at Delphi was the most famous place where the gods communed with humankind, but oracle sites were located throughout Greece. The *Argo* was built with an oracular plank from Zeus' grove at Dodona, from which the seer Mopsus came. Idmon the seer came from Delphi to speak for the gods. Since Dodona was the older oracle site, the Delphic seer is probably a later interpolation in the Jason myth (Library of Congress).

ants on the ancient prophetic title. Our Mopsus, at any rate, was independent of Jason until Pindar (or the tradition he drew on) placed him aboard the *Argo*, perhaps due to the same magnetic attraction that drafted other famous heroes, such as Heracles and Orpheus, to Argonautic service.

The *Argo*'s other seer was Idmon, and he appears to have originated in a personification of divinatory power, or as a prophetic title that would have been awarded to another character.

His name means simply "the man with second sight."[29] The existing fragments show that early Argonaut stories featured either Idmon or Mopsus, but not both, before Apollonius. The best reconstruction suggests that the *Argo* first had a prophetic plank from Dodona, followed by a version where the magic object was supplanted by a human seer, Mopsus, from that shrine. (The plank has little to do in later versions, suggesting its role was usurped.) Later, when the Oracle at Delphi eclipsed Dodona in glory, a prophet associated with Delphi's god, Apollo, came aboard, and the oracle warning Pelias of Jason's coming became the Oracle of Delphi. The seer of Apollo would be Idmon, said to be Apollo's son.[30] Still later, the ancillary seers Thestor (Idmon's son) and Amphiaraus of Thebes, a chthonic hero worshipped in Boetia, were added.

Regarding the oracular plank, there is an interesting fact. The Greeks believed that the oldest images of the gods were in fact planks. On the island of Samos, legend had it that the first cult image of Hera was a simple wooden board, and on Ikaros, a piece of rough wood represented Artemis.[31] Since we also know the Minoans carried statues of the gods on ships as protectors, the oracular plank may have originated in an attempt to convey the understanding that a god rode aboard the ship using the Dark Age understanding of what that would mean—a plank. That this plank would be associated with an oracle only makes sense, since oracles and statues were manifestations of the gods. In Epirus, the famous Oracle of Dodona provided visitors with the will of Zeus as revealed through the rustling of oak leaves, the flight of birds, and other such signs. However, the original possessor of the oracle was quite possibly an earth goddess, the pre–Mycenaean equivalent of Hera, who may have surrendered the site to Zeus around 1400 BCE when the earliest evidence of Mycenaean settlement appears. Since Hera was the protector of Jason, this makes the inclusion of a Dodona plank doubly interesting, but probably not relevant. In Mycenaean times there was likely more than one Dodona, as evidenced by passages in Homer that discuss Dodona as being on the frontier between Thessaly and Achaea, neither of which is near faraway Epirus.[32] Fragmentary material from the lost seventh book of Strabo confirms this, with Strabo noting stories from Suidas and Cineas, Thessalian antiquarians, that Zeus's temple had been transported from Scotussa to Epirus along with many priestesses, or that the sacred oak of Zeus at the Dodona of Thessaly was burned at the order of Apollo and the shrine thereafter removed to Epirus.[33] Indeed, some scholars believe this lost Dodona is the one which donated its oak to Jason, and that among the sacred rites of this oracle was the keeping of a single bare foot, like that of Jason with the one sandal.[34]

In the Greek tradition, these types of sacred places where the Olympian gods spoke to and through humans appear to exist only after the eighth century BCE or so, when the great pan–Greek oracles at Dodona and Delphi come to prominence.[35] Prior to this, "oracles" were instead associated with sacred groves and springs leading to the Underworld, the sites where the chthonic gods could be approached. At these sites, such as the Dark Age oracle of the dead at Ephyra, ghosts could be summoned and trips to the Underworld simulated mentally or physically.[36] In fact, down until the Roman era, oracles of the dead provided an experience of katabasis where the rising up of ghosts to speak prophesies became indistinguishable from the descent of the supplicant into the Underworld, a merging of the lands of the living and the dead.[37]

I would suggest that if the figures in the Jason story were originally gods (and therefore had no need of oracles), the oracles would have entered the story in part to take the place of the former deities, whose divine aspects have been removed skyward, as well as to bring the myth into conformity with Archaic and Classical understandings of the universe as the machinations of fate. The oracles thus prove the imminence and power of the otherwise now mostly absent divinities and serve the function of the chorus in Greek tragedy, commenting on the action and providing the argument of the drama.

Finally, the Argonauts visit Phineus, the seer-king of Thrace, and from him they learn the path to Colchis. His myth, however, appears to have originally been separate from that of the Argonauts,[38] though possibly parallel in some fashion. There were two men named Phineus in myth, though it would seem that a single figure stands behind both and was separated into two figures when his stories were applied to two separate sections of mythical time. The older Phineus was a brother of Cadmus, who, like his brother, journeyed around the world in search of Europa, whom Zeus abducted. He founded the kingdom in Thrace that Jason's Phineus ruled.

As scholars have noted, the earliest Phineus figure was a hubristic king blinded by the gods in retribution for sin, either blinding his own sons, discarding his wife, or plotting against Aeëtes' brother Perses, another son of the Sun.[39] Only later did the fifth century tragic poets try to burnish his image as a divinely-wronged sinner whose crime was knowing too much.[40] Strabo preserves a fragment of Ephorus the historian, who in turn quotes a lost poem attributed to Hesiod, the *Journey round the Earth* (which recalls the first Phineus' wanderings), which said that the Harpies took Phineus to the land of the milk-feeders, which have been identified with the Scythians of the Black Sea coast.[41] The sons of the Boreal Wind, Zetes and Calais, drove them off from Phineus after praying to Zeus, and the extant fragment of Hesiod's *Catalogue* detailing their adventures suggests that the *Journey* may originally have been a poem about the twins' adventures chasing the Harpies across the Greek landscape. Two variants survive indicating why the Harpies hounded Phineus, first because he showed Phrixus the path to Colchis, and second because he chose blindness with long life over a quick death, offending the gods.

The Harpies, in turn, were not originally the winged bird-women of later depiction but personifications of the storm winds. In the Archaic, and earlier, they were beautiful women (according to Hesiod), who Homer said operated in the Ocean, taking souls to Hades' servants. Having the sons of the Boreal Wind chase the personifications of the wind around earth was poetically appropriate. One can almost imagine a story in which Phineus commits a sin and proceeds around the world in desperate attempt to stay ahead of the Harpies who wish to drag him to Hades, but this leaves little trace in myth. Some form of the Phineus legend probably crossed into the Argonauts' story much later, when Jason's voyage was imagined as passing through the kingdom associated with Phineus, given variously as Thrace or in parts of Asia Minor, when the Greeks began to plot the *Argo's* path onto the geography of the Black Sea.

Serpents and Dragons

One of the animals most closely connected with seers and divination was the serpent, and the Oracle of Delphi was closely connected with the legend of Apollo and Python. The latter was a large serpent who symbolized the earth, which in the guise of Gaia was the reputed first owner of the oracle site. Apollo slew Python, whose body was said to rot beneath the oracle site, providing the imagined vapors that allowed Apollo's priestess, the Pythia, to commune with the god. Such a scene is by no means unique in world mythology, or even Greek mythology. Among the Greek heroes, Perseus kills a serpent and a serpent-woman (Medusa). Heracles kills a serpent (twice, Ladon and Hydra). Bellerophon is thought by some scholars to have originated as a dragon-slayer, later expanded into the winged lion-goat-dragon Chimera. And Cadmus, of course, killed the dragon that yielded the teeth Jason planted. Some or all of these dragons may derive ultimately from the same exceedingly old source, but the exact details are speculative.[42] In non–Indo-European cultures, the snake is frequently associated with positive traits such as fertility, the earth, and goddess figures (as it was on Crete), possibly because serpents can be seen as phallic symbols that penetrate and thus fertilize the earth. The Indo-Europeans are believed to have instead viewed the serpent as a chthonic monster whose associations with the older earth religion posed a challenge to the supremacy of the storm god or sky god. In fact, scenes of heroes killing giant serpents are among the most frequent motifs in all myth, as close to universal as any. In this regard, Jason's serpent is nothing special.

The words dragon and serpent are used interchangeably for monstrous snake-like creatures in these stories because both terms translate the Greek word *drakon* (Latin: *draco*), meaning originally serpent. The ancients envisioned dragons as a type of giant serpent, and they were distinct from the winged, pawed, fire-breathing creatures of medieval legend. The ancient view of the dragon can clearly be seen on the extant ancient images of Jason and the snake, which universally show the creature Jason battled as an oversized snake, frequently entwined around the oak holding the Golden Fleece. He is distinguished from his smaller cousins in many images by the presence of a beard. Recent scholarly efforts have attempted to demonstrate that the Greeks interpreted Pleistocene fossils, including those of mammoths in the Aegean and spinosaurs (a type of dinosaur with a dorsal fin) in Egypt, as the bones of dragons.[43] As evidence, Adrienne Mayor points to a Corinthian krater from the sixth century BCE which depicts Heracles' battle with the sea monster outside Troy. This krater shows what appears to be an ancient reptile or mammal skull eroding from a cliff instead of the expected serpent,[44] though others think it a monster emerging from the wave Poseidon sent to menace Troy.[45] However, the idea that sixth century Greeks thought fossils proved the reality of mythic creatures does not prove that the mythic creatures were inspired originally by the fossils. Another modern interpretation, finding the origin of giant serpents and dragons in exaggerated reports of real snakes, crocodiles, and whales,[46] is also interesting, but is restricted to the Hellenistic and Roman eras, and cannot speak to the origins of the earliest myths.

The motif of the battle with the serpent is common in the mythologies of most of the peoples who speak Indo-European languages, and scholars argue that it is one of the Proto-Indo-European (PIE) foundational myths, dating back to the Stone Age. Drawing from the parallel dragon-slaying stories in Hindu and Hittite myth, among others, scholars claim that in prehistoric myth, the storm god (= Teshub or Zeus) attempts to wrest a stolen treasure from the serpent, who defeats the god. The god then drinks an intoxicating beverage, giving him strength, and he defeats the dragon. This episode is closely associated, apparently, with the concept of rebirth or immortality,[47] which we have tied in other forms to the Jason story. This myth can be found in very similar forms across Indo-European cultures, notably in the

Slavic myth of the storm god Perun's battle against the serpentine underworld god Veles who lives across the great sea.[48] PIE theorists believe that priests were the repository of dragon stories, and told them of warrior kings to guarantee their immortality through fame, a valued PIE commodity.[49] Therefore, in much degraded and altered form, Jason takes the role of the god, his ointment is the equivalent of the beverage of strength, and the fleece is the dragon's treasure. Indeed, Watkins specifically argued that the Jason myth was a remembrance of the ancient PIE myth of the dragon-slayer based on Pindar's use of the shared formula of HERO-SLAY-DRAGON in the Fourth Pythian Ode[50]: "The glaring speckled dragon [...] he slew by subtlety."[51]

If this view is accepted, the similarities between Jason and other Indo-European serpent myths could derive from this earlier source, rather than direct cultural borrowing. PIE reconstructions, however, are not without a speculative element,[52] especially give the assertion that the formula equally applies to "hero slay hero," "hero slay (other) monster," and "dragon slay hero." The Greeks especially, according to Watkins, frequently substituted a second hero for the serpent (HERO-SLAY-HERO), thus rendering the monster human, or else used a different monster, such as giants, the Chimera, or a boar.[53] Watkins was primarily concerned with poetics and linguistics rather than mythology, so while his argument proves conclusively that the verb "to slay" has always been transitive, it is less helpful in seeking out the specifics of Jason's particular serpent except in the most general way. The weight of evidence seems to favor transmission of motifs from a Near Eastern, and possibly non–Indo-European, source instead of survival from the distant past.

This *ketos*, or sea-serpent, depicted on a sixth-century BCE Corinthian krater has been interpreted as either a fossil skull emerging from a cliff or, more frequently, as a serpent emerging from a gigantic wave. The large black circles are stones Hesione is hurling at the *ketos*, while at bottom an arrow shot by Heracles pierces its jaw (author's drawing).

THE SERPENT IN THE NEAR EAST

In the Near East, the serpent is sometimes associated with the chaos-monster Tiamat, which Marduk slew. However, Tiamat was, despite later opinion, not originally viewed as a serpent but as the mother of serpents, somewhat like Hera (or Gaia), who was the mother of Typhon. We have already encountered in chapter 1 several of the Near East serpent myths that may have contributed to Jason's story, including the serpent who prevents Gilgamesh from attaining immortality, the serpent entwined around a tree in an early Gilgamesh poem, the serpent or dragon Inara and Teshub slay with the help of a hero, and the dragon Baal kills. To these we might add another, the serpent who tempts Eve in the Garden of Eden. Like the snake that guards the tree of the Fleece, or more closely, that which guards the tree of Golden Apples, this serpent offers the promise of immortality through the attainment of a forbidden fruit, that of the Tree of Knowledge: "[T]he serpent said to the woman, 'You will not die. For God knows that when you eat of it your eyes will be opened, and you will be like God, knowing good and evil.'"[54] This serpent, of course, inspired the dragon of Revelation, who is identified with the Devil and the Christian Underworld, Hell.

The serpent's connection to the Underworld is also found in the frequent depiction of the gates of the Underworld as the jaws of a monster. Serpents connect to the Underworld monster through the relationship between serpents as chthonic creatures and inhabitants of the Underworld, creatures noted for their great and gaping jaws (as in Pindar's Fourth Pythian Ode). Snakes are able to dislocate their jaws to swallow prey, making them ideal symbols for a gate to the realm of the dead that opens wide enough to swallow as many as it needs to accommodate. This image is most frequently encountered in medieval Europe where it became known as the Hellmouth; however, as we have seen the image of monstrous jaws leading into the bowels of the Underworld occurred in early Sumerian poetry, describing the pit into which the dead fall before the house of the sun. Nergal, the underworld god, is also identified at times as the "demon with the gaping mouth."[55] And this image recurs in the myth of Baal and Mot (derived from an earlier story of Baal slaying the dragon), where Mot, god of the dead, is defined entirely by his ravenous jaws into which Baal descends, like Jason into the dragon's jaws. In some Ugaritic texts, Mot is likened to a serpent that holds Baal as a metaphorical lamb in his mouth. In the book of Isaiah, the Underworld of the Jews (Sheol) is likened to a mouth in a passage believed to have been influenced by the mythology of Mot: "Therefore hell [Sheol] hath enlarged herself, and opened her mouth without measure: and their glory, and their multitude, and their pomp, and he that rejoiceth, shall descend into it."[56]

A similar image recurs in the biblical Psalm 69:15: "Let not the water-flood overflow me, neither let the deep swallow me up, and let not the pit shut her mouth upon me." Here the monster of the Underworld is equated with deep water, like the Apsû waters of the Mesopotamian underworld. More closely parallel to the Jason story is that of Jonah, who sails across the sea to flee from God, a parallel noted by scholars who suggest a common origin (See chapter 11). His shipmates cast Jonah into the sea to appease God's wrath, and he is swallowed by a great fish and lives within it for three days before emerging. Interestingly, this story occurs at Joppa, on the Levantine coast, where the Greeks and Philistines said Perseus slew the dragon to rescue Andromeda. Andromeda's chains and the bones of the beast were on display to tourists, according to Pliny. In the version ascribed pseudonymously to the Hellenistic poet Lycophron, Perseus killed the serpent by being swallowed and killing it from within, a story that developed simultaneously with Heracles' own descent into the serpent's belly to save Hesione. The two stories swapped motifs during their development.[57] The stories of Perseus and Jonah possibly derive from a common source, the dragon of Baal,[58] which is in the same tradition as Jason's dragon.[59] All of these dragons, in turn, seem to derive from still more ancient dragon slaying stories of the Near East and Proto-Indo-European traditions, or perhaps the near-universal motif of monstrous serpents found worldwide.

The image of a serpent entwined around a tree are frequent in Near Eastern art. Depictions of Adam and Eve with the serpent at the Tree of Knowledge, like this 1504 piece by Albrecht Dürer, have much in common with Roman-era sarcophagus depictions of Medea and a nude Jason retrieving the Fleece. Both images were associated with the concept of death, though with opposite connotations (Library of Congress).

Among the Mesopotamians, we have already seen Ningishzida resided in the Underworld and was associated with serpents, and indeed his symbol was the coiling of two serpents around a pole. This symbol is parallel to the caduceus carried by Hermes, who took that staff with him in guiding souls to the Underworld. Early twentieth century scholars assumed that Hermes' staff derived from Ningishzida's,[60] but modern scholars are less certain about the derivation. Ningishzida was, as noted, the Lord of the Good (or True) Tree, and associated with the image of a serpent coiling around the tree of life, the same image that recurs both in the Genesis narrative and in Jason's encounter in the Grove of Ares. If we can permit ourselves to consider the Good Tree in light of the Sumerian cedars of immortality and the purifying *gis-kin* tree, we see a constellation of overlapping symbols that reflect the same complex of images in the Jason myth: immortality and purification, about which more below. Since Ningishzida was a god of healing, due to the equation of serpents with tree roots and roots with medicine, and was often conflated with Tammuz/Dumuzi, it is exceptionally appropriate for Jason the Healer to encounter a serpent entwined about a great tree, an image that is repeated consistently on pottery and in poetry depicting the achievement of the Fleece.

Interestingly, a Babylonian text from the period of Marduk's supremacy, the horned snake of Ningishzida, the basmu, was said to measure "sixty leagues"[61] or "sixty double miles."[62] It is likely that the snake's imagined size grew through time and to make him a more impressive companion to his new god, Marduk. Though obviously vastly larger, the basmu recalls the description of the serpent of Colchis in Pindar as being larger than the *Argo* itself.

THE SERPENT CULT IN GREECE

As we have seen, the Minoans may have venerated a snake goddess, and in the ruins at Mycenae, coiled snake models were found, apparently objects of cult devotion. In Athens, the Erechtheion (Erechtheum) on the Acropolis was a temple dedicated to worshipping Erechtheus, who like Ningishzida was sometimes depicted as a snake with a human head and was identified with Poseidon,[63] perhaps a memory of the earlier earth gods of the pre–Olympian pantheon. In myth, Poseidon kills Erechtheus, sending him into the earth with his trident for killing the god's son, Eumolpus. Similarly, Cecrops, the founder of Athens, was a serpent with a man's head, and within the temple of Erectheus a living snake represented Cecrops and was fed honey-cakes. The serpent also appeared beside Athena in the art of the Acropolis, symbolizing these figures. Burkert connects Poseidon-Erectheus to an ancient pattern of a god who is defeated (symbolically dead) and remains powerful beneath the earth.[64] Since this figure was identified with the snake, we once again have an underworld serpent. However, there were many other serpent cults in early Greece, the most important of which involved both a serpent and a ram's fleece. This cult worshipped an underground form of Zeus, which through the conflation of the powers within the earth (chthonic heroes and gods) and those beneath it (the Underworld) may have also been seen as a form of Hades and was certainly viewed as chthonic.

The popular and widespread Greek cult of the snake-formed chthonic god Zeus Meilichios, dating from perhaps the late Archaic period, has a close resonance with the climax of the story of Jason, including the possible overlay of Zeus imagery onto a much older earth cult, as Jane Ellen Harrison adduced in a classic 1903 study:

> The cult of the Olympian Zeus has overlaid the cult of a being called Meilichios, a being who was figured as a snake, who was a sort of Ploutos [Plutus], but who had also some of the characteristics of an Erinys [one of the Furies]; he was an avenger of kindred blood, his sacrifice was a holocaust [i.e. complete burning to ash of the animal] offered by night, his festival a time of "chilly gloom." A further element in his cult was a magical fleece used in ceremonies of purification and in the service of heroes. The cult of Meilichios is unlike that of the Olympian Zeus as described in Homer, and the methods of purification characteristic of him wholly alien. The name of his festival means "the ceremonies of imprecation"[65] [brackets added].

Most surely we can see in this a close parallel to the image of the snake in the grove of Ares, guarding the Golden Fleece that represents the soul of the hero Jason's kinsman, Phrixus. While Jane Ellen Harrison thought Meilichios was originally a snake god himself, contemporary scholars are less certain about whether Zeus imposed himself on an indigenous snake god, or whether Zeus Meilichos came to Greece fully formed.[66] The name Meilichios is sometimes thought to derive from the word for "honey,"[67] which recalls the honey-cakes used to propitiate the serpent in the Grove of Ares. However, modern theorists suspect that the Athenians adopted the cult of the chthonic snake god from the Near East, where it originated in the rites of Baal-Milik during the Dark Ages, and was much transformed.[68] The similar sound of the words for Milik and the Greek word for honey gave rise to a folk etymology and thus to the practice of making sweet offerings to the god in return for favors. It may be possible that both ideas are true, and an indigenous snake god (perhaps the ancestor of the other man-headed snake men like Erecthonius) was identified with a foreign deity during the period of oriental contact, thus bringing Zeus into the chthonic rites through his identification with Baal as storm gods.

The archaeological and philological evidence tends to favor this interpretation, given the fact that some form of Zeus had been worshipped at the altar of Meilichios in Athens since before the time of Homer, indicating that a Dark Age or even Mycenaean deity lay behind the snake god; only in Hellenistic times would the Olympian Zeus's image supersede that of the snake god in the worship of Zeus Meilichios.[69] In the Athenian festival of the Pompaia, the festival of Zeus, a ram's fleece and a staff with intertwined snakes—the symbol of the Mesopotamian chthonic god Ningishzida, who like Meilichios is also a god with snake aspects—were carried in a parade to invoke the god's aid in protecting newly planted grain.[70] As befit the mixed nature of the Olympian-chthonic hybrid human-snake god, the ram sacrificed for his fleece was killed in the manner of sacrifice to chthonic gods, but his meat was consumed in keeping with rites offered to the Olympians.[71]

THE SERPENT AND THE HEALER

While these snake cults and Near East healing snakes present the positive aspects of the snake or snake god, which may derive from the old, non–Indo-European religious ideology, the Indo-European version of the snake story is much harsher on the snake, who in these stories is not the granter of favors, healing, or purification, but the obstacle to achieving these boons. Interestingly, Watkins provides a link between the motif of the dragon-slayer and that of the medicine man or healer, the two halves of Jason. According to Watkins, the PIE myth of the slaying of the dragon, or rather its poetic formula, could be taken as a charm used for healing under the twin PIE ideas that the spoken word (incantation) is the most powerful magical force on earth, and that the serpent is the equivalent of the worm (seen as a miniature serpent) or snake, an agent of disease and the cause of human suffering:

> If the dragon or serpent is conceived of as a monstrous sort of worm, then the mythographic formula, the paean which proclaims the death of the dragon can assure by verbal magic, by the power of the spoken word, the destruction of the worm. The verbal magic is the homeopathic, analogic magic of a charm or incantation.[72]

Such imagery is found throughout the Indo-European world, from Ireland and Norway to Iran and India. Killing the serpent thus becomes cognate with curing disease, making the dragon-slayer also a healer and vice-versa. And since the healer-hero of the PIE people was also originally a god, and the serpent identified with death, the healer's attack on the serpent is the god's attack on death, and the promise of immortality through magic. The PIE healer was skilled in both the art of medical plants as well as medical formulae,[73] which immediately recalls Jason's two distinctive traits: his mastery of herbs (in the oldest myths) and his mastery of oratory. And there we have the heart of the Jason story found anew through another method of inquiry.

If this view of the PIE people is correct, the Mycenaeans would have inherited alongside the Minoan snake cult and Near East underworld serpents the Indo-European imagery of the healer slaying the serpent as a metaphor for the conquest of disease, and even death. Mycenaean Greek, of course, is an Indo-European language, and the Mycenaeans the descendants of the PIE people who migrated into the Balkan Peninsula a few centuries before their reign. We also know that the Hittites thought enough of the Mycenaeans' medicine to send for their healer god to cure their sick king, indicating a strong medical tradition. Therefore, this proposed confluence of ideas and images both for and against the serpent is not improbable, especially in light of the dual role of the serpent as chthonic god and serpentine enemy from Archaic Greece onward.

This linkage may help explain how the story of a vegetation god who dies, ventures to the Underworld, and returns became linked to a *prima facie* different story of a hero who slays the dragon; i.e., how Dumuzi and Inanna became linked to Teshub and the dragon. Both stories would have featured the idea of a healer in one sense or another, and both would have culminated in the healer's triumph over death. If the dragon-jaws of the Underworld, or the serpent of disease, became identified with the chaos dragon, then the Mycenaean Greeks or their successors may have run the stories together, linking their own dying and rising healer god to the serpent through the healer's ability to "kill" the metaphorical serpents of disease, thus externalizing the serpents within the body as literal dragons in the Underworld that the healer-hero must confront in order to stave off death and win the hand of his goddess-bride. Based on Watkins' linguistic evidence linking the transmission of the Teshub-dragon myth to Greece in the middle second millennium BCE,[74] we can propose that the core of the Jason story at Aea started to take its classic form by the end of the Mycenaean era, around 1200 BCE. In this reading, the original Jason may have indeed gained immortality from the jaws of the serpent, only to have his myth softened to conform to the more pious sentiments of Archaic and Classical Greeks, an inference we have already encountered through other lines of evidence.

With all that said, the serpent is obviously both an exceedingly complex and ambiguous symbol as well as one that is so universal as to be almost essential to a hero's adventure. It is only by reading the serpent in the context of other related symbols, including the sacred grove, purification, the land of the rising sun, and the sun god–Underworld linkage that this particular dragon's role can begin to be understood. There remains now only to account for the putative object of Jason's quest, the Golden Fleece, and how the ancient serpent-god's fleece of purification turned gold.

The Golden Fleece

The Golden Fleece is not the only time a golden sheep appears in Greek myth. In the myth of Atreus, that king of Mycenae possessed a golden lamb promised as a sacrifice to Artemis. In some versions he gave Artemis the flesh (as in a chthonic rite) but kept the fleece for himself, while in others he strangled and preserved the whole lamb. His wife made him promise that whosoever possessed the golden fleece would be king of Mycenae. She then gave the lamb to Atreus' brother Thyestes, her lover, who became king, though this judgment was reversed when the new king promised to give Atreus the throne should the sun set backward and Zeus made it so. After this dispute, Atreus boiled the sons of his brother in spite and served them to the ex-king, who was revenged many years later when his son killed Atreus and gave his father back the kingdom.[75] Thus, we have in a separate myth a usurping king, a golden fleece, a connection to the path of the sun, and boiling in a cauldron, just as we have in the story of Jason. This myth, however, has a darker cast, and though it seems to draw on the same symbolism (and possibly sources?) as Jason, it also appears to have taken these symbols in a much different direction, to which the golden lamb has become an incidental symbol of sovereignty.

The Golden Fleece is a multivalent symbol, like most in myth. It is unlikely that any one explanation will ever satisfactorily account for it, for it contains within it many threads that have been woven together into a mythic object. In this manner, the Fleece is similar to the hero Heracles, who contains within him many ancient characters, Greek and Near Eastern alike, that cannot readily be separated, and of which no one influence was the sole inspiration. However, again like Heracles, these threads of influence can be traced back, and some interesting conclusions drawn from them. Many scholars have proposed their own explanations and interpretations, which we will review in chapter 11. Here, however, I will offer my own ideas about the origins of the Golden Fleece, in keeping with the tradition that everyone who writes of Jason must forward his or her own pet theory about the Fleece, and then a decade later see it superseded by yet another, more compelling claim. My suggestion, which of course is no more definitive than any other, though I hope better supported by the extant evidence, proposes that the Fleece represents two separate objects that have become conflated into one: a ram's fleece used in rites of purification and the gold-encrusted garments donned by the divinities of the Near East upon their return from the Underworld.

THE FLEECE OF PURIFICATION

The ram is the male sheep and the leader and protector of the flock, making the ram a symbol of protection across the ancient world, including Greece, and in the Near East, where the ram's horn became a protective emblem of the Jews and a ram served as a substitute sacrifice for Isaac, much as the ram of the Golden Fleece substituted for Phrixus.[76] In a symbolic sense the ram is the equivalent of the shepherd, which as we recall was Jason's title, and reminds us of the image of Jesus carrying a ram on his shoulders in early Christian art, an image derived from Hermes carrying the young Dionysus in ram form to safety.[77] The ram plays a large role in Greek religion and rite, associated with Zeus, Hermes, Apollo, and Dionysus in Greece, and also with Baal and Ammon in the Near East. The ram Phrixus sacrificed was one of Hermes' rams, and he is the Greek god who bears the caduceus, the serpent staff of Ningishzida. At Athens, during the great festival of Zeus known as the Diasia, the chthonic Zeus Meilichios superintended an annual rite of purification during which a sacred "fleece of Zeus" was used. This fleece came from a ram sacrificed to the snake god, and the supplicant would step upon the fleece with his left foot, symbolically moving the pollution out of his body through the left side, considered the dark or evil side of the body, and onto the fleece, which was consecrated to the god and therefore a point of contact between worshipper and worshipped, and the recipient of sin, purifying the supplicant.[78]

As Harrison showed more than a century ago, this rite was an ancient one, but one whose ritual sacred fleece was far from unique. A ram's fleece was used in purification rites throughout Greece, and was likely not originally a specific aspect of the Zeus cult.[79] Similar fleeces as purification objects were used at the oracle of Amphiaraos, where the fleece of a sacrificed ram was used as bedding to induce visions; at the oracle of Calchas, where the same actions occurred; and worshippers of a "Syrian goddess" were reported to tie the fleece of a sacrificed ram around themselves as a purifying garment.[80] In a relief image, Heracles is depicted sitting on a ram's fleece to receive initiation into the Eleusinian Mysteries, which invoked the death and rebirth of Persephone, and the divine child of Iasion and Demeter. There the fleece is again a purification device for the initiate, making him ritually clean as he gained initiation. In the sixth century *Homeric Hymn to Demeter*, this fleece is described as metallic, "silvery" or "shimmering," like the Golden Fleece of Jason.[81] The fleece was therefore an essential element of ritual purification throughout Greece.[82] The reader will also recall the fleeces worn by the descendants of Athamas on Mt. Pelion during the rites performed there. Such fleeces were essential in purifying murderers after they had been sentenced for their crimes.

This fleece of purification is, however, no late development but in fact is one of the oldest attested religious rites of the Greeks. On the Mycenaean Linear B tablets from Pylos, we find a list of the offerings given to Poseidon, which in order were wheat, wine, a bull, cheese, a ram's fleece, and then honey. As Burkert noted, "Not only the combination of items, but the very order in which they are listed, agrees with Greek cultic precepts," which required offerings of grain, a libation, animal sacrifice, bloodless offerings, "and the fleece probably for purification."[83] To this we might add that the honey recalls the sweet offerings offered to chthonic powers, such as the Mycenaean earth gods would have been at this stage. It is possible that the rite of purification through contact with a ram's fleece originates in ancient beliefs about animal sacrifice, where he who sacrifices the ram wears the consecrated skin of his victim to connect with a god and in a spiritual way resurrect the animal offered to the god through the power of the divine.[84] Indeed a very clear parallel exists in Herodotus, who reported that the Zeus of Egypt, the god Ammon, had his statue at Thebes clothed once each year with a fresh fleece from a consecrated ram and his priests then bury the ram in a sacred tomb—the ram essentially *is* the god.[85]

The fragment of Hesiod's *Catalogue* mentioning the Golden Fleece says the Ram was immortal, so it is unclear whether Phrixus sacrificed it in the earliest versions. A first century BCE text attributed to Eratosthenes, the *Catasterismi*, reported that the Ram gave Phrixus his fleece before flying up to become the constellation Aries, though this may merely be an attempt to explain how a sacrificed ram ended up in the sky when sacrifice would have destroyed him. In the epic poem *Aegimius* from perhaps the seventh century BCE, the Golden Fleece is already linked to purification. In the scholia to Apollonius, the scholiast writes that "after the sacrifice he [Phrixus] purified the fleece" and entered Aeëtes' palace.[86] Logically, this should be the other way around, with the fleece purifying him who sacrificed it, but the point is still the same. However, since the Golden Fleece is not originally a part of Jason's story, and the golden ram skin Jason retrieves from Colchis appears to be an object that has been harmonized and synchronized with a formerly separate myth of Phrixus, the ram, and purification.

When the Golden Fleece entered Jason's story, perhaps by way of the Hittite *kurša* with which Phrixus' Fleece shares so many motifs (see chapter 11), it must have done so in replacement for something else, like the way Medea's cauldron may have replaced a ritual bath. I think the answer is to be found in the golden robes of royalty and Near Eastern divinities.

The Gods' Golden Garments

In Mesopotamian belief, the gods wore garments made of gold, and in ritual practice their statues were dressed in rich fabrics heavily laden with small pieces of gold on the pattern of scales used in bronze armor. Such garments are well attested in the eighth century BCE, and documentary evidence indicates their use as far back as the third dynasty in Ur, roughly the twentieth century BCE.[87] The same types of garments are seen over a geographically wide range, including areas of Asia Minor,[88] very close to the areas where the Greeks were adopting and adapting Near East beliefs and customs; and they were a hallmark of both divine and royal clothing. Such clothes were carefully prepared and usually consisted of a dyed wool base onto which golden decorations were sewn. The statue of the "Lady of Uruk" had on her garment golden stars and 688 other golden ornaments which were perhaps leaf-shaped. We know that individual garments were richly ornamented (rather than the stars representing ornaments from many gods' clothes) because a Neo-Babylonian text records 61 gold stars from a single statue's garment consigned to a goldsmith for repair. Other garments were decorated with large gold animal figures, plant shapes, or collections of golden rings,[89] and they followed the pattern of the garments worn by the Assyrian kings on relief images: a bound mantle covered with row upon row of rosettes, rings, or disks.[90] These divine garments were transported aboard sacred ships to various temples where they would adorn the gods' statues for a set time, and disputes frequently arose over the return of the expensive clothing.[91] Some scholars have even argued that the myth of Inanna's descent into the Underworld reflects the ritual whereby an old cult statue was stripped of such clothes, ritually destroyed, and replaced (or "reborn").[92] The Mycenaeans had only small statuettes, and the use of large statues seems to be an import from Mesopotamian-influenced Asia Minor at the end of the Dark Age.[93] These images, however, were generally made of carved wood, and there is no clear evidence that they wore removable, woven gold clothing, though some images were covered in gold leaf.[94] In the Mycenaean era, the Hittites, with whom they were in contact, used large divine statues made of or plated with gold or other precious metals, and these statues wore garments and were ritually cleansed and restored each year. After the fifth century BCE, the Greeks used gold (typically leaf) to cover the carved robes of the gods' statues. The robes of Athena in the Parthenon at Athens were removable for cleaning, and statues were ritually clothed with woven robes in the Classical period, a close parallel to Near Eastern rites for dressing the gods. In iconographic representations, the Hittite Sun-god of Heaven and Hittite kings both dress in priestly vestments composed of long, flowing robes. Compare, too, the fabulous Mold Gold Cape of Wales, a Bronze Age ceremonial cape in the form of sheet gold worked to look like elaborate fabric.

A wool garment covered in small gold rings immediately calls to mind the visual image of a golden fleece, whose golden rings of hair would be attached to a skin paralleling the cloth. Further, the Mesopotamians dyed the wool cloth purple to mark kingship and added the gold rings to this purple cloth. Simonides recorded a strange tradition whereby the Golden Fleece was said to be dyed purple, by which he may have meant to imply that it was a symbol of royal or divine sovereignty, since purple has always been the color of royalty and divinity. If the fleece were in fact a Mesopotamian-style sacred garment, it could be both purple and golden at the same time, with purple wool embellished with gold rings appearing like the locks of fleece on a ram's skin. Therefore, in this reading when Jason emerges from the belly of the dragon he wins the sacred vestment of royalty or divinity. He has been reborn and has gained immortality or, if he did originate in a figure like Dumuzi or Velchanos, he has regained his divinity and the rite to wear the symbol of a god's glory, the sacred robes of purple and gold. Such a reading harmonizes well with the lamb of Atreus, and interestingly, like the Fleece, this golden lamb is sometimes described as purple, and is in any event, like the gold-purple robes of the gods, a symbol of sovereignty and associated with the path of the sun and with boiling in a cauldron, just as we see in the Jason story.

This speculation has the benefit of parsimoniously accounting for the Golden Fleece without recourse to the complex theorizing that previous hypotheses have attempted, including attempts to read into the Fleece solar symbolism, remnants of Hittite religious rites, or remnants of ancient gold mining, which we will examine in chapter 11. This theory places the Fleece in a broader ritual and mythic complex and also sets it within a broader pattern of Greek adaptation of Near Eastern motifs while avoiding the literalism inherent in many theories that seek out actual rams' skins and their literal use. However, there are three issues that argue against identifying the Fleece with Mesopotamian divine robes. First, these robes are best attested in Mesopotamia only after the twelfth century BCE, before which it unclear whether the robes were completely covered in gold or merely had a few golden decorations. This would conflict with the suggestion that the Jason story dates back to Mycenaean times. Second, there is no evidence of early Greek knowledge of these divine robes, though describing the gods' clothing as golden is an Indo-European inheritance of great antiquity.[95] Third, Jason is never said to have *worn* the Golden Fleece. None of these objections is insuperable, however.

First, the chronological issue is not entirely clear-cut. Cuneiform inscriptions indicate that some form of golden robes were in use as far back as 2000 BCE and an figurine known as the Priest-King found in the Indus Valley, at Mohenjo-daro, suggest in the raised patterns on the figure's robe that the golden garments or their forerunners were possibly in use there a thousand years before.[96] The Indus Valley and Mesopotamia had a trade relationship beginning in the third millennium BCE and mutually influenced one another, with artifacts from each civilization found in the other's cities. Some of these artifacts are associated with the Third Dynasty of Ur, the same dynasty that first records the use of golden robes, around c. 2000 BCE and it is known that the Mesopotamians imported gold dust from the Indus Valley.[97] However, it is also worth noting that the Golden Fleece is not linked to Jason until the seventh century BCE, when Mimnermus refers to the "great fleece" Jason sought to obtain. Since the fleece was related only to Phrixus and not Jason in Homer[98] and Hesiod, it is quite possible that the Fleece was not the original objective of the Argonauts and is instead a symbol derived from a confluence of royal and ritual imagery, including the gods' golden robes and the fleece of purification.

To the second objection, there are several rejoinders. First, the influence of the Near East on Mycenaean and Dark Age Greece has been amply demonstrated, and though the Mycenaeans and Dark Age Greeks did not make large statues of their own, they surely were aware of Near East practices. Second, bronze statues of a Hittite god have been found in deposits from Dark Age Greece,[99] again testifying to the ongoing dissemination of Near East religious practices and customs. Although none survive, Hittite texts tell us that in the Bronze Age the gold-plated statues of the Hittite gods wore removable garments, like the Mesopotamian gods, and were associated with gold items like sun-discs, lunulae, and other golden decorations.[100] Hittite sculptures show armor made from overlapping metal scales, which were used from before the thirteenth century BCE, and such scale armor has been excavated from Hittite sites. The Hittites may therefore have clothed their gods with golden scaled armor, like the Mesopotamian gods, a fact made probable by the presence of "one jacket inlaid with gold," a "purple jacket with gold," and "two jackets embroidered in gold" listed among Hittite tablets.[101] Similar garments, apparently drawn from Near Eastern models, albeit without explicit reference to gold, appear in Homer's *Iliad* among the geographically close Trojans in the embroidered purple robes of Helen and of Andromache, and in Hesiod in the robe of the earth goddess.[102] Third, close analogs to the golden robes of the Near East gods can be found in Greek myth. In Book XVI of the *Iliad*, Achilles wears a breastplate spangled with stars, which immediately recalls the gold stars sewn onto the gods' clothes, though the one example that survives of Mycenaean armor was made of great sheets of hammered bronze rather than scales or mail. It is thought this type of armor was too heavy for most uses except when riding on chariots,[103] and lighter armor, perhaps metal sewn on leather, in the manner of Mycenaean helmets,[104] would have be used for more mobile fighting.

But beyond the direct transmission of fashion, we have seen how Greek myths have incorporated Near Eastern motifs and iconography, most noticeably in the labors of Heracles and their close relationship to the deeds of Ninurta in Near East art. If motifs such as the wearing of a lion's pelt and the slaying of a seven-headed dragon could cross the Aegean, the garbled transmission of deities' divine clothes is not *prima facie* impossible, especially if they were as close as the Hittites, with whom the Mycenaeans had contact. In fact, such an idea is strengthened by other occurrences of heroes wearing or taking divine clothing in Greek myth. Heracles famously seizes the girdle (belt) of the Amazon queen Hippolyte, which was given to her by her father Ares, was a symbol of royal sovereignty, and had magical powers. Perseus is given the helmet of Hades to aid in his fight with the Gorgon. Jason, of course, has Dionysus' robe. And of course we must mention the most important and similar object of divine clothing, the aegis of Athena and her father, Zeus. This object originated as a type of protective shawl or cape covered, as the *Iliad* says, in one hundred tightly-woven gold tassels. When Zeus shakes the aegis, storms break out and men tremble in fear, and Virgil describes the aegis around Athena's shoulders as golden and like the skin of a serpent to which tassels are attached. Here then we have an actual golden garment of the Greek gods, and it is unsurprising that scholars have frequently speculated on connections between the aegis and the Golden Fleece.[105] A possible forerunner of this divine garment can be seen on a Mycenaean ivory statue interpreted as two goddesses and a divine child from Mycenae c. 1300 BCE. The two goddesses are wrapped in just this kind of shawl, covered in tassels and heavy texturing that resembles a fleece.

The act of doffing and donning clothes as part of a sacred rite is also clearly paralleled in Greek myth and ritual. According to the Hellenistic author Euanthes, in Arcadia a young boy was led to a lake where he stripped off his clothes, hung them on an oak tree, and swam across the lake. There, he became a werewolf for nine years, after which he was allowed to swim back across the lake, remove his clothes from the oak tree and assume the mantle of manhood.[106] The idea of clothes hung upon an oak surely recalls the Fleece upon its tree, a parallel made more explicit when we recall that the sacred clothing in Thessaly's rites of Zeus Akraios, which Burkert relates to the Arcadian wolf myths,[107] was the fleece of a sacrificed ram.

Lastly, the Mycenaean tombs contain evidence that burial shrouds and other high-status clothing were sometimes covered in exactly the type of gold ornamentation seen in Mesopotamia and Anatolia. In the late Mycenaean period, such gold encrusted clothing is well attested archaeologically and artistically. Among Mycenaean trade goods was expensive wool cloth finished with sewn-on patterns of gold ornaments and beads.[108] At Sellopuolo in southwestern Greece, 148 gold rosettes were found with the burial of a woman in a position indicating that they were ornaments on a skirt. More rosettes were found near the body of a male, suggesting they were part of a burial shroud.[109] Such golden burials are quite common in Mycenaean archaeology, and it is believed that the Mycenaeans derived their gold burials from Near Eastern or Egyptian customs.[110] Tomb burials with gold shrouds disappear between 1100 and 900 BCE replaced by simple burials in clay or stone containers, or cremation, due in part to the poverty of the post–Mycenaean period.[111] It is not hard to imagine that in the impoverished early Dark Age world, memories of the gold-covered wool clothing of the Mycenaean "heroes" could contribute to the idea of the Golden Fleece, especially if in the worship of the chthonic heroes some of their ancient tomb-shrines had been opened. After all, Homer remembered the boar's tusk helmets that went out of fashion with the Trojan War. If the storytellers knew of the golden burial shrouds, this would reinforce the underworld imagery of the Jason myth still further, perhaps making a portion of the Fleece symbolism the burial shroud of the dying and rising god. Additionally, the native people of (the real) Colchis also decorated their garments with gold beads,[112] perhaps reinforcing the image of golden garments for the Greeks when they arrived in the region in the eighth century BCE.

The third objection, of course, is the strongest. Jason does not wear the Fleece, though it serves as his marriage bed in Apollonius, and we cannot immediately suspect that it was clothing. To answer this objection, we should first recall that the fleece of purification was sometimes worn as clothing, especially in the oldest contexts. We should then enter into evidence the description Pindar gives of Jason's appearance in Colchis. Pindar explicitly describes Jason as appearing like a god and wearing over his hunting tunic the skin of leopard. A leopard's fur is golden with black rosettes, making a close visual analogue to the golden garments of the gods, whose shimmering golden rings would have shown dark spots of purple among and between the gold. This costume is abandoned following Jason's embarkation, or is at least not mentioned again. Pindar again describes Jason's clothing in Colchis as "saffron in color" (κροκόεις), which is a shade of golden yellow, and Jason also removes this just before plowing the field with the fiery bulls. Since Jason's voyage is equivalent to a voyage into the land of death, these costuming changes conform to the Near Eastern pattern of a dying god whose robes are abandoned during the underworld sojourn and resumed upon rejoining the living. In the Sumerian poem "Gilagmesh, Enkidu, and the Netherworld," Enkidu is warned not to wear his clean garments in descending through the gate of Netherworld lest the dead recognize him as an interloper. In the Mesopotamian story of Inanna's descent into the Underworld to steal divine power, at the seventh gate of the Underworld "was taken, the robe of sovereignty that covered her body," in conformance with the law whereby even gods arrive in the underworld stripped of their finery.[113] This robe, called the Pala, was the mark of royal or divine status, and is the equivalent of the golden garments placed on Mesopotamian statues. Similarly, in the widely distributed Babylonian poem *Erra and Ishum* (c. eighth century BCE) Marduk descends to the Underworld when the robes of his cult image become dirty, abdicating his godly powers while his robes are purified in fire by Erra (= Nergal) and his brother Ishum. In Mesopotamian literature Dumuzi, too, is depicted in heaven as draped in the robe of sovereignty, and when the devils take him to the Underworld, they tell him specifically that he must leave behind his divine emblems: "your beautiful robes, sceptre, and sandals."[114] Presumably, these are restored to him upon his annual rebirth, just as Jason finds the Golden Fleece upon his return from the belly of the serpent. In Babylon, this is made explicit in the New Year's purification ritual of the king, who represents the sun god. Just before the festival, the king travels out from the city to the surrounding steppe where he enters a hut made of reeds (both grove and temple, like alternating references to the Grove or Temple of Ares), which represents the Netherworld, removes his royal insignia and robe, and travels along the chthonic path of the nighttime sun from west to east. At dawn, he removes his Netherworld clothes, bathes himself, resumes his royal robes, passes eastward through seven "houses" representing the seven gates leading from the Netherworld, and stands before the morning sun.[115] The king has been purified and restored to sovereignty.

Thus, upon completing his sojourn in the Underworld, Jason, too, achieves the Golden Fleece and resumes the robe of sovereignty signifying either royal or divine status. This pattern, including the attainment of a valuable robe, is seen again in Jason's sojourn on the island of Lemnos, which we have already seen is a microcosm of the Argonautic venture as a whole and may in fact have originated from the same sources. In this venture, Jason wins as a prize in combat games a sacred crimson or purple robe from the Lemnian queen Hypsipyle, which represents sovereignty over Lemnos, evidenced in the son Jason provides Hypsipyle, the son who becomes king in his absent father's stead. Significantly, in Apollonius this robe was originally the property of a god, Dionysus. (Apollonius gives Jason another robe, woven by Athena, also purple, but this does not appear in earlier versions of the story.) On Lemnos, too, is a ram's fleece offered in a purification ritual. Thus, in microcosm we see both halves of the Golden Fleece—the robe of sovereignty and the fleece of purification. It becomes easy to see how a royal purification ritual with its doffing and donning of royal robes, like the one at Babylon, could become conflated with purification fleeces.

The Mesopotamian gods' golden clothes influenced the golden robes of many Near East cultures, including the golden robes high priests in Jerusalem wore to sacrifice rams, as well as the golden robes of later Iranian kings, and through them the imperial wardrobes of the Byzantine and Holy Roman Emperors. These imperial garments survive today in the golden robes worn by the Pope.[116] It is therefore appropriate to find the myth of Jason's Fleece beloved by the same medieval men who founded the Order of the Golden Fleece and wore ritual robes descended from the very fleece Jason sailed to seize. It is to their story that we now turn.

PART FOUR

THE AFTERLIFE OF THE MYTH

9

The Knight

The Middle Ages and the Renaissance

The Greek colony of Phasis in the land of Colchis did not last forever, but it did leave a lasting legacy on the Black Sea shore. The city had long been a Greek trading port, receiving goods arriving in the Black Sea from as far away as India. Strabo described the Temple of Phrixus as a tourist attraction in the region, and beyond Colchis, where Armenia bleeds into Iran, authors including Strabo, Pliny, and Josephus placed a mountain named for Jason, the Jasonium (or Mons Jasonius), frequently identified with Mt. Damavand in the Alborz Range on the south shore of the Caspian Sea. According to Ammianus Marcellinus it was several peaks in a mountain range.[1] And of course, the region was studded with the ever-present Jasonia, those confused monuments to Jason, which like Mt. Jasonium appear to be the result of linguistic misunderstanding and wishful thinking on the part of Greek travelers. The consequence was that the entire region from Phasis through Armenia and beyond was closely associated with Jason, and remained so even after the Greek world had passed away.

This territory around Phasis fell into the orbit of Rome during the Third Mithridatic War, and was visited by Pompey in 65 BCE. The Romans turned Colchis into the provinces of Galatia and Cappadocia. A series of wars saw territory exchanged between the East Roman (Byzantine) Empire, its rivals, and independent tribal kingdoms. Parts of the territory remained Byzantine into the Middle Ages, while the majority of Colchis came together in a new kingdom, which became known as Georgia after the Persian name for the territory, *Gruzia*, in the tenth century. However, the rulers of this new kingdom on the edges of the Byzantine Empire were Christians, and they presided over a kingdom that, while Christian since the fourth century CE, was still associated with one of the pagan world's favorite heroes.

Against the superstition of paganism and its dragon-dispatching heroes like Jason and the native hero Amirani, Christian Georgia adopted a new symbol, St. George, the dragon-slayer. George was depicted in Christian iconography from the sixth century onward as a knight on horseback, and after the eleventh century he acquired a further triumph, rescuing a princess from a dragon, stories that echo (but do not necessarily derive from) pagan dragon slaying heroes, including Teshub and Perseus.[2] This saint had become enormously popular in Colchis from at least the sixth century, when he was depicted as killing a man (usually the Emperor Diocletian) rather than a dragon,[3] and his growing mythos contained exactly the right elements by the High Middle Ages to serve as Jason's replacement as the ambassador *par excellence* of the new Georgia to the wider European world. Under the militantly Chris-

194

Rogier van der Weyden's "Saint George and the Dragon" (c. 1432) depicts all of the classic elements of the myth of St. George, including his horseback slaying of the dragon, and the rescue of a princess. The story bears an uncanny similarity to Perseus' rescue of Andromeda, and in late medieval Georgia was considered a suitably Christian alternative to the popular tale of Jason and Medea, which was still attracting tourists to the region when this painting was made (National Gallery of Art).

tian Bagrationi (Bargratid) dynasty, the Christian story of the warrior saint who slew the dragon for God received official patronage and was placed on the dynasty's coat of arms. In the very land where the Greeks had placed Jason's adventures, medieval Christianity tried to replace him.

Despite this, Jason and the Argonauts remained a tourist attraction in Georgia into the Middle Ages, comingled now with Christian myths. The Spanish traveler Pero Tafur, who voyaged to Colchis and nearby Armenia in the 1430s, wrote that he visited the sites associated with the tale of the Golden Fleece during his trip, mingled now with the Christian gloss on the place called Ararat where the Mesopotamians once had their flood hero's ark come to rest:

> [I] saw the castle of Colchis where Medea lived, and the island of the Golden Fleece. [...] In this part of Armenia, there is a high mountain range called the Black Mountain, and here, they say, Noah's Ark rested after the flood.[4]

In miniature, Jason's misadventure in Georgia presents a microcosm of his myth during the Middle Ages and the Renaissance. During this era, Jason ceased being a myth tied to a living religion. Christians attempted to replace or reconfigure him in conformance with the new, changing morals and mores of the medieval world, and in the process Jason became something new. The medieval Jason was transformed into a courtly knight, the hero of medieval chivalric romance, and even a stand-in for Jesus. He was also condemned to Hell. His voyage to Colchis became enmeshed in historical reality, an event not divine but mortal, one conducted in the real word, though removed in time and space from the Western courts where his story was retold. By contrast, the Medea of the Middle Ages became still blacker and wickeder, consumed by lust and rage, attributes associated with the evils of women, and the prototype of the witch that haunted the medieval imagination and led to the great witch hunts of the early modern period. Paradoxically, she was also sometimes identified with the Virgin Mary.

The medieval Jason is defined by three major departures from the ancient myth:

- The belief, inherited from Valerius (after the rationalizing claims of Dionysus Schytobrachion), that Jason accidentally triggered the Trojan War.
- The belief that Jason's uncle Pelias was the same man as Achilles' father Peleus.
- The belief that Jason killed the serpent in Colchis and planted this serpent's teeth rather than those of the separate serpent of Cadmus.

Paradoxically, the trends that shaped Jason in the ancient world—the steady diminution of his heroic stature and the attempts to historicize his myth in terms of the Trojan War—were the same trends that assured his medieval immortality. As a seemingly real human, he could be accepted as an historical figure, unlike the more magical mythological men; and as a precursor to the Trojan War his voyage attained a seeming importance it would otherwise never have held.

The Greek East

In the eastern half of the Roman Empire, Jason and Medea remained popular until deep into the Middle Ages. In the third and fourth centuries CE, East Romans continued the practice of using images of Jason on funerary art, likening his quest to the triumph over death.

In Egypt, under Roman rule until 646, when Muslim invaders conquered it permanently, a series of relief carvings of Jason scenes were made sometime in perhaps the fourth century to decorate a tomb. The most completely preserved relief shows Jason seizing a fish-shaped Golden Fleece from the tree while an enthroned Medea feeds a magic potion to the serpent. Present in the scene are two Argonauts, two defeated Colchian guards, and in the background the ship *Argo*.[5] When much of the east had fallen to the Muslims, the Arabs gained a wealth of Greek learning and literature, preserving texts otherwise lost for many centuries. The Persian-Arabian myth cycle of Sinbad the Sailor, believed to have been first compiled in late Antiquity or the early Middle Ages, owes something to Jason, since the stories of the hero who made seven magical voyages across the sea include incidents drawn from Homer's *Odyssey*,[6] which in turn had drawn on and been inspired by the most ancient versions of the *Argonautica*.

With the breakup of the Roman Empire, the classical culture of the Greco-Roman world experienced decline. In the Greek east, the Byzantine Empire retained the Greek texts of the Jason stories, including Pindar, Apollonius, and others now lost, down until the great upheavals of the Crusades and the Turkish conquest, at which point many of these Greek classics vanished forever. We owe our knowledge of Pindar to several generations of Byzantine scholars, notably the fourteenth century scholars Thomas Magistros and Demetrios Triklinios, of whose work more than two hundred copies survive.[7] In Byzantium, ancient Greco-Roman traditions tarried longer than in the West, and our extant scholia on the *Argonautica* of Apollonius were compiled under the Byzantines, using the ancient commentaries written by Theon, Lucillus Tarrhaeus, and Sophocles (not the tragedian) in the first and second centuries CE. In the eleventh century, the Georgian-Byzantine scholar John Tzetzes used these scholia in preparing a commentary on one of Lycophron's lost poems, in which he discusses Argonautic ideas, including the assertion that the Golden Ram spoke with a human voice. The Byzantines also preserved the text of Apollonius in relatively good shape, producing a number of manuscripts and copying them as they wore out or needed duplication. However, in Late Antiquity and the early Middle Ages there were apparently a number of variant texts of the *Argonautica*, with some differences in certain line readings, and Byzantine editors selected among these and combined texts at will to produce the version known today. Scattered papyri from Egypt preserve some of the variants.[8] While most of the texts are substantively the same, the Byzantine grammarian Maximos Planudes produced a version in the thirteenth century that had many notable differences, which may derive from his study of ancient manuscripts of the poem.[9]

A Byzantine scholar named Eirenaius wrote a learned commentary on Apollonius' *Argonautica* which does not survive, and sometime around the year 500 a poet named Marianus performed a 5,608-line iambic summary of the *Argonautica*.[10] But much more interesting is the tenth century Byzantine lexicon, the *Suda*, which sought to rationalize the Jason myth by relating it to the origins of alchemy, the medieval idea that base metals could be turned into gold. According to the *Suda*, the Fleece was not a mystical animal but a mystical *book* written on skins that explained how to create gold, giving rise to the mythological name through appeal to its function, the fleece that made gold, the Golden Fleece: "This was not as stated by the poets, but was a book written on parchment describing how gold could be produced by alchemy."[11] John of Antioch in the seventh century had made the same claim, in nearly the same words, likely misunderstanding the ideas of Charax of Pergamum, who in the second century thought the Fleece was a method of writing in gold on parchment. Constantine XI's wife Eudora held this opinion as well. By happenstance, this rationalization would acquire the ring of truth in the West and serve a long life as the "vellum aureus" of alchemical investigation (see chapter 10).

That we know anything at all of the Byzantine scholarship on the *Argonautica* is due almost entirely to the chance survival of the Byzantine scholia in editions of the poem taken to Italy at the end of the Byzantine Empire. Similarly, the text of the poem exists primarily in medieval manuscripts (see chapter 10). Some lines are also found on fragmentary ancient papyri dating back to the Greco-Roman era, that while incomplete demonstrate the substantive accuracy of a tradition that preserved Apollonius' work for nearly two millennia.

In the West, however, the story was somewhat different.

The Latin West

On the European territory of what had been the Western Roman Empire, a series of Germanic kingdoms emerged and represented a change in the culture and organization of civilization on the occidental side of the continent. The old cosmopolitan Roman elite, who had been bilingual in Latin and Greek, gradually gave way to a more localized society that no longer had widespread Greek literacy. Homer fell out of fashion, and with him went Apollonius and the other Greek authors of the Jason story. Instead, the most important literary sources preserved in the West were Latin, first among them Virgil's *Aeneid*, followed by minor Latin epics on the Trojan War, including the forgery *Historia de Excidio Trioae* ("The History of the Fall of Troy"), written sometime between the fourth and seventh centuries CE under the name Dares Phrygius, a character from the *Iliad*, and claiming to be a first-person account of the Trojan War. The work begins with the story taken from Valerius Flaccus' *Argonautica*[12] that the Argonauts were mistreated by King Laomedon of Troy en route to Colchis, presaging the Trojan War. This work, despite its dubious status, became a primary source for the transmission Jason's story in the early Middle Ages, with the stopover at Troy eventually rising to the level of a First Trojan War in the medieval mind.

In the very brief and plainspoken account of Dares Phrygius, King Pelias worries that the popular and handsome Jason will drive him out of the Peloponnese (rather than Thessaly—it's the conflated Peleus' ancestral land), and promised Jason the kingdom if he retrieved the Fleece from Colchis. To this end, Pelias ordered the *Argo* built, and the Argonauts set off to claim the Fleece. Here is the rest of the story:

> Jason, when he had come to Phrygia, brought up the ship to the port of the Simoeis River. Then, they all disembarked from the ship for dry land. It was announced to Laomedon, King of the Trojans, that a ship had unexpectedly entered the port of the Simoeis River and young men had come in it from Greece. When Laomedon heard this he was disturbed, and he thought it a danger to the public if Greeks should be in the habit of landing on his shores in their ships. And so he sent word to the port for the Greeks to depart from his territory; and if they did not obey his word, then he would expel them from his territory by force. Jason and those who had come with him were deeply upset by the cruelty with which Laomedon was treating them; he had received no injury from them: and at the same time they were afraid to attempt to continue on against

the order lest they be crushed by the multitude of barbarians. As they were not ready to do battle, they boarded the ship, retreated from the land, set out for Colchis, obtained the Fleece, and returned home.[13]

This episode leads Hercules to seek vengeance against Laomedon, raiding Troy and precipitating the Trojan War, all of which is far beyond our scope but lent itself to the historical imagination of the medieval writers. As early as the seventh century, Fredigarius used Dares' version of the Jason story as part of a universal history legitimizing the Merovingian kings.

Valerius Flaccus' treatment of the Jason story should, by rights, have become the default version of the story in the Latin West, but this was not so. Anthologies of the Latin authors called *florilegia* ("gatherings of flowers") reproduced about seventy excerpts of his epic, but the complete text apparently disappeared for a thousand years until a chance rediscovery by a humanist scholar named Poggio Bracchiolini of the first half in a Swiss monastery in 1416 and the discovery of the complete text in 1429. There is evidence that a few copies of the poem circulated privately during the Middle Ages, but it was not a generally available text until it was printed in Bologna in 1474.[14] In the meantime, another source of Jason's story gained ground over the Antique originals, those compiled by the medieval mythographers.

Encyclopedias and Handbooks

With the triumph of Christianity, the Church (including Augustine and Gregory the Great) demonized the pagan gods as demons, and the Greek myths as lies. However, these gods appeared in the Roman authors included in the curriculum of Latin education, and this pagan past had to be reconciled with Christian belief so students could understand what they read without falling prey to pagan influence.[15] Attempts had been underway for centuries. In the sixth century, St. Isidore of Seville (c. 560–636 CE) compiled the *Etymologiae,* an encyclopedia of universal knowledge created from extracts from Roman literary sources edited to cast them within a Christian framework and mixed with fanciful word derivations (i.e. etymologies, hence the title). This text became so respected that it became the most important source of learning in the Latin world, replacing the texts from which it was drawn and preserving what little remained of Western knowledge of the Greek authors. Isidore spoke of Jason occasionally, referencing his alleged roles in founding Armenia via the Argonaut Armenius (a story related twice) and a confused mention of him fathering the Scythians of Asia Minor. He also references Jason's "stepson" Medus as the father of the Medes of Iran, but notes, without attempting to sort out the contradiction, that Genesis assigns the Medes to Madai.[16]

To better serve medieval students, a guide to mythology proper was needed. The West possessed the *Fabulae* of Hyginus, which treated the Jason story briefly, if somewhat unsatisfactorily. However, Hyginus covered only the Greek authors, so a comprehensive guide was needed to specifically address curriculum authors like Ovid and Virgil within a framework centered on Christianity. Such a guide would need to use moral allegory and rationalization to render the Greek myths suitable for enjoyment in the medieval Christian world. Three of these handbooks of mythology found their way into the Vatican library, where they became known collectively as the Vatican Mythographers, though the writers themselves were not likely employed by the Holy See. These books would become key sources for later authors' knowledge of Greek myths in the Middle Ages and Renaissance, but they were not necessarily true to the myths of Classical Antiquity, including Jason.

THE FIRST VATICAN MYTHOGRAPHER

The First Vatican Mythographer, writing in the eighth or ninth century CE, demonstrates the era's confusion over Greek mythological themes. In his summary of the Jason story, he is uncertain whether Jason's uncle is Pelias or Peleus (the Argonaut and father of Achilles), and he believes that the Golden Fleece came from a ram on which Jupiter ascended to heaven. He reports the late story of the Argonauts landing at Troy, as given in Valerius and Dares, and he writes that Pelias (confused, as in most medieval texts, with Peleus) and Hercules conquered Troy thereafter. At Colchis, he holds that Jason yoked bulls that the Colchians could not tame and then slew the dragon with Medea's help. Confusing Cadmus' and Jason's dragons, the Mythographer claims Jason planted the Colchian dragon's teeth and watched the men simply kill one another. This mistake would become so embedded in the Jason tradition that it would be considered the true account of Jason's three tests into the modern era. In a bit of charming color, the Mythographer writes that Medea poisoned the robes of Jason's "mistress" Glauce with toxins and "garlic," causing her to be consumed in flames. (Garlic in medieval times was considered magical, but usually to protect against poison, not as a poison itself.) "Then Medea, not putting up with the soul of Jason raging against her, fled on a winged serpent."[17]

Later in the work, he reports that Jason took Medea to Greece to have sex with her, and then asked her to restore his father to youth. Upon boiling the old man in herbs he grew young, and Liber (Dionysus), seeing the wonder, asked Medea to restore his nurses to their youth, which she did. Other stories, including Hypsipyle and Phineus, are scattered throughout the disorganized and non-chronological work.

THE SECOND VATICAN MYTHOGRAPHER

The Second Vatican Mythographer, writing not long after the First, reported that Phrixus stored the Golden Fleece in the Temple of Mars in the land of King Oeta (Aeëtes) in Colchis. Meanwhile, Pelias was said to "possess the summit of Iolcus,"[18] mixing Pelion and the city below. The Mythographer then reports that Pelias sent Jason to fetch the Fleece in hope that the dragon (rather than the journey) would kill him. Hercules, Castor, Pollux, and Tiphys are named as Argonauts, and the writer claims that the *Argo* was the first ship to sail. Because of this, in a line possibly mangled from Lucius Accius, "the earth, grieving that the previously untouched sea had become traversable, hurled rocks into the sea."[19] Seeing the sea fill up with rocks, the Argonauts launched the ship unfinished, which is why the constellation *Argo* represents only its mast and stern.

In what seems to be chronological confusion, the Mythographer reports that Jason reached Colchis, fell in love with Medea, and gave her two sons. Only then does he report Oeta's challenge to Jason and Oeta's fear that Jason would fulfill the oracle prophesying the king's death. This Mythographer again claims that the Colchian bulls were untamed by man, and he seems to also confuse Cadmus' and Jason's dragons in searching for the source of the teeth that birthed the earth-born men. He writes that lovelorn Medea put the "serpent" to sleep, and Jason killed it to extract its teeth, which he planted. Three days later (!) the army arose and attacked, but Medea enchanted them to kill each other. Having met Oeta's demands, Jason took the Fleece home with him. Medea followed, and in Italy she taught charms to the locals to send away snakes. Then she restored Aeson to youth by boiling him. She did the same to the nurses of Father Liber after he saw the wonders she worked.

Jason, however, took Glauce as a "concubine," and Medea killed her with a tunic imbued with poison and garlic, causing her to "burn with fire." Jason raged against Medea, but she killed their sons and "fled on a winged serpent."[20]

THE THIRD VATICAN MYTHOGRAPHER

The Third Vatican Mythographer does not apparently refer to Jason directly, but he does allude to Medea as a "daughter of the sun" and an embodiment of "hearing" in his attempt to relate the sun's five daughters to the five senses through a fanciful etymology of their names. Medea is said to mean "no vision" and therefore to represent hearing, while her "sister" Circe, meaning the "judgment of hands," represents touch.[21] He also mentions the Argonauts in passing in discussing the lead-up to the Trojan War, and the Golden Fleece in a discussion of the origin of the constellation Aries.

The Christian Warrior

The mythographers did their best to preserve and transmit the old pagan myths for a medieval audience, but at heart their stories were still the tales told in Greco-Roman antiquity, though in altered form. As the Middle Ages wore on, the tale of Jason and the Argonauts would escape classical mythology and enter into the medieval tradition in a new form. Jason would now become an embodiment of chivalric virtue, in short, a knight. This was not an entirely purposeful process but rather the result of two forces: first, the medieval desire to strip pagan stories of their un–Christian connotations, and second, the ethnocentric tendency of medieval writers to impose, consciously or not, the values of their society onto the stories they told. As a result, the romances told of Jason in the High Middle Ages resembled as much the Arthurian sagas or the legend cycle of Charlemagne as they did Pindar's Fourth Pythian Ode or Apollonius' *Argonautica*.

THE EPIC ROMANCES

By the twelfth century, ancient Rome was a distant memory, and the Greek past still more so. However, the aristocrats of the medieval world fancied themselves the heirs of the ancient imperial traditions, and they employed poets to sing to them of the wonders of Antiquity as mirrors of their own accomplishments. In this, they were little different than the Greek tyrants, who employed poets to sing of mythology as veiled praise of themselves. These poems of olden days were known as *romans antiques*, and typically dealt with the history of military heroes. The most influential medieval Romance to draw on the classical tradition was undoubtedly the *Roman de Troie* by Benoît de Ste. Maure (d. 1173). This forty-thousand-line epic poem, composed around 1160 in Norman French but widely translated, retold the story of the Trojan War, drawing primarily on Dares and Virgil, among other Latin sources. For Benoît and his audience, the Trojan War was a historical fact, and its prelude, the expedition of Jason, was equally an episode founded in truth.

The *Roman de Troie* devotes 1,300 lines of its early section to the story of Jason and Medea, as well as the Argonauts' mistreatment at the hands of Laomedon. In Benoît's telling, Medea is beautiful and an admirable figure, a young woman who is true in her love of Jason, though Jason's love is consciously minimized in anticipation of his later betrayal. She gives him a unique set of items drawn from medieval magical practice to help him conquer the three tasks he faces. She offers him a magical figure, a ring, a spell, ointment, and glue, the last for fastening shut (!) the mouths of the flaming bulls. However, so copious is her aid that the effect of Jason's triumph is undercut more forcefully than in any ancient epic, rendering his triumph merely the successful completion of a fixed set of mechanical exercises.[22] Jason's return to Greece is his exit from the story, yielding to Peleus, a conflated Pelias-Peleus, who leads the Greek expedition seeking vengeance against Laomedon. In extant manuscripts of the story, Jason is depicted dressed in the full armor and helmet of a medieval knight, typical of an age that viewed all history through an unchanging contemporary lens. Joseph of Exeter wrote another version of the story in 1185 as the *Ylias* (e.g., *Iliad*), also known as the *Bellum Troianum* or *De Bello Troiano*, and again included Jason as the accidental cause of the war, following Dares, whom he makes the narrator of the story. This Jason ventured forth primarily in search of personal glory.

In the thirteenth century, the Sicilian Guido de Columnis (or delle Colonne in dialect) wrote a *Historia destructionis Trioiae* (History of the Destruction of Troy), completed in 1278, under the patronage of Emperor Frederick II and based on Dares and other forgeries that claimed to be eyewitness accounts of the fall of Troy. This work, which was meant as an "allegorical counterpart" to Frederick II's crusade to recapture the Church of the Holy Sepulcher in Jersualem,[23] contained somewhat tedious passages on Jason and Medea as the initiating events precipitating the Trojan War. Guido attempted to cast the Argonauts' voyage as a historical event, with Jason as the virtuous knight and Medea a medieval witch, overcome with sexual desire and evil rage, traits medieval philosophers associated with women via the sin of Eve. Guido's work was translated into many languages, including an English adaptation as the *Troy Book* of John Lydgate (c. 1370-c. 1451), and circulated around Europe; however, the most unique version was a German translation now held in the Austrian National Library, copiously illustrated with 334 intricately-detailed painted images of the myths described. The work was created by Martin of Regensburg between 1432 and 1456, but its purpose is unknown. It remained in Martin's possession until his death, when his wife sold it for thirty pounds of silver—a princely sum—and it eventually passed into the collection of the Habsburgs.[24] An image from this book shows Jason and Medea in a bedroom, richly dressed, but appearing like teenagers rather than young adults, their heads large and bodies spindly.

Book One of the *Troy Book,* following Guido, tells the story of Jason and situates him somewhat awkwardly into the run up to the Trojan war, following Dares. Here King "Pelleus," representing both Pelias and Peleus, is presented as a good and noble ruler brought to despair by plague and pestilence. Lydgate relates the rejuvenation of "Eson" (Aeson) by Medea. Jason is introduced as a youth of exceeding beauty and bearing, in which Nature performed high art, but who, like any good medieval vassal, was outwardly the obedient servant of his liege, the king:

> For as myn auctor [Guido, whom he is translating] telleth feithefully,
> He was beloved so of old and yonge
> That thorugh the londe [land] is his honour spronge;
> But for that he was but yonge and sklender [tender],
> Of age also inly [extremely] grene and tender,
> He was committed to the governaille [governance]
> Of Pelleus, to whom withoute faille
> In everythyng he was as servisable,
> As diligent in chambre and at table,
> As evere was any childe or man.[25]

However, Jason fully intended to win back his kingdom, and Pelleus sent Jason to retrieve the Golden Fleece from King Cethes (Aeëtes) in "Colchos." Here Lydgate conflates the serpent of Cadmus with that of Colchis and imagines that Jason must sew the teeth of the dragon guarding the fleece and then kill the earthborn men to achieve the fleece, a common medieval confusion. All of this, however, exists only to introduce the Argonauts' stopover at Troy and a rather elaborate discussion of the poor treatment the Argonauts receive from the Trojans, which in this version takes place under the supervision of Jason, the "Grekys governour,"[26] which precipitates the Trojan War. This very long war scene, in the manner of the final books of Virgil's *Aeneid*, develops the brief incident of Hercules' attack on Troy, inserted rather late into the Argonaut corpus, but which would have seemed essential to medieval writers who knew the story only from the last versions produced in Antiquity.

Following this, the Argonauts, including Hercules, go to Colchis where Jason meets Medea and undertakes the triple challenges to win the Fleece. As in other versions, Medea falls in love with Jason and refers to him as a medieval knight:

> So wolde God, this yonge lusty man,
> Whiche is so faire and semly in my sighte,
> Assured were to be myn owne knyghte[27]

In Lydgate, the Greco-Roman gods are a much reduced part of the story, mentioned primarily in references to Jove, and instead it is the medieval Fortune, the personification of God's providence, who induces Medea to aid Jason and Jason to promise to serve as Medea's knight and consummate their love in marriage. Medea's aid to Jason is different than in Classical sources, including (as in Benoît) glue to fasten shut the bulls' jaws, a protective silver image, a ring of invisibility, and a document with a spell to recite before touching the Fleece. Having accomplished his goal, Jason leaves Colchis with Cethes' treasure and Medea, abandoning her along the way. He then confronts Pelleus, who yields the throne to him and provides Jason with men, described as knights, and money to seek his vengeance on the Trojans. Pelleus commands this mission and conquers Troy, thus presaging the war his son, Achilles, would conduct in the remaining books.

In these stories, Jason is cast in the role of a crusading medieval knight, reflecting the virtues treasured in an era that saw the flower of European aristocracy heading to the Holy Land to battle the infidel. The Jason of the romances sets forth on a noble quest, takes insult at poor treatment by fellow aristocrats at Troy, and yield to his liege, Peleus, in commanding a mission to seek vengeance and restore the honor of the band of knights mistreated by Laomedon. And like any good knight in shining armor, Jason battles a dragon and wins a princess, just as St. George had begun to do in the newest versions of his legend, told in the twelfth century, and serving as the model for the dragon slaying knights of medieval myth.

SAINT AND SINNER

Jason's position in the medieval imagination was problematical, however. As a pagan, he was not included among those saved by Christ, but his story appeared to have clear elements that presaged the incarnation of the Christ. As a historical figure, his deeds were therefore appropriate material for romance, but the medieval poets and scholars seemed uncertain whether to treat him as a forerunner of Jesus, with whom he shared a name, or as a sinner whose unchaste sexuality made mockery of the sublimated sexuality of courtly love, whereby knights pledged their devotion and undying love to unavailable mistresses, as well as the rules of chastity set forth by the canons of the Catholic Church. In medieval literature we find Jason as both Galahad and Lancelot, as noble exemplar of knighthood and sinful defiler of the code of chivalry. It is with some irony that for their own purposes medieval writers likened the resurrected Christ to Jason, given his own ancient (and to medieval poets, unknown) associations with dying-and-rising fertility gods and the katabasis recorded in his myth. In much the same way, Medea came to embody contradictory aspects: the wicked whore-witch and an allegorical Virgin Mary.

In his *Fourth Eclogue*, Virgil had prophesied that a new Tiphys and a new *Argo* would presage the coming of the Golden Age, with a new Golden Fleece. Since this poem was interpreted from the time of St. Augustine as a prophecy of Christ's birth due to its mention of a miraculous child, a son of God, who heralds a new dawn, it only made sense to see in Jason a parable of the Christ story. In the Introduction, we noted that the Greek name "Jason" was also used as a transliteration for the Biblical names Joshua and Jesus, and medieval writers understood that Jason's name was related to the Greek word for healing,[28] a miracle that Jesus himself frequently performed throughout the Gospels. Thus by etymology and the power of the Christian faith, Jason became a stand-in for and precursor of the Christ. Similarly, the Golden Fleece would now be understood as a version of the Lamb of God, the *agnus dei*, a symbol of Christ. The ram of Phrixus became the Lamb of God for another reason: to remove any lingering association between the (adult) ram and sexuality and fertility, subjects unfit for Christian allegory.[29] This interpretation was especially popular in the writers who attempted to Christianize the Roman poet Ovid. The works of Ovid found a new adaptation in the fourteenth century French work *Ovide moralisé*, a seventy-thousand-verse expansion of the *Metamorphoses* reinterpreting Ovid's work as Christian allegory, turning each metamorphosis into an allegory of Christ's incarnation. We have seen that Ovid made reference to the stories of Medea and Jason, and in the hands of the Christian writer of the *Ovide moralisé* Jason became, almost literally, Jesus. In his telling, Medea stood for Christ's wisdom and grace, essential for achieving the salvation symbolized in the Fleece. Similarly Peirre Bersuire's (c. 1290–1362) *Ovidius Moralizatus* depicts Medea as a symbol of the Virgin Mary, with Jason as a priest in need of her help to pass the tests set forth by Aeëtes, who represented God the Father. In another passage, Bersuire writes that Jason is Christ, with Medea as his human nature with which Christ must have congress to overcome the devil.[30] By contrast, the thirteenth century *General estoria* of Spain's King Alfonso X, a world history that reported Jason's story primarily from Ovid's accounts, attempted a more objective historiographic interpretation instead of an allegorical one.

Across medieval and Renaissance allegorical poetry, Jason became likened allegorically to Christ, with the Argonauts becoming stand-ins for the disciples. The late Spanish play *El divino Jason* (c. 1634) by Pedro Calderón de la Barca used this allegorical interpretation, likening various characters in the Jason myth to Christian concepts, with Jason as Christ, Medea standing for the soul, and Hercules as St. Peter.

However, not all medieval authors bought the virtual canonization of Jason, especially the secular courtly authors. Around 1230, the voyage of the *Argo* appeared in the French courtly epic *Roman de la rose*, with Jason depicted as "the evil trickster, the false, disloyal thief" on the grounds that all men betray the women they love.[31] The English poet John Gower (c. 1330–1408) purposely rejected the saintly interpretation of Jason in the *Confessio amantis*, making Jason a villain for breaking his oath to the sympathetic and virtuous Medea,[32] which in the medieval world was a terrible sin, since an oath sworn was a promise to God. "Thus miht thou se what sorwe it doth / To swere an oth which is noght soth / In loves cause namely."[33] (Thus might thou see what sorrow it brings to swear an oath which is not sooth in love's cause, namely.) Gower's work derived from the *Ovide* as well as the *Roman de Troie* and the other extant medieval sources, but he differs from his sources in declining to see Peleus as evil and making Jason the originator of the quest. Similarly, Geoffrey Chaucer saw in Jason a deceitful figure who badly wronged the women he seduced and left. From Guido, Joseph of Exeter, the *Troy Book*, and apparently a manuscript of Valerius Flaccus,[34] Chaucer drew his understanding of the Jason myth and used it to castigate the hero for corrupting the virtue of Hypsipyle and Medea in his *Legend of Good Women* (c. 1386–1388), a series of vignettes recording the lives of virtuous women wronged by deceitful men. Chaucer does not mince words:

> Thou rote of false lovers, duk Iasoun!
> Thou sly devourer and confusioun
> Of gentil-wommen, tender creatures,
> Thou madest thy reclaiming and thy lures
> To ladies of thy statly apparaunce,
> And of thy wordes, farced with plesaunce,
> And of thy feyned trouthe and thy manere,
> With thyn obeissaunce and thy humble chere,
> And with thy counterfeted peyne and wo.
> Ther other falsen oon, thou falsest two!
> O! ofte swore thou that thou woldest dye
> For love, whan thou ne feltest maladye
> Save foul delyt, which that thou callest love!
> If that I live, thy name shal be shove
> In English, that thy sleighte shal be knowe!
> Have at thee, Iasoun![35]

He later likens Duke Jason to a dragon who devours love, and calls him the falsest lover who ever walked the earth. Edmund Spencer (c. 1552–1595), in the *Faerie Queene* (1590) alludes to the same scenario, referring to Jason's "false faith, and love too lightly flitt."[36] Similarly, on the Continent the Italian poet Dante Alighieri (c. 1265–1321) found Jason unworthy of admiration. In his *Divine Comedy* (1308–1321), Dante placed Jason in the eighth circle of Hell, the preserve of the flatterers who used oratory to deceive. In the poem, the narrator and his guide, the Roman poet Virgil, come across a fellow who, despite being tortured, retains a lordly air. Virgil explains whom they have encountered:

> What mien he still retains of majesty!
>> 'Tis Jason, who by courage and by guile
>> The Colchians of the ram deprived. 'Twas he
>
> Who on his passage by the Lemnian isle,
>> Where all of womankind with daring hand
>> Upon their males had wrought a murder vile
>
> With loving pledges and with speeches bland
>> The tender-yeared Hypsipyle betrayed,
>> Who had herself a fraud on others planned.
>
> Forlorn he left her then, when pregnant made.
>> That is the crime condemns him to this pain;
>> And for Medea too is vengeance paid.[37]

In the *De Claris Mulieribus* ("On Famous Women," 1374) of Giovanni Boccaccio (1313–1375), Medea was all but condemned to hell as "the most cruel example of ancient wickedness," whose dark soul was equally capable of using deceitful sorcery or murderous weaponry to carry out her evil deeds.[38] By contrast, in the French poem *Epistre Othéa* (c. 1400), Christine de Pizan uses Medea as an exemplar of a moral and wise woman undone by misplaced trust born of lust for a man (Jason) who delivers to her only evil, a theme she had developed earlier in the *Epistre au dieu d'Amours* in which she described Medea as the sole reason for Jason's triumph but rewarded only with broken promises and desertion.[39]

Clearly, there was a vast gap between Jason and Medea as Christ and the Virgin and them as hell-bound sinners; yet, in the medieval imagination both sides existed simultaneously, the saint and the sinner, like the mystery of the dual nature of Christ as flesh and spirit, god and man. In medieval theology, all are born in sin, and heroism is no guarantor of divine grace. In sum, the myth of Jason was more malleable than gold, able to be bent to whatever shape a poet or scholar required, gleaming lustrously with intimations of heaven, but nevertheless mined from the corruption of the earth below.

The Glory of Kings

If the Jason myth had taken on a secular and a sacred meaning, it reflected the central conflict of medieval European high culture, the struggle between temporal and religious authority. This conflict manifested most notably in the efforts of the papacy and the Holy Roman Emperors to assert their supremacy over one another, and thus the headship of Christendom. At the more local level, the conflict was less fierce since aristocrats and bishops were often one and the same. Into this battle between church and state, the legend of the Argonauts found itself recruited to the side of royalty, but not without objection from the same religious authorities who had declared Jason a model of Christian virtue but now professed him a vile pagan. This came about because one aristocrat tried to promote Jason above an acceptable station.

Philip III, Duke of Burgundy (1396–1467) was known as Philip the Good, and he sought to expand the power and influence of his duchy by playing two great powers, England and France, off one another during the Hundred Years' War. Politically unable to accept the high honor of becoming a Knight of the Garter in England for fear of alienating France, Philip instead created his own order of knighthood in 1429,[40] which he modeled on the twin sources of Jason and the Argonauts and the knights of Arthur's Round Table (and not, as the jesting rumor would have it, for his blonde mistress's pubic hair[41]), christening it the Order of the Golden Fleece and drawing a connection between the capture of the Fleece and the order's aim of defeating the Turk to recapture Jerusalem's Church of the Holy Sepulcher.[42] Philip also saw a parallel between the Argonauts' quest for the Golden Fleece and the Arthurian knights' quest for the Holy Grail, and he was not alone. Chrétien de Troyes, the twelfth century French poet, had read Benoît's *Roman de Troie* and incorporated motifs from the Argonauts' story into his epic of Arthurian myth, including *Erec and Enide* (1170).[43] And the early twentieth century scholar C. B. Lewis believed that the Jason story, among many others from Greek myth, underlay the Arthurian cycle, proposing that classical mythology gave rise to medieval legendry, dressing up old heroes in new clothes.[44] Though many scholars disagree with these conclusions, it is nevertheless true that the medieval conception of Medea, including the specific powers assigned to her in Benoît (such as changing night to day and reversing the course of rivers), became a "staple in descriptions of Arthurian enchantresses."[45] Geoffrey of Monmouth specifically modeled Morgan le Fay on Medea (and Circe) in his *Vita Merlini* ("Life of Merlin," c. 1150), though inverting the wicked sorceress into a beneficent "fay," or magician.[46] Graham Anderson proposed in 2004 that Medea's cauldron was the precursor of the Holy Grail, with Pelias, son of the sea-god Poseidon, and his rejuvenated brother Aeson, serving as the forerunners of the Fisher King and his brother (or father) the Wounded King. In this reading, Pelias survives in Grail lore under the name Pelles, who is variously the Fisher King or the Wounded King.[47]

The Order of the Golden Fleece took as its symbol the skin of Phrixus' ram, and each of the twenty-four knights of the Order wore a golden collar from which a golden depiction of the flaccid ram's skin dangled, complete with four feet, head, and horns. In 1516, the number of knights would increase to fifty plus the sovereign of the order, the same number as there were Argonauts. To qualify as a knight, a candidate needed to exhibit great virtue and greater courage, making the order's ranks the most distinguished in Europe, eventually drawing members from the imperial and royal houses of territories from Spain to England to Austria to Hungary and beyond. Next to England's Order of the Garter, the Order of Golden Fleece was the highest rank of European knighthood.

However, as patron of a Catholic order of knighthood, Jason was less than ideal, both because he was a pagan and more especially because he broke his oath of eternal fidelity to Medea. Consequently, the bishops who served Philip began a campaign to clean up Jason's image and situate the Order firmly in the religious milieu of the times. The chancellor of the Order of the Golden Fleece, Guillame Fillastre, preached sermons likening the Golden Fleece to five fleeces known from the Bible, those of Gideon, Jacob, Mesa, Job, and David. He expanded his symbolism of the six fleeces into a book, the *Histoire de la Toison d'or.* Jason became identified with Gideon, an Old Testament figure who is associated with a fleece. In Judges, God commands Gideon to rescue Israel, but the young man is unsure of himself. He challenges God to perform two miracles to prove he is in fact the divinity. Gideon rolls a fleece onto the ground and on successive nights asks God to make the fleece damp with dew and the ground dry, and then the fleece dry with ground damp.[48] In the late Middle Ages, the fleece of Gideon became associated with the Virgin Mary in Christian allegorical thinking, with the dew representing the "moment of Christ's conception."[49] In Fillastre's mind, the Golden Fleece was nothing less than the Lamb of God, Jesus Christ, and the Order therefore His vessel to achieve humanity's salvation. Under Chancellor Jehain Germaine, Jason was formally demoted, with Gideon assuming the patronage of the Order. Philip ordered the creation in 1448 of a spectacular tapestry depicting *Gideon* and the Golden Fleece.[50]

Nevertheless, Gideon was mostly a mask hiding the pagan symbolism from the Church. In the minds of Philip and his knights, Jason was still the most prominent patron of the Order and served in parallel with Gideon. In 1454, Philip the Good laid a sumptuous feast at Lille, which was the most magnificent in living memory, according to witnesses. At this feast, Philip and the knights of the Golden Fleece swore to free the Church from the grip of the Turk, and among the elaborate festivities were four performances of the adventures of Jason, whose quest the Order took as symbolic of their own proposed crusade to the wicked east to defeat the barbarian hordes.[51]

A NEW EPIC OF JASON

To commemorate the Order of the Golden Fleece, Philip commissioned Raoul Lefèvre to compose an epic celebrating the life of Jason, and purposely salvaging his reputation from his detractors. This poem, the *Histoire de Jason* (composed between 1454 and 1467) was translated into English as the *A Boke of the Hoole Lyf of Jason* in 1477 by the printer William Caxton, and was one of the very first English language books ever printed, following a translation of Lefèvre's earlier effort, a history of the Trojan War. Lefèvre's work drew on many medieval sources, which, unfortunately, all derived from the same few original sources, namely Dares, Guido, and Benoît, so his work was in essence the epitome and completion of the medieval project to remake Jason in the image of the Christian knight. Since Lefèvre did not use ancient sources for his poem other than Justin's summary of Pompeius Trogus, who, we have seen, unusually claimed Medea and Jason reconciled and returned to Colchis, the familiar *Argonautica* of Antiquity is practically absent; all that remains of Jason's story is the origins of his quest, the stopover at Troy, and the achievement of the Fleece. As Ruth Morse noted, Lefèvre's whitewashing was challenging from the start:

> Lefèvre's defence of Jason took the form of a famous joke about labour camps under Stalin: there are no labour camps; they are a good thing anyway; and they will soon be abolished. First, Lefèvre denied the premise of the accusation: there was no oath to Medea to break, not only because she extracted it by duress (Jason was enchanted) but also because he had already made an oath to another woman. Secondly, Jason was right to leave Medea because of the wicked things that she did, and we must admire him for leaving her although because of the enchantment he was unable to stop loving her. Thirdly, he went back to her in the end. The difficulties which this contradictory welter of claims ought to have made, in fact made it possible for Lefèvre to write a coherent biographical account.[52]

The *Histoire* takes the form of a biography, modeled on those of medieval princes. The young Jason is born to an aged king Eson who entrusts the regency to Peleus. When he turns eighteen, Jason goes to Thebes to participate in a jousting tournament, where he meets the princely Sir Hercules of Thebes. Jason's performance rouses much praise from the gathered women, and Jason enters knighthood at Thessalonica at the instigation of Hercules so that both would be equals and brothers in arms. The pair adventure together, smiting the centaurs and winning Jason much fame. Peleus seeks Jason's death to avoid the poverty to which he would return upon relinquishing the regency, but Peleus knows he cannot outright murder Jason, "the grace of al the worlde" (in Caxton's translation) and retain his royal legitimacy.[53] What follows are invented medieval adventures drawn from the tradition of romance involving the chaste salvation and seduction of sixteen-year-old Queen Mirro, which were designed to show Jason as the paragon of courtly love. This involves scenes of the two lovers intercut with adventures: the slaying of a giant named Corfus, who hates love; a war against the Sclavonians and the killing of their king for trying to marry Mirro against her will; a battle with Dyomedes and killing *him*; talk about Jason's love of Mirro with the aged Sir Mopsius; dreams of love; and Eson's promise of a great wedding for the two lovers. Finally, we reach Peleus' command to fetch the Fleece, about a third of the way through the poem, when a knight tells Peleus of the island where many knights have been devoured when questing for the fleece of gold. This, Peleus thinks, is the perfect plan. To send him forth, Peleus appeals to the young, naïve, and trustful Jason's vanity, telling him at a great feast of young nobles that it saddened him that "fortune hath not giue place wher your puissau*n*ce & valor may be shewd."[54]

The assembled bachelor nobles, including Hercules, Mopsius, and Theseus, agree to join Jason to achieve greater honor through the seizure of the Fleece, and Peleus causes the *Argyne* (*Argo*) to be built. Despite repeated warnings that Peleus means him harm, Jason pushes forth valiantly. The Argonauts' first adventure on this medieval crusade was, of course, to threaten Troy with vengeance and war after Laomedon acts inhospitably. Following this, Lefèvre adds the Argonauts' visit to Lemnos, following medieval versions of Ovid's *Metamorphoses*, but the author appears to have conflated the Lemnian women with the Amazons and makes them armed and warlike. Queen Ysiphyle (Hypsipyle) comes to love Jason, who does not return her affection until the queen seduces him by stealing into his bed nude while he sleeps, inducing him to sex over his proffered objections of true love for Mirro. Nevertheless, despite their sexual congress, Jason departs for Colchos, leaving a heartbroken Ysiphyle behind with a promise to return, but which circumstances beyond his control (the sorceries of Medea) prevent him from fulfilling. The guild-ridden, sinful Ysiphyle kills herself for shame at her sexual incontinence.

A lengthy digression explains the origins of the Golden Fleece and the history of the kingship in Colchos, in excruciating detail. Apparently Mars orders a man named Apollo to found a kingdom, and to do so he builds an ark like Noah's to transport Greeks to the shore of Colchos, where a marvelous golden-fleeced sheep lives. After a colony is founded and government established, Mars teaches Apollo how to conquer the golden sheep, which is in this version a living sheep and not a dead skin. He prophesies the coming of Jason, and the secrets of defeating the magical guardians surrounding the sheep, the bulls and the dragon, are passed down from royal daughter to daughter unto the coming of Jason. This secret involved a blood rite to anoint a knight's armor to make him invincible, a mixture of glue to stop up the bulls' mouths, and a potion to defeat the "giants" who will arise from the teeth the knight must plant after slaying the serpent and returning to the glued bulls to plow a field for planting. Only then may the armored knight capture and kill the golden sheep.

With such an explicit formula for achieving the Fleece, Lefèvre accomplishes two things: First, he renders Medea's aid secondary since the knowledge came from Mars himself, but he also detracts from Jason's heroism by making him essentially a replaceable cog in a complex plot contrived by Mars.

To return us to the present, Apollo dies and becomes a (false) god, while Medea inherits the secret, giving her the knowledge needed upon Jason's arrival. Medea, of course, falls in love with Jason, and through the agency of a love spell cast by an attendant, she compels him to foreswear Mirro and love her instead. She gives him the secret to achieving the Fleece, and he wins the gold sheep following the steps outlined in the testament of Mars. He used the Fleece to wrap up the three tongues of the dragon, the metal hooves of the bulls, and their iron horns to take back with him. Oestes (Aeëtes) forbids Medea's marriage, and the story follows the familiar outlines of Seneca's tragedy, though with a twist. Medea murders her brother and uses the pieces to stop her father's pursuit. In Greece, she kills Peleus to give Jason his birthright, but restores Eson to youth to please Jason. Here is where things get weird.

Jason comes to realize that Medea is becoming an evil witch, and despite the potion that forces him to love her, he leaves her and wanders the countryside in distress. He tries to put Medea behind him by marrying Creusa at Corinth, but Medea attends the wedding feast seated on four dragons and kills everyone there save Jason himself. Jason leaves Corinth and wanders despondently until Mirro finds him and recognizes that he is enchanted. She releases him from the love spell, and blameless Jason now hates Medea for what she did, robbing him of his real love for Mirro. Eson defends his rightful daughter-in-law Medea at the witch's insistence, and the two royals go to war over the issue, leading to Mirro's demise at the hands of Achilles' friend Patroclus (!) on orders from Eson. Medea, enraged and saddened, kills her son and flees into exile. Jason and Eson eventually reconcile after many years of Jason adventuring around the world. Only then did the "noble & valiaunt prince Iason"[55] meet Medea in the woods where she had hid, reconciling with her when she vows to give up sorcery. Together, they ascend the throne in place of Jason's father and reign over the kingdom of Myrmidone, all Jason's other loves conveniently dead. They had many children and lived happily ever after.

Thus was the great epic of the Argonauts reduced to soap opera and an epic hero to a virtuous and lovelorn knight-errant. It was, in short, the culmination of the medieval *Argonautica*. Lefèvre's work was enormously popular for a century after its composition, but would lose some of its impact as the Renaissance wore on and original Greek sources came to light, contradicting medieval accounts.

JASON AND THE HABSBURGS

With the dissolution of the independence of the duchy of Burgundy, the sovereignty of the Order of the Golden Fleece passed to the duchy's new sovereigns, the House of Habsburg, which ruled both Spain and the Holy Roman Empire. The Habsburgs made a great spectacle of the Order, including its image in virtually every painting of the imperial family in Austria and their royal cousins in Spain. The Habsburgs placed the collar of the Order of the Golden Fleece around the neck of the double-headed black eagle that symbolized the Holy Roman Empire. This eagle descended from the eagle that represented Rome, and in turn from the eagle of Zeus. Thus the Habsburgs reunited the Fleece Phrixus consecrated to Zeus with the eagle that represented the god, and this piece of heraldry remained with the family after the Empire dissolved in 1806, and served as the seal of the Austro-Hungarian Empire until 1918.

The Habsburg Philip II of Spain named a warship *Argo* and painted it with scenes celebrating the Argonauts as analogues to the crusading Habsburgs and the Turkish capital of Constantinople as Colchis. He sent it to battle in 1565 against the Muslims attempting to invade Malta.[56] The Habsburgs, who ruled the Americas as Spanish kings and much of Europe as Holy Roman Emperors, purposely associated themselves with the image of Jason, and they saw themselves as embodying the prophecy of a new Golden Age that Virgil had spelled out in the *Fourth Eclogue*.[57] In 1584, Ludovico Carracci applied gold to an image of the Golden Fleece in the Palazza Fava in Bologna as part of a series of frescos known as the Jason Cycle honoring the Order of the Golden Fleece through a depiction of the Argonauts' myth.[58] The Italian artist Lorenzo Costa produced a painting called *The Ship of the Argonauts* sometime between 1480 and 1490, perhaps inspired by the recent publication of a new edition of Valerius Flaccus in the artist's hometown of Bologna.[59] Framed between two Corinthian columns of black marble, the *Argo* is seen on the image's left, in the River Phasis. It has the appearance of a small, three-masted medieval ship on which Heracles, Jason, and a handful of Argonauts stand or sit, dressed in contemporary costumes. On the right, the rocky cliffs of Colchis cascade downward toward the river, and two men on horseback view the ship.

Under the patronage of the Habsburg rulers of Spain and their ambitious rivals elsewhere in Europe, Europeans' adventures during the Age of Exploration were consciously equated with the greatest sea voyage of antiquity.[60] Luis Vaz de Camões, the sixteenth century Portuguese poet, consciously likened Vasco de Gama and his crew to modern Argonauts in his poem *Os Lusiadas* (1572).[61] When the Spanish explored South America in the sixteenth century and saw the golden richness of the Incas, they fancifully equated Peru with Colchis, and from this analogy emerged the myth of El Dorado. As in Colchis, the Inca of Peru worshipped the sun; and like Aeëtes, their king was a son of the sun. Too, the Inca associated gold with the solar deity, which conformed to the Renaissance understanding of the Golden Fleece as a solar symbol. The Spanish had also found llamas in Peru, which they interpreted as a type of sheep, and they noted that the wild savages wore their pelts as clothing. In the heart of the main temple of Viracocha in Cuzco, they found images of llamas made from gold—a veritable Golden Fleece.[62] When they heard vague rumors about a Land of Gold, *El Dorado*, could there be any doubt that they had stumbled onto the great source of wealth itself, the font of earthly gold that they believed was the hidden message of the Jason myth?

The Habsburgs, however, were not alone in appropriating Jason. When the Habsburg Emperor Charles V entered Florence in 1536, the city welcomed him with a twenty-five-foot sculpture of Jason, wearing the Golden Fleece, the symbol of His Majesty's imperial order of knighthood. On a triumphal arch in 1541, Charles simply *became* Jason, seizing the Fleece, with an inscription proclaiming his intention to restore the Golden Age.[63] Similarly, the French king Henry II (reigned 1547–1559), a rival of the Habsburgs, entered Paris in triumph after his 1549 coronation to much pomp and circumstance, including a great triumphal arch at the Gate of Saint Denis decorated in mythological themes. Farther along the road a second and third arch stood, and the third arch depicted Henry as Tiphys, the steersman of *Argo*, leading across Notre Dame Bridge to yet another arch praising the king and the French people as the new Argonauts, with the king as Tiphys steering the French toward immortality, just as they believed the prophesied new Tiphys of Virgil would steer the future Argonauts toward the same end.[64] A century later, Louis XIV, who conducted wars against the Habsburgs and schemed to place a Bourbon relative on the throne of Spain, had himself depicted as Jason in a series of paintings celebrating the king's naval prowess, virtue, courage, and glory.[65] Not for nothing did the French kings seek to associate themselves with the same myth the Habsburgs had awarded to themselves as their special imperial province.

However, upon the death of Charles II of Spain in 1700, the Order became divided between the Habsburgs, now based solely in Austria, and the new Bourbon monarchy in Spain, both of which claimed the right of succession to the Burgundian knightly inheritance. Today, the Spanish order belongs to the Bourbon king of Spain, and the Austrian to the head of the House of Habsburg. Both continue to award golden collars featuring the Fleece, but the Habsburg order is typically reserved only for members of the Habsburg family, while the Spanish order has been presented to a wider array of honorees, including a king of Thailand.

Holy Roman Emperor Charles V wears the collar of the Order of the Golden Fleece in this etching made after a portrait by Nichola Bettoni. The Order was modeled on the Argonauts, and the Habsburgs adopted it as a symbol of their sovereignty, identifying themselves with various Classical figures, including Jason and their mythic ancestor, Aeneas (Library of Congress).

We began this chapter with St. George replacing Jason in Georgia. Let us end with the opposite. On the other end of medieval world, at Laibach in Istria, now Ljubljana, the capital of Slovenia, and formerly Roman Emona (Iulia Aemona, founded 50 BCE), locals began to say sometime around the end of the Middle Ages or Renaissance (the exact time is unclear) that the city had been founded by Jason when the Argonauts fled Colchis and sailed up the Danube, carrying the *Argo* across the site of Laibach to the Adriatic. Along the way Jason encountered a dragon in a marsh and slew him. This dragon then appeared on the city's coat of arms, where it sits even today. This story, still told to tourists, is apparently the result of two mistakes: first, identifying Laibach with Nauportus, a Roman settlement that Pliny said was named for where the Argonauts "carried the boat" on their shoulders,[66] and second, a reinterpretation of the dragon of the city's patron saint, St. George, back into Jason's dragon! A competing and parallel legend, after all, situated George's dragon-slaying in the same marsh where Jason was supposed to have slain the same creature.[67] Both versions,

Cet entrée est de Monsieur le Comte de Brionne Grand Chambelan de son Altesse, representant Jason

The Jason myth was a favorite of royalty and aristocrats alike. In 1627, the Prince de Pfalzbourg organized an opulent Barriers (a joust-like tournament, but on foot) at Nancy, and the Comte de Brionne arrived in the tournament hall as Jason, in a model *Argo* surrounded by torchbearers and tritons, with the island of Colchis (with Fleece and dragon) and a temple of Mercury in tow. This etching by Jacques Callot captured the astounding scene (National Gallery of Art).

in turn, appear to be successive attempts to identify the pagan Slovene dragon-slaying healer god Kresnik, who owned the apples of immortality,[68] with figures from the wider European community, probably first George in the early medieval period of Christianization, and then Jason when Argonautic motifs were popular and the Habsburgs reigned here, after 1335, and the two stories merged.[69] This shows again how easily pagan, classical, and Christian identifications could slide into one another and how easily motifs transferred between and among myths and legends.

What can be said in favor of the medieval versions of the Argonauts and their retinue is that the persistent association of Jason with the run-up to the Trojan War saved his myth from obscurity. If not for the *Roman de Troie* or the *Histoire de Jason*, his story might have slipped entirely into the darkness that swirled through the medieval understanding of the ancient world. It is not without irony that as the medieval world gave way to the modern, Jason found himself stripped of most of his Argonauts and nearly all of his adventures, defined now by elements that were no part of his earliest myth: a reputation as a philandering seducer, the epilogue at Corinth, and, *primus inter pares*, the confrontation with Laomedon at Troy. It is also certain that the ancients would never have recognized the lovelorn knight as their ancient hero. However, this limited and restricted understanding of Jason's myth had reigned as the definitive version of the story from the sixth century to the sixteenth, influencing a thousand years of mythological understanding and a thousand years of scholarship, continuing even today, that sought out a historical reality for Jason's voyage, unconscious tribute to the medieval certainty that the *Argo* sailed real seas in a real and discoverable period of ancient history.

However, an influx of new discoveries during the Renaissance would resurrect an older version of Jason and reopen a window into the ancient Greek world that had been shut since the fall of Rome and pave the way for the modern Jason.

10

The Star

Jason in the Modern World

The fall of Constantinople in 1453 had many geopolitical consequences, but it was equally portentous in intellectual history. Between the Western invasion of Constantinople in the Fourth Crusade (1260) and the last vestiges of the Eastern Roman Empire being extinguished by the Turks two centuries later, Byzantine scholars fled the ruins of Constantine's empire and came to Europe, primarily Italy, bringing with them the fruits of Byzantine scholarship and learning. Giovanni Aurispa (1372–1460), a humanist from Sicily, travelled to Constantinople to learn Greek and study the classics. Recognizing that a wealth of ancient material was available in Constantinople that was unknown in the West, he set about purchasing as many manuscripts as he could, eventually collecting 238 codices that he took back to Italy in 1423. Among these manuscripts was the *Argonautica* of Apollonius of Rhodes, which the Byzantines had preserved by copying and recopying by hand for a thousand years, filling in corruptions and gaps by comparing and contrasting extant texts.[1] The copy Aurispa brought back with him had been made in the tenth century and contained writings from other Greek authors, including Aeschylus and Sophocles. It is known as the Laurentian manuscript and is now housed in Florence. A second version, the Guelferbytanus, was produced in the thirteenth century and reflected an early medieval version of the text that differed in some small ways from that preserved in the Laurentian text. Dozens of scattered other manuscripts and papyri preserved incomplete or fragmentary copies of the poem, some of them still different from either main text.

In these years, classical scholarship flourished, and there was a renewed interest in all things Greek and Roman. After the fall of Byzantium, Plato returned to Western Europe for the first time in a thousand years, in Latin translation in 1484 and the Greek original in 1517; and Aldus Manutius (1449–1515) among several others founded a printing press to print Greek texts of classical works that had filtered into Italy in the fifteenth and sixteenth centuries. The Byzantine scholar Janus Lascaris (c. 1445–1535) fled Constantinople at its fall and ended up in Italy where he became employed by Lorenzo de Medici. Under his auspices, Lascaris traveled to Greece in 1492 and returned to Italy with more than two hundred manuscripts brought from Mount Athos. In 1496 he published Western Europe's first Greek editions of Apollonius' *Argonautica* and Euripides' *Medea* on the press of Laurentina de Alopa in Florence. His brother, Constantine Lascaris (1434–1501), taught the *Orphic Argonautica* to his students, convinced that it was the oldest version of the story; and the philosopher Marsilio Ficino translated it into Latin, though *mihi soli*, "for me alone." We have already seen that Valerius Flaccus' *Argonautica* had been rediscovered in 1416 and 1429, and it ran through seven editions in Italy and one in Spain in the decades surrounding Columbus' voyage to America, with a total of at least sixteen editions within a century. Giovanni Battista Pio wrote a Latin hexameter conclusion to the unfinished epic for a 1519 edition, and the leading lights of the Renaissance read Valerius, enjoyed him, and alluded to the work in their own texts.[2]

For the first time since the fall of the Roman Empire, Europeans had a competing narrative—several in fact—that presented an unknown series of adventures of Jason in a light entirely different from the medieval elaborations on Dares. Suddenly, a new world had opened, and an old myth became appreciated again. It is difficult to quantify the exact effect this rediscovery of the ancient Jason had on European sensibilities, but it is evident that from this point forward the medieval Jason gradually recedes into what scholars were coming to see as a great age of darkness that separated the modern world from the glories of Antiquity. The old Jason stepped forward anew, and the ancient world triumphed over the medieval, at least partially, though not always accurately. For example, along the Dalmatian coast, the port city of Ragusa (modern Dubrovnik) became associated with the Argonauts through a historical accident. In sixteenth-century English the city's name was rendered as Aragosa, and a type of large mercantile ship used extensively by the powerful and far-flung merchants of Ragusa, the *ragusae*, in corrupted form became *argosy*. The English then etymologized backward and presumed argosy was in fact derived from *Argo*, Jason's ship, since they now knew from Apollonius that Jason had sailed the Adriatic on his return from Colchis.[3] Sill later, under the assumption of the link to *Argo*, the word argosy was applied to Apollonius' poem as a familiar English name, on aural parallel with the *Odyssey*, yielding a new definition of an argosy as an adventure, and eventually a treasury of stories. Finally, the word in this last meaning yielded *The Argosy*, the first pulp fiction magazine, founded in 1882.

E. B. Greene and F. Fawkes produced a poorly received English translation of Apollonius' *Argonautica* in 1780, as did W. Preston in 1803.[4] There was no reliable English translation of Apollonius until 1889, when E. P. Coleridge produced his version, followed in 1912 by the standard translation of R. C. Seaton.[5] Before that time, interested parties had to either read Apollonius in the original Greek, which limited the readership to possessors of elite education, or content oneself with the summaries of the Jason story presented in compendia such as Bulfinch's *Age of Fable*. Between 1912 and 1990, only one other major English translation was published, that of E. V. Rieu in 1959.[6] Only since 1990 have multiple modern translations become available. The situation with Valerius Flaccus' *Argonautica* was even worse, with no complete English translation until the standard version of J. H. Mozley in 1934. H. G. Blomfield published a partial prose translation, only Book One, in 1916, a century after Thomas Noble's verse translation of that same book.[7] David R. Slavitt produced a translation in verse in 1999, though not always true to the Latin text. The impetus for translation was less than with Apollonius because until the middle twentieth century (and even the late twentieth century in my high school), Latin was a standard element of the school curriculum. The final 300 lines of the *Orphic Argonautica* were translated into English by William Preston in 1803, but no complete translation occurred until Siegfried Pyrrhus Petrides produced a poorly-received version in 2005, and my own translation in 2011.

In the centuries between the rediscovery of Apollonius and today, there has been a veritable explosion of fictive, scholarly, and pseudoscholarly treatments of the Jason myth. It would, of course, be impossible and stultifying to catalogue them all. Instead, we will conclude our study of the epic history of Jason with three chapters examining representative or especially interesting treatments of the hero in modern contexts. This chapter will treat allegory and fiction, including mythography, literature, and the visual and performing arts. Chapter 11 will examine scholarly reactions to and theories regarding Jason and the Argonauts, and chapter 12 will look at some of the more extreme misuses to which Jason has been unfairly subjected. As our point of departure between these three threads, we will examine one area where all overlap, in the alchemical literature of the early modern period, a body of literature that used mythology allegorically in poems designed to further the pursuit of scientific knowledge of an essentially unscientific enterprise, yielding pseudo-scientific results.

The Alchemists

Alchemy began in Western Europe when Arabic treatises on the search for ways to turn base metals to gold were translated into Latin in the twelfth century. In the early modern

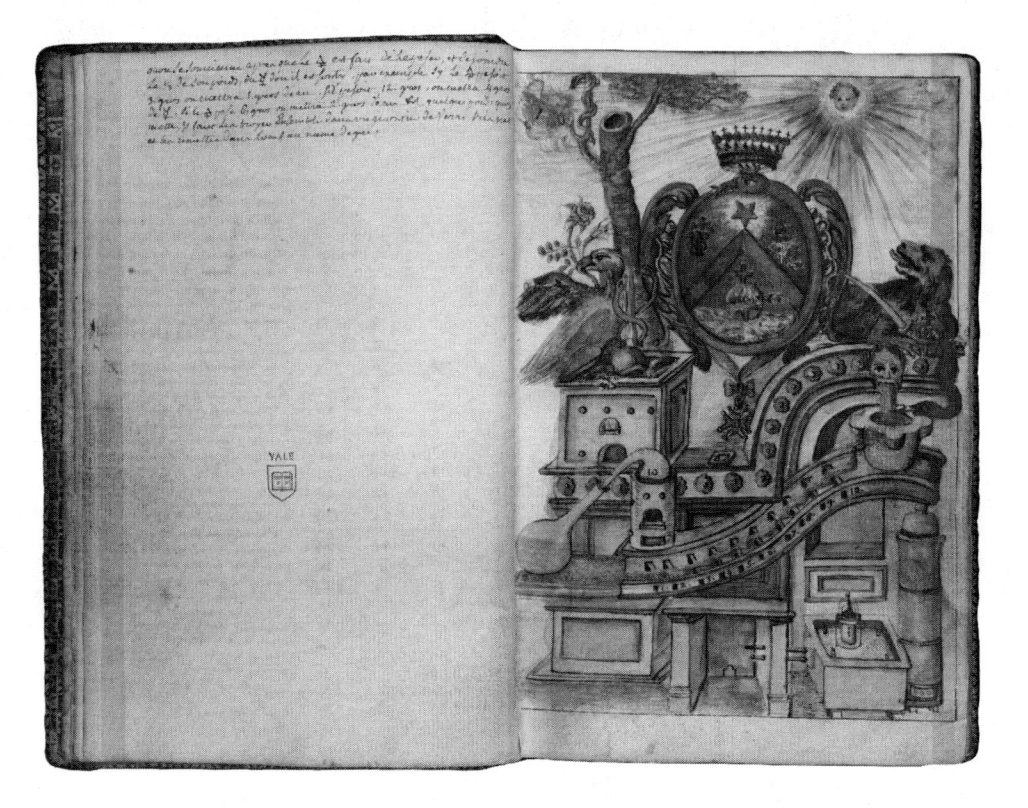

Alchemists and occultists saw in Jason's quest for the Golden Fleece and esoteric message about how to turn base metals into gold, whereby Jason's helmet or Medea's cauldron became the symbol for the scientific equipment, like that seen here in a c. 1680 French illustration, that alchemists used to combine various substances. Sir Walter Raleigh wrote that in the journey of Jason alchemists deduced nothing less than the Philosopher's Stone (Beinecke Rare Book and Manuscript Library, Yale University).

period, alchemists began to see in Greek mythology a hidden stream of knowledge that encoded alchemical principles within myths. Thus Deucalion and Pyrrah became symbols for gold and silver, the two most important metals. The *Pretiosa margarita novella* ("New Pearl of Great Price") attributed to Pietro Boni and printed in Ferrara in 1546 appears to reprint a genuine fourteenth century text traditionally dated to 1330. In it, the author interpreted stories from Ovid and other authors as alchemical allegories. Among these, Medea's cauldron became a symbol for the transformation of metals. The "dragon's teeth" Jason sewed (again conflated with the killing of the serpent) became identified with a sublimate of mercury, the old term for mercuric chloride, a solid white crystalline form of the metal used as a reagent. The armed men that sprang from the dead serpent's planted teeth were therefore the "hidden gold in Ovid."[8] Subsequently, the *Argo* came to symbolize the vessel through which experiments were conducted, and Jason's quest the process of alchemy itself.

Giovanni Pico della Mirandola (1463–1494) took full advantage of the reintroduction of the Greek *Argonautica* in seeking out the hidden meaning of Jason's quest. This he found in the Byzantine suggestion that the tale of the Golden Fleece was alchemical in nature, though hidden "under the veils of fables and the clouds of enigma."[9] He reintroduced the suggestion that the Golden Fleece was a book of alchemy, as did the humanist poet Giovanni Aurelio Augerello (1451–1524), who wrote poems on the making of gold, including "Vellus Aureum" (1505) and the much longer *Chrysopoeia* (1515). Cornelius Agrippa (1486–1535) found the whole idea absurd and attacked it in his *De incertitudine et vanitate scientiarum atque artium declamatio invectiva* ("Declamation on the Uncertainty and Vanity of the Sciences and Arts," 1526),[10] but his son Ioannes wrote a favorable poem, *Vellum aureum* (1560), that again linked Jason to the process of alchemy.[11] Chysogonus Polydorus' preface to the alchemical tracts known as *De Alchemia* (1541–1545) offered an interpretation of the entire Argonaut myth by which Jason's quest is revealed as an alchemical investigation in search of the method whereby gold may be made. From the preface of Chysogonus Polydorus,[12] the English playwright Ben Jonson (1572–1637) caused his Sir Epicure Mammon to offer the following lines in his 1610 satiric comedy *The Alchemist*:

> I have a piece of Jason's fleece, too,
> Which was no other than a book of alchemy,
> Writ in large sheepskin, a good fat ram-vellum.
> Such was Pythagoras' thigh, Pandora's tub;
> And all that fable of Medea's charms,
> The manner of our work: the bulls, our furnace,
> Still breathing fire: our argent-vive, the dragon:
> The dragon's teeth, mercury sublimate,
> That keeps the whiteness, hardness, and the biting;
> And they are gathered into Jason's helm,
> (The alembic [a type of still]), and then sowed in Mars his field,
> And thence sublimed so often, till they're fixed.[13] (brackets added)

Thus, in this reading the bulls serve as the furnace working on a still (the helmet) holding the sublimate of mercury (the dragon's teeth), boiled until what remains is alchemical gold. However, at this point the connection between Jason and alchemy is played for laughs. Nevertheless, one last alchemist took the Jason myth very seriously. This was Sir Isaac Newton, who was the father of modern physics and the co-founder of calculus but retained an active interest in alchemy and the occult throughout his life. Newton's 1728 treatise *The*

Chronology of Ancient Kingdoms Amended claimed the Argonauts' voyage to have been among the first ever undertaken by ancient man, around the time Solomon reigned in Jerusalem, and from this voyage all the signs of the zodiac took their names. His evidence was simply that the Greek constellations represented mythology down to the time of Jason (Argo Navis and Aries) and nothing after; therefore, Jason and his friends—especially Chiron—must have been the astronomers who named the stars and used the constellations to conduct the first long sea voyages (since Newton followed Valerius in making *Argo* the first seagoing ship), navigating by stellar direction.[14] He further claimed that the ancients reckoned astronomical time from the Argonautic expedition, when the Greeks first mapped the skies and from which the stars slowly deviated in their cycle through eternity.

If the alchemists wanted to use Jason to make gold, less scrupulous people found another way to get gold out of Jason. The phrase "Jason's fleece" was used in Britain from in the seventeenth to nineteenth centuries as slang for gold pieces used to defraud victims in moneychanging schemes, and down to the nineteenth century the phrase was also used for victims of swindling, punning on the verb "to fleece."[15]

Jason and Medea on Stage

The worst thing ever to happen to the reputation of Jason as an epic hero was the Corinthians' decision to adopt him and Medea as their own civic heroes. The result was a tragic mess, and though the Corinthians came to worship Medea as a goddess, poor Jason ended up as a feckless, womanizing dilettante whose misadventures at Corinth forever tainted his actions in and before Colchis. From Euripides and Seneca, the Renaissance and modern stage inherited their Medea and their Jason. In the modern period, the figure of Medea has been a source of fascination, and an unnumbered collection of adaptations of her tragedy found their way to the stage, including original plays and adaptations of Euripides' and Seneca's tragedies. By contrast, Jason was rather ill-served by drama, except primarily as adjunct to the more dynamic Medea.

The great French tragedian Pierre Corneille (1606–1684) chose as the subject of his first tragedy the myth of Medea, producing the play *Médée* in 1635. The play follows the pattern of the earlier Greek and Roman tragedies, especially that of Seneca, but adds a new element, casting Jason as a man seeking (but failing) to reinforce his heroic identity through freeing himself of Médée, while Médée seeks to achieve her own type of heroism by freeing herself of her passion for Jason and using violence to achieve self-determination.[16] Through murder and slaughter, Médée achieves the "joy" of transcendence. Corneille significantly develops Jason's character, though not for the best, making him contemplate killing the children to punish Medea and having him commit suicide at the play's end when he realizes that he will never in actuality be the type of epic hero the wider world thinks he is because he is unable to be independent, owing all his accomplishments to Médée.[17] Another French playwright, H. B. Longpierre (1659–1721), produced another *Médée* (1694) that consciously sought to be more in keeping with Euripides instead of Corneille's Seneca-infused version. Longpierre's play was popular enough to remain in production down until the time of Napoleon, and critics, including Voltaire, felt it the superior to Corneille's, which it largely eclipsed. The French emperor, in exile on St. Helena during

Euripides' play *Medea* did not just inspire later imitations. It has also been performed continuously since the Renaissance. Judith Anderson won a Tony award for her portrayal of the title character in 1947, and she reprised the role several times in the following decade. She is seen here in the role in 1959, when she performed the part for a television production (Library of Congress).

the winter of 1816–1817, read this version of the play and was inspired to read Euripides' version for comparison's sake.[18]

After stumbling on a dictionary of mythology and taking an immediate shine to the story of Medea, Austrian playwright Franz Grillparzer (1791–1872) completed a three-play cycle of the Medea story called the *Das Goldene Vleiss* (known in English as the *Golden Fleece Trilogy*). To research the cycle, he studied Apollonius and Valerius Flaccus among others.[19] The three parts he wrote included *Der Gastfreund* ("The Guest," 1818), about Phrixus; *Die Argonauten* ("The Argonauts," 1819), about Jason's acquisition of the Fleece; and *Medea* (1820), the tragedy of her failed marriage. In the first play, Phrixus brings the Golden Fleece to barbarian Colchis at the head of an invading army, having stripped the Fleece from the statue of a god at Delphi. Aeëtes kills Phrixus, in violation of the rules of hospitality, and Medea, a gentle child of nature, protests the outrage. In the second, Jason comes to seize the Fleece, and devious Aeëtes tries to poison the foreign prince, but Medea saves his life. The two fall madly in love, though Medea does not confess her feelings until Aeëtes attempts to kill Jason again. The two wed, and Jason removes her sorceress's veil, a symbolic bridal veil, to proclaim her no longer a Colchian but a woman wholly of his own people:

> Forget what thou hast heard, what thou hast seen,
> What thou hast been until this very hour.
> Æetes' daughter is now Jason's wife,
> Linked to my breast thy duty and thy right.
> And as from thee I ruthless tear this veil,
> Marked with the symbols of the powers below,
> So tear I from thee all the ancient ties
> That joined thee to this country's wickedness.
> Ye Greeks, here stands a Grecian maiden! Hail her![20]

After Jason captures the Fleece with Medea's help, he marries her aboard the *Argo*. But the Greeks do not take well to a foreign princess, and they mistreat Jason, eventually sending him and Medea fleeing to Corinth when he is suspected of murdering Pelias.

In the third play, at Corinth Medea seeks to cast aside her Colchian identity, renouncing magic and burying the Fleece in the earth. Medea finds her marriage faltering, with Jason falling for Creusa, a childhood friend. Medea sees Jason now as a man consumed by self-love, unable to return her affection:

> For him and him alone the world was made,
> And nothing lives except to prompt his deeds.
> To own in thought what may elude his clutch,
> He dares his fate and risks the fate of all.
> If glory tempts, he kills without a pang,
> And if a woman, why, he simply grasps.
> Let break what will, he has what he desires;
> Right is his deed, for what he wills is right.[21]

As in Euripides, Medea kills Creusa and the children when Jason chooses the latter woman over Medea. She bitterly confronts her husband and departs Corinth, enjoining him to "Bear, suffer, and atone."

This tragic cycle, first produced in Vienna in the Burgtheater March 26 and 27, 1821, depicts Jason as a hero only through public acclaim, who is left without this salve for his soul, and thus must face the nothingness and emptiness of human life. Medea, too, finds herself devastated by events. She takes the Golden Fleece to Delphi to dispose of the unlucky burden, and her fate is to keep living with the guilt of her actions. The work is pessimistic, implying that fate is inescapable, and to fight against it is futile. Critics have seen in it discussions of the fate of the soul, the tragedy of marriage, and the battle of the sexes. Many early critics initially praised the trilogy as among the greatest in German dramatic history, but later critics reassessed the work and found it wanting. More recent criticism focuses (but of course) on themes of colonialism and sexism in the play, the dominant issues of late twentieth century academe.[22]

The twentieth century French playwright Jean Anouilh (1910–1987) modernized the Medea story in *Médée* (1946), a play which brought to the fore themes of sensuality and sexuality, causing Medea to proclaim upon her self-declared emancipation from erotic desire for Jason, "I am no longer that woman bound to the smell of a man, that bitch in heat who waits."[23] Or, more explicitly still, Medea castigates her own shame at her sex:

> *All day long I waited for him, my legs open, maimed.... Humbly, that part of myself that he could take and give back, that middle of my womb was his ... why was I born maimed? Why have you made me a girl? Why these breasts, this weakness, this open wound in the middle of myself? Would not the boy Medea have been handsome? ... Then Jason could have come with his large and powerful hands; then he could have tried to touch me with them! Each of us with his knife—and the stronger kills the other and walks away free; ... Not this struggle where I only learned to yield, this wound I was craving for*[24] [emphasis in original].

Medea's sexual passion for Jason dies, but her embrace of evil replaces it with orgiastic energies surpassing her original sexual lust in her desire to negate her gender and assume the dominant, independent spirit associated with men. Jason, however, represents rationalism, and despite Medea's violence, he is not broken but ends the play committed to rebuilding the rational, orderly world of Corinth, one opposed in every way to the irrational and sensual world of women, even though, like twentieth century postmodern man, he has come to wonder whether reason is merely a comforting illusion in a sea of chaos. For him reason becomes its own sea of chaos, an oblivion in which to lose himself.[25]

Medea's story was also made into operas by Marc-Antoine Charpentier as *Médée* (1693), Georg Benda as *Medea* (1775), Luigi Cherubini as the comedy *Médée* (1797), Giovanni Pacini as *Medea* (1843), Saverio Mercadante as *Medea* (1851), Darius Milhaud as *Médée* (1939), and Mikis Theodorakis as *Medea* (1988). Samuel Barber produced a ballet version of *Medea* (1947) following the outlines of the tragedy, as had Jean-Georges Noverre as *Jason et Médée* in 1763, and several earlier ballets and dumb shows going back to the fifteenth century.

Against these stage performances focused on Medea stand a few devoted more to Jason. Francesco Cavalli's *Il Giasone* ("Jason") from 1649, a sexual comedy-drama loosely based on the Argonaut myth as given by Apollonius, was hailed as the most popular and widely performed seventeenth century opera.[26] In the Venetian opera, a womanizing and somewhat effeminate Jason (his part is for a castrato) sleeps his way across the Aegean and spends a full year having repeated and insatiable sex in a dark room with a Medea he cannot see while ignoring the Golden Fleece until circumstances force the lovers apart and Jason fulfills his masculine duty and seizes the Fleece. The Venetian opera theaters produced more than a dozen versions of Jason's story between 1642 and 1758, according to the existing lists of published Venetian librettos. Austrian composer Gutav Mahler (1860–1911) created *The Arg-*

JASON ET MEDEE.   BALLET TRAGIQUE.

A popular subject for the stage, the failed romance of Jason and Medea lent itself to plays, operas, and ballets. This 1781 image shows Gaétan Vestris, the famous dancer who originated the role of Jason in Jean-Georges Noverre's *Jason et Médée* (1763), performing the role in a pirated version of the ballet that Vestris opened in London without giving credit (or payment) to Noverre (Library of Congress).

onauts, though he apparently did not complete the piece and suppressed it along with many of his other early works. Austrian composer Ernst Krenek's (1900–1991) surrealistic *Der golden Bock* ("The Golden Ram," 1964) found Jason breaking through a "time barrier" to retrieve the Fleece from twentieth century American Indians on Route 66 before returning to Greece. It must surely be the only version of the story to feature a pickup truck chase and the revelation that Medea is herself the dragon, magically transformed.

Moving from opera to music, Karl Ditters von Dittersdorf (1739–1799) composed a sonata for fortepiano entitled "Jason, qui emporte la Toison d'or," and Alice Mary Smith composed "Jason, or the Argonauts and the Sirens" (1879).

Popular Mythology

The rediscovery of ancient Greco-Roman sources had spawned a great interest in mythology in Europe, prompting scholars to begin compiling and analyzing myths to discover underlying patterns. This matter we will discuss in chapter 11. The most important of these works was the 1587 *Mythologiae* of Natalis Comes (or Natale Conti, 1520–1582), the standard Renaissance work on mythology, which superseded all others (and there were many). This work rationalized the Greek heroes and gods as glorified and deified humans and served as the basis for Renaissance literary and artistic allusions to Greek myth. In parallel with these developments came the popular mythologies, compilations of Greco-Roman myths designed to furnish the literary reader with an understanding of the allusions to ancient legendry contained within classical and contemporary poetry and prose, and in the study of ancient history. They were the intellectual descendants of the Vatican Mythographers and Natalis Comes, and these guides were especially popular in the United States, a young country where mythological allusions were less prominent than in the older cultures of Europe. Sometimes the results of such guides were true to the ancient sources, as in the American writer Mary Ann Dwight's *Grecian and Roman Mythology* (1849), which carefully summarized Apollonius' *Argonautica* and Euripides' *Medea*, though not from the originals but rather from German scholars like K. O. Müller who were studying myths in the early nineteenth century. Sometimes, however, the results were less true.

The single most popular guide to Greco-Roman mythology of the modern age was Boston bank clerk Thomas Bulfinch's *Age of Fable* (1855), best known from the 1881 compilation of his antique and medieval retellings of myth, *Bulfinch's Mythology*, edited by Edward Everett Hale. Bulfinch (1796–1867) intended his work for the general reader whose mind has more practical matters to attend to than studying the "false marvels and obsolete faiths" in confusing Greek and Latin texts and dull and dry classical dictionaries, like those of John Lemprière (1788) and William Smith (1857). "Our work is not for the learned, nor for the theologian, nor for the philosopher, but for the reader of English literature, or either sex, who wishes to comprehend the allusions so frequently made by public speakers, essayists, and poets, and those which occur in polite conversation," Bulfinch wrote.[27] In short, he wished to popularize mythology for the masses, in keeping with the democratic spirit of the age. Bulfinch drew his stories of Jason and Medea primarily from Ovid ("abridged, bowdlerized, and rearranged," as one critic put it[28]), thus producing a rather unsatisfactory version of the story that left out most of the colorful adventures en route to Colchis and all of them on the return. A unique aspect of Bulfinch's enterprise was the desire to show readers the connection between myth and literature. In his discussion of Jason he points to Alexander Pope's "Ode on St. Cecilia's Day" (1708), which referenced the launching of *Argo*, the "first" ship, and the section of John Dyer's four-book epic poem on sheep-shearing and wool-weaving, *The Fleece* (1757), which talks of the Golden Fleece and the heroes who set out to find it.

Bulfinch gives equal space to the Argonauts as to Medea alone, about four pages each, and he summarizes her wickedness in only a sentence or two, noting that her actions were "too revolting" to discuss at length. Needless to say, Bulfinch's versions of myths were heavily expurgated, rendered innocuous enough for the most innocent of readers, but stripping them of much of their vitality. Nevertheless, for nearly a century Bulfinch's would be the standard version of mythology for most Americans.

This remained the case down until 1942 when the Classical scholar Edith Hamilton (1867–1963) published her *Mythology: Timeless Tales of Gods and Heroes*. Drawing on original Greek sources, Hamilton told the story of Jason concisely and accurately and in crystalline prose that captured something of the original power of the myth. Her book superseded Bulfinch's as the standard introduction to mythology and remains the most important popular work on the subject. The competing *Handbook of Greek Mythology* (1928) by H. J. Rose presented the many variants of the Jason myth, but was more scholarly than popular, becoming the standard mythology among academics. Its revision as *The Routledge Handbook of Greek Mythology* (2004) by Robin Hard, an almost completely new volume, treats myth engagingly but is too recent to have found its place as a new standard text.

The most eccentric of the popular mythologies was *The Greek Myths* (1955) of Robert Graves (1895–1985), the British poet. This compendium of retold myths offered deeply idiosyncratic interpretations, coupled with lengthy explanatory notes that were frequently misleading, inaccurate, or unsupported by evidence. Graves believed his guide to mythology was the only generally available reference work non-scholars could consult (the American works of Bulfinch and Hamilton apparently were unknown to him), and a truly revolutionary work that would situate Greek myths in the context of anthropological facts about ancient royal succession rites, as documented in Sir James Frazer's *Golden Bough* (see chapter 11), and what he presumed to be a universal belief in a three-formed moon goddess.[29]

In the case of Jason, Graves drew on outdated Victorian scholarship (see chapter 11) to claim that Jason was no figure in his own right but originally a title borne by Heracles, who in turn was originally Gilgamesh, a very reductive reading of a web of mutual influence. Jason, being only a title of a sacred king, was applied to the figure of Diomedes, though as we have seen this name was not anciently associated with Jason (see chapter 3). He further claimed Jason originally sewed the dragon's teeth in Iolcus before this adventure was transferred to Colchis. He also wrote that the Etruscan images of Jason in the dragon (which he calls a sea monster) were the inspiration for the story of Jonah and the whale (which idea, we will see in chapter 11, a Jewish scholar has resurrected), and that Jonah was (of course) the god Marduk. The long and short of it was that Graves considered Jason and Heracles to be exemplars of an ancient myth involving the initiation rituals for "sacred kingship," an office that involved plowing fields and slaying dragons, and ultimately ritual sacrifice at the end of his reign:

> The myth of Pelias and Diomedes—Jason's original name—seems to have been about a prince exposed on a mountain, reared by horseherds, and set seemingly impossible tasks by the king of a neighbouring city, not necessarily a usurper: such as the yoking of fire-breathing bulls, and the winning of a treasure guarded by a sea-monster—Jason, half-dead in the sea-monster's maw, is the subject of Etruscan works of art. His reward will have been to marry the royal heiress.[30]

Thus, in Graves's mind, the Jason story is merely a folktale magnified, essentially no different from any other tale of orphaned princes. Its epic nature he attributes to three conflated elements: First he assigns the entire story of Jason's voyage to a different myth cycle related to Cytisorus, the son of Phrixus, which became conflated with the alleged Diomedes. The "original" Argonautic journey was to the Adriatic, along the old Mycenaean amber routes, because amber was sacred to the sun and thus the origin of Aea. Never mind that the Argonauts' voyage on and about the Adriatic was a late addition (rationalizing the voyage over Ocean or up the Nile as geographic knowledge improved). Second, he claims on the authority of Simonides' purple fleece that the Golden Fleece was in fact "black fleece worn in a royal rain-making rite" of Zeus Actaeus.[31] Third, elements from a "piratical" Greek raid on the Black Sea and tales of the amber trade were grafted onto the Greek story and projected into the Black Sea, where temples of "Heracles the Healer" (i.e. the Jasonia) already existed.

Such speculations make logical sense only if we make two unsupported assumptions: first, that the myth of Jason took shape only around or after the time of Homer, congealing around a hypothetical figure named Diomedes; and second, that "Jason" was a priestly or royal title born by many figures in myth and history. These ideas were perhaps partially acceptable in the 1950s; however, critics faulted Graves from the outset. Academic reviews challenged him for his "defective scholarship"[32] for which there was "no conceivable evidence" to support his "inaccuracies, evasions, improbable analogies, and amateur etymologies."[33] It remained, unfortunately, a popular reference work, prompting the *Yale Review* to warn students away from it in 1985 lest they be misled by Graves' many "ludicrous" claims.[34] Despite these deficiencies, or perhaps because of them, Robert Graves would unwittingly give rise to decades of speculation that Jason was a space alien, as we shall see in chapter 12. He also novelized the expedition of Jason as *The Golden Fleece* (see below).

Jason in Literature and as Literature

Aside from guides to mythology, literary retellings of Greek myths were increasingly popular. Nathaniel Hawthorne presented the myth of the Golden Fleece in his *Tanglewood Tales* (1853), a mythological storybook for children. Notably, Hawthorne proposed that Chiron was actually a human who liked to pretend to be a horse, and the children of his students misunderstood the fact when their parents told them of his eccentricity. He also added some gentle fantasy back into the story, giving the oak plank of Dodona a face and a personality, something carried over into the 1963 movie version. Hawthorne preserved some of the innocence of the story by tastefully ending with the achievement of the Fleece, before the murders start. The English author Charles Kingsley devoted a lengthy section of his work *The Heroes* (1856) to presenting the Argonaut myth for children as well. The definitive version for young readers was probably Padraic Colum's Newbery-winning *The Golden Fleece and the Heroes who Lived before Achilles* (1922), a book-length retelling of the Jason story from Jason's birth down to his return to Iolcus with the Fleece, with digressions into related myths and the stories of the heroes who accompanied him. Children's versions of the myth of Jason have come along regularly since then, down to the present day, though many of the most recent of these, such as John Malam's *Jason and the Argonauts* (2004), show the influence more of the 1963 movie version (especially the depiction of the dragon's teeth yielding skeleton men) than Apollonius or Pindar. A cute version of the story was *Jeremy and the Golden Fleece* (2007) by Becky Citra, in which a boy and his cat go back in time and meet Jason and the Argonauts. Jeremy becomes captain when the ship accidentally leaves without Jason.

However, the myth of the Golden Fleece was not always bowdlerized and rendered safe for children. Dr. Nigel Spivey retold the Jason story as one of his *Songs on Bronze* (2005), an attempt to fashion in contemporary and evocative language, including brutality and sexuality, an abbreviated Greek mythology in the form of a single coherent story from creation to death of Agamemnon. Originally intended for the author's children but expanded in audience to adults unfamiliar with Greek myth, the story is well told if somewhat closer to the

Tanglewood Tales in style and tone than its author probably intended. To my taste, colloquial English and classical myth mix somewhat uneasily.

In literature, the Golden Fleece had other meanings as well. Among the tamest of these, the term "Golden Fleece" came to stand for the golden locks of a blonde woman, as when Shakespeare writes in the *Merchant of Venice* (c. 1596–1597):

> Her name is Portia, nothing undervalu'd
> To Cato's daughter, Brutus' Portia:
> Nor is the wide world ignorant of her worth,
> For the four winds blow in from every coast
> Renowned suitors, and her sunny locks
> Hang on her temples like a golden fleece;
> Which makes her seat of Belmont Colchos' strand,
> And many Jasons come in quest of her.[35]

In that play the adventure of marriage is likened to the Argonauts' quest; however, the blonde locks had another, more prurient meaning—one of which Shakespeare was not unaware— that of the pubic hair of a blonde woman. The 1976 novel *The Dead Father* by Daniel Barthelme featured an old man wandering a mythical countryside in search of the Golden Fleece in hopes of finding youth, but this fleece was in fact the pubic hair of his young daughter, which his son prevents him from touching, leading to his death. The image of the Golden Fleece as pubic hair would appear in a number of novels and short stories, many erotic, including the work of French feminist Monique Wittig (1935–2003), the anonymous erotic novel *The New Story of O* (1990), and a large number of the erotic products of the Olympia Press, the French erotic publisher (among other things) who produced the first *Story of O* (1954). Even Marilyn Monroe was alleged by a biographer to have used peroxide and a toothbrush to achieve her own perfect "golden fleece."[36] These references derive ultimately from early modern British and French slang, which apparently refer back to the scurrilous rumor about Philip the Good naming the Order of the Golden Fleece for his mistress's pubic hair in 1429.

A LITERARY HERO

While Jason had been a star on stage, after the *Histoire de Jason* he was not the hero of epic literature again until William Morris four centuries later. In the meantime, he would pop up on occasion as a mythical allusion or reference point, as in the poetry of Pope and Dyer, or the myth would be employed in service of allegory, as in Henry Ellison's "The Story of Æson Transformed by Medea: A Heathen Fable Christianly Moralized" (1844). This poem told the myth of Aeson's rejuvenation but had Medea's spell fail to make young his soul, something reserved only for God. This prompts the moral of the story: "deal not ever in forbidden things."[37] The eighteenth-century German writer Christopher Martin Wieland (1733–1813) is well known for his German translations of Shakespeare and his philosophical novels; however, he also wrote a satire that drew tangentially on Jason. *Die Abderiten, eine sehr wahrscheinliche Geschichte* (known in English as "The History of the Abderites," 1774) satirized the provincialism and small-mindedness of rural Germany by projecting the regions faults onto the city of Abdera, where Strabo had recorded that a temple of Jason stood. Wieland mocks the Abderites for raising a man to the level of a god simply by dint of him having been their ancestor. This fictional temple grew to encompass a full quarter of the city and to command great wealth and revenue, all in service of a ridiculously false god. The story was adapted by Friedrich Dürrenmatt for the radio in 1951.

The most important literary treatment of Jason in the nineteenth century was *The Life and Death of Jason* (1867, revised 1882), an epic poem by the British pre–Raphaelite socialist poet William Morris (1834–1896), today best remembered for his work in design, commemorated in a brand of paint. Morris's *Life* ran nearly four hundred pages across seventeen books (Apollonius used but four). Morris originally intended the epic to be an episode in his *Earthly Paradise*, a volume of poetry framed by the device of medieval travelers stumbling upon a hidden group of ancient Greeks and exchanging stories with them. However, the *Life* grew too large to include and was published separately, though retaining the medieval atmosphere of the other volume, a pet love of Morris's.[38] Of the story itself, however, there is little to say. It is, in essence, Apollonius' epic followed by Euripides' play, with minor changes, mostly to provide exculpatory reasons to cast Medea in a positive light as a noble heroine and emphasize the importance of unending commitment in romantic relationships.[39]

Henry James, in reviewing the poem, correctly noted that it is more correctly a poem about Medea than Jason, who becomes a secondary character as soon as the sorceress enters the story. Morris's "great stumbling-block," James wrote, "was the necessity of maintaining throughout the dignity and prominence of his hero."[40] Like Virgil with Aeneas, Morris is dissatisfied with Jason, and ultimately Morris prefers Medea to the brooding, diffident man who broke his marriage vow to her, making her the true hero, and the equal or greater actor in the Argonauts' venture. Jason, by contrast, is left, ultimately, ruined and threatening suicide:

> Ah what a shame, and what a weary load
> His life shall bear! His old love cast away,
> His new love dead upon that fearful day,
> Childless, dishonoured, must his days go by.[41]

He is saved only by a vision of his former greatness and a dream that he shall be a hero once more. Jason becomes king of Corinth, but he remains depressed until one day he recovers his will to live and begins to dream of another great adventure, one to rival the achievement of the Fleece and one that will win him back the love (!) of Medea. Regaining confidence in himself, he falls asleep beneath the rotting hulk of the *Argo*. But a chunk falls off and kills him:

> Beneath the ruined stem did Jason lie
> Crushed, and all dead of him that here can die.[42]

The people of Corinth hold splendid funeral games and sacrifice the *Argo* to Poseidon, sinking it in the sea, thus allowing the poet to rid himself of a Jason who disappointed him in his faithlessness to the apparently much more interesting and beloved Medea and had, at the last, realized and repented of his grave and unforgivable sin.

Critics took to the poem immediately, and one declared it "perhaps the most complete revitalization of a mythological world ever accomplished in English."[43] It ran through more than fifteen printings within its first forty years, testament to its popular appeal. It reigned as the longest version of the Jason myth ever committed to paper for seventy-five years, until a prose version from a familiar name became the longest Jason story ever written.

The irrepressible Robert Graves had begun his investigation of the Jason myth with his novel *The Golden Fleece* (1944), also known as *Hercules, My Shipmate* in the United States. Graves had written many historical novels before then, including *I, Claudius* (1934), and in *Golden Fleece* he followed the same template, taking Classical sources and translating them into modern forms. The story is, of course, that of Jason's quest for the Fleece, and in almost five hundred pages, Graves expands considerably on Apollonius while presenting the various Argonautic exploits in a rationalist light. In his version, Hercules is a drunken lout, magical creatures like centaurs are merely human adherents of various cults, and there is a battle looming between those beholden to the ancient earth goddess (the Colchians, etc.) and those who preach the rites of the patriarchal Olympian faith of Zeus (the Greeks). The serpent of Colchis is merely a somewhat large snake, and the whole expedition is replete with coarse bawdiness. The Golden Fleece, in his view, was a tool in religious rivalry. Intriguingly enough, Graves identified the Golden Fleece as the golden cloak worn by a statue of Zeus (as Grillparzer had done with a statue of Apollo), which agrees nicely with the suggestion proposed in chapter 8, though I had not read Graves's novel when I first developed my idea. Phrixus stole the Fleece on behalf of the earth goddess, and Jason, an acolyte of Zeus, sailed forth to bring it back.

To research the novel, Graves read the ancient sources and then purposely departed from them, in keeping with his self-described mission to upset convention (as when his *King Jesus* [1946] offered a Christ who did not die on the cross). The research for *Golden Fleece* led Graves to develop his idiosyncratic interest in Greek myths, leading to *The Greek Myths* and also his treatise *The White Goddess* (1948), which he began writing just weeks after finishing *Fleece*. In *Goddess*, Graves expands on the earth goddess from the previous novel, concluding that the most ancient European religions revolved around a three-form moon-earth goddess of birth, love, and death, symbolized in the phases of the moon and the inspiration for all true poetry. As Graves notes in the *Greek Myths*, this imagined goddess was for him the original of Medea. There is a kernel of truth here, but just barely, in the ancient earth goddess of the Near East, but the form Graves assigns her is entirely and uniquely his own. Alas, poor Jason. It is to him that we owe *The White Goddess*, through no fault of his own.

British poet Henry Treece drew on Graves's and others' accounts to produce a rationalized *Jason* in 1961, which again posited a central conflict between god- and goddess-worshippers. Told from Jason's point of view, the mythic grandeur was removed in favor of a more earthly milieu, which included a Golden Fleece that is merely Strabo's used, wet sheepskin cast off from a mining operation (see chapter 11). Still later, in 1973, John Gardner offered *Jason and Medeia*, a more than five-hundred-page epic poem that attempted to balance sympathy for Medea with sympathy for Jason, whom the author felt the Greek tragedians and modern scholars had done an injustice. Much of the poem is direct translation of the ancient authors' texts, with modern insights sprinkled throughout. At the end of this retelling of Apollonius and Euripides, Jason disappears into the sunset, sailing away in the *Argo* to chase after Medea. As with Morris and Graves, Gardner's version was longer than any classical epic, but length did not improve upon the originals.

The literary versions of Jason were sometimes moving, sometimes overwrought, but overall somewhat short of the magic of the ancient epics. One reason for this was the difficulty of capturing a lost world in modern language. But a bigger problem was the accidental legacy of the Renaissance rediscovery of Apollonius and Valerius. While those authors drew upon ancient sources, they were able to recreate the Argonauts' voyage to suit their needs because the story was fluid, changeable, and beholden to no fixed canon. By contrast, the efforts of Apollonius especially, and to a lesser extent Valerius, essentially *became* the canonical versions of the Jason story after the Renaissance, and all modern versions take their form from these examples, either following closely or purposely deviating but in any case constrained by the canonical antiquity of poems whose authors never quite meant them to be definitive. Something of the creativity of the earlier epics vanished, frozen instead in cold, dead marble like an unearthed Roman statue.

Jason Goes Multimedia

If literature had fossilized the Jason myth in a relatively fixed form, newer media would try to breathe life back into the old story by putting a simulacrum of the Golden Fleece on the silver screen and even encouraging the audience to *become* Jason in video game form. None of these efforts was wholly successful, but they were interesting attempts to update the oldest of humanity's literary genres. Just as the written epic had replaced the oral epic, so now did visual and then digital media replace the written word. And with this transfer of Jason and the Argonauts from word to image, the emphasis shifted from Jason's faithlessness back to his sex appeal on account of the inherent power of the image to overwhelm the story, and the reluctance of modern corporate productions to deny their paying audiences a happy ending.

THE BIG AND SMALL SCREENS

Among the earliest cinematic allusions to Jason and the Argonauts are the silent animated Soviet short *Argonavtebi* ("The Argonauts"), made in 1936 when Georgia was then under Soviet rule, and the film *Ogni Kolchidi* ("The Fires of Colchis") in 1941. These were not retellings of the Jason story but instead used the Argonauts as a symbol and reference point for films about the drainage of the marshes of Colchis, which is to say, the destruction of the very wetlands Apollonius had immortalized as the Plain of Circe. In the 1970s, a series of Soviet animated Greek myths depicted the Jason story in socialist-realist style. In 1986, Soviet television produced *Veselaia khronika opasnogo puteshestviia* ("The Merry Chronicle of a Dangerous Voyage"), a musical version of the *Argonautica*, which Russian cinema scholar Julian Graffy described to me as "dire." After viewing the film, I can't help but agree. The Argonaut story also served as the mythological model for Irakli Kvirikadze's Soviet Georgian film *Monanieba* ("The Swimmer," 1981), which also referenced the myth directly.[44] But these were limited releases, largely unseen in the West.

The Italian film *I giganti della Tessaglia* ("The Giants of Thessaly," 1960) featured King Giasone (Jason, played by Roland Carey) seeking out the Golden Fleece to keep Thessaly from succumbing to a volcano and barbarian invaders while the scheming Adrasto plots to seize power in Iolco. The film combined motifs from the *Argonautica* with adventures from the *Odyssey*, including an encounter with a witch and a Cyclops. Jason pulls the Fleece from a large statue. The movie's cheap special effects detracted from the rather simplified story, though the score by Carlo Rustichelli is considered one of the composer's best.

Of course, the best known and for most the definitive screen version of the Jason myth was the 1963 Hollywood sword-and-sandals epic *Jason and the Argonauts*, directed by Don Chaffey and featuring the timeless stop-motion special effects of the legendary Ray Harryhausen, who later wrote that of all his movies this was the film that most pleased him. The $3 million movie's advertising proclaimed it "The epic story that was destined to stand as a colossus of adventure!" Harryhausen was the major creative force behind the film, and he settled on the Jason story only after considering and rejecting a Perseus story (eventually to become *Clash of the Titans* in 1981), and a picture where Jason teamed up with the Arabian mythological figure Sinbad. The movie was filmed on location in southern Italy in 1961 after Harryhausen determined that Greece was too gray and bleak to effectively portray Greece on screen.[45]

In a very broad fashion the film follows the outlines of Apollonius' *Argonautica*, though with some notable differences. To provide a happy ending, the film ends with Jason and Medea sailing away from Colchis as happy lovers. As a result, adventures from the homeward journey, such as the battle with Talos, the man of bronze, are transposed to the outward journey because they make for visually interesting set pieces. Harryhausen was well aware that he was revising the myth, and in fact he began by organizing the various monsters and special effects shots in a compelling cinematic order before writing a story to link them together.[46] Oddly enough, in this Harryhausen revived the practice of the ancient poets, who freely revised and reconfigured sections of the Jason epic to suit their purposes and audiences.

In the revised version of the movie, the talking oak plank of Zeus from Dodona has become a magical figurehead of Hera who speaks to Jason (Todd Armstrong), and Jason even appears on Mt. Olympus to address the gods. Zeus (Niall MacGinnis) and Hera (Honor Blackman) use Jason as a piece on a giant game board, and Zeus has restricted Hera to aid the hero but five times. Talos becomes not the last of the race of bronze, but instead a statue forged by Hephaestus to guard the treasure of the gods. He comes to life when Hylas and Hercules steal into the treasure chamber built into the base of Talos' statue, and this episode serves to remove Hercules from the mission. While traditionally the *Argo* sailed through the Symplegades by watching a dove, in the movie gigantic Triton, son of Poseidon, rises from the sea to hold apart the rocks—not unlike Athena, who did so invisibly, in Apollonius. At Colchis, events play out somewhat differently than in the classical versions of the myth. Aeëtes imprisons the Argonauts, and only through the aid of Medea (Nancy Kovack) are they clandestinely released. The challenges of Aeëtes are eliminated, and Jason proceeds directly to the Fleece, where he kills not a serpent but the seven-headed serpentine Hydra borrowed from the myth of Heracles.

Aeëtes then tries to stop Jason's escape by planting the teeth of the Hydra (*pace*, Cadmus), which calls up from the ground seven armed skeletons (one for each of Hydra's heads) who do battle with Jason and the handful of Argonauts who had accompanied him inland. This famous four-minute sequence took four and a half months to animate and required careful planning to align the skeletons' movements perfectly with the filmed swordplay of the human actors. Though the image of Jason doing battle with the skeletons is striking, it was apparently based on a misunderstanding of the concept of the earth-born men. Harryhausen wrongly believed that "in the legend it is rotting corpses" who rise from the ground, but he worried zombie warriors would earn the film a rating that would prevent children

he 1963 production of *Jason and the Argonauts* has defined the popular understanding of the Jason myth despite its many departures from Classical sources. No single change has had more of an impact than Ray Harryhausen's mistaken interpretation of the Spartoi as reanimated corpses, which he translated into the famous skeleton warriors, seen here battling Jason (Todd Armstrong). The magnificent animation work, visible even in the lifelike poses in this still, has made these skeletons into a symbol of the Jason myth as a whole.

from attending.[47] The Spartoi of legend, of course, were not rotting zombies but living humans born from the womb of earth. The skeleton warriors of the film kill all the assembled Argonauts save Jason, who leaps from a cliff to reach the *Argo* and the Argonauts who stayed behind. Together with the Fleece and Medea, his great love, Jason sails for home, happy ending assured.

Perhaps the clearest indication of the overwhelming success of this lively and entertaining movie is the very fact that the myth of Jason forever after became known as "Jason and the Argonauts" in place of its ancient title, the *Argonautica*. There is no greater testament to the enduring influence of the 1963 movie than the adoption of its title as a synonym for the myth as a whole. Critics at the time, however, had a low opinion of the movie. *Time* complained that the producers added elements foreign to the myth such as Talos (they were, of course, wrong on that count): "The straight story of Jason's exploits, told with magic and imagination and a minimum of studio trickery, might have been delightful. This version is more bull than Bulfinch."[48] Harold Thompson, writing in the *New York Times*, called the movie an "absurd, unwieldy adventure—if that's the word" and thought the climactic battle with the skeleton men was a "comic interlude." He also complained that neither Jason nor

Medea undressed, and that Todd Armstrong was "spindly" compared to other "beefcake" actors.[49] It would only be much later, when the children who watched the movie grew up and began to celebrate the touchstones of their childhood, that the movie would be ranked a classic.

A new version of *Jason and the Argonauts* was broadcasted on NBC in the United States as a two-part miniseries in May 2000, starring Jason London as the title character. It hewed more closely to the *Argonautica* than the 1963 film, and was twice the length. To pad the time, the movie followed Jason after the achievement of the Fleece, which he won by, essentially, hurling the dragon off the side of a cliff. He, Medea, and the Argonauts voyage homeward, and the love of Jason and Medea withstands both Atalanta's confession of love for Jason and Zeus's attempts to seduce (!) Medea. The evil Pelias is killed, and Jason and Medea reign happily as the rightful monarchs of Iolcus. Like its predecessor, the TV movie earned mostly poor reviews. In 2008 NBC planned a prime-time drama called *The Argonauts* about contemporary treasure hunters propelled back in time to the age of Jason, to be filmed in the green-screen style of the then-recent Spartan-themed movie *300*. The program was never produced. However, in 2013 the BBC made Jason the star of his own fantasy-adventure series, albeit one heavily reimagined. *Atlantis* cast Jason (Jack Donnelly) as a new arrival in a parallel-universe version of the doomed city and the protagonist exploring a wealth of Greek myths in a fantasy land that is a hodgepodge of Minoan, Greek, and Persian elements. This Jason, who seems to have traveled between our world and that of Atlantis, is initially of uncertain relationship to our Jason. If not exactly true to Apollonius, the series accidentally captured something of the myth's antecedents.

Versions of the tragedy of *Medea* were filmed more than a dozen times since 1962, mostly performances of Euripides' play. Among the more interesting variants was the 1969 Italian movie version by director Pier Paolo Pasolini. This movie begins before Euripides, showing the winning of the Fleece. It depicted the Colchians as a barbarous people beholden to strange rites of human sacrifice, and the Greeks as imperialist pirates who pillage and maim at will. When the unhappy couple arrives in Corinth, Medea's revenge is depicted twice, once as a fantasy of Jason's new wife burning alive, and the second when Glauce realizes that she, like Medea, is oppressed by the Greek patriarchy and leaps to her death. The film is largely free of dialogue, and is notable for its score, drawn from North African percussion and wind instruments. Lars von Trier filmed a stark, intense, and stylized adaptation centering on Medea's emotional state. A six-episode 2005 Dutch miniseries version found Medea reimagined as the daughter of the chairman of the Dutch senate who falls in love with a scheming politician named Jason who wants to be prime minister.

BEYOND VIDEO

The myth of Jason was not limited only to motion pictures but also appeared in other media, including radio, video games, and comic books. The Australian Broadcasting Corporation had an "Argonauts Club" for children on afternoon radio from 1933 to 1972. The presenter of the program went by the name "Jason" and encouraged children to send in artwork, stories, and poems. They could advance in the club to ranks that included the "Order of the Dragon's Tooth" and "Order of the Golden Fleece" drawn from the Argonaut myth. Prior to the 2004 Olympic Summer Games in Athens, the Greek city of Volos, near ancient

Iolcus, put on a musical in the stadium where the city hosted Olympic soccer events promoting the idea, based on Pelias' funeral games, that Jason and the Argonauts were a band of athletes who participated in games that were the forerunners to the Olympics. The multimedia presentation involved music, pantomime, 3D projections, and interpretive dance to capture the story of the Argonauts.

The role-playing video game *The Rise of the Argonauts* (2008) from Liquid Entertainment and Codemasters made use of the Argonaut myth but changed many of its core elements. In this version, Jason enters his quest because his wife Alceme (his mother in ancient myth) is murdered, and Jason must convince the descendants of his "patrons" Hermes, Ares, and Athena to join the Argonauts before he can descend into Tartarus to retrieve the Golden Fleece with which he can resurrect his dead wife. Medea and Colchis are nowhere to be seen, though the removal of the Fleece to Tartarus accidentally recalls the ancient origins of the Jason story.

The Bluewater Productions five-issue title *Ray Harryhausen Presents: Jason and the Argonauts: The Kingdom of Hades* (2007–2008) follows after the events of the 1963 movie and finds the hero and his companions venturing to the realm of the dead as a vengeful Aeëtes chases the Argonauts from Colchis. In the rather shallow and unsatisfactory comic, elements from the *Odyssey* and Heracles' katabasis are drafted to fill out the adventure since the movie used all the set pieces from the *Argonautica* on its outward voyage. Here, Circe turns some Argonauts to swine and Hades takes Jason to the Underworld, where the king of the dead rather anticlimactically tells Jason he is free to go since, being mortal, he must someday return. A big fight with the skeleton men from the movie occurs, and Jason sails away from the Underworld to confront Pelias and a robot army in a sequel that was not produced as of this writing. An action figure of a glowing skeleton fighter from the comic was released, and Universal Pictures planned a movie version of *Kingdom of Hades* for 2012 that never happened. Naturally, the internet lit up with rumors of which heartthrob should play Jason. Just as Todd Armstrong and Jason London had been chosen because of their looks,[50] speculation focused mostly on the actors' appearance. In 2013, the boy hero Percy Jackson quested for the Golden Fleece on the silver screen in the *Sea of Monsters*, based on the 2006 novel from Rick Riordan's Greek mythology children's book series, though the story shared little with the Argonauts' adventure beyond the Fleece. Riordan made the Fleece into a healing object, recalling Jason's first purpose, and in later novels in the succeeding *Heroes of Olympus* series, he introduced a new Jason, a son of the Roman Jupiter.

In stripping away Jason's faithlessness and Medea's rage, and focusing on the hero as heartthrob, two millennia of mythic history had been undone, and, for entirely commercial and unintentional reasons, an older version of Jason reemerged. It was as though the Jason of the *Argo* and the Jason of Corinth and the Medea of both had split into two sets of figures, unrelated, separate. The work of the Corinthians was reversed; the angry goddess of Corinth retreated to her province, and her accidental husband returned to his. The divorce, if not quite final, was nearly complete, hero and human, saint and sinner, the two halves of Jason and Medea finally separate.

These, of course, are but a few of the many ways Jason and his myth had entered popular culture. This brief discussion barely touches on the many things named for the myth, like the *Jason* submarine that discovered the wreck of the *Titanic*, the newspapers named the *Argonaut*, and even the Ram logo of the Dodge cars, which was drawn from a statue of

Phrixus' golden ram. Nor does it touch on the people who claimed the mantle of Argonauts, such as the miners of the California Gold Rush. Nearly any story that features a great quest owes something to Jason and the Argonauts, the prototype for Homer's *Odyssey*, Virgil's *Aeneid*, and the thousand stories and works inspired by these and other epics. There is even an echo of Jason in the seemingly unrelated television series *Lost* (2004–2010). A healer, Dr. Jack Shepard, travels with a diverse group of gifted companions via a modern day *Argo*, Oceanic flight 815, across the broad sea to a fantastic island not unlike Aea full of myth, magic, mystery, and an apparent gateway to the netherworld. There he battles a serpent-shaped smoke monster, defeating it with the help of a powerful but misunderstood woman, Kate, and eventually he takes control of the golden light at the heart of the island's forest from a magical, godlike island king who tested him and his companions as "candidates" for the golden prize. And like Jason, the world of *Lost* is permeated with imagery of death, rebirth, and the netherworld beyond this life, including Jack's literal descent into an underworld and rebirth in a new world beyond.

Thus, in the twenty-first century, an ancient myth continued to be told, in ways old and new. But, a further question remained. In whatever version one heard the story of the man who sailed the seas in search of the Golden Fleece, what, exactly, did the myth mean?

11

The Symbol

Scholarly Investigations and Theories

The quest to find meaning in the story of Jason and the Golden Fleece is nearly as old as the myth itself. As we have seen, the Greeks themselves tried to explain the Argonauts' voyage with their own scholarly theories, beginning with the attempts of Herodorus and others to rationalize the story and find non-magical explanations for Jason's adventures. Some of these theories bordered on the ridiculous, such as the suggestion that the Golden Fleece was merely a man named Mr. Ram who had been skinned alive and gilded. But the impetus to seek out meaning in the constellation of symbols and ideas embodied in the myth was very serious. However, until the modern period, these efforts were doomed to fail because scholars lacked the archaeological, philological, and historical knowledge to investigate ancient history outside of the testimony of the Classical authors. In effect, early myth scholars were mostly guessing, combining intuition, ideology, and imagination, usually without supporting facts.

The medieval insistence on Judeo-Christian allegories in Greek myth gave rise to a school of thought in the Renaissance that the Greek myths were in fact pagan misinterpretations of Holy Scripture, a thought that lingered on into the Enlightenment. Various scriptural sources were proposed for the Jason story, including the story of Abraham (with the sacrifice of Isaac paralleling the Golden Fleece, and his wife and concubine the Medea tragedy), Moses, and Joshua. These theories presupposed the primacy of the Bible, which was believed to have recorded history from the beginning of time, dated to 4004 BCE with the Greeks a much later people who misunderstood the divine word. Beginning with the Enlightenment, the scholarly project began the long, slow process of applying scientific methods to the study of myth, divorcing scholarship from Christian ideology. The results however, were uneven.

My discussion of scholarly theories is by no means complete, and I can do no more than sketch the outlines of the waves of theory that have washed over Greek myth since the modern scientific study of it was inaugurated by Christian Gottlob Heyne in the eighteenth century. Fritz Graf gives a good overview of the study of myth from Heyne to the late twentieth century in his *Greek Mythology*,[1] and the interested reader should turn there for a broader overview of the evolving scholarly views of Greek myth. Nor will I be examining the vast body of literature devoted to Medea, a character whose later development derives little from the Jason story and is essentially her own myth. While nearly all of the scholarly

236

research on Jason is contained in a handful of academic articles and assorted references or chapters in works on other themes, Medea has a shelf of books devoted to her cause,[2] and I can add nothing to these except to note that scholarship has largely followed the practice of the Athenian tragedians in letting her overshadow her husband, a dedication redoubled with the rise of feminist theory in the academy.

Our concern will be primarily scholarly suggestions on the meaning of Jason, and only incidentally the bodies of theory that support them. There is no easy way to draw a bright line between ideas that are scholarly and those that are not. For example, the theory that the Jason myth began in Africa before being stolen by Greek writers could fall in either category depending on how one classifies Afrocentric ideology. For our purposes, this chapter will examine theories that were proposed by scholars, taken seriously at the time of their proposal as legitimate attempts to seek meaning in myth, and have generally accepted evidence in their favor. Chapter 12, by contrast, will look at theories that were more controversial and generally found little or no mainstream academic acceptance, though frequently were popularly acclaimed.

In the most general sense, academic theories about Jason and the Argonauts break down into two categories: theories that attempt to historicize the myth as a memory of real-life events, and theories that seek out symbolic meanings or ideological interpretations. In general, archaeologists, who work with material remains, favor the former explanation, while Classical scholars and religious scholars, who work in the realm of the mind, favor the latter hypothesis. Before exploring these two ways of reading Jason, we should first look at the work of the eighteenth-century French writer whose interpretation of Greek myth was considered close to definitive for more than a century.

Rationalism Redux

A French clergyman, the abbé Antoine Banier (1673–1741), offered rationalized interpretations of Greek myth that were the standard scholarly interpretation until the middle nineteenth century. Since this was the time of the Enlightenment, such rationalizations fit the tenor of the age, and Banier's work formed the (often unacknowledged) basis of Diderot's famed *Encyclopédie*'s sections on mythology.[3] For Banier, myths were historical events that over time acquired the trappings of fantasy, the gods nothing more than kings promoted to heaven. His *Mythologie et la fable expliqués par l'histoire* (first published in 1711; final revised edition 1738–1740) was widely translated, and in English it was known as *The Mythology and Fables of the Ancients, Explained from History*. Banier's work carefully presented the conflicting testimony of the ancient authors, including most prominent variants—the basis of the scientific study of mythology—but ran aground seeking out rationalizations in the absence of evidence, under the presumption that beneath myth must sit fact.

Banier attempted to rationalize the Jason myth following in the tradition of the euhemerist historians of antiquity. "The Voyage of the Argonauts [...] furnishes several adventures, which I shall attempt to reduce to History."[4] For him, the Argonautic expedition was a real-life event, one which travelled into the Black Sea to found colonies, and which wished to retrieve the golden prow of the ship of Phrixus, which being in the shape of a ram was taken for a Golden Fleece. Jason, clearing the seas of pirates (who were, of course, the Harpies of myth), opened the Black Sea to commerce.

Banier correctly deduced that the Argonaut myth had a relationship of sorts to the Near East, and then followed this idea by adopting the suggestion that the Greeks first wrote Jason's story in Phoenician, the language of the great sea travelers who made the most logical model for Jason's lengthy trip. The Phoenicians, he imagined, were an older people who in the guise of Cadmus gave Greeks their (Phoenician) writing. Thus, in translating ambiguous words from Phoenician to Greek, they made errors of interpretation that created a myth. He adduced a relationship via Phoenician between the words for "fleece" and "treasure," between "bulls" and "walls," and "dragon" and "bronze (or iron)," thus making Jason's quest a fairly straightforward bank robbery, breaching walls guarded by bronze-armored soldiers to steal a treasure.[5] Medea, incidentally, he believed (correctly) to have been terribly wronged by the Athenians. She was, in his opinion, a nice and blameless princess about whom malicious gossip spread.

The interested reader can of course turn to Banier to read the residuum of his rationalizations. What is perhaps more astounding than the strained explanations is the enthusiasm with which the European elite received Banier, seeing in his work a ready-made confirmation of the rationalist principles of the scientific Enlightenment projected back into myth.

Jason and the Bible

When the inevitable reaction against the euhemerist reading of myth came, it came fast and hard. During the nineteenth century a school of thinkers, influenced by the burgeoning Romantic Movement and its reaction against all things rational, celebrated the irrational in myth and saw in it allegories and symbols rather than distorted history. The longest-lived of these theories were those who attempted to revive the idea that the Greek myths were distortions of Scripture, or at least close cousins to them. By the twentieth century, the occasion would be reversed, and scholars would argue that Greek myths influenced the writers of the Bible.

THE HEBREW BIBLE

The British scholar Jacob Bryant (1715–1804) intended to prove in his *New System* (1774–1776) that Greek mythology was merely a distorted corruption of Mosaic religion, and therefore a branch of Judeo-Christian beliefs, albeit hopelessly garbled. He argued that Jason and his Argonauts were in fact originally the story of Noah and the Ark, with "ark" becoming corrupted into the word *Argo* when the Greeks borrowed the story from the Egyptians, who apparently took it from Moses. This was confirmed, Bryant noted, by Jason's use of a dove to pass through the Clashing Rocks, just as Noah released a dove to test for land after the Flood.[6]

We can give Bryant credit for noting that the Jasonia of Strabo were derived from Near Eastern temples of a different sort, but we must offer demerits for assuming the Jasonia were temples honoring Noah's Ark! According to Bryant, Jason is a mistaken identification of a divine title of God, who bore the names Jason and Argos. The proof of this is that the *Argo* shares its name with the city of Argos, which was known as Iasian (or Iason), which term must be identical with Jason, proving that Jason is a godly title for the Ark cult and, in fact, simply a Greek name for the Judeo-Christian God![7] There is a bit of truth here. Argos is called Iason or Iasian in the *Odyssey* in reference to King Iasos of Argos, son or father of Io; and it is believed now that this phrase refers to the Mycenaean ruling class, who may have called themselves Ionians, from the reconstructed Mycenaean word *Iawones*, which was linguistically distinct from the word for healer (Greek: *iasthai*, possibly also the Mycenaean *i-wa-so*) from which our Jason descends.[8] Bryant, writing long before the decipherment of Mycenaean Greek, could not have known this. However, he might well have noted that the word "ark" descends from the Old English *earc*, via the Latin *arca*, meaning a box or chest, and has no direct connection to the Greek *argos*, which derives from words meaning "swift" or "shining" or "bright," or the Hebrew for the Ark, *tebah*. Phonic similarities alone are not enough to prove a relationship.

G. F. Grotefend (1775–1853) believed that Jason was originally a Phoenician character named Joshua and his boat a Phoenician word for "long" (*Arha*). His argument was that Joshua was the Semitic equivalent of Jason and that the Phoenicians had reached such places as Lemnos and Thasos, making it probable that the myth of the Argonauts was a transmission to Greece of Phoenician sea-voyages which the Greeks later reinterpreted as entirely Greek when they "expelled" the Phoenicians from the Aegean.[9] Superficially plausible in a nineteenth century context, this thesis of course contradicts modern evidence about the Minoan and Mycenaean sea voyages and grossly overstates Phoenician influence in Greece prior to the Orientalizing Period.

However, a variation on this idea arose in the 1990s when Gildas Hamel proposed that in the story of Jonah being swallowed by a great fish "the author of Jonah plays with one of the variants of the story of Jason, or that Jonah's story, at the very least, can be placed within the nebula of variants of Jason's tale."[10] Hamel proposed that the name Jonah (Ionas in Greek) may have been selected because it was an anagram for Jason (Iason). He also saw a relationship between Jonah, meaning "dove" in Hebrew, and the dove used to guide *Argo* through the Clashing Rocks—the same dove others thought linked Jason to Noah! Even more tenuous are his identification of the fast flight of the sons of the Boreal wind with the action of Jonah "fleeing" Nineveh, and the coincidence that both the crews of Jason's and Jonah's ship are kind and pious in an era when sailors were associated with violence, rapine, and vice.

The essence of Hamel's thesis, however, rests on two pieces of evidence: The Douris cup depicting Jason emerging from the dragon's mouth in the presence of Athena, and the linguistically uncertain word *kikayon* in the Jonah story. The former evidence Hamel sees as a close parallel to God (= Athena) causing the great fish (= serpent) to disgorge Jonah (= Jason). The latter, a word referring to a plant, Hamel takes as a corruption of *kykeon*, a word used to describe Medea's herbal brews, but which was also the barley and water drink served at the Eleusinian Mysteries. He sees this as a purposeful satire of the Jason story because Jonah takes the *kikayon* to "purge" himself of his anger at a worm (this is after he leaves the fish), a reduction of Jason's magical balm to enter and withdraw from the serpent, a larger worm.

While such transmission is of course possible, Hamel himself recognizes that behind the Jonah story lies earlier Near Eastern tales of gods and monsters,[11] which somewhat negates

An influential school of thought placed the Biblical flood narrative at the headwaters of all world history and saw pagan myths as distortions of Genesis. Thus, the *Argo* became Noah's Ark and the dove that takes Jason through the Clashing Rocks turned into the dove released to find land after the flood, as seen in this illustration by Gustave Doré. Later writers attempted to turn both *Argo* and Ark into myths of the sun's passage through the water signs of the zodiac.

his grander claims of close influence and instead points to Jonah's story being one of many variants of the ancient hero and serpent story. Until someone can demonstrate uncanny parallels or clear details that drive solely from the Argonauts' tale, without resort to the types of philological sound-alike arguments, we can only note similarities and not claim solid conclusions.

THE NEW TESTAMENT

As we have seen, medieval scholars made much hay from the etymological links between Jesus and Jason, drawn from Greek transliterations of the name Yehoshua (Joshua) and an identification of the Golden Fleece with the Lamb of God. From this thin thread, medieval scholars spun elaborate allegories of Jason and Medea as various facets of Christian virtue. It is somewhat surprising that this retrograde medieval notion would find new life in the twentieth century, but it was so. In that era, the search for the "historical" Jesus was in full swing, and scholars who believed that the true Jesus was a mythological figure sought precedents for him in pagan myth. For example, Sir James George Frazer delivered his magnum opus, *The Golden Bough* (1890), which in the expanded third edition of 1906–1915 took twelve volumes to implicitly argue that Christian mythology was no different in its essentials from its pagan counterparts and Christ was just one of a worldwide collection of dying and rising gods who married earth goddesses and caused vegetables to grow. Similarly, Edwin Sidney Hartland argued explicitly in his three-volume *Legend of Perseus* (1894–1896) that classical myth, especially the impregnation of Perseus' mother by Zeus as a golden shower, was the forerunner of the Annunciation and Virgin Birth. While medieval scholars used the myth of Jason to bolster the power and majesty of Christ, their twentieth century counterparts now came to use the myth of Jason to dispel claims for the unique revelation of Christianity.

In his study of the theme of the idea of divine twins in world mythology, *Boanerges* (1913), the Cambridge Biblical scholar J. Rendel Harris (1852–1941) attempted to demonstrate the universality of twins as objects of worship and their prehistoric origins. Among these twins, he said, was once Jason, who shares, according to comparison with world myths, the common motif of rescuing the sun (the Fleece) from the Underworld dragon, who swallows it at night. Needless to say, Harris sees Jason as a solar hero (see below). Harris's heavenly twins are everywhere shipbuilders, ploughmen, and agriculturalists, all aspects associated with Jason's adventures. "Does it not seem as if the starting point for the growth of the legend as to the dragons' teeth was to be found in the simple statement that the Heavenly Ploughman or Twin taught us how to yoke cattle and attach them to the plough?"[12]

Of course, the Argonaut myth already had twins in it: Castor and Pollux, the Heavenly Twins of Greek myth, and the Boread twins as well. This Harris explains by arguing that the Greeks folded both sets of twins into a Jason myth which originally featured another set of divine twins, Jason and his "brother" Triptolemus, all of whom were identified with one another. The reasons for this are somewhat obscure but follow from his identification of Jason with the demigod Iasion, the consort of Demeter, and the relationship Iasion and Triptolemus share with the goddess, for Triptolemus, a primordial figure, was the first priest of Demeter and the man to whom Demeter gave the secret of agriculture. There is no real basis for making them twin brothers except some ancient star lore that claimed the two were the original owners of the constellation Gemini (but then the non-twins Heracles and Apollo were sometimes assigned this role, too—the constellation was so named because it has an impressive pair of bright, first magnitude stars: twins), and Harris suggests that the story of Iasion and Demeter originally belonged to Triptolemus.[13] Harris follows K. O. Müller in linking Jason, Iasion, Aeson, and Eetion as variants of the same character through shared etymology; and since Eetion was on Samothrace one of the divine twins, Jason *ipso facto* is as well.

The character of Jason Harris derived from Phoenicia (again!), the alleged origin of the Argonauts' saga, which he saw as first an ancient but simple tale of a ship that carried twins to find the sun. Specifically, he argued that Jason's first myth was of a twin who sailed in the hollow trunk of an oak tree, born of a woodpecker. This argument is etymological in nature, derived from a "variant" of the name of Jason's mother, Scarphe, which apparently had something to do with being the offspring of a woodpecker, and the idea that the oak of Dodona whose plank the *Argo* held was originally a hollow tree that served as a boat.[14] The revised cult of Jason he called "Jasonism" and considered it a subset of the cult of the Heavenly Twins. The reason for this was that the Hellenistic Greeks translated the Semitic name Joshua (and thus its derivative, Jesus) as Jason, implying through some transitive property of scholarly investigation, that Jason derived from a Semitic Joshua, which happily enough was a Hebrew (and thus Judeo-Christian) figure and not a pagan one.

To support the cult of Jason, Harris relies on the existence of Jasonia, the temples of Jason in Strabo ("unless Strabo is hopelessly inaccurate"[15]), unaware of the later suggestion that their origin lay the very different *ayazana* sites of the Persians, which were neither Jason-oriented nor associated with twins. He then suggests that the "Asian" Jason might well have been Ijasi or Ijasu, an alleged deity of Petra, who I suppose has some relationship with the season-angel Ijasusael from the Book of Enoch, but at any rate is many centuries too late to have been the origins of Jason. However, he notes further "parallels" with the name Iyasu in Ethiopia (actually an Ethiopian transliteration of Joshua) and southern Arabia. "It might mean that Jason came up from S. Arabia, instead of from Phoenicia," rendering the speculation about the Biblical Joshua as the first Jason moot.[16] The sum of his argument, however, was not to prove Jason a heavenly twin but rather to fulfill the medieval identification of Jason with Jesus. However, Harris recognized that Jason predated Jesus, so the influence must have gone from Jason to the son of God. "Is it possible that the Gospel itself has been Jasonized?" he asks, wondering inconclusively whether the balm Medea applied to Jason was the origin of the expensive unguents with which Mary of Bethany anointed Jesus.[17]

In sum, despite Harris' occasional flashes of insight into the Near Eastern (though not, in actuality, Phoenician) origins of Jason, his thesis essentially exists to prove Jason was Jesus and vice versa, providing a greater antiquity for the forerunners of the Christian faith he studied as his life's work.

JASON, THE FORERUNNER OF JESUS

In blunter fashion, the German scholar Arthur Drews attempted to link Jason to Jesus, not to improve the standing of the son of God but rather to prove him one of many like figures, all of whom are, in good German scholarly tradition, sun gods, with Christ specifically derived from an alleged sun god named Joshua whom the Greeks identified with their "solar god" Jason of the sun-fleece, all three deities representing the sun's passage through the zodiac. Drews asked why it was that the prophesied figure of Emmanuel from the Book of Isaiah should find fulfillment in a mythological figure named Jesus rather than the name Isaiah assigned him. This, he argued, was due to the influence of Jason, whose healing associations made his name ideal for a Hellenized savior-god:

> First, the fact that in the name Jesus the symbolic significance of salvation in the spiritual and bodily sense, as Isaiah attributed it to the servant of God, was perceived more clearly, especially among the dispersed Jews. Jaso (from *iasthai*, to heal) was the name of the daughter of the saver and physician Asclepios. He himself was in many places worshipped under the name of Jason.

Thus we read in Strabo that temples and the cult of Jason were spread over the whole of Asia, Media, Colchis, Albania, and Iberia, and that Jason enjoyed divine honours also in Thessaly and on the Corinthian gulf, the cult of Phrixos, the ram or lamb, being associated with his (I, 2, 39). Justin tells us that nearly the whole of the west worshipped Jason and built temples to him (xlii, 3), and this is confirmed by Tacitus (*Annals*, vi, 34). Jason was also supposed to be the founder of the Lemnic festivity, which was celebrated yearly at the beginning of spring, and was believed to impart immortality to those who shared in it. Jasios (Jasion) was called Asclepios, or the "mediating god" related to him in this respect, and the conductor of souls, Hermes, at Crete and in the famous mysteries of Samothracia, which enjoyed the greatest repute about the beginning of the present era, and were frequented by high and low from all the leading countries. Here again the idea of healing and saving is combined in the name, and would easily lead to the giving of the name to the savior of the Jewish mystery-cult. Epiphanius (*Hæres*, c, xxix) clearly perceived this connection when he translated the name Jesus "healer" or "physician" (*curator, therapeutes*). It is certain that this allusion to the healing activity of the servant of God and his affinity with the widely known Jason contributed not a little to the acceptance of the name of Jesus and to its apparent familiarity in ancient times.[18]

Since the honors described above were a standard part of the Greek hero cult and an obvious reference to the Jasonia, these are not evidence of the worship of a pre–Christian savior god as much as the importation of eastern cult practices under a Greek name. Needless to say, Asclepius' daughter's name, Iaso ("Healing"), derives from the same word as Jason, but this does not make them, or Asclepius, the same figure. I frankly have no idea why Drews thought the ancients worshipped Asclepius as Jason unless it was a confusion of an epithet for the physician in his healing capacity, or confusion over their joint tutelage to Chiron, or even over the Jasonia and the shrines of Asclepius. Based on this, Drews concluded that Jesus was a mythological figure akin to Jason whose worship stretched back before his alleged "life."

The essential problem with this theory is the idea that the etymological relationship between healing and Jason (from the same root) and the one between Joshua and Jesus (from Yehoshua) transfers by the transitive property of scholarship to the phonic relationship of Jason as the transliteration of Joshua into Greek. The Greeks rendered Joshua as Jason because that's how it sounded to them, not for more esoteric reasons. The most ancient Jason was surely associated with healing, but that was many centuries before Jesus, and had the Greeks intended to identify Christ, or Joshua, with the hero of the *Argo*, surely they would have transliterated the name as Jason. But this they did not, spelling Joshua and Jesus both as Iēsoūs in the Greek translation of the books of Moses (the Septuagint). Jason is a variant version found in the New Testament, possibly from Hellenized Jews who adopted the closet Greek name to their Hebrew one. Indeed, Flavius Josephus reports just such a case, when a Jewish high priest named Jesus adopted the Hellenized name Jason in 175 BCE.[19] Critics were dismissive of Drews' theory of a prehistoric Joshua-Jason cult from the first. In the *American Journal of Theology*, Shirley Jackson Case wrote:

> But when one asks for the evidences of a Joshua cult among the Jews, he finds no answer. Again, is there anywhere in Judaism an intimation that Joshua was ever the hero about whom messianic hopes were built? Here also evidence fails; and as for a resemblance between the Jesus of the gospels and this alleged cult-god, Joshua, it lies merely in the identity of name—a feature of no importance when one recalls the frequency of the name among the Jews.[20]

This criticism applies equally to the alleged Jason-Jesus link, a holdover from medieval scholarship that continued long past the end of the Middle Ages. Absent any other evidence of linkage, a similarity in name is little more than suggestive.

If this were not enough, another school of thought claimed that one of the four rivers flowing out of the Garden of Eden in the Bible was the Phasis from Jason's Colchis. According to this theory, which has been offered regularly for three centuries, Eden is located in Armenia, and the Phasis is identical with the first river of Eden: "The name of the first is Pison [or Pishon]: that is it which compasseth the whole land of Havilah, where there is gold."[21] The evidence is paltry, but twofold. First, Pishon looks like Phasis if one squints. Second, Havilah, since it is a land of gold, must therefore be Colchis, for where else would one find gold than in the land of the Golden Fleece? This idea, like so many connected with Jason, relies on the supposition that ancient stories have a real and literal geographic origin. Russell E. Gmerkin offered the theory again in 2006 with an elaborate explanation of how the Greek authors of the Jason story provide insight into the rivers of Eden by showing that the author of Genesis 2 drew on a Near Eastern tradition shared by the Jason myth whereby the world's waterways were connected to the encircling Ocean, thus explaining how it was that one of the rivers of Eden, the Gihon, originating in Mesopotamia, could be imagined to stretch as far as Cush (usually associated with Ethiopia, but thought by some Islamic scholars to be the Hindu Kush), which it encircled. By the transitive property of scholarship, the fact that Jason sailed from the Phasis to the Ocean to the Nile allows us to imagine the rivers Pishon and Gihon as the Phasis and the Nile,[22] and apparently Jason as once again a hero in a biblical landscape.

The Symbolic Hero

Given the contortions scholars undertook to link Jason to the Bible, it is refreshing to note that the symbolic interpretations offered by the German scholars of the nineteenth century are gloriously simple, and at least partially in agreement with the complex interpretation I have offered in this book. Taking the myth in isolation, these scholars proposed that it was essentially a fertility myth, with the actors playing various parts. K. O. Müller argued that the Jason myth derived from the rites of Zeus Laphystius, whom we have met before. In this version, Jason is a god of healing, Medea is a form of Hera, and the Golden Fleece is Zeus' promise of reconciliation. This theory is plausible but falters because it considers the myth only in the context of Classical Greece, and not the broader Near Eastern world to which it belongs. The German archaeologist Peter Wilhelm Forchhammer (1801–1894) believed Greek myths recorded weather phenomena, and therefore the Jason story was the tale of a fertility and healing god (Jason) who carried a rain cloud (the Fleece) to the land of the sun, whose heat had burned the land. Even nineteenth-century scholars recognized this theory was problematic at best. Ulrich von Wilamowitz-Moellendorff (1848–1931), the German classical scholar, believed, as I have endeavored to show, that the Jason myth was at heart a descent into the underworld, a katabasis, a theory that dates back at least to Virgil[23] and was reiterated by Fontenrose in the 1950s.

THE SOLAR HERO

The most influential explanation of Jason was the myth as solar allegory. This theory derives from a complex web of investigation that essentially follows this form: Sir William

Jones (1746–1794) noted the similarity of the ancient Sanskrit language of India to Latin and Greek, an Indo-European family of languages. From this theory was born the idea that a distinct race had spoken the common ancestor of the Indo-European tongues, and this group was the Aryan race, from the Sanskrit for "civilized." Today they are known as the Proto-Indo-European people to escape the associations with nineteenth and twentieth century scientific racism. Comparative mythologists, in turn, attempted to reconstruct the religion of the Aryans by examining Indian and Greco-Roman mythology. From this, they deduced, wrongly it turns out, that the sun was the first and universal Aryan god, a glorious and golden image fitting for a civilized master race who ruled over those who worshipped snakes and earth and other dirty things.

In terms of the Jason myth, the Fleece is a solar symbol, with its journey to Colchis representing the setting sun and its recovery the rising sun. Or else, the voyage was a trip to the place of the rising sun (to find out, Paley thought, why it rises[24]), and Aeëtes and Medea, through their relationships to Helios, self-evident solar symbols, as with everything in their kingdom. In another version, the Fleece, removed from the ram, becomes the sunset, perhaps identical to the sunset "red cloth" of Latvian myth. The tree on which it hangs, the tree of life, represents the night sky, from which Jason, as solar hero, retrieves the Fleece and causes the sun to be reborn as the dawn. To the German philologist F. Max Müller, who specialized in Indian religion, the solar hero is the Vedic sun god Vivásvân, corrupted into the name Jason by poor transliteration and later erroneously identified as "healer," who brings the sun back from the clutches of night.[25] In the theory of Sir G. W. Cox, the entire myth complex derives from a Proto-Indo-European root, the letter *i*, which represented a "loud" color, such as violet, which stood for the dawn and therefore proves that Jason's myth is solar, with Jason as the sun and the Golden Fleece representing the gold-tinted clouds of the dawn.[26] However, Paley noted objections to the theory:

> There are some persons who read with utter incredulity the attempts of learned men to show that many of the legends of classical antiquity—even the Achilles and the Ulysses of Homer—may be readily explained by the ideas and the symbolism of a primitive sun-worship. [...] "Everything," they object, "was the sun, according to your view." And the reply is not an irrational one: "Yes, everything *was* the sun, at a time and in a nation where the all-powerful and beneficent giver of light and heat engaged all the prayers and all the aspirations of the human race." [...] [W]hat symbolism can they embody if they are *not* stories about the sun?[27]

The solar theory, as applied to Jason, is at least partially correct. There is definitely a solar *element* to it, though obviously I differ from the solar theorists in relating the solar element to the ancient sun god's *underworld* aspect. The solar theory was popular with scholars who sought a symbolic explanation for Jason, but it gradually waned as new research cast doubt on the claim that the sun god was the first and universal Aryan deity.

A competing claim, eventually championed by Sir James George Frazer, attributed Greek myths to fertility rites. One nineteenth century theory argued that Jason and Cadmus were both fertility gods associated with Demeter, and the sewing of the dragon's teeth descended from a fertility rite of Demeter that involved the ritual throwing of stones to guarantee a good harvest. Again, there is partial truth here, too, and we cannot ignore the echoes of the dying and rising gods in Jason's story, though, once more, they are not the only element at work. A slightly different theory, by John Kenrick, instead substituted bronze for solar gold and suggested the myth was really about metallurgy, with Jason as Hephaestus, the fiery bulls as the smith's bellows and forge, and Medea representing technical knowledge of the smith's art transmuted into mythological magic.[28] The early modern alchemists would have been proud.

THE PSYCHOLOGICAL HERO

Among the Victorians, Andrew Lang, the journalist and scholar of myths, argued that the story of Jason, defined only as a mortal who defeats a powerful man to marry his daughter, was nearly universal among the world's people, told originally of an anonymous character and later personalized in Greece. It was for him certainly no solar myth, nor nature myth, nor the result of the gradual corruption of real life adventures, as other scholars claimed. He saw Jason reflected in a Samoan tale of a man who sails to the island of the song god and defeats his tests through the aid of his daughter, winning her hand in marriage, and also in an Algonquin myth and a Scottish one, too. The core elements of Jason's myth, being known in the Americas and the Pacific, and among the Finns and in Asia, proves that it is no Indo-European creation but one of exceedingly primitive age.

> We must suppose, therefore, either that all wits jumped and invented the same romantic series of situations by accident, or that all men spread from one centre, where the story was known, or that the story, once invented, has drifted all round the world. [...] The story will have been carried hither and thither, in the remotest times, to the remotest shores, by traders, by slaves, by captives in war, or by women torn from their own tribe and forcibly settled as wives among alien peoples. [...] By all these agencies, working through dateless time, we may account for the diffusion, if we cannot explain the origin, of tales like the central arrangement of incidents in the career of Jason.[29]

Lang was, of course, half right. Elements of the Jason story spread into Greece from the Near East, and outward from it. But there are many cultures, like the Samoan and North American, that had no contact with these areas and knew no Greek myth. Instead, their versions derived from the universality of marriage rites, and another true human universal, the neurological and psychological workings of the human mind, an idea twentieth century scholars would explore.

At least one early scholar apparently believed that the Golden Fleece referred to the pubic hair of a blonde (i.e. Aryan) woman, in the manner of British and French slang.[30] This suggestion was echoed in the work of the American psychoanalyst Leon Balter, who in 1969 used the sexual theories of Sigmund Freud to read the Fleece as the pubic hair of Jason's mother, the serpent as the (phallic) father, and the Clashing Rocks as a fanged vagina threatening to castrate Jason (but of course).[31] Carl Jung, Freud's protégé and rival, took the symbolic reading still further and held that the Argonauts' voyage over water represented the unconscious, into which one would journey to encounter monsters and achieve insight into the self, achieving the Golden Fleece, which symbolizes the attaining of the unattainable, by having the hero expose himself to the abyss that is the female—the monstrous feminine that is both Medea and the dragon.[32] Jung believed in a collective unconscious shared by humanity, within which sat archetypical images, such as the hero-savior, the shared heritage of mankind. This theory, derived from psychology and a dash of mysticism, is remarkably close to the neurobiological views of David Lewis-Williams (see chapter 1), though Lewis-Williams's theories require no mystical or collective forces since mythic symbols are to him derived from the evolved wiring of the brain.

From the matrix of Freud and Jung and Frazer grew the most popular interpretation of myth, Joseph Campbell's monomyth, explained in his *Hero with a Thousand Faces* (1949) as a basic underlying pattern through which all myths of the hero's journey could be diagrammed. Predicated on the rituals of rites of passage, this involved at its core *separation*, *initiation*, and *return*. Campbell explained that hero myths, including Jason's, could be reduced to the following formula:

> *A hero ventures forth from the world of common day into a region of supernatural wonder: Fabulous forces are there encountered and a decisive victory is won: The hero comes back from this mysterious adventure with the power to bestow boons on his fellow men.*[33] (emphasis in original)

Campbell divides this basic structure into seventeen stages, which are too tangential to our discussion to go into here. Suffice it to say that the pattern involves such themes common to the Jason story as the call to adventure, the crossing of thresholds (such as the sea), dramatic tests of the hero, the love of a woman, atonement with (or defeat of) a father figure, the stealing of a prize, a flight from the supernatural forces, and a return flight to the world of reality. Campbell used the Jason myth only incidentally in the book, to illustrate the threshold via the Clashing Rocks, and the flight of return via the challenges at Colchis (which one might have presumed would be the "tests") and the return voyage to Greece. Nevertheless, Campbell's theory clearly fits the Jason myth. I do not believe this is due entirely to some mysterious "power of myth" or universal secret for understanding the first cause of creation encoded in myth, as Campbell did. Instead, I find more persuasive the theory that such patterns emerge from the neurological events experienced during altered states of consciousness—as in the shaman's journey (see chapters one and three). It is uncanny how closely this neurobiological phenomenon parallels biologically the patterns of myth deduced from studies of literature and psychology. The implication is that they are one and the same.

That the Jungian archetypes and Campbell's monomyth can be explained by appeals to the neurological makeup of the human mind can help us to incorporate two other major theories about Jason into our understanding of the myth: the idea that Jason's adventure symbolizes a rite of initiation and that his was a shaman's journey. The latter idea we explored in chapter 3. Though not the first to propose the initiation theory, Fritz Graf is its most prominent proponent,[34] and in his view the Argonauts' age, around twenty, mark them as adolescents on the brink of adulthood. Some of the older adults on the ship are the maternal uncles of other Argonauts, reflecting the important role of these relatives in initiation rites of adulthood. (But surely these characters were added later and therefore reflected the cultural practices of those who wrote them into the story.) Because Jason is a prince, his rite of initiation is not simply that of a boy to a man but rather of a group of aristocrats entering the class of royal warriors. "Not a shamanistic background, then, lies behind this myth, but that of archaic initiatory rituals—more specifically, the initiation of aristocratic warriors."[35] In this matrix, Medea "can be understood as initatrix," a role that originated with her formerly divine status as a one-time goddess figure.[36] Graf believes that Medea was first the goddess-helper of the Jason story and was later replaced with Aphrodite and Hera.

In support of his claims, Graf notes the similarity between the Argonauts' journey and the initiation rites of Cretan youths as reported in the fourth century BCE. He describes these rites as a boy's journey into the woods with a group of peers and an older man who is his lover. Graf notes the erotic nature of the relationship of Heracles and Hylas as a reflection of this practice. This, however, does not quite match the facts. First, the oldest Jason myths belie no evidence of an older male lover (Heracles was added later). Second, when more fully described, the ritual is quite different in form. The older lover "kidnaps" the boy, and his friends give chase. The man and boy vanish into the woods for two months of feasting, hunting, and loving, culminating in the boy's acceptance into the company of men, symbolized by a new robe. He and his companions then formed a cohort employed in sport and hunting until marriage.[37] Certainly such rites share elements with Jason's myth (the Fleece could stand for the robe), but it does not seem so close a match as to say that the myth derived from "archaic initiatory rituals." This is especially true in situations, like Jason's, where there is no known cult or group to which the myth was attached, and no plausible method by which it could be ritually applied.

Such ideas derive, ultimately, from a group of Cambridge scholars known as the ritualists who believed that Greek myths were all the magical stories told during religious rituals, which predated myths and created myths to explain the rituals. This position was modified over the years, but not entirely abandoned. But even if Graf's position were true, what insight does it provide other than to say that initiations were conceived as journeys into death and rebirth? It tells us nothing of the myth's multiplicity of meanings or symbolic import. Happily, initiation rites, purification rites, and the monomyth share in common the architecture of descent and return found in the neurobiology of the human mind, allowing us to see these theories as partial truths, reflecting an essentially human pattern of storytelling rather than the imagined survival of culturally-bound ritual practice across millennia.

THE UNDERWORLD AGAIN

More recently, efforts have been made to situate Jason within the context of the Greek epic hero. In the 1970s, the Hungarian scholar Karl Kerényi agreed that Jason's journey was essentially a voyage to the Underworld, with Aeëtes representing a god of death, equated (via the disputed derivation of his name as Aides, from the word for earth) with Hades himself.[38] Kerényi, however, argued that Jason's tasks in Colchis were later additions meant to associate him with epic heroes such as Cadmus, and that the original goal involved neither bulls nor earthborn men nor even a dragon, but instead simply retrieving the Fleece from the King of Death. Kerényi also discussed the ways Jason's quest could not but end badly since the un-heroic hero could not accomplish his task without a woman's help, meaning that he must invariably fall into fatal ruin.[39] This argument is logical if we assume that the Jason story was primarily and originally the story of the voyage of the *Argo* and that Medea was always Jason's helper, but as we have seen a better argument can be made for the voyage as a secondary motif, developed primarily following Greek colonization of the Black Sea, with Medea gradually assuming a role she did not first possess.

In discussing the epic hero, Dean A. Miller held at the turn of the millennium that Jason's story is essentially a quest for treasure, onto which was grafted the motif of the rightful king. In agreeing with Kerényi that Jason's trip was to the Underworld (or, in his terminology, the Otherworld, which can be a land of death or an alternate reality, sometimes confused), he adds the further coda that Jason returned from the Otherworld with an "evil destiny," a result of a typical epic-heroic myth pattern where voyages to the Otherworld produce great rewards or great suffering.[40] In his view, heroes who do not measure up to full heroic character must pay a penalty for daring to seek out the Otherworld, and Jason, therefore, is no true hero but a man (whom he describes as "dense"[41]) who suffers for taking on a quest too great for him and is saddled with Medea.[42] However, as we have seen, the "evil destiny" in Corinth was almost certainly a much later addition and cannot be taken as the original conclusion to the Jason story. Like many applications of universal theories, Miller's suffers from assuming that the Standard Version of the Jason myth represents the story in its original and fixed form, rather than as a summation of a fluctuating and multivalent myth.

The trouble with many of the symbolic approaches is that they reduced complex and potent mythic symbols to simple causes—or worse, treated symbols in isolation. As I hope that I showed in Part Three, it is only by considering mythic symbols in the context of the myth itself, Greek mythology as a whole, and the broader mythic world to which Greek mythology belongs that we can begin to appreciate the multiple meanings of symbols and the multivalent influences and meaning that give them their power. These ideas, however, were positively rich with imaginative potential compared to the second group of scholarly theorists who read Jason's journey as a distorted record of actual Mycenaean era voyages to the gold mining regions of the eastern Black Sea on or about 1400 BCE.

The Gold Rush

All scholarly theories that claim that the Jason story derived from real-life Mycenaean voyages into the Black Sea trace their origins back to the rationalizing speculations of Strabo. Strabo described the mining techniques of the Soanes, a "dirty" group of people in the highlands of the Caucasus above the coastal Black Sea colony of Dioscurias:

> In their country the winter torrents are said to bring down even gold, which the Barbarians collect in troughs pierced with holes, and lined with fleeces; and hence the fable of the golden fleece.[43]

In another passage, Strabo speculated on the real reason for Jason's mission:

> Æetes is generally believed to have reigned in Colchis, the name is still common throughout the country, tales of the sorceress Medea are yet abroad, and the riches of the country in gold, silver, and iron, proclaim the motive of Jason's expedition, as well as of that which Phrixus had formerly undertaken.[44]

In short, they went in search of treasure. But note: Strabo claims no proof of this other than the association of Colchis with metals, and Strabo's own imagination. As a supplement, Pliny noted a century later that the region around Colchis was famed for its mineral wealth in both gold and silver.[45] This explanation is superficially plausible (it must be, or Strabo, clearly a very intelligent man, would not have suggested it), and if the Golden Fleece is entirely divorced from its mythic context it might well agree with Strabo's theory. But Strabo was writing in the rationalizing tradition, not in the modern scientific one. His explanation was not grounded in interdisciplinary research into mythology, history, archaeology, and anthropology but instead in a seemingly harmonious coincidence between a gold panning technique and a mythic image. Strabo also suggested that Jason must have been a historical figure because otherwise there would be no Jasonia, and he further held that the same temples proved that Jason conducted an unrecorded campaign into Armenia and Media (Persia).

357. "We have It Rich." - Washing and panning gold. Rockerville, Dak. Old-timers, Spriggs, Lamb and Dillon at work. Photo and copyright by Grabill, 1889.

Strabo believed that the Golden Fleece originated in early efforts to pan gold from the waters near Colchis. Similar methods remained in use in the nineteenth century, when the California Gold Rush miners of 1849 became known as Argonauts after this interpretation of Jason's myth. Later gold miners, like these seen here in 1889, strained water to separate out gold, much as the Colchians had done thousands of years earlier (Library of Congress).

Though I certainly do not mean to demean Strabo, his rationalizing conclusions cannot be accepted at face value without confirmatory evidence since so many were clearly imaginative or based on Greco-Roman assumptions modern scholarship has shown false.

Nevertheless, generations of scholars have accepted Strabo's claim uncritically. In the eighteenth-century masterpiece *The Decline and Fall of the Roman Empire*, Edward Gibbon combined Strabo's and Pliny's claims and concluded that the gold of ancient Colchis lured the avaricious Argonauts, who are therefore little more than treasure hunters raiding the wealthy mines of foreign potentates, with the Golden Fleece merely the rag with which peasants panned for gold:

> The waters, impregnated with particles of gold, are carefully strained through sheep-skins or fleeces, but this expedient, the groundwork perhaps of a marvellous fable, affords a faint image of the wealth extracted from a virgin earth by the power and industry of ancient kings. Their silver palaces and golden chambers surpass our belief; but the fame of their riches is said to have excited the enterprising avarice of the Argonauts.[46]

There is nothing here not found in Strabo and Pliny, and no more reason to suspect it true because Gibbon repeated their claims uncritically, though more baldly than Strabo's speculation (he cites Strabo and Pliny in his notes for the passage); yet, seventeen centuries later, the same speculation was repeated again as fact.

And on it went. In 1927, John A. Scott used Gibbon as confirmation of Strabo to argue that gold panning was the origin of the Fleece myth, apparently unaware that Gibbon drew his information from Strabo, and that Strabo was merely rationalizing. Scott did add that contemporary gold-panning in Asia Minor was conducted the same way, burning the gold-laden fleeces to free the gold collected from rivers.[47] Arthur F. Taggart then reintroduced Strabo's theory in 1947, arguing that science proved the Fleece must have been a gold-mining technique since the greasiness of a sheep's fleece was an ideal method for capturing gold, rendering Jason a thief raiding an ancient gold refinery. Strabo's theory has adherents today. After the discovery of the oldest known gold mine in the Caucasus at Sankdrissi in Georgia in 2004, archaeologists determined that the mine had been in operation since 3000 BCE and had been trading gold across Georgia since 2500 BCE. The scientists used laser ablation inductively coupled plasma mass spectrometry, a complex method of analyzing trace minerals in gold, to connect gold artifacts back to their source. However, French physicist Maria Filomena Guerra believes that the gold was not originally mined but instead panned from rivers using fleeces, a theory she bases on both documented local practice and, of course, Strabo's gloss on the myth of the Golden Fleece. She began testing gold from Mycenaean tombs in Volos, near Iolcus, with particle-induced x-ray emission x-ray fluorescence, a non-invasive technique, to prove that the gold came from Georgian rivers.[48] As of this writing, Guerra had not been able to demonstrate that the Mycenaean gold was Georgian, only that is had been panned in a river[49]—somewhere—but even if she documents a connection it no more proves Jason's journey to Colchis than the amber used by the Mycenaeans would "prove" trips to Britain and the Baltic. Trade routes do not necessarily imply the movement of peoples, only goods.

So here we are in the modern world still chasing after a speculation offered by an ancient author two millennia earlier. This theory, however, has logical problems, many of which derive from the fact that it considers the Golden Fleece as an object in isolation, separate from the myths of Phrixus and Jason through which it was developed:

- Nowhere in either myth is the Fleece linked to mining, panning for gold, or the acquisition of mineral wealth, except as Aeëtes' lucky charm. Neither is it associated with rivers, only the Hellespont (and, in older versions where the ram swam, the Aegean).
- Greek myths are told of (and mostly for) aristocrats—kings, princes, and warriors—not of common folk, and if the Fleece were merely the rag used by peasants panning for gold it would hardly be a fit subject for upper class mythology. Nowhere else are the tools of the peasant (as opposed to the high status specialist, like the blacksmith) celebrated and commemorated as a central facet of myth, excepting of course farming implements, which in the ancient world were simply universal.
- To take the myth as historical, one must accept that the Golden Fleece was *originally Greek*, meaning that the alleged gold it represented went from Greece *to Colchis* and was not therefore the gold mined in that distant land.
- This point is moot anyway, since Colchis was not Jason's original destination, but rather the imaginary land of Aea, which was the sun-kingdom and quite possibly the Underworld.

When considered within the broader context of the Argonaut myth, the Golden Fleece seems much less likely to have originated in a damp mining rag, which, I can only imagine, must have looked somewhat less spectacular than recent writers have implied.

The Royal Fetish

The other major rationalizing explanation for the Golden Fleece is the one given by Jan Bremmer, who rightly rejected the idea that the Fleece was merely a mining rag. For Bremmer, the Fleece was instead the Hittite cult object known as the *kurša*, a theory proposed by Volkert Haas in the 1970s and A. H. Sayce in 1930. Bremmer identifies the kurša as a fleece that was sewn into a bag and used to carry objects when hunting. An elaborate form of the kurša was nailed to a tree as part of a ritual, and one was hung up in the temple of the war god, which Bremmer suggests gave rise to the Fleece's association with the "temple" of Ares—though it was usually the Grove of Ares in Greek myth. The kurša served as a symbol of the gods, and at the annual Purulli fertility festival where the myth of Teshub and dragon (including the aid given by Inara and a human hero) was performed, six news kuršas of goat leather were inaugurated, to replace the previous years' bags. This, Bremmer suggests, was the ritual that the Greeks transformed into the myth of Jason and the Golden Fleece when they heard—but did not see—stories of this magic bag and reinterpreted it as a living animal in a ritual environment.[50]

Thus, the similarities between the Hittite Purulli and the Jason story are:

- A long journey. Jason travels to Colchis across the sea by ship; the celebrants of the Purulli travel from city to city before reaching Nerik where the ritual is performed.
- The identification of a shaggy object made from an animal's skin with protection, divinity, royal power, and fertility.
- The slaying of a serpent. Jason kills the guardian of the Fleece with the help of Medea, and the festival reenacted or recited Teshub's triumph over the dragon through the aid of Inara and a human hero.
- A (sacred) marriage. Prince Jason marries Princess Medea (once a goddess), and Teshub's marriage to a goddess is reenacted by the Hittite king and queen.

Of course, a problem with this identification is that Jason is not a storm god, and it is unclear by what route a story of the storm god, the equivalent of Zeus, would descend on a character more closely associated with healing.

Scholars of Hittite language and culture also dispute the association of kurša and Fleece, at least partially, noting two key differences between the Hittite magic hunting bag and the Fleece of Jason. First, the kurša was not gold in color, though it may occasionally have had a gold disc attached to it. (Bremmer suggests that the "gold" was added to replace its forgotten sacred function.) Second, the kurša was *not* a fleece. According to Jaan Puhvel, "Nor is 'fleece' the dominant sense in the texts (the normal term being ^{SIG}*esri*- [...] *kursa*- meant specifically 'skin(bag)' [...] with some metonymic extension to other pliable containers (wicker, reed)..." (Some of the kurša bags made from goat skins retained the goat's long hair.) Puhvel does dutifully note, though obviously without being convinced, that the "talismanic aura" of the kurša might derive anciently from a sheepskin and therefore relate to the Golden Fleece.[51] In Hittite usage, the kurša is almost certainly a bag (in Hittite art, it retains no animal parts and has a large handle, and one Hittite text specifies that it and a sheep's fleece are distinct), often used in hunting in addition to ritual, a pliable container that held items, whether sacred or secular, and thus very different in form *and* function from the Golden Fleece, which to my mind compromises the idea of the kurša as the sole, or primary, origin of the

Fleece. The kurša is connected with much older sets of words, all dealing with bags (and not fuzzy ones), ultimately yielding the English word purse.[52] Even Bremmer noted that the Hittite kurša was not exclusively a ram's skin but could be made from the hide of oxen, sheep, or goats.

Calvert Watkins argued that the Greeks incorporated the kurša into their mythology as the aegis of Athena, which was originally a protective garment made of goatskin covered in a hundred woven gold tassels, since both are described in their respective cultures as shaggy and play protective roles. Based on the fact that Homer describes the aegis as tufted, the same word Pindar used to describe the Fleece, Watkins suggests a common origin for aegis and Fleece—the kurša.[53] I am not convinced, especially since the wording may simply be coincidence, or even Pindar consciously evoking Homer rather than a descendant of a prehistoric progenitor.[54] The myth of Perseus shows that the

The Hittite *kurša*, or skin-bag, was believed to have great magical power, to hold the essence of fertility, and was sometimes worshiped as a god. Scenes like this one from a Hittite rhyton dated to 1400 BCE, in which the kurša is seen dangling below a quiver on a sacred tree, may have inspired the Golden Fleece hanging upon an oak tree in the Jason myth, according to some scholars (author's drawing).

Greeks knew the kurša as a bag, for Perseus places Medusa's head in a tufted bag, the *kibisis* (possibly from kurša), a silver hunting bag with golden tassels in literature,[55] but usually a simple bag or sack in art. The implication of this would be that if there were a connection between *kibisis,* kurša, aegis, and Fleece, it might in fact go back to a common source of all four.[56] But this is to say only that animal skins are sacred because they are sacred to the gods, which is really saying nothing at all since sacred animals are as old as the human imagination. The most parsimonious reading, as far as I can tell, is that the Golden Fleece (a ram's skin), Athena's aegis (a tufted goat skin), and the kurša (a bag made from many different skins) must, as Puhvel suggested, all derive from the ancient association of sheepskins with the sacred and the divine. A direct connection would be unnecessary since these beliefs were already ancient in Greece and may have been inherited from the Neolithic, though certainly the Greeks modeled the poetic forms used with the aegis on Hittite texts about kurša, implying that those two, if not the Fleece, had motifs that transferred from one to the other.

While I see the reasoning behind the theory that the kurša gave rise to the Golden Fleece, and it is as close to persuasive as any theory yet proposed, I cannot get past the major differences between the two: that the kurša was not golden and the Fleece was not a bag. I am willing to accept, however, that the Fleece may derive in part from the golden aegis, or a common source, and that the aegis probably had a relationship to the kurša in that the aegis was once imagined as bag-like. However, even granting all this, there simply must be a reason that both aegis and Fleece are gold, while the kurša is not. For that, I see a much closer connection between the golden garments of the Near Eastern gods than the hunting bag they carried with them, though both were apparently part of a Hittite god's sacred equipment and may have been conflated in the transmission from Anatolia to Greece. If the kurša stands behind the Jason myth it cannot have done so in isolation, and it must have come as part of a package with other symbols at some point so long in the past that it was effectively absorbed into a constellation of Mycenaean symbolism related to fleeces, golden robes, and the gods—long before the Jason myth formed.

Of the Purulli festival, there is an interesting connection to the ideas I have already put forward about the chthonic and underworld associations of the Jason story. Prior to the Indo-European Hittites, the Purulli festival belonged to the Hattians, down to between 2000 and 1700 BCE in various locations, and they envisioned the gods as living under the earth rather than in the sky.[57] The oldest Purulli festival, therefore, had a decidedly chthonic aspect and was intended to appease the deities within the ground. The king was given symbolic charge over a "river of the watery abyss" which was a passage to the Underworld.[58] If the Mycenaeans therefore had encountered this older version of the Purulli, or chthonic elements of it survived among the Hittites longer than the "official" textual versions suggest, then this would go a long way toward resolving the distance between the Hittite festival of the sky-oriented storm god and the obviously chthonic and Underworld nature of the Jason myth.

Thus, we can see how the Greeks could have come to associate this ritual, with its fleece bag, dragon-slaying, and attendant helper goddess, with their own myth of the serpent-slayer who descended into the Underworld, for as we proposed in chapter 3, there appear to be two layers to the Jason story, and the older one was most likely Mycenaean and Minoan, to which the Hittite story became attached and incorporated. Robin Lane Fox suggested the period of contact was the eighth century, but at that period the Greeks brought over the story of Teshub and the dragon as Zeus and Typhon. It seems unlikely that they would have brought the myth to Greece twice simultaneously yet so divergently. Jason must have come earlier, either in Mycenaean times, or perhaps from an Indo-European source antecedent to both.

Other minor theories seeking a real-life origin for the Fleece have explained the Fleece as an object used for rain magic, a type of Georgian sheep with yellowish wool, and, if not gold, then a representation of the *amber* trade. None of these explanations was particularly convincing. The yoked bulls had their own literalist interpretation, too. Proto-Indo-European linguist Saul Levin, taking the Jason myth quite literally, assumed that the two bulls Jason yokes at Colchis essentially record prehistoric animal husbandry techniques. The fiery bulls simply represent un-castrated bulls whose aggressiveness has not been tamed, "an old memory from before the discovery" that castration made bulls docile enough to plow fields. Further, this same theory argued, based entirely on Jason's two bulls, that the ancients tamed *two bulls simultaneously* as their standard practice of husbandry.[59] Levin, however, admits that Jason is the only Greek example of this alleged practice.

A Voyage to Nowhere

Having explained Jason's adventures in Colchis with appeals to real-life rituals and actions, it was only natural that literalists would turn to Jason's voyage to Colchis and see in it a literal record of a Bronze Age sea voyage. To this bit of historical sleuthing, we owe, again, Strabo, with an assist from medieval scholars and Heinrich Schliemann. Strabo, of course, had claimed that Jason's voyage was indubitably real since "the Jasonia are evidence of the expedition of Jason," as are the cities who claimed him as their founder.[60] Further, the medieval writers had accepted Jason as a historical figure, one who was intimately tied to the Trojan War, which was without doubt a historical event, for did not the authority of Dares, Valerius Flaccus, and Diodorus Siculus so attest? As we have seen, down to the nineteenth century, the voyage of the Argonauts was reported as a factual event due to the testimony of Strabo and the scholars of the Middle Ages, such as the passage from Royal Robbins quoted in chapter 2, which presumed that the Argonauts sailed in 1263 BCE (remarkably close to the actual date of the Mycenaean Age, in fact) to seize treasure from the Black Sea. Therefore, when Schliemann excavated at Troy and Mycenae and proved that the Trojan War had a basis in geographical—if not martial—fact, archaeologists and antiquarians cast about for another myth that archaeology might prove real. And they found Jason.

The German scholar W. Schwartz proposed in 1893 that the Argonauts' sea trip was a merchant's trade voyage promoted to epic status, which echoed the same suggestion given in the encyclopedia edited by the French theologian Jean le Clerc two centuries earlier, the *Bibliothèque universelle et historique* (1686–1693). Other Victorian scholars had suggested that Phoenician sea voyages were origin of the Argonauts' venture, again related to trade missions. Among the more fanciful attempts at rationalization was the Victorian speculation that the Clashing Rocks Jason passed going to (or from) Colchis were in fact giant icebergs, which would have the property of seeming like jostling rocks and would be unfamiliar to the Greeks, since they are absent from the Aegean. These icebergs were thought to constitute evidence of a real voyage into the Black Sea, and one writer thought the icebergs in the Jason story might have been a mythic memory of the Ice Age![61] More recent scholarship attempted to explain the Symplegades as the result of an earthquake-induced tsunami that moved rocks, or as an optical illusion seen during a ground swell, when winds displace the waters of the sea significantly, along with boats floating on them, making fixed points like rocks seem to move relative to the aquatic observer.[62] Why this freak occurrence should be commemorated for millennia is unclear, but Herodorus would be proud.

The foremost early proponent of the antiquity of Greek myth, Martin Nilsson, changed scholarly understandings of mythology when he concluded in the 1930s that Greek myth had Mycenaean origins, a theory quickly accepted. He believed that the Jason story was Mycenaean in origin based on the prominence of Iolcus in Mycenaean times. This, he believed, helped answer a conundrum in the Argonaut myth. Jason travelled to Colchis to retrieve the Fleece of Phrixus because Phrixus was a kinsman, from Orchomenus, whose inhabitants, the descendants of the legendary King Minyas, were called Minyans. The Argonauts, too, were traditionally called Minyans, but they did not live in Orchomenus. To solve this problem, Apollonius had made Jason and his men descendants of Minyas' daughters, rather than his sons, who remained in Orchomenus. According to Nilsson, the Argonauts were deemed Minyans because that was the half-forgotten name of the people who inhabited Thessaly in Mycenaean times, only partly remembered by later Antiquity as the people of a single city instead of the entire region of Boetia and Thessaly. The imaginative genealogies of Jason and his companions, therefore, "were invented in order to give a reason for the traditional phrase describing the Argonauts as Minyans."[63] If Iolcus had been a real and powerful Mycenaean city, then it stood to reason, others would claim, that the voyage from there had been every bit as real as its starting point.

Janet Ruth Bacon was the most prominent of the scholars who claimed a historical reality for the *Argo*'s adventure. In her *Voyage of the Argo* (1925), Bacon attempted to find the "historical" Jason using many of the same methods that scholars had applied to the search for the historical Jesus, by removing everything unoriginal and everything impossible: "Though it is reasonable to doubt that the Argonauts really dashed between the Clashing Rocks or pursued malevolent spirits through the air, it does not therefore follow that they did not make the voyage at all."[64] She dismissed any connection between Phrixus and Jason as a later conflation of myths, and she correctly peeled away many of Jason's adventures as folk tales that had become attached to a spine of truth. Others, such as the stopover on Lemnos, she felt had a historical origin. She then dismissed the magical elements of the story, including Aeëtes and Medea, whom she regarded as later additions. This left her with what she presumed to be the truth: that the voyage of the *Argo* was a mythologized memory of a Bronze Age voyage from Iolcus to the Black Sea, around 1400 BCE and the many different return routes proposed by ancient authors were all ancient amber trails, accounting for the Fleece, which represented the riches that flowed into Greece from the east. Thus, just as the *Iliad* could be reduced to the stones of Troy, so too could the *Argonautica* be reduced to the waves of the Black Sea. This is the rough equivalent of arguing that Christianity was "really" a set of additions and distortions to a straightforward account of Roman judicial practices; it somewhat misses the point.

Bacon's literary excavations discarded the wrong half of the myth. As we have seen, the myth of the healer who battles the serpent came before the elaboration of his voyage to reach the dragon. When Bacon stripped out the mythic elements to expose the historical truth, she did uncover a historical set of voyages, but they were not Jason's. These were the voyages to the Black Sea the Archaic Greeks themselves made and added to the mythic tale of Jason as they retold and adapted an old myth to the new circumstances of Black Sea exploration. After all, to apply another literalist interpretation, if the Fleece really descends from the Purulli festival of Anatolia, then it could not have been the object of a Black Sea voyage, since no such journey is required to reach Anatolia. The Jason myth, despite medieval beliefs to the contrary, did not belong the historicizing myths of the Trojan Cycle or the legends of Alexander. The Argonauts are older than that, closer in spirit to the myths of Perseus and Heracles, whose stories are clearly mythological and not folk memories of ancient history. Just as Schliemann had identified the wrong layer of Troy as Homer's city, Bacon excavated a layer of myth in a stratum a bit higher than she thought and missed the mythic origins of Jason.

Bacon's thesis was highly influential and, more or less, has stood as the standard interpretation of the Jason myth among archaeologists, if not Classical scholars, down to the present day. Nearly every contemporary published discussion of Jason makes reference to the hypothetical Bronze Age voyages, and this is due primarily to Bacon. In tandem with the thesis that Argonauts crossed into the Black Sea was a scholarly debate on whether such crossings were possible at all in the Bronze Age. In a famous 1948 article, Rhys Carpenter argued that Greeks could not have entered the Black Sea prior to the seventh century BCE because they did not yet possess the fifty-oared boat, the *pentekonter*, which was necessary to make sufficient gains against the powerful current of the Bosporus. It was, in short, impossible to move against the current with small, Dark Age boats. Only when the new ship had been invented, he said, did the fairy tale of the *Argo* become geographically associated with penetration of the Black Sea.[65] This idea, in turn, received challenges from scholars who demonstrated that the Bosporus, while difficult, was in fact navigable.[66] In no way did this really affect the Jason myth, however, since even the earliest dates for Greek navigation, in the eighth century BCE, came long after the Mycenaeans began telling the Jason story, though it obviously impacts the date at which the myth took on the coloring of a Black Sea quest. In 1976, Robert Drews proposed that in the ninth or eighth centuries BCE, the Greeks learned about the gold and iron of the Caucasus from the Anatolian kingdom of the Uratians, who traded with a land called Qulha that *might* have been Colchis,[67] which in turn prompted the first Black Sea voyages—including voyages by Medea's adopted home of Corinth—which became embedded in the Jason myth.

In 1984, the British historian and explorer Tim Severin, who has made a career out of recreating ancient voyages, tried to prove that Bronze Age Greeks could have sailed to Colchis. He built a replica of a 52-foot Mycenaean-style galley ship with room for twenty oarsmen based on iconographic evidence, such as the vase painting discussed in chapter 2, and he and his crew sailed the ship from Volos (Iolcus) to Poti in Soviet Georgia, taking a little less than three months to make the trek. In Georgia, Severin witnessed peasants panning for gold with a sheep's fleece and concluded from Strabo's rationalization that he had found the Golden Fleece.[68] Severin chose the era of 1250 BCE for the style of his ship because he followed the legend that Jason was the father of Euneus, who was alive in the Trojan War, which he believed happened around 1200 BCE. However, just because a journey was *possible* did not mean it actually occurred.[69] One could, in theory, sail a ship from Greece to Guyana (I think someone named Columbus had an idea like that), but this does not prove that Mycenaeans explored the Amazon.

Nevertheless, the idea of a real Mycenaean-era voyage has become the default explanation of the Argonaut myth. In 1980, the Colombian ambassador and historian Mauricio Obregón retraced the Argonauts' journey by sailboat and plane to get a feel for its geography and concluded that the *Argo*'s voyage, along with Odysseus' and many others, was based on a real-life journey. Just before his death in 1998, Obregón attempted to rationalize each stage of the *Argo*'s voyage and provide not just a proposed route for the trip but also an explanation of how the ship would have overcome all the challenges of geography posed by following in general plan the paths laid out by ancient authors, who, apparently, simply remembered Jason's itinerary for a thousand years.[70] In 2005, British historian Michael Wood broadcast a BBC/PBS television series *In Search of... Myths and Heroes*, with a companion volume of the same name. The series covered four myths, and the Golden Fleece episode combined a travelogue of the Aegean and Black Seas with an overview of scholarship on the Argonaut myth. After exploring the archaeological evidence for Greeks on the Black Sea shore, Wood travelled to Georgia where he found what he considered the "true" origin of the Golden Fleece. It was, of course, the same wet sheepskins that Strabo rationalized about more than two thousand years before.

Clearly, for the rationalizers and the literalists, the Jason myth is not much more than a story about some pirates who sailed the high seas to steal for themselves some wet rags crusted with gold. The problem I have with this method of approaching myth is that it reduces an imaginative and majestic system of storytelling and understanding the world to an algorithm. In their view, myths are faulty memories and distortions of real events, places, and people which the ancients repeated slavishly and unimaginatively from generation to generation, accruing minor changes, distortions, and misinterpretations as the game of Chinese telephone progressed until we have the wild phantasmagorias of today. These, in turn, can be projected backward to understand the first cause of the myth, a natural or human event.

But this view denies the power of the human imagination and the ability of ancient people to think symbolically and to engage the world at a creative, imaginative, and, yes, even fictional level. It also denies the power of mythic heroes, rendering them irrelevant impositions on history. Surely, when the painters of the Paleolithic placed composite creatures and bird-men on the walls of their caves they were not reporting literal events but were thinking imaginatively and creatively (and possibly under the influence of hallucinogens). We must be able to afford the Greeks the same privilege; their mythology, while rationalized in the Classical era more than any other myth system, originates in the same world of symbols and imagination as any other. We owe it to the Greeks to see their myths in the context where they were created. And even if some episodes in myth began as worldly objects or events, their power lies not in their mundane origins but in the realm of the imagination to which they belong.

This denial of human imagination, assuming the ancients were fundamentally different from us, slavish reporters of whatever they stumbled across by chance, is the motivating force behind the last group of theories we will examine, the ones that send Jason into outer space.

12

The Astronaut

Jason in Outer Space

The euhemerists and the rationalizing writers of antiquity had tried to find meaning in the Jason myth, and they did so by looking for human or natural phenomena that could explain the symbols and ideas in the myth that seemed too improbable to be real—presupposing in doing so that some level of literal truth undergirded the mythic story. The scholarly successors to these camps perpetuated some of these rather free-form interpretive techniques. Thus, at various times writers proposed Jason's mission was "really" a trade mission, or the Clashing Rocks icebergs, or the Golden Fleece a book of alchemy. If scholarly opinion could countenance such theories, then it would only stand to reason that those who followed more extreme interpretations of the human past would find no objection to applying their own euhemerist or rationalized interpretations of myth, proceeding from their own unique assumptions about history. Beyond this, exponents of certain ideologies and belief systems perverted or abused the Jason myth in support of their specific ends. What nearly all the theories in this chapter share are a superficial understanding of the Jason myth, an ignorance of its development, and an equation of the *Argonautica* of Apollonius with some sort of official form of the story that can be used, by itself, to derive hidden truths encoded not in the poem but in the most ancient layers of the myth.

This chapter will examine theories serious and silly, ideological and idiotic proposed by people who really should have known better. Though they may teach us nothing about Jason or his myth cycle, they do provide a chilling insight into the way the past can be rewritten to support whatever beliefs one wishes it to confirm.

A Hero in Spirit

We will begin with an old pseudoscience, the idea that the stars determine our fates. Surprisingly, the idea of personalized, zodiac-based horoscopes dates only to around 500 BCE when the Babylonians began the practice.[1] They viewed the stars of Aries not as a ram but as a human (see below). Nevertheless, modern astrologers saw a link between Aries the constellation and Jason the hero through the Golden Fleece. Where Hellenistic scholars had used myths to explain the constellations in the night sky, modern astrologers reversed the equation and deduced that the stars under which a person is born influence their lives according to the patterns in the myths associated with them. Liz Green, who claims that astrology is a guide to one's fate, discussed the connection between those born under the sign of Aries and the mythic patterns in the story of Jason. For her, Jason's is an archetypical myth in which a young man overcomes powerful father figures through the help of his soul, represented by a sacred female, which empowers him to overthrow the old order. But Jason—and all born under Aries—suffer because they are too fiery to give proper reverence to their souls. Jason got bored with what he had (Medea), in her view, and simply wanted more and more to feed his ego. Therefore, Jason dies disgraced:

> I am not suggesting that the ignominiouss end of Jason is necessarily the fate of Aries. But his problem certainly is. It is ironic [...] that the young hero who battles the old Terrible Father to inaugurate a new order should repudiate his own inner feminine self in order to court the very collective power which he had previously undergone his quest to fight. [...] [B]y the end of his story, [Jason] has become himself the Terrible Father, and the *nemesis* which dogs him is that his own children are killed. On an inner level, perhaps this sad ending to a glorious tale is a necessary passage for Aries, before a new cycle begins and a new quest arises for a new fleece.[2]

Such ideas were a strange mixture of astrological nonsense, Joseph Campbell's monomyth, and feminist theory, all of which would, as we will see, reappear repeatedly in fringe theories about the Argonaut myth.

But, if one preferred, one could have a more literally godlike Jason if one is willing to accept some linguistic mixing and matching and resurrect the old idea that the pagan gods were part of an ancient sun cult. In *Suns of God* (2004), Acharya S (Dorothy M. Murdock) followed the almost two-century-old scholarly hypothesis of K. O. Müller which suggested that the Samothracian figure Eetion was the same as Jason due to shared etymology, and noted correctly that both Christianity and Greek paganism had mystery cults and secret doctrines. Acharya S was unaware, however, that the (real) Samothracian Mysteries were not original to the Argonauts' tale but added later, probably in substitution for the mysteries of the Cabeiri on Lemnos, which would likely have appeared in older versions of the myth. The author then went still further, conflating this (speculative) etymological connection with the Greeks' own transliteration of Yeshua into Jason, combining the completely separate ideas of etymology and transliteration into one conflated confectionary of speculation: "... 'Eetion,' the founder of the Samothracian mysteries is another name for Jason, i.e. Jesus. Hence Eetion/Jason is a pre–Christian Jesus who instituted some of the most famous mysteries, which in actuality differ little from the later Christian mythos and ritual."[3] That all of this was derived from Arthur Drews' *The Witnesses to the Historicity of Jesus* shows just how deeply the desire to provide any type of alternative support for Christian beliefs, even under the guise of New Age paganism, truly runs.

In 1994, playwright and screenwriter J. Nigro Sansonese offered a mystical take on the Argonauts' voyage based on the premise that Proto-Indo-Europeans had a religion based on shamanic trances, and that the myths of the peoples they spawned encoded shamanic trance material within them. This would superficially seem close to either Jung's collective unconscious or Lewis-Williams's idea of the neurobiological origins of myths in altered states of consciousness, such as trances. But unfortunately Sansonese means his trances to be encoded literally, including the nostrils used for rhythmic breathing. The fifty Argonauts represent for him the five senses, and the voyage to Colchis a "journey into trance, a withdrawal of the senses from the world." The *Argo* is therefore an "esoteric cranium" into which the senses retreat, just as in trance vision, smell, etc. turn off and retreat into the skull. The rowing of the Argonauts represents "alternate nostril breathing" in meditation, since the oars move along one side of the ship (= skull) and then the other. A great deal of more nasal-sinus imagery follows, since apparently the sinuses are the primary inspiration for ancient myth-makers.[4] The core idea is sound enough, given what we know about shamans and altered states of consciousness, but the elaboration and expression of the idea come close to the sublimely ridiculous.

A whiff of the ridiculous also hung over the more polemic uses to which the Jason myth has been twisted.

Mythic Propaganda

In two very different ways, propagandists looking to sell an ideology employed the Jason story as a mythic backdrop against which the superiority of modern society could be measured. The Soviet Union used Jason to demonstrate the greatness of its collective farming, while some feminists used Jason to criticize patriarchal society. In both cases, the myth had polemical value because it seemed useful as a tool against the negative aspects of Western civilization.

THE ARYAN GRAIL KNIGHTS

In the previous chapter I discussed the nineteenth-century theory that the Indo-European languages derived from a people known as the Aryans. The Victorians assumed that these people would have had a natural superiority over the races they conquered and must therefore have had a superior civilization, bringing the gifts of culture to India, Persia, and Greece. There was, of course, a very small step between these Aryans and the racist assumption that the Aryans were a milky white master race. The Nazis adopted this position as their official ideology; but unlike earlier scholars who placed the Aryan homeland in Eurasia (where Proto-Indo-Europeans are today still argued to have originated), the Nazis claimed that the Aryans originated in the mystical polar land of Thule before descending into Germany and spreading eastward before returning to the German homeland from Eurasia. They took great pains to show that the non–Aryan (i.e. non–German) cultures of the world were "really" Aryan or derived from Aryan sources, including Greece.

Heinrich Himmler of the SS oversaw the Nazis' effort to recreate the past in German style, and the medievalist SS Lt. Otto Rahn investigated the Holy Grail, arguing that it was in fact not a Christian relic but an Aryan one, a set of tablets inscribed with ancient Germanic runes which were identical with the medieval philosopher's stone, the key to the magic of alchemy. Now, since the Golden Fleece had been said by some of the alchemists and the tenth century Byzantines to have been a book of alchemy, in some contexts it began to be argued that the Fleece was identical with the philosopher's stone, and both were the sacred rune-strewn tablets of the master race. Rahn himself believed that the Argonaut legend, the Grail legend, and other tales all derived from an ancestral memory of journeys to the Aryan homeland, Thule, in an era when the North Pole was warm and welcoming. Rahn believed the Argonauts sailed in the North Atlantic, all the better to reach Thule.

In the 1988 novel *Focault's Pendulum*, Umberto Eco attributed the identity of Fleece and Grail to Rahn and then fancifully connected both to a Nazi super-weapon. Genealogist and alien theorist Laurence Gardner reaffirmed the identity of the two mystical ideas in his *Bloodline of the Holy Grail* (1996), which attempted to prove that his sponsor, a pretender to the British throne, was descended from Christ. Gardner later linked Christ to gold-eating aliens who were his ancestors. And of course conspiracy theorists saw in the knightly Order of the Golden Fleece a cover story for adepts seeking out the Grail and its occult secrets. Dutch journalist Philip Coppens claimed that the Golden Fleece was really the star Canopus, which apparently has some mystical connection to gold in ancient Egypt, because that star is in the constellation of Argo Navis,[5] which is of course Jason's boat. All of this was related to the Holy Grail and alchemy, tracing its origins, he said in *The Canopus Revelation* (2004), to Osiris' sacred ark (the constellation Argo Navis, of course, following Jacob Bryant's original identification) that ferried the dead and which allowed Osiris to gain resurrection and believers to commune with the god via a "star gate" around Canopus to become immortal themselves. I suppose it is at least mildly interesting that Fontenrose saw Jason's *Argo* as a ship of the dead, and the Egyptians saw the constellation Argo Navis as one, too; or at least it would be if the Egyptians had recognized Argo Navis as a constellation prior to the coming of the Greeks, which cannot be proved.[6]

The idea that the quest for the Fleece inspired the quest for the Grail was not new; it had been suggested since the nineteenth century, and the Argonaut myth had served as a template for medieval Grail poets like Chrétien de Troyes. What was new was the linkage of Fleece, Grail, alchemy, conspiracy, and aliens.

COMRADE JASON

In the Middle Ages Colchis had been absorbed into Georgia, and Georgia fell to the Russian Empire in 1801. Upon the Communist revolution of 1917, Georgia passed to the Soviet Union, eventually promoted to a full Soviet Socialist Republic. The Soviets adopted the Jason myth as a symbol of the glory and greatness of Communist rule over Colchis. We have already seen the movies the Soviets made to that end. In his popular 1948 work on the Communist empire, *Soviet Russia: The Land and Its People*, Nicholas Mikhailov wrote: "The inhabitants of Soviet Colchis have no need for a Golden Fleece, their gold is in the wonderful land that has been made so fertile by the climate and the toil of generations of farmers."[7] More to the point, Soviet educators in the 1940s taught students for ideological reasons that the true meaning of the Golden Fleece was that it represented the golden wheat growing in Colchis,[8] which they used as a propaganda tool to promote Soviet collective farms and provide collective farmers in the USSR's most fertile region with a noble and honorable mythic past. In this view, the hated West, represented by Jason, had come to the glorious land of the Soviets because of their inherent superiority in farming even in the most ancient of days. It hardly hurt that the dictator of the Soviet Union, Joseph Stalin, was from Georgia himself. However, it should not be thought that only the Soviets saw their political reflection in Colchis; European archaeologists of the era tended to favor the work of Judith Bacon, which identified the Golden Fleece with the amber trade and conveniently connected the Argonauts back to the heart of Western Europe, the source of ancient amber.

After the fall of the Soviet Union, the new Republic of Georgia inherited the Argonauts as its mythic history, but still a tool of the state, given official status because of its utility to a particular power structure—almost the antithesis of the vitality, adaptability, and multivalent meanings of ancient myth. Georgian scholars have attempted to connect the Argonauts to many aspects of Georgian history and have promoted the idea that the Greek language derived from an early Georgian language (both are Indo-European tongues, though most scholars deny a direct derivation of one from the other), its myths from Georgian myths. According to Tbilisi University professor Gia Kvashilava of the grandly named Aia-Colchis Center for the Colchian-Iberian Ethno-Cultural Scientific Research, on uncertain evidence of his own decipherment of the undeciphered Linear A, the Minoans spoke Colchian.[9] Today, the Argonaut story is a tourist draw. In the coastal city of Batumi, in Colchis, a large statue of Medea stands on a pedestal in Freedom Square in the center of the city. The elongated female figure presents the Golden Fleece, gilded, in her right hand. Unveiled by Georgia's president in 2007, the 1 million Georgian lari (about $500,000) sculpture by Davit Khmaladze was intended to commemorate "the person who brought Georgia closer to Europe," according to the city's mayor.[10] Apparently, they have forgiven her for abandoning Colchis.

JASON AND THE PATRIARCHY

Georgia was not alone in celebrating Medea; feminists adopted her as their own. We have already mentioned the medieval upset over Jason's faithlessness, and this thread found its way into contemporary feminist interpretations of the Jason myth. I have previously mentioned that an overwhelming amount of scholarly work has focused on Medea. At the extreme end of this spectrum sit certain feminist theories which I emphasize are by no means mainstream. I include one particular version under unsupported theories because it is extreme enough to serve almost as parody of feminist literary readings. This particular theory, from former lawyer turned writer Craig S. Barnes, attempts to read the Jason myth as a sustained attack on feminine power, which he believes had been embodied in an earth-based, matriarchal goddess religion prior to the coming of the Zeus-worshipping Indo-Europeans and their oppressive, patriarchal culture designed to force free and independent women into unhappy, slave-like marriages (as though the Indo-Europeans were only men, or the people they encountered only women). Myths like that of Jason existed solely to establish "sons in their property rather than daughters in their fertility," through male adventurers deemed "the heroes of the early patriarchy." Specifically, Jason existed to "disparage women-centered culture."[11]

Barnes argued that Medea was a representative of the "old religions" that the Greeks feared for their feminine power. Jason must retrieve the Golden Fleece, seen as a "patriarchal charter" of kingship that evil males cut from a "spiritually conscious" ram, from the naughty feminists in order to legitimate his Indo-European supremacy over the goddess peoples. In this view, such feminist, matrilineal outposts as Lemnos must be passed by to reach another outpost of patriarchy, Colchis, to prove Jason's right to kingship by returning to the homeland of the Indo-European peoples and the font of male-supremacist ideology.[12]

As with nearly every theory we have examined, there is a core of truth: that within the Jason story are remnants of the older layers of Aegean or Near Eastern religious traditions, before the supremacy of Zeus, including a time when an earth goddess was a powerful focus of religious life; and that archaeological evidence indicates no differentiation between the status of men and women at that time, implying a more equal society. But this kernel has been fertilized and watered until it blossomed into a theory more exuberant than evidence can support. This is no examination of ancient attitudes toward gender relations and the ideal organization of society; it is contemporary political ideology masquerading as scholarship and projected onto a past that operated under very different rules from contemporary Western society.

Sailing to Atlantis

If the Soviets and extreme feminists sought to adopt the Argonaut story as proof of their alternatives to Western capitalist, patriarchal society, another group would desperately try to use Jason to bolster that same society by employing him as a prop for imperialist and colonialist ideologies remade in new clothes. The European empires of the modern era had incorporated an ideology of superiority that found its roots in scientific racism, Aryan supremacy, and the raw authority of European military rule over subject peoples. That many, if not most, of the most bizarre ideas about Jason's myth and mission originated in the nineteenth century is no coincidence; they were derived from and reflected the imperial and colonial ideology of empire, even if their latter-day proponents are unaware of this and adamantly deny any such connection.

The European empires collapsed in the twentieth century, but the ideologies they left behind—specifically the idea that native peoples were incapable of monumental achievements—continued on. Divorced from the imperial context, the idea of a superior group who gave culture and civilization to the inferior races was etherealized and projected backward in time to a civilization like Atlantis, outward toward non–European cultures such as sub–Saharan Africa, or upward toward space aliens. We will begin with Atlantis and parallel lost civilizations.

OFF TO THE AMERICAS

Surprisingly, the monuments of nineteenth-century pseudoscience and silliness, Helena Blavatsky's theosophical treatises and Ignatius Donnelly's study of *Atlantis: The Antediluvian World*, contain only the barest references to the Argonauts, a situation doubly surprising in the latter case since a supposed record of an epochal sea voyage would be just the sort of "evidence" that a writer would love to use to support the reality of Atlantis as a maritime power. However, in seeking Atlantis, William Stephens Blacket claimed in 1884 that Colchis was in Peru, the Inca were the true denizens of Colchis, and Jason trained with Chiron among the Maya on the strength of old Classical dictionaries rather than primary sources. Archaeology would prove these speculations off by about two thousand years.[13] This situation is probably due to the lack of English translations of Apollonius' *Argonautica* and therefore the relative obscurity of the details of the Jason myth beyond Classical scholars. With only a general idea of the story from mythological guidebooks, most purveyors of pseudoscience dared not make statements that a consultation of the ancient texts could contradict. Once good quality translations became available, suddenly Jason became a voyager to lost Atlantis.

Megalithic architecture reminiscent of Mycenaean style and the solar religion of Tiwanaku in Bolivia, embodied in the Gate of the Sun seen here, convinced Henrietta Mertz that the Argonauts' sun-kingdom of Colchis was actually at this Andean site. Earlier speculators also identified Colchis with Peru, where the Inca had enormous reserves of gold. However, there is no evidence of any connection between Greece and prehistoric America. The Inca and the Tiwanaku people were thousands of years too late to have been part of the Argonauts' adventure (Library of Congress).

Henriette Mertz (1898–1985) was a World War II-era code breaker and a patent attorney. She turned in the 1960s to solving the mystery of the ancient past and "discovered," like Blacket before her, that the ancient Greek myths were garbled discussions of actual voyages to the New World. Thus, unaware of Homer's borrowings from body of Argonaut myths, she took the *Odyssey* at face value and claimed Odysseus sailed into the North Atlantic, placing Scylla and Charybdis in Nova Scotia's Bay of Fundy. She also argued that Jason and the Argonauts sailed across the Atlantic Ocean to South America, travelling down the continent's coast to reach the Rio de la Plata in Argentina, up which they sailed to reach the Paraguay River, which carried them upland to the Altiplano in Bolivia, where they encounter the ancient monumental stone city of Tiwanaku, whose golden treasures were the Golden Fleece.

The logical leaps are staggering. First, there being no definitive catalog of the Argonauts' travels, and their most common forms arrived at through accretion and poetic license, any assumed textual basis for this fantasy is entirely the subjective interpretation of the author. It would also be an astonishing feat for the Argonauts to have encountered

Tiwanaku, since archaeology holds that the city was but a tiny agricultural village in 1500 BC and only built its monumental stone structures after 500 CE Nevertheless, Mertz's claims were repeated by credulous writers for decades, with the fringe history writer and *Ancient Aliens* pundit David Hatcher Childress, who never met a myth he failed to take literally, calling her work "scholarly" and chiding "myopic scholars" for daring to place Jason's voyage in the Black Sea, "a nearby location that every local sailor would have visited, and hardly the stuff of epic voyages to the ends of the world."[14] How little Childress knows of the Greek world or the gradual expansion of geographic knowledge between the Bronze Age and today.

At least, however, these authors were generally close to the Late Bronze Age. The Russian writer Nicholas A. Zhirov gathered masses of data in 1970 to "prove" Atlantis existed. He concluded, based again on the assumption that Apollonius' poem is synonymous with the Platonic ideal of the Jason myth, or at least its original form, that the Argonauts entered the Black Sea around 3000 BCE the last time that the Bosporus was geologically dangerous enough to give rise to the myth of Clashing Rocks[15]—never mind that these rocks were only associated with that location millennia later!

Apropos of nothing, the Latvian-born law professor Andis Kaulins, who once claimed on his self-titled website to be the "best in the world—ever"[16] (seriously) at deciphering ancient mysteries that hated "scholars and experts" cannot, proposed that the ancients had used astronomy to measure the world and encoded their advanced science in the myth of Jason and the Argonauts on the supposition that the Greek word *argos* meant "earth" and "clay" as well as "ship." Under this idea, Jason and the Argonauts were scientists who travelled the world to map its surface (as Newton had thought), recording their findings on megalithic stones across Great Britain, including maps of unexplored continents such as Africa. All this was done under the supervision of Merlin the Magician, who (but of course) was also King Narmer of Egypt and the Greek Asclepius and thus rode on the *Argo* (!). According to Kaulins, the Argonauts were (emphasis his) "the *first men* to ever conduct a *geodetic survey of earth by astronomy*."[17]

JASON VS. THE VOLCANO

In 1969 J. V. Luce and James Watt Mavor both published books arguing (apparently independently) that Atlantis was Minoan Crete and that Apollonius of Rhodes encoded a memory of the eruption of the volcano that destroyed the island of Thera around 1600 BCE the event that triggered the "end of Atlantis."[18] This evidence takes the form of the bronze man Talos, whom both viewed as representing the volcano on Thera since the bronze giant, crafted by the volcano god Hephaestus, threw rocks at the Argonauts just as the volcano spewed pumice, his hot flowing ichor representing lava. This shows an astounding lack of insight into the origins and development of the Talos myth, and also begs us to ask whether the Cyclops Polyphemus must therefore also be a volcano since he too threw rocks. But what then of the actual volcanoes in Greek myth? Both authors further correlate the Thera eruption to the legend of the Argonaut Euphemus, whom Triton gave a clod of earth to found an island, which became Thera. A small island has recently appeared in the crater left by the volcano's devastation of Thera. Mavor writes: "Geologically, there is good reason to believe that similar growth also took place before the great eruption, and this is what the Argonauts may have seen."[19] Even as a rationalization, there seems to be a vast gap between growing a clod of earth into the island of Thera and the growth of the existing island—which at any rate would have taken place on a geological timescale and simply could not be "seen" to grow by a passing ship. But, in the eternal maxim that no idea ever truly dies, this one continues to be repeated even today despite the overwhelming evidence that Atlantis was entirely the product of Plato's imagination.[20]

INTO AFRICA

If some Atlantis theories were mythologized versions of Western colonialism, another set of theories sought to reverse the equation and ascribe the triumphs of the West to the world's oppressed people in a bid to correct the power imbalance. Early on the Afrocentrist Drusilla Dunjee Houston claimed that the Golden Ram had been an airplane invented by Ethiopians, who were also the "black" people of Colchis.[21] Afrocentric theorists took at face value the statements of Herodotus about Egyptians in Colchis (repeated by Apollonius, with a colorful detail about hieroglyphs and stone-carved sea maps),[22] and on no more evidence than the ancient historian's word—and often in the face of facts—they recreated Jason and the Argonauts as a testament to the Greeks' cognitive debt to the "superior" cultures of Africa, especially Egypt. These theorists combined Herodotus' observation that the Colchians had Egyptian ancestors with the conventional adjective used to describe the Colchians and the peoples of the east—black—to conclude that Africans settled Colchis. In the most ancient sources, the farthest east is considered the home of "black" people because it is where the sun rose, burning the skins of those who lived closest to the sun, a description Apollonius repeats. However, in ancient times it was well known that the people surrounding the Greek colony of Phasis, the Colchians, were fair of skin like the other peoples of the Caucasus Mountains. The conventional description of "black" (actually "dark") skin referred to the old mythological conception of black people living in the farthest east (and also west) where the sun came closest to the earth. The same word was also used to describe the olive complexion of some Greeks, who today would be classified as "white."

The Afrocentric scholar John G. Jackson, author of *Man, God, and Civilization* (1972), mostly refuted his own argument in 1987 in answering a sympathetic interviewer's question about the presence of Africans in Colchis:

> The ancient Egyptians invaded [Colchis] under a pharaoh known as Sesostris. An Egyptian army under this pharaoh established a colony there. This area has been called the 'Black Soviet' because there are so many Black people living down there. Of course they tell you in the history books that these people are the descendants of slaves that the Russians imported in the Middle Ages. But if this territory was settled by the Egyptians in ancient times, then these people are probably their descendants.[23]

The slipshod scholarship is evident in the reliance on Herodotus as the primary source for the Egyptian presence in Colchis, as well as the rejection of conventional understanding of the African presence in Georgia. There are no widespread black populations, only a small population, perhaps as few as thirty individuals, as conceded even by those most sympathetic to the idea that Africans and Colchians are one.[24] Obviously, as Martin W. Lewis and Kären Wigen so astutely noted, for these few Africans to have been remnants of an Egyptian army of the Bronze Age, we would need to assume an army primarily of Africans, including black women, who lived thousands of years in a land of non–Africans without ever interbreeding and while maintaining a viable reproductive population within their group, which by the twentieth century numbered between thirty and two hundred.[25] The so-called "Black Colchians" themselves knew the truth and told those willing to listen: They were a remnant population of Ottoman-era slaves. Early ethnographies and genealogies confirmed this fact, and archaeology says no different.[26]

Sesostris was probably based on the exploits of Ramses II, Sensuset I, and the Nubian conquests of the Middle Kingdom pharaoh Senusret III (c. 1870–1831 BCE), around whom the deeds of the Middle Kingdom coalesced as a composite semi-legendary figure.[27] However, no modern resarcher has found any evidence of an Egyptian pharaoh conquering lands any farther north than the Euphrates, and the Afrocentrist scholars seem largely uninterested in investigating Herodotus' composite Sesostris, simply presuming that the story is *prima facie* true—a hallmark of pseudoscience—and that the pharaoh must be one of the four pharaohs Senusret, whose names were transliterated into Greek as Sesostris. Like so much in Herodotus, this story is an exaggeration combined with a dose of myth. Unfortunately, this myth still finds uncritical adherents today.

As a consequence of the Afrocentric belief that the Colchians were Egyptians, and the facile equation of Egypt (a Near East culture) with all of Africa (a geographic expression with several distinct and unrelated cultural regions), some Afrocentric scholars have sought to portray Jason and the Argonauts as an adventure derived from Egyptian sources, thus proving Greece's inferiority to African culture. This manifested in a strange article by R. A. Jairazbhoy who attempted to argue that most elements in the Jason story are Egyptian in nature. First, he claims that the Golden Ram overseen by a watchful serpent is an image that "occurs nowhere else" but on the prow of a ship belonging to Ramses III (reigned c. 1186–1155 BCE), where a ram's head was overseen by a sacred serpent, a uraeus, used in Egyptian royal iconography.[28] He then links the Golden Fleece to Egyptian worship of the sacred ram of Ammon, again on Herodotus' word. Aeëtes as the son of Helios is likened to the "exclusive title in antiquity of the Pharaohs of Egypt," the son of the Sun.[29] He concludes by, correctly (!) noting that the land of Aea is connected to the sun god and exists on the edge of Ocean. He then mistakenly links both to Ramses III's ram-headed boat and the Egyptian belief in an all-encompassing river Ocean.

Needless to say, the children of the Near East's other sun gods would be shocked to know that only the pharaohs were ever named sons of the Sun. The Greeks had not just Aeëtes as the child of the sun but also Phaëton. Some Mesopotamian kings counted themselves as children of Shamash, the sun god, and went by the name "son of the sun," along with symbolic filial relationships to other gods. All this is to say that the Afrocentric interpretation gets one thing right and many things very wrong. The theorists correctly see in Jason's story a common Near Eastern heritage of symbols and ideas, including solar imagery and ram imagery. But they fail in their preconceived notion that Egypt is the font of such images. Therefore, they neglect to go farther and seek out any sort of demonstrable connection between the myth and the Egyptians. This they cannot prove, and the weight of scholarly evidence favors Mesopotamian, Levantine, and Anatolian influence on Greek myth before that of Egypt, despite Herodotus' claims about the Egyptian origins of Greek culture and religion.[30]

The ancient Greeks said that the Golden Ram was placed among the stars as the constellation Aries, seen here in an 1825 illustration, and astrologers applied its name to a house of the zodiac. However, the original zodiac of the Babylonians viewed the constellation as the "Agrarian Worker," who was later associated with Dumuzi, the dying and rising shepherd-consort of Inanna. It is through him that the constellation became a sheep and then the Golden Ram (Library of Congress).

THE STAR-SEEKER

Two authors who cannot be accused of failing to take a cross-cultural view of mythology are Giorgio de Santillana, a professor of the history of science at MIT, and Hertha von Dechend, a German scientist and professor, neither of whom were experts in ancient history or mythology before claiming to have discovered in *Hamlet's Mill* (1969) that all world mythologies derived from a single, highly advanced scientific civilization around 4000 BCE. This they derived from the notion that most world mythologies are primarily astronomical in character and describe precession, which refers to the fact that due to the slight wobble of the earth's axis, the position of the stars in the sky appears to rotate backward about one degree of arc every seventy-two years relative to a fixed point on the horizon, completing a circuit roughly every twenty-six thousand years. This means that every few millennia, the sun will appear to rise against a new constellation of the zodiac thanks to the slow drifting of the stars.

Mercifully, most of their complex mythological mess is far beyond our scope. Suffice it to note that the authors assume that because the Argonauts were after the Golden Fleece of a "ram" their mission was "undertaken in all probability to introduce the Age of Aries,"[31] which in astrological terms coincided with the Bronze Age. Never mind that the familiar set of twelve equally divided zodiac constellations cannot be shown to go back much before seventh century BCE Babylon,[32] and other cultures assigned different creatures and whole constellations to the sky[33]—or that Aries was not at first a ram at all but a human character known officially as the "Hired Man" or "hireling." Ironically, the Babylonians eventually saw Aries as Dumuzi, the dying-and-rising god, but they had only created the constellation around 1500 BCE it is not especially ancient. Apparently Dumuzi's status as a shepherd, possibly along with a cuneiform pun between the abbreviations for "Hired Man" and "ram," contributed to the transformation of Aries into a ram when adopted into the Greek astronomical system, which developed in the form we know it today no earlier than 540 BCE.[34]

That the Greeks envisioned their myths written in the stars proves not that star scientists designed the myths but that the Greeks projected their myths into the sky, and also that bulls (Taurus), serpents (Draco), and boats (Argo) are fairly common objects. If characters from the *Argonautica*, including the *Argo*, Heracles, Castor and Pollux, a ram, a bull, etc., are in the sky, it is much more likely that the fame of the myth identified them with Babylonian constellations the Greeks adopted relatively late than that a secret cabal from a lost civilization designed a myth from characters they sprinkled among the stars and kept the knowledge secret for millennia. After all, Jason and Medea are absent from the night sky, and one might reasonably expect these most important figures to have, well, *figured* into the celestial scheme if the Argonaut myth were that important to the skies.

Jason in Outer Space

If de Santillana and von Dechend could imagine Jason as intimately tied to the drama of the stars, it surely should surprise no one that authors less scrupulous than they would seek to connect Jason to the most celestial of the twentieth century's pantheon of imaginary beings, space aliens. Beginning in the 1960s a series of writers began claiming that ancient history, especially monumental architecture and sacred texts, was really the record of visitations from advanced beings from distant galaxies who, depending on the writer, civilized humanity, built pyramids, mined the earth for gold, or genetically engineered the human race. Forms of this theory had been around for many years; Helena Blavatsky's followers imagined spiritual beings from Venus coming to earth to civilize men, though they were closer to angels than aliens. The modern version of the story was little more than colonialist-imperialist myth-making projected into space. The essence of this theory was twofold: First, that ancient monuments were too perfectly constructed and their stones too heavy for "primitive" savages to have hewn and built; and second, that these primitive savages were unimaginative clods whose mythology simply recorded for all time literal records of the arrival and departure of alien spaceships and the advanced technology they brought. Needless to say, only the so-called "ancient astronaut theorists" had the brilliance to understand the aliens on their own level.

THE SIRIUS MISERY

The foremost practitioner of this theory was the Swiss hotelier Erich von Däniken; however, he initially concerned himself primarily with Egypt and the Americas, and it was another writer, Robert Charroux, who first shot Jason into space, claiming in 1972 that the Golden Ram was an alien airship whose wreckage, the Fleece, the Colchians venerated.[35] On the heels of this, in 1976, Robert Temple (b. 1945) published *The Sirius Mystery*, which he had begun at the age of 22. This book claimed that a group of African tribesman, the Dogon, knew before Western scientists that the star Sirius is in fact two stars that orbit each other, a fact they inherited from their ancestors, the Argonauts, who brought it to Africa on their wanderings, having learned it from the Sumerians, who in turn derived it from amphibious extraterrestrials from a planet orbiting Sirius. These space frogs pretended to be gods, and they were worshipped as Oannes, the Babylonian fish-man hybrid deity recorded by Berossus.[36] It is beyond our scope to evaluate the entirety of Temple's thesis except to note that more recent studies of the Dogon failed to confirm any anomalous knowledge of Sirius among the tribe,[37] so the house of cards he built upon that foundation cannot stand.

The allegedly esoteric knowledge the space frogs gave the Sumerians was that their home star was a double star, containing a bright Sirius A, and a smaller, darker Sirius B which orbits Sirius A in a period lasting fifty years. For Temple, the *Argo* represents the orbit of Sirius B, with the fifty Argonauts corresponding to the fifty years. These Argonauts, originally nameless, are therefore identical to the fifty Annunaki of Sumerian myth (never mind that their number is usually not fifty), who are also symbols for Sirius B. He also argued that Jason's quest was inherently Egyptian, involving "sacred puns" that transformed straightforward Egyptian terms into Greek through fanciful descriptions of the picture-based hieroglyphics used to write them. Thus he equates the Greek word for "fleece" with the Egyptian term for the sun god Horus, the terms for dragon's teeth with a hieroglyphic pun for the "Goddess Sirius," etc. Needless to say, Temple also imagines that the *Argo* is related to the Ark, and that both derive from an Egyptian term meaning "the end of things," the conclusion of Sirius B's orbit. On the authority of Herodotus, Temple links Colchis and Circe to Egypt, and he derives great pleasure from some amateur etymologies intended to provide the Egyptian origin of Circe's name. However, Temple also believed that Jason was a late intruder in a myth that was told earlier of Heracles, and before that of Briareus, a fifty-headed monster, who (of course) is also Sirius B. Temple also, perhaps partly contradicting himself, identifies Jason with Gilgamesh, who in the oldest Sumerian sources also had fifty companions, who are once again the fifty years of Sirius B in their purest form, as the space frogs had given it to the Sumerians themselves.[38]

All of this was presented with a plethora of footnotes and a patina of scholarship, leading many who should have known better to take Temple's work quite seriously. The paucity of his true scholarship was evident in the fact that Temple's citations to the Argonaut myth derived entirely from Robert Graves's faulty *Greek Myths*, on whose authority Temple proclaimed the identity of Jason, Heracles, Briareus, and Gilgamesh—subtlety and complexity be damned. Worse, Temple confuses Graves's retelling of Jason for some sort of "official" version of the myth, though it would seem logical that any ancient Sumerian space science should best be preserved in the *oldest* Jason myths, not in the homogenized modern forms.

It is simply inconceivable how one could take a modern retelling of a late version of a Greek myth as incontrovertible evidence that the Dogon are the flesh-and-blood descendants of Jason's Argonauts, but there you have it. Apparently when Jason landed in Libya, he left behind colonists who migrated southward, preserving of Greek culture only the secret knowledge that the space frogs whispered about the double nature of the star Sirius—not the Greek language, not Greek myth, not writing, only the secret of the space frogs. This is proved not by the Dogon but because Robert Graves quoted an anthropologist who claimed that the *neighbors* of the Dogon came to Ghana due to migrations of *non-Greeks* southward from Libya after Greek colonization. Temple expands Graves's citation beyond the evidence:

> There is something incredible in the survival of the Argonauts in the obscure reaches of the French Sudan. These people, which I assume must include the Dogon as well as their immediate southern neighbors [...], seem to be descendants of Lemnian Greeks who claimed to be the grandsons of the actual Argonauts. It almost seems too amazing to be true, that we should have begun this book by considering a strange African tribe, then considered similar Sirius traditions in the Mediterranean stemming from Ancient Egypt, and then be led back again to the African tribe whom we discover to be directly descended from the Mediterranean peoples privy to the Sirius complex![39]

That, in essence, is the definition of circular reasoning. Temple's own statements proved their falsity; their logic is ridiculous. His argument rests entirely on false or incorrect etymologies, Robert Graves's view of myths, and a heavy dose of gullibility. Nevertheless, in a dark and disturbing development, Temple's book-length discussion of Jason and the Argonauts and space aliens was for many years the single longest and most detailed popular interpretation and analysis of the Jason myth readily accessible to non-academic readers. Hidden behind the veneer of scholarship, the misuse and abuse of the myth went largely unnoticed amidst the battles over the existence or non-existence of amphibious space frogs, who still have adherents today. *The Sirius Mystery*, with poor Jason roped inside, is a standard reference work for New Age and UFO writers, who believe, even today, that it is a monument of scholarly investigation.

INVASION OF THE ALIEN ROBOTS

Robert Temple's book was disturbing because it had pretensions to scholarship and wore its linguistic erudition as a badge of pride, bolstered by the author's trumpeted membership in such groups as the Royal Astronomical Society and Classicist organizations, which he declined to reveal to readers were actually open to anyone who paid the entrance fee. No such troubles cloud the blue skies of Erich von Däniken's world. Since the 1960s, he has published dozens of books "investigating" the "mystery" of ancient astronauts, but it was only in 1999 that he turned his attention to Greece and brought Jason into his elaborate, if highly speculative and sometimes fraudulent,[40] world of extraterrestrial secrets.

In *The Odyssey of the Gods: The Alien History of Ancient Greece* (1999, English translation 2000), von Däniken uses the tale of Jason as a springboard for his exploration of aliens in ancient Greece. For von Däniken, the "gods" of Greece were aliens, and Greek myths are the records of their actions. He has no truck with the idea that the Argonauts went on a voyage "in the quest of a ridiculous bit of fur."[41] On his unshakeable faith that myth recorded literal history, von Däniken asserts that the Golden Fleece was in fact an airplane or helicopter belonging to the alien astronaut Hermes. The sleepless dragon is "really" a robot with always-vigilant motion sensors, which von Däniken oddly thinks spew fire. Medea's ointment for Jason is a futuristic "heat shield." That the *Argo* has a pilot fascinates the author, who, unaware that the term applied to ships before airplanes, thinks it is a veiled reference to the *Argo*'s origins as an alien flying machine. The talking beam from Dodona is obviously a communication device to the alien mother ship. Jason was raised by a mutant horse-man created by rebel aliens who genetically engineered hybrid monsters. And of course Talos is a robot built by aliens. The irrepressible David Childress seemed to agree in *Technology of the Gods* (2000). I could go on listing these imaginary correlations, but they are obviously nothing more than a fancied similarity between an ancient word or image and some piece of twentieth-century technology, free-association of a fact-free sort. That did not stop the History Channel from broadcasting these ideas as fact, without rebuttal, in a 2010 episode of *Ancient Aliens* that told viewers thundering Zeus was a laser-wielding alien, the gods' palace on Olympus a flying saucer, and mythic monsters extraterrestrial genetic experiments.

The theme of Talos as a robot is perennially popular, mostly due to Ray Harryhausen's depiction of him as one in the 1963 *Jason* movie, though scattered references to him as a robot seem to begin in 1950s science fiction magazines. (There is, of course, a difference between saying he is akin to a modern robot, as those writers and some scholars do, and saying he was a real, extant robot built by aliens or Atlanteans.) A 2007 book by Brian Haughton called him "the first fully operational robot in history," though attributing the claim to unnamed "proponents" who calculated Talos' top speed at 155 miles per hour to make his three daily circuits of Crete.[42] Never mind that his status as metallic was ancient linguistic confusion over being the last survivor of the Bronze Age, not originally made from bronze; and never mind that he was probably first a Cretan sun god and not an artifact of alien technology. A. B. Cook more parsimoniously explained the poetic description of vein and ichor as an image of the lost wax bronze-casting technique, whereby core of the mold of a bronze statue was extracted through holes in the soles of the statue's feet, the bronze support pin holding the whole together being analogous to Talos' single vein. Thus, when the poets decided Talos was a man of bronze, they chose to envision him as a gigantic bronze statue in the manner in which the ancients were accustomed to creating such statues.[43]

In the 1996 book *Architects of the Underworld*, Bruce Rux reported that not only was Talos a robot, but he is one of a series of alien-crafted automatons dating back to ancient Sumer. These robots came to earth on UFOs, and the myth of Jason and the Argonauts is, in his view, intimately connected with worldwide myths of dying-and-rising gods and the division of the world between the eastern lands of men and the western underworld beyond the River Ocean. This is not, however, the land of the dead across the great sea that we have explored in this volume. Instead, "Since 'sea' or 'ocean' can also mean '[outer] space,' and there is no up or down in space, it is certainly possible that this Underworld is actually beneath the earth—another planet."[44] Because this Underworld is associated with the west and the color red (usually thought to be the sunset) it must therefore be the planet Mars, home to alleged alien monuments. The aliens' robots, masquerading as gods, promote the bodily resurrection of the dead through cloning and take tissue samples into deep space for cloning (since bodily transport requires too much fuel) so the dead may live with them amidst power and glory forever and ever. Red is closely associated with white and black in alien cosmology, so therefore, such figures as (and I am not making this up) the Red Cross, the country of Japan, Easter Island's statues, and Santa Claus are all part of the aliens' secret plans directed from their Martian base.[45] Poor Jason was apparently a distorted memory, since *Argo* = Ark, of Noah's or Utnapishtim's space ark fleeing Mars for earth at the time of cosmic destruction of that planet's habitable surface. Naturally, Rux claims that Jason the

Healer was the equivalent of Jesus, with Colchis's Grove of Ares proving the divine extra-terrestrials' link to the red planet Mars.[46] Both Colchis and Mars share monumental sym-bolism, since Colchis was an Egyptian colony under the protection of the falcon (thanks, Herodotus), and Mars has a hawk-sphinx sculpture on the pyramid fields of Cydonia, some-thing NASA tries very hard to prevent the common folk from knowing, claiming such mon-uments are merely natural phenomena or artifacts of low resolution photography. The nerve!

Naturally, UFO researchers are certain that such organizations as NASA, the Illuminati, and the Freemasons are working together to prevent the aliens' ancient secrets from getting out to the general public. These conspiracy theorists have read much into the JASON Group, an advisory body of scientists established by the United States government in 1960 and orig-inally named Project Sunrise. Mildred Goldberger, the wife of a founding member, thought the moniker was bland and proposed naming the group after an adventuresome hero to rep-resent the group's quest for scientific knowledge. From this, conspiracy theorists led by the right-wing ufologist Milton William Cooper have imagined a shadowy "JASON Society" whose mythological patron was carefully selected to reinforce its clandestine ties to the Illu-minati, a global elitist conspiracy which they see as the Cosmic Serpent, and also to extra-terrestrials. Such theorists believe President Dwight Eisenhower commissioned the JASON Group and JASON Society to uncover the truth about alien visitations (which is ridiculous, since the government already had the information from the Roswell spaceship, according to the same theorists!) and prepare America for contact with outer space. The thirty-two mem-ber Society's leaders are alleged to be the Majestic 12 (MJ-12), who run the government's extraterrestrial liaison program, according to documents that must be true because they were posted on the internet.[47] The Society killed John F. Kennedy, using his own chauffeur to shoot him in Dallas, when he found out about their activities, which they had been clan-destinely funding by running the world's drug cartels, with the side benefit of using the drugs to eliminate unwanted minority groups.[48]

According to Cooper's internet posting, under the leadership of the JASON Society, one in every forty Americans has been abducted by aliens and implanted with sinister tech-nology, apparently under a plan approved by President George H. W. Bush. The conspiracy silenced Cooper in 2001, when he was killed in a shootout with Arizona police attempting to arrest him on a complaint that he threatened passersby with a gun. As Nicholas Goodrick-Clarke noted, such conspiracy theories related to the Illuminati reflect a real fear among cer-tain groups that "the awesome power of interlocking elites" is being used in ways they do not understand to shape their lives without their consent, and identifying such actors is an important tool for forging a group identity through a shared mythology.[49]

The maddening thing about the extreme theories of Jason and the Argonauts is that most had a little grain of truth buried in them. Bruce Rux's ideas emerge from a plausible reading of the Jason myth as a type of katabasis, but then they run off the rails imagining the Underworld as an actual, real-life rocket trip into deep space with alien robot pilots. Robert Temple's theories were predicated on the sensible observation of Near East influence on the Jason story, but then fly off the handle in presuming an origin for it in amphibious space frogs from Sirius. J. Nigro Sansonese noticed the similarity of Jason to the dreamscape of altered states of consciousness, but then expanded the idea into a ridiculous theory about nostrils. Craig S. Barnes correctly intuited the Indo-European and non–Indo-European min-gling of elements in the Jason story, but then spun them into an ideological battle between patriarchy and matriarchy that was in all likelihood quite secondary to other forces and factors in Bronze Age cultural transformation.

In their strange and twisted way, however, these extreme theories attempted to recapture something of the power and magic of ancient myth that had been lost in the scholarly and scientific arguments that such stories were little more than distorted history or primitive superstition or nature worship. The grand progress of science had stripped the supernatural of much of its force, and more than a few observers have noted that extraterrestrials and UFOs have taken the place of angels and Greek gods as both a modern mythology and a method by which individuals can experience transcendence and a sense of the divine in a world increasingly beholden to materialist forces.[50] The belief in aliens allowed a subset of believers to imbue ancient texts with new power, though at the cost of rendering their symbolic and spiritual meanings into cruder, literal records of extraterrestrial visitation. The aliens were substitute gods in an age of science, the supernatural made material.

In the end, therefore, the oddest of the modern interpretations of the Jason myth did the most to overturn three millennia of scholarly investigation that had stripped the magic and wonder from the story. These alien-inspired theories, as improbable and ridiculous as they may seem, called back to a different age, when the gods still walked the earth and the world was alive with magic and power. At some time, on some dark Bronze Age night, someone started to tell a tale of a hero who set out on a voyage over the sea and battled monsters to win the hand of a goddess. It was an old story, and familiar, but this time something was a little different, and for some unfathomable reason we will never know, Jason set off on an epic voyage over the seas and across the millennia.

Conclusion

The myth of Jason, like those of so many Greek heroes, lacks a truly heroic ending. Valerius Flaccus died without providing one, and Apollonius of Rhodes chose to end his *Argonautica* with the Argonauts' return to Greece rather that tell the story through to the sad end. Pindar has no interest in the story's end, irrelevant as it was to his purpose. Instead, we are left with two final images of Jason. The kinder version, he sits beneath the rotting hull of the *Argo* dreaming of past glories when a chunk of the old ship falls off and crushes him to death. In the other, distraught over the deaths of his fiancée and children at the hands of Medea, he kills himself in desperation and grief. Few of the Greek heroes had heroic fates. Theseus lost popularity in Athens and died when Lycomedes of Syros pushed him off a cliff. Achilles died when the cowardly Paris struck him in the heel with an arrow—and dead Achilles had to spend eternity in Elysium with Medea as wife. Bellerophon tried to scale Olympus and was punished by spending the rest of his miserable life a lonely, blind cripple. In his inglorious end, Jason was therefore something of a typical Greek hero, though it is perhaps a small mercy that the Greeks married off his wife to dead Achilles.

But the heroes' ends were only reflections of the end of every human life—to die, of old age, in battle, of accident, or by the hand of another or oneself. Heroes, Burkert wrote, "are not generally imagined as old, grey, and ugly, but in the full force and perfection of youth."[1] The death of a hero was largely an afterthought, a tale added to a hoary legend to give the mythic hero the semblance of biography and to explain how he came to take up residence in the Underworld, where he might wield chthonic power and bring blessings unto the land and the people. "It is some extraordinary quality that makes the hero; something unpredictable and uncanny is left behind and always present."[2] Thus, when the Greeks went to the Jasonia (devoted by the Greeks to Jason, whatever their origin) to pay their respects to the great hero of the *Argo*, they imagined themselves honoring the glorious youth who seized the Golden Fleece, not the broken man who died beneath his ship. Like a modern movie star, the hero was forever frozen at the moment of his supreme triumph.

Summing up the Story of Jason

One reason the Greeks struggled to end the lives of their heroes might well be because the traditional stories from which the well-known Greek myths grew did not contain complete biographies of the characters but instead told only of their core adventures. For Jason, this may be doubly true since we have seen evidence that the earliest Jason originated in the hero or god who died each year and was resurrected to forever remarry the earth goddess Hera. If that is the case, then there was no original ending to the Jason story because the story never ended. The yearly death and rebirth of the hero *was* the story, part of the cyclical flow of nature, the rhythms of the environment in which the story was told and the audience lived. Only in rendering this mythic hero more human as the Greeks rationalized and naturalized their mythology did the logistics of storytelling demand details of Jason's life and a final, permanent death.

THE CORE STORY

So what can we say of life of the Jason myth? The story's birth is shrouded in shadow, but some of the threads that went into the weaving of the tapestry have become somewhat clearer. After surveying the many versions of the Jason myth, its position within Greek mythology as a whole, and its relationships to the adjacent myth cycles of the Near East, we can point to several distinct streams that merged to form the core of the story we know today:

- The myth of the god or hero who dies each year for the Great Goddess of nature (the Mycenaean Hera) and is reborn to contract a sacred marriage to her.
- The Proto-Indo-European (or perhaps even universal) figure of the hero who slays a serpent associated with chaos and the Underworld.
- Imagery from Near Eastern sources, including the Underworld role of the sun in Mesopotamia and possibly the Hittite dragon-slaying spring festival of Purulli.

The most perplexing question is determining to what degree Jason draws from each of these sources. Was he primarily the Indo-European serpent slayer? Or did he gain that identity secondarily, beginning life instead as a pre–Indo-European fertility god? Was his myth an indigenous development in Greece, or did he travel to Greece from the Hittite lands? I believe that Jason's close relationship with Hera and the fact that his adventure has, at least from Hesiod's day, always been associated with marriage to a goddess argues in favor of his indigenous development as the Great Goddess's annually resurrecting consort, one of a spectrum of such figures stretching from Mesopotamia through Anatolia to the Mediterranean. The serpent slaying must have come later, an Indo-European overlay associated with the transformation of heroic myths associated with the goddess into forms more acceptable to the new religion headed by the storm god-sky god synthesis as the supreme Zeus and his retinue. In place of the hero's original descent into the Underworld, the serpent of death replaces whatever he would have first found beneath the earth.

It is one thing, of course, to note that the similarities between a Greek myth and Near East myths. It is another to propose some plausible way whereby the Greeks came to incorporate into their mythology such diverse elements as the golden garments of the Mesopotamian gods or the Mesopotamian sun god with his earth-plowing knife and bull men. Fortunately, most of this work has been done for us. It has been plausibly established that the Greeks borrowed iconographic ideas about Ninurta for Heracles, and for him, too, they borrowed adventures once associated with Gilgamesh. We know as well that the earliest *Argonautica* contained echoes of Gilgamesh. We also know that the Hittites had incorporated into their mythology much that came from Mesopotamia, and that the Mycenaeans were in contact with the Hittites. Other Anatolian peoples also shared the Mesopotamian inheritance, and by any number of routes such ideas and imagery could have come into Greece in the Mycenaean era, just as it would again in the second wave, during the Orientalizing Period, a thousand years later. There is therefore little controversy in suggesting a relationship between the Jason myth and Near Eastern sources.

To imagine how it might have gone is of course to speculate. It is entirely possible to imagine Mycenaean Greeks encountering a Babylonian cylinder seal with a strange image of the sun god Shamash brandishing his curved knife to cut through the mountains of the east while his bull men open the gates of the sun and these Greeks trying to learn what the image showed. In some garbled way they could have gotten the story from people whose language and culture they barely understood or purposely misunderstood (as the Greeks would later do with the *ayazana*/Jasonia), with the sun becoming a son of the sun, his knife turning into a plow, and the bull men becoming the bulls that pulled the plow to cut through the ground at the gates of the sun. When they asked where these events took place, they would have heard about the sun's palace at the Gate of Aya and Inanna in the farthest east, and possibly that those gates led down to the Underworld where the sun reigned as judge. From this, perhaps, came Aeëtes and his court at Aea and the persistent undercurrent of necromancy and Underworld imagery lurking beneath Aea's solar surface. Surely, if the Mycenaeans understood these gates to stand over the Underworld, the act of digging a furrow into the earth's surface must therefore, as in the necromantic rites Odysseus performed, give entrance to the Underworld and those that dwell within. Was this the first story of the earth-born men?

Of course, we need not posit such a specific transmission. It is possible that Shamash and his iconography were part of the common stock of pre–Indo-European religious imagery in the Aegean; however, the close linguistic similarity between the dawn land of Aea and the Mesopotamian dawn goddess Aya, noted by M. L. West and others, tends to support the idea of influence, perhaps mediated through the Hittites.

It is also surely interesting to see that in the Near East rites of sacred marriage were enacted for so many of the figures associated by scholars with the Jason myth. Teshub had his sacred marriage to his pre–Indo-European consort at the Purulli festival each year. The new year also brought the sacred marriage of Shamash with Aya, Velchanos with the Minoan Great Goddess, and Hera with her hero. Innana and Dumuzi in all their myriad forms similarly enacted this rite. That Jason and Medea do as well again reinforces the idea of an ancient, pre–Indo-European pattern of sacred marriages stretching across the Aegean into the Middle East, the vestiges of which remained in Jason's marriage to Medea even after the Zeus-worshippers had rebuilt so much of Greek religion in their image. It would be tempting, though unsupportable, to suggest that Jason's unhappy divorce was the result of the Zeus cult's ongoing campaign to demote, degrade, and devalue the remnants of the former goddess, which the Medea figure almost certainly once was. The Great Goddess had been broken into Hera, Athena, and Aphrodite, and even Medea. Her divine consort had been changed to a hero and then human. And, as Hesiod told us, "the will of great Zeus was fulfilled."

THE ADDITIONS

Contrary to many archaeologists' opinions, the weight of the evidence suggests that the story of the hero's journey predates its localization in the Black Sea. The Greeks of the Dark Age lived in a world that they understood through appeals to myth, and when they ventured into the Black Sea, it was only natural that they should interpret those voyages in terms of stories they already knew. When they reached Colchis at the far east of what they must have originally thought was the River Ocean and found a land where the locals worshipped a sun god and told stories of a hero who slew a serpent, it was only natural to associate this place with Jason and his voyage to the magical dawn land across the eastern ocean, just as Gibraltar would someday be identified with the magical western pillars where Heracles stole Geryon's cattle.

Once this identity was established, the geography of the Black Sea became part and parcel of the Jason myth, and stories told of the islands and settlements between Iolcus and Colchis merged into Jason's story. There is, of course, no way to know now, but I would suspect that at least some of the men assigned to the *Argo* as sailors were originally the Mycenaean heroes of whatever set of long-vanished adventures were first attached to the ship's voyage, brought aboard when their myths fell into Jason's orbit. Bits of these memories remain. Hylas is largely considered to have once been a vegetation god. Poeas may have been the original slayer of Talos. The Boreadae, Zetes and Calais, were almost certainly part of an independent myth chasing the Harpies from Phineus. However, most of the ancient Mycenaean hero myths are lost beyond recovery, and we can only speculate about what types of adventures the men placed aboard the *Argo* originally encountered before Jason claimed them as his own and Homer raided this catalogue of deeds for the *Odyssey*. Following the Homeric cattle raid, new heroes and new adventures entered Jason's orbit, including Heracles, Orpheus, Theseus, and the other famed heroes of Greece. All of these were embellishments of the earliest Jason adventure of course.

Jason's adventures upon his return from Colchis were additions, too. The rejuvenations of Aeson and Pelias were probably constructed from Jason's own one-time death and resurrection. The tragedy at Corinth is the joint result of Corinth's attempt to appropriate a hero as patron of their nautical prowess and the Athenian tragedians' desire to make Corinth look bad. These stories became dominant only because the purposely reconstructed versions of the Athenian stage gradually became hoary with age and respected enough to become canon.

THE MEANING OF THE MYTH

Those who have sought to interpret the myth of Jason and uncover its original meaning have tended to err on two counts. First, more often than not they take the myth as it was told in Apollonius as reflective of the myth as it was always told. True, we have no way of knowing the exact content of the myth as it was known to Homer; but this does not make interpretations based on one particular late version of the story especially accurate. Second, and more important, interpreters of all stripes tend to assume that a myth has a single point of origin and thus a single meaning behind its symbols. Thus, for Janet Ruth Bacon the point of origin was a Mycenaean voyage to the Black Sea. The symbols were therefore nothing but distortions of this historical event. For the solar theorists, the point of origin was Aryan solar mythology. All of the symbols therefore had a single meaning: the sun. For Jan Bremmer, the origin was the Purulli festival, and the symbolic meaning accordingly Hittite. For Fritz Graf, the origin was initiatory and therefore the symbols related to the rites performed to welcome warriors into adulthood.

Such reductionist views presume that myths and symbols have power because they have a specific meaning, when just the opposite is true. A myth is powerful because it is flexible, mutable, and applicable to many circumstances and purposes. The symbols contained within, whether they be the Golden Fleece, the serpent, or the ship, are powerful because they contain within them *multiple* meanings derived from centuries of accretion and tradition. The search for a single origin for such multivalent symbols as the Fleece is probably fruitless because to become powerful such symbols must derive from *many* sources and bring within them many reflections and memories. If a symbol had only one origin and only one specific meaning, there is no reason for it to exist; the thing itself could stand naked. The symbols that survived Antiquity did so because they were conflations of multiple ideas run together by time and chance to increase their dramatic and sacred potential.

As we have seen, nearly every element of the Jason story seems to point toward at least one ancient meaning standing behind the myth: an encounter with and triumph over the forces of death. But this does not negate the other meanings or strip them of their power, for certainly there are in the Jason stories elements of solar imagery, initiatory and ritual reflections, shamanic experiences, and even real sea voyages—because all of these layers are part and parcel of the culture in which the myth was invented, expanded, told, and retold. But wrapped up in the language of sacred marriage is the ancient pre–Indo-European belief in the goddess's dying-and-rising consort who descends to the Underworld each year and returns to wed the goddess. Jason's myth, as Apollonius and Virgil knew, represented just such a journey, even if he did not explicitly harrow hell like Heracles or Theseus. But as we have seen, even these figures incorporate within their myth cycles elements of former descents into the Underworld that had been transformed and translated into less infernal forms. It is therefore with some irony that the medieval allegorists likened Jason to Jesus, since Jason must, as the Douris cup shows us, have experienced a descent into the jaws of death and a rebirth, just as Jesus died and was resurrected. However, if this were the ancestral line of Jason, it is, in the end, only a partial parent. The myth of Jason is not the story of "Jason and the Argonauts" until it takes its recognizable form, sometime in the centuries before Homer. And by then, its symbols are pregnant with possibility and a multiplicity of meanings.

If I choose to see the Jason story as primarily a katabasis related to a vegetation or healing god and his divine goddess, this is no more than the spine on which so many other aspects hang, accretions drawn from the cultural practices of Mycenaean, Dark Age, Archaic, Classical, and Hellenistic Greeks. Each succeeding culture left its mark on the myth, providing ideas and elements unique to the time and place in which they were told. Only when the story assumed the dimensions recognizable to us can we call this the Jason myth; and many and varied were the parent streams that flowed into its river. Thus, in the end, most interpretations of the Jason myth share a partial truth; they are explications of one or more of the many overlapping and interlaced layers that make up a story that beneath its relatively placid and straightforward surface contains within it an intellectual and religious history of more than a thousand years of Mycenaean and Greek ideas about life, the gods, and man's place in the world and the cosmos.

Disembarking from the Argo

To close out the epic adventure of the myth of Jason, Medea, and the Argonauts, I would like to speak to the paradox of the myth of Jason as it has come down to us. The great scholar G. S. Kirk, as we have noted, complained that the Jason myth was "enthralling but bland, even superficial."[3] C. J. Mackie wrote that the Greek poets had turned Jason into "a rather bland figure" who must have differed markedly from the oral traditions about him.[4] Yet at the same time we read that the Argonaut myth was among the ancient world's best loved, and even Homer speaks of the story as one widely circulated and wildly popular. Surely we cannot suppose that the ancients enjoyed stories that were "bland" and "superficial." It is therefore not just possible but probable that the earliest Jason was more exciting, more dynamic, more—heroic—than the literary figure who lives on under his name. The versions of the story we have are very late, written a thousand years after the story may have originated. The versions we have in Diodorus, Apollodorus, and even Apollonius are homogenized, rationalized, revised, and blended—in short, the rough edges and interesting bits of tradition have been averaged out, leaving only the least common denominator.

The great tragedy of the Jason myth is that no poet equal to Homer sang of him in the Homeric age, that no great *Argonautica* became canonized alongside the *Iliad* and the *Odyssey*. Had this occurred, we would have had not just the myth as known to Homer but the constellation of cultural traits and values, perhaps even back into the Mycenaean era, that informed the story. Instead, Jason floated along as a popular oral tale, of no fixed version, changing and mutating with Greek culture down unto the Hellenistic era.

Yet we sense in the evidence that has come down to us a tension between the "popular" Jason myth and the elite poets who operated in Greek literary culture. Homer clearly knew of Jason and chose to minimize him, almost with a whiff of disapproval. The iconographic evidence records exciting and magical adventures the Archaic and Classical poets appear to have purposely rejected or dramatically transformed. I think the reason for this is because the Argonaut story reflects religious ideas that belonged to another time and were no longer in favor among the elite of Dark Age and Archaic Greece. The earliest Jason stories reflect a time when Hera was far more powerful than she would be in Classical Greece, when she was an earth goddess and could even have headed the pantheon of gods in some places. The earliest Jason stories also reflect a culture where humans and chthonic gods interacted closely, and humans could wield near-divine supernatural powers, including Jason's own powers of extraordinary healing. We know that in the *Iliad* Homer (or, perhaps more likely, the Dark Age poets whose stories he drew upon) purposely transformed Hera from a powerful and beneficent earth goddess to the angry but subordinate consort of the all-powerful Zeus. Similarly, Hesiod too takes great pains to place Zeus supreme above a much diminished Hera.

This, then, must be the reason that the Jason story found no great Homeric epic—he was too closely associated with the old, Mycenaean-era worship of Hera, a hero closely entwined with a chthonic goddess and the unsettling supernatural powers associated with the old religion. Such subjects were clearly inappropriate for the pious poets of Zeus. Only when a way could be found to transform the popular hero into a Greek worthy of Zeus's divine grace could Jason form a suitable subject for the highest levels of elite poetry. This, I would suggest, accounts for the origins of Medea, a pointedly non–Greek figure who derived from the earth goddess (who, of course, was now also alien to Greek religion) and could absorb the unwelcome, impious aspects of Jason's supernatural power. Through this innovation, the story of Jason could be welcomed back into the fold of elite myths. But something had been lost.

In the attempt to reach into the dragon's belly and resurrect the Jason of ancient myth, we are confronted with a chasm between the Mycenaean faith and that of Homer, between the religion of Hera and that of Zeus, between the gods who live in the earth and those who live in the sky. Jason's voyage, then, is at one level a voyage between the lands of the living and the dead, and at a larger level a voyage between the earliest human faith and the powerful new religious order dawning across the Western world. Wherever the storm god went, from Greece to Persia to India, even down into Israel where he would take the name Yahweh, the storm god came to reign supreme, replacing the worship of Hera, Ishtar, Ashtoreth, Astarte, and all her kith and kin. When Jason left Iolcus, he did so with the aid of Hera. When he returned from Colchis, he had come back with the Golden Fleece dedicated to the glory of Zeus and had brought back to Greece the symbol of the supremacy of a powerful and terrible new god.

I can do no better than to end this book with the words Apollonius used to end his own version of Jason's story when the Argonauts reached the safety of Pagasae in Greece:

> Be gracious, race of blessed chieftains! And may these songs year after year be sweeter to sing among men. For now have I come to the glorious end of your toils; for no adventure befell you as ye came home from Aegina, and no tempest of winds opposed you; but quietly did ye skirt the Ceeropian land and Aulis inside of Euboea and the Opuntian cities of the Locrians, and gladly did ye step forth upon the beach of Pagasae.[5]

Let us then remember Jason and his Argonauts this way, as triumphant heroes, flush with the exultation of victory, a band of happy warriors. For them, the Golden Fleece was a boon achieved, and in the end this is the reason the Jason myth has survived century upon century, millennium upon millennium, for the quest for the Golden Fleece is the archetypical journey, the prize we hope to win, the promise of glory that lies within us all. Through the medium of myth, we can all strive to be Jason and achieve, for a moment, a small piece of the heroism that marks the closest approach a human may make to the divine. Ours may be the Golden Fleece, whatsoever it may mean to us, and with it, a bit of the reflected glory of the gods.

Appendix:
Selected Lists of Argonauts

The Argonauts
According to Apollonius of Rhodes

Jason

Acastus, Admetus, Aethalides, Amphidamas, Amphion, Ancaeus, Ancaeus (2), Argus, Arius, Asterion, Asterius, Augeas, Butes, Calais, Canthus, Castor, Cepheus, Clytius, Coronus, Echion, Erginus, Eribotes, Euphemus, Eurydamas, Eurytion, Eurytus, Heracles, Hylas, Idas, Idmon, Iphiclus, Iphiclus, Iphitus, Iphitus (2), Laocoön, Leodocus, Lynceus, Meleager, Menoetius, Mopsus, Nauplius, Oileus, Orpheus, Palaemon, Peleus, Periclymenus, Phalerus, Phlias, Polydeuces (Pollux), Polyphemus, Talaus, Telamon, Tiphys, Zetes.

The Argonauts
According to Valerius Flaccus

Jason

Acastus, Admetus, Aethalides, Amphidamas, Amphion, Ancaeus, Argus, Asterion, Asterius, Butes, Calais, Canthus, Castor, Cepheus, Clymenus, Deucalion, Echion, Erginus, Eribotes, Euphemus, Eurytion, Eurytus, Heracles, Hylas, Idas, Idmon, Iphiclus, Iphis, Iphitus, Leodocus, Lynceus, Meleager, Menoetius, Mopsus, Nauplius, Nestor, Oileus, Orpheus, Peleus, Periclymenus, Phalerus, Philctetes, Phlias, Polydeuces, Polyphemus, Talaus, Telamon, Tiphys, Tydeus, Zetes.

The Argonauts
According to Apollodorus

Jason

Acastus, Actor, Admetus, Amphiarus, Ancaeus, Argus, Ascalaphus, Asterius, Atalanta, Augeas, Autolycus, Butes, Caeneus, Calais, Castor, Cepheus, Erginus, Euphemus, Euryalus, Eurytus, Heracles, Hylas, Ialmenus, Iphiclus, Iphitus, Laertes, Leitus, Lynceus, Meleager, Menoetius, Orpheus, Palaemon, Peleus, Peneleus, Periclymenus, Phanus, Poeas, Polydeuces, Polyphemus, Staphylus, Telamon, Theseus, Tiphys, Zetes.

The Argonauts
According to Hyginus' *Fabulae*

Jason

Acastus, Actor, Admetus, Aethalides, Amphidamas, Amphion, Ancaeus, Ancaeus, Argus, Asclepius, Asterion, Asterius, Augeas, Butes, Caeneus, Caeneus (2), Calais, Castor, Cepheus, Clytius, Coronus, Deucalion, Echion, Erginus, Eribotes, Euphemus, Eurydamas, Eurymedon, Eurytion, Eurytus, Heracles, Hippalcimus,

Hylas, Idas, Idmon, Iolaus, Iphiclus, Iphiclus (2), Iphitus, Iphitus, Laocoön, Lynceus, Meleager, Menoetius, Mopsus, Nauplius, Neleus, Oileus, Orpheus, Palaemonius, Peleus, Periclymenus, Perithous, Phaleros, Philoctetes, Phliasus, Phocus, Pirithous, Pollus (Pollux), Polyphemus, Priasus, Telamon, Theseus, Tiphys, Zetes.

Plus three whose names are partially or wholly missing:

[Missing text]thersanon, son of Helios and Leucothoe
[Missing text], Thestius' daughter
[Missing text]ixition, of Cerinthus

The Argonauts

According to the *Orphic Argonautica*

Jason

Acastus, Admetus, Aethalides, Amphidamas, Amphion, Ancaeus, Argus, Arius, Asterion, Asterius, Augeas, Butes, Calais, Canthus, Castor, Cepheus, Coronus, Echion, Erginus, Euphemus, Eurydamas, Eurytion, Eurytus, Heracles, Hylas, Idas, Idmon, Iphiclus, Iphiclus (2), Iphitus, Leodocus, Lynceus, Meleager, Menoetius, Mopsus, Nauplius, Oileus, Orpheus, Palaemon, Peleus, Periclymenus, Phalerus, Phlias, Polydeuces (Pollux), Polyphemus, Talaus, Telamon, Tiphys, Zetes.

Chapter Notes

Introduction

1. Emmet Robbins, "Jason and Cheiron: The Myth of Pindar's Fourth Pythian," *Phoenix* 29, no. 3 (1975): 205.

2. Homer, *The Odyssey,* 12.69–72, trans. George Herbert Palmer (Boston: Houghton Mifflin, 1921), 182.

3. See, for example, Ken Dowden, *The Uses of Greek Mythology* (London: Routledge, 1992), and Martin Persson Nilsson, *The Mycenaean Origins of Greek Mythology* (Berkeley: University of California Press, 1932).

4. Nilsson, for example, suggested Heracles' story dated back to the Mycenaean period and may have represented the exploits of a king, and many have noted the similarities between Heracles and Gilgamesh, positing that the latter influenced the stories and depictions of the former. Walter Burkert suggested Heracles was a Neolithic story in origin.

5. G. S. Kirk, *The Nature of Greek Myths* (Hammondsworth: Penguin, 1982), 163.

6. Like any myth, the Jason story has many variants. What I have chosen to call the Standard Version makes use of the most familiar and repeated variants, but is by necessity my own selection among them. A fuller treatment of the many variants as well as the ancient sources upon which they are founded can be found in Robin Hard, *The Routledge Handbook of Greek Mythology* (London: Routledge, 2004), 377–400. Subsequent chapters of this book will explore the major variants as they change through time, but it would be impossible, if not exhausting, to rehearse each variation, no matter how small, when they do not contribute to our understanding of the changing nature of the myth.

7. For a discussion of the multiple meanings of myth, see G. S. Kirk, *The Nature of Greek Myths* (Hammondsworth: Penguin, 1982), especially chapter 1.

8. C. J. Mackie, "The Earliest Jason: What's in a Name?" *Greece and Rome 48,* no. 12 (2001): 4.

Chapter 1

1. Whether the so-called "hobbit," *Homo floresiensis,* discovered in 2003, is a distinct species of small-statured human or the result of disease is still controversial, though evidence as of this writing seems to favor the species designation. The Siberian human species, the Denisova hominin, is currently known from two small bones and two teeth with a distinct genetic code, and little more can be said about it until more evidence comes to light.

2. A very concise argument against Neanderthal language is presented in Michael Shermer, *Science Friction: Where the Known Meets the Unknown* (New York: Henry Holt, 2005), 167.

3. David Lewis-Williams, *The Mind in the Cave* (New York: Thames & Hudson, 2002).

4. Lewis-Williams, *Mind in the Cave,* 144–148.

5. The word "shaman" derives from the Siberian Tungus word for "ecstatic" and has been applied by anthropologists to ritual practitioners across cultures who engage in the complex of behaviors described below.

6. Miranda and Stephen Aldhouse-Green, *The Quest for the Shaman* (London: Thames & Hudson, 2005), 10–15.

7. Andrew Curry, "Göbekli Tepe: The World's First Temple?," *Smithsonian*, November 2008, http://www.smithsonianmag.com/history-archaeology/gobekli-tepe.html?c=y&page=1

8. David Lewis-Williams and David Pearce, *Inside the Neolithic Mind* (London: Thames & Hudson, 2005), 157.

9. Curry, "Göbekli Tepe."

10. Benjamin W. Fortson, *Indo-European Language and Culture: An Introduction* (Malden, Mass.: Blackwell, 2004), 40–43.

11. Fortson, *Indo-European Language and Culture,* 17–18, 29.

12. Peter Jackson, "Light from Distant Asterisks: Toward a Description of Indo-European Religious Heritage," *Numen* 49, no. 1 (2002): 63–64.

13. Fortson, *Indo-European Language and Culture,* 22–23.

14. Calvert Watkins, *How to Kill a Dragon* (Oxford: Oxford University Press, 1995), 301.

15. Watkins, *How to Kill a Dragon,* 299–300.

16. See chapter 8, esp. note 52.

17. Robin Lane Fox, *Travelling Heroes in the Epic Age of Homer* (New York: Knopf, 2008), 173.

18. See, for example, M. L. West, *The East Face of Helicon: West Asiatic Elements in Greek Poetry and Myth* (Oxford: Oxford University Press, 1997) and Walter Burkert, *The Orientalizing Revolution: Near Eastern Influence on Greek Culture in the Early Archaic Age* (Cambridge: Harvard University Press, 1992).

19. West, *East Face of Helicon*, 5.

20. M. L. West, "*Odyssey* and *Argonautica*," *Classical Quarterly* 55, no. 1 (2005): 62–64.

21. On Sumeria, see Harriet Crawford, *Sumer and the Sumerians*, 2nd ed. (Cambridge: University of Cambridge Press, 2004).

22. The surviving Sumerian tales share the same general outlines as the episodes of the Akkadian epic, but they differ in both their details and their emphasis, as Samuel Noah Kramer discovered in piecing the Sumerian material together in the 1930s and 1940s. The exact differences are beyond the scope of this book, but the interested reader can find an entertaining overview in Kramer's *In the World of Sumer: An Autobiography* (Detroit: Wayne State University Press, 1986), 79–84. The differences might profitably be compared to the changes between Saxo Grammaticus' medieval "Life of Amleth" and Shakespeare's magisterial play, *Hamlet*.

23. Steven Mitchell, *Gilgamesh: A New English Version* (New York: The Free Press, 2004), 1.

24. For example, Gerald K. Gresseth, "The Gilgamesh Epic and Homer," *Classical Journal* 70 (1974–1975): 1–18.

25. For example, K. Meuli, *Odyssee und Argonautika* (Utrecht, 1974; orig. publ. Berlin, 1921), as cited in Mackie, "The Earliest Jason," 15, n. 13; and West, "*Odyssey* and *Argonautica*," 39–64, who notes the idea was first proposed by the German scholar A. Kirchhoff in 1869.

26. A. R. George, *The Babylonian Gilgamesh Epic: Introduction, Critical Edition and Cuneiform Texts,* vol. I (Oxford: Oxford University Press, 2003), 127–135.

27. West, "*Odyssey* and *Argonautica*," 64.

28. M. L. West, "Phasis and Aia," *Museum Helveticum* 64, no. 4 (2007): 196–197; see chapter 4, note 90 for additional discussion.

29. West, "*Odyssey* and *Argonautica*," 62–63.

30. Walter Burkert, *Structure and History in Greek Mythology and Ritual*, originally 1979 (Berkeley: University of California Press, 1982), 80–83; on Heracles' debt to Gilgamesh and other Near East figures, see Burr C. Brundage, "Herakles the Levantine: A Comprehensive View," *Journal of Near East Studies* 17, no. 4 (1958): 225–236, but note that many of his conclusions cannot be supported in light of modern evidence.

31. Burkert, *Structure and History*, 83.

32. The Warka Vase from 3000 BCE found at Uruk has been interpreted as depicting the marriage of Inanna and Dumuzi, but not all scholars agree. Otherwise, the gods are attested from the third millennium. Unfortunately, the vase was shattered in the 2003 looting of Iraq's National Museum, though the fragments were to be restored.

33. N. K. Sandars, trans., *Poems of Heaven and Hell from Ancient Mesopotamia* (New York: Penguin, 1971), 129–131.

34. Bruce Satterfield, "Dumuzi," in *Gods, Goddesses and Mythology* (volume 4), edited by C. Scott Littleton (Tarrytown, NY: Marshall Cavendish, 2005), 449; Thorkild Jacobsen, *The Harps that Once...: Sumerian Poetry in Translation* (New Haven: Yale University Press, 1987), 5, n. 6.

35. Samuel Noah Kramer, "Cuneiform Studies and the History of Literature: The Sumerian Sacred Marriage Texts," *Proceedings of the American Philosophical Society* 107 (1963): 485–527.

36. Susan Deacy, *Athena* (New York: Routledge, 2008), 20.

37. Ezekiel 8:14, "Then he brought me to the door of the gate of the LORD'S house which was toward the north; and, behold, there sat women weeping for Tammuz" (King James Version).

38. Burkert, *Structure and History*, 108–110.

39. Burkert, *Structure and History*, 111.

40. Trevor Bryce, *Life and Society in the Hittite World* (Oxford: Oxford University Press, 2002), 136.

41. Susanne Görke, "Hints and Temple Geography and Cosmic Geography from Hittite Sources," in *Heaven on Earth: Temples, Ritual, and Cosmic Symbolism in the Ancient World*, ed. Deena Ragavan, University of Chicago Oriental Institute Seminars No. 9 (Chicago: University of Chicago Press, 2013), 47.

42. Gary Beckman, "Gilgamesh in Hatti," *Hittite Studies in Honor of Harry A. Hoffner, Jr. on the Occasion of His 65th Birthday,* edited by Gary Beckman, Richard Beal, and Gregory McMahon (Winona Lake, Ind.: Eisenbrauns, 2003), 37–58.

43. Charles Allen Burney, *Historical Dictionary of the Hittites* (Lanham, Maryland: Scarecrow Press, 2004), 138; Bryce, *Life and Society in the Hittite World*, 146–147.

44. Bryce, *Life and Society in the Hittite World*, 211, 213.

45. *ANET*,[3] 128, column b; the translation is my adaptation of several standard sources, which vary in details, particularly whether the bag *symbolizes* or actually *contains* its boons.

46. Joseph Eddy Fontenrose, *Python: A Study of Delphic Myth and Its Origins,* 1959 (reprint, Berkeley: University of California Press, 1980), 121–125.

47. Fontenrose, *Python*, 121–122.

48. Fortenrose, *Python*, 124–125.

49. Jan N. Bremmer, *Greek Religion and Culture, the Bible, and the Ancient Near East* (Leiden/Boston: Brill, 2008), chapter XV.

50. Richard J. Clifford, "The Roots of Apocalypticism in Near Eastern Myth," *The Encyclopedia of Apocalypticism*, Vol. 1: *The Origins of Apocalypticism in Judaism and Christianity*, edited by John. J. Collins (New York: Continuum, 2000), 22–23

51. Clifford, "Roots of Apocalypticism," 23.

52. Clifford, "Roots of Apocalypticism," 23–25.

53. Alberto Ravinell Whitney Green, *The Storm-God in the Ancient Near East* (Winona Lake, Ind.: Eisenbrauns, 2003), 203.

54. Patricia Turner and Charles Russell Coulter, *Dictionary of Ancient Deities* (Oxford: Oxford University Press, 2001), 172.

55. Glenn Markoe, *The Phoenicians* (Berkeley: University of California Press, 2000), 112; also Fox, *Travelling Heroes*, 67–68.

56. For the Phoenicians, their achievements, and their religion, see Markoe, *The Phoenicians*.

57. Fontenrose, *Python*, 307.

58. Alternately, Athena or Ares sows the dragon's teeth for Cadmus to fight, and in the version of Hellanicus only five warriors rose up. In contrast to the version given above, other variants hold that Athena asked for the teeth to be sown so that Cadmus would have helpful citizens for Thebes, but in their confusion the Spartoi instead slaughtered one another (Robin Hard, *The Routledge Handbook of Greek Mythology* [London: Routledge, 2004], 296).

59. West, *The East Face of Helicon,* 57.

60. Markoe, *The Phoenicians,* 112.

61. Diodorus Siculus, *Library of History,* 1.85.5.

62. On Osiris, see Bojana Mojsov, *Osiris: Death and Afterlife of a God* (Malden, Mass.: Blackwell, 2005)

63. Susan Redford and Donald B. Redford, "The Cult and Necropolis of the Sacred Ram at Mendes," in *Divine Creatures: Animal Mummies in Ancient Egypt,* ed. Salima Ikram (New York: American University in Cairo Press, 2005), 165–166; Geraldine Pinch, *Egyptian Mythology: A Guide to the Gods, Goddesses, and Traditions of Ancient Egypt* (Oxford: Oxford University Press, 2002), 114–115.

64. The following discussion of Homer, his history, and his sources follows the argument in Barry B. Powell's *Homer* (Malden, Mass.: Blackwell Publishing, 2004), a concise overview of the current scholarly consensus on Homer and his world.

65. Andrew Dalby, in *Rediscovering Homer* (New York: Norton, 2006), for example, argued, unpersuasively I think, that Homer was a woman.

66. *Iliad* 10:260–5.

Chapter 2

1. The term "Achaean" has several uses. Homer's Achaeans referred to all Greeks, likely the Mycenaeans; however, in later centuries the Achaeans were one of four tribal divisions in Classical Greek culture, traced to Achaeus, their mythical founder, one of the four sons of the progenitor of the Greeks, Hellen, son of Deucalion and Pyrrah, the only humans to survive the great flood.

2. Adrienne Mayor, *The First Fossil Hunters: Paleontology in Greek and Roman Times* (Princeton: Princeton University Press, 2000), chapter 3.

3. Strabo, *Geography* 11.2.38.

4. Strabo, *Geography,* 1.2.39; *The Geography of Strabo,* trans. Horace Leonard Jones (London: William Heinemann, 1918), 167.

5. Fox, *Travelling Heroes,* 176; citing J. Markwart, *Südarmenien und die Tigrisquellen nach griechischen undarabischen Geographen* (Vienna, 1930).

6. Royal Robbins, *The World Displayed in Its History and Geography; Embracing a History of the World from the Creation to the Present Day* (New York: W. W. Reed, 1830), 30, 40–41.

7. J. N. L. Myers, *Homer and His Critics* (London: Routledge and Keegan Paul, 1958), 124–129.

8. Rodney Castleden, *The Mycenaeans* (London: Routledge, 2005), 2.

9. Myers, *Homer,* 124–129.

10. Myers, *Homer,* 132.

11. The site was occupied beginning c. 3000 BCE with numerous layers of settlement, conventionally labeled Troy I-Troy IX, with some layers having subdivisions. The controversy over which was the Troy of Homer is beyond the scope of the present work, but is usually identified as the apparently war-ravaged Troy VIIa (c. 1300–1190 BCE), rather than Schliemann's candidate, Troy I or Troy II.

12. William C. Morey, *Outlines of Greek History* (New York: American Book Company, 1903), 92.

13. Martin P. Nilsson, *The Mycenaean Origin of Greek Mythology* (Berkeley: University of California Press, 1932), 28.

14. Arnold Walter Lawrence and Richard Allan Tomlinson, *Greek Architecture,* 5th ed. (New Haven: Yale University Press, 1996), 37–42.

15. Kirk, *Nature of Greek Myths,* 155.

16. Susan Lupack, "Minoan Religion," in *The Oxford Handbook of the Bronze Age Aegean,* ed. Eric H. Cline (Oxford: Oxford University Press, 2010), 258.

17. Castleden, *Minoans,* 125; Paula J. Perlman, "Invocatio and Imprecatio: The Hymn to the Greatest Kouros from Palaikastro and the Oath in Ancient Crete," *The Journal of Hellenic Studies* 115 (1995): 161–167.

18. Nanno Marinatos, *Minoan Kingship and the Solar Goddess: A Near Eastern Koine* (Urbana: University of Illinois, 2010), chapter 13.

19. Stephanie Lynn Budin, *The Ancient Greeks: An Introduction* (Oxford: Oxford University Press, 2004), 226–227.

20. Marija Gimbutas, *The Living Goddesses,* revised by Miriam Robbins Dexter (Berkeley: University of California Press, 2001), 134–139.

21. Castleden, *Mycenaeans,* 143.

22. Rodney Castleden, *The Knossos Labyrinth: A New View of the 'Palace of Minos' at Knossos* (London: Routledge, 1990), 112–113, 139. Unfortunately, his view rests on identifying the bull Poseidon sent to Minos (which fathered the Minotaur) with the bull form of Zeus during the rape of Europa by falsely applying the description of Zeus in Moschus' Hellenistic poem *Europa* as a bull with solar imagery to Poseidon's bull, which rose from the sea.

23. Marinatos, *Minoan Kingship and the Solar Goddess,* 166.

24. Martin Persson Nilsson, *The Minoan-Mycenaean Religion and Its Survival in Greek Religion,* 2nd rev. ed. (New York: Biblo and Tannen, 1928), 374n15; Burkert, *Greek Religion,* 23.

25. Dietrich, *Origins of Greek Religion,* 115–117.

26. Castleden, *Minoans,* 114–115.

27. Burkert had no doubt they were goddesses, but Marinatos believes them to be Near Eastern-style snake handlers. Two of the most famous faience figurines from Knossos were reconstructed from fragments during Arthur Evans' excavations, and many of the snakes depicted on the two figurines were added by Danish artist Halvor Bagge.

28. Burkert, *Greek Religion,* 30.

29. Bruce Lincoln, *Death, War, and Sacrifice: Studies in Ideology and Practice* (Chicago: University of Chicago Press, 1991), chapter 5.

30. Brendan Burke, "Mycenaean Memory and Bronze Age Lament," in *Lament: Studies in the Ancient Mediterranean and Beyond,* ed. Ann Suter (Oxford: Oxford University Press, 2008), 79–80.

31. Burke, "Mycenaean," 77.

32. Castleden, *The Mycenaeans,* 186.

33. Castelton, *The Mycenaeans,* 187.

34. Castleden, *The Mycenaeans,* 187; Samuel Mark, *Homeric Seafaring* (College Station: Texas A&M University Press, 2005), 106–107.

35. James C. Wright, "The Formation of the Mycenaean Palace," in in *Ancient Greece: From the Mycenaean Palaces to the Age of Homer,* eds. Sigrid Deger-Jalkotzy

and Irene S. Lemos (Edinburgh: Edinburgh University Press, 2006), 7–52.

36. Bernard Clive Dietrich, *The Origins of Greek Religion* (Berlin and New York: de Gruyter, 1974), 38–39.

37. Castleden, *The Mycenaeans*, 146.

38. Dietrich, *Origins of Greek Religion*, 38–39.

39. Dietrich, *Origins of Greek Religion*, appendix III.

40. Dietrich, *Origins of Greek Religion*, 311–313; Nilsson, *Mycenaean Origin*, 33–34.

41. Susan Lupak, "Mycenaean Religion," in *The Oxford Handbook of the Bronze Age Aegean,* ed. Eric H. Cline (Oxford: Oxford University Press, 2010), 271.

42. Fritz Graf, *Apollo* (New York: Routledge, 2009), 67; Ian Rutherford, *Pindar's Paeans: A Reading of the Fragments with a Survey of the Genre* (New York: Oxford University Press, 2001), 16.

43. Walter Burkert, *Greek Religion,* trans. John Raffan (Cambridge: Harvard University Press, 1985), 140.

44. Burkert, *Greek Religion*, 131–132.

45. Joan V. O'Brien argued for the primacy of Hera in the Mycenaean pantheon because the earth goddess had led the Minoan pantheon and was a goddess with aspects in heaven, on earth, and in the underworld. She correctly notes poetic references to the superiority of Hera over Zeus, though this does not necessarily contradict the claim (see below) that Poseidon headed the Mycenaean pantheon, as Zeus was not yet king of the gods (*The Transformation of Hera: A Study of Ritual, Hero, and the Goddess in the* Iliad [Landham, Maryland: Rowman and Littlefield, 1993]).

46. The Two Queens have also been variously interpreted as Demeter and Persephone, Posidaeja (a female form of the name Poseidon) and Iphimedeia (a nymph), and the Cretan sisters Ariadne and Pasiphae. Castleton suggests Hera and Athena as the two queens based upon the identification of those goddesses with two goddesses appearing jointly on a fresco at Mycenae (*Mycenaeans*, 143–144).

47. The first part of his name derives from the Mycenaean *Potei-*, meaning lord, but it is open question whether the "da" syllable refers to the earth or something else entirely (Burkert, *Greek Religion*, 136).

48. Burkert, *Greek Religion*, 136.

49. Castleden, *Mycenaeans*, 143–144; Yves Bonnefoy, *Greek and Egyptian Mythologies,* trans. Wendy Doniger (Chicago: University of Chicago, 1992), 80–81.

50. Burkert, *Greek Religion*, 139.

51. Similarly, in the *Iliad* Poseidon is remembered as the god especially favoring the Achaean (Mycenaean) effort to attack and defeat Troy, another possible echo of Poseidon's original position at the head of the Mycenaean pantheon.

52. Castleden, *The Knossos Labyrinth*, 174.

53. Euripides, *Orestes* 789 and 1377, with scholia.

54. *Etymologicum Gudianum*, s.v. Zagreus.

55. Michael C. Astour, *Hellenosemitica* (Leiden: E. J. Brill, 1967), 195–204.

56. Castleden, *Mycenaeans*, 154–156.

57. Hesychius, *s.v.* Talos; Apollodorus, *Library* 1.9.26; the connection between Talos and the sun gained its modern form from A. B. Cook, who argued that Talos was originally a sun god and later was identified with Zeus; however, not all scholars agree and prefer alternative explanations. (A. B. Cook, *Zeus: A Study*

in Ancient Religion, vol. 1: Zeus, God of the Bright Sky [Cambridge: Cambridge University Press, 1914], 719, 728.)

58. Curtis Neil Runnels and Priscilla Murray, *Greece before History: An Archaeological Companion and Guide* (Stanford: Stanford University Press, 2001), 147.

59. Walter Burkert, *Homo Necans: The Anthropology of Ancient Greek Sacrificial Ritual and Myth,* trans. Peter Bing (Berkeley: University of California Press, 1983), 113.

60. Runnels and Murray, *Greece before History*, 147.

61. D. H. French, "Late Chalcolithic Pottery in North-West Turkey and the Aegean," *Anatolian Studies* 11 (1961): 99–141.

62. Vassiliki Adrimi-Sismani, "The Palace of Iolkos and Its End," in *Ancient Greece: From the Mycenaean Palaces to the Age of Homer*, eds. Sigrid Deger-Jalkotzy and Irene S. Lemos (Edinburgh: Edinburgh University Press, 2006), 465.

63. Adrimi-Sismani, "The Palace of Iolkos," 467.

64. Adrimi-Sismani, "The Palace of Iolkos," 467.

65. Adrimi-Sismani, "The Palace of Iolkos," 468.

66. Adrimi-Sismani, "The Palace of Iolkos," 468.

67. Ingrid E. M. Edlund-Berry, "The Ritual Destruction of Cities and Sanctuaries," in *Murlo and the Etruscans: Art and Society in Ancient Etruria,* eds. Richard Daniel De Puma and Jocelyn Penny Small (Madison: University of Wisconsin Press, 1994), 18.

68. Edlund-Berry, "Ritual Destruction," 16–26.

69. Didorus Siculus 1.79.4, with archaeological excavations reported in Edlund-Berry, "Ritual Destruction," 27n22.

70. Catherine Morgan, "The Early Iron Age," in *A Companion to Archaic Greece,* eds. Kurt A. Raaflaub and Hans van Wees (Malden, Mass.: Blackwell, 2009), 49.

71. Castleden, *Mycenaeans*, 185–186.

72. Castleden, *Mycenaeans*, 191–195.

73. Stephan Hiller, "Mycenaeans and the Black Sea," in Robert Laffineur and Lucien Busch, eds., *Thalassa: L'Egée préhistorique et la mar* (Liège: Univerité de Liège, 1991), 206–217.

74. Peter James and Nick Thorpe, *Ancient Mysteries* (New York: Ballantine Books, 1999), 399–400. Known as the Maine Penny, the coin of Olaf Kyrre (c. 1060 CE was found in situ and with Native American artifacts buried in a farmer's field during an archaeological excavation. The coin had a puncture hole and is believed to have been used as a pendant, worn by Native Americans and traded from Norse settlements in Greenland across the Arctic and down the eastern seaboard of Canada until it reached Maine. Its date places it after the abandonment of L'Anse aux Meadows, the Viking settlement in Newfoundland, implying it came to Maine via a different route.

75. Castleden, *Mycenaeans*, 183.

76. Castleden, *Mycenaeans*, 201–217, but see reservations in Thomas G. Palaima, "Ilios, Tros and Tlos: Continuing Problems with to-ro, to-ro-o, to-ro-wo, to-ro-ja, wi-ro and a-si-wi-ja/a-si-wi-jo," in *STEFANOS ARISTEIOS Festschrift fur Stefan Hille zum 65. Geburtstager,* eds. Felix Lang, Claus Reiholdt, and Jörg Weilhartner (Vienna: Phoibos Verlag, 2007).

77. Castleden, *Mycenaeans*, 218–225.

78. Pausanias, *Description of Greece* 2.16.5 and 2.25.8.

79. Burkert, *Greek Religion*, 50–52.

80. Thomas R. Martin, *Ancient Greece: From Prehistoric to Hellenistic Times* (New Haven: Yale University Press, 2000), 38–39.

81. This transition has spawned many theories about Indo-European invasions, the replacement of proto-feminist goddess worshipping equalitarian societies with hierarchical patriarchy, etc. However, the evidence indicates no revolutionary instant replacement of the ancient earth goddess with the Indo-European storm god, or one people with another. The Mycenaeans themselves spoke an Indo-European language yet did not apparently recognize the supremacy of Zeus. Instead, the transition to the supposedly typical Indo-European pattern of hierarchy and male dominance in both religion and culture appears more gradual, stretching from the Mycenaean period through the Dark Ages, substantively complete by the time Homer assembled his poems, and quite likely indicative of Dark Age peoples turning to Near East, especially Hittite, models to revitalize their religion in the wake of the Mycenaean collapse and the manifest failure of the old gods and the old ways. New patterns were needed to remake society when a vanished elite and the symbols and ideology they promoted had so utterly and totally failed.

82. Hesiod, *Theogony*, 178ff., in *Hesiod: The Homeric Hymns and Homerica*, trans. Hugh G. Evelyn-White (London: William Heinemann, 1920), 93.

83. Hard, *Routledge Handbook of Greek Mythology*, 35.

84. Dietrich, *Origins of Greek Religion*, 63.

85. First proposed in Alexander Hislop's anti–Catholic tract, *The Two Babylons* (1853). The theory is highly speculative but has some scholarly support today, as in A. P. Bos, *Cosmic and Meta-Cosmic Theology in Aristotle's Lost Dialogues* (New York: E. J. Brill, 1989), 11, n. 26. The etymology of Cronus has never satisfactorily been explained, and the relationship between Cronus and the Semitic *km* or *qm* is only one possible interpretation. Hislop, however, used the identification to argue that Cronus was an historical king of Babylon, which is virtually impossible. Bos, by contrast, connects the horns to the forks in lightning rather than bulls' horns, though one could easily stand for the other.

86. Bos, *Cosmic*, 9–10.

87. Valerius Probus, commentary on Virgil's *Georgics* at 3.92; Apollonius, *Argonautica* 2.1231–41; Hyginus, *Fabulae* 138; Hesiod, *Theogony* 1001–2; Pindar, *Pythian* 6.22. See also Hard, *Routledge Handbook of Greek Mythology*, 73.

88. Burkert, *Greek Religion*, 138.

Chapter 3

1. G. S. Kirk, *Myth: Its Meaning and Functions in Ancient and Other Cultures*, originally published 1970 (London: Cambridge University Press, 1998), 177–178.

2. G. S. Kirk, *The Nature of Greek Myths* (Harmondsworth: Penguin, 1982), 160.

3. Henry D. Ephron, "The Jēsŏn Tablet of Enkomi," *Harvard Studies in Classical Philology* 65 (1961): 60.

4. Kirk, *Nature of Greek Myths*, 162.

5. Carol G. Thomas, *Finding People in Early Greece* (Columbia: University of Missouri Press, 2005), 73;

Thomas G. Palaima, "Ilios, Tros and Tlos: Continuing Problems with to-ro, to-ro-o, to-ro-wo, to-ro-ja, wi-ro and a-si-wi-ja/a-si-wi-jo," in *STEFANOS ARISTEIOS Festschrift fur Stefan Hille zum 65. Geburtstager,* eds. Felix Lang, Claus Reiholdt, and Jörg Weilhartner (Vienna: Phoibos Verlag, 2007), 199n.17.

6. Natalis Comes (*Mythologiae* 6.8) misread the word δολόμηδες in the scholia to Apollonius of Rhodes at 3.26 as a proper name, and later writers, such as the Abbé Banier in the 1700s, either misread or misinterpreted Dolomedes as Diomedes, probably in light of the late myth in which Diomedes (not Jason) slays the Colchian dragon when the dragon comes looking for the Golden Fleece and the fact that seventeenth century editions of Comes (the edition Banier would have consulted) contained a typographical error misprinting Diomedes for Dolomedes. These writers then back-cited the source to the Pindar scholia (*ad vers.* 211) rather than their true source, Comes; and the story was repeated uncritically down to the present day. (See Winifred Warren Wilson, "Jason as 'Dolomedes,'" *Classical Review* 24 [1910]: 180.) My thanks to M. L. West for providing me with some of this information.

7. Indeed, so little sense did this at first seem that nineteenth century philologists attempted to relate Jason's name to that of the Indian sun-god Vivásvân in an attempt to prove a solar connection and origin for Jason (see chapter 11 and F. Max Müller, *Contributions to the Science of Mythology,* vol. II [London: Longmans, Green, and Co., 1897], 437).

8. The reference occurs in the *Catalogue of Women*, whose author is traditionally given as Hesiod but may have been the work of another. See chapter 4 for discussion.

9. Frederick A. G. Beck, *Greek Education: 450–350 BC* (Frome, Somerset: Butler & Tanner, 1964), 49–51.

10. Sinclair Hood, *The Arts in Prehistoric Greece,* orig. 1978 (New Haven: Yale University Press, 1994), 111.

11. Ian Morris, *Archaeology as Cultural History: Words and Things in Iron Age Greece* (Malden, Mass.: Blackwell, 2000), 250.

12. There are many other proposed derivations for the centaur, including the Greek stem *–auros*, meaning "water" and the Vedic "gandharva," which were nature spirits. It has also been argued that the Greeks invented centaurs from folk memories of seeing mounted horsemen, conflating rider and steed, much as the Aztecs would do during the Spanish Conquest. This is, however, an unnecessary complexity given the frequency with which animal-human hybrids are depicted in shamanic art going back to the Paleolithic, as we have seen.

13. Mackie, "Earliest Jason," 4.

14. Mackie, "Earliest Jason," 7.

15. Because the image does not contain Jason's name, it is not absolutely certain it is he in the images, but the similarity in composition to other images of Jason with his name inscribed, and the presence of the Golden Fleece makes the identification probable (Mackie, "Earliest Jason," 10).

16. Apollonius, *Argonautica* 4.155, Seaton, p. 305.

17. Mackie, "Earliest Jason," 12. By contrast, Daniel Ogden argued that such claims were "unnecessary speculation" and that the vase simply recorded Jason being

vomited by the dragon because Medea had covered him in anti-dragon unguent. (Ogden, *Drakon: Dragon Myth and Serpent Cult in the Greek and Roman Worlds* [Oxford: Oxford University Press, 2013], 58–59.)

18. Pindar, *Pythian* 4 158–159 (new system), 282–283 (old system).

19. Mackie, "Earliest Jason," 13.

20. This view was popular with the German scholars of comparative mythology in the early twentieth century. For more modern discussions of Jason's descent to Hades, symbolic or otherwise, see Fontenrose, *Python*, 305–306 and appendix 1; Richard Hunter, *The Argonautica of Apollonius* (Cambridge: Cambridge University Press, 1993), 184.

21. Kathleen Jenks, "Phobos," in *Gods, Goddesses, and Mythology*, ed. C. Scott Littleton (Tarrytown, NY: Marshall Cavendish, 2005), 1121; Fontenrose, *Python*, 329.

22. Apollodorus, *Library* 1.9.16, believed to be derived from Pherecydes.

23. Satterfield, "Dumuzi," 449.

24. Kenton L. Sparks, *Ancient Texts for the Study of the Hebrew Bible: A Guide to the Background Literature* (Peabody, Mass.: Hendrickson, 2005), 128–129.

25. Turner and Coulter, *Dictionary of Ancient Deities*, 172.

26. Jeremy Black and Anthony Green, *Gods, Demons, and Symbols of Ancient Mesopotamia: An Illustrated Dictionary* (Austin: University of Texas, 2003), 140.

27. B. Alster, "Tammuz," in *Dictionary of Demons and Deities in the Bible*, 2nd ed., edited by K. van der Toorn, Bob Becking, and Pieter Willem van der Horst (Leiden: Brill, 1999), 832.

28. Turner and Coulter, *Dictionary of Ancient Deities*, 346.

29. Robbins, "Jason and Cheiron," 210 n. 16. Brelich sought to attach every Greek hero to healing power as one of nine core elements of a mythic hero, but most scholars feel he overstated his schemata, which reflect common concerns of aristocratic Greeks as much as the essential elements of a hero. See H. L. Rose, "Who Were the Heroes?," *The Classical Review* 10 (1960): 48–50.

30. Quoted in Emmet Robbins, "Jason and Cheiron: The Myth of Pindar's Fourth Pythian," *Phoenix* 49, no. 3 (1975): 210 n. 16.

31. Kirk, *Nature of Greek Myth*, 119–120.

32. Ian Rutherford, *Pindar's Paeans* (Oxford: Oxford University Press, 2001), 16.

33. R. Arnott, "Mycenaean and Minoan Medicine and Its Near Eastern Contacts," in *Magic and Rationality in Ancient Near Eastern and Greco-Roman Medicine*, edited by H. F. J. Horstmanshoff and M. Stoll (Leiden: Brill, 2004), 168.

34. Arnott, "Mycenaean and Minoan Medicine," 169.

35. Mackie, "Earliest Jason," 14.

36. For example, *The New International Encyclopedia* wrote, "Much points to an original divinity sunk to heroine" in the entry on Medea in 1930. Hesiod makes Medea a goddess in *Theogony* 956–962, counted among the immortals. However, Cicero used Medea in *De natura deorum* (3.19) as an example of an ambiguously divine figure whose status depends on how one chooses to count the children and grandchildren of gods.

37. Argument to Euripides' *Medea*.

38. Aldhouse-Green and Aldhouse-Green, *Quest for the Shaman*, 15.

39. Yulia Ustinova, *Caves and the Ancient Greek Mind: Descending Underground in Search for Ultimate Truth* (Oxford: Oxford University Press, 2009), 152–3, n. 619.

40. Aldhous-Green and Aldhous-Green, *Quest for the Shaman*, 10–15.

41. Mimnermus, quoted in Strabo, *Geography* 1.2.40; see also West, "*Odyssey* and *Argonautica*," 41.

42. Lewis-Williams, *The Mind in the Cave*, 145.

43. Pindar, *Pythian* 4, 79–80 (new system), 140–141 (old system).

44. Susan A. Stephens, *Seeing Double: Intercultural Poetics in Ptolemaic Alexandria* (Berkeley: University of California Press, 2003), 201.

45. Sandars, *Poems of Heaven and Hell from Ancient Mesopotamia*, 160.

46. Deacy, *Athena*, 20.

47. Aldhouse-Green and Aldhous-Green, *Quest for the Shaman*, 143–147; for discussion of the literature and additional evidence, see Ustinova, *Caves and the Ancient Greek Mind*, 47–51.

48. Fritz Graf, "Orpheus: A Poet among Men," in Jan V. Bremmer, ed., *Interpretations of Greek Mythology* (Beckenham, Kent: Croom Helm, 1987), 95–99. Graf argued that the Argonauts were a brotherhood of initiates entering into the cult of aristocratic warriors. I disagree with Graf that a warrior initiation is necessarily at odds with interpreting the story as a shaman/priest's journey. The shaman is protector of his community, and it is in no way a contradiction to argue that a shamanic-style journey may have been part of the initiation rights for kings or warriors, as is known to have occurred in Egypt and among the Native American "vision quest" traditions.

49. M. L. West, *Indo-European Poetry and Myth* (Oxford: Oxford University Press, 2007), 168.

50. Ken Dowden, *Zeus* (New York: Routledge, 2006), 9–10, 28–30.

51. Dowden, *Zeus*, 28.

52. West, *Indo-European Poetry and Mythology*, 243–244.

53. Dennis D. Hughes, *Human Sacrifice in Ancient Greece* (New York: Routledge, 1991), 186–187; see also Walter Burkert's *Homo Necans*.

54. Herodotus, *The Histories* 7.197, trans. Alfred Dennis Godley, volume III (London: William Heinemann, 1920), 513–514.

55. Hughes, *Human Sacrifice in Ancient Greece*, 93–94.

56. Hughes, *Human Sacrifice in Ancient Greece*, 95.

57. Heraclides 2.8, quoted in Burkert, *Homo Necans*, 113.

58. The Greek conceptions of the shepherd as leader differ from the Hebrew conception, in which the king's role as shepherd is based on an analogy with God's role as shepherd. The Greeks instead analogized from a (superior) man shepherding (inferior) animals. (Robin Osborne, "The Religious Contexts of Ancient Political Thought," in Ryan K. Balot, ed., *A Companion to Greek and Roman Political Thought* [Malden, Mass.: Blackwell, 2009], 120).

59. Johannes Haubold, *Homer's People: Epic Poetry*

and Social Formation (Cambridge: Cambridge University Press, 2000), 17–20.

60. "I am Hammurabi, Enlil's chosen shepherd [...] the shepherd of the people, whose achievements bring glory to Ishtar." (Hammurabi's Code, P4, in M. E. J. Richardson, *Hammurabi's Laws: Text, Translation, and Glossary*, originally published 2000 [London: T&T Clark International, 2004], 31, 39.).

61. Joan V. O'Brien notes that Hera's mythology includes a great deal of material from earlier earth goddess traditions, including her role as mother of serpents, that other traditions reassigned to Gaia, reinforcing the identification between Hera and the earth goddess discussed in this book (*The Transformation of Hera: A Study of Ritual, Hero, and the Goddess in the* Iliad [Landham, Maryland: Rowman and Littlefield, 1993], 100–102.)

62. O'Brien, *Transformation of Hera*, 205. This is based, O'Brien says, on etymology and Hera's links to Jason, whom she sees as a "Minyan" (northern Mycenaean) figure.

63. O'Brien, *Transformation of Hera*, 127, 206.

64. O'Brien, *Transformation of Hera*, 127, 162.

65. Morris, *Archaeology as Cultural History*, 233. "Hero" and "Hera" are etymologically connected, regardless of whether there was a specific deity named Heros.

66. O'Brien specifically notes the Dark Age and Archaic cult of Hera had associations with heroes, of whom she was the special protector, and connects these to her Mycenaean cult.

67. O'Brien, *Transformation of Hera*, 121.

68. Homer, *Odyssey* 5.125f.; Hesiod, *Theogony* 969–974. Interestingly Demeter would give Plutus a chariot pulled by serpents, just like the one Medea would use, another link between Medea and the original earth goddess of myth.

69. Fontenrose, *Python*, 315 n. 75; Müller, *Orchomenos und die Minyer*, 260.

70. Noel Robertson, *Religion and Reconciliation in Greek Cities: The Sacred Laws of Selinus and Cyrene* (Oxford: Oxford University Press, 2010), 165. Scholars are divided whether heroes represent humans mythologized and partially deified or whether they represent former deities who became increasingly human. There is no consensus, and the best guess is that the "heroes" are a hodgepodge of ex-gods, promoted humans, and some who are entirely fictional inventions. It is worth noting that the line between hero and god is not clear (this is especially true cross-culturally), and it may only have been later that distinctions emerged in the telling of hero stories.

71. Louise Bruit Zaidman and Pauline Schmitt Pantel, *Religion in the Ancient Greek City,* trans. Paul Cartledge, 1989 (Cambridge: Cambridge University Press, 2002), 179–180.

72. Walter Burkert, *Greek Religion,* trans. John Raffan (Cambridge: Harvard University Press, 1985), 205–206. Note that older generations of scholars thought that Zeus-worshipping Indo-European Greeks simply replaced earth-worshipping pre–Greek peoples. This simplistic version is not the case, since sky gods and earth gods are attested in both groups. The difference is that older belief systems placed their gods in the sites of their function (the earth goddess in the earth, the weather god on a mountain, etc.) while the new religion

that developed in the Dark Ages separated the gods from the earth and removed them to Olympus, eventually rendering them (especially Zeus) transcendent rather than imminent.

73. B. C. Dietrich, *Origins of Greek Religion,* orig. 1974 (reprint, Bristol: Bristol Phoenix Press, 2004), 115–116.

74. These symbols can also be read as symbols of the earth goddess herself, including the bulls as fire symbols (related to the fire-god Typhon, son of an early form of Hera), the earth men as earth symbols, and the dragon representing the goddess' role as mother of serpents. Given the identity of Poseidon, the sun, and the bull, I have chosen to read these as symbols of male gods; however, the interchangeability of the earth god and goddess in early practice cannot be entirely discounted. Cf. O'Brien, *Hera*, 94–102.

75. Dietrich, *Origin of Greek Religion*, 17.

76. Dietrich, *Origin of Greek Religion*, 18–19.

Chapter 4

1. Kirk, *The Nature of Greek Myths*, 160.

2. Thomas, *Finding People in Early Greece*, 77–79. In the same period the formerly nameless mountain on which Prometheus was chained became localized in the Caucasus when the Greeks became aware of the story that the Georgian hero Amirani had been chained to a mountain there as divine punishment, but no one supposes the myth reflects Bronze Age travels to central Asia. Instead, it clearly reflects Greek efforts to match their myths to those they encountered in their eighth century travels. This should give pause to those who uncritically assume the Argonauts originated in Bronze Age epic voyages. This also supports the idea (see below) that the Greeks came to identify Aea with Colchis as part of the same process that matched Prometheus to Amirani since the latter's myths were obviously known to the Greeks, who matched elements from them to their gods more or less at will without seeking a perfect one-to-one correlation.

3. Robert Van De Noort, "Argonauts of the North Sea: A Social Maritime Archaeology for the Second Millennium BC," *Proceedings of the Prehistoric Society* 72 (2006): 279

4. Van De Noort, "Argonauts of the North Sea," 279.

5. Van De Noort, "Argonauts of the North Sea," 282.

6. Strabo, *Geography* 1.2.38. Demetrius argued that Homer knew only that Jason voyaged out into the Ocean and was therefore ignorant of the Black Sea in general and Colchis in particular.

7. In *Theogony* (746–751) night and day greet each other at a single point, the bronze gateway to Tartarus, the deepest Underworld, and rise and set from there at intervals.

8. Dimitri Nakassis, "Gemination at the Horizons: East and West in the Mythical Geography of Archaic Greek Epic," *Transactions of the American Philological Association* 134, no. 2 (2004): 215–233.

9. In the nineteenth century, F. Max Müller suggested that Jason's journey was originally to the west based on his reading of Mimnermus as suggesting the

sun's rays would logically "rest" in the west (i.e. at night) and the theory that Homer's Aea (Aeaea) in the west predated the one in the east, which is not likely the actual case (*Contributions to the Science of Comparative Mythology*, 437–438). Carl Robert argued in *Die Griechische Heldensagen* (1920) that Jason's journey occurred in the west before being relocated to the east based on the assumption that the clashing rocks were always identified with the Bosporus. If so, the Argonauts could not have encountered them while returning from Colchis (as they do in Homer) unless they travelled to Colchis by going west and circumnavigating the world. However, as shown below, the evidence instead supports the idea that the rocks were formerly mythical and were only later identified with the Bosporus after the Greeks explored the Black Sea in the seventh and sixth centuries BCE. If the *Argonautica* took place in the cosmic geography preserved in Hesiod, where east and west were the same, then this argument is moot since there was but one Gate of the Sun and the Underworld.

10. Homer, *Odyssey* 11.13–15; trans. Palmer.

11. Of course, the Cimmerians may have existed in myth long before the real people of the Black Sea were encountered. The important point is that the Greeks must have viewed the Black Sea as part of Ocean for a time, or they would not have connected the Cimmerians with the sea's northern coast.

12. Terry G. Jordan-Bychkov and Bella Bychkova Jordan, *The European Culture Area: A Systematic Geography* (4th ed.) (Lanham, Maryland: Rowman and Littlefield, 2002), 2–3.

13. Stephan Hiller, "Mycenaeans and the Black Sea," in *Thalassa: L'Égée préhistorique et la mer* (Aegaeum 7), 206–217.

14. Gocha R. Tsetskhladze, "Greek Colonisation in the Black Sea Area: Stages, Models and Native Population," in *The Greek Colonisation of the Black Sea Area: Historical Interpretation of Archaeology,* edited by Gocha R. Tsetskhladze (Germany: Steiner, 1998): 13–14; A. J. Graham, "Pre-Colonial Contacts: Questions and Problems," in *Collected Papers on Greek Colonization* (Boston: Brill, 2001), 34–36; Otar Lordkipanidze, "The Golden Fleece: Myth, Euhemeristic Explanation and Archaeology," *Oxford Journal of Archaeology* 20, no. 1 (2002): 18.

15. A. J. Graham, "The Date of the Greek Penetration of the Black Sea," in *Collected Papers on Greek Colonization* (Boston: Brill, 2001), 113–138.

16. Graham, "Date," 129–130.

17. Tzetskhladze, "Greek Colonisation," 10–15.

18. Maya Vassileva, "Greek Ideas of the North and East: Mastering the Black Sea Area," in *The Greek Colonisation of the Black Sea Area: Historical Interpretation of Archaeology,* edited by Gocha R. Tsetskhladze (Germany: Steiner, 1998): 69–77.

19. David Braund, "Writing and Re-Inventing Colonial Origins: Problems from Colchis and the Bosporus," in *Greek Colonisation of the Black Sea Area: Historical Interpretation of Archaeology,* edited by Gocha R. Tsetskhladze (Germany: Steiner, 1998): 289–290.

20. W.E.D. Allen, *Georgia and Its People* (London: Routledge 1932, reissue 1971), 37–39. The Georgians also had gods derived from the Zoroastrian and Mithraic pantheons, but those influences arrived centuries after our period.

21. Peter Nasmyth, *Georgia: In the Mountains of Poetry* (New York: St. Martin's Press, 1998), 45–46.

22. David Hunt, "The Association of the Lady and the Unicorn, and the Hunting Mythology of the Caucasus," *Folklore* 114, no. 1 (2003): 83. This figure was chained to a mountain as punishment from a god, leading Greeks to associate Amirani's mountain of punishment with the mountain to which Prometheus was chained. In all other respects, however, the two figures are very different, indicating that the Greeks matched *elements* of their myths to those found in Colchis, not whole stories or even entire characters. Thus, they may well have identified Jason with Amirani's slaying of the dragon without necessarily equating Jason with Amirani one-to-one. But, for the opposing view, see D. M. Lang and G. M. Meredith Owens, "*Amiran-Darejaniani* and Its English Rendering," *Bulletin of the School of Oriental and African Studies, University of London* 22 (1959): 464–466. The authors caution that the Georgian material is medieval in date and may well represent Greek myths that have been folded into Georgian legends. Thus, Prometheus may have come to the Caucasus and influenced Amirani's story.

23. On the common Proto-Indo-European origins of Georgian and Greek mythology, see Kevin Tuite, "Achilles and the Caucasus," *Journal of Indo-European Studies* 26, no. 3 (1998): 289–344. However, I disagree with his conclusion that the Greeks and Caucasians were in contact in the Mycenaean period, and am uneasy with the somewhat circular argument of "reconstructing" Bronze Age versions of Greek and Caucasian myths by applying Proto-Indo-European theories and concepts and thus deducing from the reconstructions startling similarities. Nevertheless, Tuite presents some interesting comparisons and an intriguing Russian theory that Achilles was himself originally the dragon in a primitive version of a battle with the storm god (Zeus) based on his serpentine and chthonic ancestors, which imply a substitution of the hero Achilles for the ancient dragon at some early date.

24. A. Kirchoff, *Der Composition der Odyssee* (Berlin: Verlag von Wilhelm-Hertz, 1869), 84–86.

25. F. A. Paley, "Pre-Homeric Legends of the Voyage of the Argonauts," *The Dublin Review* (1879): 164–182. Paley treats Apollonius as though he never read Pindar and Homer, leading him to faulty conclusions about elements in the various poems that he believed were "independently" drawn from an ancient oral tradition.

26. West, "*Odyssey* and *Argonautica*," 57–58.

27. Homer, *Iliad* 7.464ff.

28. Mackie, "Earliest Jason."

29. Walter Burkert, "Jason, Hypsipyle, and New Fire at Lemnos: A Study in Myth and Ritual," *The Classical Quarterly* (New Series) 20, no. 1 (May 1970): 1–16.

30. Burkert, *Greek Religion*, 281.

31. Burkert, "Jason, Hypsipyle, and New Fire," 9–10. Aeschylus specifically connected the Argonauts and Cabeiri.

32. Castleden, *Mycenaeans*, 83.

33. Wood, *In Search of Myths & Heroes*, 100.

34. Thomas, *Finding People in Early Greece*, 65.

35. Alfred Heubeck and Arie Hoeckstra, *A Commentary on Homer's* Odyssey, Volume II: Books IX–XVI (Oxford: Clarendon Paperbacks, 1990), 121.

36. The Symplegades and Planctae are sometimes

considered separate, and Apollonius, to make his story agree with Homer, separates them, placing one at the Bosporus and the other in the west. This, however, is a late tradition. For Homer's usage see discussion in Heubeck and Hoeckstra, *Commentary on Homer's Odyssey*, 121.

37. Homer, *Odyssey* 12.69–72, *op. cit.*, 182.

38. West, "*Odyssey* and *Argonautica*," 40.

39. West, "*Odyssey* and *Argonautica*," 41–42.

40. *Odyssey* 12.61–65.

41. West, "*Odyssey* and *Argonautica*," 45, citing a fragment of Pherecydes preserved in scholia.

42. West, "*Odyssey* and *Argonautica*," 45.

43. Judith Yarnall, *The Transformation of Circe: The History of an Enchantress* (Urbana: University of Illinois, 1994), 31. Yarnall notes that Circe shares a mastery of animals and a mortal consort (Odysseus) with other earth goddesses.

44. Strabo, *Geography* 1.2.40.

45. West, "*Odyssey* and *Argonautica*," 47.

46. Graf, "Orpheus: A Poet among Men," 97.

47. West, "*Odyssey* and *Argonautica*," 53. West also notes the existence of a Cape Aia (Aea) in the same Crimean location, but can find no evidence to support the antiquity of the name.

48. Nakassis, "Gemination," 225.

49. G. S. Kirk believed Odysseus' underworld vision was an interpolation and not derived from the *Argonautica*. This would actually be in keeping with the theory that the *Argonautica* was originally an underworld trip in itself, since in that case no explicit necromantic underworld conjuring would be necessary (*Homer and the Epic* [Cambridge: Cambridge University Press, 1965], 172).

50. Homer, *Odyssey* 11.14f., *op. cit.*, p. 160.

51. Eustabius, commentary on *Odyssey* 12.129.

52. N. K. Sandars (trans.), *Poems of Heaven and Hell from Ancient Mesopotamia* (Penguin, 1971), 115.

53. West, *East Face of Helicon*, 153.

54. Robert Lamberton, *Hesiod* (Hermes Books, 1988), 15–16.

55. Friedrich Solmsen, *Hesiod and Aeschylus,* 1949 (Ithaca: Cornell Paperbacks, 1995), 49–51.

56. Richard Hunter, introduction to *The Hesiodic Catalogue of Women: Constructions and Reconstructions,* ed. Richard Hunter (Cambridge: Cambridge University Press, 2005), 2–3.

57. Also translated as "Zeus-cherished king," or "high bred."

58. This phrase is also translated less discretely as "He made her submit to his passion" (Hesiod, *Theogony, Works and Days, and Shield,* trans. Apostolos N. Athanassakis [Baltimore: Johns Hopkins University Press, 2004], 36) or "In wifely duty to Jason" (Hesiod, *Works of Hesiod and the Homeric Hymns,* trans. Daryl Hine [Chicago: University of Chicago Press, 2005], 87).

59. Hesiod, *Theogony* 993–1002, in *Hesiod, the Homeric Hymns, and Homerica,* trans. Hugh G. Evelyn-White (London: William Heinemann, 1920), 153. Some scholars believe this passage is a later interpolation, based on the appearance of Medeus, who can otherwise only be securely attested from the sixth century, but this opinion is by no means universal.

60. Hesiod, preserved in Eratosthenes, *Catasterisms* 19.

61. Scholiast on Homer, at *Odyssey* 12.69, in Hesiod, *Hesiod*, 163.

62. Alcimede: Apollonius, *Argonautica* 1.233, Hyginus, *Fabulae* 14, and *Odyssey* scholia at 12.69, citing Pherecydes; Amphinome: Diodorus, *Library* 40.50.2; Arne: Tzetzes, scholia on Lycophron at 872; Eteoclymene: Apollonius scholia at 1.230, citing Stesichorus; Polymede: Apollodorus, *Library* 1.9.16; Polymela: *Odyssey* scholia at 12.70; Polypheme: Apollonius scholia at 1.45, citing Herodorus; Rhoeo: Tzetzes, *Chiliades* 6.96; Scarphe: Tzetzes, scholia on Lycophron at 872; and Theognete: Apollonius scholia at 1.45, citing Andron.

63. There is debate over whether all the fragments derive from the original poem devoted to Hesiod, or whether some come from another substantively similar poem from the same tradition. Known as the *Megalai Ehoiai* and the *Catalogue of Women* to distinguish them, it is unclear whether these were two separate poems or one a revised and expanded version of the other. For our purposes, we may treat them as reflecting traditions from the same era, no matter their original relationship. For discussion, see Giovan Battista d'Alessio, "The *Megalai Ehoiai*: A Survey of the Fragments," in *The Hesiodic Catalogue of Women: Constructions and Reconstructions,* edited by Richard Hunter (Cambridge: Cambridge University Press, 2005), 178–216.

64. Scholiast on Apollonius of Rhodes at *Argonautica* 1.45.

65. *Catasterisms* 19.

66. Scholiast on Apollonius, at *Argonautica* 2.181, trans. in Hesiod, *Hesiod*, 177. These variants likely derived from the *Megalai Ehoiai* and the *Catalogue* separately.

67. Ephorus in Strabo, *Geography* 7.3.9: trans. in Hesiod, *Hesiod*, 179.

68. Scholiast on Apollonius at *Argonautia* 2.296 and 297, trans. in Hesiod, *Hesiod*, 181.

69. Philodemus, *On Piety* 10; Strabo, *Geography* 1.2.35; scholiast on Apollonius' *Argonautica* at 4.259 and 4.284. Hesiod also mentions the Phasis in *Theogony* 340.

70. West, "Phasis and Aia," 196.

71. At *Argonautica* 4.892.

72. At *Argonautica* 1.128.

73. Jonathan S. Burgess, *The Tradition of the Trojan War in Homer and the Epic Cycle* (Baltimore: Johns Hopkins University Press, 2001), 8.

74. For discussion of the many dating problems, see Burgess, *Tradition of the Trojan War*, 9–12.

75. Trans. in Hesiod, *Hesiod,* 527.

76. At line 273, trans. in Hesiod, *Hesiod*, 535.

77. Bruce Karl Braswell, *Commentary on the Fourth Pythian Ode of Pindar* (Berlin/New York: De Gruyter, 1988), 8.

78. Thomas, *Finding People in Early Greece*, 73.

79. Scholiast on Apollonius at *Argonautica* 3.587, trans. in Hesiod, *Hesiod*, 271.

80. Bremmer, *Greek Religion and Culture,* chapter XV.

81. D. S. Robertson, "The Flight of Phrixus," *The Classical Review* 54, no. 1 (1940): 1–8.

82. Strabo, *Geography* 1.2.40, *op. cit.*, vol. 1, 171, 173.

83. Herodorus, who drew on the *Naupaktia*, states Heracles was not an Argonaut, apparently on this poem's authority (Victor J. Matthews, "Naupaktia and Argonautika," *Phoenix* 31, no. 3 [Autumn 1977]: 197).

84. Matthews, "Naupaktia and Argonautika," 194.

85. Matthews, "Naupaktia and Argonautika," 205.

86. The standard interpretation of this phrase is "all the heroes aboard the *Argo*" followed by their names, but Matthews argues that a recitation of such a list would have made the poem unwieldy, and proposes this alternative reading. "Naupaktia and Argonautika," 195.

87. Matthews, "Naupaktia and Argonautika," 202.

88. Moses Hadas, "A Tradition of a Feeble Jason?," *Classical Philology* 31, no. 2 (1936): 167.

89. Matthews, "Naupaktia and Argonautika," 199. Matthews again suggests that Corinth made Hera a part of Jason's myth, but this seems impossible since Homer was well aware of her role at least a century before Eumelus.

90. Burkert, *Structure and History,* 10; West, *East Face of Helicon,* 407 and "Odyssey and Argonautica," 62. But in "Phasis and Aia," 196–197, without resolving the contradiction, West further proposes an Indo-European derivation, though to my mind an unsatisfactory one whereby he traces *Aia* back through several hypothesized layers to *h_2eus, a Proto-Indo-European word. But since Greek has an Indo-European-derived word for dawn, *eos*, this implies the existence of proto-*Aia* before the two words diverged without leaving any trace outside the Jason myth and the Homeric elements (Circe's Aeaea) derived from it, not even in other myths of Helios.

91. Obviously, this is parallel to the Etruscan practice of asking the gods' permission to destroy a city, which we examined in chapter 2.

92. Alain Blomart, "Transferring the Cults of Heroes in Ancient Greece: A Political and Religious Act," in *Philostratus's* Heroikos: *Religion and Cultural Identity in the Third Century*, eds. Ellen Bradshaw Aitken and Jennifer K. Berenson Maclean (Leiden: Brill, 2004): 87–88, 93.

93. M. L. West, "'Eumelos': A Corinthian Epic Cycle?," *The Journal of Hellenic Studies 122* (2002): 130–131.

94. Pausanias, *Description of Greece* 2.3.10–11, trans. W. H. S. Jones (London: William Heinemann, 1918), 265.

95. Diogenes Laertius, "Life of Epimenides" 5, in *The Lives and Opinions of Eminent Philosophers,* trans. C. D. Young (London: George Bell and Sons, 1901), 51.

96. Pausanias, *Description of Greece* 2.3.7.

97. Sarah Iles Johnson, "Corinthian Medea and the Cult of Hera Akraia," in *Medea*, eds. James J. Clauss and Sarah Iles Johnson (Princeton: Princeton University Press, 2004), 44–70.

98. Hesiod, *Theogony* 450, 452; trans. in *op. cit.,* 109.

99. *Etymologicum Magnum*, s.v. Cyllarus; Athenaeus, *Deipnosophistae* 4.172; Zenobius, *Proverbs* 1.173; Braswell, *Commentary on the Fourth Pythian Ode,* 12–13.

100. Scholia at *Argonautica* 4.814–5; Benjamin Acosta-Hughes, *Arion's Lyre: Archaic Lyric into Hellenistic Poetry* (Princeton: Princeton University Press, 2010), 168.

101. Acosta-Hughes, *Arion's Lyre,* 165.

102. Scholia to Euripides, *Medea* line 5; trans. in Acosta-Hughes, *Arion's Lyre,* 199.

103. Acosta-Hughes, *Arion's Lyre,* 200.

104. Acosta-Hughes, *Arion's Lyre,* 202, esp. n. 97.

105. Scholia at *Argonautica* 4.814–5; Acosta-Hughes, *Arion's Lyre,* 203–205.

Chapter 5

1. Burkert, *Greek Religion,* 209.

2. Burkert, *Greek Religion,* 210.

3. D. L. Toye, "Pherecydes of Syros: Ancient Theologian and Genealogist," *Mnemosyne* (4th series) 50 (1997): 547.

4. Pherecydes' fragments on Argonaut themes are primarily found in the scholia to Apollonius and Pindar. Of particular relevance are the scholia to Apollonius at 1.4, 1.1290, 2.411, 3.1178, 4.156, 4.223, and 4.228, as well as the scholia to Pindar at *Pythian* 4.133. From the last I have translated the line about Hera's idea.

5. Braswell, *Commentary on the Fourth Pythian Ode,* 19.

6. Plutarch, "Life of Theseus" 29.

7. Stanley Mayer Burstein, *Outpost of Hellenism: The Emergence of Heraclea on the Black Sea* (Classical Studies Vol. 14) (Berkeley: University of California Press, 1976), 2.

8. Gilbert Murray, *A History of Ancient Greek Literature* (New York: Appleton and Company, 1903), 127.

9. Herodotus, *Histories* 7.62.

10. Herodotus, *Histories* 1.2.

11. Herodotus, *Histories* 4.179.

12. Herodotus, *Histories* 7.193.

13. Frank J. Nisetich, introduction to *Pindar's Victory Songs* by Pindar, trans. Frank J. Nisetich (Baltimore: Johns Hopkins University Press, 1980), 7–12.

14. Dio Chrysostom, *Orations* 37.15.

15. Robbins, "Jason and Cheiron," 205.

16. Robbins, "Jason and Cheiron," 205–206.

17. Robbins, "Jason and Cheiron," 208–213.

18. Pindar, *Pythian* 4, 79ff. (new system), 139ff. (old system), trans. in *The Extant Odes of Pindar,* trans. Ernest Myers (London: Macmillan, 1904), 72.

19. M. L. West suggests that Pindar's description of the single sandal and Pelias' reaction is the remnant of an ancient Indo-European rite for inaugurating kings, based on an early modern Irish analogy in which a claimant surrenders a shoe as a mark of candidacy and receives a new one upon assuming office, but this seems rather uncertain in the absence of additional parallels (*Indo-European Poetry and Myth* [Oxford: Oxford University Press, 2007], 419).

20. Pindar, *Pythian* 4, 118f. (new system), 210f. (old system), trans. in *Extant Odes,* 73.

21. Pindar, *Pythian* 4, 237f. (new system), 422f. (old system), trans. in *Extant Odes,* 77.

22. Braswell, *Commentary on the Fourth Pythian Ode,* 161.

23. Thomas K. Hubbard, *The Pindaric Mind: A Study of Logical Structure in Early Greek Poetry* (Leiden: Brill, 1985), 95

24. Gilbert Norwood, *Pindar,* Sather Classical Lectures, vol. 19 (Berkeley: University of California Press, 1945), 39.

25. Jennifer Neils, "Reflections of Immortality: The Myth of Jason on Etruscan Mirrors," in Richard Daniel De Puma and Jocelyn Penny Small, eds., *Murlo*

and the Etruscans: Art and Society in Ancient Etruria (Madison: University of Wisconsin Press, 1994), 192.

26. On Etruscan afterlife beliefs: Nancy Thompson de Grummond, *Etruscan Myth, Sacred History, and Legend* (Philadelphia: University of Philadelphia Museum of Archaeology and Anthropology, 2006), 209. On Etruscan golden sheep: Macrobius, *Saturnalia* 3.7.2.

27. Mackie, "Earliest Jason," 10.

28. Neils, "Reflections of Immortality," 193.

29. Neils, "Reflections of Immortality," 191.

30. George Dennis, *The Cities and Cemeteries of Etruria*, Vol. II, 3rd ed. (London: John Murray, 1883), 88.

31. de Grummond, *Etruscan Myth*, 117.

32. Richard Seaford, *Dionysus* (London: Routledge, 2006), 76–81.

33. Alexandra Carpino, "Greek Mythology in Etruria: An Iconographic Analysis of Three Etruscan Relief Mirrors," in *Etruscan Italy: Etruscan Influences on the Civilization of Italy from Antiquity to the Modern Era*, ed. John Franklin Hall (Salt Lake City: Brigham Young University Press, 1996), 77–80.

34. Pausania, *Description of Greece* 5.17.5–5.19.10.

35. Cynthia King, "Who Is That Cloaked Man? Observations on Early Fifth Century B.C. Pictures of the Golden Fleece," *American Journal of Archaeology* 87, no. 3 (1983): 386–387. King also sees the snake on the krater as a penis and Jason as infibulated to prevent erection, but the snake looks rather snake-like to me.

36. Gisela M. A. Richter, "Jason and the Golden Fleece," *The Metropolitan Museum of Art Bulletin* 30, no. 4 (1935): 87.

37. Hadas, "Feeble Jason," 168.

38. Timothy Gantz, "The Aischylean Tetralogy: Attested and Conjectured Groups," in *Aeschylus*, edited by Michael Lloyd (Oxford: Oxford University Press, 2007), 66.

39. Sophocles, *The Dramas of Sophocles Rendered into English Verse: Dramatic & Lyric*, trans. Sir George Young (London: J. M. Dent, 1906), 328.

40. Sophocles, *Dramas of Sophocles*, 329.

41. Sophocles, *Dramas of Sophocles*, 329.

42. Quoted in Macrobius, *Saturnalia* 5.19.8; my translation.

43. Emily A. McDermott, *Euripides'* Medea: *The Incarnation of Disorder* (Pennsylvania State University, 1989), 20–24. Neophron is dated in ancient sources to either before Euripides or living during the reign of Alexander the Great. McDermott believes Neophron came after Euripides and imitated him, while some ancient authors accused Euripides of plagiarizing Neophron. Unfortunately, the question cannot be resolved given current evidence.

44. Euripides, *Medea* 475f., trans. in *The Plays of Euripides*, Vol. 1, trans. Edward P. Coleridge (London: George Bell and Sons, 1906), 45–46.

45. Euripides, *Medea* 908f., trans. *op. cit.,* 57–58.

46. Euripides, *Medea* 1069f., trans. *op. cit.*, 62.

47. Marianne McDonald, "Medea as Politician and Diva: Riding the Dragon into the Future," in *Medea*, edited by James J. Clauss and Sarah Iles Johnson (Princeton: Princeton University Press, 1997), 297–324. McDonald sees Medea as a heroic figure who chooses to invert male heroic ideology by enacting her triumph through the feminine realm of family.

48. Robert B. Palmer, "An Apology for Jason: A Study of Euripides' *Medea*," *The Classical Journal* 53, no. 2 (1957), 49–55.

49. Dracontius, *Carmina minora* 10; Fritz Graf, "Medea: The Enchantress from Afar: Remarks on a Well-Known Myth," in *Medea*, edited by James J. Clauss and Sarah Iles Johnson (Princeton: Princeton University Press, 1997), 26.

50. Malcolm Bell, "A Coptic Jason Relief," *Gesta* 18, no. 1 (1979): 48. This inference is based on the scholia to Apollonius and several Roman and medieval Jason images that show several Argonauts and defeated soldiers beside the tree holding the Fleece.

51. Kirk, *The Nature of Greek Myths*, 104–107.

52. 4.40–56.

53. Palaephatus, *On Unbelievable Tales* 30, trans. Jacob Stern (Wacunda, Illinois: Bolchazy-Carducci, 1996), p. 61.

54. Diodorus Siculus, *The Historical Library* 4.55.1; trans. G. Booth (London, 1814), 267.

55. Photius, *Bibliotecha* 190. Photius, in summarizing Ptolemaeus calls him Ptolemy Hephaestion. Most modern scholars identify this figure with Ptolemaeus Chennus, about whose serious or satirical intent scholars are divided.

56. *Catasterismi* 35.

57. Steven Jackson, "*Argo*: The First Ship?," *Rheinisches Museum für Philologie* 140 (1997): 255.

58. Catullus 64.11; Valerius Flaccus, *Argonautica* 1.273–276; *Orphic Argonautica* 64f.

59. R. J. Clare, *The Path of the Argo: Language, Imagery, and Narrative in the* Argonautica *of Apollonius Rhodius* (Cambridge: Cambridge University Press, 2002), chapter 1.

60. For example, Virginia Knight, *The Renewal of Epic: Responses to Homer in the* Argonautica *of Apollonius* (Leiden: Brill, 1995); Robert V. Albis, *Poet and Audience in the* Argonautica *of Apollonius* (Lanham, MD: Rowman & Littlefield, 1996); Margaret Margolies DeForest, *Apollonius'* Argonautica: *A Callimachean Epic* (Leiden: Brill, 1994), and Clare, *The Path of the Argo*.

61. Apollonius Rhodius, *Argonautica* 3.453ff., trans. R. C. Seaton (London: William Heinemann, 1912), 225.

62. Apollonius, *Argonautica*, 3.957; trans. *op. cit.*, 259.

63. Apollonius, *Argonautica*, 3.1015f., trans. *op. cit.*, 263, 265.

64. Apollonius, *Argonautica* 4.1773f., trans. *op. cit.*, 415.

65. Longinus, *On the Sublime*, 33.1, trans. A. O. Prickard (Oxford: Clarendon Press, 1906), 61–62.

66. Quintilian, *Institutes of Oratory*, 10.1.54, in *Quintlians's Institutes of Oratory: Or, the Education of an Orator*, Vol. 2: trans. John Selby Watson (London: George Bell and Sons, 1905), 258.

67. R. L. Hunter, "'Short on Heroics': Jason in the *Argonautica*," *The Classical Quarterly* (New Series) 38, no. 2 (1988): 436; Steven Jackson, "Apollonius' Jason: Human Being in an Epic Scenario," *Greece & Rome* 39, no. 2 (1992): 155.

68. Jackson, "Apollonius' Jason," 158. Apollonius has Jason use the Theseus story to influence Medea, leaving out Theseus' abandonment of Ariadne, an irony readers would savor, knowing the outcome of Medea's story.

69. Hunter, "Short on Heroics," 443.

70. Hunter, "Short on Heroics," 451–452.

71. Jackson, "Apollonius' Jason," 161.

72. Horace, *Epistles*, epistle 2.156, translation in Horace, *The Satires and Epistles of Horace: A Modern English Verse Translation,* trans. Smith Palmer Bovie (Chicago: University of Chicago Press, 2002), 254.

73. Hyginus, *Fabulae* 12 and 13.

74. *Fabulae* 13 and 22.

75. Marie Tanner, *The Last Descendant of Aeneas: The Hapsburgs and the Mythic Image of the Emperor* (New Haven: Yale University Press, 1993), 6.

76. Seneca, *Medea* lines 140–143, in *Seneca's Tragedies,* vol. I, trans. Frank Justice Miller (London: William Heinemann, 1918), 239.

77. Seneca, *Medea*, lines 1026–1027, trans. *op. cit.,* p. 315.

78. Inga-Stina Ewbank, "The Fiend-Like Queen: A Note on 'Macbeth' and Seneca's 'Medea,'" in *Shakespeare Survey 19: Macbeth,* ed. Kenneth Moore, orig. 1966 (Cambridge: Cambridge University Press, 2002), Shakespeare also drew on both Ovid's and Seneca's depictions of Medea to model *Macbeth's* weird sisters and their brew.

79. Sanja Pilopović, "A Contribution to the Study of the Jason Sarcophagus from Viminacium," *Starinar* no. 53–54 (2003–2004): 65–78.

80. R. L. Hunter, *The Argonautica of Apollonius* (Cambridge: Cambridge University Press, 1993), chapter 7; Damien Nelis, *Vergil's Aeneid and the Argonautica of Apollonius Rhodius* (Leeds: Francis Cairns, 2001).

81. Nelis, *Vergil's Aeneid and the Argonautica of Apollonius Rhodius,* chapter 6.

82. Scott McGill, *Virgil Recomposed: The Mythological and Secular Centos in Antiquity* (Oxford: Oxford University Press, 2005), 31–32.

83. Andrew Zissos, *Valerius Flaccus' Argonautica Book 1: A Commentary* (Oxford: Oxford University Press, 2008), xxiv-xxv.

84. Alan Cameron, *Greek Mythography in the Roman World* (Oxford: Oxford University Press, 2004), 64.

85. *Institutio Oratoria* 10.1.90.

86. Gaius Valerius Flaccus, *Argonautica* 7.91–95 (my trans.).

87. A. J. Kleywegt, *Valerius Flaccus: The Argonautica, Book 1: A Commentary* (Leiden: Brill, 2005), xii.

88. Hard, *Routledge Handbook of Greek Mythology,* 193–194.

89. For discussion, see W. K. C. Guthrie, *Orpheus and Greek Religion,* originally 1952 (Princeton: Princeton University Press, 1993).

90. Hermann Frankel, review of *Die orphischen Argonautika in ihrem Verhaltnis zu Apollonios Rhodios* by Helmut Venzke, *The American Journal of Philology* 65, no. 4 (1944): 394.

91. *Orphic Argonautica* 898f. (my trans.).

92. J. R. Bacon, "The Geography of the *Orphic Argonautica*," *The Classical Quarterly 25,* no. 3/4 (1931): 179.

93. Jan N. Bremmer, *The Rise and Fall of the Afterlife* (London: Routledge, 2002), 15; Giovanni Reale, *A History of Ancient Philosophy: From the Origins to Socrates,* trans. John R. Catan (Albany: State University of New York Press, 1987), 15.

94. Jean-René Jannot, *Religion in Ancient Etruria,* trans. Jane K. Whitehead (Madison: University of Wisconsin Press, 2005), 52, 71.

95. The poem was widely derided as everything from "tame" to "dreary" by Classical scholars, and so low was its reputation that it was not translated into English until the twenty-first century. It's not that bad and is, in places, quite enjoyable, especially in its infernal and underworld motifs.

96. Kirk, *Nature of Greek Myths,* 169–173.

97. Strabo, *Geography,* 11.14.12.

98. Strabo, *Geography,* 6.1.1; however, Pliny (*Natural History* 3.9) places this on the other side of the river Silaris, in Picentia. Archaeology proved Strabo right in 1934 when the Heraion at Foce del Sele was discovered on the left bank of the river, where Strabo had placed it. The site contains Corinthian-style pottery, suggesting another connection to Jason myths.

99. Trudy Ring, Robert M. Salkin, and Sharon La Boda, eds., *International Dictionary of Historic Places,* Vol. 3: Southern Europe (Chicago: Fitzroy Dearborn, 1995), 509.

100. N. G. L. Hammond, "Alexander and Armenia," *Phoenix* 50, no. 2 (1996): 135.

101. Strabo, *Geography* 11.14; Justin, *Epitome* 42.2–3.

102. Tacitus, *Annals* 6.34.

103. Justin, *Epitome* 42.2, trans. in *Justin, Cornelius Nepos, and Eutropus,* trans. John Selby Watson (London: Henry G. Bohn, 1853), 279.

104. Justin, *Epitome* 42.3, trans. in *op. cit.,* 279.

105. Xenophon, *Anabasis* 6.2

106. Robin Lane Fox, introduction to *The Long March: Xenophon and the Ten Thousand,* ed. Robin Lane Fox (New Haven: Yale University Press, 2004), 29.

Chapter 6

1. Averil Cameron and Judith Herrin, *Constantinople in the Early Eighth Century: The* Parastaseis syntomoi chronikai*: Introduction, Translation, and Commentary*, Columbia Studies in the Classical Tradition Vol. 10 (Leiden: Brill, 1984), vii.

2. Ronald E. Papin, *The Vatican Mythographers* (New York: Fordham University Press, 2008), 4–10.

3. Bernadette Filotas, *Pagan Survivals, Superstitions, and Popular Cultures* (Toronto: Pontifical Institute of Medieval Studies, 2005), 97

4. A fact long recognized. See, for example, Edwin Sidney Hartland, *The Legend of Perseus: A Study of Tradition in Story, Custom, and Belief*, vol. 3 (London: David Nutt, 1896), 158–159.

5. Nilsson, *Mycenaean Origins,* 40–43.

6. Daniel Ogden, *Perseus* (Oxon: Routledge, 2008), 4

7. For additional discussion of the thematic and incidental parallels, see Ogden, *Perseus,* 63–65.

8. Ogden, *Perseus,* 68–69.

9. Lycophron, *Alexandra* 834–42.

10. Ogden, *Perseus,* 8.

11. Homer, *Odyssey* 11.634–5, trans. *op. cit.,* p. 179.

12. Clark Hopkins, "Assyrian Elements in the Perseus-Gorgon Story," *American Journal of Archaeology* 38, no. 3 (1934): 347.

13. Edward Phinney, Jr., "Perseus' Battle with the Gorgons," *Transactions and Proceedings of the American Philological Association* 102 (1971): 446–447.

14. Cf. Zeus displaying himself to Semele in his full glory and her subsequent destruction.

15. Kirk, *Nature of Greek Myths*, 148; Hard, *Routledge Handbook of Greek Mythology*, 108; but note that Ogden disagrees and suggests the name refers to the king's desire to receive many presents at the feast he throws, and the episode in general to have only a superficial relationship to the underworld (*Perseus*, 50).

16. Kirk, *Nature of Greek Myths*, 150.

17. Fontenrose, *Python*, 296–299.

18. Hard, *Routledge Handbook of Greek Mythology*, 337.

19. Hunter, "Short on Heroics," 449–450.

20. Kirk, *Nature of Greek Myths*, 155; Castleden, *Knossos Labyrinth*, 107.

21. Hunter, "Short on Heroics," 450; Henry J. Walker, *Theseus and Athens* (Oxford: Oxford University Press, 1995), 89–90.

22. Nilsson, *Mycenaean Origins*, 171–174.

23. Hard, *Routledge Handbook of Greek Mythology*, 254–255.

24. Kirk, *Nature of Greek Myths*, 177–179.

25. Burkert, *Structure and History*, 93–94.

26. Frederick E. Brenk, "The Herakles Myth and the Literary Texts Relating to the Myth of Ninurta," *Relighting the Souls: Studies in Plutarch, in Greek Literature, Religion, and Philosophy, and in the New Testament Background* (Stuggart: Steiner, 1998), 200; Brundage, "Herakles the Levantine."

27. Bremmer, *Interpretations of Greek Mythology*, 14–16.

28. West, *The East Face of Helicon*, 471.

29. *Iliad* 5.392–404; Nilsson, *Mycenaean Origins*, 203–204.

30. Bruce Lincoln, "The Indo-European Cattle-Raiding Myth," *History of Religions* 16, no. 1 (1976): 55–56.

31. Kirk, *Nature of Greek Myths*, 190; cf. Ken Dowden, *The Uses of Greek Mythology* (1992; reprint, London: Routledge, 2000), 98.

32. Nakassis, "Gemination," 226–227.

33. Watkins, *How to Kill a Dragon*, 464–468.

34. West, *The East Face of Helicon*, 471.

35. R. Roux, *Le problème des Argonautes: Recherches sur les aspects religieux de la légende* (Paris: E. de Boccard, Editeur, 1949), 41.

36. Kirk, *Nature of Greek Myths*, 192; Nilsson *Mycenaean Origin*, 214.

37. Apollonius, *Argonautica* 4.1396; for Lethe: see *The Argonautika*, expanded ed., trans. Peter Green (Berkeley: University of California Press, 2007), 345, note for lines 1396–1405.

38. Nilsson thought the process worked the other way round, with what he believed was a common Mycenaean men's name, Heracles, giving rise later by folk etymology to the idea that Hera was involved in a story once told about a vassal to the Mycenaean king. Of course, this then raises the question of whence came the name Heracles, which returns us to supposing the name derived from the goddess (*Mycenaean Origin*, 211).

39. West, *The East Face of Helicon*, 471.

40. Diodorus Siculus, *Library of History* 4.39.2; Brundage, "Herakles the Levantine," 227.

41. Kirk, *The Nature of Greek Myths*, 216–217.

42. Cf. to the Christian Jesus who is primarily viewed in one of three ways: as a god who became a man, as a man who either himself or through his followers was elevated to a god, or as a fictional creation designed to appropriate and reconfigure Jewish messianic beliefs. However, no matter his origin, the messianic ideology and Jewish mythology existed before Jesus. Similarly, the mythic actions assigned to heroes likely predated them, too.

43. David R. Kinsey, *The Goddesses' Mirror: Visions of the Divine from East and West* (Albany: State University of New York Press, 1989), 133, 136.

44. In the nineteenth century and occasionally thereafter, it was suggested that Ares originated as a dying and rising vegetation god (cf. his Roman counterpart Mars, who oversaw agriculture), which if true would make his sacred grove Jason's own, as Jason was himself compared to Ares in Pindar, suggesting that the serpent is therefore Jason's mythic double, who as per Joseph Campbell must be reconciled to the hero to win the goddess. However, there is little evidence to support Ares as a vegetation deity (see William Crook, "The Binding of a God: A Study in the Basis of Idolatry," *Folk-Lore* 8, no. 4 (1897): 351).

45. Marylin B. Arthur, "The Curse of Civilization: The Choral Odes of the *Phoenissae*," *Harvard Studies in Classical Philology* 81 (1977): 168; Fontenrose, *Python*, 142–145.

46. Apollonius, *Argonautica* 3.1265–67; see James Joseph Clauss, *The Best of the Argonauts: The Redefinition of the Epic Hero in Book 1 of Apollonius'* Argonautica (Berkeley: University of California Press, 1993), 84–85.

47. *Argonautica* 3.1282–83.

48. Adrian Room, *Placenames of the World* (Jefferson, NC: McFarland, 2006), 290.

49. Hard, *Routledge Handbook of Greek Mythology*, 380.

50. West, *The East Face of Helicon*, 407.

51. West, *The East Face of Helicon*, 407; "Phasis and Aia," 196–197.

52. Graf, "Medea," 32–33.

53. West, *The East Face of Helicon*, 407; "Phasis and Aia," 196–197.

54. Indeed, Michael C. Astour concurred on this point in his study *HellenoSemitica* (Leiden: Brill, 1967), 286–88.

55. West, *The East Face of Helicon*, 407.

56. West, "*Odyssey* and *Argonautica*," 45.

57. West, *The East Face of Helicon*, 408; Astour, *HellenoSemitica*, 286.

58. West, *The East Face of Helicon*, 409–10.

59. Emma Griffiths, *Medea* (Abingdon: Routledge, 2006), 32.

60. Griffiths, *Medea*, 69.

61. *Encyclopedia Britannica*, 9th ed. (1894), s.v. "Medea."

62. Graf, "Medea," 37–38.

63. Griffiths, *Medea*, 30–31.

64. Fontenrose, *Python*, appendix 1.

65. Hard, *Routledge Handbook of Greek Mythology*, 112–113.

66. Pausanias, *Description of Greece* 10.28.2, trans. in *op. cit.*

67. Fontenrose, *Python*, 480–481.

68. Fontenrose, *Python*, 477–480.

69. Fontenrose, *Python*, 481.

70. Fontenrose, *Python*, 482.

71. Fontenrose, *Python*, 483–484.

72. Better known in English as "the dead travel fast" from Bram Stoker's *Dracula* and Rudyard Kipling's "The Phantom Rickshaw."

73. Job 9:26.

74. Arthur Bernard Cook, "The European Sky-God," *Folklore* 15 (1904): 270.

75. Watkins, *How to Kill a Dragon*, 383–385.

76. S. Davis, "Argeiphontes in Homer—The Dragon Slayer," *Greece and Rome* 22, no. 64 (1953): 34.

77. Fontenrose, *Python*, 485.

78. Lincoln, *Death, War, and Sacrifice*, chapter 5.

Chapter 7

1. "Erebus" is related to a series of Semitic words referring to the west as the land of the setting sun, and thus of incipient "darkness"—a recurrence of the confluence of solar and underworld imagery (Mark Munn, *The Mother of the Gods, Athens, and the Tyranny of Asia: A Study of Sovereignty in Ancient Religion* [Berkeley: University of California Press, 2006], 180n2).

2. Homer, *Odyssey* 11.13f., trans. in *op. cit.*, pp. 160, 161.

3. Kirk, *Homer and the Epic*, 171–172.

4. Knight, *The Renewal of Epic*, 34–35.

5. Knight, *The Renewal of Epic*, 34.

6. Paul Dräger, "Response," *Bryn Mawr Classical Review*, February 26, 2003, http://bmcr.brynmawr.edu/2003/2003-02-26.html

7. Gocha R. Tsetskhladze, *Pichvnari and Its Environs: 6th C BC-4th C AD* (Besançon, France: Presse Universitaires Franc-Comtoisses, 1999), 1–15.

8. Thomas, *Finding People in Early Greece*, 73; J. T. Hooker, *Linear B: An Introduction* (Bristol Classics Press, 1980), 165; Jan Driessen, "The Arsenal of Knossos (Crete) and Mycenaean Chariot Forces," in *Archaeological and Historical Aspects of West-European Societies*, ed. Marc Lodewijckx (Leuven: Leuven University Press, 1996), 485–486. The text of the tablet, Sd 4403, deals with chariot wheels, so it is unclear what relationship Colchis would have. The alternate reading that a man named Kokida had a wheel workshop seems to better fit the context.

9. Hiller, "Mycenaeans and the Black Sea," 214.

10. Neal Ascherson, *Black Sea* (New York: Hill and Wang, 1996), 7.

11. Herodotus, *Histories* 2.104–105.

12. For discussion see Chapter 12 and R. A. Jairazbhoy, "Egyptian Civilization in Colchis on the Black Sea," in *African Presence in Early Asia*, eds. Runoko Rashidi and Ivan Van Sertima (New Brunswick: Transaction, 1988), 61–64.

13. Giorgij Shamba, "On the Track of Abkhasia's Antiquity," *The Abkhazians: A Handbook*, ed. George B. Hewitt (New York: St. Martin's Press, 1988), 56.

14. Margalit Finkelberg, *Greeks and Pre-Greeks: Aegean Prehistory and the Greek Heroic Tradition* (Cambridge: Cambridge University Press, 2005), 152. Finkelberg connects these presumed migrants to the myth of Jason's seer Mopsus, who was said to have wandered across Asia founding towns populated by Greek migrants.

15. Philip Kohl, "Caucasian Bronze Age," *Encyclopedia of Prehistory*, Volume 4: Europe, eds. Peter N. Peregrine and Melvin Ember (New York: Human Relations Area Files, 2001), 36.

16. Nino Lordkipanidze, "Medea's Colchis," in *Wine, Worship, and Sacrifice: The Golden Graves of Ancient Vani* by Darejan Kacharava and Guram Kvirkvelia, ed. Jennifer Y. Chi (Princeton: Princeton University Press, 2008), chapter 1.

17. Leonid Serebyanny, "Mixed and Deciduous Forests," *The Physical Geography of Northern Eurasia*, edited by Maria Shahgedanova (Oxford: Oxford University Press, 2002), 241–242.

18. Tsetskhladze, *Pichvnari*, 99–100.

19. Michael Wood, *In Search of Myths and Heroes: Exploring Four Epic Legends of the World* (Berkeley: University of California Press, 2005), 117, 120. Gate guardians were not especially rare in the ancient world, so there is not much to read into this. Mesopotamian temples featured statues as guardians of gates, including human-headed bulls, lions, and sphinxes. Images of Artemis and Hecate were sometimes used as guardians of gates in homes and temples, since the virgin Artemis was considered incorruptible and Hecate was a patroness of gates.

20. Hiller, "Mycenaeans and the Black Sea," 213–214.

21. "[At] her [Ereshkigal's] exalted, unalterable command, Biblu, the butcher of the underworld, shall deliver thee to the gatekeeper Lugalsula, that he may lead [thee] out through the gate of Ishtar (and) Aya." ("The Underworld Vision of an Assyrian Prince," in *The Gilgamesh Epic and Old Testament Parallels*, 2nd ed., by Alexander Heidel, 1949 [Chicago: University of Chicago Press, 1963], 134.) The text dates from the Neo-Assyrian period, around the seventh century BCE, but must have referred to an older geography of the underworld since the Gate, unlike concepts believed original to the poem, is not explained and must have been in the reader's common knowledge.

22. Hesiod, *Theogony* 746–751, trans in *op. cit.*, 133.

23. Nakassis, "Gemination," 230.

24. M. L. West, *Indo-European Poetry and Mythology* (Oxford: Oxford University Press, 2007), 394.

25. William Brede Kristensen, *The Meaning of Religion: Lectures in the Phenomenology of Religion*, trans. J. B. Carman (The Hague: Martinus Nijhoff, 1968), 65.

26. Sarah Immerwahr, "Death and the Tanagra Larnakes," in *The Ages of Homer: A Tribute to Emily Townsend Vermeule*, edited by Jane B. Carter and Sarah P. Morris (Austin: University of Texas Press, 1998), 117.

27. Immerwahr, 116–117.

28. Michael J. Clark, *Flesh and Spirit in the Songs of Homer: A Study of Words and Myths* (Oxford: Oxford University Press, 1999; reprint 2002), 6.

29. Homer, *Odyssey* 24.6f., trans. in *op. cit.*, 365.

30. LeRoy G. Holm, Jerry Doll, Eric Holm, Juan Pancho, and James Herberger, *World Weeds: Natural Histories and Distribution* (New York: John Wiley and Sons, 1997), 92.

31. *The Epic of Gilgamesh,* tablet 12, trans. N. K. Sanders (London: Penguin, 1972), 92.

32. Stephanie Dalley, *Myths from Mesopotamia: Creation, the Flood, Gilgamesh, and Others* (Oxford: Oxford University Press, 1989), 163–164.

33. Wayne Horowitz, *Mesopotamian Cosmic Geography* (Eisenbrauns, 1998), 293.

34. Horowitz, *Mesopotamian Cosmic Geography*, 293.

35. Burney, *Historical Dictionary of the Hittites*, 301.

36. A. D. H. Bivar, "Religious Subjects on Achaemenid Seals," in *Mithraic Studies*, volume 1, edited by John R. Hinnels (Manchester: Manchester University Press, 1975), 102–103.

37. Mehmet-Ali Ataç, "The 'Underworld Vision' of the Ninevite Intellectual Milieu," *Iraq* 66 (2004): 68.

38. H. D. Galter, "Hubur," in *Dictionary of Deities and Demons*, eds. Van der Toorn, Becking, and Van der Horst, 431.

39. *Poems of Heaven and Hell*, 115.

40. Black and Green, *Gods, Demons, and Symbols of Ancient Mesopotamia*, 140.

41. Thorkild Jacobsen, *The Treasures of Darkness: A History of Mesopotamian Religion* (New Haven: Yale University Press, 1976), 7.

42. Kirk, *The Nature of Greek Myths*, 260–261.

43. Astrid Lindenlauf, "The Sea as a Place of No Return in Ancient Greece," *World Archaeology* 35 (2003): 416–433.

44. West, "*Odyssey* and *Argonautica*," 45.

45. Apollonius, *Argonautica* 3.201f., trans. in *op. cit.*, 209.

46. Frederic J. Simoons, *Plants of Life, Plants of Death* (Madison: University of Wisconsin Press, 1998), 294.

47. Malcolm Campbell, *A Commentary on Apollonius Rhodius* Argonautica *III, 1–471* (Leiden: Brill, 1994), 194.

48. West, "*Odyssey* and *Argonautica*," 39.

49. Paley, "Pre-Homeric Legends of the Voyage of the Argonauts," 179. However, Paley seems to treat Apollonius as working independently of Homer, and does not recognize the clear borrowings the former made from the latter, arguing that no author could make such "barefaced plagiarisms." Paley in general seemed unaware that Greek poets had access to and recycled ideas from earlier Greek authors, also wondering how Pindar and Apollonius chanced to hit upon similar details. The mind boggles.

50. M. L. West, *Indo-European Poetry and Myth* (Oxford: Oxford University Press, 2007), 97.

51. Erwin Cook, "Near Eastern Sources for the Palace of Alkinoos," *American Journal of Archaeology* 108, no. 1 (2004): 43–77.

52. Peter E. Knox, "Phaeton in Ovid and Nonnus," *Classical Quarterly* (new series) 38 (1988): 541–543.

53. Bivar, "Religious Subjects," 103.

54. Cedric H. Whitman, "Hera's Anvils," *Harvard Studies in Classical Philology* 74 (1970): 42n.11.

55. Dominique Colon, "Iconographic Evidence for Some Babylonian Cult Statues," in *Die Welt der Götterbilder*, edited by Brigitte Groneberg and Hermann Spieckermann (Berlin: Walter de Gruyter, 2007), 60–61.

56. Edwin Oliver James, *The Tree of Life: An Archaeological Study* (Leiden: Brill, 1966), 118.

57. M. L. West, *Indo-European Poetry and Mythology* (Oxford: Oxford University Press, 2007), 372.

58. Jeremy McInerney, *The Cattle of the Sun: Cows and Culture in the World of the Ancient Greeks* (Princeton: Princeton University Press, 2010), 103.

59. Nakassis, "Gemination," 226–227.

60. Lincoln, "The Indo-European Cattle Raid," 62.

61. H. J. Rose, "Chthonic Cattle," *Numen* 1, no. 3 (1954): 213–227.

62. Rose, "Chthonic Cattle," 226.

63. McInerney, *The Cattle of the Sun*, 48–49.

64. *Poems of Heaven and Hell from Ancient Mesopotamia*, 142.

65. Kirk, *The Nature of Greek Myths*, 158.

66. Sir Hugh Lloyd Jones, *The Further Academic Papers of Sir Hugh Lloyd Jones* (Oxford: Oxford University Press, 2005), 216.

67. Daniel Ogden, *Magic, Witchcraft, and Ghosts in the Greek and Roman Worlds: A Source Book* (Oxford: Oxford University Press, 2002), 182.

68. Sarah Iles Johnston, *Restless Dead: Encounters between the Living and the Dead in Ancient Greece* (Berkeley: University of California Press, 1999), 88.

69. Johnston, *Restless Dead*, 89.

70. Bryce, *Life and Society in the Hittite World*, 185.

71. Apollonius, *Argonautica* 3.1391–2, trans. in *op. cit.*, 289.

72. Ogden, *Magic, Witchcraft, and Ghosts*, 93.

73. E.g. Juius Africanus, *Cestus* 18, trans. in Ogden, *Magic, Witchcraft, and Ghosts*, 183.

74. Kirk, *Nature of Greek Myths*, 91; G. S. Kirk, *Myth: Its Meaning and Function*, 238–251. Kirk thought the transformation of imaginative and crude Greek myths began in the Neolithic, but this would place the impetus prior to our evidence for the earliest myths, and it would be difficult to propose a transmission of myths for three thousand unbroken years.

75. Lucian, *Menippus* 10, trans. in Ogden, *Magic, Witchcraft, and Ghosts*, 185.

76. Christine Sourvinou-Inwood, "Early Sanctuaries, the Eighth Century and Ritual Space: Fragments of a Discourse," in *Greek Sanctuaries: New Approaches,* edited by Nanno Marinatos and Robert Hägg (London: Routledge, 1993), 3.

77. Castleden, *Mycenaeans*, 55.

78. Pierre Bonechere, "The Place of the Sacred Grove (*Alsos*) in the Mantic Rituals of Greece: The Example of the *Alsos* of Trophonios at Lebadeia (Boeotia)," in *Sacred Gardens and Landscapes: Ritual and Agency,* ed. Michael Conan (Washington: Dumbarton Oaks Research Library and Collection/Harvard University Press, 2007), 23.

79. Bonechere, "Place of the Sacred Grove," 24.

80. Teanarus: Hyginus, *Fabulae* 79; Colonus: Sophocles, *Oedipus at Colonus*; Bonechere, "Place of the Sacred Grove," 20.

81. Homer, *Odyssey*, 10.510f., trans. in *op. cit.*, 157.

82. Pausanias, *Description of Greece*, 3.26.6–7.

83. Bivar, "Religious Subjects," 103.

84. Eric S. Rabkin, *Mars: A Tour of the Human Imagination* (Westport, Conn.: Praeger, 2005), 9.

85. Henry O. Thompson, *Mekal: The God of Beth-Shan* (Leiden: Brill, 1970), 125.

86. Stephanie Dalley, *The Legacy of Mesopotamia* (Oxford: Oxford University Press, 1998), 116.

87. Graham Cunningham, *Deliver Me from Evil: Mesopotamian Incantations 2500–1500 BC* (Rome: Ed-

itrice Pontifico Instituto Biblico, 1997, reprint 2007), 56.

88. Adapted from trans. by Reginald Campbell Thompson, *The Devils and Spirits of Babylonia, vol. 1: Evil Spirits* (London: Luzac and Co., 1903), liv. Thompson originally translated "netherworld" as "earth," but for clarity I have adjusted this and other lines to agree with modern translations. See, e.g., Ewa Wasilewska, *Creation Stories of the Middle East* (London: Jessica Kingsley, 2000), 167.

89. James, *The Tree of Life*, 166.

90. James, *Tree of Life*, 212.

91. Burkert, *Greek Religion*, 200–201.

Chapter 8

1. Derek Collins, *Magic in the Ancient Greek World* (Malden, Mass.: Blackwell, 2008), 29.

2. Collins, *Magic in the Ancient Greek World*, 29.

3. Collins, *Magic in the Ancient Greek World*, 31.

4. Mackie, "Earliest Jason," 13–14.

5. Demosthenes, *Against Aristogiton* 25.79–80; Plutarch, "Life of Demosthenes" 14.5; Harpocration, s.v. "Theoris"; Collins, *Magic in the Ancient Greek World*, 134-139.

6. Hesiod, *Theogony* 411f., trans. in *op. cit.*, 109.

7. Apollonius, *Argonautica* 3.1026f., trans. in *op. cit.*, 265.

8. Burkert, *Greek Religion*, 78.

9. *Odyssey* 3.464. Ritual bathing and anointing of heroes by women occur at least eight times in the *Odyssey*.

10. John Boardman, *The Archaeology of Nostalgia: How the Greeks Re-Created Their Mythical Past* (New York: Thames & Hudson, 2002), 41, 86. This view, however, presupposes a very literal encoding of reality into myth that is demonstrated with few other artifacts the Greeks may have uncovered. Typically, as Boardman himself notes, strange objects, once discovered, were used to support preexisting myths rather than give rise to new stories.

11. T. T. Duke, "Murder in the Bath: Reflections on the Death of Agamemnon," *The Classical Journal* 49, no. 7 (1954): 325–330.

12. Ezekiel 24:1–14; discussion in Dale F. Launderville, *Spirit and Reason: The Embodied Character of Ezekiel's Symbolic Thinking* (Waco, Texas: Baylor University Press, 2007), 118–120.

13. For Enki: *Atrahasis* 1.4.206–26; for Marduk: *Enuma Elish* tablet 6; cf. Berossus in Eusebius, *Chronicle* 5.4.4; Launderville, *Spirit and Reason*, 47.

14. Apollodorus, *Library* 1.9.26.

15. R. F. Willetts, *Cretan Cults and Festivals* (London: Routledge & Keegan Paul, 1962), 52, 100–102; Cook, *Zeus*, vol. 1, 719, 728.

16. The word *poias* means grass and also refers to a type of red poppy.

17. Martin Robertson, "The Death of Talos," *The Journal of Hellenic Studies* 97 (1977): 158–160.

18. Martti Nissinen, *Prophets and Prophesy in the Ancient Near East* (Writings from the Ancient World) (Atlanta: Society for Biblical Literature, 2003), 6

19. Nissinen, *Prophets*, 18–19.

20. Nissinen, *Prophets*, 36.

21. Bryce, *Kingdom of the Hittites*, 219.

22. Bryce, *Kingdom of the Hittites*, 374.

23. Lane Fox, *Travelling Heroes*, 212.

24. Lane Fox, *Travelling Heroes*, 214.

25. Michael Attyah Flower, *The Seer in Ancient Greece* (Berkeley: University of California Press, 2008), 43.

26. Lane Fox, *Travelling Heroes*, 216–217.

27. Flower, *The Seer*, 44.

28. Lane Fox, *Travelling Heroes*, 215; Sarah Iles Johnston, *Ancient Greek Divination* (Malden, Mass.: Wiley Blackwell, 2008), 82.

29. Pierre Grimal, *The Dictionary of Classical Mythology*, trans. A. R. Maxwell-Hyslop (Malden, Mass.: Blackwell, 1996), 228.

30. Hyginus, *Fabulae* 14; *Orphic Argonautica* 185–7; Zissos, *Valerius Flaccus'* Argonautica, 187.

31. Burkert, *Greek Religion*, 89. On Samos, Hera also received offerings of small wooden boats, interpreted as gifts from sailors, perhaps another connection between Hera and Jason.

32. Homer cites Thessalian geographic features like the river Titaressus in describing Dodona (*Iliad* 2.748–54); see discussion in David Evans, "Dodona, Dodola, and Daedala," in *Myth in Indo-European Antiquity*, ed. Gerald James Larson (Berkeley: University of California, 1974), 105.

33. Strabo 8.5.20 and 7.7.12 with the corresponding following section of the Strabo *Epitomes*, usually given among the first fragments from Book VII, but varying by editor; Stephanus of Byzantium, s.v. "Dodona."

34. Evans, "Dodona," 107–108, 111–112.

35. Burkert, *Greek Religion*, 114.

36. Burkert, *Greek Religion*, 114.

37. Daniel Ogden, *Greek and Roman Necromancy* (Princeton: Princeton University Press, 2001), xxi.

38. Knight, *Renewal of Epic*, 170.

39. Donald Normal Levin, *Apollonius'* Argonautica Re-Examined (Leiden: Brill, 1971), 151–153.

40. Virgil would do the same with Laocoön, who in Greek myth was killed by serpents for having sex, either in a sanctuary or against the vows of his priesthood. Virgil had him killed instead for defying the gods and warning the Trojans not to accept the Trojan Horse. The recurring theme is the diminution of sexual motifs from myth in favor of more cerebral crimes.

41. Strabo, *Geography* 7.3.9.

42. Fontenrose attempted to link the dragon myths in *Python* (183), and Watkins derives Python's and Typhon's name from the same source in *How to Kill a Dragon* (460–463).

43. Mayor, *First Fossil Hunters*, 127–139

44. Mayor, *First Fossil Hunters*, 155–162.

45. Ogden, *Perseus*, 95.

46. Richard B. Sothers, "Ancient Scientific Basis of the 'Great Serpent' from Historical Evidence," *Isis* 95, no. 2 (2004): 220–238.

47. Fortson, *Indo-European Language and Culture*, 26.

48. See chapter 9, note 68 for discussion of Perun and Veles and their similarity to Jason and the dragon.

49. Fortson, *Indo-European Language and Culture*, 29.

50. Watkins, *How to Kill a Dragon*, 365.

51. Pindar, *Pythian* 4, 444–5 (old system); 249–50 (new system); trans. in *The Extant Odes of Pindar*, 77.

52. Contamination through borrowing and random chance cannot be entirely eliminated, and some aspects of the reconstructed PIE mythology may reflect common images from altered states of consciousness as much as specific PIE cultural traits. "Thematic similarity may be striking enough, but should not be taken as a proof of heredity unless the notion of secondary creation or loan appears less convincing" (Jackson, "Light from Distant Asterisks," 63). I find myself unable to conceive how else to express the idea of killing a dragon without stating it plainly. Or, in the words of Carol F. Justus, "But how is the theme SLAY ADVERSARY ([with] WEAPON) of peculiarly [Indo-European] inheritance, and not the epitome of a culture that started over five thousand years ago when [non–Indo European] Sumerian Gilgamesh slew his Ancient Near East monster, Humbaba?" (Carol F. Justus, review of *How to Kill a Dragon* by Calvert Watkins, *Language* 73, no. 3 [1997]: 640).

53. Watkins, *How to Kill a Dragon*, 366–369, 374–375.

54. Genesis 3:4–5.

55. John J. Rogers, "Origins of the Ancient Constellations, I: The Mesopotamian Traditions," *Journal of the British Astronomical Association* 108 (1998): 12.

56. Isaiah 5:14; John Day, *Yahweh and the Gods and Goddesses of Canaan* (London: Sheffield Academic Press, 2002), 185–188.

57. Ogden, *Perseus*, 92–94.

58. John Day, *God's Conflict with the Dragon of the Sea: Echoes of a Canaanite Myth in the Old Testament* (Cambridge: Cambridge University Press, 1985), 111.

59. Perseus' battle with the Gorgon is apparently the core of his story, while the Andromeda-dragon story was tacked on later, as a synchretization of two different dragon-slaying stories.

60. A. L. Frothingham, "The Babylonian Origin of Hermes the Snake-God, and of the Caduceus," *The American Journal of Archaeology* 20, no. 2 (1916): 175–211.

61. Horowitz, *Mesopotamian Cosmic Geography*, 35.

62. Alasdair Livingstone, *Mystical and Mythological Explanatory Works of Assyrian and Babylonian Scholars* (Oxford: Oxford University Press, 1986; reprint, Eisenbraun, 2007), 91.

63. Burkert, *Homo Necans*, 157.

64. Burkert, *Homo Necans*, 157–158.

65. Jane Ellen Harrison, *Prolegomena to the Study of Greek Religion* (Princeton: Princeton University Press, 1903), 28.

66. Gerald V. Lalonde, *Horos Dios: An Athenian Shrine and Cult of Zeus* (Leiden: Brill, 2006), 47.

67. Lalond, *Horos Dios*, 45.

68. Lalond, *Horos Dios*, 46.

69. Erika Simon, *Festivals of Attica: An Archaeological Commentary* (Madison: University of Wisconsin Press, 1983), 13.

70. Simon, *Festivals of Attica*, 14.

71. Simon, *Festivals of Attica*, 14.

72. Watkins, *How to Kill a Dragon*, 521.

73. Watkins, *How to Kill a Dragon*, 537.

74. Watkins, *How to Kill a Dragon*, 448–459. This is based on Greek poetic versions of the myth of Typhon which use the word "lash" in regard to the monster. This term comes from a word for "thong," equivalent to the "cord" used to bind the dragon in a version of the Hittite dragon myth recorded in specific word forms used around 1500 BCE Typhon derives at least in part from the Hittite dragon myth, as apparently does Jason's own serpent.

75. Apollodorus, *The Library*, Epitome 2.10–14.

76. Genesis 22:1–19. In both stories a distraught father agrees to sacrifice his son because he believes a god demands it, and in both situations the divine figure dramatically countermands the order of sacrifice, resulting in the substitution of a ram.

77. Also the origin of the image of St. Christopher carrying the Christ child. Cf. their Greek names: Hermes Kriophoros (the ram bearer) vs. Christophoros (the Christ-bearer).

78. Robert Parker, *Miasma: Pollution and Purification in Early Greek Religion* (Oxford: Oxford University Press, 1983; reprint: Clarendon Press, 2003), 376.

79. Harrison, *Prolegomena*, 23–24.

80. Amphiaraos: Pausanias, *Description of Greece* 1.34.2–5; Calchas: Strabo, *Geography* 6.3.9; Syrian goddess: Lucian, *De Syria Dea* 35; Harrison, *Prolegomena*, 27–28.

81. *Homeric Hymn to Demeter* 192–198. This term is variously translated as "shimmering" (Walter Burkert), "glistering" (Andrew Lang), "silvery" (Hugh Evelyn White), or "silver" (Jules Cashford). The Greek ἀργύφεος can mean either "silver-white" as in the color of wool, or "silver-shining," as in glittery and metallic.

82. Burkert, *Greek Religion*, 78.

83. Burkert, *Greek Religion*, 46.

84. Burkert, *Greek Religion*, 65.

85. Herodotus, *Histories* 2.42.

86. Scholiast on Apollonius' *Argonautica* 3.587; trans. in Hesiod, *Hesiod*, 271.

87. A. Leo Oppenheim, "The Golden Garments of the Gods," *Journal of Near Eastern Studies* 8, no. 3 (1949): 180.

88. Oppenheim, "Golden Garments," 181.

89. Oppenheim, "Golden Garments," 177.

90. Oppenheim, "Golden Garments," 179.

91. Oppenheim, "Golden Garments," 179n.21.

92. Giorgio Buccellati, "The Descent of Inanna as a Ritual Journey to Kutha?," *Syro-Mesopotamian Studies* 4, no. 3 (1982): 3–7.

93. Burkert, *Greek Religion*, 89.

94. Burkert, *Greek Religion*, 89–90.

95. West, *Indo-European Poetry and Myth*, 153–154.

96. Oppenheim, "Golden Garments," 188.

97. Jane McIntosh, *The Ancient Indus Valley: New Perspectives* (Santa Barbara: ABC-CLIO, 2008), 182–188.

98. The Hellespont appears often in Homer (*Iliad* 15.233, for example), so he must have had some version of the myth where Helle falls from the ram.

99. Burkert, *Greek Religion*, 90.

100. *KUB* 9.17, §4 , in Gregory McMahon, *The Hittite State Cult of the Tutelary Deities,* Oriental Institute of the University of Chicago Assyriological Studies 25 (Chicago: University of Chicago Press, 1991), 219, 221, in which a statue of a god is clothed for a procession; CTH 375, §4, 13", 17", 22", in Itamar Singer, *Hittite*

Prayers (Leiden: Brill, 2002), 41–42, presenting Arnuwanda I's lament that the Kaska had destroyed the gods' statues, took the gold, and stole their garments. Therefore, the gods' statues must have had clothes to wear, clothes valuable enough to want to haul away along with other gold and silver items with which they are listed.

101. Jaan Puhvel, *Hittite Etymological Dictionary, Vol. 6: Words Beginning with M* (Berlin: De Gruyter, 2004), 108.

102. H. A. Shapiro, "Jason's Cloak," *Transactions of the American Philological Association* 110 (1980): 266–267.

103. Rodney C. Woosnam-Savage and Anthony Hall, *Brassey's Book of Body Armor* (Dulles, Virginia: Brassey's, 2001), 24.

104. Castleden, *Mycenaeans*, 122.

105. Calvert Watkins, "A Distant Anatolian Echo in Pindar: The Origin of Aegis Again," *Harvard Studies in Classical Philology* 100 (2000): 6; Thomas Day Seymour, *Life in the Homeric Age* (New York: Macmillan, 1908), 649.

106. Pliny, *Natural History* 8.34; Burkert argued in *Homo Necans* that this story was a survival of ancient sacrificial rituals (87–88).

107. Burkert, *Homo Necans*, 113–114. Burkert thought Phrixus' Golden Fleece an importation into Jason's myth.

108. Castleden, *Mycenaeans*, 72.

109. Nancy C. Wilke, "The MME Tholos Tomb," in *Excavations at Nichorea in Southwest Greece, Vol. II: The Bronze Age Occupation*, edited by William A. McDonald and Nancy C. Wilkie (Minneapolis: University of Minnesota, 1992), 271.

110. Castleden, *Mycenaeans*, 74–75.

111. Christina Souyoudzoglou-Haywood, "Burial Practices," in *Encyclopedia of Ancient Greece,* edited by Nigel Guy Wilson (New York: Routledge, 2006), 135. Some early Dark Age burials reused Mycenaean gold ornaments.

112. Kohl, "Caucasian Bronze Age," 35.

113. *Poems of Heaven and Hell,* 141.

114. *Poems of Heaven and Hell,* 160.

115. Claus Ambos, "Temporary Ritual Structures and Their Cosmological Symbolism in Ancient Mesopotamia," in *Heaven on Earth: Temples, Ritual, and Cosmic Symbolism in the Ancient World*, ed. Deena Ragavan, University of Chicago Oriental Institute Seminars No. 9 (Chicago: University of Chicago Press, 2013), 247–8. The ritual is known from seventh century BCE documents but is almost certainly much older.

116. Oppenheim, "Golden Garments," 191–192.

Chapter 9

1. Ammianus Marcellinus, *Roman Antiquities* 6.28; A. Houtum-Schindler, "Notes on Demavend," *Proceedings of the Royal Geographic Society* 10 (1888): 85–89.

2. Christopher Walter, *The Warrior Saints in Byzantine Art and Tradition* (Aldershot, UK: Ashgate, 2003), 121–122.

3. Walter, *Warrior Saints*, 122. The dragon motif George apparently took over from St. Theodore, with

whom he was frequently paired in Byzantine art. George was first recorded as fighting a dragon in an eleventh century Georgian manuscript. St. George also absorbed elements of pagan sun worship, which echoes Aeëtes in an indirect way.

4. Pero Tafur, *Travels and Adventures 1435–1439,* trans. Malcolm Letts (1926, reprint London: RoutledgeCurzon, 2005), 63–64. The alleged site of Noah's Ark at Jabal Judi had previously been associated with the ark of the Mesopotamian flood hero, as Berossus reported (Eusebius, *Praepartio Evangelica* 9) and had been a Judeo-Christian tourist attraction since the Classical Age (Flavius Josephus, *Antiquities of the Jews*, 1.3; Epiphanius, *Panarion* 1.18). From Babylonian times down to the Byzantine era believers came to collect bits of "bitumen" as souvenirs and to view the site of one Ark or another, including the Emperor Heraclitus (Theophilus of Edessa, preserved in Agapius, *Universal History*).

5. Bell, "Coptic Jason Relief," 45–52.

6. The encounter with Polyphemus the Cyclops is included wholesale, and another incident strongly recalls elements of the Circe and Lotus-Eaters stories.

7. E. B. Fryde, *The Early Paleologian Renaissance (1261-c. 1360)* (Leiden: Brill, 2000), 276, 296.

8. Fryde, *Early Paleologian Renaissance*, 24–25.

9. Fryde, *Early Paleologian Renaissance*, 231

10. D. P. M. Weerakkody, "Apollonius Rhodius, c. 295–215 BC," in *The Encyclopedia of Ancient Greece*, ed. Nigel Guy Wilson (London: Routledge, 2006), 66.

11. *Suda*, s.v. "Deras"; trans. by H.C. Bolton, "The Golden Fleece and Alchemy," *Notes & Queries*, July 1886, 114.

12. Zissos, "Reception of Valerius Flaccus' *Argonautica*," 169.

13. Dares Phrygius, *Historia de Excidio Trioae* 3 (my trans.).

14. Zissos, "Reception of Valerius Flaccus' *Argonautica*," 170, 173.

15. Pepin, *Vatican Mythographers,* 4.

16. Isidore, *Etymologiae* 9.2.46, 58, and 65.

17. First Vatican Mythographer 25 (my trans.).

18. Second Vatican Mythographer 135.

19. Second Vatican Mythographer 136 (my trans.); cf. Cicero, *De natura deorum* 2.88–90, quoting Lucius Accius wherein *Argo* is compared to a rock plunging into the sea in a war between Earth and Neptune.

20. Second Vatican Mythographer 138.

21. Third Vatican Mythographer 116.

22. This observation, which occurred to me on reading the poem, was also and earlier made by Evelyn Mullally in *The Artist at Work: Narrative Techniques in Chrétien de Troyes* (Philadelphia: American Philosophical Society, 1988), 27.

23. Tanner, *Last Descendant of Aeneas*, 150.

24. "Guido de Columnis: The Trojan War," *Faksimile Verlag*, http://www.faksimile.ch/pdf/Troja_e.pdf

25. John Lydgate, *Troy Book: Selections,* edited by Robert R. Edwards (Kalamazoo, Michigan: Medieval Institute Publications, 1998), 1.162–171.

26. Lydgate, *Troy Book* 1.968.

27. Lydgate, *Troy Book* 1.2038–2040.

28. Frank A. Domínguez, *The Medieval Argonautica* (Studia Humanitatis) (Potomac, Maryland: José Porrúa Turanzas, 1979), 80.

29. Domínguez, *The Medieval Argonautica*, 78.

30. Florence Percival, *Chaucer's Legendary Good Women* (Cambridge: Cambridge University Press, 1998), 206.

31. Guillame de Lorris and Jean de Meun, *The Romance of the Rose,* 3rd ed., trans. Charles Dahlberg (Princeton: Princeton University Press, 1995), 229.

32. Katherine McKinley, "Lessons for a King from Gower's *Confessio amantis,*" in *Metamorphosis: The Changing Face of Ovid in Medieval and Early Modern Europe,* edited by Allison Keith and Steven Rupp (Toronto: Center for Reformation and Renaissance Studies, 2007), 127.

33. John Gower, *Confessio amantis* 5.4223–4225, in *The Complete Works of John Gower: English Works,* ed. G. C. Macaulay (Oxford: Clarendon Press, 1901), 62.

34. Zissos, "Reception of Valerius Flaccus," 171.

35. Geoffrey Chaucer, *Legend of Good Women,* 1368–1383; ed. Walter W. Skeat (Oxford: Clarendon Press, 1889), 72.

36. Edmund Spencer, *The Faerie Queene*, Book II, canto XII, in *The Second Book of the Faerie Queene,* edited by Thomas J. Wise (London: George Allen, 1895), 511.

37. Dante Alighieri, *The Inferno* 18.85–96, trans. James Romanes Sibbald (Edinburgh: David Douglas, 1884), 134–135.

38. Percival, *Chaucer's Good Women*, 205.

39. Marilynn Robin Desmond and Pamela Sheingorn, *Myth, Montage, & Visuality in Late Medieval Manuscript Culture: Christine de Pizan's* Epistre Othèa (Ann Arbor: University of Michigan Press, 2006), 8–10.

40. The date is variously given as 1429 or 1430, with the discrepancy due to some historians choosing to use the Gregorian calendar date (1430) rather than the Julian calendar date (1429) in use in Philip's day.

41. A popular but apocryphal story claimed that Philip named the order after the golden hair of his mistress Maria von Crombrugge in revenge for his nobles making fun of their romance. Another version says that the Fleece was chosen to honor Burgundy's wool industry, which used the symbol of the Fleece since the Crusades. Their Fleece differed from Classical depictions by showing a hoisted standing ram rather than a flaccid fleece. This version was incorporated into the Order's collar and also appears on Brooks Brothers' clothing after the Flemish model.

42. Tanner, *Last Descendant of Aeneas*, 57. Not all historians agree on this point. Richard Vaughn notes that there is no trace in contemporary records of Philip connecting the Golden Fleece to a crusade, and this may be a post hoc rationalization, or even a pious myth concocted as the Order grew in prestige (Richard Vaughn, *Philip the Good: The Apogee of Burgundy* [Woodbridge: Boydell Press, 2002, reprint 2004], 162).

43. Mullaly, *The Artist at Work,* 27, 96.

44. C. B. Lewis, *Classical Mythology and Arthurian Romance* (London: Milford, 1932), 99, 295–296. Lewis appears to have recognized common mythological patterns between Celtic and Greek myth that today scholars would interpret as shared survivals of Proto-Indo-European myth with some minor contamination from later Greco-Roman contact. The more recent work of

C. Scott Littleton and Linda A. Malcor attributes the origins of the Arthur cycle to ancient Iranian myth brought to Europe in the Roman era (see *From Scythia to Camelot: A Radical Reassessment of the Legends of King Arthur* [New York: Garland, 2000]). Arthurian, Celtic, (some) Greek, and Iranian myths, of course, are Indo-European in origin and need not necessarily have a physical connection with Iran across three thousand years to retain such parallels.

45. Carolyne Larrington, *King Arthur's Enchantresses: Morgan and Her Sisters in Arthurian Tradition* (London: I.B. Tauris, 2006), 9.

46. Larrington, *King Arthur's Enchantresses*, 8.

47. Graham Anderson, *King Arthur in Antiquity* (London: Routledge, 2004), 104. Anderson misidentifies the fathers of Pelias and Aeson, making Poseidon Aeson's father. Correctly identified as Poseidon's son, Pelias' identification with the Fisher King becomes stronger.

48. Judges 6:36–40.

49. Barbara Haggh, "The Order of the Golden Fleece," *Journal of the Royal Musical Association* 121, no. 2 (1996): 268–269.

50. Vaughn, *Philip the Good*, 162.

51. Arjo Vanderjagt, "The Princely Culture of the Valois Dukes of Burgundy," in *Princes and Princely Culture 1450–1650,* volume 1, edited by M. Gosman, A. MacDonald, and A. Vanderjagt (Leiden: Brill, 2003), 60–61.

52. Ruth Mores, "Problems of Early Fiction: Raoul Lefèvre's 'Histoire de Jason,'" *The Modern Language Review* 78, no 1 (1983): 37.

53. William Caxton, *The History of Jason translated from the French of Raoul Le Fevre,* edited by John Munro (London: Early English Text Society/Oxford University Press, 1913), 13.

54. Caxton, *History of Jason*, 70.

55. Caxton, *History of Jason*, 197.

56. Tanner, *Last Descendants of Aeneas*, 5, 8.

57. Tanner, *Last Descendants of Aeneas*, 7.

58. Creighton E. Gilbert, *Caravaggio and His Two Cardinals* (University Park, Pennsylvania: Pennsylvania State University Press, 1995), 52–53.

59. Andrew Zissos, "Reception of Valerius Flaccus' *Argonautica,*" *International Journal of the Classical Tradition* 13, no. 2 (2006): 175.

60. Jean Pierre Sanchez, "El Dorado and the Myth of the Golden Fleece," *The Classical Tradition and the Americas,* edited by Wolfgang Haase and Meyer Reinhold. (Berlin and New York: Walter de Gruyter, 1993), 362.

61. Zissos, "Reception of Valerius Flaccus' *Argonautica,*" 176.

62. Sanchez, "El Dorado," 369–375.

63. Tanner, *Last Descendant of Aeneas*, 156.

64. Lawrence M. Bryant, *The King and the City in Royal Parisian Entrance Ceremony: Politics, Ritual, and Art in the Renaissance* (Geneva: Libraire Droz, S.A., 1986), 59, 196.

65. Carl Goldstein, "Louis XIV and Jason," *The Art Bulletin* 49, no. 4 (1967): 327–329.

66. Pliny, *Natural History* 3.22.

67. F. S. Copeland, "Slovene Folklore," *Folklore* 42 (1931): 421n.19.

68. Fanny S. Copeland, "Slovene Mythology," *The*

Slavonic and East European Review 11 (1933): 638–639; Tomo Vinšćak, "On 'Strige,' 'Štriguni' and 'Krsnici' on Istrian Peninsula," *Studia Ethnologica Croatica* 17 (2005): 221–235. Skilled in magic and the art of healing, the divine prince Kresnik was associated with the rebirth of nature in the spring, like the vegetation gods of the ancient world. Like Jason, this god angered his wife by taking up with another woman, and he died as a result. In turn, he may derive from the Slavic storm god Perun, who each year battles Veles, a bull-horned serpentine earth god of death from the Underworld, just like Jason and so many others. To the death god's realm across the sea the fertility god of the Slavs travelled back and forth each year, and in celebration of Veles' rites men wore sheepskins and wool in honor of his identification with rams and sheep (!). The reasons for identifying this Proto-Indo-European-derived figure with Jason or St. George are correspondingly obvious. The identification with St. George dates from Christianization in the medieval period, and the Jason story probably from a later period when classical mythology was en vogue.

69. In Ljubljana, Kresnik, Jason, and George often seem hopeless jumble of influences and counter-influences, which is perhaps why most discussions of the Ljubljana dragon simply attribute his source to an undated "ancient legend" of Jason or George and leave it at that. In reviewing the documentation, it appears that the medieval story of St. George and the dragon from Laibach merged at some point with the classical story of Jason carrying the *Argo* from nearby (and vanished) Nauportus, yielding a combination story with Jason slaying the dragon by the time folklorists started collecting stories from the region in the nineteenth century.

Chapter 10

1. Fryde, *Early Paleologian Renaissance*, 23.
2. Zissos, "Reception of Valerius Flaccus' *Argonautica*," 173–174.
3. Peter D. Jeans, *Seafaring Lore and Legend: A Miscellany of Maritime Myth, Superstition, Fable, and Fact* (Camden, ME: International Marine/McGraw-Hill, 2004), 65–66.
4. R. C. Seaton, in Apollonius, *The Argonautica*, xiv.
5. D. P. M. Weerakkody, "Apollonius Rhodius, c. 295–215 BC," in *The Encyclopedia of Ancient Greece*, ed. Nigel Guy Wilson (London: Routledge, 2006), 66.
6. Weerakkody, "Apollonius," 66.
7. Zissos, "Reception of Valerius Flaccus' *Argonautica*," 179.
8. Thomas Willard, "The Metamorphoses of Metals: Ovid and the Alchemists," in *Metamorphosis: The Changing Face of Ovid in Medieval and Early Modern Europe*, edited by Allison Keith and Steven Rupp (Toronto: Center for Reformation and Renaissance Studies, 2007), 153–154.
9. Willard, "Metamorphoses of Metals," 156.
10. Willard, "Metamorphoses of Metals,"
11. Zweder von Martels, "Augurello's *Chrysopoeia* (1515)—A Turning Point in the Literary Tradition of Alchemical Texts," *Early Science and Medicine* 5, no. 2 (2000): 193.

12. Supriya Chaudhuri, "Jason's Fleece: The Source of Sir Epicure Mammon's Allegory," *Review of English Studies* 35, no. 137 (1984): 71.
13. Ben Jonson, *The Alchemist* 2.1.89–104, edited by H. C. Hart (London: De La More Press, 1903), 33. This edition is slightly modernized in spelling and punctuation.
14. Sir Isaac Newton, *Chronology of Ancient Kingdoms Amended* (London: J. Tonson, 1728), 83–86.
15. Jonathon Green, *Cassell's Dictionary of Slang*, 2nd ed. (London: Weidenfeld & Nicolson, 2005), 789.
16. William O. Goode, "Médée and Jason: Hero and Nonhero in Corneille's *Médée*," *The French Review* 51 (1978): 804.
17. Goode, "Médée and Jason," 809.
18. F. G. Healy, *The Literary Culture of Napoleon* (Geneva: Librairie de Droz, 1959), 111.
19. Gustav Pollak, *Franz Gillparzer and the Austrian Drama* (New York: Dowd, Mead & Company, 1907), 76.
20. Translated in Pollak, *Franz Gillparzer*, 90.
21. Pollak, *Franz Gillparzer*, 94.
22. Ian F. Roe, *Franz Gillparzer: A Century of Criticism* (Columbia, SC: Camden House, 1995), 43–48.
23. Charles R. Lyons, "The Ambiguity of the Anouihl 'Medea,'" *The French Review* 37, no. 3 (1964): 313.
24. Lyons, "Ambiguity," 313.
25. Lyons, "Ambiguity," 317.
26. Ellen Rosand, *Opera in Seventeenth Century Venice: The Creation of a Genre* (1991, paperback reprint: Berkeley: University of California Press, 2007), 276–277, n.39.
27. Thomas Bulfinch, *Bulfinch's Mythology* (New York: Crown, 1979), vi, vii-viii.
28. Marie Sally Cleary, "Bulfinch's Mythology," *Humanities* 8, no. 1 (1987): 12–15.
29. Michel W. Pharand, "Greek Myths, White Goddess: Robert Graves Cleans up a 'Dreadful Mess,'" in *Graves and the Goddess: Essays on Robert Graves's* The White Goddess, edited by Ian Firla and Grevel Lindop (London: Associated University Presses, 2003), 184–186.
30. Robert Graves, *The Greek Myths* (New York: Penguin, 1993), 581.
31. Graves, *Greek Myths*, 584.
32. H. J. Rose, Review of *The Greek Myths* by Robert Graves, *The Classical Review* 5, no. 2 (1955): 208.
33. J. Macpherson, Review of *The Greek Myths* by Robert Graves, *Phoenix* 21, no. 1 (1958): 17.
34. Pharand, "Greek Myths," 184.
35. Shakespeare, *The Merchant of Venice* 1.1.166–176.
36. Roger Kahn, *Joe and Marilyn: A Memory of Love* (New York: Morrow, 1986), 63. Kahn was not the only biographer to so designate that part of Monroe's anatomy; however, it is beyond our scope to provide a fuller bibliography.
37. Henry Ellison, *The Poetry of Real Life: A New Edition, Much Enlarged and Improved* (London: G. Willis, 1851), 279.
38. Alfred Noyes, *William Morris* (London: Macmillan, 1908), 41–42.
39. On Morris's views of Medea, sources, and interest in promoting the sanctity of monogamy, I am indebted to Florence S. Boos, "Medea and Circe as 'Wise' Women in the Poetry of William Morris and Augusta Webster," in *Writing on the Image: Reading William Morris*, ed.

David Latham (Toronto: University of Toronto Press, 2007), 43–60.

40. Review of *The Life and Death of Jason: A Poem* by William Morris, *North American Review* 105, no. 217 (October 1867): 690.

41. William Morris, *The Life and Death of Jason: A Poem*, 9th ed. (New York: Longmans, Green, and Co., 1897), 17.1180–1184, p.369.

42. Morris, *Life and Death of Jason*, 17.1337–1338, p. 375.

43. Noyes, *William Morris*, 55.

44. Except for the 1970s animated version, I owe all of the information about Soviet Jason movies to Prof. Julian Graffy of the School of Slavonic and East European Studies at University College, London (personal communication, May 31, 2010).

45. Ray Harryhausen and Tony Dalton, *Ray Harryhausen: An Animated Life* (New York: Billboard Books, 2004), 152.

46. Harryhausen and Dalton, *Ray Harryhausen*, 151.

47. Harryhausen and Dalton, *Ray Harryhausen*, 159.

48. *Time*, July 19, 1963.

49. Harold Thompson, "Jason and Argonauts Seek Golden Fleece at Loew's State," *New York Times*, August 8, 1963, p. 19.

50. Armstrong had never been a lead actor before, and his voice ended up being dubbed by another actor when executives felt his American accent clashed too harshly with the mostly British cast.

Chapter 11

1. Fritz Graf, *Greek Mythology: An Introduction*, trans. Thomas Marier (Baltimore: Johns Hopkins University Press, 1996), chapters 1 and 2.

2. Among the books discussing Medea are Emma Griffiths' *Medea* (2006), a scholarly overview; *Medea: Essays on Medea in Myth, Literature, Philosophy and Art* edited by James Joseph Clauss and Sarah Iles Johnson (1997), a collection of articles exploring several facets of the character; Ruth Morse, *The Medieval Medea* (1996), about the witch in the Middle Ages; and Amy Wygant's *Medea, Magic, and Modernity in France: Stages and Histories, 1553–1797* (2007), about the reception and use of Medea's image in early modern France, just to start. Against these, there are no recent books covering Jason excepting two classes: those treating him as a part of a larger work, or literary criticism of a specific ancient poem, such as those of Pindar, Apollonius, or Valerius Flaccus. As far as I can determine, excepting the self-published *The Image of Jason in Early Greek Myth* by Simon Spence in 2010, no English-language book on Jason has appeared since Dominguez's *Medieval Argonautica* in 1979 and before that none at all. Clearly, modern scholars agree that Medea is the more fascinating figure.

3. Robert D. Richardson, "Antoine Banier," in *The Rise of Modern Mythology, 1680–1860*, edited by Burton Feldman and Robert D. Richardson (Bloomington: University of Indiana Press, 1972), 86–67.

4. Antoine Banier, *The Mythology and Fables of the Ancients, Explained from History* (London: A. Millar, 1740), 30.

5. Banier, *Mythology and Fables*, 42.

6. Jacob Bryant, *A New System; or, an Analysis of Ancient Mythology*, 3rd ed., Vol. III (London: J. Walker, 1807), 54.

7. Bryant, *A New System*, 412–413.

8. Alfred Heubeck and Arie Hoeckstra, *A Commentary on Homer's* Odyssey, Volume III: Books XVII–XXIV (Oxford: Clarendon Paperbacks, 1992), 64–65.

9. Rendel Harris, *Boanerges* (Cambridge: Cambridge University Press, 1913), 232.

10. Gildas Hamel, "Taking the *Argo* to Nineveh: Jonah and Jason in a Mediterranean Context," *Judaism* 44, no. 3 (1995): 342.

11. Hamel, "Taking the *Argo* to Nineveh," 351.

12. Harris, *Boanerges*, 339.

13. For Iasion and Triptolemus as Gemini, see Hyginus, *Astronomica* 2.22. There is an interesting connection, thematically at least, between Jason (if not Iasion) and his alleged brother. To spread agriculture throughout the land Triptolemus plowed fields with Demeter's chariot drawn by dragons, and a mortal tried to do the same, yoking the dragons, but plummeting to his death (in the manner of Phaëton). Incidentally, scholars now believe Triptolemus was once an agricultural deity who degraded into a satellite of Demeter, much as I have proposed Jason himself had done in another context.

14. Harris, *Boanerges*, 230.

15. Harris, *Boanerges*, 364.

16. Harris, *Boanerges*, 366.

17. Harris, *Boanerges*, 371.

18. Arthur Drews, *The Witnesses to the Historicity of Jesus*, trans. Joseph McCabe (London: Watts & Co., 1912), 196–197.

19. Flavius Josephus, *Antiquities of the Jews* 12.237.

20. Shirley Jackson Case, "The Historicity of Jesus: An Estimate of the Negative Argument," *The American Journal of Theology* 15 (1911): 29.

21. Genesis 2:11. One prominent early advocate of the theory was Joseph Pitton de Tournefort, the French botanist, in his posthumous *Relation d'un voyage du Levant* (1717).

22. Russell E. Gmirkin, *Berossus and Genesis, Manetho and Exodus: Hellenistic Histories and the Date of the Pentateuch* (New York: T & T Clark International, 2006), appendix D. Flavius Josephus first proposed the identification of the Gihon and the Nile, but the Nile is identified by a different Hebrew word than the Gihon, suggesting to most scholars that the latter is a different river, perhaps the Araxes of Armenia among many other suggestions. The Pishon has also been identified with many other rivers, including the Ganges by Flavius Josephus, the Nile (!) by Rashi, and the Uizhun by Egyptologist David Rohl. The long and short of it is that no one knows, and these suggestions are merely guesses.

23. R. L. Hunter, *The* Argonautica *of Apollonius* (Cambridge: Cambridge University Press, 1993), 186.

24. Paley, "Pre-Homeric Legends," 167.

25. Müller, *Contributions to the Science of Comparative Mythology*, 436–440. Müller was admittedly lost in trying to understand the meaning of Aea, which he speculatively linked to the Vedic word for the quarter moon, *ayava*. This is especially ironic since Aea, derived most likely from the dawn goddess Aya, is the one place in the Jason myth that has an actual and demonstrable link to the sun!

26. Sir George W. Cox, *The Mythology of Aryan Nations,* new ed. (London: Keegan, Paul, Trench & Co., 1887), 382–388.

27. Paley, "Pre-Homeric Legends," 167–168.

28. John Kenrick, *The Egypt of Herodotus* (London: B. Fellows, 1841), 281–282.

29. Andrew Lang, *Custom and Myth,* new edition (London: Longmans, Green, and Co., 1893), 101–102.

30. O. A. Wall, *Sex and Sex Worship (Phallic Worship)* (St. Louis: Mosby, 1920): 550. I have been unable to find what "writers" Wall claimed considered this theory valid. He may have been referring to the slang term, but he discusses the theory alongside legitimate ideas, such as the solar theory.

31. Leon Balter, "The Mother as Source of Power: Three Greek Myths," *Psychoanalytic Quarterly* 38 (1969): 266–271.

32. Jung referred to Jason only a few times in passing in his works and lectures; I am here summarizing from these references and some of his broader mythic theories.

33. Joseph Campbell, *The Hero with a Thousand Faces* (1949; reprint, New York: MJF Books, undated), 30.

34. Ironic since his earlier writing disclaimed a direct connection between myth and ritual but saw them as sharing atmosphere and structure.

35. Graf, "Orpheus," 98.

36. Graf, "Medea," 40–41.

37. Strabo, *Geography* 10.4.20–21; Burkert, *Greek Religion,* 261.

38. K. Kerényi, *Goddesses of Sun and Moon* (Dallas: Spring Publications, 1979), 12.

39. K. Kerényi, *Heroes of the Greeks,* trans. H. R. Rose (New York: Thames & Hudson, 1978), 264–266.

40. Dean A. Miller, *The Epic Hero* (Baltimore, MD: Johns Hopkins University Press, 2000), 156.

41. Miller, *Epic Hero,* 169.

42. Miller, *Epic Hero,* 170.

43. Strabo, *Geography,* 11.11.19, trans. in *op. cit.,* vol. 2, p. 229.

44. Strabo, *Geography,* 1.2.40, trans. in *op. cit.,* vol. 1, p. 72.

45. Pliny, *Natural History* 33.15.

46. Edward Gibbon, *The History of the Decline and Fall of the Roman Empire,* ed. J. B. Bury, vol. IV (London: Methuen & Co., 1901), 372.

47. John A. Scott, "The Origin of the Myth of the Golden Fleece," *Classical Journal* 22, no. 7 (1927): 541.

48. Emiliano Feresin, "Fleece Myth Hints at Golden Age for Georgia," *Nature* 448 (August 2007): 846–847.

49. Maria Filomena Guerra, "Sur les traces de l'or antique : analyse élémentaire de bijoux et monnaies," June 1, 2010: http://culturesciences.chimie.ens.fr/dossiers-experimentale-analyse-article-Or_Antique_Guerra.html

50. Jan N. Bremmer, *Greek Religion and Culture, the Bible, and the Ancient Near East* (Leiden/Boston: Brill, 2008), chapter XV.

51. Jaan Puhvel, *Hittite Etymological Dictionary, Vol. 4: Words Beginning with K* (Berlin: De Gruyter, 1997), 274.

52. Puhvel, *Hittite Etymological Dictionary,* Vol. 4, 274.

53. Watkins, "A Distant Anatolian Echo in Pindar," 6.

54. Braswell, *Commentary on the Fourth Pythian Ode of Pindar,* 318, who notes Pindar's familiarity with Homeric vocabulary.

55. Pseudo-Hesiod, *Shield of Heracles* 223–4; but Apollodorus omits the tassels in *Library* 2.4.2.

56. Billie Jean Collins places the origins of the Jason myth in Mycenaean encounters with Hittite culture in Late Bronze Age Anatolia. This is doubly problematic because while Jason is known to Homer and associated with Mycenaean Iolcus, the Golden Fleece cannot be tied to his myth until Mimnermus around 630 BCE—more than six centuries later—and may not have been original to his myth. ("Hittite Religion and the West," *Pax Hethitica: Studies on the Hittites and Their Neighbours in Honour of Itamar Singer,* eds. Yoram Cohen, Amir Gilan, and Jared L. Miller [Weisbaden: Harrassowitz Verlag, 2010], 63.)

57. Green, *The Storm-God in the Ancient Near East,* 149.

58. Fox, *Travelling Heroes,* 297.

59. Saul Levin, *Semitic and Indo-European II: Comparative Morphology, Syntax and Phonetics* (Amsterdam: John Benjamins, 2002), 526–527.

60. Strabo, *Geography* 11.14.13.

61. Paley, "Pre-Homeric Legends of the Voyage of the Argonauts," 174–175. He further argues that the rocks must be icebergs because they are described by the ancients as "blue" and icebergs would stop moving when they hit the mouth of the Bosporus and got stuck, just like Jason's rocks. "Nothing ... but the iceberg theory will really satisfy the conditions of the legend." Sir George G. Cox also adopted this theory on the authority of Paley in his *Mythology of Aryan Nations,* 386–387 n.3. There is obviously a degree of contradiction in asserting that Jason and the Fleece are symbols of the sun and clouds while the Clashing Rocks must have had a basis in real life cloaked in myth.

62. William F. Pickard, "The Symplegades," *Greece & Rome,* second series, 34, no. 1 (1987): 1–6.

63. Nilsson, *Mycenaean Origin,* 141.

64. Janet Ruth Bacon, *The Voyage of the Argonauts* (London: Methuen & Co., 1925), 108.

65. Rhys Carpenter, "The Greek Penetration of the Black Sea," *American Journal of Archaeology* 52, no. 1 (1948): 1–10.

66. Benjamin W. Labaree, "How the Greeks Sailed into the Black Sea," *American Journal of Archaeology* 61, No. 1 (1957): 29–33.

67. Robert Drews, "The Earliest Greek Settlements of the Black Sea," *Journal of Hellenic Studies* 96 (1976): 30–31.

68. Tim Severin, *The Jason Voyage: The Quest for the Golden Fleece* (London: Hutchinson, 1985).

69. Cf. Thor Heyerdahl's *Kon Tiki* voyage, which attempted to prove that South Americans settled the Pacific islands of Polynesia. His raft made the trip from Peru to the Tuamotu Islands, but archaeology has demonstrated that in fact the influence went the other way: The Polynesians sailed to South America.

70. Mauricio Obregón, *Beyond the Edge of the Sea: Sailing with Jason and the Argonauts, Ulysses, the Vikings, and Other Explorers of the Ancient World* (New York: Random House, 2001), chapters 4 and 5.

Chapter 12

1. James J. Rogers, "Origins of the Ancient Constellations: II. The Mediterranean Traditions," *Journal of the British Astronomical Association* 108, no. 2 (1998): 82.

2. Liz Green, *The Astrology of Fate* (Boston: Red Wheel/Weiser, 1984), 180.

3. Acharya S, *Suns of God: Krishna, Buddha, and Christ Unveiled* (Kempton, Illinois: Adventures Unlimited Press, 2004), 506.

4. J. Nigro Sansonese, *The Body of Myth: Mythology, Shamanic Trance, and the Sacred Geography of the Body* (Rochester, Vermont: Inner Traditions, 1994), 216–219.

5. The constellation of Argo Navis is ancient, dating back into the Bronze Age. It was the largest constellation in the night sky, but French astronomer Nicolas Louis de Lacaille considered it unwieldy and broke it into three constellations in 1752: Carina (the heel), Puppis (the poop deck), and Vela (the sails). A fourth, Pyxis (the compass), was in ancient times considered the ship's mast but is now counted as an independent constellation.

6. Modern scholars have been unable to correlate Egyptian constellations to modern ones, and Egypt apparently had relatively poor astronomy compared to Babylon and Greece, making any zodiac or star theories reliant on alleged Egyptian master astronomers rather suspect. (Otto Neugebauer, *A History of Ancient Mathematical Astronomy,* vol. 1 [Heidelberg: Springer-Verlag, 1975], 561–563).

7. Nicholas Mikhailov, *Soviet Russia: The Land and Its People,* trans. George H. Hanna (New York: Sheridan House, 1948), 140.

8. James P. Mitchell, *Our Good Neighbors in Soviet Russia* (New York: Noble and Noble, 1945), 150.

9. Gia Kvashilava, "On Decipherment of the Phaistos Disk and Linear A Inscriptions in Colchian Language," *Aia-Colchis,* 2013, http://www.scribd.com/gia_kvashilava.

10. *Lonely Planet,* http://www.lonelyplanet.com/georgia/adjara/batumi/sights/446195>.

11. Craig S. Barnes, *In Search of the Lost Feminine: Decoding the Myths that Radically Reshaped Civilization* (Golden, Colorado: Fulcrum Publishing, 2006), 160–161, 210.

12. Barnes, 113–120.

13. W. S. Blacket, *Researches into the Lost History of America* (London: Trübner & Co., 1884), 199, 303–306.

14. David Hatcher Childress, *Lost Cities of Atlantis, Ancient Europe & the Mediterranean* (Kempton, Illinois: Adventures Unlimited Press, 1996), 142–143.

15. N. Zhirov, *Atlantis: Atlantology—Basic Problems* (Honolulu: University Press of the Pacific, 2001), 97–98.

16. He later revised this claim to merely being "one of the best in the world." http://www.andiskaulins.com/academics

17. Andis Kaulins, *Stars, Stones and Scholars: The Decipherment of the Megaliths* (Victoria, BC: Trafford, 2003), 5, 99.

18. J. V. Luce, *The End of Atlantis: New Light on an Old Legend* (New York: McGraw-Hill, 1969), 148–151;

James Watt Mavor, *Voyage to Atlantis: The Discovery of a Legendary Land* (Rochester, Vermont: Park Street Press, 1969; reprint 1996), 49–50.

19. Mavor, *Voyage to Atlantis,* 49–50.

20. For discussion of Atlantis, its origins in Plato's philosophy, and the history of the quest for the imaginary continent, see Paul Jordan, *The Atlantis Syndrome* (Sparkford: Sutton Publishing, 2003).

21. Drusilla Dunjee Houston, *Wonderful Ethiopians of the Cushite Empire* (Oklahoma City: Universal Publishing, 1926), 4–6.

22. Herodotus, *Histories* 2.104; Apollonius, *Argonautica* 4.257–293.

23. John G. Jackson quoted in James E. Brunson and Runoko Rashidi, "Sitting at the Feet of a Forerunner: An April 1987 Meeting and Interview with John G. Jackson," in *African Presence in Early Asia,* eds. Runoko Rashidi and Ivan Van Sertima (New Brunswick: Transaction, 1988): 198.

24. Patrick T. English, "Cushites, Colchians, and Khazars," *Journal of Near Eastern Studies* 18, no. 1 (1959): 49–53. The article, frequently cited in Afrocentric literature, commits the fallacy of assuming that the prehistory of a non–Greek people can be deduced entirely from Greco-Roman sources unrelieved by archaeology or ethnology.

25. Martin W. Lewis and Kären Wigen, *The Myth of Continents: A Critique of Metageography* (Berkeley: University of California Press, 1997), 257n.66.

26. Lewis and Wigen, *The Myth of Metageography,* 257n.66.

27. Ian Shaw, *The Oxford History of Ancient Egypt* (Oxford: Oxford University Press, 2000), 154; Phiroze Vasunia, *The Gift of the Nile: Hellenizing Egypt from Aeschylus to Alexander* (Berkeley: University of California Press, 2001), 78n.6.

28. Jairazbhoy, "Egyptian Civilization," 61.

29. Jairazbhoy, "Egyptian Civilization," 61.

30. Herodotus, *Histories* 2.4, 6.53–55.

31. Giorgio de Santillana and Hertha von Dechend, *Hamlet's Mill: An Essay Investigating the Origins of Human Knowledge and Its Transmission through Myth,* original: 1970 (Boston: Nonpareil, 1998), 318.

32. However, Aries may have been a constellation in Babylon around 1500 BCE (as the "Hired Man"), which is still far too late for the theory presented in *Hamlet's Mill.* See Rogers, "Origins of the Ancient Constellations I."

33. James J. Rogers, "Origins of the Ancient Constellations: II. The Mediterranean Traditions," *Journal of the British Astronomical Association* 108, no. 2 (1998): 79.

34. Rogers, "Origins of the Ancient Constellations I," 27; Rogers, "Origins of the Ancient Constellations II," 81.

35. Robert Charroux, *The Mysterious Unknown,* trans. Olga Sieveking (London: Neville Spearman, 1972), 210.

36. Eusebius, *Chronicon* 1.3–5.

37. See W. E. A. Van Beek, "Dogon Restudied: A Field Evaluation of the Work of Marcel Griaule," *Current Anthropology* 32, no. 2 (1991): 139–167. For Temple's misuse of the Jason myth, see also my article "Golden Fleeced: Robert Temple's Misuse of the Argonaut Myth in the *Sirius Mystery,*" *eSkeptic,* May 5, 2010.

For a broader discussion of Temple and other ancient astronaut theorists, I offer the interested reader my earlier work *The Cult of Alien Gods: H. P. Lovecraft and Extraterrestrial Pop Culture* (Amherst, NY: Prometheus, 2005). For the scientific reasons Sirius does not match Temple's claims, see J. B. Holberg, *Sirius: Brightest Diamond of the Night Sky* (Berlin: Springer, 2007), 181–184.

38. Robert Temple, *The Sirius Mystery: New Scientific Evidence of Alien Contact 5,000 Years Ago* (Rochester, Vermont: Destiny Books, 1998). Temple scatters his Argonaut ideas throughout the book, and I have extracted and presented them in somewhat more coherent fashion than the author himself.

39. Temple, *Sirius Mystery*, 222.

40. Von Däniken admitted at one point that he had altered or exaggerated some of his "evidence" for the book *The Gold of the Gods* (1972), including the existence of laser-carved caves filled with gold tablets, calling it "theatrical effect" (Erich von Däniken, interview with Timothy Ferris, *Playboy*, August 1974, 58).

41. Erich von Däniken, *Odyssey of the Gods: The Extraterrestrial History of Ancient Greece,* trans. Matthew Barton (Shaftesbury: Element Books, 2000), 4. I will kindly assume the confusion over mythological names, assuming Minerva and Athena are two separate goddesses for example, is the fault of poor translation since other passages seem garbled beyond even von Däniken's usual incoherence.

42. Brian Haughton, *Hidden History: Lost Civilizations, Secret Knowledge, and Ancient History* (Franklin Lakes, NY: Career Press, 2007), 216.

43. Cook, *Zeus,* vol. 1, 723.

44. Bruce Rux, *Architects of the Underworld: Unriddling Atlantis, Anomalies of Mars, and the Mystery of the Sphinx* (Berkeley, California: Frog Ltd., 1996), 364.

45. If you don't believe me, see Rux, *Architects of the Underworld,* 366–369.

46. Rux, *Architects of the Underworld,* 393.

47. Michael Barkun, *A Culture of Conspiracy: Apocalyptic Visions in Contemporary America* (Berkeley: University of California Press, 2006), 93.

48. John Lawrence Reynolds, *Secret Societies: Inside the World's Most Notorious Organizations* (New York: Arcade, 2006), 290–291.

49. Nicholas Goodrick-Clarke, *Black Sun: Aryan Cults, Esoteric Nazism, and the Politics of Identity* (New York: New York University Press, 2002), 285–286.

50. For example, see Thomas E. Bullard, "UFO Abduction Reports: The Supernatural Kidnap Narrative Returns in Technological Guise," *Journal of American Folklore* 102, no. 404 (1989): 147–170.

Conclusion

1. Burkert, *Greek Religion,* 208.

2. Burkert, *Greek Religion,* 208.

3. Kirk, *The Nature of Greek Myths,* 163.

4. Mackie, "Earliest Jason," 12.

5. Apollonius, *Argonautica* 4.1773–1781, trans. *op. cit.,* 415.

Bibliography

Primary Sources

Apollodorus. *The Library*. Trans. Sir James G. Frazer. London: William Heinemann, 1921.

Apollonius. *Argonautica*. Trans. R. C. Seaton. London: William Heinemann, 1912.

_____. *The Argonautika*. Expanded ed. Trans. Peter Green. Berkeley: University of California Press, 2007.

Banier, Antoine. *The Mythology and Fables of the Ancients, Explained from History*. London: A. Millar, 1740.

Bulfinch, Thomas. *Bulfinch's Mythology*. New York: Crown, 1979.

Caxton, William. *The History of Jason translated from the French of Raoul Le Fevre*. Ed. John Munro. London: Early English Text Society/ Oxford University Press, 1913.

Chaucer, Geoffrey. *Legend of Good Women*. Ed. Walter W. Skeat. Oxford: Clarendon Press, 1889.

Dante Alighieri. *The Inferno*. Trans. James Romanes Sibbald. Edinburgh: David Douglas, 1884.

Dares Phrygius. *Historia de Excidio Trioae*. Ed. Ferdinand Meister. Leipzig: B. G. Teubneri, 1873.

De Lorris, Guillame and Jean de Meun. *The Romance of the Rose*. 3rd ed. Trans. Charles Dahlberg. Princeton: Princeton University Press, 1995.

Diodorus Siculus. *The Historical Library*. Trans. G. Booth. London, 1814.

Diogenes Laertius. *The Lives and Opinions of Eminent Philosophers*. Trans. C. D. Young. London: George Bell and Sons, 1901.

Euripides. *The Plays of Euripides*. Vol. 1. Trans. Edward P. Coleridge. London: George Bell and Sons, 1906.

Gower, John. *The Complete Works of John Gower: English Works*. Ed. G. C. Macaulay. Oxford: Clarendon Press, 1901.

Graves, Robert. *The Greek Myths*. New York: Penguin, 1993.

Herodotus. *The Histories*. Trans. Alfred Dennis Godley. London: William Heinemann, 1920.

Homer. *The Iliad*. Trans. W. G. Caldcleugh. PhHesiod. *Hesiod, the Homeric Hymns, and Homerica*.

Trans. Hugh G. Evelyn-White. London: William Heinemann, 1920.

_____. *Theogony, Works and Days, and Shield*. Trans. Apostolos N. Athanassakis. Baltimore: Johns Hopkins University Press, 2004.

_____. *Works of Hesiod and the Homeric Hymns*. Trans. Daryl Hine. Chicago: University of Chicago Press, 2005.

iladelphia: J. B. Lippincott & Co., 1870.

_____. *The Odyssey*. Trans. George Herbert Palmer. Boston: Houghton Mifflin, 1921.

Horace. *The Satires and Epistles of Horace: A Modern English Verse Translation*. Trans. Smith Palmer Bovie. Chicago: University of Chicago Press, 2002.

Isidore of Seville. *The Etymologies of Isidore of Seville*. Trans. and eds. Steven A. Barney, W. J. Lewis, J. A. Beach, Oliver Berghof. Cambridge: Cambridge University Press, 2006.

Jacobsen, Thorkild. *The Harps that Once...: Sumerian Poetry in Translation*. New Haven: Yale University, 1987.

Jonson, Ben. *The Alchemist*. Ed. H. C. Hart. London: De La More Press, 1903.

Justin, et al. *Justin, Cornelius Nepos, and Eutropius*. Trans. John Selby Watson. London: Henry G. Bohn, 1853.

Longinus. *On the Sublime*. Trans. A. O. Prickard. Oxford: Clarendon Press, 1906.

Lydgate, John. *Troy Book: Selections*. Ed. Robert R. Edwards. Kalamazoo, Michigan: Medieval Institute Publications, 1998.

Maio, Angelo, ed. *Classicorum auctorum e Vaticanus codicibus editorum*. Vol. III. Rome: Vatican, 1831.

Mitchell, Steven (trans.). *Gilgamesh: A New English Version*. New York: The Free Press, 2004.

Morris, William. *The Life and Death of Jason: A Poem*, 9th ed. New York: Longmans, Green, and Co., 1897.

Orpheus. *Orphei Argonautica, hymni et libellus de lapidbus*. Ed. Johann Matthias Gesner. Leipzig, 1764.

Ovid. *Metamorphoses*. Trans. Rolfe Humphries. Bloomington: Indiana University Press, 1955.

Palaephatus. *On Unbelievable Tales*. Trans. Jacob Stern. Wacunda, Illinois: Bolchazy-Carducci, 1996.

Pausanias. *Description of Greece*. Trans. W. H. S. Jones. London: William Heinemann, 1918.

Pindar. *The Extant Odes of Pindar*. Trans. Ernest Myers. London: Macmillan, 1904.

_____. *Pindar's Victory Songs*. Trans. Frank J. Nisetich. Baltimore: Johns Hopkins University Press, 1980.

Pliny the Elder. *Natural History*. Vol. VI. Trans. John Bostock and H. T. Riley. London: Henry G. Bohn, 1857.

Quintilian. *Quintilians's Institutes of Oratory: Or, the Education of an Orator*. Vol. 2. Trans. John Selby Watson. London: George Bell and Sons, 1905.

Richardson, M. E. J., trans. *Hammurabi's Laws: Text, Translation, and Glossary*, originally published 2000. London: T&T Clark International, 2004.

Sandars, N. K., trans. *The Epic of Gilgamesh*. London: Penguin, 1972.

_____, trans. *Poems of Heaven and Hell from Ancient Mesopotamia*. London: Penguin, 1971.

Seneca. *Seneca's Tragedies*. Vol. I. Trans. Frank Justice Miller. London: William Heinemann, 1918.

Sophocles. *The Dramas of Sophocles Rendered into English Verse: Dramatic & Lyric*. Trans. Sir George Young. London: J. M. Dent, 1906.

Spencer, Edmund. *The Second Book of the Faerie Queene*. Ed. Thomas J. Wise. London: George Allen, 1895.

Strabo. *The Geography of Strabo*. Trans. Horace Leonard Jones. London: William Heinemann, 1918.

Tafur, Pero. *Travels and Adventures 1435–1439*. Trans. Malcolm Letts. Orig. 1926. Reprint London: RoutledgeCurzon, 2005.

Valerius Flaccus. *Argonautica*. Trans. J. H. Mozley. Loeb Classical Library, Vol. 286. Cambridge: Harvard University Press, 1928.

Secondary Sources

Acosta-Hughes, Benjamin. *Arion's Lyre: Archaic Lyric into Hellenistic Poetry*. Princeton: Princeton University Press, 2010.

Aitken, Ellen Bradshaw, and Jennifer K. Berenson Maclean, eds. *Philostratus's Heroikos: Religion And Cultural Identity in the Third Century*. Leiden: Brill, 2004.

Albis, Robert V. *Poet and Audience in the* Argonautica *of Apollonius*. Lanham, MD: Rowman & Littlefield, 1996.

Aldhouse-Green, Miranda, and Stephen Aldhouse-Green. *The Quest for the Shaman*. London: Thames & Hudson, 2005.

Allen, W.E.D. *Georgia and Its People*, orig. 1932. Reissue, London: Routledge, 1971.

Anderson, Graham. *King Arthur in Antiquity*. London: Routledge, 2004.

Arthur, Marylin B. "The Curse of Civilization: The Choral Odes of the *Phoenissae*." *Harvard Studies in Classical Philology* 81 (1977): 163–185.

Ascherson, Neal. *Black Sea*. New York: Hill and Wang, 1996.

Astour, Michael C. *Hellenosemitica*. Leiden: E. J. Brill, 1967.

Ataç, Mehmet-Ali. "The 'Underworld Vision' of the Ninevite Intellectual Milieu." *Iraq* 66 (2004): 67–76.

Bacon, Janet Ruth. "The Geography of the *Orphic Argonautica*." *The Classical Quarterly* 25, no. 3/4 (1931): 172–183.

_____. *The Voyage of the Argonauts*. London: Methuen & Co., 1925.

Balot, Ryan K., ed. *A Companion to Greek and Roman Political Thought*. Malden, Mass.: Blackwell, 2009.

Balter, Leon. "The Mother as Source of Power: Three Greek Myths." *Psychoanalytic Quarterly* 38 (1969): 266–271.

Barkun, Michael. *A Culture of Conspiracy: Apocalyptic Visions in Contemporary America*. Berkeley: University of California Press, 2006.

Barnes, Craig S. *In Search of the Lost Feminine: Decoding the Myths that Radically Reshaped Civilization*. Golden, Colorado: Fulcrum Publishing, 2006.

Beck, Frederick A. G. *Greek Education: 450–350 BC*. Frome, Somerset: Butler & Tanner, 1964.

Beckman, Gary, Richard Beal, and Gregory McMahon, eds. *Hittite Studies in Honor of Harry A. Hoffner, Jr. on the Occasion of His 65th Birthday*. Winona Lake, Ind.: Eisenbrauns, 2003.

Bell, Malcolm. "A Coptic Jason Relief." *Gesta* 18, no. 1 (1979): 45–52.

Black, Jeremy and Anthony Green. *Gods, Demons, and Symbols of Ancient Mesopotamia: An Illustrated Dictionary*. Austin: University of Texas, 2003.

Blacket, W. S. *Researches into the Lost History of America*. London: Trübner & Co., 1884.

Boardman, John. *The Archaeology of Nostalgia: How the Greeks Re-Created Their Mythical Past*. New York: Thames & Hudson, 2002.

Bonnefoy, Yves. *Greek and Egyptian Mythologies*. Trans. Wendy Doniger. Chicago: University of Chicago Press, 1992.

Bos, A. P. *Cosmic and Meta-Cosmic Theology in Aristotle's Lost Dialogues*. New York: Brill, 1989.

Braswell, Bruce Karl. *Commentary on the Fourth Pythian Ode of Pindar*. Berlin/New York: De Gruyter, 1988.

Bremmer, Jan N. *Greek Religion and Culture, the Bible, and the Ancient Near East*. Leiden/Boston: Brill, 2008.

_____, ed. *Interpretations of Greek Mythology*. Beckenham, Kent: Croom Helm, 1987.

_____. *The Rise and Fall of the Afterlife*. London: Routledge, 2002.

Brenk, Frederick E. *Relighting the Souls: Studies in Plutarch, in Greek Literature, Religion, and Philosophy, and in the New Testament Background.* Stuggart: Steiner, 1998.

Brundage, Burr C. "Herakles the Levantine: A Comprehensive View." *Journal of Near East Studies* 17, no. 4 (1958): 225–236.

Bryant, Jacob. *A New System; or, an Analysis of Ancient Mythology.* 3rd ed. Vol. III. London: J. Walker, 1807.

Bryant, Lawrence M. *The King and the City in Royal Parisian Entrance Ceremony: Politics, Ritual, and Art in the Renaissance.* Geneva: Libraire Droz, S.A., 1986.

Bryce, Trevor. *Kingdom of the Hittites.* New Edition. Oxford: Oxford Unviersity Press, 2006.
_____. *Life and Society in the Hittite World.* Oxford: Oxford University Press, 2002.

Buccellati, Giorgio. "The Descent of Inanna as a Ritual Journey to Kutha?" *Syro-Mesopotamian Studies* 4, no. 3 (1982): 3–7.

Budin, Stephanie Lynn. *The Ancient Greeks: An Introduction.* Oxford: Oxford University Press, 2004.

Bullard, Thomas E. "UFO Abduction Reports: The Supernatural Kidnap Narrative Returns in Technological Guise." *Journal of American Folklore* 102, no. 404 (1989): 147–170.

Burgess, Jonathan S. *The Tradition of the Trojan War in Homer and the Epic Cycle.* Baltimore: Johns Hopkins University Press, 2001.

Burkert, Walter. *Greek Religion.* Trans. John Raffan. Cambridge: Harvard University Press, 1985.
_____. *Homo Necans: The Anthropology of Ancient Greek Sacrificial Ritual and Myth.* Trans. Peter Bing. Berkeley: University of California Press, 1983.
_____. "Jason, Hypsipyle, and New Fire at Lemnos: A Study in Myth and Ritual." *The Classical Quarterly* (New Series) 20, no. 1 (May 1970): 1–16.
_____. *The Orientalizing Revolution: Near Eastern Influence on Greek Culture in the Early Archaic Age.* Cambridge: Harvard University Press, 1992.
_____. *Structure and History in Greek Mythology and Ritual,* originally 1979. Berkeley: University of California Press, 1982.

Burney, Charles Allen. *Historical Dictionary of the Hittites.* Lanham, Maryland: Scarecrow Press, 2004.

Burstein, Stanley Mayer. *Outpost of Hellenism: The Emergence of Heraclea on the Black Sea* (Classical Studies Vol. 14). Berkeley: University of California Press, 1976.

Cameron, Alan. *Greek Mythography in the Roman World.* Oxford: Oxford University Press, 2004.

Cameron, Averil, and Judith Herrin. *Constantinople in the Early Eighth Century: The* Parastaseis syntomoi chronikai: *Introduction, Translation, and Commentary.* Columbia Studies in the Classical Tradition, Vol. 10. Leiden: Brill, 1984.

Campbell, Joseph. *The Hero with a Thousand Faces,* orig. 1949. Reprint; New York: MJF Books, undated.

Campbell, Malcolm. *A Commentary on Apollonius Rhodius* Argonautica *III, 1–471.* Leiden: Brill, 1994.

Carpenter, Rhys. "The Greek Penetration of the Black Sea." *American Journal of Archaeology* 52, no. 1 (1948): 1–10.

Carter, Jane B., and Sarah P. Morris, eds. *The Ages of Homer: A Tribute to Emily Townsend Vermeule.* Austin: University of Texas Press, 1998.

Case, Shirley Jackson. "The Historicity of Jesus: An Estimate of the Negative Argument." *The American Journal of Theology* 15 (1911): 20–42.

Castleden, Rodney. *The Knossos Labyrinth: A New View of the "Palace of Minos" at Knossos.* Routledge: London, 1990.
_____. *The Minoans: Life in Bronze Age Crete.* London: Routledge, 1993.
_____. *The Mycenaeans.* London: Routledge, 2005.

Charroux, Robert. *The Mysterious Unknown.* Trans. Olga Sieveking. London: Neville Spearman, 1972.

Chaudhuri, Supriya. "Jason's Fleece: The Source of Sir Epicure Mammon's Allegory." *Review of English Studies* 35, no. 137 (1984): 71–73.

Childress, David Hatcher. *Lost Cities of Atlantis, Ancient Europe & the Mediterranean.* Kempton, Illinois: Adventures Unlimited Press, 1996.

Clare, R. J. *The Path of the Argo: Language, Imagery, and Narrative in the* Argonautica *of Apollonius Rhodius.* Cambridge: Cambridge University Press, 2002.

Clark, Michael J. *Flesh and Spirit in the Songs of Homer: A Study of Words and Myths.* Oxford: Oxford University Press, 1999; reprint 2002.

Clauss, James Joseph. *The Best of the Argonauts: The Redefinition of the Epic Hero in Book 1 of Apollonius'* Argonautica. Berkeley: University of California Press, 1993.

Clauss, James J., and Sarah Iles Johnson, eds. *Medea.* Princeton: Princeton University Press, 1997.

Cleary, Marie Sally. "Bulfinch's Mythology." *Humanities* 8, no. 1 (1987): 12–15.

Cline, Eric, ed. *The Oxford Handbook of the Bronze Age Aegean.* Oxford: Oxford University Press, 2010.

Cohen, Yoram, Amir Gilan, and Jared L. Miller, eds. *Pax Hethitica: Studies on the Hittites and Their Neighbours in Honour of Itamar Singer.* Weisbaden: Harrassowitz Verlag, 2010.

Colavito, Jason. *The Cult of Alien Gods: H. P. Lovecraft and Extraterrestrial Pop Culture.* Amherst: Prometheus, 2005.
_____. "Golden Fleeced: Robert Temple's Misuse of the Argonaut Myth in the *Sirius Mystery.*" *eSkeptic,* May 5, 2010.

Collins, Derek. *Magic in the Ancient Greek World.* Malden, Mass.: Blackwell, 2008.

Collins, John. J., ed. *The Encyclopedia of Apocalypticism, Vol. 1: The Origins of Apocalypticism in Judaism and Christianity.* New York: Continuum, 2000.

Conan, Michael, ed. *Sacred Gardens and Landscapes: Ritual and Agency.* Washington: Dubmarton Oaks Research Library and Collection/Harvard University Press, 2007.

Cook, A. B. "The European Sky-God." *Folklore* 15 (1904): 264–315.

_____. *Zeus: A Study in Ancient Religion. Vol. 1: Zeus, God of the Bright Sky.* Cambridge: Cambridge University Press, 1914.

Cook, Erwin. "Near Eastern Sources for the Palace of Alkinoos." *American Journal of Archaeology* 108, no. 1 (2004): 43–77.

Copeland, Fanny S. "Slovene Folklore." *Folklore* 42 (1931): 405–446.

_____. "Slovene Mythology." *The Slavonic and East European Review* 11 (1933): 631–651.

Cox, Sir George W. *The Mythology of Aryan Nations,* new ed. London: Keegan, Paul, Trench & Co., 1887.

Crawford, Harriet. *Sumer and the Sumerians,* 2nd ed. Cambridge: University of Cambridge Press, 2004.

Crook, William. "The Binding of a God: A Study in the Basis of Idolatry." *Folk-Lore* 8, no. 4 (1897): 325–355.

Cunningham, Graham. *Deliver Me from Evil: Mesopotamian Incantations 2500–1500 BC.* Rome: Editrice Pontifico Instituto Biblico, 1997; reprint 2007.

Curry, Andrew. "Göbekli Tepe: The World's First Temple?" *Smithsonian,* November 2008, http://www.smithsonianmag.com/history-archaeology/gobekli-tepe.html?c=y&page=1

Dalby, Andrew. *Rediscovering Homer.* New York: Norton, 2006.

Dalley, Stephanie. *The Legacy of Mesopotamia.* Oxford: Oxford University Press, 1998.

_____. *Myths from Mesopotamia: Creation, the Flood, Gilgamesh, and Others.* Oxford: Oxford University Press, 1989.

Davis, S. "Argeiphontes in Homer—The Dragon Slayer." *Greece and Rome* 22, no. 64 (1953): 33–38.

Day, John. *God's Conflict with the Dragon of the Sea: Echoes of a Canaanite Myth in the Old Testament.* Cambridge: Cambridge University Press, 1985.

_____. *Yahweh and the Gods and Goddesses of Canaan.* London: Sheffield Academic Press, 2002.

De Grummond, Nancy Thompson. *Etruscan Myth, Sacred History, and Legend.* Philadelphia: University of Philadelphia Museum of Archaeology and Anthropology, 2006.

De Puma, Richard Daniel, and Jocelyn Penny Small, eds. *Murlo and the Etruscans: Art and Society in Ancient Etruria.* Madison: University of Wisconsin Press, 1994.

De Santillana, Giorgio, and Hertha von Dechend. *Hamlet's Mill: An Essay Investigating the Origins of Human Knowledge and Its Transmission through Myth,* orig. 1970. Boston: Nonpareil, 1998.

Deacy, Susan. *Athena.* New York: Routledge, 2008.

DeForest, Margaret Margolies. *Apollonius' Argonautica: A Callimachean Epic.* Leiden: Brill, 1994.

Deger-Jalkotzy, Sigrid, and Irene S. Lemos, eds. *Ancient Greece: From the Mycenaean Palaces to the Age of Homer.* Edinburgh: Edinburgh University Press, 2006.

Dennis, George. *The Cities and Cemeteries of Etruria.* Vol. II, 3rd ed. London: John Murray, 1883.

Desmond, Marilynn Robin, and Pamela Sheingorn. *Myth, Montage, & Visuality in Late Medieval Manuscript Culture: Christine de Pizan's Epistre Othèa.* Ann Arbor: University of Michigan Press, 2006.

Dietrich, Bernard Clive. *Origins of Greek Religion.* Berlin and New York: de Gruyter, 1974.

Domínguez, Frank A. *The Medieval Argonautica* (Studia Humanitatis). Potomac, Maryland: José Porrúa Turanzas, 1979.

Dowden, Ken. *The Uses of Greek Mythology,* orig. 1992. Reprint, London: Routledge, 2000.

_____. *Zeus.* New York: Routledge, 2006.

Dräger, Paul. "Response." *Bryn Mawr Classical Review,* February 26, 2003, http://bmcr.brynmawr.edu/2003/2003-02-26.html

Drews, Arthur. *The Witnesses to the Historicity of Jesus.* Trans. Joseph McCabe. London: Watts & Co., 1912.

Drews, Robert. "The Earliest Greek Settlements of the Black Sea." *Journal of Hellenic Studies* 96 (1976): 18–31.

Duke, T. T. "Murder in the Bath: Reflections on the Death of Agamemnon." *The Classical Journal* 49, no. 7 (1954): 325–330.

Ephron, Henry D. "The Jēsön Tablet of Enkomi." *Harvard Studies in Classical Philology* 65 (1961): 39–108.

Ellison, Henry. *The Poetry of Real Life: A New Edition, Much Enlarged and Improved.* London: G. Willis, 1851.

English, Patrick T. "Cushites, Colchians, and Khazars." *Journal of Near Eastern Studies* 18, no. 1 (1959): 49–53.

Feldman, Burton and Robert D. Richardson, eds. *The Rise of Modern Mythology, 1680–1860.* Bloomington: University of Indiana Press, 1972.

Feresin, Emiliano. "Fleece Myth Hints at Golden Age for Georgia." *Nature* 448 (August 2007): 846–847.

Filotas, Bernadette. *Pagan Survivals, Superstitions, and Popular Cultures.* Toronto: Pontifical Institute of Medieval Studies, 2005.

Finkelberg, Margalit. *Greeks and Pre-Greeks: Aegean Prehistory and the Greek Heroic Tradition.* Cambridge: Cambridge University Press, 2005.

Firla, Ian, and Grevel Lindop, eds. *Graves and the Goddess: Essays on Robert Graves's* The White Goddess. London: Associated University Presses, 2003.

Flower, Michael Attyah. *The Seer in Ancient Greece.* Berkeley: University of California Press, 2008.

Fontenrose, Joseph Eddy. *Python: A Study of Delphic Myth and Its Origins,* 1959. Reprint, Berkeley: University of California Press, 1980.

Fortson, Benjamin W. *Indo-European Language and Culture: An Introduction.* Malden, Mass.: Blackwell, 2004.

Fox, Robin Lane. *Travelling Heroes in the Epic Age of Homer.* New York: Knopf, 2008.

_____, ed. *The Long March: Xenophon and the Ten Thousand.* New Haven: Yale University Press, 2004.

Frankel, Hermann. Review of *Die orphischen Argonautika in ihrem Verhaltnis zu Apollonios Rhodios* by Helmut Venzke. *The American Journal of Philology* 65, no. 4 (1944): 393–398.

French, D. H. "Late Chalcolithic Pottery in North-West Turkey and the Aegean." *Anatolian Studies* 11 (1961): 99–141.

Frothingham, A. L. "The Babylonian Origin of Hermes the Snake-God, and of the Caduceus." *The American Journal of Archaeology* 20, no. 2 (1916): 175–211.

Fryde, E. B. *The Early Paleologian Renaissance (1261-c. 1360).* Leiden: Brill, 2000.

George, A. R. *The Babylonian Gilgamesh Epic: Introduction, Critical Edition and Cuneiform Texts.* Vol. I. Oxford: Oxford University Press, 2003.

Gibbon, Edward. *The History of the Decline and Fall of the Roman Empire.* Vol. IV. Ed. J. B. Bury. London: Methuen & Co., 1901.

Gilbert, Creighton E. *Caravaggio and His Two Cardinals.* University Park, Pennsylvania: Pennsylvania State University Press, 1995.

Gimbutas, Marija. *The Living Goddesses.* Revised by Miriam Robbins Dexter. Berkeley: University of California Press, 2001.

Gmirkin, Russell E. *Berossus and Genesis, Manetho and Exodus: Hellenistic Histories and the Date of the Pentateuch.* New York: T & T Clark International, 2006.

Goldstein, Carl. "Louis XIV and Jason." *The Art Bulletin* 49, no. 4 (1967): 327–329.

Goode, William O. "Médée and Jason: Hero and Nonhero in Corneille's *Médée.*" *The French Review* 51 (1978): 804–815.

Goodrick-Clarke, Nicholas. *Black Sun: Aryan Cults, Esoteric Nazism, and the Politics of Identity.* New York: New York University Press, 2002.

Graf, Fritz. *Apollo.* New York: Routledge, 2009.

_____. *Greek Mythology: An Introduction.* Trans. Thomas Marier. Baltimore: Johns Hopkins University Press, 1996.

Graham, A. J. *Collected Papers on Greek Colonization.* Boston: Brill, 2001.

Green, Alberto Ravinell Whitney. *The Storm-God in the Ancient Near East.* Eisenbrauns, 2003.

Green, Jonathon. *Cassell's Dictionary of Slang.* 2nd ed. London: Weidenfeld & Nicolson, 2005.

Green, Liz. *The Astrology of Fate.* Boston: Red Wheel/Weiser, 1984.

Gresseth, Gerald K. "The Gilgamesh Epic and Homer." *Classical Journal 70* (1974–1975): 1–18.

Griffiths, Emma. *Medea.* Abingdon: Routledge, 2006.

Grimal, Pierre. *The Dictionary of Classical Mythology.* Trans. A. R. Maxwell-Hyslop. Malden, Mass.: Blackwell, 1996.

Gosman, M., A. MacDonald, and A. Vanderjagt, eds. *Princes and Princely Culture 1450–1650.* Vol. 1. Leiden: Brill, 2003.

Groneberg, Brigitte, and Hermann Spieckermann, eds. *Die Welt der Götterbilder.* Berlin: Walter de Gruyter, 2007.

Guerra, Maria Filomena. "Sur les traces de l'or antique : analyse élémentaire de bijoux et monnaies." June 1, 2010. http://culturesciences.chimie.ens.fr/dossiers-experimentale-analyse-article-Or_Antique_Guerra.html

"Guido de Columnis: The Trojan War." *Faksimile Verlag.* http://www.faksimile.ch/pdf/Troja_e.pdf

Guthrie, W. K. C. *Orpheus and Greek Religion,* originally 1952. Princeton: Princeton University Press, 1993.

Haase, Wolfgang, and Meyer Reinhold, eds. *The Classical Tradition and the Americas.* Berlin and New York: Walter de Gruyter, 1993.

Hadas, Moses. "A Tradition of a Feeble Jason?" *Classical Philology* 31, no. 2 (1936): 166–168.

Haggh, Barbara. "The Order of the Golden Fleece." *Journal of the Royal Musical Association* 121, no. 2 (1996): 268–270.

Hall, John Franklin, ed. *Etruscan Italy: Etruscan Influences on the Civilization of Italy from Antiquity to the Modern Era.* Salt Lake City: Brigham Young University, 1996.

Hamel, Gildas. "Taking the *Argo* to Nineveh: Jonah and Jason in a Mediterranean Context." *Judaism* 44, no. 3 (1995): 341–359.

Hammond, N. G. L. "Alexander and Armenia." *Phoenix* 50, no. 2 (1996): 130–137.

Hard, Robin. *The Routledge Handbook of Greek Mythology.* London: Routledge, 2004.

Harris, Rendel. *Boanerges.* Cambridge: Cambridge University Press, 1913.

Harrison, Jane Ellen. *Prolegomena to the Study of Greek Religion.* Princeton: Princeton University Press, 1903.

Harryhausen, Ray and Tony Dalton. *Ray Harryhausen: An Animated Life.* New York: Billboard Books, 2004.

Hartland, Edwin Sidney. *The Legend of Perseus: A Study of Tradition in Story, Custom and Belief.* 3 vols. London: David Nutt, 1894–1896.

Haubold, Johannes. *Homer's People: Epic Poetry and Social Formation.* Cambridge: Cambridge University Press, 2000.

Haughton, Brian. *Hidden History: Lost Civilizations, Secret Knowledge, and Ancient History.* Franklin Lakes, NY: Career Press, 2007.

Healy, F. G. *The Literary Culture of Napoleon.* Geneva: Librairie de Droz, 1959.

Heidel, Alexander. *The Gilgamesh Epic and Old Testament Parallels,* 2nd ed., orig.1949. Chicago: University of Chicago Press, 1963.

Heubeck, Alfred, and Arie Hoeckstra. *A Commentary on Homer's* Odyssey. Volume II: Books IX-XVI. Oxford: Clarendon Paperbacks, 1990.

_____. *A Commentary on Homer's* Odyssey. Volume III: Books XVII-XXIV. Oxford: Clarendon Paperbacks, 1992.

Hewitt, George B., ed. *The Abkhazians: A Handbook.* New York: St. Martin's Press, 1988.

Hinnels, John R., ed. *Mithraic Studies.* Vol. 1. Manchester: Manchester University Press, 1975.

Holberg, J. B. *Sirius: Brightest Diamond of the Night Sky.* Berlin: Springer, 2007.

Holm, LeRoy G., Jerry Doll, Eric Holm, Juan Pancho, and James Herberger. *World Weeds: Natural Histories and Distribution.* New York: John Wiley and Sons, 1997.

Hood, Sinclair. *The Arts in Prehistoric Greece,* orig. 1978. New Haven: Yale University Press, 1994.

Hooker, J. T. *Linear B: An Introduction.* Bristol: Classics Press, 1980.

Hopkins, Clark. "Assyrian Elements in the Perseus-Gorgon Story." *American Journal of Archaeology* 38, no. 3 (1934): 341–358.

Horowitz, Wayne. *Mesopotamian Cosmic Geography.* Winona Lake, Ind.: Eisenbrauns, 1998.

Horstmanshoff, H. F. J. and M. Stoll, eds. *Magic and Rationality in Ancient Near Eastern and Greco-Roman Medicine.* Leiden: Brill, 2004.

Houston, Drusilla Dunjee. *Wonderful Ethiopians of the Cushite Empire.* Oklahoma City: Universal Publishing, 1926.

Houtum-Schindler, A. "Notes on Demavend." *Proceedings of the Royal Geographic Society* 10 (1888): 85–89.

Hubbard, Thomas K. *The Pindaric Mind: A Study of Logical Structure in Early Greek Poetry.* Leiden: Brill, 1985.

Hughes, Dennis D. *Human Sacrifice in Ancient Greece.* New York: Routledge, 1991.

Hunt, David. "The Association of the Lady and the Unicorn, and the Hunting Mythology of the Caucasus." *Folklore* 114, no. 1 (2003): 75–90.

Hunter, Richard. *The Argonautica of Apollonius.* Cambridge: Cambridge University Press, 1993.

_____, ed. *The Hesiodic Catalogue of Women: Constructions and Reconstructions.* Cambridge: Cambridge University Press, 2005.

_____. "'Short on Heroics': Jason in the *Argonautica.*" *The Classical Quarterly* (New Series) 38, no. 2 (1988): 436–453.

Ikram, Salima, ed. *Divine Creatures: Animal Mummies in Ancient Egypt.* New York: American University in Cairo Press, 2005.

Jackson, Peter. "Light from Distant Asterisks: Toward a Description of Indo-European Religious Heritage." *Numen* 49, no. 1 (2002): 61–102.

Jackson, Steven. "Apollonius' Jason: Human Being in an Epic Scenario." *Greece & Rome* 39, no. 2 (1992): 155–162.

_____. "*Argo*: The First Ship?" *Rheinisches Museum für Philologie* 140 (1997): 249–257.

Jacobsen, Thorkild. *The Treasures of Darkness: A History of Mesopotamian Religion.* New Haven: Yale University Press, 1976.

James, Edwin Oliver. *The Tree of Life: An Archaeological Study.* Leiden: Brill, 1966.

James, Henry (unsigned). Review of *The Life and Death of Jason: A Poem* by William Morris. *North American Review* 105, no. 217 (October 1867): 688–692.

James, Peter, and Nick Thorpe. *Ancient Mysteries.* New York: Ballantine Books, 1999.

Jannot, Jean-René. *Religion in Ancient Etruria.* Trans. Jane K. Whitehead. Madison: University of Wisconsin Press, 2005.

Jeans, Peter D. *Seafaring Lore and Legend: A Miscellany of Maritime Myth, Superstition, Fable, and Fact.* International Marine/McGraw-Hill, 2004.

Johnston, Sarah Iles. *Ancient Greek Divination.* Malden, Mass.: Wiley Blackwell, 2008.

_____. *Restless Dead: Encounters Between the Living and the Dead in Ancient Greece.* Berkeley: University of California Press, 1999.

Jones, Sir Hugh Lloyd. *The Further Academic Papers of Sir Hugh Lloyd Jones.* Oxford: Oxford University Press, 2005.

Jordan, Paul. *The Atlantis Syndrome.* Sparkford: Sutton Publishing, 2003.

Jordan-Bychkov, Terry G., and Bella Bychkova Jordan. *The European Culture Area: A Systematic Geography,* 4th ed. Lanham, Maryland: Rowman and Littlefield, 2002.

Justus, Carol F. Review of *How to Kill a Dragon* by Calvert Watkins. *Language* 73, no. 3 (1997): 637–641.

Kacharava, Darejan, and Guram Kvirkvelia. *Wine, Worship, and Sacrifice: The Golden Graves of Ancient Vani.* Ed. Jennifer Y. Chi. Princeton: Princeton University Press, 2008.

Kaulins, Andis. *Stars, Stones and Scholars: The Decipherment of the Megaliths.* Victoria, BC: Trafford, 2003.

Keith, Allison, and Steven Rupp, eds. *Metamorphosis: The Changing Face of Ovid in Medieval and Early Modern Europe.* Toronto: Center for Reformation and Renaissance Studies, 2007.

Kerényi, K. *Goddesses of Sun and Moon.* Dallas: Spring Publications, 1979.

_____. *Heroes of the Greeks.* Trans. H. R. Rose. New York: Thames & Hudson, 1978.

King, Cynthia. "Who Is That Cloaked Man? Observations on Early Fifth Century B.C. Pictures of the Golden Fleece." *American Journal of Archaeology* 87, no. 3 (1983): 385–387.

Kinsey, David R. *The Goddesses' Mirror: Visions of the Divine from East and West.* Albany: State University of New York, 1989.

Kirchoff, A. *Der Composition der Odyssee.* Berlin: Verlag von Wilhelm-Hertz, 1869.

Kirk, G. S. *Homer and the Epic.* Cambridge: Cambridge University Press, 1965.

_____. *Myth: Its Meaning and Functions in Ancient and Other Cultures,* originally published 1970. London: Cambridge University Press, 1998.

_____. *The Nature of Greek Myths.* Hammondsworth: Penguin, 1982.

Kleywegt, A. J. *Valerius Flaccus: The* Argonautica, *Book 1: A Commentary.* Leiden: Brill, 2005.

Knight, Virginia. *The Renewal of Epic: Responses to Homer in the* Argonautica *of Apollonius.* Leiden: Brill, 1995.

Knock, A. D. "Notes on Beliefs and Myths." *The Journal of Hellenic Studies* 46, no. 1 (1926): 47–53.

Knox, Peter E. "Phaeton in Ovid and Nonnus." *Classical Quarterly* (new series) 38 (1988): 536–551.

Kramer, Samuel Noah. "Cuneiform Studies and the History of Literature: The Sumerian Sacred Marriage Texts." *Proceedings of the American Philosophical Society* 107 (1963): 485–527.

_____. *In the World of Sumer: An Autobiography.* Detroit: Wayne State University Press, 1986.

Kristensen, William Brede. *The Meaning of Religion: Lectures in the Phenomenology of Religion.* Trans. J. B. Carman. Martinus Nijhoff, 1968.

Labaree, Benjamin W. "How the Greeks Sailed into the Black Sea." *American Journal of Archaeology* 61, No. 1 (1957): 29–33.

Laffineur, R., and L. Basch, eds. *Thalassa: L'Égée préhistorique et la mer* (Aegaeum 7). Liìge, Belgium: University of Liìge, 1991.

Lalonde, Gerald V. *Horos Dios: An Athenian Shrine and Cult of Zeus.* Leiden: Brill, 2006.

Lamberton, Robert. *Hesiod.* New Haven: Yale Yniversity Press, 1988.

Lang, Andrew. *Custom and Myth,* new edition. London: Longmans, Green, and Co., 1893.

Lang, D. M., and G. M. Meredith Owens. "*Amiran-Darejaniani* and Its English Rendering." *Bulletin of the School of Oriental and African Studies, University of London* 22 (1959): 454–490.

Lang, Felix, Claus Reiholdt, and Jörg Weilhartner, eds. *STEFANOS ARISTEIOS Festschrift fur Stefan Hille zum 65. Geburtstager.* Vienna: Phoibos Verlag, 2007.

Larrington, Carolyne. *King Arthur's Enchantresses: Morgan and Her Sisters in Arthurian Tradition.* London: I.B. Tauris, 2006.

Larson, Gerald James, ed. *Myth in Indo-European Antiquity.* Berkeley: University of California, 1974.

Latham, David, ed. *Writing on the Image: Reading William Morris.* Toronto: University of Toronto Press, 2007.

Launderville, Dale F. *Spirit and Reason: The Embodied Character of Ezekiel's Symbolic Thinking.* Waco, Texas: Baylor University Press, 2007.

Lawrence, Arnold Walter, and Richard Allan Tomlinson. *Greek Architecture,* 5th ed. New Haven: Yale University Press, 1996.

Lefkowitz, Mary R. "The Pindar Scholia." *American Journal of Philology* 106 (1985): 269–282.

Levin, Donald Normal. *Apollonius'* Argonautica *Re-Examined.* Leiden: Brill, 1971.

Levin, Saul. *Semitic and Indo-European II: Comparative Morphology, Syntax and Phonetics.* Amsterdam: John Benjamins, 2002.

Lewis, C. B. *Classical Mythology and Arthurian Romance.* London: Milford, 1932.

Lewis, Martin W., and Kären Wigen. *The Myth of Continents: A Critique of Metageography.* Berkeley: University of California, 1997.

Lewis-Williams, David. *The Mind in the Cave.* New York: Thames & Hudson, 2002.

Lewis-Williams, David, and David Pearce. *Inside the Neolithic Mind.* London: Thames & Hudson, 2005.

Lincoln, Bruce. *Death, War, and Sacrifice: Studies in Ideology and Practice.* Chicago: University of Chicago Press, 1991.

_____. "The Indo-European Cattle-Raiding Myth." *History of Religions* 16, no. 1 (1976): 42-65.

Lindenlauf, Astrid. "The Sea as a Place of No Return in Ancient Greece." *World Archaeology* 35 (2003): 416–433.

Littleton, C. Scott, ed. *Gods, Goddesses and Mythology.* Tarrytown, NY: Marshall Cavendish, 2005.

_____, and Linda A. Malcor. *From Scythia to Camelot: A Radical Reassessment of the Legends of King Arthur.* New York: Garland, 2000.

Livingstone, Alasdair. *Mystical and Mythological Explanatory Works of Assyrian and Babylonian Scholars.* Oxford: Oxford University Press, 1986; reprint, Eisenbraun, 2007.

Lloyd, Michael, ed. *Aeschylus.* Oxford: Oxford University Press, 2007.

Lodewijckx, Marc, ed. *Archaeological and Historical Aspects of West-European Societies.* Leuven: Leuven University Press, 1996.

Lordkipanidze, Otar. "The Golden Fleece: Myth, Euhemeristic Explanation and Archaeology." *Oxford Journal of Archaeology* 20, no. 1 (2002): 1–38.

Luce, J. V. *The End of Atlantis: New Light on an Old Legend.* New York: McGraw-Hill, 1969.

Lyons, Charles R. "The Ambiguity of the Anouihl 'Medea.'" *The French Review* 37, no. 3 (1964): 312–319.

Mackie, C. J. "The Earliest Jason: What's in a Name?" *Greece and Rome* 48, no. 12 (2001): 1–17.

Macpherson, J. Review of *The Greek Myths* by Robert Graves. *Phoenix* 21, no. 1 (1958): 15–25.

Markoe, Glenn. *The Phoenicians.* Berkeley: University of California Press, 2000.

Marinatos, Nanno. *Minoan Kingship and the Solar Goddess: A Near Eastern Koine.* Urbana: University of Illinois, 2010.

_____ and Robert Hägg, eds. *Greek Sanctuaries: New Approaches.* London: Routledge, 1993.

Martin, Thomas R. *Ancient Greece: From Prehistoric to Hellenistic Times.* New Haven: Yale University Press, 2000.

Matthews, Victor J. "Naupaktia and Argonautika." *Phoenix* 31, no. 3 (Autumn 1977): 189–207.

Mavor, James Watt. *Voyage to Atlantis: The Discovery of a Legendary Land.* Rochester, Vermont: Park Street Press, 1969; reprint 1996.

Mayor, Adrienne. *The First Fossil Hunters: Paleontology in Greek and Roman Times.* Princeton: Princeton University Press, 2000.

McDermott, Emily A. *Euripides' Medea: The Incarnation of Disorder.* University Park: Pennsylvania State University, 1989.

McDonald, William A., and Nancy C. Wilkie, eds. *Excavations at Nichorea in Southwest Greece. Vol. II: The Bronze Age Occupation.* Minneapolis: University of Minnesota Press, 1992.

McGill, Scott. *Virgil Recomposed: The Mythological and Secular Centos in Antiquity.* Oxford: Oxford University Press, 2005.

McInerney, Jeremy. *The Cattle of the Sun: Cows and Culture in the World of the Ancient Greeks.* Princeton: Princeton University Press, 2010.

McIntosh, Jane. *The Ancient Indus Valley: New Perspectives.* Santa Barbara: ABC-CLIO, 2008.

McMahon, Gregory. *The Hittite State Cult of the Tutelary Deities.* Oriental Institute of the University of Chicago Assyriological Studies 25. Chicago: University of Chicago Press, 1991.

Mikhailov, Nicholas. *Soviet Russia: The Land and Its People.* Trans. George H. Hanna. New York: Sheridan House, 1948.

Miller, Dean A. *The Epic Hero.* Baltimore, MD: Johns Hopkins University Press, 2000.

Mitchell, James P. *Our Good Neighbors in Soviet Russia.* New York: Noble and Noble, 1945.

Mojsov, Bojana. *Osiris: Death and Afterlife of a God.* Malden, Mass.: Blackwell, 2005.

Moore, Kenneth, ed. *Shakespeare Survey 19: Macbeth,* orig. 1966. Cambridge: Cambridge University Press, 2002.

Mores, Ruth. "Problems of Early Fiction: Raoul Lefèvre's 'Histoire de Jason.'" *The Modern Language Review* 78, no 1 (1983): 34–45.

Morey, William C. *Outlines of Greek History.* New York: American Book Company, 1903.

Morris, Ian. *Archaeology as Cultural History: Words and Things in Iron Age Greece.* Malden, Mass.: Blackwell, 2000.

Morse, Ruth. *The Medieval Medea.* Woodbridge: Boydell and Brewer, 1996.

Mullally, Evelyn. *The Artist at Work: Narrative Techniques in Chrétien de Troyes.* Philadelphia: American Philosophical Society, 1988.

Müller, F. Max. *Contributions to the Science of Mythology,* vol. II. London: Longmans, Green, and Co., 1897.

Müller, Karl Otfried. *Orchomenos und der Minyen.* Breslau: Josef Max und Comp., 1844.

Munn, Mark. *The Mother of the Gods, Athens, and the Tyranny of Asia: A Study of Sovereignty in Ancient Religion.* Berkeley: University of California Press, 2006.

Murray, Gilbert. *A History of Ancient Greek Literature.* New York: Appleton and Company, 1903.

Myers, J. N. L. *Homer and His Critics.* London: Routledge and Keegan Paul, 1958.

Nasmyth, Peter. *Georgia: In the Mountains of Poetry.* New York: St. Martin's Press, 1998.

Nakassis, Dimitri. "Gemination at the Horizons: East and West in the Mythical Geography of Archaic Greek Epic." *Transactions of the American Philological Association* 134, no. 2 (2004): 215–233.

Nelis, Damien. *Vergil's* Aeneid *and the* Argonautica *of Apollonius Rhodius.* Leeds: Francis Cairns, 2001.

Neugebauer, Otto. *A History of Ancient Mathematical Astronomy.* Vol. 1. Heidelberg: Springer-Verlag, 1975.

Newton, Sir Isaac. *Chronology of Ancient Kingdoms Amended.* London: J. Tonson, 1728.

Nilsson, Martin Persson. *The Mycenaean Origins of Greek Mythology.* Berkeley: University of California Press, 1932.

_____. *The Minoan-Mycenaean Religion and Its Survival in Greek Religion,* 2nd rev. ed. New York: Biblo and Tannen, 1928.

Nissinen, Martti. *Prophets and Prophesy in the Ancient Near East* (Writings from the Ancient World). Atlanta: Society for Biblical Literature, 2003.

Norwood, Gilbert. *Pindar.* Sather Classical Lectures, Vol. 19. Berkeley: University of California Press, 1945.

Noyes, Alfred. *William Morris.* London: Macmillan, 1908.

Obregón, Mauricio. *Beyond the Edge of the Sea: Sailing with Jason and the Argonauts, Ulysses, the Vikings, and Other Explorers of the Ancient World.* New York: Random House, 2001.

O'Brien, Joan V. *The Transformation of Hera: A Study of Ritual, Hero, and the Goddess in the* Iliad. Landham, Maryland: Rowman and Littlefield, 1993.

Ogden, Daniel. *Drakon: Dragon Myth and Serpent Cult in the Greek and Roman Worlds.* Oxford: Oxford University Press, 2013.

_____. *Greek and Roman Necromancy.* Princeton: Princeton University Press, 2001.

_____. *Magic, Witchcraft, and Ghosts in the Greek and Roman Worlds: A Source Book*. Oxford: Oxford University Press, 2002.

_____. *Perseus*. Oxon: Routledge, 2008.

Oppenheim, A. Leo. "The Golden Garments of the Gods." *Journal of Near Eastern Studies* 8, no. 3 (1949): 172–193.

Paley, F. A. "Pre-Homeric Legends of the Voyage of the Argonauts." *The Dublin Review* (1879): 164–182.

Parker, Robert. *Miasma: Pollution and Purification in Early Greek Religion*. Oxford: Oxford University Press, 1983; reprint: Clarendon Press, 2003.

Pepin, Ronald E. *The Vatican Mythographers*. New York: Fordham University Press, 2008.

Percival, Florence. *Chaucer's Legendary Good Women*. Cambridge: Cambridge University Press, 1998.

Peregrine, Peter N., and Melvin Ember, eds. *Encyclopedia of Prehistory. Volume 4: Europe*. New York: Human Relations Area Files, 2001.

Perlman, Paula J. "Invocatio and Imprecatio: The Hymn to the Greatest Kouros from Palaikastro and the Oath in Ancient Crete." *The Journal of Hellenic Studies* 115 (1995): 161–167.

Phinney, Edward, Jr. "Perseus' Battle with the Gorgons." *Transactions and Proceedings of the American Philological Association* 102 (1971): 445–463.

Pickard, William F. "The Symplegades." *Greece & Rome*, second series, 34, no. 1 (1987): 1–6.

Pilopović, Sanja. "A Contribution to the Study of the Jason Sarcophagus from Viminacium." *Starinar* no. 53–54 (2003–2004), 65–78.

Pinch, Geraldine. *Egyptian Mythology: A Guide to the Gods, Goddesses, and Traditions of Ancient Egypt*. Oxford: Oxford University Press, 2002.

Pollak, Gustav. *Franz Gillparzer and the Austrian Drama*. New York: Dowd, Mead & Company, 1907.

Powell, Barry B. *Homer*. Malden, Mass.: Blackwell Publishing, 2004.

Puhvel, Jaan. *Hittite Etymological Dictionary, Vol. 4: Words Beginning with K*. Berlin: De Gruyter, 1997.

_____. *Hittite Etymological Dictionary. Vol. 6: Words Beginning with M*. Berlin: De Gruyter, 2004.

Raaflaub, Kurt A., and Hans van Wees, eds. *A Companion to Archaic Greece*. Malden, Mass.: Blackwell, 2009.

Rabkin, Eric S. *Mars: A Tour of the Human Imagination*. Westport, Conn.: Praeger, 2005.

Ragavan, Deena, ed. *Heaven on Earth: Temples, Ritual, and Cosmic Symbolism in the Ancient World*. University of Chicago Oriental Institute Seminars No. 9. Chicago: University of Chicago Press, 2013.

Rashidi, Runoko, and Ivan Van Sertima, eds. *African Presence in Early Asia*. New Brunswick: Transaction, 1988.

Reale, Giovanni. *A History of Ancient Philosophy: From the Origins to Socrates*. Trans. John R. Catan. Albany: State University of New York Press, 1987.

Reynolds, John Lawrence. *Secret Societies: Inside the World's Most Notorious Organizations*. New York: Arcade, 2006.

Richter, Gisela M. A. "Jason and the Golden Fleece," *The Metropolitan Museum of Art Bulletin* 30, no. 4 (1935): 86–88.

Ring, Trudy, Robert M. Salkin, and Sharon La Boda, eds. *International Dictionary of Historic Places. Vol. 3: Southern Europe*. Chicago: Fitzroy Dearborn, 1995.

Robbins, Emmet. "Jason and Cheiron: The Myth of Pindar's Fourth Pythian." *Phoenix* 29, no. 3 (1975): 205–213.

Robbins, Royal. *The World Displayed in Its History and Geography; Embracing a History of the World from the Creation to the Present Day*. New York: W. W. Reed, 1830.

Robertson, D. S. "The Flight of Phrixus." *The Classical Review* 54, no. 1 (1940): 1–8.

Robertson, Martin. "The Death of Talos." *The Journal of Hellenic Studies* 97 (1977): 158–160.

Robertson, Noel. *Religion and Reconciliation in Greek Cities: The Sacred Laws of Selinus and Cyrene*. Oxford: Oxford University Press, 2010.

Roe, Ian F. *Franz Gillparzer: A Century of Criticism*. Columbia, SC: Camden House, 1995.

Rogers, John J. "Origins of the Ancient Constellations: I. The Mesopotamian Traditions." *Journal of the British Astronomical Association* 108 (1998): 9–28.

_____. "Origins of the Ancient Constellations: II. The Mediterranean Traditions." *Journal of the British Astronomical Association* 108, no. 2 (1998): 79–89.

Room, Adrian. *Placenames of the World*. Jefferson, NC: McFarland, 2006.

Rosand, Ellen. *Opera in Seventeenth Century Venice: The Creation of a Genre*, orig. 1991. Paperback reprint: Berkeley: University of California, 2007.

Rose, H. L. "Chthonic Cattle." *Numen* 1, no. 3 (1954): 213–227.

_____. Review of *The Greek Myths* by Robert Graves. *The Classical Review* 5, no. 2 (1955): 208–209.

_____. "Who Were the Heroes?" *The Classical Review* 10 (1960): 48–50.

Roux, R. *Le problème des Argonautes: Recherches sur les aspects religieux de la legend*. Paris: E. de Boccard, Editeur, 1949.

Runnels, Curtis Neil, and Priscilla Murray. *Greece before History: An Archaeological Companion and Guide*. Stanford: Stanford University Press, 2001.

Rutherford, Ian. *Pindar's Paeans*. Oxford: Oxford University Press, 2001.

Rux, Bruce. *Architects of the Underworld: Unriddling Atlantis, Anomalies of Mars, and the Mystery of the Sphinx*. Berkeley, California: Frog Ltd., 1996.

S, Acharya. *Suns of God: Krishna, Buddha, and Christ Unveiled*. Kempton, Illinois: Adventures Unlimited Press, 2004.

Sansonese, J. Nigro. *The Body of Myth: Mythology, Shamanic Trance, and the Sacred Geography of the Body*. Rochester, Vermont: Inner Traditions, 1994.

Scott, John A. "The Origin of the Myth of the Golden Fleece." *Classical Journal* 22, no. 7 (1927): 541.

Seaford, Richard. *Dionysus*. London: Routledge, 2006.

Severin, Tim. *The Jason Voyage: The Quest for the Golden Fleece*. London: Hutchinson, 1985.

Seymour, Thomas Day. *Life in the Homeric Age*. New York: Macmillan, 1908.

Shahgedanova, Maria, ed. *The Physical Geography of Northern Eurasia*. Oxford: Oxford University Press, 2002.

Shapiro, H. A. "Jason's Cloak." *Transactions of the American Philological Association* 110 (1980): 263–286.

Shaw, Ian. *The Oxford History of Ancient Egypt*. Oxford: Oxford University Press, 2000.

Shermer, Michael. *Science Friction: Where the Known Meets the Unknown*. New York: Henry Holt, 2005.

Simon, Erika. *Festivals of Attica: An Archaeological Commentary*. Madison: University of Wisconsin Press, 1983.

Simoons, Frederic J. *Plants of Life, Plants of Death*. Madison: University of Wisconsin Press, 1998.

Singer, Itamar. *Hittite Prayers*. Leiden: Brill, 2002.

Solmsen, Friedrich. *Hesiod and Aeschylus*, orig. 1949. Ithaca: Cornell Paperbacks, 1995.

Sothers, Richard B. "Ancient Scientific Basis of the 'Great Serpent' from Historical Evidence." *Isis* 95, no. 2 (2004): 220–238.

Sparks, Kenton L. *Ancient Texts for the Study of the Hebrew Bible: A Guide to the Background Literature*. Peabody, Mass.: Hendrickson, 2005.

Stephens, Susan A. *Seeing Double: Intercultural Poetics in Ptolemaic Alexandria*. Berkeley: University of California Press, 2003.

Suter, Ann, ed. *Lament: Studies in the Ancient Mediterranean and Beyond*. Oxford: Oxford University Press, 2008.

Tanner, Marie. *The Last Descendant of Aeneas: The Hapsburgs and the Mythic Image of the Emperor*. New Haven: Yale University Press, 1993.

Temple, Robert. *The Sirius Mystery: New Scientific Evidence of Alien Contact 5,000 Years Ago*. Rochester, Vermont: Destiny Books, 1998.

Thomas, Carol G. *Finding People in Early Greece*. Columbia, Missouri: University of Missouri Press, 2005.

Thompson, Harold. "Jason and Argonauts Seek Golden Fleece at Loew's State." *New York Times*, August 8, 1963, p. 19.

Thompson, Henry O. *Mekal: The God of Beth-Shan*. Leiden: Brill, 1970.

Thompson, Reginald Campbell. *The Devils and Spirits of Babylonia. Vol. 1: Evil Spirits*. London: Luzac and Co., 1903.

Toye, D. L. "Pherecydes of Syros: Ancient Theologian and Genealogist." *Mnemosyne* (4th series) 50 (1997): 530–560.

Tsetskhladze, Gocha R. *Pichvnari and Its Environs: 6th C BC-4th C AD*. Besançon, France: Presse Universitaires Franc-Comtoisses, 1999.

———, ed. *The Greek Colonisation of the Black Sea Area: Historical Interpretation of Archaeology*. Germany: Steiner, 1998.

Tuite, Kevin. "Achilles and the Caucasus." *Journal of Indo-European Studies* 26, no. 3 (1998): 289–344.

Turner, Patricia and Charles Russell Coulter. *Dictionary of Ancient Deities*. Oxford: Oxford University Press, 2001.

Ustinova, Yulia. *Caves and the Ancient Greek Mind: Descending Underground in Search for Ultimate Truth*. Oxford: Oxford University Press, 2009.

Van Beek, W. E. A. "Dogon Restudied: A Field Evaluation of the Work of Marcel Griaule." *Current Anthropology* 32, no. 2 (1991): 139–167.

Van De Noort, Robert. "Argonauts of the North Sea: A Social Maritime Archaeology for the Second Millennium BC." *Proceedings of the Prehistoric Society* 72 (2006): 267–287.

Van der Toorn, K., Bob Becking, and Pieter Willem van der Horst, eds. *Dictionary of Demons and Deities in the Bible,* 2nd ed. Leiden: Brill, 1999.

Vasunia, Phiroze. *The Gift of the Nile: Hellenizing Egypt from Aeschylus to Alexander*. Berkeley: University of California Press, 2001.

Vaughn, Richard. *Philip the Good: The Apogee of Burgundy*. Woodbridge: Boydell Press, 2002; reprint 2004.

Vinšćak, Tomo. "On 'Štrige,' 'Štriguni' and 'Krsnici' on Istrian Peninsula." *Studia Ethnologica Croatica* 17 (2005): 221–235.

Von Däniken, Erich. *Odyssey of the Gods: The Extraterrestrial History of Ancient Greece*. Trans. Matthew Barton. Shaftesbury: Element Books, 2000.

Von Martels, Zweder. "Augurello's *Chrysopoeia* (1515)—A Turning Point in the Literary Tradition of Alchemical Texts." *Early Science and Medicine* 5, no. 2 (2000): 178–195.

Walker, Henry J. *Theseus and Athens*. Oxford: Oxford University Press, 1995.

Wall, O. A. *Sex and Sex Worship (Phallic Worship)*. St. Louis: Mosby, 1920.

Walter, Christopher. *The Warrior Saints in Byzantine Art and Tradition*. Aldershot, UK: Ashgate, 2003.

Wasilewska, Ewa. *Creation Stories of the Middle East*. London: Jessica Kingsley, 2000.

Watkins, Calvert. "A Distant Anatolian Echo in Pindar: The Origin of Aegis Again." *Harvard Studies in Classical Philology* 100 (2000): 1–14.

———. *How to Kill a Dragon*. Oxford: Oxford University Press, 1995.

West, M. L. *The East Face of Helicon: West Asiatic Elements in Greek Poetry and Myth*. Oxford: Oxford University Press, 1997.

_____. "'Eumelos': A Corinthian Epic Cycle?" *The Journal of Hellenic Studies* 122 (2002): 109–133.

_____. *Indo-European Poetry and Myth*. Oxford: Oxford University Press, 2007.

_____. "*Odyssey* and *Argonautica*." *Classical Quarterly* 55, no. 1 (2005): 39–64.

_____. "Phasis and Aia," *Museum Helveticum* 64, no. 4 (2007): 193–198.

Whitman, Cedric H. "Hera's Anvils." *Harvard Studies in Classical Philology* 74 (1970): 37–42.

Willetts, R. F. *Cretan Cults and Festivals*. London: Routledge & Keegan Paul, 1962.

Wilson, Nigel Guy, ed. *Encyclopedia of Ancient Greece*. New York: Routledge, 2006.

Wilson, Winifred Warren. "Jason as 'Dolomedes.'" *Classical Review* 24 (1910): 180.

Wood, Michael. *In Search of Myths and Heroes: Exploring Four Epic Legends of the World*. Berkeley: University of California Press, 2005.

Woosnam-Savage, Rodney C., and Anthony Hall. *Brassey's Book of Body Armor*. Dulles, Virginia: Brassey's, 2001.

Wygant, Amy. *Medea, Magic, and Modernity in France: Stages and Histories, 1553–1797*. Aldershot: Ashgate Publishing, 2007.

Yarnall, Judith. *Transformations of Circe: The History of an Enchantress*. Urbana: University of Illinois, 1994.

Zaidman, Louise Bruit, and Pauline Schmitt Pantel. *Religion in the Ancient Greek City,* trans. Paul Cartledge, orig. 1989. Cambridge: Cambridge University Press, 2002.

Zhirov, N. *Atlantis: Atlantology—Basic Problems*. Honolulu: University Press of the Pacific, 2001.

Zissos, Andrew. "Reception of Valerius Flaccus' *Argonautica*." *International Journal of the Classical Tradition* 13, no. 2 (2006): 165–186.

_____. *Valerius Flaccus'* Argonautica *Book 1: A Commentary*. Oxford: Oxford University Press, 2008.

Index

323